M000307735

HASIDISM REAP

Proceedings of the International Conference of the Institute of Jewish Studies in memory of

JOSEPH G. WEISS

University College London, 21–23 June 1988

The Institute of Jewish Studies, privately funded and dedicated to the promotion of the academic study of all aspects of Jewish culture, was founded by Alexander Altmann in Manchester in 1954. Following Altmann's appointment to the Chair of Jewish Philosophy and History of Ideas at Brandeis University in the USA, the Institute was transferred to London, where, while retaining its autonomous status, it was located at the Department of Hebrew and Jewish Studies of University College London.

The Institute supports individual research projects and publications, and its annual programme of events includes series of public lectures, research seminars, symposia, and one or more major international conferences whose proceedings are published

THE LITTMAN LIBRARY OF JEWISH CIVILIZATION

Dedicated to the memory of

LOUIS THOMAS SIDNEY LITTMAN

who founded the Littman Library for the love of God
and as an act of charity in memory of his father

JOSEPH AARON LITTMAN

and to the memory of

ROBERT JOSEPH LITTMAN

who continued what his father Louis had begun

יהא זכרם ברוך

'Get wisdom, get understanding:
Forsake her not and she shall preserve thee'

PROV. 4: 5

The Littman Library of Jewish Civilization is a registered UK charity
Registered charity no. 1000784

HASIDISM REAPPRAISED

Edited by

ADA RAPOPORT-ALBERT

The Littman Library of Jewish Civilization
in association with Liverpool University Press

The Littman Library of Jewish Civilization
in association with Liverpool University Press
4 Cambridge Street, Liverpool L69 7ZU, UK

www.liverpooluniversitypress.co.uk/littman

Managing Editor: Connie Webber

Distributed in North America by
Oxford University Press Inc., 198 Madison Avenue,
New York, NY 10016, USA

First published 1996
First published in paperback 1998

© *The Littman Library of Jewish Civilization 1996*

All rights reserved.
No part of this publication may be reproduced,
stored in a retrieval system, or transmitted, in any form or by
any means, without the prior permission in writing of
The Littman Library of Jewish Civilization

The paperback edition of this book is sold subject to the condition
that it shall not, by way of trade or otherwise, be lent, re-sold, hired out or
otherwise circulated without the publisher's prior consent in any
form of binding or cover other than that in which it is published
and without a similar condition including this condition
being imposed on the subsequent purchaser

Catalogue records for this book are available from the
British Library and the Library of Congress

ISBN 978-1-874774-35-8

Publishing co-ordinator: Janet Moth
Copy-editing: Tamar Berkowitz, Jackie Pritchard, and Connie Webber
Index: Meg Davies
Design: Pete Russell, Faringdon, Oxon.

Printed in Great Britain by
CPI Group (UK) Ltd, Croydon, CR0 4YY

Preface

THE present volume grew out of an international conference entitled 'The Social Function of Mystical Ideals in Judaism: Hasidism Reappraised', which was held by the Institute of Jewish Studies at University College London on 21–3 June 1988. The idea for the conference was conceived in a series of discussions with my friends Professors Rachel Elior and Immanuel Etkes of the Hebrew University in Jerusalem. Together we formed an organizing committee and proceeded to invite to London virtually every scholar known to us to be actively engaged in research and writing on hasidism. While we realized that we could not hope to be exhaustive, our intention was to be as comprehensive as possible—to include contributions from specialists in a variety of disciplines, from multiple centres of scholarship, and to cover between us the widest possible chronological, geographical, methodological, and thematic span. The preparations generated considerable excitement: it was to be the very first major international conference dedicated specifically to the study of hasidism, and we all felt that the time for it was ripe; we hoped to capture something of the sense we shared of having reached a certain turning-point in our collective understanding of the subject.

The turning-point was occasioned by the convergence primarily of two factors. On the one hand the libraries and archives of eastern Europe were becomining increasingly accessible. The new data that were becoming available were prompting a re-evaluation of what had been for several generations of historians the received notion of the background, origins, and nature of hasidism. On the other hand, the passing away in 1982 of Gershom Scholem, who had pioneered the academic study of Jewish mysticism and whose approach had dominated the field for at least a half a century, was followed, perhaps inevitably, by a revision of his entire scholarly enterprise. Every one of his 'major trends in Jewish mysticism' was beginning to attract critical scrutiny, and it was becoming clear that his regnant interpretation of hasidism—the 'last phase' of the kabbalistic tradition—was no exception.

The coincidence of these two revisionist processes has had considerable implications for the study of hasidism, and the present volume, like the conference that inspired it, constitutes one of its landmarks. It signals a certain redefinition of scope, a response to the challenges of new methodologies and data, a fresh awareness of underlying ideological issues, and an overall shift of outlook on a subject whose historiography has been almost as colourful and as controversial as its own expression in history.

The relationship between the conference and the volume is not quite a straightforward one. Not all the lectures delivered at the conference were included in the volume, and some of the chapters were specially commissioned for the volume from colleagues who were not able to take part in the conference. Many of the contributions eventually submitted for publication were substantially expanded, updated, and elaborated versions of the conference papers, but some chapters retain their original conference flavour. This is especially true of those which address wider issues in a programmatic way and point to new directions of research. Overall, the result is a broad view of divergent opinions and approaches encompassing areas of common consent alongside dissent among a team of scholars engaged in dialogue with one another as well as with the historiographical tradition within which they stand. It acquires coherence from the common endeavour to shed new light on the singular phenomenon of hasidism.

The conference was dedicated to the memory of Joseph G. Weiss—one of the most original and influential historians of the hasidic movement, who was Professor of Jewish Studies at University College London and director of the Institute of Jewish Studies under whose auspices the conference was being held. We were pleased to have among us for many of the sessions his widow, Erna Weiss, and his son, Amos. They were able to meet again Joseph Weiss's friends and colleagues, and to become acquainted with a younger generation of scholars who, whether or not they had studied with him directly, all regarded themselves as Joseph Weiss's students. Indeed, it was precisely this personal dimension of the occasion that prompted 'Ora'—Professor Sara Ora Heller Wilensky, who attended the conference as a non-participating guest—to contribute to the volume her private collection of letters from Joseph Weiss—a close friend and fellow student of kabbalah under Scholem in Jerusalem. Subsequently, as the manuscript of the volume was being prepared for publication, Erna Weiss was kind enough to review the English version of 'Joseph Weiss: Letters to Ora', and to supply some additional biographical details. I should like to thank her for her interest and help.

Many other individuals and organizations have facilitated the publication of the volume, and this is the opportunity to acknowledge their help and to express my gratitude to all of them. The Institute of Jewish Studies, which convened the conference and thereby generated the volume, supplied generous financial assistance for the translation of some of the chapters into English and other technical preparations. I would like to thank its chairman, Dr Manfred Altman, and its director, Professor Mark Geller, for their constant friendship and support. Thanks are due also to the Institute for Polish–Jewish Studies at Oxford and to its director, Professor Antony Polonsky, for the award of a generous grant towards translations into English, and for the initial undertaking to publish the volume as a special issue of the Institute's Journal *Polin*, then published by Blackwell Publishers. Subsequent doubts as to the future of *Polin* required us to seek an alternative solution. This inevitably delayed publication, but finally the volume found a new 'home' in the Littman Library. I should like to thank the editors of the Littman Library, especially Professor Jonathan Israel, and its managing editor, Connie Webber, for their commitment to the publication of the volume. Connie Webber, who was closely involved with every stage of preparation, is responsible for the much enhanced accessibility and usefulness of the volume through her insistence that it should include a detailed index covering themes as well as personal names and a single comprehensive bibliography—the latter an unusual feature in such a complex, multi-author work, but a contribution that will be of great benefit to those working in the field. Thanks are due also to other members of the Littman team: Jackie Pritchard who copy-edited the volume together with Connie Webber and Tammy Berkowitz, who also compiled the bibliography; Meg Davies, who indexed it; Pete Russell, who designed it, and Janet Moth, who co-ordinated and checked everyone's input and dealt tirelessly with a large range of matters. Dalia Tracz, the Jewish Studies librarian at University College London, answered innumerable bibliographical queries with patience, generosity, and good cheer, as did Professor Chimen Abramsky, who was an invaluable resource, especially during the preparation of the bibliography. Acknowledgement is due to the translators from Hebrew into English: Chapter 2 was translated by Connie Webber and Ada Rapoport-Albert; Chapters 6, 13, and 16 were translated by Morris Hoffman; Chapter 18 was translated by Philip Simpson and Ada Rapoport-Albert. Professors Rachel Elior and Immanuel Etkes offered advice and help at all stages, and I am delighted to offer them now this volume, the final product of our joint London venture, as a token of personal friendship and professional respect.

Finally, and with great sadness, I must mark the passing away of a distinguished contributor to the volume, Professor Shmuel Ettinger. One of the leading modern Jewish historians of our time, teacher and mentor to a whole generation of scholars, and a proud product and lifelong student of east European Jewry, he died in London on 22 September 1988. His contribution to the volume is drawn from an unpublished manuscript kindly made available to us by his family in Israel.

London A.R.-A.
1996

Contents

❧

PART I

JOSEPH G.WEISS AS A STUDENT OF HASIDISM

PART II

TOWARDS A NEW SOCIAL HISTORY OF HASIDISM

PART III

THE SOCIAL FUNCTION OF MYSTICAL IDEALS IN HASIDISM

PART IV

DISTINCTIVE OUTLOOKS AND SCHOOLS OF THOUGHT WITHIN HASIDISM

PART V

THE HASIDIC TALE

PART VI

THE HISTORY OF HASIDIC HISTORIOGRAPHY

PART VII

CONTEMPORARY HASIDISM

Notes on Contributors

JACOB BARNAI is Associate Professor of Jewish History at the University of Haifa. He is editor of *Hasidic Letters from Eretz-Israel* (Heb.) (Jerusalem, 1981), and author of *The Jews in Palestine in the 18th Century* (Tuscaloosa, 1992) and *Historiography and Nationalism* (Heb.) (Jerusalem, 1995).

ISRAEL BARTAL is Associate Professor of Jewish History at the Hebrew University, Jerusalem. He is the author of *Exile in the Land of Israel* (Heb.) (Jerusalem, 1995), co-author of *Poles and Jews: A Failed Brotherhood* (Hanover and London, 1993), and co-editor of *Hasidism in Poland* (Heb.) (Jerusalem, 1994).

JOSEPH DAN is Gershom Scholem Professor of Kabbalah at the Hebrew University, Jerusalem. His publications include *The Esoteric Theology of Ashkenazi Hasidism* (Heb.) (Jerusalem, 1968), *The Hasidic Story: Its History and Development* (Heb.) (Jerusalem, 1975), *Jewish Mysticism and Jewish Ethics* (Seattle and London, 1986), and *The Unique Cherub Circle* and *On Sanctity* (both forthcoming).

RACHEL ELIOR is Professor of Jewish Thought at the Hebrew University, Jerusalem. Her publications include *The Theory of Divinity of Hasidut Habad* (Heb.) (Jerusalem, 1982) and *The Paradoxical Ascent to God: The Kabbalistic Theosophy of Habad Hasidism* (New York, 1993).

IMMANUEL ETKES is Professor of Modern Jewish History at the Hebrew University, Jerusalem. His publications include *From Esoteric Circle to Mass Movement: The Emergence of Early Hasidism* (Heb.) (Tel Aviv, 1991) and *Rabbi Israel Salanter and the Muscar Movement* (Philadelphia, 1993).

SHMUEL ETTINGER was, at the time of his death in September 1988, Emeritus Professor of Modern Jewish History at the Hebrew University, Jerusalem. His publications include *Modern Antisemitism* (Heb.) (Israel, 1979), and two posthumously published collections of essays: *History and Historians* (Heb.) (Jerusalem, 1992) and *On the History of the Jews in Poland and Russia* (Heb.) (Jerusalem, 1994).

MORRIS M. FAIERSTEIN is Jewish Chaplain to the US Air Force in Europe. His publications include *All is in the Hands of Heaven: The Teachings of Rabbi Mordecai Joseph Leiner of Izbica* (New York, 1989), and *Jewish Mystical Autobiographies* (forthcoming).

ROLAND GOETSCHEL is University Professor and director of the Institute of Jewish Studies at the University of Paris (Sorbonne). His publications include *Meir Ibn Gabbai: Le Discours de la Kabbale Espagnole* (Louvain, 1981), *La Kabbale* (Paris, 1985), and *Abravanel: L'Homme d'État et le philosophe* (forthcoming).

ARTHUR GREEN is Philip W. Lown Professor of Jewish Thought at Brandeis University. He is the editor of *Jewish Spirituality* (2 vols.; New York, 1986–7), and author of *Tormented Master: A Life of Rabbi Nahman of Bratslav* (Alabama, 1979), and of various other studies on hasidism and kabbalah, including *Keter: The Crown of God in Early Jewish Mysticism* (forthcoming).

ZEEV GRIES is Senior Lecturer in the Department of History at Ben-Gurion University of the Negev. His publications include *Conduct Literature (Regimen Vitae): Its History and Place in the Life of Beshtian Hasidism* (Heb.) (Jerusalem, 1989) and *The Book in Early Hasidism* (Heb.) (Tel Aviv, 1992).

KARL ERICH GRÖZINGER is Professor of Comparative Religion and Jewish Studies at Potsdam University. His publications include: *Musik und Gesang in der Theologie der frühen jüdischen Literatur* (Tübingen, 1982) and *Kafka and Kabbalah* (New York, 1994).

MOSHE HALLAMISH is Alexandre Safran Professor of Kabbalah at Bar Ilan University. His publications include *Path to the Tanya* (Heb.) (Tel Aviv, 1987) and *Introduction to Kabbalah* (Heb.) (Jerusalem, 1992).

GERSHON HUNDERT is Professor of Jewish Studies and History at McGill University. He is the editor of *Essential Papers on Hasidism* (New York, 1991) and author of *The Jews in a Polish Private Town: The Case of Opatow in the Eighteenth Century* (Baltimore, 1992).

MOSHE IDEL is Professor of Jewish Thought at the Hebrew University, Jerusalem. His publications include *Kabbalah: New Perspectives* (New Haven, 1988) and *Hasidism: Between Ecstasy and Magic* (New York, 1995).

LOUIS JACOBS is rabbi of the New London Synagogue and Visiting Professor in the Department of Religion, Lancaster University. His publications include *Hasidic Prayer* (London, 1972) and *Jewish Mystical Testimonies* (New York, 1976).

JACOB KATZ is Emeritus Professor of Jewish History at the Hebrew University, Jerusalem. His publications include *Tradition and Crisis* (New York, 1961; 1993), *Out of the Ghetto* (Cambridge, Mass., 1973), and an autobiography, *With My Own Eyes* (Hanover and London, 1995).

NAFTALI LOEWENTHAL is Honorary Research Fellow and Adjunct Lecturer in the Department of Hebrew and Jewish Studies, University College London. His publications include *Communicating the Infinite: The Emergence of the Habad School* (Chicago, 1990) and *Hasidism and Modernity* (forthcoming).

DANIEL MEIJERS is Professor of Anthropology at the Free University of Amsterdam. His publications include *Ascetic Hasidism in Jerusalem: The Guardian-of-the-Faithful Community of Mea Shearim* (Leiden, 1992); he has also published various studies on the anthropology of modern Judaism.

YEHOSHUA MONDSHINE is Senior Librarian and researcher of Hebrew manuscripts at the Jewish National and University Library in Jerusalem. His publications include *Migdal oz* (Kfar Habad, 1980), *Shivḥei haBesht: Ketav yad* (Jerusalem, 1982), and *Kerem Habad* (5 vols.; Kfar Habad, 1986–92).

GEDALIAH NIGAL is Professor in the Department of Literature of the Jewish People at Bar Ilan University. His publications include *The Hasidic Tale: Its History and Topics* (Heb.) (Jerusalem, 1981) and *Magic, Mysticism and Hasidism* (Northvale and London, 1994).

MENDEL PIEKARZ lives in Jerusalem. His publications include *Ideological Trends of Hasidism in Poland during the Interwar Period and the Holocaust* (Heb.) (Jerusalem, 1990) and *Between Ideology and Reality: Humility, Ayin, Self-Negation and Devekut in Hasidic Thought* (Heb.) (Jerusalem, 1994).

ADA RAPOPORT-ALBERT is Lecturer in Jewish History in the Department of Hebrew and Jewish Studies, University College London. She is the editor of *Essays in Jewish Historiography* (1988), co-editor of *Jewish History: Essays in Honor of Chimen Abramsky* (London, 1988), and the author of various studies on the history of hasidism.

MOSHE J. ROSMAN is Associate Professor of Jewish History at Bar Ilan University. His publications include *The Lord's Jews: Magnate–Jewish Relations in the Polish–Lithuanian Commonwealth during the 18th Century* (Cambridge, Mass., 1990); he is currently writing a book on Israel Baal Shem Tov and early hasidism.

BRACHA SACK is Associate Professor of Jewish Thought at Ben-Gurion University of the Negev. She is the author of *The Kabbalah of Rabbi Moshe Cordovero* (Heb.) (Beer Sheva, 1995), and of various studies on the history of Jewish mysticism.

YOSEPH SALMON is Associate Professor of History at Ben Gurion University of the Negev. His publications include *Religion and Zionism: First Encounters* (Heb.) (Jerusalem, 1990) and *The Return to Zion* (Heb.) (forthcoming).

CHONE SHMERUK is Emeritus Professor of Yiddish Literature at the Hebrerw University, Jerusalem, and frequent Visiting Professor at the universities of Warsaw, Cracow, and Lodz. His publications include *Yiddish Literature in Poland: Historical Studies and Perspectives* (Heb.) (Jerusalem, 1981) and *The Illustrations in Yiddish Books in the Sixteenth and Seventeenth Centuries* (Heb.) (Jerusalem, 1986).

SARA ORA HELLER WILENSKY is Sir Isaac Wolfson Professor Emeritus of Jewish Thought at the University of Haifa. She is co-editor of *Studies in Jewish Thought* (Heb.) (Jerusalem, 1989), and author of *The Philosophy of Isaac Arama* (Heb.) (Jerusalem and Tel Aviv, 1956) and of various studies on the dialectical relations between Jewish philosophy and kabbalah.

ELLIOT R. WOLFSON is Professor of Hebrew and Judaic Studies and director of religious studies at New York University. His publications incude *Through a Speculum that Shines: Vision and Imagination in Medieval Jewish Mysticism* (Princeton, 1994), *Along the Path: Studies in Kabbalistic Myth, Symbolism, and Hermeneutics* (Albany, NY, 1995), and *Circle in the Square: Studies in the Use of Gender in Kabbalistic Symbolism* (Albany, NY, 1995). He is the editor of the *Journal of Jewish Thought and Philosophy.*

Introduction

ADA RAPOPORT-ALBERT

HASIDISM is a movement of Jewish spiritual revival which began in southeastern Poland during the second half of the eighteenth century and came to be characterized by its charismatic leadership, mystical orientation, and distinctive pattern of communal life. It became controversial during the last quarter of that century, when the Lithuanian rabbinic establishment denounced it as a heretical sect and conducted a militant campaign to eradicate it. In the early decades of the nineteenth century it again encountered belligerent hostilities, this time in Galicia, where Jewish Enlightenment activists, in collaboration with the Austrian authorities, campaigned to coerce it into compliance with their programme of radical Jewish reforms. In spite of all this, hasidism spread rapidly throughout eastern Europe and became, by the second half of the nineteenth century, a mass movement aligned with other sectors within Orthodox Judaism in resisting secularization and modernity. It survived the long series of traumas that eastern European Jewry suffered from the 1880s until the end of the Second World War, to become established during the postwar years in all the major centres of Jewish population in Israel and the West, where it forms a vital and distinctive element of Orthodox Jewish life.

More than any other movement or school of Jewish spirituality, hasidism has attracted the attention of scholars who have offered widely divergent interpretations, often ideologically charged, of its doctrines and extraordinary popular appeal. Since the beginnings of modern Jewish historiography in the nineteenth century, the movement has been variously portrayed: as a reactionary barrier to Jewish progress and political emancipation in Europe; as a revolutionary expression of social, material, and spiritual discontents on the part of the alienated Jewish masses of eastern Europe; as a conservative force in Jewish life which prevented the disintegration of traditional values and institutions in the face of secularization and modernity; as a radical challenge from within the tradition to the established value-system and its decaying institutional framework; as a national–messianic revival which both anticipated and facilitated the political ideology of Zionism; as a movement of popular mysticism which sanctified the concrete and the mundane by denying their very reality; or as the arena for the most authentic encounter in Judaism between God and man precisely within the freshly affirmed reality of the concrete and the mundane. It has even been construed as the first feminist revolution in Judaism! Whether celebrating or decrying the undeniable success of hasidism, all have acknowledged its vitality and vigour; none could dispute its traditionalist Jewish flavour; and few but its most ardent opponents and denigrators could resist the urge to discover within it their own extraneously inspired philosophical or political sensibilities: if Zionism, socialism, religious existentialism, or feminism could be shown to have been anticipated in the intrinsically Jewish phenomenon of hasidic revival, they could be promoted as authentically Jewish orientations for the regeneration of the Jewish people in the modern era. All this has turned hasidism into an interesting subject of enquiry, not only in its own right but also as a fraught historiographical issue which reflects the clash of rival ideologies marking the transition to modernity in the history of European Jewry.

Whether explicitly, in the chapters identified as 'historiographical', or implicitly, throughout the chapters which trace the evolution and characteristic physiognomy of the hasidic movement as such, the present volume addresses the history of hasidism as a complex of historical and historiographical considerations. It sets out to reappraise what we know and understand about hasidism not only in the light of fresh historical data but also in response to the changed existential circumstances and the shifting ideological and intellectual bearings that have prompted the pursuit of new historical data and led to the re-examination of interpretative models constructed by previous generations of historians.

The dedication of the conference and this volume to the memory of Joseph Weiss provided the opportunity to assess his contribution to the study of hasidism in relation to the circumstances that shaped his life and intellectual development. Throughout Part I, which is fittingly devoted to this topic, Weiss's close but anxious relationship with his teacher Gershom Scholem stands out as a crucial factor. It has implications for the wider consideration of Scholem's impact on the entire field of kabbalistic and hasidic scholarship in the twentieth century, a field which, in the aftermath of Scholem's demise, is undergoing revision and has generated considerable controversy and debate. Some of the participants in this debate have adopted Weiss as their tragic precursor in the struggle to establish a certain measure of freedom from the overpowering influence of Scholem's methodology and underlying historiosophical stance. In Weiss's time, they felt, during the 1940s and 1950s, such a struggle was doomed to failure, and it thwarted his career. Readers may gauge for themselves the extent to which this perception of the relationship between Scholem and Weiss is compatible with the insights of two closely involved observers, and above all with Weiss's letters, of which it forms a recurrent theme.

Whether or not he was a frustrated revisionist, Weiss undoubtedly belonged to the Scholem school which interpreted hasidism as a dialectical response to the Lurianic kabbalah and the Sabbatean heresy that proceeded from it. By implication, he followed Scholem in placing hasidism primarily in its kabbalistic context and explaining the most distinctive features of the movement in reference to a certain range of theological and spiritual stimuli. And yet his seminal studies of 'pre-' and early hasidism, as well as his exposition of its Bratslav branch, reveal a heightened sensitivity to socio-historical, sociological, and psychological factors, all of which he saw as having crucial importance in determining the spiritual constitution of the hasidic leadership in its formative years. In this respect Weiss anticipated the collective endeavour in the present volume to transcend the disciplinary divides that have fragmented our understanding of hasidism, addressing its many facets—mystical, literary, linguistic, historical, sociological, and so on—not as discrete subjects of enquiry but as interrelated components of a coherent, if complex, whole.

Part II re-evaluates the conditions from which hasidism emerged, the factors that facilitated its rapid expansion, and the mechanisms by which this was achieved. Until relatively recently, most historians of eastern European Jewry set the rise of hasidism in the context of crisis—the disintegration and final collapse of traditional modes of Jewish life in Poland on the eve of its own disintegration, partitions, and effective political demise. The crisis began with the mid-seventeenth-century Cossack-led peasant uprising in the Ukraine, which Jewish historiography has labelled 'the massacres of 1648–9'. The Jews, who bore much of the brunt of the events, suffered unprecedentedly large-scale losses in life, wealth, and property, and witnessed the total devastation by the rebels of several well-established Jewish communities in the region. These events and their aftermath have been construed as a turning-point: following two centuries of prosperity and growth, Polish Jewry was now seen as being set on an irreversible course of economic, political, and spiritual decline. The most comprehensive and authoritative presentation of the rise of hasidism against this dire background was Simon Dubnow's, and his view still reverberates through much of the scholarly as well as the popular literature on hasidism. It has its origins in nineteenth-century Jewish histriography in Germany, where the pioneering Jewish historians described the 'new hasidim' in terms drawn almost exclusively from the hostile accounts of the movement written by Jewish Enlightenment authors from eastern Europe who were actively engaged in anti-hasidic agitation; they in turn had drawn on the anti-hasidic polemical writings of the rabbinic opponents of the movement in Lithuania. The early historiography of hasidism was thus permeated by the several strands of ideological antagonism that the movement had aroused in its early opponents. Moreover, the anti-hasidic biases that the German Jewish historians had assimilated uncritically from their sources were reinforced by their own intellectual and cultural distaste for the eastern European phenomenon of hasidism. This sprang from their devaluation of the emotional piety and mystical imagination associated with hasidism, qualities which were at odds with their own sober religiosity and rationalist cast of mind. To their Western bourgeois sensibilities, hasidism appeared to be obscurantist, uncivilized, and crass, and it came to epitomize what they perceived as the depravity of eastern European Jewry as a whole.

A proud eastern European Jew himself, Dubnow came out against this legacy of German Jewish disdain for eastern European Jewry and hasidism. Nevertheless, its residual influence on his own approach is evidenced not only by his relative insensitivity to the 'supernatural' or 'irrational' elements of hasidic spirituality but above all in his sense that hasidism must be seen to have emerged from conditions of extreme adversity. The implication was that the rise of hasidism was symptomatic of a certain pathology; that it would have been inconceivable in more auspicious political, economic, and cultural circumstances. Moreover, Dubnow's pessimistic view of the condition of Polish Jewry in the first half of the eighteenth century was undoubtedly coloured, at least to some extent, by his own bitter experience of the plight of eastern European Jewry during the latter part of the nineteenth century and the first half of the twentieth. He had lived through the most violent upheavals and ruptures this Jewish community had ever experienced and was a victim of its final liquidation by the Nazis. His reconstruction of the background to the rise of hasidism must therefore be seen in the context of both the historiographical tradition to which he belonged and the tragic historical circumstances of his own lifetime.

In recent years, with the growing accessibility of archival materials within the former Soviet Union and its satellite states, the history of the Jews in eastern Europe has become the subject of revision. A new generation of historians, mostly born after the last war, who had not shared personally in the predicaments of east European Jewry, are examining the subject afresh, and their findings so far seem to point to a modified picture of the adverse conditions from which hasidism emerged. Far from the drastic material and spiritual impoverishment which, according to Dubnow and his historiographical tradition, marked the decline of Polish Jewry in the course of the eighteenth century and preconditioned the rise of hasidism, the economic and cultural circumstances of the Jews within the regions and during the very period in which hasidism began are shown to have been not altogether unfavourable. While it would be wrong to underestimate the impact of the mid-seventeenth-century crisis, it should be recognized that conditions of crisis cannot persist for as long as a century without some form of accommodation. Barring such 'final solutions' as mass expulsion or total extermination, which clearly did not occur in this case, rehabilitation must, and did, take place within a few decades; so that by the middle of the eighteenth century, hasidism was emerging in a more hospitable environment than had previously been assumed.

The implications of this revision, which have been far-reaching, are explored here by some of its leading pioneers. They put in question Dubnow's depiction of hasidism as a 'natural' response, on the one hand to external forces of unrelenting exploitation and oppression, and on the other hand to internal conditions of spiritual bankruptcy and communal–organizational collapse; they challenge the notion that the founders of hasidism were anti-establishment figures who clashed with an 'old regime' of corrupt communal leaders, disfunctional institutions, and a fossilized value-system which they strove to overturn. Rather than being necessarily oppositional, the relationship between hasidism and the institutions of communal government emerges as complementary, at times collaborative, and based on a shared commitment to much of the traditional value-system as well as on practical common concerns. New light is also shed on the dynamics of the organizational structure within which hasidism operated as a movement—a subject which was formerly neglected by most historians of hasidism who, drawing uncritically on naïvely anachronistic hagiographical sources, have tended to project latter-day norms of social organization on to the loose organizational patterns in which hasidism was first formed and which it continued to modify until it eventually generated what has come to be recognized as its characteristic mould. An equally neglected field, the social history of hasidic printing, is here explored in a pioneering study which focuses on the transition from the oral communication of hasidic lore—always the strongest determinant of hasidic identity and experience—to the often haphazard and rarely authoritative form in which this lore was disseminated in writing, and eventually in print. Until we become better acquainted with the motivations and modes of operation of the hasidic managing editors who, more than the majority of the hasidic masters themselves, were responsible for the evolution of hasidic *texts*, our understanding of hasidism as a historical phenomenon—wholly dependent as it is on our access to its textual traditions—will be limited by the unknown quality of its mediation.

Part III engages with what has long been recognized as a defining characteristic of hasidism: the 'paradox of solitude and communion' whereby, in Scholem's words, 'he who has attained the highest degree of spiritual solitude, who is capable of being alone with God, is the true centre of the community'. Hasidism is distinguishable from all other schools of Jewish esoteric spirituality and mysticism in having fused together two diametrically opposed poles of human experience: intensely personal, reclusive, mystical flight from the world, and robust involvement in mundane human affairs. But this fusion is only one expression of the dialectical dynamics that are paradigmatic in hasidism and may be discerned in every aspect of its religious teaching and function in society. The contributions to this part of the volume explore, from various perspectives, the hasidic interplay of dialectical mystical paradigms and the patterns of social behaviour which they at once both mirror and shape. The range of polarities noted, and the rich variety of their modes of interaction and fusion, is dazzling: it includes the integration in the doctrine of the zaddik of two conflicting earlier models of leadership; the multifaceted paradox of 'being and non-being' which is inherent in the divine nature, and thus governs and energizes every aspect of the created universe; the polarities of exile and redemption which are fused through the device of charging the social reality of itinerancy with the symbolic meaning of both the wanderings of exile and the redemptive dimension of sexual union; the dialectical tension between the present and the past as it is expressed in the sense of rivalry between the intensity of revelation now and the authority of revelation then; the interaction of conflicting (élitist as against popular) models of personal redemption; and the conflation of élitist and popular norms in the ambivalently charged concept of mystical union, *devekut*. It is the tension generated by all these polarities, and the energy released by their unprecedented fusion, that have empowered the hasidic leadership and infused the entire movement with the vitality that has turned it into a powerful historical force.

Part IV presents a sample of individual approaches to hasidism. Their clear distinctiveness highlights the difficulty inherent in any attempt to define the core of common beliefs and practices that lends the movement coherence. From its earliest beginnings, hasidism accommodated a variety of distinct and at times conflicting opinions, directions, and personal styles of spirituality which could, and occasionally did, lead to inter-hasidic rivalries, bitter divisions, and controversies. The movement sprang from a tradition in which the notion of any singular source of supreme authority had been alien for centuries; it never generated mechanisms for the imposition of uniformity and control from any nominal centre of its own. The initial absence of any centralized framework of government in early hasidism was accentuated by the rapid proliferation of hasidic schools and the expansion of the movement to outposts which lay well beyond its region of provenance. These processes brought hasidism into contact with a diversity of local customs and existential conditions that lent it a rich variety of distinctive local characteristics. Against this background of diversity, it is instructive to observe some of the shared concerns and mutual influences that link the individual hasidic masters to one another and to their common kabbalistic legacy. Among the distinctive hasidic approaches reviewed here, the endeavour to anchor emotional, spiritual, and mystical values in the traditional halakhic framework and ethical teaching of Judaism stands out as a common conservative trend: rather than divorcing the liberating personal experiences of ecstasy, vision, equanimity, or self-abnegation from such ostensibly prosaic norms as academic study or routine communal prayer, the hasidic masters preserve the connection with all the texts and formal institutions of traditional Judaism precisely by locating in them the greatest capacity for personal spiritual transformation. They charge the established concepts and practices with new meanings, so that Torah study, while remaining an intellectual discipline, can become a meditative exercise or a vehicle for theurgic action of cosmic dimensions: humility—primarily an ethical concept—may signify mystical self-abnegation, and the set prayers are capable of providing the opportunity for some to subdue and for others to sanctify the forces of evil which constantly threaten to distract the individual from his contemplation of God. While this link with the traditional norms injects them with fresh rigour, it also endows the hasidic vocabulary with a certain elasticity which enables the spiritual masters to stress the exclusive nature of their own experience while at the same time connecting it to the experience of the ordinary hasidim.

Part V focuses on the literary genre of the tale, which has become a hallmark of the hasidic tradition, and is arguably the most authentic expression of its distinctive ethos. It has been the subject of controversy between two important modern exponents of hasidism: Martin Buber, who anthologized a vast number of hasidic tales and analysed hasidism on that basis; and Gershom Scholem, who argued that the tales provided only a limited insight into the least distinctive aspects of the essential hasidic experience. Scholem grounded his presentation primarily in an analysis of the speculative doctrines of the movement, which were published long before the publication of the earliest collections of tales, and were clearly considered the preferred vehicle for the dissemination of hasidism in its first period of expansion. This controversy features as a historiographical issue in its own right in Part VI of the volume, but it underlies the analysis here, which implicitly challenges the juxtaposition of the speculative teachings and the tales as two wholly distinct bodies of literature, reflecting two wholly distinct sets of concerns and sensibilities. This juxtaposition served both Buber and Scholem as a common point of departure, despite their conflicting evaluations of each of the two genres. The contributions to this part of the volume suggest an affinity between the tales and the speculative teachings. They demonstrate that the earliest teachings contain the nuclei of many hasidic tales, and that the telling of tales formed an integral part of the early dissemination of hasidism. Special attention is paid to the first published collection of tales. *In Praise of the Baal Shem Tov*, which is scrutinized for evidence of discrete stages of recension, each representing a distinctive conception of the ideal hasidic leader as it was thought to have been embodied in the personality of the Besht.

In Part VI some of the most influential interpretations of hasidism are subjected to critical analysis. The literature of the Jewish Enlightenment in eastern Europe is shown to have been responsible not only for much of the distortive bias against hasidism that for so long marked its historiography, but also for preserving a great deal of perceptive insight about the movement and the context in which it is to be understood. The historiography of the hasidic immigrations to Erets Yisrael is reviewed and found to have been partly the product of the rival ideological motivations of the historians of the old yishuv. An analysis of the conflicting interpretations of hasidism by Martin Buber and Gershom Scholem highlights a surprising number of assumptions and premisses on which they were tacitly agreed, while proposing an alternative approach to the study of hasidism, which links it to important strands of kabbalistic tradition previously excluded from view. Finally, the recently discovered unpublished history of Polish hasidism by Yitzhak Schiper, written during the last year of his life in the Warsaw ghetto and presumed lost since his death in the Majdanek concentration camp in 1943, is introduced here for the first time in English, and assessed in the context of subsequent developments in the postwar historiography of hasidism—some of which he appears to have anticipated with remarkable intuition.

Part VII, which contains only two contributions, reflects a certain imbalance in twentieth-century hasidic scholarship: it has tended to concentrate on the early history of hasidism but has paid little attention to more recent or contemporary developments. This is in direct contrast with the preference for genealogies, popular biographies, and histories of contemporary hasidism which characterizes the prolific output of intrahasidic historiography. Implicit in the scholarly concentration on early hasidism is the sense, on which there has been a virtual consensus, that while the movement had begun as a genuine spiritual revival, it soon degenerated into a vulgar personality cult, devoid of any original religious ideas but providing ample opportunity for an avaricious, imperious leadership to exploit its naïve following and to delude it with extravagant claims. This sense, which has led many scholars to conclude their histories of the movement in the middle of the nineteenth century at the latest, is now increasingly recognized to stem either from an idealized depiction of early hasidism that overlooks or misconstrues some of its features, or from a view of late hasidism which is blinkered by inapposite value-judgements. In this latter view there is a failure to note not only such original thought as does continue to develop in the later stages, but also the numerous expressions of hasidic creativity and enterprise in various spheres of activity within the modern world. Part VII, therefore, is a gesture towards redressing the balance of scholarship. It contains an analysis of the remarkably effective postwar rehabilitation of the hasidic movement and calls for a re-evaluation of its early beginnings in the light of this modern success. The other contribution to this part of the volume places hasidism in the context of contemporary Orthodoxy, and proceeds to differentiate it from other divisions within this variegated sector of modern Judaism.

The volume concludes with two authoritative overviews of hasidic scholarship in recent decades. They survey past trends, identify current preoccupations, and propose new directions for future research.

If the thrust of the volume is revisionist, this is a measure of the impressive scope and quality of the legacy of past scholarship with which it grapples; but it is equally a measure of hasidism's capacity to continue to excite the imagination and curiosity of successive generations of scholars.

PART I

JOSEPH G. WEISS AS A STUDENT OF HASIDISM

ONE

Joseph G. Weiss: A Personal Appraisal

JACOB KATZ

THE idea of dedicating a conference on hasidism to the memory of Joseph Weiss is entirely appropriate. Although historians before and after him have engaged in the study of the hasidic movement and its teachings, and some may have contributed more to its elucidation, I doubt if any were as fascinated and absorbed by it as he was. He was committed to studying hasidism, and particularly the hasidism of Bratslav, not only intellectually but also emotionally, and—dare I say it—existentially.

I shall not spell out in detail Weiss's material contribution to the study of hasidism because I am not sufficiently familiar with all the relevant aspects of this vast field. What I can offer instead is an attempt to characterize his methodological approach and the quality of his achievements.

Anyone acquainted with Weiss's opus will have observed that most of his publications are predicated on a meticulous analysis of the relevant sources, on the basis of which he then attempts to substantiate the thesis of the article in question. His groundwork is thus of a philological nature based on intimate acquaintance with the nomenclature employed by the hasidic authors. These drew their terminology from the vast literature of the aggadah and homiletics, medieval philosophy and kabbalah, allowing themselves at the same time to deviate from and revise the original meanings. Correct interpretation of the hasidic sources therefore requires due attention to the terms employed in them and their historical background, an enterprise whose success depends upon continual rereading and examination of the texts. Weiss recognized this: he once told me that in order to be sure of one's handling of the sources, one should peruse all the relevant texts every year. From the fact that he returns again and again to the basic sources of hasidic history and teachings in his publications and constantly offers new insights into the intentions of their authors, I suspect that he tried to live up to this.

I said that most of Weiss's articles were philologically based. Most, but not all. Some of them are no doubt informed by close study of the relevant sources but do not specifically mention them; rather, they are bold generalizations offering most important insights. In one such article, 'Hasidism of Mysticism and Hasidism of Faith', one of his earliest publications, he dismisses the then prevailing monolithic conception of the whole hasidic movement as endowing religion with emotion, in contradistinction to the prevailing rigour of legalistic rabbinism. Weiss focused instead on the differing directions within the hasidic movement. The most telling differentiation he found was in the way of trying to achieve nearness to God, whether through the mystical union with

Him, *devekut*, or through dialectical justification of faith in Him. His classification of the various hasidic groups in these terms yielded some rather surprising results. Thus, the Habad movement, which had been regarded as rationally based because of the systematic exposition of its lore in its main tractate, the *Tanya*, was now defined by Weiss as belonging to the mystical trend. Bratslav hasidism, on the other hand, which, because of the erratic behaviour of its founder and the opaque character of his homilies and tales, had been considered a mystical movement was now classified as faith-oriented. These surprising statements were initially presented as mere contentions; it took Weiss the better part of his scholarly career to substantiate them, especially the thesis concerning Bratslav hasidism.

The key to the fruitfulness of Weiss's approach is to be seen precisely in the recourse to such refined and sophisticated differentiations. Weiss belonged to the small group of young scholars of the 1930s and 1940s whom I would call revisionists because of their outspoken tendency to improve upon the naïve historical approach of their predecessors, who though in command of the relevant sources had relied only on their own common sense in their analysis and presentation. The revisionists, in contrast, applied methodological tools appropriate to the object of their research. Thus, Weiss explicitly referred to the necessity of applying the nomenclature of comparative religion in dealing with the phenomena of kabbalah and hasidism. I remember most vividly the impression that his criticism of Benjamin Klar's edition of *Megilat Ahima'ats*, published in *Ha'aretz* in February 1946, made on me. Klar, in his comments on the published text, had tried to explain the presumption that mysticism had flourished in Byzantium in the High Middle Ages, but not in Babylonia, on the grounds that, in the latter, Jews had lived in relative tranquillity, while in the former they had been persecuted. Hardship, according to this theory, encouraged the flight into mysticism; peace and quiet generated rationalism. Klar was a well-established scholar and a highly esteemed one, but as far as interpretative tools were concerned he definitely belonged to the traditionalist school. Joseph Weiss, though still a student, ridiculed this simplistic formula and showed easily that it led to misrepresentation of the facts: mysticism was evident in Babylonia no less than in Byzantium.

The use of scholarly terminology is, of course, no guarantee of the correct interpretation of historical sources or the understanding of historical processes. These depend on applying the terminology in a manner appropriate to the subject. It was in this that Joseph Weiss excelled. Not only was he careful to choose the right scholarly terms for the phenomenon at hand, but he attempted to coin new terms as the need arose; he transcended the vocabularies of religious thinkers by translating them into the idiom of scholarly disciplines. Thus, he characterized the theology of Mordecai Joseph of Izbica as religious determinism, and the psychological state of mind of R. Nahman of Bratslav as a fascination with limits. His interpretative apparatus was never a mere mechanical translation of the fluid, imprecise, and often inconsistent language of the hasidic sources into the rigorous terminology of one scholarly discipline or another. Rather, it offered fresh insights and supplied a wider context in which the hasidic sources could assume new meaning.

The choice of proper interpretative tools does not in itself make the historian, however. He also needs the capacity to reconstruct with accuracy the reality reflected in his sources. Even if this reality is of an abstract nature, such as the evolvement of ideological trends or religious attitudes, the reader should not get the impression that the historian is merely manipulating the sources. He should feel that he is a witness to events or mental processes that happened or existed at a certain time in the past. Weiss achieves such mirroring of the past, I think, in all his historical writings, even when they touch upon the most subtle mental events. For example, when dealing in his article on 'The Beginnings of Hasidism' with the problem of *maḥshavot zarot*—that is, the distraction of the devotional intentions of worshippers through profane reflections—Weiss succeeds in showing us real people struggling with their temptations. This is even more pronounced when his descriptions relate to individual people; I refer particularly to the various episodes he describes in the life of R. Nahman of Bratslav, and especially his insightful reconstruction of the biography of R. Nathan Sternhartz, the devoted follower, servant, and secretary of R. Nahman.

Weiss's single-minded attention to the history of hasidism in general and of the Bratslav branch in particular has often been attributed to his innate affinity with this mystical trend in Judaism. Some have even hinted at a certain congruence between Weiss's life and that of his hero, R. Nahman, who was recently correctly described by Arthur Green as the 'tormented master'. I have no quarrel with this observation. What I am sceptical about is the contention that Weiss's commitment to his subject and putative personal consequences of that were psychologically predetermined. The biographical data available to us cast great doubts on this interpretation.

Weiss was born in Budapest in 1918. He attended the Jewish gymnasium—an excellent secondary school—and used other opportunities to broaden his Jewish and general European education. As I gather from his own recollections, preserved in his correspondence with Gershom and Fania Scholem in his last years, his family belonged to the Neolog community, though he himself, having lost his father in his early teens, took an interest in all varieties of religious activity of the large Jewish community in the capital. On finishing school he entered the rabbinical seminary and the university, but in 1939, after one year, he went to live in Palestine. In the same year he published his first article, in his mother tongue, Hungarian, in the literary periodical *Libanon*.

I have reason to believe that Weiss was later somewhat embarrassed by this article. It is indeed the typical premature production of a daring young intellectual, but none the less it testifies to his broad horizons and his budding originality. The essay is called 'The Baroque in Jewish Literature', and its main thesis is that the infusion of Jewish life by the dynamic conceptions of Lurianic kabbalah, displacing as they did the static system of Moses Cordovero, corresponded with baroque tendencies in the non-Jewish world. The novel assumption underlying this view is that, despite the obvious social and cultural separation between Jews and non-Jews at that time (unlike the active search for contact at the time of the Enlightenment), the spiritual trends emerging among them displayed some common features. Although this earlier contact was subdued and possibly even clandestine, Weiss claimed, it was demonstrably present.

In view of Weiss's later intellectual and scholarly development, it would be useful to know whence he derived his information about the two trends of kabbalah while still in Budapest. He must have read some of the main tests of both Cordoverian and Lurianic kabbalah, and also some of their modern elaborations. The name of Gershom Scholem is not mentioned, but knowing Weiss's comprehensive reading habits and the fact that Scholem's publications were available through the fine library of the rabbinical seminary, it is reasonable to assume that Scholem had not escaped Weiss's attention. However, to conclude from this that Weiss entered the Hebrew University with the idea of becoming a pupil of the great expert on kabbalah and hasidism would be unwarranted. Such an assumption is in fact contradicted by direct and indirect evidence.

Weiss no doubt became acquainted with Scholem very soon after his arrival in Jerusalem, yet in his first two years he preferred other Judaic subjects: history, philosophy, and medieval poetry. The obituaries about him mention Yitzhak Ber and Julius Guttmann as his teachers, along with Scholem, and it is known that he held Ber and Guttmann in high esteem. But he must have also studied with David Yellin, professor of medieval *piyutim*, and also with Haim Schirmann, then a guest lecturer at the Hebrew University. They may have introduced him to the world of medieval Hebrew poetry, but their interest in the subject was limited to its philological and historical aspects, while Weiss was accustomed, from his European education, to a more sophisticated interpretation of poetry; I once heard him say scathingly of Yellin that he had three aesthetic categories—'beautiful', 'rather beautiful', and 'extremely beautiful'.

Weiss himself focused not only on the aesthetic side of poetry but also on its sociological function. Prompted by this approach, his first major article, printed in 1948, was entitled *Courtly Culture and Courtly Poetry: Towards the Understanding of the Hebrew Poetry of Spain* (*Tarbut ḥatsranit veshirah ḥatsranit: Berurim lehavanat shirat sefarad ha'ivrit* (Jerusalem, 1947)). In this small treatise, Weiss's perceptive analysis of the secular poetry of the Golden Age of Spain reconstructed the social environment and cultural climate that lay behind it. What is important in the present context is the note he appended to this essay: 'These pages are a mere project and outline of a comprehensive description of the poetry of Sefarad.' In other words at the time of its composition, which no doubt preceded its publication by several years, Weiss intended to dedicate himself to the study of medieval poetry. This is at least circumstantial evidence for a delay between Weiss's arrival in Jerusalem and his becoming a student of Gershom Scholem.

The second and direct proof for this state of affairs comes from Weiss's literary estate, which contains his correspondence with Gershom Scholem and various notes on their relationship written in the last years of Weiss's life. These documents are now held at the Leo Baeck Institute in Jerusalem, which is preparing the Scholem correspondence for publication. In one of the notes, Weiss expressly mentions 1941 as the year when he began to study kabbalah as a major subject. Before that, he had participated in one or two of Scholem's seminars to enlarge the scope of his education, and he mentions an episode indicating that Scholem had made some effort to enlist him among his students. A collector of kabbalistic works, Scholem was often offered books that he already possessed. One day, a copy of Joseph Gikatilla's *Sha'arei orah*, the kabbalistic classic, happened to arrive at the time of the seminar, and Scholem asked Weiss if he would be interested in buying it. Weiss understood this question, at least in retrospect, as a suggestion on Scholem's part that he immerse himself in the subject-matter of the book. Weiss declined. He resisted the temptation for the time being, but in relating the episode in his typical mystically minded fashion, he interpreted it as an omen of what had to happen. He was destined to become a student of kabbalah and a follower of its master, Gershom Scholem.

Weiss considered his encounter with Scholem as a fateful turn in his life. It was indeed. It induced him to dedicate his mind to the study of mystical movements past and present and at the same time tied him to the personality of a towering and overwhelming figure. Had he kept to his original intention and studied medieval poetry, a field that by its very distance in time and lack of emotional content was less prone to encourage personal identification, he would have been spared a psychological entanglement that was to dominate his life. He would also have had a more independent terrain for his academic achievements. This is of course no more than a hypothesis; much of Weiss's quixotic behaviour—his eternal self-examination, his wavering, and his inability to make rational decisions in his personal life—was, as he would freely admit, deeply ingrained in his personality. They might have surfaced even without the encounter with mysticism and its master. But, subjectively, the encounter with Scholem unquestionably coloured much of Weiss's intellectual and existential experiences.

The relations between the two men went far beyond the usual ties between student and teacher. To understand this, one must also know something abut Scholem's mentality, character, and temperament. Scholem's gigantic intellectual creativity was paired with a passion for imparting his insights to people whom he found receptive to his scholarly findings, and especially to younger people. Those who lived up to his expectations were privileged to enter into a personal relationship with him. This meant enjoying access to the Scholem home, a prominent social centre for intellectuals. Students of this status may have felt distinguished, but this gave them no licence to be complacent in their academic achievements. Scholem had the rare ability to separate academic evaluation and personal relations, as Weiss was to learn.

Scholem regarded Weiss as his most able student. He declared this publicly at the celebration of his sixtieth birthday, though Weiss was not present. Even as early in Weiss's career as the late 1940s, Scholem employed Weiss as a kind of scholarly secretary, dictating to him his *Reshit hakabalah*. Scholem refers to this joint activity with Weiss in one of his letters to him, and Weiss told me in all modesty that he had contributed to the wording and formulation of Scholem's seminal tractate. Though Scholem clearly had a high appreciation of Weiss, when the latter delivered his doctoral thesis and Scholem found it in need of correction and completion, he returned it to him unhesitatingly.

The doctoral thesis itself has its history, which can be reconstructed on the basis of records in the archives of the Hebrew University. Its original title was 'The Dialectic Doctrine and Faith of Rabbi Nahman of Bratslav'. Having worked on this thesis for years, Weiss found that without going back to the teaching of the Baal Shem, it was impossible to ascertain the novelty in the teachings of his grandson, R. Nahman. He therefore asked, with Scholem's consent, to change his title to 'The Original Teachings of the Baal Shem Tov', and began collecting quotations given in the name of the Baal Shem in the writings of his successors from first editions of the relevant texts. But when the east of Jerusalem fell to the Arabs in Israel's War of Independence and the books of the university library became inaccessible, he was unable to pursue this course of study and thus returned to his original title.

Scholem found parts of Weiss's thesis most original and well substantiated, and was full of praise for his scholarly potential. But other parts he regarded as being unfounded and speculative, and thus he regretfully rejected it.

This decision must have been most painful for Weiss. He learnt of it in London, where he had moved some time after the war with his new wife, who was also a student of Scholem. The move may have been prompted by the hardships of Israel at that time, but it was also undoubtedly an attempt by Weiss to distance himself from Scholem's overpowering presence. Scholem, for his part, clearly recognized the necessity of the move and tried, through his many connections, to help his student establish himself. He was instrumental in securing an invitation for Weiss to the Jewish Theological Seminary in New York as a guest lecturer, a plan that Weiss first actively pursued but ultimately rejected without in fact having reasonable grounds for doing so. On Scholem's recommendation, Weiss received the prestigious Warburg Prize from the Hebrew University, which permitted him to stay on in London. Weiss later found a part-time job at University College, and soon also became affiliated with the Institute of Jewish Studies that Rabbi Alexander Altmann had recently established in Manchester.

It was at this juncture and in this context that my intermittent acquaintance with Weiss became a continuous and intimate relationship. Having taken my first sabbatical from the Hebrew University at Altmann's institute in 1956/7, spending half of the time in Manchester and half in London, I had plenty of opportunity to discuss both scholarly and personal problems with Weiss, and also to observe his performance as a lecturer.

The Institute in Manchester had no students. Its only academic activity was a kind of staff seminar once a week or once a fortnight. Weiss's seminars were always based on analysis of a hasidic text, but were at no time restricted to its mere interpretation. Rather, they served as an occasion for discussing major problems of hasidic life as illustrated by the text under discussion. To this day, I recall the discussions conducted by Weiss in his halting yet highly stimulating manner as an intellectual experience.

In the many private conversations I had with Weiss, I enjoyed his humour and his sharp yet non-malicious judgements of people. These conversations also showed me his capacity for self-doubt, his anxieties about his capacities and achievements, his apprehensions about future calamities, and his inability to cope with the everyday problems imposed upon him by the fact of his marriage having broken down. He was unable to plan ahead, preferring rather to enjoy what the present moment was offering. I repeatedly discussed with him the possibility of his return to Israel, which, in view of his scholarly interest and expertise, would have been appropriate and, given the expansion of academe there, seemed likely to be offered to him. He had half a dozen answers why the opportunity would never arise and why, even if it did, he could not and would not be able to accept.

In point of fact, opportunities for his return did arise, as is obvious from Scholem's letters to Weiss. Scholem also regarded Weiss's return to Israel as a precondition for the full fruition of his talents, and thought of ways and means of realizing it. When the Hebrew University contemplated establishing a department of comparative religion in the 1950s, Scholem discussed with Weiss the possibility of his joining it. Later, in the early 1960s, Scholem entertained the idea of partial retirement and turning over some of his teaching duties to Weiss. With his retirement in 1965 approaching, he prepared a memorandum for the university authorities in which he named Weiss as one of the best candidates to succeed him. Weiss turned a deaf ear to all these suggestions, as well as to others from Bar-Ilan and Tel Aviv universities. The formal reason he gave was that he was capable of teaching hasidism only, while his appointment would require him to lecture on kabbalah in general or on the history of religion. But in view of Scholem's contrary opinion, Weiss's refusal must be regarded as merely a rationalization of his reluctance to extricate himself from his current predicament.

Subjectively, Weiss indeed saw his situation as one of extreme predicament, but objectively he had no reason to be discontent with his position. He had received his doctorate from University College in 1961 partly on Scholem's recommendation. He had consequently been appointed as a reader, and he had in 1967 become a full professor. His scholarly output, though always slow, was steady, and gained him a growing reputation among his peers. In 1964 he had been invited, again on Scholem's recommendation, to lecture at the yearly international meeting of the Eranos Conference on comparative religion in Ascona. He was a welcome guest at conferences on Jewish studies wherever these took place. In the meantime, his personal status, too, took a turn for the better with his second marriage, an occasion at which all his friends genuinely rejoiced.

The trouble was that Weiss gradually lost his capacity to evaluate his situation, replacing reality with the world of his imagination. It was a world full of threats to his academic status and even to his life. He wrote to Scholem, who did what he could to help him. On the basis of his correspondence with Scholem the process that led to his tragic end can be reconstructed, but the details are perhaps better left undisturbed in the archives. For his friends and admirers and those who are aware of his existence only through the mirror of his writings, it is proper to remember him as he was in his early days—the handsome man, beaming even when silent, and sparkling with wit and acumen whenever he spoke. *Yehi zikhro barukh*—may his memory be for a blessing.

TWO

Joseph Weiss: Letters to Ora

SARA ORA HELLER WILENSKY

To my son Uriel Joseph
with love

INTRODUCTION

I

THE twenty letters that Joseph Weiss sent to me in Cambridge, Massachusetts, over the years 1949 to 1968, published here for the first time in English translation,[1] offer an insight into Weiss's spiritual constitution and into the extraordinary friendship that developed between him and Professor Gershom Scholem, its vicissitudes notwithstanding.

The letters date back to the years when Weiss was an ardent student of Scholem's at the Hebrew University of Jerusalem and continue through the years he spent in England—in Leeds, Manchester, and Oxford, and finally in London, where he became a professor in the Department of Hebrew and Jewish Studies at University College London.

The letters are of value not only for the personal and biographical details they contain, but also because they contribute to a deeper understanding of Weiss's scholarly work, while at the same time enriching our knowledge of intellectual life in Jerusalem and in the Jewish academic community of the 1950s. Undoubtedly, however, their greatest importance is that they afford us a new perspective on Weiss's complex personality and add a unique and personal dimension to his scholarly bequest.

Joseph Weiss's letters are unusually frank. They speak of the changing circumstances of his life—his torments, deliberations, despair, fears, guilt, scepticism, disappointments, and changing moods; his poverty and alienation, particularly during his unsettled period in England in the early 1950s. There are hints of his ambivalence towards Diaspora Jews in England and towards the State of Israel, and we see his response, wounded and sarcastic, to the criticism of his bold new approach to the study of hasidism.

Professor Sara Ora Heller Wilensky was known as Ora in her youth in Jerusalem.

[1] The Hebrew originals were published as: 'Igrot Gershom Scholem veYosef Weiss el Orah', accompanied by a biographical essay entitled 'Gershom Scholem veYosef Weiss: Sipur yerushalmi', in N. Zach (ed.), *Igra: Almanakh lesifrut ve'omanut*, 3 (1990–1), 37–88.

But what Weiss's letters reveal most clearly is his life-long love for Scholem, and his anguish at the schism that divided them in the early 1950s. The complexity of the relationship echoes through the letters, even in apparently minor details. For example, Weiss generally refers to Scholem not by name but by a variety of other appellations—'Rabbenu Gershom', 'our master', 'our teacher' 'the teacher', and 'my teacher'. By contrast, Professor Julius Guttmann, whom Weiss respected and liked simply as a teacher, is fondly referred to throughout as *guttmannenu* ('our Guttmann').

Weiss's letters are written in a rich Hebrew, rooted in the language of his Jewish sources but marked by a mood of despondency. They are severely self-critical, self-deprecating, and even self-denigrating, with occasional flashes of wry humour and bitter irony.

I decided to publish the letters as a result of attending the conference whose proceedings this volume represents and meeting there Joseph Weiss's widow Erna and their son Amos. It was this that prompted me to make public a friendship that dated back to my Jerusalem days, and thereby to honour the memory of a cherished friend.

II

The friendship between Joseph Weiss and myself began in 1942, at the Hebrew University,when we both attended Gershom Scholem's seminar on the kabbalah of R. Moses Cordovero. Weiss was then a shy young man of 24, with blond hair, a pale complexion, light blue eyes, an upturned nose, and thin, sensitive lips. He spoke a flowery Hebrew with a Hungarian accent, his sentences long and tortuous and peppered with foreign words. He exuded the personal charm of a restless intellectual well versed in European literature and philosophy.

Scholem's seminars were held in the evenings at his home in Abarbanel Street in Reḥaviah. After the seminar—an intellectual treat for us all—Joseph would accompany me on foot to my home in Bar-Kokhba Street in Jerusalem's Mekor Barukh neighbourhood. We used to study Cordovero's *Pardes rimonim* together, trying to get to grips with the mystical symbolism and the philosophical implications of his pantheistic teaching and talking a great deal about 'our Rabbi Gershom'—*Rabbenu* Gershom, as Weiss called him—who aroused in both of us admiration and tremendous curiosity.

Much has been written about Gershom Scholem, and it is not my intention to reiterate here things that have already been said about his life, his works, or his ideas. Nevertheless, in order to dispel at least one of the myths that have proliferated around his personality, I should like to mention that he maintained a relationship of constant dialogue with his students. Scholem displayed an attitude of intense personal involvement, openness, and generosity towards this select group of ardent young scholars. He was understanding, affectionate, and attentive at all times. His home—a meeting place for Jerusalem's intellectuals—was always open to us, and his wife Fania used to invite us to join the frequent gatherings of friends that she arranged.

Scholem was generous with his time and treated us as friends. For example, on his birthday, which fell on 5 December and coincided with mine, we would exchange gifts. One year we gave him a box of chocolates (his proverbial sweet tooth was well known to us), and he gave me a copy of Joseph Gikatilla's *Sha'arei orah* (the Lemberg 1858 edition), a book that helped to open up for me the language and symbols of kabbalah. (Joseph Weiss, who was engrossed even at that time in existential philosophy, gave me Kierkegaard's *Fear and Trembling* in English translation and a dozen red roses.)

From time to time, Scholem used to walk with Joseph and me in the narrow streets of the Old City, to the *beit midrash* of the Beit-El kabbalists. On the way we would talk about his favourite writers (Kafka in particular), about new work on the history of mysticism, about his colleagues at the university (especially Martin Buber), and about current issues of the day. However, close relations such as these were possible only while his students remained fledglings nestling in his shadow. When they left the nest and tried to make their independent and distinctive mark in the world, or dared to differ from him and go their own way, the relationship became more complex, charged with dialectical tension, subject to 'ascents and descents', and interrupted by long periods in which the master would 'conceal his countenance' from them.

III

There is no need for me to provide here a biographical account of Joseph Weiss;[2] this is the subject of Jacob Katz's contribution to the present volume. Nevertheless, I should like to highlight a number of facts that are of particular relevance to these letters.

Joseph Weiss was born in Budapest, Hungary, on 10 August 1918. Joseph, or George as he was then known, was an only child, and his father died when he was 18 years old, having left home and abandoned his family long before. This left a strong mark on Joseph's sensitive personality. After completing his schooling at the Budapest gymnasium, he continued his studies at the rabbinical seminary in Budapest and the Department of Semitic Languages and Philosophy at Budapest University. He found himself intensely attracted to Jewish studies, and this spurred him to leave Hungary for Erets Yisrael in order to become involved in the movement for national spiritual revival. He arrived in 1940 and registered as a student at the Institute of Jewish Studies at the Hebrew University. His intention was to specialize in Hebrew literature, especially Hebrew poetry of the medieval period; but his encounter with Gershom Scholem and the world of kabbalah proved to be a decisive turning point in his life.

To me it seems that Joseph Weiss was totally captivated by Scholem's charms, and that his entire life from then on revolved around his great love for the man whom he considered his mentor, his spiritual father, and the 'root of his soul'. Fired by a longing for the father who had abandoned him, it was a love that knew no bounds: all-embracing, demanding, and requiring total attention. At times it was marked by outbursts of jealousy and terror at the slightest sign of rejection on the part of the teacher whom he regarded as a father-figure.

[2] See the obituaries published after Weiss's death: H. H. Ben-Sasson, 'Yosef Weiss, zal: An Obituary' (Heb.), *Zion*, 34 (1969), 261–4; G. Scholem, 'The Neutralization of the Messianic Element in Early Hasidism' (first delivered as a memorial lecture at the Institute of Jewish Studies, University College London), *Journal of Jewish Studies*, 20 (1969), 25–6, repr. in id., *The Messianic Idea in Judaism* (London, 1971), 176–202; S. Stein and R. Loewe, 'In Memoriam Joseph George Weiss', *Journal of Jewish Studies*, 20 (1969), 1–3.

Scholem, for his part, was particularly fond of Weiss and recognized his worth (he was to mark him out as his successor to the chair in kabbalah at Jerusalem). None the less, he treated Weiss with some restraint, and from time to time was either critical or ambivalent in his attitude to him. It may be that Scholem's restraint and reservations can be attributed to the trauma that he himself experienced at this time (1940) with the suicide of a much loved and admired friend, Walter Benjamin. Or it may have been that Scholem was put off by an awareness of Weiss's subconscious desire to adopt him as a loving father-figure, because his problems with his own father were unresolved, and he was unwilling to play the part.

Nevertheless, it must be noted that Scholem supported and helped Weiss in a variety of ways. From the letters we learn, for example, that it was thanks to Scholem's recommendation that Weiss received the prestigious Warburg Prize, which saved him from having to earn his living by working in the Schocken Library and allowed him to devote all his time to writing his doctorate on R. Nahman of Bratslav. But in 1950 ideological and methodological differences that had developed between them caused a crisis in their relationship. Scholem was extremely critical of the doctoral dissertation that Weiss had submitted and demanded significant changes. It seems that he regarded Weiss's existentialist and phenomenological approach as undermining his own historical-philological method. Indeed, Scholem's attitude to Weiss's work on hasidim was ambivalent: in his letter to me of 17 December 1952, he faulted Weiss for his unhistorical approach and for his tendency to overstate his case and overinterpret his sources. At the same time he praised his persuasive analytical insights and described his observations as original and remarkable:

> Mr Weiss, whose article on R. Naḥman you praise,[3] is extremely talented; I hope his endeavours turn out to be rewarding to us all. It seems to me, however, that his theories tend to be over-speculative (and I have struggled in vain to moderate his stylistic excesses). Now it seems that he is going from one extreme to the other, having abandoned existentialist philosophy only to discover other issues entirely, all equally interesting and equally doubtful. Read his article in the first issue of *Zion*, a major work on the beginnings of Hasidism in which he tries to prove a totally new theory, that Hasidism developed as a response to the 'professional problems' of a circle of failed preachers.[4] His idea is wonderful, and the analysis is both elegant and persuasive, but at the same time I cannot accept it. The truth is that the path I opened in the study of kabbalah by its very nature attracts others who are inclined to follow it far less cautiously than I have done, and though philological sense can be an excellent tool and is indispensable for the study of any mysticism, philological ingenuity can be a hindrance to success. Weiss's world is one in which chronology has no meaning and everything is stood on its head; it is precisely this that gives him a strange thrill and fills him with inexplicable pleasure. In any event I find what he has to say of great interest, even if the truth may be diametrically opposed to some of his arguments. [Hebrew original in *Igra*, 59–60.]

Weiss interpreted Scholem's critical remarks as a personal rejection, and it cut him to the core. One night, after a bitter and trenchant argument with Scholem, he decided to

[3] See 'Ha"kushiya" betorat R. Naḥman miBraslav', *Alei ayin: Minḥat devarim liShelomo Salman Schocken* (Jerusalem, 1948–52), 245–91.

[4] See J. Weiss, 'Reshit tsemiḥatah shel haderekh haḥasidit', *Zion*, 16 (1951), 46–105, repr. in A. Rubinstein (ed.), *Perakim betorat haḥasidut vetoledoteihah* (Jerusalem, 1977), 122–81.

cut his losses and leave the country. 'He stole from Jerusalem at the dead of night,' was how Scholem put it; 'I went without saying goodbye,' was Weiss's version. But from Weiss's letters to me it becomes apparent that a passion to go abroad to pursue the study of mysticism and comparative religion had taken hold of him long before, and that he had fought bitterly on this point with Scholem. According to Weiss, Scholem was offended by his desire to leave and tried to dissuade him. It seems that Weiss's desire to go abroad derived principally from his wish to free himself from the situation of 'total dependence' in which he felt that Scholem had placed him, and from his ambition to achieve self-determination and be 'a free man'. Spurred by these urges, he decided to purchase his freedom at any price, even at the cost of his doctorate. He remarks in his letter dated 8 January 1951:

> The relationship between disciple and master has been very discordant recently . . . but I stand firm on my right to self-definition as a free man . . . Time and distance may either heal the terrible rift between us or else lead to a total break . . . I shall do everything I can, short of abandoning my freedom, in order to allow Scholem to maintain a congenial relationship with me—something as essential to me, now as then, as the air itself.[5]

Weiss's doctoral dissertation, entitled 'The Dialectic Doctrine and Faith of Rabbi Nahman of Bratslav', was submitted to the Senate of the Hebrew University in December 1950. R. Nahman's doctrine of faith was discussed in four chapters from four different perspectives: epistemological, ontological, reflexive, and existentialist. In Gershom Scholem's letter of 14 March 1951 to the Hebrew University's Postgraduate Students Committee—an instructive letter in many respects—he praises the first three chapters as 'an important and *very original* [Scholem's emphasis] contribution to our understanding of R. Nahman's thought', but totally rejects the fourth chapter: 'I find the fourth chapter essentially without foundation . . . and I am absolutely unwilling to follow him on this.' Particularly pertinent are Scholem's concluding remarks:

> Since the author has left the country I see no way of discussing the matter with him personally, as the situation requires in order that the work be put right and meet with my approval. I am not prepared to conduct such a difficult discussion in writing . . . If Mr Weiss intends to stay abroad . . . I would recommend that the work be referred back to him. I do this with much regret and a sense of disappointment since I consider Mr Weiss to be a highly gifted man.

Why did Gershom Scholem reject the fourth (existentialist) chapter of Weiss's thesis and state that he was unwilling to 'follow him'? It seems that he considered Weiss's interpretation of R. Nahman's doctrine to be biased, in that he was reading the existentialist ideas of Kierkegaard and Heidegger into the text without finding any support for this in the Bratslav sources.[6] The 'original sin' of interpreting hasidic texts subjectively, for which Gershom Scholem never forgave Martin Buber,[7] surfaced here anew and

[5] Letter 5, below, p. 25. See also Letters 4 and 6.

[6] See Scholem's letter of 14 Mar. 1951 to the Postgraduate Students Committee at the Hebrew University and the comments he wrote in the margins of Weiss's doctoral dissertation, both of which are to be found in the Gershom Scholem Library at the Hebrew University of Jerusalem.

[7] See G. Scholem, 'Perusho shel Martin Buber laḥasidut', *Amot*, 1 (1962–3), 42–89; id., 'Martin Buber's Hasidism: A Critique', *Commentary*, 32 (1961), 305–16; id., 'Buber and Hasidism', *Commentary*, 33 (1962), 162–3.

aroused his strong opposition. Moreover, it is not impossible that Weiss's hasty departure from the country despite Scholem's objections had hurt Scholem's feelings badly. In any event, he decided to take a hard line and in his letter to the Postgraduate Students Committee dated 21 March 1951 he rejected Weiss's doctoral dissertation: 'After prolonged deliberation I have come to the conclusion that I cannot accept this work in its present form.' It was this that caused the 'rift', as Weiss termed it, between the two men.

IV

Weiss and his wife Miriam arrived in England in December 1950. Their first few years were unsettled; they moved from place to place—Leeds, Manchester, Oxford, and London. But altogether this was a period of many hardships for Weiss—problems of employment, of poverty, and of adapting to the strange environment; his wife's illness and eventual return to Israel, and finally their divorce; his depression, vacillation between religious faith and agnosticism, and problems of identity, loneliness, and alienation. But through all these difficulties, the main source of suffering he reported in his letters to me was the 'rift' or 'disastrous relations' between him and 'Rabbenu Gershom'. He blamed himself, and only himself, for the 'whole crazy affair'; he had betrayed his teacher and broken the bonds of discipleship: 'After all, I am one of the university's more stubborn and rebellious sons', he wrote with bitter irony (Letter 5, 8 January 1951). But his chief fear was that the relationship between them would come to a 'total break'; Scholem was as essential to him 'as the air itself'. When he learnt that Scholem had recommended him for a scholarship to the Jewish Theological Seminary in New York he was truly overjoyed, not so much at the news of the scholarship as at the knowledge that, in spite of his misconduct, Scholem was still behind him. He described his mixed feelings as 'joy at his goodness, and sorrow at my own wickedness' (Letter 6, 13 March 1951).

Weiss's concern for Scholem could be touching. For example, in the condition of economic austerity that prevailed in Israel at that time, he feared that Scholem might be short of food and suggested discreetly that I should send food parcels to our teacher. In a different vein, since he was aware of my own correspondence with Scholem, Weiss made a point of asking from time to time that I should spare Scholem all knowledge of his inner doubts, his equivocations, and his suspicions.

In his early letters, Weiss expresses reservations about the complacent Jewish community of England, to which any ideas of kabbalah and hasidism are totally alien, and he complains of the noise and bustle of London ('the damned city', as he refers to it). Disappointed by his experiences in England, lonely, and alienated, he writes occasionally of his longing to return 'home', that is, to Jerusalem.

It seems that Weiss 'sentenced himself' to years of exile in the Diaspora as a penance; he even signed one of his letters 'A Friend in Exile' (Letter 5, 8 January 1951). In his later letters, however, he claimed that his geographical exile expressed his existential exile: 'my place in international society is on the periphery—that's where I feel I belong' (Letter 16, 14 January 1957).

His only friend in England at that time was the Orientalist Samuel M. Stern, a fellow native of Budapest who was living in Oxford and who was to become world-famous as a scholar of Islamic culture. The strong link that had bound them together since their youth in Budapest had been forged into a lifelong friendship in Jerusalem, in the years when both were studying at the Hebrew University and Stern was a member of our circle in Jerusalem.[8] Weiss gives a sarcastic account of how Stern's application for employment at the Hebrew University went unanswered, prophesying that the day would come when the university would find itself knocking in vain on Stern's door (see Letter 11). Little did he know how true his prophecy would turn out to be. Similarly, his ironic remarks on the appointments procedure at the Hebrew University are very telling of the way the university was run in those days (see Letter 4).

Weiss wanted very much to continue his studies in Oxford but was unable to do so for lack of means. In 1954 he was appointed to a teaching position in the Department of Hebrew (later Hebrew and Jewish Studies) at University College London, but even in London he continued to be preoccupied with 'Rabbenu Gershom', ever awaiting from afar the slightest sign of recognition and approval from him.

Scholem spent the summer of 1954 at the Warburg Institute in London and the rift between them mended during this time.[9] At Scholem's recommendation Weiss was invited to attend an international conference on the study of religion which was held in Marburg (1959). There he met Erna, who converted to Judaism and became his second wife and the mother of his only child, Amos. Again at Scholem's recommendation, Weiss was awarded a Ph.D. by the University of London (1961) and was invited to lecture at the Eranos Conference in Ascona (1963).

At long last, Weiss was beginning to enjoy academic recognition and esteem. He became director of the Institute of Jewish Studies at University College London, editor of the prestigious *Journal of Jewish Studies*, and in 1966 he was appointed full professor at University College. When Gershom Scholem retired from the Hebrew University in 1966, he recommended to the Senate of the University that they invite Joseph Weiss to take his place as Professor of Kabbalah. Weiss had meanwhile (1962) given a series of guest lectures in Jerusalem on Bratslav hasidism, and the lectures had drawn large and enthusiastic audiences and had considerable impact. At Scholem's recommendation, then, the dean of the Faculty of Humanities at the Hebrew University came to meet Weiss in London and offered him Scholem's position at the university. He met with a firm refusal.[10]

I remember my last meeting with Joseph Weiss, during the World Congress of Jewish Studies in Jerusalem in August 1965. It was late at night, and we were walking through the painfully familiar streets of Reḥaviah—Ben-Maimon Boulevard, Rashba, Ramban, Ibn Shaprut, and Abarbanel. Weiss, somewhat depressed, talked about the many 'enemies' who he felt were out to get him, and about his loneliness in London. I told him of my plan to go back to Israel for good and of my longing for Jerusalem. He tried to dissuade me from my plan, declaring perhaps only half in jest, that a life of

[8] Stern dedicated his book *Les Chansons mozarabes* (Palermo, 1956; Oxford, 1964) to his friend Joseph Weiss. On the friendship between them, see A. M. Habermann, 'Shenei talmidei ḥakhamim shehalekhu le'olamam', in id., *Anshei sefer ve'anshei ma'aseh* (Jerusalem, 1974), 206–9.

[9] According to Scholem in a letter to me from London dated 28 July 1954.

[10] According to Prof. J. Prawer, then dean of the faculty.

alienation in the Diaspora was more appropriate for the intellectual than a 'normal' life in Israel. Suddenly, as if out of nowhere, Gershom Scholem himself appeared in our path and gazed at us in surprise. The three of us continued to walk together in an embarrassed silence. It was the last time we would do so.

In the later years of Weiss's life his health began to fail. His last letter to me was written in July 1968, when his condition was poor. He congratulated me on the bar-mitzvah of my son, Uriel Joseph, and tried to recapture distant memories of my wedding in Jerusalem which he had attended together with Gershom Scholem. He expressed the hope that we would meet at the Congress in Jerusalem in the summer of 1969—'if the Lord decrees that I live till then'. But in the end he himself decreed that he should not: on 25 August 1969, aged 51, he killed himself. I was at that time on the high seas, on a passenger vessel from Boston to Haifa that was carrying me back home after an absence of more than twenty years. On my return to Israel I learned the bitter news of Joseph Weiss's suicide from Gershom Scholem.

Weiss's suicide hurt Scholem very badly. Shortly before his death Weiss had sent an emotional letter to 'Rabbenu Gershom'—in retrospect, a farewell letter—in which he confessed his love for him: 'I love you with every fibre of my sick soul.'[11] At a memorial lecture for Weiss that was held in London, Scholem delivered a moving eulogy:

> I considered him in many ways the closest of my pupils, and the dialogue between us, a dialogue in the true sense of a term so much abused nowadays, went on for nearly thirty years.[12]

Gershom Scholem took upon himself the responsibility for preserving Weiss's scholarly legacy. He transferred Weiss's unpublished manuscripts to Jerusalem, and, thanks to his efforts and dedication to the task, an edition of Weiss's collected writings on Bratslav hasidism was published posthumously, including some previously unpublished material.[13] The remainder of his works on hasidism were published in English in the Littman Library by Oxford University Press, edited by David Goldstein.[14]

V

It is not my intention to attempt here an appreciation of Weiss's scholarly contribution to the study of hasidism, a task for which I do not feel qualified. However, I should like to comment briefly on the principles and methodology underlying his interpretation of Bratslav hasidism, as these shed light above all on his own personality and his faith.

The character of R. Nahman of Bratslav, the 'paradoxical zaddik' who 'stands on the boundary', fascinated Joseph Weiss right from the start of his scholarly career; this is clear both from his first book, *Ma'aglei si'aḥ*,[15] and from his personal association with Bratslav hasidism in Jerusalem. Weiss considered R. Nahman to be the forerunner of that trend of thought which modern philosophy has termed religious existentialism. In

[11] According to Fania Scholem.

[12] See Scholem, 'Neutralization of the Messianic Element', 25.

[13] See J. G. Weiss, *Meḥkarim bahasidut Braslav*, ed. M. Piekarz (Jerusalem, 1974).

[14] Id., *Studies in Eastern European Jewish Mysticism* (Oxford, 1985).

[15] See id., *Ma'aglei si'aḥ: Leket siḥot vehanhagot shel R. Naḥman miBraslav* (Tel Aviv, 1947).

his opinion, the key concern in Bratslav thinking was the question of ascertaining religious faith: from what does man derive the certainty of his faith? According to Weiss, R. Nahman was aware of all the rational reasons why not to believe, and claimed that these must be overcome by means of an existential decision—the product of free will. Weiss claimed that the 'paradoxical faith' of R. Nahman 'derived from the dialectical contradiction between faith and reason'.[16] Accordingly, faith is man's confrontation of the denial of faith by reason with his own 'existential resistance to this denial'—a resistance which amounts to 'metaphysical stubbornness, to believe in spite of the obvious'. Weiss argues that R. Nahman's paradoxical faith is faith born of freedom, since it is man's stand on the confrontation between faith and reason that earns him the status of freedom. It was this existentialist, Kierkegaardian interpretation of R. Nahman's perception of faith, with which Weiss himself clearly identified, that led to the criticism from many quarters that Weiss's interpretation was subjective.

Weiss's interpretation was based on a methodological assumption which underlay his approach to the whole of Bratslav thought: R. Nahman's teachings cannot be separated from his autobiography since, as all the Bratslav homilies and tales revolve around the central figure of R. Nahman himself, 'there is not a single word in all the tales which does not refer to the character of the man, Nahman of Bratslav'.[17] For Weiss, this methodological assumption is also the key to the speculative teachings of Bratslav, which he considered to be a 'mythological autobiography'. R. Nahman's teachings, he wrote, 'revolve around his personal experience—his entire work is but an interpretation of his life, of his mythological autobiography. As we know, there is not a single word, either in the tales or in *Likutei Moharan* and the rest of the Bratslav literature, that does not refer to R. Nahman himself.'[18]

Weiss identified with R. Nahman the 'paradoxical zaddik' and with his existentialist faith. He saw in R. Nahman a reflection of his own soul and of the agitations of his own spiritual life. R. Nahman's afflictions of the soul, his 'falls' (sins), his cycles of 'ascent and descent', his fear of sinking into 'the darkness of insanity', his identity problem, and the laws governing the dialectical tension between faith and heresy, asceticism and sensuality, were for Weiss a reflection of the conflicts in his own soul. Recasting Weiss's own words, one might almost say that there is not a single idea of R. Nahman of Bratslav which cannot be construed as referring to Joseph Weiss.[19]

Weiss's essays on Bratslav hasidism are marked by evident literary ability, originality, and interpretative prowess. They reveal his penetrating psychological discernment, often reinforced by psychoanalytical insight. Furthermore, they uncover the affinity between Bratslav thought and modern intellectual concerns. Weiss laid the foundations for the phenomenological approach to the study of hasidism, and his existentialist reading of the Bratslav texts has served as the basis for much of the subsequent research on R. Nahman of Bratslav.

[16] Weiss, 'Ha"kushiya"', 109–49.

[17] Id., 'Iyunim bitefisato ha'atsmit shel R. Naḥman miBraslav', in id., *Meḥkarim*, 152. (Originally published in *Tarbiz*, 27 (1958)—an issue dedicated to Gershom Scholem on his 60th birthday.)

[18] Id., 'Ko'aḥ hamoshekh shel hagevul', in id., *Meḥkarim*, 108.

[19] Weiss's identification with R. Nahman aroused considerable criticism—see e.g. M. Piekarz, *Ḥasidut Braslav* (Jerusalem, 1972), 9–10.

VI

In the following pages, Joseph Weiss's twenty letters to me appear in chronological order. They have been reproduced in full, except that in rare instances I have deleted a name or a sentence where I thought it necessary to protect someone who is still living; such omissions have been marked by [. . .]. I have added notes where names or other details alluded to in the text seemed to require clarification.

I would like to express my thanks to Dr Ada Rapoport-Albert for her valuable suggestions and numerous bibliographical notes.

This introduction was completed in Jerusalem on 25 August 1989, twenty years to the day since Joseph Weiss died. May his memory be blessed.

THE LETTERS

I

Jerusalem, 21 Ḥeshvan 5550
13 November 1949

Dearest Ora,

Attack is the best defence—isn't that so, Ora? Your attack on the silence from my end is thus all too easy to explain. But custom has it that the one who travels is the one who writes, and he who knows, knows, and this is how it should be.

I see from your letter with great satisfaction, however, that all the scandal and gossip has reached you—admittedly with some delay, but the fact that you heard it from the best of all raconteurs is surely some compensation! Of gossip-mongers such as these it is said, they set their mouth in America, and their tongue walketh through the Holy Land.

But to get on with the things that matter: I am close (???) to finishing my doctorate, the subject of my thesis being the authentic texts of the Baal Shem Tov.[20] In October I was awarded a two-year Warburg scholarship, and the chances are good that it will be extended to five years. Having resigned from the Schocken Library (which is why your letter took some time to reach me),[21] I no longer have to get up early to 'enter the gates of the nobles', which is in itself a blessing.

My own writing is in a sorry state. Of all the things I am working on only one small piece has been published, and that I sent you a few days ago. The others—including the material that Dr Glatzer saw in New York[22]—lie around gathering dust, and I have almost given up hope of ever getting them published.

Miriam passed the second paper of her final exams the day before yesterday, and I hope that she will pass the third within the year.[23] She's with her parents in Tel Aviv at the moment, recovering from the exhausting business of revision.

That's the news from our end. I'm hungry for the slightest crumb of information about you and your work. I didn't manage to get anything at all out of your sister on this; she has always avoided giving straight answers. In any event, your address is most awe-inspiring! Is Harvard College attached to Harvard University? Is there any truth in the rumour that once reached me to the effect that you are writing your doctorate under Professor Wolfson?[24] What's it on?

I finish with a request. Our teacher[25] submitted an article on *devekut* in hasidism (in fact, a chapter from his new book) to one of the American periodicals—I've forgotten which, although I think it's published by Columbia University.[26] It should have been

Letters translated by Connie Webber and Ada Rapoport-Albert.

[20] The original title suggested by Gershom Scholem, later changed at Weiss's request.

[21] For a period of some two years Weiss was employed by Salman Schocken as a Research Assistant to H. Brody at the Schocken Institute Library.

[22] Nahum Glatzer, who was at that time an editorial adviser to Schocken Books in New York.

[23] Miriam Wiener, Weiss's first wife. She was a student of Jewish philosophy and kabbalah at the Hebrew University.

[24] Harry Austryn Wolfson, Professor of Hebrew Literature and Philosophy at Harvard University.

[25] The references to 'Our Teacher' and 'R. Gershom' or 'Rabbenu Gershom' are to Gershom Scholem.

[26] This was 'Devekut, or Communion with God', first pub. in the *Review of Religion*, 14 (1949–50), 115–39, and subsequently repr. in Scholem, *The Messianic Idea*, 203–27.

published in the October issue but hasn't reached here yet. As you have easy access to scholarly periodicals, please do me the favour of looking it up in your library and sending it to me as soon as possible; and may the Lord bless you for so doing.

Write and you'll be written to!

Yours, in earnest quest of friendship and collegiality,
Joseph

2

Jerusalem, 15 March 1950

Dear Ora,

I'm writing in what for me are troubled times, so I won't write much. When things are easier, I promise I'll write again—even without waiting for your reply, should it be late in coming. My relations with our teacher have become extremely paradoxical, and I am trying hard to avoid a public explosion.*

In the meantime the *Review of Religion* has arrived, the January 1950 issue (14; 2), with the article I mentioned in my last letter. I don't know how easy it will be for you to get hold of it (I fear that single issues are not available for purchase), but if you can't, please take it upon yourself to make a photocopy of the article; I've heard that this is not as expensive in America as it is here.

I have a second request for you too: an article by my friend Dr Taubes appeared in Paul Weiss's *Journal of Metaphysics*,[27] in one of the issues that came out last summer. If you could send me a copy of the issue I would be most grateful, but on no account should you make a photocopy of the article—it's not sufficiently important to me to warrant that. Have you received my pamphlet on courtly culture?[28] I shall soon be sending you the paper I gave at the [Hebrew] University's Congress of Jewish Studies three years ago, which I am publishing in honour of our Guttmann's 70th birthday.[29] On 15 April Guttmann will be 70, Ora! He's been very ill for months—had several operations. They've sent him home from hospital now, but there's been no improvement. He would certainly be *very* happy to get a letter of congratulations from you for his 70th birthday! Overcome your laziness and surprise him with a nice letter! Here we're getting ready to lecture (what else?) in his honour—a series of lectures to be held at the university, with me your humble servant among the fortunates invited to speak. Some three months have gone by since I received the invitation from the Jubilee Committee, but I haven't given them an answer yet. I have some doubts about the project as a whole, and may not lecture after all—writing in the Festschrift should be enough to cover my debt to Guttmann. But perhaps I'm wrong [. . .][30]

The Bialik Institute has now commissioned a similar work from me in three volumes, *Mishnat ḥasidim* (The teaching of hasidism). Luckily for me, Scholem has never taught hasidism, except for his lectures in America a year ago, which are to be pub-

[27] Jacob Taubes, who subsequently became Professor of Jewish Studies and the Sociology of Religion at the Free University in West Berlin.

[28] Joseph Weiss, *Tarbut ḥatsranit veshirah ḥatsranit* (Jerusalem, 1947).

[29] Professor Yizhak Julius Guttmann. The lecture was entitled 'Ḥasidut shel mistikah vaḥasidut shel emunah'. It appeared in Hebrew in 1953, and a revised English version, 'Contemplative Mysticism and "Faith" in Hasidic Piety', appeared in the *Journal of Jewish Studies*, 4: 1 (1953), repr. in id., *Eastern European Jewish Mysticism*.

[30] One sentence in the original letter is omitted here.

lished in book form. What I learn from his book I'll be able to cite, but I'm delighted that there's no heritage of 'oral law' from him that I might have been tempted to use as the basis for my book. Instead it will be set in a typological mould (which you will be able to see from my paper in honour of Guttmann, as mentioned above).

Well, I'm very busy; 'the Holy Spirit had hardly departed when they said that the Divine Presence would only rest where there is joy', etc. [Shab. 30*b*]. This is a condition which I have not fulfilled yet, by force of circumstance no less than by choice.

Be well,
Joseph

Miriam asks after you. She's coming back from Tel Aviv today *by train*; there are trains again between Tel Aviv and Jerusalem!

*NB. Don't mention this comment of mine in your letter to him.

3

[*Jerusalem*], *Erev Shavuot 5710* [*1950*]

Dear Ora,

When Miriam and I left the day before yesterday to celebrate the Shavuot holiday in Tel Aviv, I took your last letter with me with the intention of answering all your questions about Professor Guttmann's condition. If I had moved myself to write the same day, as I had originally planned, my report would have been of no value, for yesterday, while we were in Tel Aviv, we heard on the radio that he had taken his last breath. I therefore cut short my stay in Tel Aviv and rushed to Jerusalem to pay my final respects. He was buried this afternoon, and I pen these lines still under the spell of the funeral.

These last weeks, the doctors had given up hope that Guttmann would regain his former strength. Some ten weeks ago, Guttmann himself told one of us that his illness 'had entered its final stage'. So he knew. Last week he was barely conscious much of the time, and only rarely fully conscious and awake. He passed away on Friday night, before dawn of the 4th of Iyar. Today we buried him in the new cemetery in Sanhedria; the Mount of Olives is in Arab hands, so for the last two years burials have taken place within the city proper.

Mrs Guttmann was very brave—but then, she's known for several weeks now that no human intervention could save him.

Miriam and I became closer to him only after we finished his course; Miriam in particular was a regular visitor at their home, and he for his part was very fond of her. (Even so, I left Miriam behind in Tel Aviv; I thought it would be easier for her not to take part in the funeral of one so dear to her.)

When you lecture to your students in Boston on Jewish philosophy you will doubtless recall that your first introduction to the subject came from him; it is to be hoped that the foundations he laid have not been completely lost under Wolfson's influence.

You ask my opinion of Wolfson: I have no *opinion* of him because I have read only a few of his books, but I do have an attitude towards him. He is a Spinozan idealist through and through, a believer in the ultimate harmony of the world—one of those towering giants from the last generation at whose harmonious spiritual world the young can only wonder.

Best wishes, Yours
Joseph

Miriam sends warm regards.

4

Jerusalem, 6 November 1950

Hello dear Ora,

You asked a lot of questions in your letter, and from your questions it is clear that the paths of Jerusalem are still as familiar to you as the streets of Boston. And particularly the paths of the University! We are still cut off from the library on Mount Scopus, and this of course has implications in every area: a slow but steady decline (sometimes it seems a fast but steady decline) in the spiritual and political standard of living.

Several names have indeed been put forward to take the place of our teacher Guttmann of blessed memory. Wolfson, it seems, was not approached at all, on account of his age and his ideas. However, the chair has been offered throughout the Diaspora, and many potential candidates have been wooed. They seem particularly keen to have someone from abroad. A year ago (Guttmann was to have retired in 1951) they offered it to Professor Leo Strauss,[31] who has written several ingenious papers on medieval philosophy (Maimonides, Judah Halevi), but he refused to come. The chair was then offered to Professor [George] Vajda of Paris, but he too turned it down. It was not offered to Efros,[32] whom you mentioned in your letter, because he came here and indicated that he would be willing to take up the post—and that rules him out completely (although, in truth, one should add to the above fault that the guest lecture he gave here was extremely weak). Simon Rawidowicz's name was put forward, but it is expected here that he would decline—rumour has it that he has been appointed Professor of Hebrew Literature at Brandeis University. It seems that in the end they will appoint Dr Altmann,[33] an orthodox rabbi from Manchester in England. Since he is a rabbi, and since moreover he was here and hinted at his willingness to come—two black marks against him—he would be considered only as a candidate of last resort. Professor Heinemann, who has been living in Jerusalem for the past fifteen years, was ignored as if he were as invisible as the air itself. Consideration was also given to the merits of Dr Pines, an important but somewhat retiring scholar who has written some extremely valuable and perceptive essays on medieval philosophy (Arabic and Jewish); the content of his guest lecture was indeed superb, but his delivery was such a total disaster that his name was struck off the list of candidates. The same pattern repeats itself every time someone retires—this year Buber and Epstein retire from teaching, and

[31] Leo Strauss had been appointed to the Chair of Political Science at the University of Chicago in the previous year.

[32] Israel Efros, who was the Professor of Jewish Philosophy and Modern Hebrew Literature at Dropsie College, Philadelphia.

[33] Alexander Altmann, who later founded the Institute of Jewish Studies in Manchester. The Institute was transferred to London in 1959, with Altmann's appointment to a chair at Brandeis University in the USA, and Joseph Weiss became its Director at University College London.

there's no one to replace them. Bringing in some of the younger people who were trained here (those you mentioned in your letter) is not only a question of helping the individuals concerned but a vital and unavoidable need. And you don't have to worry yourself wondering whether my turn will come too—I am not in the habit of paying my respects by calling on the inner circle of professors on every sabbath and festival, and appointments depend chiefly on this. Yesterday, however, I received a hint from R. Gershom (with whom my relations have improved recently since I finished my doctorate) that in another few years a Department for the Study of Religion will be established, that the university may perhaps be interested in the services of Dr Weiss, and so on—although I don't hold out much hope after what I have seen of the appointments business. At this point I am interested not in general promises for the future, but in a framework that would allow me to go abroad for further study. Scholem wants me to spend another year in Jerusalem, arguing with him over every letter of my wretched thesis. I, however, would prefer to travel before I get the degree, and I may well do so at my own expense—and despite his opposition.

I was delighted to hear (from you and from highly reliable sources) that you are going from strength to strength. Here there have been some rumours about [Ora] Wilensky and Brandeis University—are these premature, perhaps?

I recently came across a German periodical, *Zeitschrift für Religions und Geistesgeschichte*, 1, 1 (Marburg, 1948), with an article by the strange Jewish scholar Schoeps on philosemitism in the seventeenth century.[34] From page 31 on it describes the pre-Adamite theories which, as far as I can recall, were mentioned in Wilensky's Ph.D. thesis.[35] I am citing the above in case he would like to see a new approach to a problem he once dealt with, however marginally.

By the time I hear from you it's more than likely that we shall already be in Europe. We'll probably work as teachers in a town in England somewhere, and we hope to spend a little while in Paris first. My address in the coming months will therefore be: J. Weiss, c/o I. Wiener, 110 rue de Rennes, Paris 6. I simply said to myself, 'Bow down, that we may go over' [Isa. 51: 23]—even if it costs me my Ph.D.!

With warm regards from Miriam and me,
Joseph

5

Leeds, 8 January 1951

Dear Ora,

Your letter of 27 January was like water to a dying man! From this you may infer that there are still dear friends whose letters inspire me to recite the Benediction on Deliverance. I am deeply grateful for what you wrote and for your interest in my fate. I shall therefore answer your questions one by one, and in order.

Over the last two months I have received letters from all corners of the world (New York, Boston, Jerusalem) from friends who had heard that the Schechter Institute has decided to award me a prize (or a prize of sorts, for it seems that the conditions of the prize include my having to give some hours of instruction at the teachers' seminary).[36] But while my friends congratulated me (those in New York also asked whether I

[34] Hans Joachim Schoeps, who taught religious and intellectual history at the University of Erlangen.
[35] Mordecai Wilensky, my husband, then Professor of Jewish History at Hebrew College, Boston.
[36] The Jewish Theological Seminary in New York.

wanted them to arrange somewhere for me to stay, and so on) I, the recipient of the prize, knew nothing about it whatsoever. To put you in the picture, the formal communication of the Schechter decision was conveyed through the [Hebrew] University (seemingly in November, when I was already in Leeds), and more precisely through the professor under whom I wrote my doctoral dissertation. I do not know the details of the negotiations between Scholem and the Schechter Institute, but the fact is that I have not yet received the slightest official indication, either from Jerusalem or from New York, and there are grounds for my supposition—almost certainly justified—that the decision has been revoked, suspended, or consumed in the ceremonial burning of leaven in the Lurianic kabbalistic sense. My senses have sharpened in recent years (Aharon Street isn't far from Abarbanel Street),[37] and I generally don't make mistakes in such matters. After all, I am one of the university's more stubborn and rebellious sons, and a traitor to my teacher . . . The relationship between disciple and master has been very discordant recently: the former has begged the latter for five years now to send him abroad to study, and the request was taken as a personal insult. That's the general background to a thousand intricacies which neither time nor space permit me to go into. My prime guilt, I am convinced, is that I do not accord our teacher the reverence due (because I seek to learn from others too); things are pretty bad. You know all too well and can attest to my regard for him (a regard that has remained basically unchanged in the five years since you and I saw each other), but I stand firm on my right to self-definition as a free man. He demands that his students give him total subservience; admittedly he rewards this subservience well, but I cannot render this service, not even for this reward.

After a long period of indecision with the pendulum swinging this way and that, I saw no alternative but to take the question of studying abroad into my own hands and accepted the first offer that chanced my way. Leaving Jerusalem offers promises and risks. Time and distance may either heal the terrible rift between us or else lead to a total break. The Lord will have mercy. I shall do everything I can, short of abandoning my freedom, in order to allow Scholem to maintain a congenial relationship with me—something as essential to me, now as then, as the air itself. I finished my doctorate before I left and submitted it to the university (on the dialectical teaching of R. Nahman of Bratslav), but of course it hasn't yet been approved (although I've heard rumours from Jerusalem that Scholem's initial reaction was that it was the best thesis ever written in kabbalah). My instincts tell me that the approval of my doctorate will not go smoothly, but time will tell.

Warmest congratulations to you, Ora, on your own doctoral dissertation—it's finished, then! Well done. I very much hope you won't forget me when you send copies to your friends. When is that likely to be?

The volume in Guttmann's memory, if it ever comes out, will include a series of lectures given by his students (and other, younger scholars who were not directly his students) in celebration of his birthday. I am one of the contributors, but at the time of my departure from Jerusalem the entire project seemed uncertain . . . In any event, Wolfson's involvement in this project is totally out of the question.

You ask about my work at Leeds University: in fact, my work and the University of Leeds are totally removed from each other! I was hired from Jerusalem simply to be a teacher of beginners at the Talmud Torah of the Leeds Jewish congregation. I teach

[37] Both are in the Reḥaviah quarter of Jerusalem. Scholem lived in Abarbanel Street and Weiss in Aharon Street (now Haran Street).

the Hebrew alphabet, a few pieces of liturgy from the *siddur*, and a few verses from the Pentateuch. My pupils are children aged 5 to 11. Because of a number of disappointments I have had here, as regards both the hours of work and the pay, it is virtually impossible for me to think about continuing in Religious Studies here; and moreover the standard of the university here is very low—say, like the Hebrew University will be in ten years' time. However, in the little spare time I have, I continue with my academic activities, working on my book *Mishnat ḥasidim* (which I have already mentioned to you),[38] but it will be very difficult for me to honour my commitment to the Bialik Institute as regards the timetable for submitting the manuscript.

Miriam accompanied me on my journey to England and is now teaching with me in the same institution. She also signed up for some courses at the university, in contemporary English literature. I've also been to a few lectures, not so much for the lectures themselves but more to speed up my acquisition of skills in English. We realized very quickly that Leeds isn't for us: neither the university nor its library are what I would choose by preference. The institution we work in isn't what we hoped for either. We shall try to move to London as soon as possible, perhaps even during the present academic year.

As to next year, I don't have any definite plans. Much depends on how R. Gershom reacts to my thesis, which has yet to be approved. You're lucky, Ora, that you can choose freely between the many opportunities that are open to you. My own position is quite different: I would be happy with more modest offers than any you have received. Perhaps you may get wind of (or dare I say it, please make it your business to look out for) some small job in the great United States that would be more congenial for me than teaching in the Leeds Talmud Torah. Of course, I don't yet have my doctorate (and may not for a long time yet), but my head does bear the crown of an MA in Jewish history from the Hebrew University. Perhaps there's a vacancy in one of the teachers' seminaries? I can't commit myself in the first instance to more than a year, though. The Schechter Institute would of course have been ideal, the best and most convenient way to get a taste of America—perhaps even an opportunity to further my studies and have access to a decent library. But the idea was put under wraps even before it saw the light of day. (Please do me the favour of keeping this request of mine from R. Gershom's ears—in fact, it's better that he should know nothing at all of our correspondence.)

And finally: my mother has told me about your gift of a packet of coffee, which arrived after we had left for England, and said that she was keeping it for us till we got back. Many thanks, Ora, for the coffee itself, but doubly so for your concern for us.

Pass on my regards to Mordecai, and write as soon as you can to a friend in exile—

Joseph

Dear Ora,

Please accept my congratulations, too, on finishing your thesis, as well as my warmest regards. In future I'll mend my ways and write more.

Miriam

[38] See above, Letter 2.

6

Leeds, 13 March 1951

Dear Ora,

I received your letter only yesterday but am replying immediately, spurred to action by a mixture of sorrow and joy, to correct the mistake I made in my last letter in accusing R. Gershom of holding up the Schechter invitation. A few days ago I received the official letter from them inviting me to come for two years—'on the recommendation of Professor Scholem' . . . Imagine how thrilled I was, not at the prospect of New York (my stay in England has taught me not to expect too much of being abroad), but at being wrong about Scholem. He hadn't spoiled my chances, *even after my spiteful departure* without taking leave of him! On the contrary—he helped me yet again. (A thought passes through my mind: maybe he helped me in order to rid himself of me once and for all?) But as I say, my joy is mingled with sorrow—joy at his goodness, and sorrow at my own wickedness. Now I must write to him—and I keep putting it off, for it is seven times more difficult than writing to you. I might have got to the bottom of this crazy affair if we could talk about it face to face, but by letter it's impossible. Of course the gossip-mongers of Jerusalem continue to pursue their calling, despite my being far away—and there are of course those who even now prefer there to be a rift between us, just as they did when I was still in Jerusalem, and they tell me all sorts of stories about what R. Gershom did when the Schechter business came up last year with the arrival of Dr Davis in Jerusalem.[39] And as we know, slander is always the mirror-image of the truth! How many misunderstandings have arisen as a result of malicious tale-bearers, and how many are simply based on false deductions from the truth? And how can it all be put to rights? I still don't know exactly what his attitude is— perhaps his support for the Schechter proposal says nothing about his overall attitude to me? Questions, questions, questions . . .

The first priority, however, is for us to go back as soon as possible (and this for several reasons),[40] even sooner than I had originally thought—I hope to be back at home [in Jerusalem] between Pesach and Shavuot. My frame of mind on returning will be completely different from what it was when I left. Miriam suffers very much from the cold climes of these parts, and my own enthusiasm for being abroad has abated so much that my very acceptance of the scholarship is now in question. The Schechter scholarship will enable me to study in comfort for a couple of years, but I doubt that I'll learn anything new in America. I feel myself a little too old to learn anything new. The years pass, and even if they don't finish us entirely, they leave their mark. Perhaps it would be better if I didn't go to New York at all, but stayed in Jerusalem—albeit in less comfortable conditions—and concentrated on my work. After all, Miriam won't go to New York with me, and what will I do on my own in America? I'm not really interested in the adventures that a new country has in store—my experience in England was quite enough. I was astonished, however, to read in your letter that Miriam could earn $3,500 a year, but even that doesn't really warrant serious consideration at the present time.

If I didn't shrink from paradoxical formulations, I would say that it was precisely my stay in England and the possibility of going to the United States that have enabled me to feel so certain about the return home. Be that as it may, I'll answer Schechter in the

[39] Moshe Davis, who was then Provost of the Jewish Theological Seminary in New York.

[40] The main reason may well have been his wife's illness, which began at this time in Leeds.

affirmative so as not to slam the door in my own face (and don't spoil my chances by spreading the news of my prevarications in America). Perhaps in the end I'll go just for a year; that would also be something. As the sages have already said, one should always aim to end on a positive note; at which point I end this hasty letter.

In friendship,
Joseph

7

London, 15 Elul 5711
[*September 1951*]

Dear Ora!

The troubles we had in Leeds—some the work of God and others of man's doing—left me dumbstruck. We managed to leave Leeds in the early summer and are now in London, our suitcases packed, half prepared to sail home and half prepared to spend another year in England.

For a variety of reasons I have had to forgo my trip to the States, so our meeting in the autumn in America, Ora, is not to be. But there is indeed a possibility that we shall stay here for a year, in London or in Oxford; we'll know in another few weeks. We'd already given the shippers almost all our things when I was informed that the Hebrew University would award me a scholarship to stay in England (R. Gershom working behind the scenes). Meanwhile, the factors affecting the decision whether to return immediately or to stay another year have become so complicated that I can't accept the university's offer immediately, but I hope I won't have to forgo yet another chance to spend some time in libraries and universities. If we stay, it could well be more worthwhile to go to Oxford, and there of course I would get to know a university of a type completely different from anything I've ever seen before.

The stupid way in which I left Jerusalem seems to have antagonized everyone. R. Gershom may have forgiven me, but probably not completely. As with his support for me at the Schechter Institute last year, his support for my candidacy for the present scholarship doesn't really say much in this regard. By the way, I've just heard that he was very ill last month, and that although he is better now he is not completely better yet. I think that the food crisis in Israel is very bad for his recovery: it's having a bad enough effect on people who are healthy. I am of the opinion that those of his students who are overseas must take steps to ensure that his table lacks nothing. Perhaps you can help too? I should say, though, that I am reluctant to take the responsibility for encouraging you to send him food parcels, for who knows how he'll react?

What are you doing at the moment, Ora, and what's happening with your Ph.D.? Should I have added 'Dr' to the address I wrote on the envelope?

Now that I have released myself from the yoke of hard labour in Leeds, I am free to get on with my work on hasidism and am collecting material for a piece on ecstasy in early hasidism; perhaps I'll be able to finish that by the time a decision is finally reached as to whether we stay or go back.

I don't get much news from the Hebrew University. It seems that Dr Altmann, the rabbi of Manchester who studied under the late Guttmann, has been invited to give some guest lectures in Jewish philosophy. If they eventually appoint him, the subject will be in good hands [. . .] he knows a lot and he's a good teacher. Academically, Dr

Pines (who has been living in Jerusalem for some fifteen years, earning his living in all sorts of ways that strain both body and mind) is certainly superior, but Pines was rejected because he's not a good lecturer. The students protested vehemently, saying, 'if we don't understand Dr Pines we'll simply ask him again' (after all, in Jewish philosophy there aren't the great hordes of students that there are in literature courses, for example). But their protests were to no avail, and Pines had to go back to translating Arabic newspapers for the Ministry of Foreign Affairs. Meanwhile, Roth has left[41]—the country as well as the university—and Dr Jonas, who had spent fifteen years in Jerusalem before he was made a professor in Canada, was appointed in his place.[42]

Greetings from both of us to both of you; may you be blessed with all the blessings that the coming New Year can bring.

Joseph

PS. About the food for Scholem: I am in two minds as to whether it's better to send a parcel or a dollar cheque, as permitted under the new scheme. A cheque would be quicker, but it might hurt his pride; the decision is not straightforward.

8

Oxford, 27 September 1951

Dear Ora,

A few days after I wrote to you from London, I received the letter you wrote at the beginning of September and sent to Israel: in other words, our letters crossed.

With regards to having your book published in Israel: as I haven't been in Israel for nine months, I don't know the situation exactly, but things are clearly very bad. There's no paper to be had except at extortionate prices on the black market, and printers' charges have gone up because everything has got so alarmingly expensive. Your question isn't entirely clear to me. I understand that the Littauer Foundation will cover the costs of printing (which are very high), so what else do you need of a publisher? Can't Harvard publish the book in Israel in *Hebrew*? In my opinion, that would be the best solution. If the Israeli publisher isn't putting any money into it but only lending its name, Harvard is surely a better name than that of any other publisher. As to the idea of publishing in Hebrew—Wolfson of course has no idea about the real state of affairs intellectually in Israel. After all, no one will take any interest in the book (which is no reflection on you!), and sales will be far less than if it were published in English! You know the 'intellectual' community in Israel, and you must take into consideration too that since last year no one in Israel is interested in anything at all other than parcels from America or the rations that are distributed—or, more frequently, not distributed. The situation now seems to be much worse than when I left. The news that comes through from letters and conversations is really quite shocking—perhaps not so much the shortage of food in Israel (which is no small thing), but more the shortage in other areas . . . though these things are well known. I don't know where our salvation will come from.

[41] Professor Leon Yehuda Roth, who was the first incumbent of the Chair of Philosophy at the Hebrew University.

[42] Hans Jonas, the philosopher and historian of gnostic religion, who left Israel for Canada in 1949 and eventually became Professor of Philosophy at the New School for Social Research in New York. His appointment to succeed Leon Roth at the Hebrew University never materialized.

But back to our own concerns. I doubt if the Bialik Institute, for example, will be willing to publish your book; they are interested more in works surveying entire fields (such as the late Guttmann's history of Jewish philosophy, or R. Gershom's history of kabbalah, which I've heard they're publishing, and so forth). The Bialik Institute would of course be a very good place to publish, since they are affiliated to the powers that be at the Jewish Agency, and *they've got paper*. Schocken is completely defunct, and the other publishers are of no significance and won't give their black-market paper to a book that won't sell 2,000 copies in the first year. Thus, I can't see any possibility of publishing in Israel, even if the Littauer Foundation is covering the cost (which will be *ten times* more than in America); moreover, the distance involved just makes everything more difficult. (For example, my work on R. Nahman of Bratslav, which was accepted for publication by Schocken in 1947, has yet to be published; and that's but one example among many.) I recommend wholeheartedly that you *publish in America* (perhaps in Hebrew, but why?) if you want to see your book in print in a comfortably human time-span.

It may be that my geographic separation from Israel makes the situation look worse than it is, but that's the impression I've got from letters and conversations.

It seems that we shall stay here in England till next year; for the time being we'll live in London, and I'll travel up to Oxford two or three times a week to go to lectures. Perhaps in the second or third term we'll move to Oxford. In any event, I want to see what I can study in three areas—early Christianity, Christian mysticism of the Middle Ages, and the English Revivalist movement of the seventeenth and eighteenth centuries. I might have to leave out that last subject if time does not permit. I hope that more serious contact with the world of non-Jewish mysticism will have an invigorating influence on my own work.

And what's happening with you, Ora, now that you've been 'doctorated'? What comes next? Are you going to start research on something new, and if so in what area? As I said in the letter I wrote two weeks ago, our coming to America (rather, my coming; there was no mention of Miriam in the Schechter plan at all) is no longer on the cards, and I'm pleased to be staying here a little longer. I've already told you to whom credit is due for that! I have no further news as to how he is, but it seems there's no need for concern.

Miriam is in London at the moment; we may move to Oxford, but uncertainty as to our address is *no excuse for not writing*, for any letter sent to L. Gertner, 77 Great Russell Street, London WC1[43] will reach me in a day, even if we're not in London.

So forgive me for the limited information I am able to furnish, and also for the length of my letter. Miriam asks after you, and I sign off with the traditional greeting for the New Year: 'May you be inscribed and sealed for a good life.'

Joseph

9

Oxford, 20 August 1952

Dear Ora,

I no longer know who owes whom a letter; since we came to Oxford, everything's got confused. I think I recently sent you a rather depressing letter about publishing your book in Israel; I now retract everything I then wrote. I hope that the optimistic climate

[43] Levi Gertner was Director of Education of the World Zionist Organization in London at that address.

of America outweighed my own pessimism, that everything turned out well, and that publication of your book in Hebrew is going ahead. I know of only one press [in Israel] that's reliable, and that's the Cohen Press in Jerusalem (that will suffice as a postal address); although I doubt whether the standard of their typesetting is up to that of Harvard University. (Cassuto's books on the Torah, which I'm sure you'll be able to find in your library, were printed there.)

My own doings are few and depressing, so let's go on to what you're doing. What's happening now that you've got the doctorate? Rawidowicz wrote and told me of your visit, and what he had learnt about me from you, but his letter was rather ambivalent.[44] I hope any gossip you passed on was favourable.

My wretched study of R. Nahman—the one I wrote eight years ago, if you remember—has at long last been published,[45] and of course it's now old hat even to its author. The next issue of *Zion* should contain my paper on the beginnings of hasidism;[46] perhaps you'd like a copy? Since you wrote that Mordecai is editing a historical anthology of the hasidic movement, perhaps it will interest him too. If one has something good to sell, one has to make sure the world knows about it—isn't that the case? Anyway, that's the end of my literary career.

Finkelstein was in Israel, and on his way back to America he came through here and invited me to meet him.[47] Not five minutes after we met he offered me a research fellowship and invited me to America, together with my wife. The invitation is for several years, so as to allow me to work comfortably. For personal reasons I was forced to refuse, but truth be told it gave me no small measure of happiness (within the limits of the portion of happiness allotted to me in the forty days before I was born) that there is somewhere where people think, albeit mistakenly, that I can do something in this world. For to me it is absolutely clear that there is nothing I am capable of, and the last year in Oxford has proved to me conclusively that it's all over, that I have nothing more to say. Even so, other people's illusions are a salve to the soul.

I haven't even learnt English here properly, and have made no progress at all in other things. The work that's being published now is still from the good old days.

I find it difficult to write to you after we haven't seen each other for such a long time—I don't know if my words reach you in the way they should, or whether they are weary from covering a distance that is greater than mere geography would imply. You once said something deep about Scholem's volubility being nothing more than a way of concealing his silence. However, I find it difficult to talk for that purpose. Will you be coming to England or to Israel in the near future?

The month of Elul is upon us, and I send you my best wishes: may you be blessed with salvation and mercy, together with the writer of these words.

Joseph

PS. Tishby has got married, and from what I hear he has married his student. (In this, too, he follows his master) [. . .]

[44] Professor Simon Rawidowicz. Cf. above, Letter 4.

[45] This was 'Ha"kushiya"'.

[46] See Weiss, 'Reshit tsemiḥatah shel haderekh haḥasidit'.

[47] Professor L. Finkelstein, Chancellor of the Jewish Theological Seminary in New York.

10

Oxford,
Rosh ḥodesh Tevet 5713 [*1953*]

A stream of greetings to you, Ora!

I'm writing to you belatedly—very belatedly—and for this I apologize. In my favour, and in my own defence, let it be said that the postcard you sent from a fishing village at the beginning of August (by surface mail) never arrived. All I got was an airmail letter dated 3 September 1952, to which I am at long last replying.

Thank you for the reference from the *Akedat Yitsḥak*.[48] I have distanced myself, perhaps mistakenly, from dealing with R. Nahman and his world, but it seems I'll have to get back to him one of these days, I hope only from a purely academic standpoint. I knew of course about paradoxical faith in Christianity—it was in fact the source of my inspiration, even if Thomas[49] is very much of a moderate in this respect; there are, as we know, Christian theologians far more extreme than he is from whom one can learn about the world of faith.

What's happening with your book and the Bialik Institute? They are normally quite prompt in such matters. Shall we see it finished soon? I was supposed to have already let them have the manuscript of the first volume of the history of hasidic thought (i.e. covering the first three or four generations only), but you know how slowly I work.

You, on the other hand, seem to be going from strength to strength: the doctorate, a book, other books, a research associateship at Harvard. What next?

Life in Oxford, objectively speaking, is very good. I've got a grant for the coming year, and one can't complain at the British. I have little contact with the Jews here, though; I almost wrote 'thank God'. Among non-Jews one can still find people interested in mysticism, but among the Jews no one takes an interest in kabbalah. We've got to accustom ourselves to the idea that Judaism is now completely finished. Should one be sorry about it?

I haven't managed to send Rawidowicz a paper yet; I have been bogged down in a thousand things that had nothing to do with the academic world and research. I sent an offprint of my *Zion* article off by surface mail.

Be well. Greetings to both of you from your loving friend,
Joseph

11

Oxford, 4 Nisan 5713
[*March 1953*]

Dear Ora,

So many of our letters recently have crossed in the mail that it's impossible to know who owes whom a letter, but I am giving you the benefit of the doubt (if only a very slight doubt) and taking upon myself the duty of renewing the correspondence—even if this is contrary to all the kabbalistic teachings on the mystery of the 'stirring from

[48] By R. Isaac Arama, the 15th-cent. Spanish philosophical preacher who was the subject of my doctoral dissertation.

[49] Thomas Aquinas, the 13th-cent. Catholic theologian.

below', namely from the divine attribute of Malkhut (kingship), namely, from the female aspect, etc. (Need I say more?)

So, I have decided not to be silent or hold back lest, Heaven preserve us, I should contribute by my silence to the disruption of scholarly discourse. Here goes, then.

A few weeks ago I visited the Holy Community of Birmingham in the Kingdom of England, 'and the lines are fallen to me in pleasant places' [Ps. 16: 6]—I had the opportunity of making the acquaintance of a veritable student of Torah, Rabbi Chaim Pearl, may the Almighty preserve him, a young man who ministers to the aforesaid community and is also engaged in the study of the *Akedah.*[50] Of course I made mention of you and sang the praises of your glorious work. He was eager to know more of your work and the progress of its publication (I heard about the Bialik Institute in Jerusalem), and so on and so forth. I gave him your address at Harvard; perhaps he has written to you, or perhaps in his great modesty he expects to hear from you first, for I promised to inform you of his interests and his address. Thus, if he has not yet written to you, I would most earnestly and humbly request that you write to him without further delay; my own letter to you has already been postponed unduly and I pray that the good Lord will forgive me for this.

If the meagre amount of time at your disposal permits such things, do please write to me too and let me know how your work is getting on and whether publication is now taken care of, in Jerusalem or elsewhere, and so on. Here in Oxford I met Helen Rivlin of Harvard,[51] who claims to know you—although it seems only slightly, for I did not manage to learn anything but the most general things from her, things about your work and your achievements that I already knew from you. What are you *really* doing?

Do you remember Samuel Stern,[52] my friend from Budapest–Jerusalem? Tall, of dark complexion, wears glasses, an Arabic specialist? After having spent the last five years at Oxford, he's now been invited to be Professor of Arabic at the famous old university at Leiden in Holland. He refused the invitation, it seems for rather complicated reasons. When he finished his doctorate at Oxford he had written to Jerusalem and enquired as to whether he might be able to find some sort of employment there (not, Heaven forbid, as a professor). In fact, he wrote two letters to two professors. One didn't reply at all, the second wrote a rather evasive reply, so he stayed here. In another five years they'll be running after him with letters of invitation to Jerusalem, and they'll be most deeply offended it he turns them down.

Now Dr Pines occupies the throne formerly occupied by our very own Guttmann, of blessed memory, but of course I don't have to tell you that if it weren't for R. Gershom Scholem and for the refusal of every single scholar invited from abroad, he would still be killing time translating in the Censor's Office or the Ministry of Foreign Affairs. Yet in Jerusalem, no one had ever doubted his ability!

You may have seen the attack that the hasidim made on me and my article in *Zion*: only hasidim, it seems, are allowed to study hasidism; I didn't imbibe hasidism with my mother's milk (I'm lucky that they don't know what milk I *did* suck) so I am unfit to study the subject.[53] At least I now know that there are people who read what I have to say—if not always with great comprehension, then with sufficient attention to discover mistakes and things that render me unfit to be a serious scholar. That's also something:

[50] The *Akedat Yitsḥak* of Isaac Arama.

[51] An American scholar who wrote her doctorate on Islamic culture at Oxford.

[52] The well-known Arabist S. M. Stern, who was a close friend of Weiss. See above, pp. 15–16.

[53] See H. Lieberman, 'Keitsad ḥokerim ḥasidut beYisrael?', *Bitsaron*, 14, 27: 3 (1953), 165–73, repr. in id., *Ohel Raḥel* (3 vols.; New York, 1980–4), i. 1–11.

I mean, bearing in mind the present state of the 'wisdom' of Israel,[54] even that's a consolation.

I've heard that there's great consternation that R. Gershom may be elected president of the University (he hasn't refused to let his name go forward), which would put an end to kabbalah research in our generation. I must say I'm very surprised that he's let this ambition turn his head. I still hope my information is inaccurate or out of date, or was wrong from the very beginning, or that at least he won't be elected. If he is elected it will be a tragedy for Jewish studies—need I say more?

I must finish now; let me wish you all the best for the forthcoming festival [Passover],

Your friend,
Joseph

12

[Oxford] After Yom Kippur 5714
[September 1953]

Dear Ora,

My greeting comes to you a little late, but it comes none the less! What news do you have at the moment? I have none to speak of, other than a few biographical details: I have been offered an appointment at the University of London as of the coming academic year, and it's quite possible that I will also get a part-time appointment somewhere else. At London I would not of course be lecturing on the subject of my research because it isn't part of the regular curriculum, but the part-time appointment would be a research and teaching position primarily in my own field, which is why I am interested in it. I hope that these developments will have a positive effect on me and accelerate my research and so forth.

Which leads me to the next topic. I've just managed to take a quick look at what Mordecai wrote about the critique of *Toledot Ya'akov Yosef*,[55] and I found what he said *extremely important*. It sits *very well indeed* with my own views about the origins of hasidism as a desperate attempt to come to terms with the problem of 'straying thoughts' through an ideology of 'raising them', and I would greatly like to have an *offprint* of Mordecai's article if he has any left. For the moment and the foreseeable future, my address for correspondence is Oxford. Do please plead with Mordecai not to turn me away empty-handed!

Did you hear anything from a Rabbi Chaim Pearl,[56] who wants to do some work on the *Akedah*? He wrote to me some months ago and asked for your address and so forth.

I hope to go back to working on hasidism in the coming years, after having distanced myself somewhat from this topic recently.

[54] Weiss is making an ironic pun on the Hebrew name of the *Wissenschaft des Judentums* (Science of Judaism) school of historiography.

[55] M. Wilensky, 'Bikoret al sefer *Toledot Ya'akov Yosef*', in *The Joshua Starr Memorial Volume* (New York, 1953), 183–9.

[56] Rabbi Chaim Pearl did indeed write to me. At his request I sent him a copy of my doctoral dissertation on R. Isaac Arama (1951) and of the book I published in Hebrew (1956) which was based on it. See below, n. 67.

What news do you hear from Jerusalem? And how is your sister, whom I met in Jerusalem some five or six years ago? When do you intend to visit Israel?

Scholem is in Switzerland, amusing himself with the Eranos circle, where he has found a receptive audience for his ideas. He does not concur with their Jungian orientation, but somehow, in spite of himself, etc.

Yours, with every good wish,
Joseph

13

London, 20 March 1954

Dear Ora,

Last week I received from Oxford the microfilm you requested in your letter (don't blame me for the delay—I sent it on to America as soon as it arrived). I hope Mordecai finds it useful, and that the manuscript contains good variant readings. Meanwhile I have reread the piece he sent me (on the critique of *Toledot Ya'akov Yosef*) and was delighted with what I found in it.[57] I look forward impatiently to seeing the complete book.[58] I have always focused my work on the history of hasidic ideas, and have paid no special attention to the hasidic–mitnaggedic controversy. Mordecai's publication has opened my eyes, and I am now convinced that a number of hasidic *teachings* can be explained in terms of the polemic with the mitnaggedim. I am thinking of publishing 'addenda' to my article on the beginnings of hasidism[59] (isn't the literary genre of the addendum pathetic?), where I shall use what I have learnt from Mordecai's paper. In any event, I await the book, and hope to hear soon that it has been submitted for publication!

(Incidentally, I sent the microfilm to your address at Harvard, Ora, since I could not lay my hands on your last letter with the Boston address. It went by ordinary surface mail, and by the time you receive this letter you should have had it. Please let me know whether it arrived safely.)

Meanwhile it has transpired that writing about hasidism is a dangerous occupation. Rabbi Lieberman, the librarian of the Lubavitcher Rebbe, launched his attack,[60] and was followed in the offensive by the eminent and well-known writer and 'scholar' Eliezer Steinman, who has been publishing his findings both in Israel and abroad. R. Gershom has just written to me as follows: 'Mr Steinman has published a book entitled *Mibe'er hahasidut* which contains a whole chapter devoted to an attack on me and my students (unnamed) for vilifying hasidism in our scholarly investigations.[61] He had earlier published the same dramatic and idiotic chapter in *Molad*,[62] and the editors have invited us to reply. I wonder if it might not be worthwhile, for the benefit of the spiritual well-being of the readers, to engage in a little polemic.' So, if he does not wish to

[57] See above, n. 55.

[58] This was eventually published as M. Wilensky, *Ḥasidim umitnaggedim* (2 vols.; Jerusalem, 1970).

[59] See above, n. 46.

[60] See above, n. 53.

[61] E. Steinman, *Be'er haḥasidut* (10 vols.; Tel Aviv, 1951–62). Scholem is referring to the 'First Series', the unnumbered volume subtitled *Torot vesiḥot shel shiv'at haro'im* (n.d.), last chapter, 'Tiyulim befardes haḥasidut', 339–98, esp. s. 4, 'Bedikat ḥamets bemishnat haḥasidut', 363–72, which had previously appeared in *Molad*, 11: 65–6 (1953), 259–67.

[62] Steinman, 'Bedikat ḥamets'.

become a target for the arrows of Mr Steinman and his gang, Mordecai must be very careful not to take sides in his account of the polemic between hasidism and mitnaggedism. I saw a rather silly article by the same scholar in the American *Hado'ar*.[63] And by the way, I hear that a year ago Aharon Zeitlin published an article in America against my paper on the beginnings of hasidism (probably in Yiddish, but I'm not sure).[64] I haven't seen this article, and would be extremely grateful to you if you could find it for me so that I can read what he has to say. I assume that you can do this more easily in America. I have already enquired in Israel, but no one there knows anything about it.

With all best wishes,
Joseph

14

[*London*], *10 August 1955*

Dear Ora,

For once I'm writing in pen and ink, as our fathers did in the age before the discovery of typewriters. And that's to mark the occasion of your good news, which reached me with such *great delay*, about the birth of your Uri Joseph, in the celebration of which I join most wholeheartedly!

How is your book on the *Akedat Yitsḥak*, and how is Mordecai's book on the anti-hasidic polemics? Please explain to him that many people are waiting eagerly for a book like this, and I the least among them; publication is imperative. For example, I am at present gathering information on the practice of smoking (and particularly of smoking a pipe) among the early hasidim; a collection of all the polemical literature would make my search much easier! I just recently sent a short article to press and shall of course let you have an offprint when it appears; you may find it of interest. Have you not yet received the Zeitlin paper that Mordecai read a year ago, in which my work on hasidism was pulled to pieces?[65] Even things like this hold their pleasures; why do you deny suffering from those to whom it rightly belongs?

R. Gershom is coming to Europe for the Eranos meeting, after which he will come to London and will speak at the university here. But he refuses to address the Patristic congress in Oxford in the autumn, which is a shame because the Judaistic case will then not be put forward by anyone of any stature. But he simply doesn't care: the paltry fare of international conferences on religion and science—or, more accurately, on the science of religion—holds no interest for him.

We heard that Helen Rivlin has been asked to come to Harvard,[66] following the appointment there of Professor Gibb from Oxford; please convey congratulations and best wishes to her on my behalf until I can find the strength to write, and may this be as acceptable and pleasing to her as if I had written myself—which I still intend to do.

May everything be well with you and your household and your firstborn,

Joseph Weiss

[63] Id., 'Ha'im hayah rabbi Yisrael Ba'al Shem Tov lamdan?', *Hado'ar*, 34: 16 [1536] (19 Feb. 1954), 301–2. Steinman polemicizes with 'modern scholars' without mentioning anyone by name. His main arguments are against the thesis which links hasidism to Sabbateanism. I am grateful to Prof. Rachel Elior for her help in locating the references here and in the previous note.

[64] I have not been able to locate Zeitlin's article.

[65] See above, n. 64. [66] See above, n. 51

15

London, 3 October 1956

Dear Ora,

Thank you very much for those few lines—few indeed!—with which you thought to fulfil your letter-writing obligations to me. I could have responded in kind by writing you a few words of greeting for Rosh Hashanah, and thereby fulfilled my own obligations . . . I should like to congratulate you on the publication of your book by the Bialik Institute.[67] Keeping your promise of sending me a copy will bring blessings upon your soul. I am always happy to see that one of our *ḥavurah*[68] is working, and God is my witness that I am not too jealous. On the contrary, I think that others are fulfilling my obligations for me. My attitude to my own scholarly potential has entered a phase of total resignation. In any event, in London no one expects very much from me, so I'm not a source of disappointment to anyone; in Manchester, on the other hand, they do expect wonders of me[69] but haven't yet realized that wonders are quite beyond me.

I was in Switzerland for five weeks in the summer, but didn't enjoy myself particularly. It was my first visit, but even the fantastic scenery was no compensation for being shaken about in a car in travelling from place to place. Then until last week I was in Oxford, in the house of some friends who went abroad and left me a house full of books and pictures and drawings, and two lovely cats. The quiet and calm of that beautiful city always bring similar quiet and calm to my soul. Which is not the case at all in London, a damned city full of masses of people and noise. I don't know what I shall do this year—I so hate being in London that I dream up all sorts of fantastic plans to get away.

What are you working on at the moment? Your son doubtless constitutes an obstacle to your regular quest for knowledge, but at least he is a worthy obstacle. And what is Mordecai working on? I am still awaiting the collection of historical documents on hasidism. The importance of such a work has recently become only too clear to me.

Wishing you both all the very best in the coming year,
Yours, as ever, in friendship,
Joseph

16

Oxford, 14 January 1957

Dear Ora,

Having come here at the beginning of the winter holiday they call the Festival of the Birth of Christ the Messiah, I've stayed here the whole time, and I'm still staying here, in this wonderful town, travelling up to London two days in each week and to Manchester two days in each fortnight. But things that look good on paper are not always so good in reality. It's not only the bothersome business of travelling from city to city—the physical disturbance, that is—but also the mental disturbance of not-

67 Sara Heller Wilensky, *R. Yitsḥak Arama umishnato* (Jerusalem, 1956).

68 The circle around Scholem in Jerusalem.

69 The reference is to Prof. Alexander Altmann, who was rabbi of Manchester at the time, and who had founded there and directed the Institute of Jewish Studies where Weiss was employed in a part-time research post. See n. 33 above.

being-settled-anywhere-in-the-world. Thank you for your kind words about my so-called achievements in London and Manchester. I had wanted to succeed in Oxford, but there I failed: Chaim Rabin, who had been at Oxford, was appointed to a professorship at the Hebrew University of Jerusalem, and I was a candidate for his Oxford post—but in the end I didn't get it. And I can't even complain, for the man appointed was in fact a far better candidate than I![70]

Tomorrow I have to go up to London and I won't be able to get back to Oxford next week because of a lecture and some other matters, so I feel myself even more disoriented than usual—splitting oneself geographically is worse than any other split I know. My books are all in London, so each week I bring here only what I need for the week. None the less, I managed to write a paper that both I and others were rather pleased with, on the phenomenology of tardiness in reciting the Shema and other prayers, a widespread hasidic custom that the mitnaggedim denigrated. Having finished it I went up to London feeling very happy, with the paper and all the notes on which it was based—source citations, and so on—in the pocket of my coat. I then left my coat in my room when I went down to the staff room for a cup of coffee. I didn't shut the door of my room, and when I came back there was no coat and no paper and no notes and no citations: years of reading in libraries [had just disappeared]. The coat had been stolen—and with it the envelope I'd left in the pocket. What's done is done and can't be undone, but it *was* an important piece of work.

Which brings me to the next topic. To give myself a treat, I brought your valuable study with me to Oxford.[71] But then my dear friend Samuel Stern came along (you may remember him from Jerusalem—his main field of interest is Arabic—and if you don't, Helen Rivlin knows of him, even if she may not have met him personally; he's got quite a reputation as one of the leading scholars in the field, and was even invited to lecture in Harvard for three months next year). In short: Stern came and took the book. He's delighted with it and never puts it down, so I, meanwhile, am still waiting to read it.

I was stunned* to hear of your escape plans,[72] but your logic is persuasive. Certainly, American Jewry is not devoid of smugness and self-indulgence, but aren't there also non-Jews in America? I am very isolated in England, for our English brethren, the Jews who live in the palaces of London, are not to my liking; I have chosen to live as far from them as I can. On the other hand, it's clear to me that I am no Englishman, I don't want to be English, and indeed cannot be English, and I have maintained my Israeli nationality for some years now. My sociological place in international society is on the periphery—that's where I feel I belong. I have no need to be integrated in a large, organized society (which, reading between the lines, is what you aspire to), but I am in need of a small group of intimate friends. This is totally impossible in London because of the distances involved, and particularly as I live in a neighbourhood where I don't know a soul. It might have been possible in Oxford, but the price to be paid for dragging oneself from place to place was too high, and in any case one can't continue dragging oneself around for ever. This feeling of alienation stems of course from the

[70] The candidate appointed was Dr David Patterson.

[71] Cf. above, n 67.

[72] This is a reference to my intention to come to Jerusalem at Gershom Scholem's invitation, in order to teach at the Department of Jewish Philosophy and Kabbalah of the Hebrew University (between 1957 and 1959).

collapse of my home life,[73] which has been the dominant factor in my life in recent years, for better or for worse. It's a sorry state of affairs.

Very much yours,
Joseph

Questions:

1 Will you be going to Jerusalem for the Congress?[74] If so:
2 Will you go via England or direct from America?

My regards to: (a) Regesch and Fania;[75] (b) Mordecai; and (c) Helen Rivlin.

*Not stunned, only sorry; J. W.

17

London, 19 Shevat 5721
5 February 1961

Dear Ora,

Your letter has been lying on my desk for a long time. Counting it as personal correspondence, I allowed myself to put it on one side, and that initial delay has just gone on and on. In the midst of the maelstrom of duties into which Altmann's departure has thrown me,[76] I find it difficult to keep up to date with my personal correspondence. I was planning to go to Jerusalem this winter, as last year, but had to cancel at the last minute to attend the annual meeting of the Institute to which I have become totally enslaved. My departure is now postponed till next summer, and my visit then will overlap with the World Congress of Jewish Studies which is due to take place in Jerusalem, as you probably know. Are you or Mordecai—or both of you—taking part?

You asked about Scholem in your last letter. We were in Marburg together in September, for a conference on the study of religion, and then we spent some more time together in Zurich. Fania was operated on in Zurich while Scholem was in Marburg, and he didn't find out about the operation until after it was all over. The operation was successful, but I hear that since returning to Jerusalem she has been in pain again, although this apparently has nothing to do with her operation.

We are expecting Scholem here soon, once the second term in Jerusalem is over. He's going to spend some six months in London, mostly doing research but also a little teaching (he's giving a few seminars). From his last letter I understand that he is not going to take part in the Congress next summer. You must have seen his new English book on the Merkavah literature which was published recently in America.[77]

You ask about Dror: after a long spell of terrible suffering, of which you probably knew, she finally died.[78] During a period of remission between attacks she was in London for a while, and we talked a great deal. I knew that these were to be my last conversations with her, but she did not, or perhaps she knew without realizing it. By the time

[73] Weiss is alluding to the breakdown of his first marriage.

[74] The World Congress of Jewish Studies that took place in the summer in 1957.

[75] Regesch—an acronym of Reb Gershom Scholem; Fania—his wife.

[76] See above, n. 33.

[77] This was Gershom G. Scholem, *Jewish Gnosticism, Merkabah Mysticism, and Talmudic Tradition* (New York, 1960).

[78] Dror Oron, an author and translator of classical Greek literature into Hebrew. She died of cancer.

I arrived in Jerusalem last winter she was no longer alive; my last letter to her arrived on the day of her funeral. Halkin and Fuks both spoke at the memorial service, and hundreds of people came.[79]

I would like to hear about your work at the Brandeis Institute.[80] On my own research there is nothing to report since it simply does not exist: ever since I was harnessed to the wagon of the Institute (which has now transferred to London), all my energies go into administrative work. The general impression everywhere is that the enterprise has been successful beyond all expectations, certainly beyond my own, although, as you know, I have always been a pessimist.

With all best regards, Yours,
Joseph

18

[*London*], *First day of* seliḥot
[*23 September 1962*]

Dear Ora,

Your letter dated the first day of *ḥol hamo'ed* Sukkot has been lying on my desk for a whole year (a constant reminder of my failure to meet my obligations). Now that the Days of Penitence are upon us, I am putting aside all the worldly chores which have kept me busy all year long at my job (or rather the various jobs which have been thrust upon me, and which I do unwillingly) to make time to write a few words to you.

I must also ask you to take note that we have drawn down a holy soul from the heavenly treasury of souls; who knows, it may turn out to be the soul of the messiah.[81]
I was in Switzerland during the summer, in Ascona, for the Eranos meeting at which R. Gershom lectured on 'Commentary as a Basic Category in Judaism'.[82] He made a tremendous impression on the gentiles and even more so on the Jews—ignoramuses who did not expect anything of the kind.

Regards to Mordecai. Yours with all best wishes
for deliverance and indeed mercy during these Days of Mercy,
Joseph

19

[*London*] *12 July 1963*

Dear Ora,

I was truly delighted with your offprint on *Sha'ar hashamayim* (through I had already read the paper in *Tarbiz*.[83] Getting the offprint as well as your new address is a

[79] Simon Halkin, then Professor of Hebrew Literature at the Hebrew University; Alexander Fuks, then Professor of Ancient History and Classics at the Hebrew University.

[80] The Institute for Advanced Judaic Studies at Brandeis University, directed by Prof. Alexander Altmann. Between 1960 and 1963 I was a Research Associate of the Institute.

[81] Weiss's second wife, Erna, had recently given birth (on 8 Jan. 1962) to their son Amos.

[82] The lecture was published as G. Scholem, 'Tradition und Kommentar als religiöse Kategorien in Judentum', *Eranos Jahrbuch*, 31 (1962), 19–48; pub. in Eng. as 'Tradition and Commentary as Religious categories in Judaism', *Judaism*, 15: 1 (1966), 23–39.

[83] See S. O. Heller Wilensky, 'Lishe'elat meḥabero shel sefer *Sha'ar hashamayim* hameyuḥas leAvraham ibn Ezra', *Tarbiz*, 32 (1963), 278–95.

good omen for the future of our correspondence!

This year, in fact this summer, I face a difficult task—to lecture at the Eranos meeting.[84] Who am I to stand where my elders and betters have stood and to address so august an assembly? As always, I shall need assistance from on high.

Your friend,
Joseph Weiss

20

London, 21 July 1968

My dearest Ora,

An hour or so ago I happened to pick up a copy of *Hado'ar* dated 25 Sivan and saw an announcement congratulating Mordecai and Sara Wilensky on the barmitzvah of their son Uri Joseph. I don't know and have never known the name of your son,[85] but I do know a Mordecai Wilensky with a wife called Ora. And here the angel in charge of things remembered and forgotten opened up a small window through which I could see your wedding in Jerusalem—how many years ago? I don't remember. And the rabbi who officiated at the ceremony—who was it? Perhaps Rabbi Zvi Pesah Frank, of blessed memory, then chief rabbi of Jerusalem—reading the *ketubah* the whole way through, from which I learnt that your full name is Sara Ora (till then I had known only of Ora Heller). All this led me to surmise that the congratulatory announcement printed in *Hado'ar* was intended for you. But that was not all: the announcement was directed to a couple in Chicago, and it was signed by Yehuda and Hanna Rosenthal. Now, Yehuda Rosenthal I know, both personally and through his writings, even if the name of his wife, Hanna, is unknown to me. And the Rosenthal I know is a professor at the same institution that Mordecai teaches (or taught) at—yet another clue.

So if the conclusion I have reached is correct, you have my congratulations too; do please write a few lines to let me know if my detective work is accurate.

Will we meet next summer in the Congress in Jerusalem? It is my intention to go, if the Lord decrees that I live till then.

In greetings and friendship,
Joseph

[84] The lecture was published as J. G. Weiss, 'Eine spätjüdischer Utopie religiöser Freiheit', *Eranos Jahrbuch*, 32 (1964), 235–80, pub. in Eng. as 'A Late Jewish Utopia of Religious Freedom', in id., *Eastern European Jewish Mysticism*, 209–48.

[85] But see above, Letter 14.

PART II

TOWARDS A NEW SOCIAL HISTORY OF HASIDISM

THREE

The Conditions in Jewish Society in the Polish-Lithuanian Commonwealth in the Middle Decades of the Eighteenth Century

GERSHON DAVID HUNDERT

WHAT is the place of hasidism in the religious history of the eighteenth century? Is there any use in macrohistorical discussions that seek to incorporate hasidism within the general body of widespread movements of religious emotionalism, enthusiasm, revival, or quietism that swept across western Europe and New England between about 1730 and 1760? The latter movements are usually interpreted as a popular rejection of the cold logic of the Newtonian Enlightenment championed by the educated preachers of the age.[1]

The leader of what in New England was called the Great Awakening, a movement that began in 1740, was Jonathan Edwards. The movement was condemned by the Harvard faculty as an orgy of emotions; they dismissed it with contempt as mere enthusiasm (and no word in their vocabulary was more opprobrious). The historian Perry Miller has claimed that the Great Awakening could only properly be understood in its American context and, indeed, only in terms of the particular development of the beliefs and values of the Protestant churches of New England.[2] At issue, in his view, was those Christians' quest for the saving experience that was eluding them. Edwards addressed this increasingly urgent problem and struck a responsive chord in the following way, according to Miller: 'By 1740, the leader had to get down amongst them and bring them by actual participation into an experience that was no longer private and privileged but social and communal.'[3] This passage is, of course, so strikingly reminiscent of the remarks of Gershom Scholem and others about the social function of mystical ideals as to be remarkable.

Like most of the others who have raised this question, I am not prepared to argue, in the absence of systematic study, that Wesleyan Methodism, the Great Awakening, or the schismatic groups in the Russian Church discussed by Ysander were, together with

[1] See e.g. W. R. Ward, 'The Relations of Enlightenment and Religious Revival in Central Europe and in the English Speaking World', in Derek Baker (ed.), *Reform and Reformation: England and the Continent* (Oxford, 1979); id., 'Power and Piety: The Origins of Religious Revival in the Early Eighteenth Century', *Bulletin of the John Rylands University Library of Manchester*, 63 (1980), 231–52.

[2] Perry Miller, *Errand into the Wilderness* (New York, 1964).

[3] Ibid. 154.

hasidism, part of some general movement.[4] Nor am I prepared to argue that there is more than a superficial similarity of one to the others, however striking and unexpected some of those similarities may be. The custom among historians has been to make some vague reference to the *Zeitgeist* and to leave it at that; what I am suggesting here is that some further consideration be given to this problem.

The historians of seventeenth- and eighteenth-century New England have interesting methods and modes of analysis. I quote again the remarks of Miller on the Great Awakening, but I think that in fact they apply equally well to hasidism: 'the social historian . . . has difficulty dealing with [the Great Awakening of 1740] . . . this eruption came from sources which elude more sociological analysis'.[5] Indeed, one must take into account demographic developments, economic conditions, the degree of physical security, class conflict, the stability of communal institutions and the family, and so on in any discussion of the beginnings of hasidism. No one of these factors, however, nor indeed all of them together, adequately explains why a movement of spiritual enthusiasm and religious revival struck such a responsive chord among the Jews of Poland–Lithuania.

I should like now to take up two or three of these socio-historical topics in turn. First, about demographic conditions. Even though we lack precise data, it is clear that the rate of growth of the Jewish population in Poland was faster than that of their Christian neighbours. The proportion of Jews in the population of the Polish Commonwealth probably at least doubled between 1672 and 1772. It is important to emphasize that the proportion of Jews living in villages increased during this period to a maximum of one-third, peaking at this level during the third quarter of the eighteenth century. From that time on, the number and proportion of Jews in villages constantly diminished. In other words, throughout the period, a substantial majority of Jews lived in the cities and towns. Further, an unknown number of village Jews were only temporarily rural; they either maintained residence in towns, or returned to the towns after the expiry of their *arenda* contracts.[6]

Here, I would mention a strong impression I have, but have been unable so far to measure in any meaningful way, namely, that the Jewish population was highly mobile. If new opportunities arose in a neighbouring town, or even a distant one, there was little reluctance to move. It seems to have been not at all uncommon for people to move several times in the course of a lifetime from one town to another. But this, as I say, remains for the moment merely an impression.

There is one other aspect related to demography that I cannot resist raising for discussion in this forum, even though I have written about it briefly elsewhere.[7] A number

[4] Torsten Ysander, 'Zur Frage der religionsgeschichtlichen Stellung des Hasidismus', *Studien zum bestischen Hasidismus in seiner religionsgeschichtlichen Sonderart* (Uppsala, 1933), 327–413.

[5] Miller, *Errand into the Wilderness*, 153.

[6] G. D. Hundert, 'On the Jewish Community in Poland during the Seventeenth Century: Some Comparative Perspectives', *Revue des études juives*, 152 (1983), 364–5.

[7] Id., 'Shekiat yirat kavod bikehilot Beit Yisrael bePolin–Lita', *Bar Ilan*, 24–5 (1989), 47–9; id., 'Jewish Children and Childhood in Early Modern East Central Europe', in D. Kraemer (ed.), *The Jewish Family: Metaphor and Memory* (New York, 1989), 81–94. And see Louis Jacobs, 'Honour thy Father: A Study of the Psychology of the Hasidic Movement', in M. Zohar and A. Tartakower (eds.), *Hagut ivrit be'Eiropah* (Tel Aviv, 1969), 136–43.

of scholars have postulated that, in its early days, hasidism had a special appeal to youth. If this is correct, it may well be related to the rapid expansion of the Jewish population in the following way.

It seems very likely that the expansion of Jewish numbers was a result not of a higher birth rate but of a lower death rate. Particularly, the rate of infant mortality among the Jewish population seems to have been lower. In these conditions, the proportion of young people in the Jewish population would constantly expand; the society as a whole would be younger rather than older.

Now, I should like to apply the following reasoning:

1. In conditions of social, economic, and political stability, the natural tensions between generations, even in periods of expansion, can be channelled in a way that does not threaten the stability of the family and the community. That is, authority and discipline within the family tend to reflect the authority and the stability of broader social, economic, and political institutions. Certainly this was the case in the conditions of rapid growth but social and political stability and relative economic prosperity in Poland during the second half of the sixteenth century.

2. When, however, social, economic, and political conditions are unstable, generational tensions are more likely to take more threatening forms, both within individual families and in communities and society at large. I would argue that this latter situation characterized most of the eighteenth century. It is true that sometimes these struggles were between contending parties of people of roughly the same social class, but in other cases, surely the majority, the revolts are known to have been led by artisans, and I suspect by young artisans. In a growing but relatively unstable society, it should be remembered, the number of potential leaders also grows. There will be more pressure to revolve the offices of leadership among a larger and larger pool of aspirants.

3. In this way, the artisan revolts and other violent disputes in east European Jewish communities should be understood as arising from a number of factors, one of which was rapid demographic growth.

4. By extension, then, can we not say that the loosening of Jewish social stability, accompanied by a lessening of deference to social institutions that were increasingly no longer effective, which was characteristic of the middle decades of the eighteenth century—can we not say that these factors created conditions in which defiance and generational conflict could extend to rejection of norms of behaviour and of traditional institutional authority?

To illustrate briefly the cogency of this position, let me recall for you some familiar passages from the attacks on the early hasidim: 'constantly, they insult the angels of God [rabbis], and act crazily'; 'turning over, heads down and legs up like the clowns'; 'they seduce children, bringing them to disobey their parents and steal their property'.[8]

I am not arguing that generational conflict is the explanation for the genesis of hasidism, or for the remarkable receptivity to it in Jewish society. I am saying that

[8] M. Wilensky, *Ḥasidim umitnaggedim* (2 vols.; Jerusalem, 1970), i. 59, 68, 282. And see B. Dinur, *Bemifneh hadorot* (Jerusalem, 1955), 160.

generational conflict is a neglected filament in the web of explanation of this movement. The topic should be pursued, in spite of the methodological difficulties inherent in the term 'generation'.

I should like to turn now to my third subject and say a word about the physical security of Jews in Polish-Lithuanian society during the middle decades of the eighteenth century. Here, I should stress one point, following a remark made by Professor Jacob Goldberg.[9] If we ask what group or class of people suffered more loss of life, by a factor of ten at least, than any other as a result of persecution during the eighteenth century, the answer is women. According to Janusz Tazbir and Bohdan Baranowski, the execution of witches by burning and other means reached huge proportions in Poland–Lithuania during the eighteenth century. The precise figures are not clear; estimates range between 1,000 and 10,000.[10] It is true that there were during the same period more ritual murder trials than previously. The loss of Jewish lives at Uman may come to mind here, but that event deserves careful analysis to uncover what measure of specific anti-Jewish animus played a role in the battle and its aftermath.

I am arguing that the Jews' sense of insecurity during this period, as described by the older historiography, has been exaggerated—a classic instance of the lachrymose presentation of the Jewish historical experience.

Finally, I should like to say something about the economic situation of Polish-Lithuanian Jewry during the middle decades of the eighteenth century.[11] Here the emphasis should be on the complexity of the picture. Beginning around 1740, the Polish economy resumed a halting recovery that had been interrupted by the Great Northern War, which had led to about four decades when both the political and the economic situation reached a nadir of anarchy and stagnation. After the death of Sobieski and the outbreak of the Northern War, the dimensions and the velocity of trade were reduced. More and more Christian town-dwellers turned to agriculture; indeed, there is a literature on the 'agrarianization' of Polish towns during this period. After about 1740, grass continued to grow in the streets of some towns, but others, by contrast, displayed considerable dynamism. Market days and fairs began to be more numerous and more active. By 1750, grain exports reached totals approaching those of the first half of the seventeenth century.

The pace of recovery of the Polish economy accelerated during the third quarter of the eighteenth century. For the first time, the Polish state began to intervene in an effort to ameliorate the conditions of commerce: roads and waterways were improved; internal tariffs and tolls were abolished; weights and measures were standardized. The funds of wealthy magnates and of the new private banks were invested in manufacturing on a significant scale. By this time, Warsaw had become the centre of Polish commerce

[9] Jacob Goldberg, 'The Attitude of Polish Society toward the Jews in the Time of the Enlightenment', in J. Micgiel, R. Scott, and H. B. Segel (eds.), *Proceedings of the Conference on Poles and Jews: Myth and Reality in the Historical Context* (New York, 1986), 72.

[10] Janusz Tazbir, 'Procesy o czary', *Odrodzenie i Reformacja w Polsce*, 23 (1978), 152–75; Bohdan Baranowski, *Procesy czarownic w Polsce w XVII i XVIII wieku* (Lodz, 1952); M. Dabrowska-Zakrzewska, *Procesy o czary w Lublinie w XVII i XVIII wieku* (Lublin, 1947). And see the materials assembled in *Nietolerancja i zabobom w Polsce w XVII i XVIII w.* (Warsaw, 1950), 119–87.

[11] G. D. Hundert, 'The Role of the Jews in Commerce in Early Modern Poland–Lithuania', *Journal of European Economic History*, 16 (1987), 245–75.

and banking, and Brody a major emporium of international trade. The configuration of the reconstruction of Polish commerce, however, was altered by each successive partition when the territories of the Commonwealth were incorporated by Russia, Austria, and Prussia.

From the late Middle Ages, Polish commerce had been largely in the hands of people who were not ethnic Poles. In the thirteenth century large-scale trade was dominated by Germans, while in the second half of the fourteenth century Italian merchants began to play an important role. This was particularly noticeable during the ensuing two centuries in Poznan, Cracow, and Lublin. During the same period, Armenians dominated international commerce in the south-eastern territories. Scots were characteristically pedlars from the fifteenth century, although some became great merchants; Dutch and English traders were active in Poland at the same time. After the *potop* in the middle of the seventeenth century, this conglomerate of nationalities became less conspicuous as they were assimilated. Although there was a new penetration by west European and especially German merchants during the eighteenth century, it was with the progressive disappearance of the non-Polish merchants that Jews began to be virtually a decisive element in Polish commerce. During the eighteenth century, Jews shared in the ruin of some towns and in the prosperity of others. In the middle decades of that century we find high levels of unemployment and under-employment and many of the unskilled Jewish poor on the roads. We find increasing proportions of artisans in Jewish communities, a culture and society that esteemed commerce more highly than working with one's hands. Yet we also find that the Jewish share of Polish commerce, by every measure, increased dramatically. This is true even though some of the older literature may exaggerate the Jews' dominance, and even though the very largest commercial houses were in the hands not of Polish Jews but mainly of non-Polish merchants from German-speaking lands. And further, Jewish commercial activities were characterized typically by small quantities and rapid turnover.

At this juncture, I should like to share some new data which, I believe, present the beginnings of a realistic picture of the Jewish share of Polish commerce during the decades that interest us.

In the Archive of Old Acts in Warsaw, there is a series of books recording the payments of internal tariffs by merchants in about sixty localities during the years 1764–7.[12] These notebooks contain in sum about 45,000 entries. Almost every one of these entries includes the name of the merchant, the quantity, type, and value of the goods he carried, and whether he was travelling out of the country, into the country, or within the country. Now, there are all sorts of potentially interesting manipulations of these data, but my own study of them has only just begun.

For now, I think a very crude measure will suffice to indicate the general situation. In twenty-three toll stations in all sections of the country during the years 1764–7, payments were collected from 11,485 merchants, of whom 5,888 or 51.25 per cent were Jews. While, for technical reasons (namely, that not all of the items in all of the entries are priced), I cannot present the figures as yet, I can say that the value of the Jews' goods did not exceed this proportion of just over 50 per cent.

[12] Warsaw, Archiwum Glowne Akt Dawnych, Archiwum Kameralne III.

On the basis of these figures, then, about half of Polish domestic and international commerce was in Jewish hands. This proportion corresponds to the percentage of Jews among the urban population of the country. Thus, one should not describe Polish Jewry in a general way during the middle decades of the eighteenth century as impoverished. It is true that the number and proportion of poor had increased, but a significant proportion was succeeding in finding means of support.

To summarize the points made here:

1. The place of hasidism in the religious history of the eighteenth century ought to be reconsidered not only in light of the questions about the schismatic groups in the Orthodox Church raised by Ysander, but also in light of the general revivalist currents in western Europe.
2. The social historian cannot explain hasidism, which belongs to the context of the development of the east European religious mentality in the eighteenth century.
3. Social history does, however, point to some significant questions that ought to be explored further. One of these is the role of youth and generational conflict in the beginnings of the movement, and not only in its beginnings.
4. A realistic recovery of the situation of the Polish-Lithuanian Jewry in the eighteenth century shows that neither the economic nor the security conditions were such as to warrant their use as causal or explanatory factors in the rise and reception of hasidism.

FOUR

Social Conflicts in Międzybóż in the Generation of the Besht

MOSHE J. ROSMAN

THE question of the connection between strains in Jewish society and the development of hasidism has attracted the attention of historians for generations. For many years it was common to posit the rise of hasidism as somehow related to a putative social crisis in the Polish Jewish community.[1] Over the last three decades, some have downplayed this connection and portrayed early hasidism as essentially a movement with a religious message that was not socially activist and did not see resolving social problems as one of its aims.[2] More recently, Gershon Hundert has suggested that hasidism may have derived its early vitality from the generation gap that resulted from a population explosion within eighteenth-century Polish Jewry and subsequent economic dislocations. According to this view, hasidism may have been in large part a movement of the disaffected young.[3]

My own approach to this question, following the general method I have been trying to develop for the study of early hasidism, is to ask: what was the situation in Międzybóż, the place where it all began? Whatever generalizations one makes about the Baal Shem Tov and early hasidism, it seems reasonable to expect to find concrete examples in the sources stemming from the place where he was most active. If, then, social

In this chapter Polish forms of place-names are used; for equivalent forms see the index.

[1] See M. Rosman, 'An Exploitative Regime and the Opposition to it in Międzybóż *c.*1730', in S. Almog *et al.* (eds.), *Transition and Change in Modern Jewish History: Essays Presented in Honor of Shmuel Ettinger* (Jerusalem, 1987), pp. xi–xvi and the studies cited there; esp. S. Dubnow, *Toledot haḥasidut* [Tel Aviv, 1930–1] (Tel Aviv, 1960), 8–36; and B. Dinur, 'Reshitah shel haḥasidut viyesodoteihah hasotsialiyim vehameshiḥiyim', in id., *Bemifneh hadorot* (Jerusalem, 1955), 100–43.

[2] S. Ettinger, 'The Hasidic Movement: Reality and Ideals', in H. H. Ben-Sasson and S. Ettinger (eds.), *Jewish Society Through the Ages* (New York, 1971), 251–66, orig. pub. in *Cahiers d'histoire mondiale: Journal of World History*, 11: 1–2 (1968), 251–66, repr. in G. D. Hundert (ed.), *Essential Papers on Hasidism* (New York, 1991), 226–43, and studies cited there; see also G. Scholem, 'Demuto hahistorit shel R. Yisrael Baal Shem Tov', *Molad*, 18: 144–5 (1960), 354–6, repr. in id., *Devarim bego* (Tel Aviv, 1975); A. Rapoport-Albert, 'God and the Zaddik as the Two Focal Points of Hasidic Worship', *History of Religions*, 18:4 (1979), 313–21, repr. in Hundert (ed.), *Essential Papers*, 299–329; I. Etkes, 'Hasidism as a Movement: The First Stage', in B. Safran (ed.), *Hasidism: Continuity or Innovation?* (Cambridge, Mass., 1988), 5–22; and Y. Hisdai, 'The Origins of the Conflict between Hasidim and Mitnagdim', in Safran (ed.), *Hasidism*, 36–7.

[3] G. D. Hundert, 'Some Basic Characteristics of the Jewish Experience in Poland', *Polin*, 1 (1986), 29, repr. in A. Polonsky (ed.), *From Shtetl to Socialism: Essays from Polin* (London, 1993); id., 'Shekiat yirat kavod bikehilot Beit Yisrael bePolin-Lita', *Bar Ilan*, 24–5 (1989), 47–9.

conflict had a role in preparing the ground for the establishment of the new movement, or affected the Baal Shem Tov's activities, this should be evident in the sources from Międzybóż. These can be found in the Czartoryski Library in Cracow where the archive of the Czartoryski family, the owners of the town, is located.

In the work I have done so far on this subject, I have noted the prevalence of social controversy in Międzybóż in the years preceding as well as during the Besht's sojourn there.[4] My objective here is to describe some of the forms the conflicts took, to characterize the alignment of various social groups in the town, and to suggest implications that these may have had for the Besht's status in the town and for the development of early hasidism.

Discussions of social conflict in the Jewish communities of eighteenth-century Poland generally tend to consider the phenomenon in terms of the élite class versus the 'common people'. According to the usual construction, rich, politically powerful individuals, particularly those with close ties to Polish magnates, monopolized control over the institutional resources of the Jewish community in order to benefit themselves and exploit or oppress the poor and powerless.[5] There is evidence that, to some extent, this paradigm fits the circumstances of the Jews in Międzybóż during the time of the Besht's residence there.[6]

The earliest clear example of this phenomenon in the available sources stems from c.1730. A man by the name of Icko Ognisty, who worked as the factor of the lessee-administrator of Międzybóż, Jan Dessier, was notorious for his rapacious activities—both in collaboration with Dessier and on his own behalf. He defrauded widows, expropriated merchandise from artisans, extorted payments from various people, accused people falsely in court, and generally harassed and intimidated the inhabitants of the town.[7] Ognisty was eventually punished, but he was not the last to try to lord it over Międzybóż.

In sources dating from around 1740, one of the most prominent characters is Wolf Abramowicz, a factor who served the noblemen administrators of Międzybóż and sold supplies to various army units. At times, he held office as one of the four elders (Polish *kwartalny*, Hebrew *roshim*) of the Jewish community,[8] possibly with the active support of the Polish administration.[9] In addition to supplying merchandise to powerful Poles, Wolf provided them with information about activities within the Jewish community that were of interest to them. For example, he told about disputes between various factions in the community and about petitions—no doubt containing complaints

[4] Rosman, 'Exploitative Regime', pp. xvii–xxx; id., 'Międzyboż veRabi Yisrael Ba'al Shem Tov', *Zion*, 52 (1987), 177–89; Eng. trans. in Hundert (ed.), *Essential Papers*, 209–25.

[5] Dinur, 'Reshitah shel haḥasidut', 100–10, 131–8; R. Mahler, *Toledot haYehudim bePolin* (Merhavya, 1946), 415; B. D. Weinryb, *The Jews of Poland* (Philadelphia, 1972), 282.

[6] The Besht lived in Międzybóż from approximately 1740 until his death in 1760 (see Dubnow, *Toledot haḥasidut*, 51, 69; Scholem, 'Demuto', 337, 342; and Rosman, 'Besht', 186–7). The sources utilized in this article originate mainly from the period *c.*1720–1750.

[7] Rosman, 'Exploitative Regime', pp. xix–xxix; cf. Hundert, 'Jewish Experience', 43–7.

[8] Biblioteka Czartoryskich, Cracow (henceforth: BC), Ewidencja (henceforth: EW) 40, 41 *passim*.

[9] See BC 4080 15*b* *c.*1741, which notes that the latifundium owner's administrator has the right to choose one of the four elders. Wolf's membership in the *kahal*'s ruling group might, then, have resulted directly from his close relationship with the administrators.

about the Polish administrators—being sent directly to the Czartoryskis as the magnate owners of Międzybóż.[10]

Wolf not only reported on disputes and petitions, but also recommended specific responses for the Polish authorities.[11] There are accusations that he took advantage of his powerful position to advance his own interests and harm those of others. In a petition of 1741, the Jewish butchers' guild of Międzybóż complained that Wolf tried to extort a pay-off from the guildmaster, Leyba, who was seeking permission from the *kahal* to build a barn near his home; attempted to force Leyba to sell him and his partners tallow and skins; apparently pocketed a fine levied against his brother-in-law for beating this same Leyba; and beat several butchers who ran foul of him and had another (unjustly) placed in the stocks.[12]

Assuming that this petition is credible, Wolf Abramowicz can be seen to have followed in the footsteps of Icko Ognisty. Like him, Wolf served the local Polish officials, gained a place of authority in the community, intimidated people, used strong-arm tactics to get his way, and specifically targeted the butchers' guild and its members as objects of his exploitation.

Other people with direct though less entrenched ties to the Polish officials were the *arendators*, who farmed taxes, tolls, customs duties, and other revenues and controlled mills, liquor-manufacturing appliances, and other facilities—all by lease arrangement with the Czartoryskis.[13] Their goal, of course, was to expand the range of enterprises they controlled and to maximize the revenues they collected. This often created a conflict of interest between them and the town's small-scale merchants, artisans, and innkeepers—Christians as well as Jews. If prices and fees were raised, it was the latter group that would have to pay the increased rates; and if a monopoly were expanded their rights to trade freely would be curtailed.

In 1742, for example, the *arendators* contracted with Czartoryski's representative to add to their monopoly the right to serve liquor in the town on the sabbath and holidays.

[10] BC 5948 l.38568, Sinicki to Walicki?, 25 June 1745; BC 5929 l.33449, Rapacki to Walicki, 26 June 1745. In these letters, the lower-level officials Rapacki and Sinicki used information supplied by Wolf to report to their superior Walicki, the general administrator for Międzybóż. These reports concerned petitions being sent to the Czartoryskis with regard to a dispute between the *arendators* and the *kahal* in which the town rabbi was prepared to take the side of the *kahal* (see below on such disputes and on the rabbi's situation). Wolf had also reported that a Jewess named Manasterna had gone to petition the Czartoryskis, evidently with a complaint against Walicki. In BC 5931 l. 33988, Rosciszewski to Walicki?, 10 July 1745, Rosciszewski told how Wolf (and the rabbi) had assured him that a certain petition did not originate in the official community institutions of Międzybóż, but was the product of some malcontents who sent it from a neighbouring locale.

[11] According to the letters cited in the previous note, Wolf recommended preventing the *arendators* from sending their petition and insisted that R. Hirsz Leybowicz's contract for the rabbinate not be renewed.

[12] BC EW 41, Punkta Cechu Rzezników Zydowskich Międzyboskiego przeciwko Judce, Leybce Niesmacznemu, Jankielowi Arendarzom, y Wolfowi Abramowiczowi . . . 14 Oct. 1741. For some of these acts Wolf claimed to be exercising his authority as 'elder of the month' (that is, rotating chairman of the *kahal* administration). In at least one of these instances, however, the petitioners pointed out how Wolf himself admitted that a different 'elder of the month', Chaskiel, would not have imposed the same punishment during his term of office.

[13] For details see: BC EW 40 1743, Kontrakt na aręde mieyska Międzyboska z targowym pro A' 1743 za summe 28,800; see also M. J. Rosman, *The Lords' Jews* (Cambridge, 1990), 106–20.

This elicited a strong protest from the *kahal* on behalf of the poor innkeepers, who claimed that such a move would eliminate a major portion of their livelihood and do them incalculable damage.[14] Merchants and artisans often tried to avoid paying duties and breached commercial rules designed as protectionist measures for the *arendators*. Such practices are reflected in the *arendators*' complaint in 1745 that evasive practices employed by those bringing merchandise to the market in the town were detrimental to the market and fairs. They also claimed that the artisan guilds' tariffs were so high as to discourage merchants from bringing outside merchandise for sale in Międzybóż, thereby reducing the duties that the *arendators* could collect.[15] When, in 1746, there was a shortage of bread in Międzybóż, the head of the bakers' guild claimed that it was because his guild had been ruined by the 'extortion of the *arendator*' (*zdzierstwem arendarskim*) and one of the administrators confirmed that the *arendator* had confiscated grain from the baker.[16]

The *arendators* had the upper hand because the Polish authorities gave them the right to confiscate contraband merchandise and even to arrange for the imprisonment or fining of anyone who violated their rights.[17] Such power lent itself to abuse, and the rabbi of Międzybóz may well have been correct when, in 1744, he denounced the *arendator* Leybka as a 'tyrant' and urged Czartoryski's commissioner, Walicki, to 'liberate the poor people from his hand'.[18]

This rabbi, Hirsz Leybowicz, himself apparently had a good working relationship with the magnate's men as well as with the local priest. He also can be considered in the category of those who derived influence from these ties. When the leaders of the Jewish community, including Wolf Abramowicz, decided not to renew his appointment as rabbi in 1744, he appealed to Walicki to force the community to keep him on. He even asked the priest, Losowski, to write a letter of recommendation on his behalf.[19]

Direct ties to the Poles were not the only source of powerful position in Międzybóż. The *akcyzniki*, those who leased from the *kahal* the excise taxes to which it was entitled, also wielded a significant degree of control in the community. Rather than remit the lease fee to the *kahal* in a lump sum, they paid it off by settling the financial obligations of the *kahal* as these became due. This meant that it was they who effectively controlled the purse-strings. Anyone who was owed money, such as the salaried employees of the *kahal*—the rabbi, the cantor, and so on—would suffer if for any reason the

[14] EW 87 1742, Petition signed by Międzybóż *kahal* and *pospulstwo*; EW 41, Torn document in Hebrew and Polish, dated 20 Tevet 5403 and 31 Mar. 1743; cf. BC 5825 l. 13594, Grętkowski to Walicki?, 30 Mar. 1745. For background on the problem of Jews serving liquor on the sabbath when work is prohibited, see H. H. Ben-Sasson, 'Statutes for the Enforcement of the Observance of the Sabbath in Poland and their Social and Economic Significance' (Heb.), *Zion*, 21 (1956), 188–90, 199–200.

[15] BC EW 41 1745, Punkta do WW Pana and Rezolucya na tą supplikę (see points 3–5).

[16] BC 5913 l.29489, Pęsky to ?, 17 Feb. 1746. According to the EW 40 1743 contract (see above, n. 13), the bakers had to buy all of their wheat from the *arendators* for more than the market price.

[17] BC EW 40 1743, contract; BC EW 41, Rezolucya na tą supplikę (point 3); BC 5931 l.33997, l.33999, Rosciszewski to Walicki, 21, 27 Feb. 1746. On powerful *arendators*, see: M. J. Rosman, 'The Relationship between the Jewish Arrendator and the Polish Nobleman: The Other Side' (Heb.), in N. Gross (ed.), *Hayehudim bakalkalah* (Jerusalem, 1985), 237–43.

[18] BC 5870 l.21169, Leybowicz to Walicki, 21 Dec. 1744.

[19] BC 5870 l.21168, l.21169, Leybowicz to Walicki, 2 Apr., 21 Dec. 1744; BC 5929 l.33449, Rapacki to Walicki, 26 June 1745; BC 5931 l.33988, Rosciszewski to Walicki?, 10 July 1745. On the possible involvement of the Besht in the attempt to unseat this rabbi, see below.

akcyzniki decided to postpone payment.[20] The *akcyzniki*'s tax-collecting authority also allowed them direct power over other people. The system that had evolved by the late 1730s was that every Thursday or Friday each merchant, shopkeeper, innkeeper, and butcher had to report to the *akcyzniki*, under threat of excommunication (*pod becheyrim*), what his turnover had been the previous week. The *akcyzniki* would then assess his tax. The exercise of their discretion in this matter could easily have been perceived as unfair by those who were dunned.[21] Also, the system was unwieldy and conducive to lying. By 1744 the system was revamped and merchants, shopkeepers, and artisans were being assessed a predetermined sum—set by officials of the *kahal* (innkeepers continued to be charged according to what they sold in practice, and butchers according to what they slaughtered).[22]

The *kahal* itself in Międzybóż was accused of disdaining the needs of those on the lower rungs of the socio-economic scale and representing the interests of the élite only. The *kahal* controlled the granting of residence rights, the apportionment of the tax burden, and the distribution of seats in the community synagogue. These decisions were important determinants of economic status and social prestige for the people who lived in the community. Various documents imply that in these matters the poorer shopkeepers and artisans were at a disadvantage.

In a petition to one of Czartoryski's senior officials, Manaszko Dubienski described himself as 'a poor shopkeeper here in Międzybóż who, having suffered much harm at the hands of the powerful members of the *kahal*, is appealing to the kindness of Your Most Powerful and Gracious Lordship'. Manaszko claimed that although he did not even own his own home, and made his living from a small shop where he sold skins, boots, and 'other small items', he was assessed 90 zloty—the same amount as some international merchants who travelled several times a year to Germany and traded in imported luxury goods worth tens of thousands. The *kahal* members, according to Manaszko, played favourites with their colleagues and friends and overburdened the poor.[23]

In 1741 the butchers' guild petitioned the Polish authorities concerning their synagogue.[24] They noted how they had refurbished the synagogue at their own expense and had even consented at one point to share it with the tailors' guild[25] until the latter could set up their own place of worship. When they did this, however, the *kahal* insisted that the butchers exchange their synagogue for the (presumably plainer) one that the tailors had acquired. The butchers refused, and for two years the *kahal* prohibited the use of their synagogue. Finally, after accepting a payment of five golden ducats from the tailors,[26]

[20] EW 41 contains a list of payments made by *akcyzniki*. On this payment order system in general, see Rosman, *The Lords' Jews*, 128–30.

[21] BC EW 41 1739, Akcyza contract; EW 41 1740, Taxy kontraktowanu kahalu; BC 5778 l. 5250, Ciesielski to Walicki, 28 Mar. 1745. For a case of alleged trumped up tax on the part of the *akcyzniki* see EW 41 1741, Petition of the Jewish butchers' guild.

[22] BC EW 41 1744, Akcyza contract.

[23] BC EW 87, Petition of Manaszko Dubienski to J. Wolinski.

[24] BC EW 41 1741, Petition of the Jewish butchers' guild.

[25] The arrangement was that on alternate sabbaths members of one of the guilds would receive all of the honours given out during the service.

[26] This equals 90 zloty. In this period in the town of Brzezany a small wooden house cost 50 to 80 zloty. If this is a reliable guide, then five ducats seems like a reasonable price to pay for a one-room small wooden synagogue (which this building probably was).

the *kahal* took possession of the butchers' building by force and gave it to the tailors, ordering the word 'butchers' to be scratched off the sign at the front.[27] In consequence, the butchers were now asking the Polish administration to restore their synagogue to them and allow them to appoint a rabbi who would judge them, in effect granting them a large degree of autonomy from the *kahal.*

The butchers were not the only group to want to set up its own congregation. On 24 November 1741 a Polish court document took note of the fact that Osior Moszkowicz and his companions had begun private prayer services. Like the butchers' synagogue, the establishment of this separate *minyan* was probably connected to the fact that the members of this group were not given ritual honours—or the social respect that the conferring of such honours represented—in the main synagogue.[28] It is obvious from a set of rules governing the distribution of honours in the synagogue, dating from 1745, that these were at a premium, and that the *kahal* leaders were apt to monopolize them.[29] The fact is that more than honours were in short supply in the Międzybóż synagogue: due to an influx of newcomers the place was overcrowded, and some new arrivals were taking the seats of established community members.[30] Others were occupying temporarily free seats without paying for a permanent seat of their own as was customary.[31]

The overcrowding in the synagogue was just a reflection of a more basic problem. Many of the new settlers in Międzybóż were poor and did not pay taxes.[32] This means that they also could not have paid the initiation fee that Jewish communities normally required before granting newcomers the right of residence (*ḥerem hayishuv*).[33] These people were not only sitting in the synagogue contrary to accepted custom, they were unlawfully settled in the town. By 1743 the problem had become serious, and the Polish administrator Wolinski ordered the community to form a committee to regularize the seating assignments in the synagogue and sell any remaining empty places. He further authorized the committee to make up a list of those who possessed the formal right of residence in Międzybóż. Those 'foreign and poor' Jews who were in the town illegally would be expelled. The *kahal* submitted a list of potential expellees numbering over thirty persons, composed mainly of people in low-paying occupations like candle-makers, tailors, carters, and musicians.[34]

[27] Another case where it is specified that the *kahal* has the power to prohibit the use of a guild's synagogue by its members as a result of a conflict between the guild and the *kahal* is preserved in the minute book of Włodawa; see B. D. Weinryb, *Texts and Studies in the Communal History of Polish Jewry*, Proceedings of the American Academy for Jewish Research 19 (New York, 1951); Włodawa Hebrew section, document no. 10.

[28] BC EW 80/1, Dekret, 24 Nov. 1741. The identity of this group is not at all clear; but it is unlikely that this was a separate group of hasidim or kabbalists because such a group was already apparently supported by the *kahal*; see Rosman, 'Besht', 187. Cf. Jacob Katz, *Masoret umashber* (Jerusalem, 1958), pub. in Eng. as *Tradition and Crisis*, trans. B. D. Cooperman (New York, 1993), 153–5, 177–8.

[29] BC EW 41, Kopia punktow.

[30] Rosman, 'Besht', 181, 183.

[31] BC EW 41, Order of Wolinski, 28 Mar. 1743. A seat in the synagogue was considered real estate that could be bought, sold, and inherited; see Katz, *Tradition and Crisis*, 153.

[32] BC EW 41 Wolinski Order, 28 Mar. 1743.

[33] Katz, *Tradition and Crisis*, 88–9.

[34] BC EW 41, Specifikatia Żydów Międzyboskich . . . (There is no indication of whether or not the expulsion was executed.)

The material from Międzybóż not only presents examples of how élites bore down on the lower classes in the 1730s and 1740s, but also indicates some of the ways in which those who were pressed by the establishment responded. The impression given by Polish sources, although they are obviously weighted in this direction, is that one of the most frequent forms of protest was petitioning the Polish authorities to step in and restrain the arrogant exercise of power by one of the sources of authority in the Jewish community.[35] Sometimes the protest was much more direct and took a violent form. For example, in 1731 the butchers, in cooperation with the *kahal*, tried to poison Ognisty.[36] There also was a tendency by those who viewed themselves as victims of discrimination to attempt to escape the control of the élite by setting up parallel institutions such as their own synagogue and their own rabbinic court.[37]

So the Polish material would seem to confirm that the social situation in Międzybóż at the time of the Besht was congruent with what historians working on the basis of Jewish sources have taught us to expect. Powerful individuals in various roles took advantage of those low on the ladder. There was a social gap, and there are signs of enmity between ruler and ruled, rich and poor, the élite and the lower classes.

The élite groups that I have singled out—factors who worked for the Polish administrators, *arendators* of the magnate's rights, *akcyzniki* of the *kahal*'s income, and the *kahal* itself—were not mutually exclusive. Icko Ognisty, Wolf Abramowicz, and the various types of lessees often served on the *kahal* in diverse capacities;[38] and a lessee of the magnate one year could, in theory at least, become a lessee of the *kahal* the next. This overlapping makes it tempting to accept the paradigm with which we began—a monolithic establishment versus 'the people'—as a sufficient description of the social situation in the Międzybóż community in this period. In reality however, this relationship was not the only one at work.

I noted earlier that when Wolf wanted to punish a certain butcher he said that he could not do it at the present time because Chaskiel and not he, Wolf, was currently the *kwartalny*.[39] Moreover, in protesting against Ognisty, the butchers tried in cooperation with the *kahal* to poison him. Similarly, the *kahal* made appeals to the Polish owners of Międzybóż against Ognisty or the *arendators* on behalf of those who were victimized.[40] The *kahal*, then, was capable, at least some of the time, of standing up for the interests of the common man. Resistance did not necessarily have to take the form of appeal to some outside authority or of overtly anti-establishment violent behaviour.

The body that was supposed to represent the best interests of the entire community

[35] See petitions of this type in EW 41 and EW 87.

[36] Rosman, 'Exploitative Regime', p. xxv; cf. Hundert, 'Shekiat yirat kavod', 43–4.

[37] The request of the butchers and the private prayer services in the house of Osior, cited above, are examples of this.

[38] In n. 9 I cited the 1741 rule granting the magnate's administrator the right to appoint one of the four *kahal* elders. Also, according to the 1743 contract for the general *arenda* of Międzybóż (n. 13), the *arendator* of the town would automatically become one of the elders. It is not clear whether these two provisions were in force at the same time; and if they were, whether they were just different ways of stating the same thing.

[39] BC EW 41 1741, Punkta Cechu Rzezników Żydowskich . . . ; cf. n. 12 above.

[40] BC EW 87 1742, Petition of *kahal* and *pospulstwo*; BC 3822, no. 76, pp. 335–6, petition of the *kahal* v. Ognisty; EW 80/1, Kopia Dekretu Rabina Skahalem.

—the *kahal*—sometimes did just that. There were apparently at least semi-institutionalized safeguards to ensure that this would be the case. Taxpaying members of the community who did not serve as members of the *kahal* had influence on its actions through a body referred to in the sources as the *pospulstwo* ('plebs'), which seems to have exercised an advise and consent function. When the *kahal* acted against the general interest, the *pospulstwo* could protest. Important decisions were announced and conflicts resolved by joint committees made up of an equal number of members from the *kahal* and the *pospulstwo*. A document of 1741 seems to imply that the *pospulstwo* was guaranteed representation among the *kwartalny*.[41]

This means that the pattern of exploitation of the weak by the strong was inconsistent; the non-élite were not without representation and the means to resist.[42] Moreover, not only is the pattern of the exploitation inconsistent, it is not the only paradigm of social conflict. The protest by the *kahal* against the *arendator*'s newly acquired monopoly over the sale of alcohol on the sabbath and its involvement in the machinations against Ognisty demonstrate that the *kahal* might go against the factor or the *arendator*: the interests of those in power did not necessarily coincide. The most common type of intra-élite conflict was between the two classes of *arendator*: those who leased the incomes of the magnate, and those who leased the excise tax from the *kahal*. Several sources report one group protesting that the prerogatives of the other were infringing on their profits.[43] There were also conflicts between candidates competing for the same lease.[44]

The non-élite group was also not an undifferentiated, harmonious whole. This is demonstrated in two of the cases mentioned above: the butchers' synagogue being ceded to the tailors, and the people without formal residence rights overcrowding the synagogue. The tailors were obviously on better terms with the *kahal* than were the butchers, and initiated, or at least cooperated with, the attempt to dispossess the butchers' guild of its synagogue. It was 'the Jews of Międzybóż'—not just the élite—who complained about the overcrowding and usurpation of places in the synagogue. A joint committee of the *kahal*, the *pospulstwo*, and the rabbi drew up the list of those who were legitimate inhabitants of the town.[45] In other words, not surprisingly, many of the non-élite were also interested in expelling the 'foreign and poor' Jews.

Thus in Międzybóż there were several vectors in the vortex of social confrontation. In addition to élite versus plebeians, there were also different versions of élite versus

[41] Rosman, 'Besht', 182–3; BC 4080 15*b*. (This is in addition to the provision in the same document allowing the magnate's administrator to appoint one of the four elders; see nn. 9 and 38.)

[42] See Rosman, 'Exploitative Regime', pp. xxvii–xxix.

[43] BC EW 87, Supliki of Akcyzniki and Arendators; EW 41, Suplika do WImP Woyskiego Rawskiego; EW 41, Punkta do WWPana, pts. 7–9; BC 5931 l. 33994, Rosciszewski to Walicki?, 31 Dec. 1745; BC 5948 l. 38562, Sinicki to Walicki?, 9 June 1745. Other types of *arendator* also fought with each other, e.g. EW 41, Punkta do WWPana, pt. 5; EW 87, 16 Feb. 1739.

[44] BC EW 87, Suplika of Akcyzniki to Wolinski; BC 5758 l. 483, Badyński to ?, 25 Nov. 1745. Apparently part of the reason for Wolf and his brother harming poor Leyba the butcher (see above) was that doing so would lower the income of their rivals the 'current *akcyzniki*'; EW 41 1741, Punkta Cechu Rzezników Żydowskich. Compare Dov Ber b. Shmuel of Linits (Luniets), *Shivḥei haBesht* [Kopys, 1814], pub. in Eng. as *In Praise of the Baal Shem Tov*, trans. D. Ben-Amos and J. R. Mintz (Bloomington, Ind., 1970), 128, 200–1.

[45] BC EW 41, Order of Wolinski, 28 Mar. 1743 and Specifikatia Żydów Międzyboskich . . .

élite as well as artisan versus artisan and poor versus poorer. The array of power relationships was not rigid; alignments could shift.[46]

It is well to keep the complexity of the patterns of social conflict in mind when attempting to characterize the Baal Shem Tov's position in Międzybóż. As I have pointed out elsewhere, he was not an anti-establishment figure. On the contrary, he was supported by the establishment to the end of his days in Międzybóż, and such support apparently was extended to his son after his death.[47]

Another indication of the Besht's respected status within the official, normative Jewish community is contained in a responsum cited by Dinur some forty years ago.[48] This responsum begins with the testimony of Mordekhai b. Judah Leib, called *ne'eman* (trustee) of Międzybóż.[49] Mordekhai testified how some spoiled flesh could not be separated from the lung of a freshly slaughtered cow and the butcher was sent to bring the rabbi to examine the lung and decide whether the animal was kosher or not. The rabbi came and said that he would have to refer to his books (the continuation of the responsum indicates that later the rabbi declared the animal kosher). Following Mordekhai's testimony the next passage reads:

> In our presence, the court signed below, our teacher, the aforementioned Mordekhai, related all that is written above as testimony and then wrote all of this in his own handwriting and signed it with his very own signature. Therefore we have confirmed it and substantiated it as is proper. Signed, Israel BeSh [Baal Shem] from Tluste; and signed, Moses Joseph *magid meisharim* [preacher] of Międzybóż.[50]
>
> And behold regarding all of the foregoing we have requested from the rabbi, the great light, the light of Israel, the glory of the generation whose holy name we glorify, our teacher, Meir [R. Meir of Konstantynów, a leading rabbi of the time], may God protect and bless him, to inform us as to his opinion in this matter. Did the teacher [rabbi] do the right thing or not to permit the cow? And due to the size of the fire that became a torch because of this, etc., we therefore trust in him that he will consider our words so as to inform us as to what he thinks about this and may there be therein peace from now and forever.

The 'we' who are challenging the Międzybóż rabbi's decision and asking the question of R. Meir are the two signatories to the testimony: the Besht and the preacher (who probably was close to the Besht).[51] R. Meir acknowledged the Besht as the chief questioner by addressing his response as follows:

[46] Cf. Ettinger, 'The Hasidic Movement', 254, '. . . among the rabbis and the ritual slaughterers and the wandering preachers, some are connected with the ruling group and some are against it'.

[47] Rosman, 'Besht', 187–8; cf. Etkes, 'Hasidism as a Movement', 15–17, 21; and Ettinger, 'The Hasidic Movement', 254–5, 260.

[48] Dinur, 'Reshitah shel haḥasidut', 205–6. The responsum, addressed to R. Meir of Konstantynów, son of the famous R. Jacob Emden, appears in Haim b. Berish Rapoport, *She'elot uteshuvot mayim ḥayim* (2 vols., Zhitomir, 1857), Yoreh de'ah, i, no. 27.

[49] The title *ne'eman* denotes a *kahal* official, often a treasurer; but here, in view of the context, perhaps it means official communal slaughterer.

[50] The first signatory is obviously the Besht, who had moved from Tluste to Międzybóż. Moses Joseph is probably the person referred to as Joseph Maggid Meisharim in both Polish and Jewish sources; see Rosman, 'Besht', 177–8 nn. 4–5.

[51] It is evident from *Shivḥei haBesht* that the Besht had great respect for Joseph the preacher; see *In Praise*, 125–6, 206–7.

Champion in Judea and Israel! *He whose success has been witnessed by both high and low*. He provides balm and medicament to the person without strength. He is great in Babylonia and famous in Tiberias and has prevailed in all things.[52] The great sage, the eminent rabbi, famous for his good name, our teacher Israel, may God protect and bless him. And of all his colleagues, all of them beloved rabbis, the great and eminent sage, our teacher Gershon,[53] may God protect and bless him; and those whom I don't know [by name] I greet; may they all be granted the highest blessing.

The Besht's question challenged a controversial decision made by the rabbi of Międzybóz, referred to here as R. Falk, in the area of *kashrut*. R. Meir agreed with the questioners that the rabbi had erred and should have declared the cow unkosher, in line with a long-accepted precedent set by R. Moses Isserles in the sixteenth century.

As Dinur says, this source makes it clear that the Besht and his group were not on the margins of normative Jewish society, much less in opposition to it. The 'trustee' and 'preacher' of the community were associated with the Besht, and R. Meir praised and blessed his entire circle. Moreover, the honorifics applied to the Besht by R. Meir, the scion of a very important rabbinic family, indicate that the Besht was a person of some fame and worthy of the respect of scholars.

Dinur also observed that the ramifications of this responsum went beyond the issue at hand. The questioners themselves indicated that this had become a great controversy that necessitated an urgent response, which they hoped would re-establish peace. Near the end of his response R. Meir implied that the rabbi's job was hanging in the balance: if the rabbi admitted his mistake all would be well but 'if he is steadfast in his rebellion, as Maimonides decreed, his fate is decided . . . He should not build an altar for himself to destroy the words of the classic scholars by whose instruction we live and who are our guides.'

This background puts the Besht's position in this controversy in an interesting light. If the rabbi was to be dismissed for a ruling that contravened established tradition and was too lenient, then it was the Besht who was defending established precedent and advocating stricter application of the law. It should also be noted that leniency in *kashrut* decisions was bound to find favour with the poorer elements in the community: carcasses discarded or sold as non-kosher reduced the supply of kosher meat and raised its price. This incident presents a dimension of the Besht not usually emphasized by the interpreters of the hagiographic stories about him in *Shivḥei haBesht*.[54] It makes it difficult to portray him as a totally populist figure, irreconcilably alienated from the rabbinical and political establishment. Although the identification cannot be confirmed, if this is the same episode referred to in Polish sources dating from 1744 and 1745 concerning an attempt on the part of the *kahal*, Wolf Abramowicz, and Leybka the *arendator* to depose the town's rabbi, then the Besht's ties to the élite may have been

[52] 'Great in Babylonia and famous in Tiberias' is an expression originating in the Talmud, Meg. 6*a*, and connoting great fame and admiration throughout the Jewish world.

[53] This is R. Abraham Gershon of Kutow, the Baal Shem Tov's brother-in-law and a prominent talmudist and kabbalist in Podolia who emigrated to the Land of Israel in 1747. See A. J. Heschel, *The Circle of the Baal Shem Tov: Studies in Hasidism*, ed. S. H. Dresner (Chicago, 1985), 44–97.

[54] M. J. Rosman, 'The Quest for the Historical Ba'al ShemTov', in *Tradition and Crisis Revisited* (in press). Actually, there are stories in *Shivḥei haBesht* which portray the Besht as rather strict in ritual matters, e.g. Ben-Amos and Mintz, *In Praise*, 90–1, 195, 254–5—but cf. 192.

very close indeed.[55] On the other hand, support of members of the élite on a particular question does not necessarily imply alignment with them on all issues, as I have attempted to demonstrate above.

Moreover, the Besht had ties to the other factors in the social equation of Międzybóż. Some stories in *Shivḥei haBesht* imply that the Besht had meaningful relationships with certain powerful members of the nobility, and even with local clergymen.[56] Given the power that connections with this type of people could confer, such associations may have given him a certain degree of independence in his dealings with the *kahal* and men like Wolf Abramowicz.[57] It is also obvious that the Besht's spiritual qualities gained him the admiration and even devotion of many of the learned kabbalists with whom he came into contact.[58] Finally, his healing powers prompted 'the entire world' (in the words of *Shivḥei haBesht*) to come to him, and his ecstatic mode of prayer apparently exercised a profound impact on those who observed him and attracted the common man to him as well.[59] Not only were there spheres of activity of which the Besht stood at the centre,[60] the Besht maintained links with the various social circles of the town.

Social conflict did not give rise to hasidism; but at the time that the Besht lived in Międzybóż there were conflicts and a lack of communal concord. The cross-currents of controversy were complex. Within this complexity, the Besht seems to have managed to avoid identifying fully with any one constituency. Instead, through the various facets of his personality and his activities, he apparently established relationships with all components of Międzybóż society. This may have been the beginning of a tradition of hasidic leadership whereby the zaddik represented a force for unity in an increasingly disharmonious community. Hasidism eventually came to espouse alternative institutions of leadership, prayer, and social organization that may have been welcomed by the

[55] Dinur, 'Reshitah shel haḥasidut', 206, claimed that his association with the establishment represented an early stage in the Besht's career and that later he aroused opposition; but in my opinion there is no proof for such an assertion. The Polish sources imply that cordial relations were maintained between the Besht and the *kahal* of Międzybóż until his death; see Rosman, 'Besht', 187–8. For the Polish sources that touch on the rabbi's dismissal see n. 19. Dinur, 'Reshitah shel haḥasidut', 206, conjectured that the responsum dates from *c.*1744. Its *terminus ad quem* is *c.*1747, the year when Gershon of Kutów—addressed by R. Meir as present in Międzybóż—emigrated to the Land of Israel. Since the Polish documents which concern the rabbi's dismissal date from 1744 and 1745 it would seem that the responsum and these Polish letters are talking about the same incident. The responsum, however, calls the rabbi in question Falk, while the Polish documents speak of one Hirsz Leybowicz (that is Zevi [or Hirsch] b. Judah [or Aryeh] Leib). It may be that the man's personal name was Zevi (in Yiddish: Hirsch) Falk b. Judah (or Aryeh) Leib or Zevi Hirsch b. Judah (or Aryeh) Leib Falk and that the Polish and Hebrew sources simply refer to him in different ways. (There is at least one confirmed example of this phenomenon, Israel b. Rubin Ritfin, called in Polish sources Rubinowicz, and in Hebrew sources Israel Ritfin; see Rosman, *The Lords' Jews*, 154–5.) It is also possible that the printed responsum (as opposed to the Polish manuscript letters written by Hirsz Leybowicz and others who knew him) is mistaken. Interestingly, according to the Polish sources, it was Rabbi Hirsz Leybowicz who once tried to put himself in the role of defender of the common people against the 'tyrant' *arendator* Leybka (see n. 18) and, as already noted, leniency in *kashrut* decisions was potentially a populist position.

[56] See *In Praise* 129, 193, 241–2, 248, 253; Rosman, 'Besht', 186.

[57] Compare how Hirsz Leybowicz attempted to fight his dismissal by the powers that be in the community by appealing to Walicki and the priest Losowski; see above, n. 19.

[58] Etkes, 'Hasidism as a Movement' 11–15, Heschel, *The Circle*, 11–13, 48–9, 120–1; Scholem, 'Demuto', 339, 340, 344.

[59] Etkes, 'Hasidism as a Movement', 17.

[60] Ibid. 7.

disaffected, and to appeal to both mystic and legalist.[61] Yet the hasidim continued to participate in the official life of the *kahal*.[62] This stance may well have had its roots in the Baal Shem Tov's connections to all the points on the social spectrum.

[61] Ettinger, 'The Hasidic Movement', 255.
[62] Ibid. 265; Katz, *Tradition and Crisis*, 210–11.

FIVE

Hasidism and the *Kahal* in Eastern Europe

SHMUEL ETTINGER

ALTHOUGH the subject has featured in numerous histories of eastern European Jewry in the modern era, we do not as yet possess a thorough and unbiased analysis of the relationship between the hasidic movement and the institutions of Jewish communal organization in eastern Europe during the period in which hasidism began. The main obstacle has been the dislocation and probable destruction of the bulk of the evidence—the minute books (*pinkasim*) in which community councils (*kehalim*) as well as the various 'societies' (*ḥevrot*) which operated within their organizational framework had kept their records for centuries. Many hundreds of Jewish communities existed in the region and came under the influence of the hasidic movement during the latter part of the eighteenth century. This influence must have left its mark on communal records, but only a small number of the original documents is known to have survived. Some *pinkasim*, still available to scholars prior to the two world wars, were subsequently lost or destroyed, with the result that we are now left with only a few selections of documents, compiled at best by professional historians but in some cases by amateurs, or else quotations from various *pinkasim* which are scattered in a variety of historical publications.

These selections from the documents are by no means representative; they were often made by editors eager to avoid controversial issues and to suppress what they judged to be unsavoury facts. Moreover, in some of the extant *pinkasim*, as in that of the Society [for the Study of] Talmud and Mishnah (Ḥevrah Shas Umishnayot) in the Lithuanian community of Radoshkovichi, all the anti-hasidic regulations were blotted out once the controversy between the hasidim and their opponents had died out.[1] From others, as from the *pinkas* of the community council of Shargorod, it seems that the

Prof. Shmuel Ettinger died in London on 22 Sept. 1988—only three months after the 'Hasidism Reappraised' conference and before completing the preparation of his conference lecture for publication. I am grateful to his family, and to Prof. Israel Bartal of the Hebrew University, for locating, and making available for inclusion in the present volume, the unpublished manuscript of this paper. The paper required some stylistic modifications as well as the insertion of bibliographical references, which were totally absent from the original manuscript. For help in locating some of these, thanks are due to Prof. Chimen Abramsky: a lifelong and intimate friend of Prof. Ettinger, he was able to draw on the immense powers of memory and erudition which he shared with his late friend, to identify some of the less obvious sources cited or mentioned in the paper. [A.R.-A.]

[1] See I. Halpern, 'Ḥavurot letorah umitsvot vehatenu'ah haḥasidit behitpashtutah', in id., *Yehudim veyahadut bemizraḥ Eiropah* (Jerusalem, 1969), 319–20.

hasidim had torn out the pages which related to, or which contained the signatures of, leading hasidic personalities in order to keep them as holy relics. Some of the *pinkasim* may still exist in what was until recently the Soviet Union or in private hands, but they have not so far become available for inspection. For this reason, sweeping generalizations and far-fetched assumptions have been made about the subject on the basis of insufficient documentation.

Another difficulty arises from the fact that, to this day, few scholars have been able to address hasidic history in a detached manner. The tradition of militant opposition to hasidism on the one hand, and of uncritical, sentimental empathy and apologetics on the other hand, has left an indelible mark on the historiography of the hasidic movement. One can discern the influence of either neo-hasidic romanticism or the hostile legacy of mitnaggedism and Haskalah even in important scholarly studies of hasidism. This problem is exacerbated by the scarcity of communal records and other concrete historical documentation, which has led the historians to rely very heavily on literary sources such as the sermons of the hasidic leaders or the hagiographical tales about them. From these problematic sources—homiletic writings and didactic tales which may be theologically, ethically, and even poetically charged but which can hardly substitute for plain archival documentation—the historians were able to extract the 'evidence' in support of virtually any view they might have wished to advance concerning the relationship between hasidism and Jewish communal organization. Thus, for example, the literary sources, supported by inadequate documentary materials, were often construed as evidence indicating special hasidic concerns with such issues as social injustice or the desire to democratize the institutions of communal government, a view which has been shown to be totally unfounded.[2] Another body of problematic literary sources on which the historians were forced to rely all too heavily, but which may well have distorted their understanding of the relationship between hasidism and traditional communal organization, was the overtly polemical literature of both the mitnaggedim and the maskilim. For these reasons, a brief review of the history of scholarly research on Hasidism may in itself shed some light on the subject under discussion.

The first two historians who attempted to explain in modern scholarly terms the success of the hasidic movement and its impact on Jewish society were Ilya Orshanski (1846–75) and Sergey Bershadski (1850–96), the former a young militant campaigner for Jewish emancipation and integration in Russian society, the latter a Gentile historian who was brought up in an anti-Jewish environment but became not only an important historian of Russian Jewry but also a supporter of the cause of Jewish equality. Both, however, saw in Jewish legal and social autonomy the burdensome legacy of the Middle Ages, an obsolete remnant of the Polish political tradition which had prevented the Jews from integrating into an enlightened modern Russia. (Bershadski was even willing to consider a biased memorandum, full of anti-Jewish innuendoes and openly expressed hostility, which was submitted in 1773 by M. V. Kakhovskii, the then Governor of Mogilev province, to the Governor-General of Belorussia, Count Z. G. Chernyshev, as a genuine 'characterization of the Kahal administration . . . by a knowledgeable and

[2] See I. Halpern, 'Yaḥaso shel R. Aharon hagadol miKarlin kelapei mishtar hakehilot', *Zion*, 22 (1957), 86–92, repr. in id., *Yehudim veyahadut*, 333–9.

unbiased observer'.) From this point of view, neither Bershadski nor Orshanski could understand why the great majority of Russian Jews continued to consider all government intervention in internal Jewish affairs as persecution, and they looked upon all developments in Jewish communal organization during the century prior to their own time as a long process of degeneration and decline, the inevitable disintegration of an archaic system and its decaying institutions.[3]

The modern historians of eastern European Jewry and hasidism were all distinguished by their Jewish nationalist rather than integrationist ideological orientation (including S. Dubnow, P. Marek, B. Dinur, R. Mahler, and J. Katz). Not only had they witnessed the survival of Jewish communal organization in eastern Europe throughout the nineteenth century and well into the twentieth, but at least some of them had even considered this same organizational structure a possible basis for the regeneration of Jewish life in the modern world; yet paradoxically they continued to use Bershadski's analysis uncritically. They still spoke about the disintegration, be it functional or structural, of Jewish communal institutions in the course of the eighteenth century; they observed the emergence of new forms of communal leadership in place of the old moribund ones; and thus they gave rise to the school of thought which explained the emergence of hasidism primarily as a response to the collapse of the traditional institutions of Jewish communal life in eastern Europe.

It was the important contribution of Isaac Levitats to show that the historical frameworks of Jewish communal organization continued to function in Russia at least until the formal dissolution of the *kahal* in 1844,[4] and, at any rate, long after the beginning and rapid spread of hasidism in the second half of the eighteenth century and the early decades of the nineteenth. Hasidism did not, then, owe its success primarily to the fact that it was able to fill an alleged communal-organizational vacuum; other factors must have facilitated at least the initial stages of its expansion and growth.

There is no doubt that the polemical, anti-hasidic writings of the final decades of the eighteenth century had influenced the historians' perception of early hasidism and its scale of operation during the lifetime of Israel Besht. Some polemicists and critics had claimed that by the time of his death in 1760 he had amassed a following of no less than 10,000,[5] suggesting the existence of a radical popular movement undermining the traditional order of Jewish communal life. In fact we know that the Besht's circle of followers was small, spiritually motivated, and devoid of any clear social or political orientation. What its members had in common was some previous mystical-pietistic experience which had led them to the Besht. It seems that the circle was closed, offering little access to outsiders, and that any influence which the Besht might have had on the larger public was in his capacity of *ba'al shem*—a popular healer. According to the *Shivḥei haBesht*, it was for this very reason that the circle of mystics with which he became associated did not at first hold him in high esteem. There are signs of tension within the circle, even direct antagonism to the Besht, and possibly some rivalry over the leadership (as between Nahman of Kosov and the Besht), but there is no concrete

[3] See I. Orshanski, *Yevrei v Rossii* (St Petersburg, 1877), 177–243.

[4] See I. Levitats, *The Jewish Community in Russia, 1772–1884* (New York, 1943), 123 ff.

[5] See e.g. Israel Loebel, 'Yedi'ot meheimanot al kat ḥadashah bePolin veLita hamekhunah ḥasidim' (Heb. trans. of the German original) in M. Wilensky, *Ḥasidim umitnaggedim* (2 vols.; Jerusalem, 1970), ii. 326.

evidence of any public or institutional opposition to its activities. Even the circumstances in which R. Jacob Joseph of Polonnoye was dismissed from his rabbinical post in Shargorod are not clear, and the affair may not have been connected at all to his association with the Besht as a hasid.

On the other hand, some of the doctrines which were to become the hallmarks of later hasidism were evident already in the Besht's teachings and his life. These included the claim that the future redemption of Israel was dependent on the diffusion of his own teaching; the demand that a mystic should serve as communal leader and be responsible for both the spiritual and the material well-being of the community; the 'organistic' conception of the relationship between the leader and the community—the notion that all the constituent parts of the Jewish people function as a single organism and are accountable to one another; the condemnation of the ascetic withdrawal of the mystic from public life as serving no positive purpose but rather nourishing the divine attribute of harsh judgements and constraint (*din*); the definition of the task and obligation of the leader as the elevation of the common people to a higher level of existence by infusing spiritual meaning into their mundane lives (the doctrine of 'worship through corporeality'). In addition, a number of the social and religious practices of later hasidism appear to have been customary already in the circle of the Besht: the protection of individual monopoly rights (*arenda*) to prevent economic rivalry within the Jewish community; the insistence on the use of specially sharpened knives by ritual slaughterers; and the 'redemption' or 'ransom' of Jewish tenants from incarceration by the Polish estate owners for failure to pay rent or other pecuniary offences. All these activities are attested in the circle of the Besht, and while we do not hear of any opposition to them, there is no evidence either to suggest that the Besht and his associates were collaborating in such matters with the communal institutions of the *kahal* and its agencies.

The position changed once hasidism began to emerge as a significant social movement during the 1760s and 1770s, under the leadership of the Great Maggid, Dov Ber of Mezhirech. According to the testimony of one of the most virulent opponents of hasidism, David of Makow (Makow Mazowiecki), 'In the year 1766, R. Berush of Mezhirech became famous, and a number of rabbis and eminent scholars (*ge'onim*) came to visit him. A few of them then adopted some of his ways.'[6] This implies a degree of cooperation between Dov Ber of Mezhirech and at least some members of the existing rabbinic leadership of the communities; it represents the ascent of a hasidic leader to a position of authority within, rather than in the face of, the established communal-organizational order. In the same year, 1766, a dispute occurred between two Jewish residents of the Volhynian town of Starokonstantinov who each claimed exclusive rights over the manufacture of copper utensils. When one of the parties refused to appear before the rabbinical court, R. Dov Ber threatened both with excommunication, and he barred the entire community from all commercial dealings with them until they reconciled themselves to the decision of the court. In their ruling on the matter, the rabbi of Rovno together with the town's Maggid referred respectfully to 'the letter sent by the famous hasid, Rabbi Dov, may his light shine, the Maggid of the holy com-

[6] See David of Makow's letter in Wilensky, *Ḥasidim umitnaggedim*, ii. 235.

munity of Mezhirech', and even stated explicitly that 'We, the undersigned court, agree with the statement of the hasid . . .'[7] Clearly, it was not R. Dov Ber's official status as the maggid of a neighbouring Jewish community (he had signed the letter as 'Preacher (*maggid meisharim*) of Greater Mezhirech and Korets') but rather his reputation as a hasid and spiritual master that lent weight to his opinion in this case.

Dov Ber of Mezhirech's reputation was to grow as his disciples and emissaries began to spread hasidism further afield. The evidence of the Kantian philosopher Solomon Maimon—one of the earliest 'neutral' accounts of hasidic activities at that time—should be treated with caution since it was written decades after the events described, when the author had cut all his connections with eastern European Jewish life. Nevertheless, it seems that Maimon was recalling authentic events and impressions when he described in his autobiography 'a young man of twenty two, of very weak bodily constitution, lean and pale', who

> travelled in Poland as a [hasidic] missionary. In his look there was something so terrible, so commanding, that he ruled men by means of it quite despotically. Wherever he came he inquired about the constitution of the congregation, rejected whatever displeased him and made new regulations which were punctiliously followed. The elders of the congregation, for the most part old respectable men, who far excelled him in learning, trembled before his face.[8]

Several scholars commenting on this passage have suggested that the young man described in it should be identified with one of the Maggid's closest disciples, Aaron of Karlin, a hasidic leader in his own right who had added his signature and stamp of approval to a set of communal ordinances (*takanot*) in Solomon Maimon's Lithuanian home town of Nesvizh (although at the time, in 1769, Aaron of Karlin must have been 33, not 22 years old as reported by Maimon). Some have found in this particular set of ordinances, whose effect was to prohibit double taxation, evidence of the novel, democratic sensibility which is alleged to have distinguished the hasidic leadership from the established communal leadership of the *kahal*. The ordinances guaranteed some protection to the poor and made further rises in the level of taxation dependent on the collective agreement of all the taxpaying members of the community. However, as I. Halpern has shown convincingly,[9] there was nothing novel or extraordinary about the ordinances of Nesvizh, and even the invitation extended by the local community council to the hasidic emissary Aaron of Karlin to act as one of the signatories to their amended ordinances was in line with the established practice of soliciting the formal approval of such procedural changes from any important visitor who happened to be 'in town'. The significance of the incident, overlooked by many, is not only that it corroborates Solomon Maimon's report by presenting a hasidic emissary as one who was considered prominent enough to be honoured in this way by the local *kahal*, but also that it establishes the fact that Aaron of Karlin was acting on the authority of 'our teacher . . . the learned sage of the whole *golah* (diaspora), the Maggid of the holy com-

[7] For the collection of letters and fragments of letters relating to this incident see Isaac b. Leib Landau, *Zikaron tov* [Piotrkow, 1892], 68–9. For the letters by and about the Maggid of Mezhirech see p. 68, letters 2 and 4. Cf. C. Shmeruk, 'Haḥasidut ve'iskei hahakhirut', *Zion*, 35 (1970), 187.

[8] Solomon Maimon, *The Autobiography of Solomon Maimon*, trans. J. Clarke Murray (London, 1954), 177 n. 1.

[9] See 'Yaḥaso shel R. Aharon Hagadol miKarlin kelapei mishtar hakehilot'.

munity of Mezerich'.[10] It was possible, then, for the Maggid of Mezhirech to be described at that time as a universally acknowledged leader in the official *kahal* records of a Jewish community in Lithuania. The fact is that we do not possess a single record of opposition either to Dov Ber of Mezhirech or to hasidism dating from the period when his popularity as a hasidic leader was at its height, and when his emissaries were establishing new centres of hasidism in Lithuania, Belorussia, and all other parts of Poland. On the contrary, as we have seen, the evidence suggests that the Maggid's reputation and authority as a hasidic leader were readily acknowledged by all. This was also the impression of Solomon Maimon, who claimed that 'the fact that this sect spread so rapidly, and that the new doctrine met with so much approbation, may be very easily explained. The natural inclination to idleness and a life of speculation on the part of the majority who from birth are destined to study . . . these are sufficient to make this phenomenon intelligible.'[11]

It seems that we have sufficient reason to conclude that, contrary to the opinion of a number of historians, neither the revolutionary or radical religious teachings of the new movement, nor its alleged opposition to the oligarchic structure of the traditional leadership institutions of the *kahal*, were the reason for the eruption of the anti-hasidic polemic of 1771–2; rather, it was the personal intervention of Elijah, the Gaon of Vilna, that brought it about. The Gaon of Vilna, who was not a communal officer as such (although he was supported by the community chest), and who was described in all the documents of the polemic as 'the hasid'—a mystically oriented pietist—was himself the moving force behind the campaign to eradicate the heretical 'sect' (*kat*) of the hasidim, a violent campaign which lasted for a quarter of a century.

The first initiative to oppose hasidism may have come from the leaders of the community of Shklov,[12] but it did not gain wider support until the Gaon of Vilna was mobilized to lend it his personal authority. The Gaon had detected heretical elements in such hasidic writings as were available to him, and he called for the excommunication of all the followers of hasidism and their total exclusion from the body of the Jewish community. On his authority, a circular letter to this effect was distributed throughout Poland. As a result, a number of important communities (such as Brody) issued their own writs of excommunication; an anthology of anti-hasidic proclamations and other polemical writings was published (*Zemir aritsim veḥarvot tsurim*); and in some communities a violent campaign of persecution was launched against all those who were suspected of belonging to or even sympathizing with the sectarians. It is not impossible that the emigration to the Holy Land in 1777 of a group of hasidim headed by one of the oldest disciples of the Maggid of Mezhirech, R. Menahem Mendel of Vitebsk, was connected with this wave of persecutions. All these events have been described in the scholarly literature, on the basis of the careful analysis of the extant polemical tracts.

It is important, however, to highlight some other aspects of the polemic which may shed new light on the question of the relations between the hasidic movement and the *kahal* organizations during the period from 1772 on. Notably, neither the *kahal* of

[10] See W. Z. Rabinowitsch, *Lithuanian Hasidism* (London, 1970), 12.

[11] Maimon, *Autobiography*, 172.

[12] See Wilensky, *Ḥasidim umitnaggedim*, i. 29.

Vilna nor its rabbi and rabbinical court took any extreme measures against their congregants who were known to be associated with hasidism, a group headed by an illustrious scholar who also served as the preacher of the community at that time. In fact, so restrained was the response of the official leadership of the community that the Gaon of Vilna was moved to reproach them 'for being so lenient in their judgement', stating: 'If the matter was left to me, I would do to them what Elijah the prophet had done to the prophets of Ba'al.'[13] Similarly, in Pinsk, as Nadav's study has shown,[14] neither the rabbi of this important community—one of the major Jewish communities of Lithuania—R. Raphael, a leading rabbinic authority who later became rabbi of Hamburg, nor the *kahal* officials took any part in the persecution of the hasidim of the town in 1772. Even more significantly, they appointed a hasidic leader, Levi Isaac (later of Berdichev) as their communal rabbi *after* the start of the Vilna-led campaign against the hasidim. As P. Marek has observed:

> From above they sent out circular letters forbidding any contact with the sectarians, including the demand to refrain from offering them help or shelter, while down below, in Gorodok, Liozno, Mezhirech, Medzibezh and many other communities and sub-communities, the heretics were not only accepted and admitted but they were being appointed to the important and well paid positions of rabbis and preachers.[15]

Indeed, at the very time at which the calls for the excommunication of the hasidim were being issued, the most famous Hasidic personality after the death of the Maggid of Mezhirech, R. Jacob Joseph of Polonnoye, was serving as rabbi of Polonnoye—one of the most important Jewish communities in Volhynia. Another Volhynian community, the largest of them (Dubno), entered in 1778 into a formal agreement with R. Jacob Joseph 'and his faction' whereby, should they succeed in obtaining the release ('redemption') from incarceration of a number of Jews from one of the villages in the vicinity before the Jewish New Year, the community would pay them an annual fee of 50 zloty for the next four years.[16] The agreement was signed by the town's rabbi, and it shows quite clearly that, at the height of the controversy against the hasidic movement, a non-hasidic community did not have any reservations about employing the services of a hasidic group and its leader in a field of action ('redemption of captives') in which the hasidim seem to have acquired the reputation of being particularly expert.

The campaign against hasidism erupted again following the publication in 1780 of the first hasidic book, Jacob Joseph of Polonnoye's *Toledot Ya'akov Yosef.* In it he attacked the rabbis who exploited their learning to gain prestige or material wealth, and he deplored the decline of moral standards in the community as a whole. But if we compare this book, which attracted so much hostility, with the vast library of moralistic works published in Poland during the eighteenth century, many of them directing equally critical remarks at the rabbinical leadership and communal institutions and yet failing to inspire any official opposition, we are forced to conclude that the publication of R. Jacob Joseph's book could not have triggered off the second stage of the anti-hasidic campaign during the early 1780s.

[13] Ibid. 66.

[14] See M. Nadav, 'Kehilot Pinsk–Karlin bein ḥasidut lehitnaggedut', *Zion*, 34 (1969), 98–108.

[15] P. Marek, 'Vnutrennyaya bor'ba v yevreistve v XVIII veke', *Yevreiskaya Starina*, 12 (1928), 130.

[16] See Shmeruk, 'Haḥasidut', 191; H. S. Margolies, *Dubna rabati* (Warsaw, 1910), 118–19.

In general, any comparison between the critique of the social order which is to be found in hasidic writings and in non-hasidic or pre-hasidic homiletic works respectively would reveal that the issue of social justice did not occupy an important position in hasidic thought.[17] This might have resulted from the particular emphasis which hasidism placed on the principle of trust in divine Providence (*bitaḥon*), and on the ability of the zaddik to release the flow of abundance (*shefa*) from Heaven to earth—a basic component of the hasidic doctrine from the outset. It seems clear, at any rate, that neither social nor institutional issues were at the heart of the second controversy between the hasidim and their opponents, and that, moreover, these issues were not conceived as being central to the controversy by either of the parties at the time. If Jacob Joseph of Polonnoye and his book were condemned, this was for entirely different reasons which may have included, for example, the disclosure in the book of the hasidic belief that the prophet Ahijah the Shilonite was the personal teacher of Israel Besht. Ahijah the Shilonite was traditionally viewed as the personal teacher of the prophet Elijah, who was himself regarded as the precursor of the messiah. The association of the Besht with the messianically charged figure of Ahijah of Shiloh may have provoked the opponents of hasidism, in much the same way as the Gaon of Vilna considered it an affront that the term hasid should be applied to the Maggid of Mezhirech. The Gaon's disciples were claiming that he himself enjoyed direct contact with the prophet Elijah, and he might have been provoked by the hasidic claim to the same prophetic source of authority. The controversy may have been triggered off by another feature of the book *Toledot Ya'akov Yosef*: in defiance of convention, it was published without the approbation of any rabbinic authority. This omission alone might have turned an otherwise inoffensive publication into a provocative challenge to traditional authority, implicitly claiming the autonomous power to introduce new modes of worship and novel pietistic norms—a claim which soon became a major issue in the controversy. It was, after all, precisely this issue that was to feature prominently in the series of questions addressed in 1784 to Levi Isaac of Berdichev (then rabbi of Zelechow) by Abraham Katzenellenbogen, the rabbi of Brisk. The underlying question throughout was: who gave the hasidim the authority to depart from the custom which Ashkenazi Jews had kept for generations?[18] (Notably, the same departures from Ashkenazi custom—the adoption of the Sefardi liturgical rite of the Ari and the wearing of white dress on the sabbath and festivals—were tolerated and even respected so long as they were confined to the exclusive group of 'approved' mystics in the *kloiz* of Brody.[19])

The last and most acrimonious phase of the controversy took place near the end of the Gaon of Vilna's life and shortly after his death (in 1797). By this time even he was forced to admit that the attempts to suppress the heresy of hasidism had proved to be futile. It seems that he could not be reconciled to this failure. His last testament to his disciples and followers was to urge them to embark on one final campaign against the rebellious 'sect'. Paradoxically, the outcome of this final endeavour was the complete

[17] See Y. Shachar, *Bikoret haḥevrah vehanhagat hatsibur besifrut hamusar vehaderush bePolin bame'ah hayod ḥet* (Jerusalem, 1992); M. Piekarz, *Biyemei tsemiḥat haḥasidut: Megamot ra'ayoniyot besifrei derush umusar* (Jerusalem, 1978), 377–83.

[18] See Wilensky, *Ḥasidim umitnaggedim*, i. 123–31.

[19] See ibid. 47–8.

take-over by the local hasidim, assisted by the Russian authorities, of all the institutions of communal leadership in the mitnaggedic stronghold of Vilna. The background to this turn of events is as follows. For over thirty years the Jewish community of Vilna had been torn by a bitter struggle between two feuding parties, the community council (the *kahal*) and the town's rabbi, Samuel b. Avigdor. On several occasions the Polish authorities (Lithuania was still a part of Poland at that time) were invited to intervene by one or another of the parties. The rabbi was supported against the *kahal* by the representatives of the common people, mostly artisans, of whom the most outstanding and able was one Simon b. Wolf. The struggle ended with the death of the rabbi of Vilna and the incarceration of his supporters. When the campaign against the hasidim was renewed at around the same time, their regional leader, Shneur Zalman of Lyady, was imprisoned in 1798 by the Russian authorities (Lithuania had by now been annexed to Russia in the third partition of Poland of 1795), having been denounced as a dangerous agitator by the leaders of the Vilna *kahal*. After a short period of incarceration he was found innocent and released. The hasidim proceeded to exploit this advantage. They used their influence on certain Russian officials to press, in February 1799, for new elections to the *kahal* leadership. They must have gained the support of the common people of Vilna, who had been opposing their own *kahal* for decades, so that the newly elected leadership of the community was now entirely hasidic.[20] Interestingly, the new *kahal* did not introduce any procedural or structural changes to advance any particular hasidic interest or cause, and this seems to have been the standard practice wherever the Hasidim succeeded in being elected to positions of communal leadership within the framework of the *kahal*.

The hasidic attitude to the *kahal* and its functions was distinguished from that of other opposition groups within the community precisely by the absence of any antagonism to the existing frameworks of communal organization. In contrast to the hasidim, the dissenting 'common people' were demanding the curtailment or even the complete abolition of the judicial and economic powers of the *kahal*. Simon b. Wolf, their spokesman in Vilna, wrote to the Polish Sejm at the end of 1789, outlining his plan for reforming the status of the Jews. He proposed that the Jewish community should be legally defined as an estate among other estates of the Polish kingdom, but that their internal communal institutions should be divested of their authority in all secular matters.[21] The same sentiments were expressed by a group of Jews in the Lithuanian town of Shavli (Siauliai), who wrote in May 1790: 'We declare that we require neither rabbi nor community council . . . they rob us of our last pennies to advance their own interests . . . If the government were to divest them of their powers, greater tranquillity would prevail.'[22]

The two feuding camps in Vilna finally reached a compromise and learnt to coexist alongside each other by the beginning of the nineteenth century.[23] Some historians have tried to explain the cessation of hostilities at this stage as the result of sheer fatigue,

[20] See ibid. 210–22; I. Klausner, *Vilna bitekufat HaGa'on* (Jerusalem, 1942), 27–45.

[21] See Klausner, *Vilna*, 274–80; id. 'Hama'avak hapenimi bikehilot Rusiah veLita vehatsa'at Rabbi Shimon b. Wolf letikunim', *He'avar*, 19 (1972), 54–73.

[22] See P. Marek, 'Krizis yevreiskovo samoupravliennie i khasidism', *Yevreiskaya Starina*, 12 (1928), 88–90, quoting S. Bershadski, *Litovskie yevrei* (St Petersburg, 1883), 46–8.

[23] See Wilensky, *Ḥasidim umitnaggedim*, i. 235–6.

or else a sign of recognition by both parties that a common enemy, the Enlightenment, was now posing a greater threat to them both. But the Haskalah movement as an active spiritual and social force was still a distant prospect on the horizon of eastern Europe, even in Austrian Galicia. The experience of the feud in Vilna must be seen primarily in the context of the long-drawn-out internal struggles and disputes which occurred in numerous communities throughout the region during this period. Social tensions and antagonism had become a regular feature of communal life, and it is against this background that the mitnaggedic campaign against hasidism (as well as the various internal hasidic disputes between individual leaders and schools) should be considered. Shmeruk's study of ritual slaughter and hasidism has demonstrated the importance of the income from this source to the managers of community budgets, and pointed out that it played a crucial part in establishing the legitimacy of the hasidim in relation to both *kahal* authorities and government officials:

This fiscal interest gradually paved the way for the recognition granted to hasidism by the governing institutions of the *kahal*. It turned the hasidim into a legitimate element of the community, even where they formed only a small minority of the population. Where the State was to take over the traditional functions of the *kahal*, it pursued the selfsame policy in regard to hasidism.[24]

An important factor contributing to the reconciliation between the feuding camps was the basic affinity between their respective concepts of communal functions, institutions, and organization. The hasidic movement did not aspire to create new frameworks of Jewish self-governing institutions or to promote any new model of communal leadership. Rather, it endeavoured to gain influence and ultimately control over the existing institutional framework within which it operated quite effectively.

As early as 1802, the newly elected *kahal* of Vilna included among its members both hasidic and mitnaggedic representatives, and within a short time it recognized the rights of the two distinct hasidic communities of the town, Habad and Lyakhovichi (Lachowicze), to maintain their own separate prayer groups (*minyanim*).[25] At the end of 1805, the Burial Society of Igumen (Cherven) recorded in its minute-book the decision 'to allow the leaders of the honest and God-fearing men, the followers of R. . . . Shneur Zalman [of Lyady], to buy a plot of land within the grounds of the synagogue, in order to build on it [their own] *beit midrash*'.[26] A similar development, noted by Halpern and dating from the period following the eruption of the controversy between hasidim and mitnaggedim, is reflected in the extant minute book of the Society [for the Study of] Talmud and Mishnah (Ḥevrah Shas Umishnayot) in the community of Radoshkovichi.[27] During the final years of the eighteenth century, while the controversy was at its height, a special regulation was adopted by the society, designed to exclude from its membership all those who were known to have hasidic inclinations. Between the years 1801 and 1804, every new member had to undertake on admission to the society not to attend any hasidic prayer group, not to visit any hasidic *rebbe*, and altogether to dissociate himself from hasidism.[28] This regulation was modified somewhat in 1805, and by

[24] See C. Shmeruk, 'Mashma'utah haḥevratit shel hasheḥitah haḥasidit', *Zion*, 20 (1955), 69.
[25] See Klausner, *Vilna*, 24–5.
[26] See Marek, 'Vnutrennyaya', 164.
[27] See Halpern, 'Ḥavurot letorah umitsvot', 323–5.
[28] See ibid. 322.

1809 it was effectively reversed. The minute-book reads as follows: 'Now we realize that the above-mentioned ordinance is no longer tolerable to the majority of the community. It may lead to public disgrace, heated disputes, and quarrels . . . For this reason the society has agreed to abrogate this ordinance, and every one of its members is hereby warned, on penalty of the strictest ban of excommunication, that the ordinance is not to be enforced any longer.'[29] The same trend is observable in Minsk and elsewhere.[30]

In 1800 the civil governor of Lithuania, Ivan Friesel, presented a memorandum to the Russian government which contained a Jewish 'project'—a set of proposals for the reform of Jewish life in Russia. One of these called for the introduction of strict government controls over the religious teachings of the Jews, on the grounds that the main source of corruption in Jewish life was the teaching of the new hasidic masters. But the Committee for the Organization of Jewish Life created by Tsar Alexander I in 1802 did not share this view. One of the clauses of its 1804 Statute read as follows: 'If in any particular locality a division of sects should occur, and the rift between them should be so deep as to prevent the one from sharing its prayer-house with the other, then one of the sects should be allowed to build its own prayer-house and to elect its own rabbis, so long as there remains only one *kahal* in each locality.'[31] This granted formal recognition to what had already become the effective practice of many communities.

As we have seen, the hasidic movement did not attempt to alter the structure and functions of the *kahal* administration. It did not campaign for social reform or for the implementation of democratic procedures within the institutions of Jewish communal government. It did not set out to represent the particular interests of either 'village Jews' (*yishuvniks*) or the 'common' townspeople, the artisans or—as some historians have argued—the itinerant 'secondary intelligentsia' of eastern European Jewry.[32] All one can say is that some of the religious doctrines and social activities associated with hasidism did at times attract the support—either on an ad hoc basis or more permanently—of some of these and perhaps other interest groups. The common townspeople, for example, would often join forces with the hasidim in the struggle against the official leadership of the *kahal*, traditionally recruited exclusively from the ranks of the scholarly-wealthy élite. This collaboration was facilitated by the appeal to the common people of such hasidic doctrines as the principle of the 'organic' unity of all Israel whereby 'the entire world [that is, the Jewish people] is called "one figure"; the common people are its feet, the zaddikim "the eyes of the congregation", etc.';[33] or the doctrine of the 'descent' of the zaddik for the sake of his 'ascent' by means of which he 'elevates' the entire congregation with him.[34] These doctrines raised the importance and self-esteem of the lower strata, and provided some theoretical grounds on which to

29 Ibid.

30 See Wilensky, *Ḥasidim umitnaggedim*, i. 263; Shmeruk, 'Mashma'utah', 69–70.

31 Wilensky, *Ḥasidim umitnaggedim*, i. 295; Shmeruk, 'Mashma'utah', 71.

32 See J. G. Weiss, 'Reshit tsemiḥatah shel haderekh haḥasidit', *Zion*, 16 (1951), repr. in A. Rubinstein (ed.), *Perakim betorat haḥasidut vetoledoteihah* (Jerusalem, 1977), 125–32.

33 Jacob Joseph of Polonnoye, *Toledot Ya'akov Yosef* [Korets, 1780] (Jerusalem, 1966), on 'Vayetse', 22*d*.

34 See Weiss, 'Reshit tsemiḥatah shel haderekh haḥasidit', 145–64; S. H. Dresner, *The Zaddik* (New York, 1960), 148–90.

base their demand for a greater say in the management of communal affairs. More concretely, the direct involvement of the hasidic leaders in social and economic life encouraged certain classes and groups, particularly those on the periphery of communal life, to turn to them rather than to the *kahal* officials for guidance and help. Their interests had been neglected by the official *kahal* leaderships, weakened in many localities by the perennial tension between major communities and small, peripheral ones, by the increasingly heavy financial demands placed upon them by the Polish nobility, and by the inner struggles amongst various pressure groups within the communities they governed. By contrast, the hasidic leaders concerned themselves with the day-to-day problems of those whose interests the *kahal* authorities had failed to represent. This was expressed, for example, in their endeavours to protect the rights of Jewish *arendators* and to eliminate economic rivalry amongst the 'village Jews' and innkeepers,[35] or their special commitment to the 'redemption of captives'—raising funds on behalf of individual Jews who had been imprisoned for failing to meet their fiscal obligations to the Polish estate owners.[36] All these activities and concerns are attested in the literary and documentary sources of early hasidism.

In the final years of the eighteenth century, for example, a number of hasidic leaders, including Mordecai of Chernobyl, employed the full weight of their personal prestige and authority to endorse the established rights of certain individuals to a specific source of livelihood, protecting them from unfair competition.[37] Similarly, sometime before 1815, the hasidic leader Zevi Hirsch of Zhidachov demanded from the *kahal* authorities that a certain ritual slaughterer whom he considered to be unfit be removed from office. He warned: 'If you disobey, you should know that I shall enlist the support of all the zaddikim of our generation, from both the immediate vicinity and far afield, such as the holy master, the Maggid of Kozienice, and my teacher [the Seer] of Lublin, as well as my teacher R. Mendel of Rymanow. All were my personal teachers, and they authorized me to teach the Law to God's own people.'[38] In 1798 the Baal Shem Tov's grandson, Moses Hayyim Ephraim of Sudylkow, entered into a formal agreement with 'the chiefs of the holders of *arenda* in the neighbouring villages' whereby they would 'submit to his authority in all that he might say', and he would 'help them with his teaching [Torah] and his prayer which effectively aids all who cleave to him', in return for 6 zloty out of every thousand of their income.[39] According to rumour and oral tradition, Jewish informers to the Russian authorities during the oppressive regime of Tsar Nicholas I were persecuted and in some cases even assassinated by fellow Jews on the authority of some hasidic leaders who had taken it upon themselves to punish the 'traitors' and to relieve the Jewish community of their extortionist reign of terror. There is no doubt, for example, that the trial, imprisonment, and eventual escape to

[35] See Shmeruk, 'Haḥasidut', 182–9.

[36] See ibid. 189–92.

[37] See Isaac b. Leib Landau, *Zikaron tov*, 69, letter 9.

[38] Israel Berger, *Eser orot* [Piotrkow, 1907], 153; Shmeruk, 'Mashma'utah', 71 n. 104.

[39] For the original Heb. text of the letter see A. Kahana, *Sefer haḥasidut* (Warsaw, 1922), 304. For the Eng. trans. of the relevant passage see S. Ettinger, 'The Hasidic Movement: Reality and Ideals', in H. H. Ben-Sasson and S. Ettinger (eds.), *Jewish Society through the Ages* (New York, 1971), 251–66, orig. pub. in *Cahiers d'histoire mondiale: Journal of World History*, 11: 1–2 (1968), 251–66, repr. in G. D. Hundert (ed.), *Essential Papers on Hasidism* (New York, 1991), 236.

Austria of the zaddik Israel of Ruzhin were connected with such an assassination of a Jewish informer in Ushitsa in 1838.[40]

The direct, personal involvement of all these hasidic leaders with the difficulties and practical needs of individual Jews contrasts sharply with the distant, impersonal operations of the *kahal* authorities. Clearly, the hasidic leaders were fulfilling functions which the *kahal* institutions were unable to fulfil, even though, at one time, they might have been expected to fulfil them, either within the framework of the old central councils of Poland and Lithuania or within the institutions of each autonomous *kahal*. The authority now exercised by the hasidic leader altered the inner structure of communal government and changed the balance of power within it. The office of rabbi—traditionally the highest seat of scholarly and spiritual authority (although this had diminished in many communities as a result of inner tensions and conflicts)—was reduced to the level of technical expertise in matters relating to ritual law and rabbinic learning. In addition, the office of *maggid*—preacher—gradually disappeared from many communities which came under hasidic control. Both the spiritual authority of rabbinic office and the moral authority of the *maggidim* were now subsumed under the authority of the hasidic zaddik. In communities whose membership comprised both hasidim and mitnaggedim, the two seats of authority—communal rabbi and hasidic *rebbe*—coexisted side by side, but the split had clearly loosened the leadership's grip on individuals.

In the light of this, there is truth in Gottlober's observation that the Haskalah movement succeeded in penetrating eastern Europe precisely through the towns in which communal authority had split as a result of the struggle between hasidim and mitnaggedim.[41]

[40] See S. Dubnow, *History of the Jews in Russia and Poland* [3 vols.; Philadelphia, 1916–20] (New York, 1975), ii. 84 ff., 121.

[41] Abraham Ber Gottlober, *Zikhronot umasa'ot*, ed. R. Goldberg (2 vols.; Jerusalem, 1976), ii. 121.

SIX

Hasidism after 1772: Structural Continuity and Change

ADA RAPOPORT-ALBERT

1. THE PROBLEM

THE YEAR 1772 is generally regarded as a critical one, or at least an important turning point, in the history of hasidism. Three decisive events took place in that year which altered both the ideological and the organizational course on which the movement had originally embarked. The spring brought with it the first outbreak of bitter hostilities between the mitnaggedim and the hasidim in Vilna, whence the dispute quickly spread to other Jewish communities in Lithuania and Galicia. During the summer months Belorussia was annexed to Russia, and Galicia to Austria, in the first partition of the disintegrating kingdom of Poland; as a result, parts of the Jewish (and hasidic) community in Poland which until then had formed a single cultural and political entity found themselves arbitrarily separated. At the end of the year, in December, the supreme leader of hasidism, R. Dov Ber, the Maggid of Mezhirech, died without leaving an 'heir' to take charge of the movement in his place.

In the light of this historic combination of circumstances, the scholarly literature on hasidism has tended to divide the history of the movement, especially from the point of view of its organizational structure, into two periods separated by a clear line of demarcation: (*a*) from the foundation of the movement to the death of the Maggid of Mezhirech, the period of centralized leadership under a single universally acknowledged head (first the founder, Israel Baal Shem Tov (the Besht), and then his disciple and successor, the Maggid of Mezhirech); (*b*) the period beginning immediately after the death of the Maggid in 1772, which was marked by the onset of decentralization: the leadership split up, and the movement began to function as a loose affiliation of distinct communities connected, it is true, by the common legacy of the Besht and the Maggid of Mezhirech, but independent of each other, and each led by its own zaddik.

This periodization scheme underlies every major historical study of hasidism. Explicit discussions of it, however, have been scarce and lacking in rigour, since the organizational development of hasidism, as distinct from the evolution of its doctrines, has not received much critical scholarly attention. Processes of organizational change, inasmuch as they are observed at all, are treated casually, and up to now no systematic attempt has been made to identify their causes.[1]

[1] See e.g. S. Dubnow, *Toledot hahasidut* [Tel Aviv, 1930–1] (Tel Aviv, 1960), 87, 126; S. A. Horodecky, *Hahasidut vehahasidim* (4 vols.; Tel Aviv, 1928–43), i. 83, 102; ii. 8; M. Teitelbaum, *HaRav*

It is surprising that the many historians who posited such an abrupt and extensive change in the organizational structure of hasidism as this transition, following the death of the Maggid, from central leadership to a multiplicity of independent centres showed so little curiosity as to its causes. In most cases they contented themselves with the assumption that the son of the Maggid, R. Abraham ('the Angel'), either did not want or was not competent to succeed to his father's place, and that therefore the leadership passed to a group of the Maggid's disciples and became fragmented.[2] The late Shmuel Ettinger, who did recognize the decentralization of the hasidic leadership after the death of the Maggid of Mezhirech as an intriguing historical question, labelled it a paradoxical element in the formation of the movement:

miLiadi umifleget Ḥabad (2 vols.; Warsaw, 1910), i. 32; A. Rubinstein, 'Perakim betoledot haḥasidut' (under the heading 'Hasidut'), in *Hebrew Encyclopaedia*, xvii (1965), 758, 764, repr. in A. Rubinstein (ed.), *Perakim betorat haḥasidut vetoledoteihah* (Jerusalem, 1977), 242, 245.

[2] As e.g. in Dubnow, *Toledot haḥasidut*, 213. It is hardly necessary to point out that this assumption alone is not enough to explain the fragmentation of the leadership after the death of the Maggid. As hasidic history itself demonstrates, in later generations, once the leadership had become a hereditary institution, the absence of any suitable candidate for the succession did not necessarily entail a break in the dynasty; witness the cases in which infants served as heads of hasidic communities or a son-in-law, brother, or pupil was found to continue the leadership of the community and preserve its particular identity. So, too, with regard to the transmission of the leadership from the Besht to the Maggid and from the Maggid to his disciples, it is customary to assume that R. Zevi, the son of the Besht, was unsuited for office, and that therefore the Maggid was elected or appointed to succeed his master; and that after the death of the Maggid his office was divided among several of his disciples as a result of the 'refusal' of his son R. Abraham to take his father's place. In both cases (and in some others too), this is no more than an anachronistic application of expectations that the son would inherit the zaddik's position. It is clear that in the first generations of hasidism this expectation had not yet gained currency. It does, indeed, appear that R. Zevi was unfitted for leadership, in spite of the attempts of hagiography to present him as a most saintly man. And R. Abraham 'the Angel', too, appears to have shunned public affairs and led the life of an ascetic kabbalist in the manner of earlier generations, rather than that of a hasidic leader of the new type. But there is no doubt that the unsuitability of both for the role of leader was not regarded, at the time, as precipitating a crisis or upsetting any established procedures so far as concerns leadership. I propose to deal with this fully elsewhere. And see below, 89 ff. and 94 ff.

Quite the opposite view has been taken in the internal historiography of Habad produced in recent generations. Most of this is the work of the *admor* Joseph Isaac Schneersohn (the sixth *admor* of the Habad dynasty, father-in-law and predecessor of the late *admor* Menahem Mendel Schneerson who died in 1994). On his historiographical writings and their historical value, see: Rachel Elior, 'Viku'aḥ Minsk', *Meḥkerei Yerushalayim bemaḥshevet Yisrael*, 1: 4 (1981–2), 181–3; Z. Gries, 'Mimitos le'etos: Kavim lidmuto shel R. Avraham miKalisk', *Umah vetoledoteihah* (2 vols.; Jerusalem, 1984), ii. 130–1 n. 41; Ada Rapoport-Albert, 'Hagiography with Footnotes: Edifying Tales and the Writing of History in Hasidism', *History and Theory*, Beiheft 27: *Essays in Jewish Historiography* (Wesleyan University, 1988), 137 ff. And see also below, n. 76, and s. 6 of the present chapter. The *admor* Joseph Isaac Schneersohn repeatedly treats the first stages in the development of the hasidic movement as if they were governed by the regular procedures, sound organizational structure, and relative institutional stability which are characteristic of Habad. In his writings both of the sons with doubtful qualifications for the succession—the son of the Besht and the son of the Maggid—are credited with short periods in office as supreme leaders of hasidism, each immediately after the death of his father. On the year-long leadership of R. Zevi, the son of the Besht, see R. Joseph Isaac Schneersohn, 'Avot haḥasidut', in *Hatamim* [Warsaw, 1936] (Kfar Habad, 1975), i(*b*). 140 (ch. 6); and cf., by the same author, *Sefer hazikhronot* (2 vols.; Kfar Habad, 1985), i, ch. 9, 390–41. On the two years' leadership of R. Abraham 'the Angel', son of the Maggid, see the *admor* Joseph Isaac's letter of 1935 to his daughter Mushka, in Raphael Nahman b. R. Barukh Shalom Hakohen, *Shemu'ot vesipurim meraboteinu hakedoshim* (3 vols.; Kfar Habad, 1974–7), iii. 10–11, repr. in *Igrot kodesh me'et kevod kedushato admor moreinu verabeinu harav R. Yosef Yitsḥak nuḥo eden miLubavich* (12 vols.; Brooklyn, NY, 1982–5), iii. 162–3. And see below, n. 76.

Rabbi Dov Ber of Meseritz, the Great Maggid, the well known figure called by his disciples the 'Rabbi of all the sons of the Diaspora', who was a leader of authoritarian views . . . directed the movement into . . . decentralization. He set up group after group with a pupil at the head of almost every one, with the result that after his death there was no single agreed leader of the movement.[3]

In his search for an answer to this question Ettinger suggested that 'the tradition of autonomous activity in the local Jewish communities must have assisted the decentralizing tendency in the movement',[4] and he was undoubtedly right in this. But his answer itself raises new, and equally intriguing, questions: if hasidism emerged on a landscape of which autonomous units of communal organization had traditionally formed a natural feature, why, then, did it adopt in its initial stages such an 'unnatural' framework of central control, and why did it abandon this novel structure immediately after the death of the Maggid?

In order to give these questions proper consideration, the assumptions from which they have sprung must be examined first: did hasidism really undergo a swift and clear-cut transition from centralized organization to a loose association of autonomous units? In other words, was the leadership centralized in the first place? Did the death of the Maggid really create a void, and was it only because no suitable successor could be found that this void came to be filled by a group of the Maggid's disciples? Was it only at this stage that the process of decentralization was set in train?

There is no doubt that hasidism did eventually develop as a thoroughly non-centralist movement, and that it has remained so up to the present day. The sphere of influence of each zaddik, though not formally fixed, was well defined and jealously guarded, just like the formal boundaries of the *kehalim*[5] or—and this factor should not be under-

[3] See S. Ettinger, 'The Hasidic Movement: Reality and Ideals', in H. H. Ben-Sasson and S. Ettinger (eds.), *Jewish Society through the Ages* (New York, 1971), 251–66 (orig. pub. in *Cahiers d'histoire mondiale: Journal of World History*, 11: 1–2 (1968), 262, repr. in G. D. Hundert (ed.), *Essential Papers on Hasidism* (New York, 1991), 238).

[4] Ibid.

[5] The principle of the multiplicity of hasidic courts was accepted by most hasidic leaders and their followers (see s. 7 below), but the encroachment of one zaddik on the sphere of influence of another was not tolerated, and when it did occasionally occur, whether accidentally or by design, it led to serious clashes. A case in point was that of R. Asher of Karlin. After the death of his master R. Solomon, in 1792, he spent some time at the courts of R. Baruch of Medzibezh and R. Israel of Kozienice. On his return, he was at first reluctant to settle in Karlin again, for fear, it seems, of the anti-hasidic activity of R. Avigdor of Pinsk (who had been dismissed from his position as local rabbi, apparently in 1793). He therefore settled temporarily in Zelechow, where he occupied the position of town rabbi for a time. Zelechow, however, 'belonged' to R. Levi Isaac of Berdichev, and on this account a dispute arose between him and R. Asher. As a result of this R. Asher was obliged to move from Zelechow to Stolin, whence he returned to Karlin. See W. Z. Rabinowitsch, *Lithuanian Hasidism* (London, 1970), 49, 69. Similarly, in the 1780s, Karlin hasidism experienced a period of crisis. Under the pressure of the campaign by the mitnaggedim against Lithuanian hasidism on the one hand, and, on the other hand, faced with the growing influence of R. Shneur Zalman of Lyady in Lithuania and in Karlin itself in particular, R. Solomon of Karlin was forced to remove his court from Karlin and look for a new place of residence. According to hasidic tradition, he first tried to settle in the small town of Beshenkovich in Belorussia, where there was a small concentration of his hasidim. This town adjoined the area of influence of R. Shneur Zalman of Lyady, and R. Solomon was obliged to seek his permission to settle there. R. Shneur Zalman attached several conditions to his consent. R. Solomon refused to accept all of them, abandoned his plan to settle in Belorussia and moved to Ludmir. See ibid. 35; H. M. Hielman, *Beit rabbi* [Berdichev, 1903] (Tel Aviv, n.d.), 128 n. *b*. Another territorial clash involved R. Shneur Zalman of Lyady and R. Baruch of Medzibezh. On this, see below,

estimated—the oft-disputed boundaries of the independent estates of the Polish aristocracy in eighteenth-century Poland.[6] Ettinger pointed out that the boundaries of the autonomous units which together constituted the expanding hasidic movement did not match the traditional areas of jurisdiction of the *kehalim*. The various hasidic fraternities drew their membership from extensive regions which might include any number of established *kehilot*, some of them large and important, while the leaders of these hasidic fraternities might be resident in remote little towns, away from the major traditional seats of rabbinic authority.[7] But in spite of the fact that the boundaries of the two types of autonomous unit—those within the regime of the *kehalim* and those which constituted the hasidic movement—did not correspond, it is clear that we are dealing with two equally non-centralist systems. The independence of the various hasidic courts from each other found expression not only in the exclusive relationship of each hasidic fraternity to its own zaddik and his particular teachings but also in the realm of everyday life: for example, as was shown by Chone Shmeruk, each court had its own *shoḥet*, and meat slaughtered by a 'foreign' hasidic *shoḥet* was regarded as if slaughtered by a non-hasidic *shoḥet*.[8]

Since, as all agree, hasidism ultimately adopted a highly fragmented organizational structure, it is particularly important to re-examine its structure in the earliest stages, during which it is generally assumed to have been highly centralized. How far was

pp. 109–13. The well-known dispute between R. Aryeh Leib, the Shpola Zeide, and R. Nahman of Bratslav also appears to have been the result of encroachment on a neighbour's preserves, R. Nahman having entered the Zeide's area of influence by settling in Zlatopol just before Rosh Hashanah 5560 (1800). See 'Mekom yeshivato unesi'otav', *Ḥayei Moharan* (Jerusalem, 1947), s. 11, 54–5.

[6] On the disintegration of the kingdom of Poland, a process which began in the 17th cent. and reached its climax in the partitions of the 18th cent., see S. Kieniewicz *et al.* (eds.), *History of Poland* (Warsaw, 1968), 223–4; N. Davies, *God's Playground: A History of Poland* (2 vols.; Oxford, 1981), i. 492–546; O. Halecki, *A History of Poland* (London, 1978), 177–213; W. Reddaway *et al.* (eds.), *The Cambridge History of Poland* (2 vols.; New York, 1978), ii. 1–176. During that period, while central government in other European countries such as France and Austria was being strengthened, the kingdom of Poland underwent a process of decentralization. The elected kings, their army, and the central parliament of the state—the Sejm—gradually lost their power, and in practice the landowning aristocracy, with their private armies and their local parliaments, ran the affairs of the state as they saw fit.

On the tradition of non-centralist Jewish communal organization which prevailed in Europe from the beginning of the second millennium, see e.g. S. W. Baron, *The Jewish Community* (2 vols.; Philadelphia, 1945), i. 206, 231, 326, 372; ii. 20. There were several attempts to set up centralist institutions above the level of the individual community councils, the best known of these being the Council of Four Lands and the Council of the Land of Lithuania which branched off from it. During the period of their existence these councils succeeded in imposing their central authority, but not without a certain measure of strain and opposition on the part of the *kehilot*, who were not happy to sacrifice their traditional sovereignty. See on this H. H. Ben-Sasson, *Hagut vehanhagah* (Jerusalem, 1959), 38–9; I. Levitats, *The Jewish Community in Russia, 1772–1884* (New York, 1943), 71–91; see also J. Katz, *Tradition and Crisis*, trans. B. D. Cooperman (New York, 1993), orig. pub. in Hebrew as *Masoret umashber* (Jerusalem, 1958), 122–34, and esp. 129–31. It must be remembered that, in parallel with the dwindling power of the central Polish government, the central councils of the Jewish communities grew weaker from the second half of the 17th cent. and during the 18th cent., until they were abolished by government order in 1764. See Dubnow, *Toledot haḥasidut*, 20–1. The hasidic movement, therefore, was born into an environment which was marked by the disintegration of centralized organizational frameworks, whether we consider the decline of the Polish monarchy or the collapse of the Jewish Council of Four Lands.

[7] See Ettinger, 'The Hasidic Movement', 262.

[8] See C. Shmeruk, 'Mashma'utah haḥevratit shel hasheḥitah haḥasidit', *Zion*, 20 (1955), 70–1.

leadership of the hasidic movement in fact concentrated at that time in the person of the Besht and, after him, the Maggid of Mezhirech?

2. THE LEADERSHIP IN THE TIME OF THE BAAL SHEM TOV

The method by which hasidism recorded its spiritual debt to its two first and most profoundly revered leaders has to some extent obscured the facts. Hasidic literature consistently presents the Besht as the founder and sole leader of the movement in his day, exercising supreme control from the centre. The following quotation, chosen almost at random from among dozens of similar passages, clearly reflects the traditional hasidic evaluation of the Baal Shem Tov's leadership:

The rabbi, our teacher, R. Israel Ba'al-Shem-Tov, of blessed memory, father of the hasidim and chief of those holy zaddikim the light of whose Torah and righteousness has continued to shine up to the present day, and all the zaddikim there have been since the time of the Besht, of blessed memory, have but drawn from the well of his instruction. And even though his disciples have gone their various ways, nevertheless they all drink their fill from his unfailing source alone; all are his disciples and the disciples of his disciples who cast their light on the world to teach the people the ways of the Lord, to love Him and fear Him with heart and soul.[9]

Similarly *Shivḥei haBesht* declares:

The crown of Israel's glory, the rabbi, our teacher R. Israel Ba'al-Shem-Tov, may his merit protect us and all Israel, and his holy and pure disciples who dwelt in his shadow and sheltered under his wings and sat in the dust of his feet, to drink in his words with thirst.[10]

[9] *Seder hadorot heḥadash* (Lublin, 1927), 5.

[10] From the title-page of Dov Ber b. Shmuel, *Shivḥei haBesht* (Berdichev edn., 1815), and also (with slight variations) in the Kopys edn., 1814. Facsimiles of the two title-pages were included in B. Mintz's edition of *Shivḥei haBesht* (Tel Aviv, 1961). The well-known statement of R. Menahem Mendel of Vitebsk: 'Thus it was that the word of God was given to the Ba'al Shem. He was the one. None of the ancients were like him, nor will there be any like him upon earth', which was quoted in the printer's preface to the 1814 Kopys edn. of *Shivḥei haBesht* (p. 2 in the English edn. *In Praise of the Baal Shem Tov* (Bloomington, Ind., 1970)), was clearly taken by the printer as a declaration of the unique 'greatness and glory' of the Besht, in the spirit of the hagiographical evaluation of the Besht's leadership which became prevalent in later hasidism. At first sight this statement appears, then, to provide conclusive evidence, dating from relatively close to the time of the events in question—some twenty-five years after the death of the Besht—as to his unique status within the organizational framework of the hasidic leadership of his day. But it is doubtful if this was the intention of R. Menahem Mendel of Vitebsk. His statement needs to be examined in its original context rather than being severed from it, as it is in R. Israel b. Isaac Jaffe's introduction to the Kopys edn. of *Shivḥei haBesht*. R. Menahem Mendel's statement occurs in his letter of 1786, addressed from Tiberias to R. Jacob of Smela (Samilian), who was in charge of fund-raising for the benefit of the hasidic community in Erets Yisrael. In response to R. Jacob's personal request that he should intercede (with Heaven) on his behalf in the matter of 'children', R. Menahem Mendel launched into an attack on 'some great men among the zaddikim of our generation' who acceded to requests from their hasidim with regard to this. He stressed his strong objection to the claims of some of his colleagues in the hasidic leadership to perform miracles for their followers. It is in this polemical context that his remarks on the Besht appear: only the Besht could act in this way and alter the laws of nature; no one after him had been granted these powers, and it would be better if the zaddikim of the generation gave up this contemptible practice: 'But to return to the matter of his request for children: having seen the fervency of his prayer and his prostration before us and his strong pleas . . . I was covered in shame. For am I in the place of God? [cf. Gen. 30: 2] Thus it was that the word of God was given to the Baal Shem. He could

The whole of *Shivḥei haBesht* reflects this attitude when it portrays all the Baal Shem Tov's associates as his subservient disciples, repeatedly emphasizing not only their spiritual inferiority to him but also their willing recognition of this fact (even if they were sometimes slow to appreciate his full spiritual stature). But this picture is incomplete and somewhat distorted. In a series of biographical studies A. J. Heschel sketched the characters of several members of the Besht's circle on the basis of *Shivḥei haBesht* and other sources which are independent of it. These studies call for re-evaluation of R. Phinehas of Korets, R. Nahman of Kosov, R. Isaac of Drogobych, and others, and the complex pattern of their relations with the Besht. It is clear that they were not merely 'disciples' humbling themselves before their master and 'sitting in the dust of his feet to drink in his words with thirst' but charismatic figures in their own right, charged with enormous spiritual power and claiming the same freedom of access to the upper worlds as the Besht himself.[11] Dinur and Weiss have furnished further support for this assessment of the Besht's circle in the first generation of hasidism.[12] *Shivḥei haBesht* itself drops occasional hints on the position of the Besht in the circle of his intimates which depart from the express tendency of that book to glorify him and exalt him above all his contemporaries. It describes R. Nahman of Kosov, for example, as a man who headed his own circle of hasidim and who opposed and even persecuted the Besht. The scene in which he finally acknowledges the spiritual stature of the Besht and appears to be submitting to his authority in fact refers to a test of the pneumatic powers of the Besht forced upon him by R. Nahman, whose own powers were already tried and tested.[13] Only after the Besht had passed this test was R. Nahman ready to treat him as a colleague and an equal:

The rabbi, our teacher and rabbi, Nahman of Kosov, was an opponent of the Besht. (I heard that the Besht stems from the soul of King David, may he rest in peace, and the rabbi, our

decree and it would come to pass. He was the one. None of the ancients were like him, nor will there be any like him on earth, even though some of the great ones among the zaddikim in our generation are big talkers and make such claims. That is not how I see myself . . .' (*Peri ha'arets* [Zhitomir, 1867] (Jerusalem, 1970), 60; also pub. in J. Barnai, *Igrot ḥasidim me'Erets Yisrael* (Jerusalem, 1980), *Igeret* 35, 154). This polemical statement, which evokes the unique spiritual stature and supernatural powers of the Besht in order to condemn the practice of miracle-working which was becoming the hallmark of popular zaddikism at that time, is certainly not to be taken as hard evidence of the status of the Besht within the overall structure of the hasidic leadership of his time.

[11] See A. J. Heschel, *The Circle of the Baal Shem Tov*, ed. S. H. Dresner, Studies in Hasidism, (Chicago, 1985).

[12] See B. Dinur, *Bemifneh hadorot* (Jerusalem, 1955), 159–70. An Eng. transl. of parts of Dinur's study appeared in Hundert (ed.), *Essential Papers*, 159–72; 203–8. See J. Weiss, 'Reshit tsemiḥatah shel haderekh haḥasidit', *Zion*, 16 (1951), 46–9 (repr. in Rubinstein, in *Perakim betorat haḥasidut vetoledoteihah*, 122–5); J. Weiss, 'A Circle of Pneumatics in Pre-Hasidism', *Journal of Jewish Studies*, 8 (1957), 199–213 (repr. in id., *Studies in Eastern European Jewish Mysticism* (Oxford, 1985), 27–42). M. Piekarz, in *Biyemei tsemiḥat haḥasidut: Megamot ra'ayoniyot besifrei derush umusar* (Jerusalem, 1978), 22–33, criticizes the methodology and conclusions of Heschel and Weiss in these studies. His criticisms, particularly those dealing with their analysis of the traditions relating to R. Nahman of Kosov, are justified for the most part, but do not invalidate their observations on the network of personal relationships and the balance of power among the members of the circle, with which we are here concerned.

[13] *Shivḥei haBesht*, ed. Mintz, 136–7; ed. S. A. Horodecky [Berlin, 1922] (Tel Aviv, 1947), 93–5; *In Praise*, 208–10. This is of course a standard motif in *Shivḥei haBesht* and in hagiographic literature in general. The accounts lay stress on the dramatic transition from a hostile, suspicious, or dismissive attitude to one of admiration for the saintly man, which was experienced sooner or later by most of his associates. See J. Dan, *Hasipur haḥasidi* (Jerusalem, 1975), 123–8.

teacher and rabbi, Nahman stems from the soul of King Saul, may he rest in peace. Therefore Rabbi Nahman always hated this David.)

Once the Besht said: 'The rabbi, our teacher and rabbi, Nahman, pursues me to kill me.' (It is known that in bowing down [*nefilat apayim*] there is the *kavvanah* of killing one's enemies.) 'But with the help of God he will not get me.'

Once the disciples of our teacher and rabbi, Nahman, went to their rabbi and said to him: 'Why is it that all the world goes to the rabbi, the Besht, and everyone praises him highly? Why don't you come to an agreement and learn his true nature so that we will know where the truth lies. Why let him be a snare for us?'

He listened to their words and he went to the holy community of Medzibozh to the rabbi, the Besht, who received him with great honour. Afterwards, both of them entered a special room, and everyone was excluded from the room save one who hid himself in a certain place. The rabbi, our teacher and rabbi, Nahman, said: 'Israel, is it true you say that you know people's thoughts?'

He said to him: 'Yes.'

He said to him: 'Do you know what I am thinking now?'

The rabbi answered: 'It is known that thought is not fixed. It wanders from one point to another and is continually transformed. If you concentrate your thought on one thing, then I will be able to know.'

The rabbi, our teacher and rabbi, Nahman, did so.

The Besht said: 'The name of YAHWEH is in your thoughts.'

The rabbi, our teacher and rabbi, Nahman, said: 'You would know this anyhow, for I must always keep this thought. As it is written: "I have set the Lord [YAHWEH] always before me [Ps. 16: 8]." Whenever I remove all thought and concentrate on one thing, the name of the Presence is before my eyes.'

The Besht said: 'But there are several holy names, and you could have concentrated on any that you like.'

Then the rabbi, our rabbi and teacher, admitted that it was as the Besht had said. After that they discussed the secrets of the Torah.[14]

Even after R. Nahman recognized the spiritual powers of the Besht, he did not humble himself before him. It appears that he continued to maintain a circle of his own followers and these were inclined to be scornful of the Besht in spite of the improvement in the personal relations between him and their master.[15] According to *Shivḥei haBesht*,

[14] *Shivḥei haBesht*, ed. Mintz, 149–50; ed. Horodecky, 92; *In Praise*, 234–5. This tale is missing in the Yid. edn. of *Shivḥei haBesht* [Korets, 1816] (Jerusalem, 1965) and in the manuscript version published by Y. Mondshine (Jerusalem, 1982).

[15] *Shivḥei haBesht* relates how 'Harav Moharan [R. Nahman of Kosov] once heard some of his people [*anashav*] speaking ill of the Besht . . .' (text according to ed. Mintz, 150). Horodecky (p. 93) reads: 'Harav Moharan once heard some of his intimates [taking the abbreviation *an"sh* as = *anshei shelomo*, but see below]', and the Eng. version, *In Praise*, offers: 'our own people' (p. 236) (evidently taking the same abbreviation as '*anshei shelomeinu*'). This tale, too, does not appear either in the Yid. version or in the Mondshine edn. Examination of the first editions yields *an"sh* in the Kopys and Berdichev prints of 1814 and 1815 respectively, and *anash*[*av*] in the Laszczow edition of 1815. The Mintz edition therefore corresponds to the Laszczow text, and the Horodecky edition to the Kopys and Berdichev versions. It is clear from the context that the reference is to R. Nahman's intimate associates, *anshei shelomo*, the 'disciples' who regarded him as 'their master', as we are told in the other tale quoted above, and not to the collective *anshei shelomeinu*, 'our people', as the English version has it, for what is in question is the opposition of a particular group to the Besht. The version *anashav*, 'his people', appears to be the better one, and of course the '*an"sh*' of the Kopys edn. can also be interpreted as '*anshei shelomo*' ('his . . .') and not necessar-

R. Nahman rebuked his people 'for speaking ill of the Besht', and described his relations with the Besht in these terms:

The quarrel between the Besht and myself is a very old one. It is the quarrel that was between King Saul and David, may they rest in peace, and the quarrel that was between Hillel and Shammai. How can you dare to butt into it?[16]

Although *Shivḥei haBesht* seeks to glorify the status of the Besht as sole leader, the image of R. Nahman of Kosov emerges from between the lines as a pneumatic personality in his own right, independent of the Besht and not subject to his authority.[17]

Unlike such men as R. Nahman of Kosov and R. Phinehas of Korets, who had their own circles of disciplines and regarded themselves as colleagues of the Besht, R. Aryeh Judah Leib, the Mokhiaḥ (preacher) of Polonnoye, accepted the Besht as his teacher, as is shown by all the stories about him in *Shivḥei haBesht*. All the same, according to those accounts, R. Aryeh Judah Leib was gifted with a power 'to annul judgements'

ily as '*anshei shelomeinu*' ('our . . .'). I am grateful to Professor Rachel Elior, who kindly checked the text of the editions not available to me in London libraries from the copies in the National Library in Jerusalem.

16 *Shivḥei haBesht*, ed. Mintz, 151; ed. Horodecky, 93; *In Praise*, 236–7. In the Yid. edn. of *Shivḥei haBesht* the tale appears in a somewhat extended version, but without the comparison of the dispute between R. Nahman and the Besht to the dispute between Saul and David/Hillel and Shammai. See pp. 31*b*–32*a* of that version. A. Ya'ari, 'Shetei mahadurot yesod shel Shivḥei haBesht', *Kiryat sefer*, 39 (1964), 554–5, compares the Yid. and Heb. versions of this tale, and the conclusion which he draws from this comparison supports the conclusion of his article as a whole, namely that this Yid. version is independent of the Heb. version and may even be the earlier of the two. For this reason he assumes that the passage missing in the Yid. edn. is a later addition to the Heb. version of the tale. But see Y. Mondshine's critical remarks on Ya'ari's study in the introduction to the Mondshine edn. of *Shivḥei haBesht*, 22–47. In any event, in all the versions of the tale R. Nahman of Kosov and the Besht are portrayed as equals.

17 Weiss, in his article 'A Circle of Pneumatics', drew a character sketch of R. Nahman of Kosov's 'holy fraternity' (*ḥavurta kadishta*). Unlike Dinur, who regarded R. Nahman as the leader of this fraternity (see Dinur, *Bemifneh hadorot*, 160–1), Weiss emphasizes that R. Nahman of Kosov did not serve as leader of the group in any sense comparable to the institutionalized leadership of the zaddik which was developed in the hasidic movement later on. Rather, R. Nahman belonged to a *pre-hasidic* circle of ascetic kabbalists gifted with supernatural spiritual powers. Weiss was inclined to identify this circle with the exclusive circle known as the 'hasidim' of Kutow which also numbered among its members R. Moshe, head of the rabbinical court of Kutow, and R. Gershon, the brother-in-law of the Besht (see Weiss, 'A Circle of Pneumatics', 203 ff.). Weiss's analysis of the complex of relations between the various members of this group of pneumatics serves well to clarify the links between the circles of kabbalists and Sabbateans of that period and the early hasidic masters who emerged from within their ranks, but the resultant chronology is not compatible with the facts. The term 'pre-hasidism' which Weiss coined is helpful as a typological category but chronologically misleading. It implies that those circles of kabbalists and pneumatics preceded the foundation of the hasidic movement by the Besht. But in fact they operated contemporaneously, and to some extent overlapped, with the Besht and his associates in hasidism. All the information we have about those circles and the individuals who were active in them relates to the same period as that in which the Besht was active. Moreover, according to hasidic tradition, it was precisely the members of those circles who were the early disciples of the Besht, his intimates, and his colleagues. As we have seen, not all of them humbled themselves before him and accepted him as their leader. In fact, it appears that the relations between him and them were not unlike those outlined by Weiss in his descriptions of the pre-hasidic circles in his article. The difference between those 'pre-hasidic' circles of kabbalists and the circle in which the Besht operated consists only in the active involvement of the Besht's circle with the wider public and their mundane affairs, as contrasted with the reclusiveness of the fraternities of the Kutow type. The conclusion this invites is that the activity of the Besht among the members of his circle, as it is described in the works of R. Jacob Joseph of Polonnoye and in *Shivḥei haBesht*, likewise belongs to the 'pre-hasidic's stage from the point of view of its leadership structure, in which there is not yet an institutionalized court and a single zaddik who is the focus of all its activities. See more on this below.

which was not inferior to that of the Besht, and which, in one case at least, exceeded it and was exercised in order to render ineffective an action taken by the Besht in the upper worlds.[18] In another incident it was said of the Mokhiaḥ that he heard a proclamation by a heavenly herald which led him to foretell the destruction of Shargorod. The Besht, who was present, 'shouted at the Preacher and said: "Fool, do you, too, hear heralds?" ',[19] but later admitted to R. Jacob Joseph of Polonnoye: 'You may think that the *Preacher* was lying, Heaven forbid, but it is true that he heard a herald's voice.'[20] It is clear, therefore, that the Mokhiaḥ of Polonnoye could hear heavenly proclamations and exert influence in the upper worlds just like his master, the Besht. Clearly, he was not 'one of the common people' or 'a man of matter', to use the terminology employed by hasidism, from its beginnings, to describe the ordinary hasid and to distinguish him from the zaddik, the 'man of form' or the leader, who was 'a man of the spirit'.[21]

Later hasidic tradition could hardly fail to recognize this. In spite of its anachronistic tendency to turn the Besht into a latter-day zaddik in all respects and to present his intimates as his subservient disciples and 'courtiers', it does not deny those 'disciples' their status as charismatic figures quite like the Besht himself:

And in this generation, too, it has been revealed that the Besht had the Holy Spirit and the revelation of Elijah and other exalted spiritual qualities, and he disclosed the secrets of the Torah to his disciples (may their souls rest in Paradise) who also had the Holy Spirit, as, for example, his brother-in-law R. Gershon of Kutow and R. Nahman of Kosov and his other famous disciples, the marvellous greatness of whose deeds was recognized by all who saw them and whose prayer was heard from afar, and at the end of his days he handed on the principles of the Torah to the holy rabbi, R. Dov of Mezhirech, who had the Holy Spirit, which he attained by means of great affliction as we have explained; and now, in this generation, all the zaddikim are his [presumably the Besht's] disciples and we drink his waters.[22]

We see, then, that the picture of the Besht's circle, even as portrayed in *Shivḥei haBesht* and later hasidic tradition, is far removed from the typical image of the hasidic court in which one spiritually outstanding personality dominates a congregation of ordinary hasidim who, by their very nature, are 'common people' from the spiritual point of view (though not necessarily from the point of view of education, intellectual capacity, material wealth, or anything else) and who are totally dependent on the personality of the leader and his mediation to realize their own spirituality. Rather, the whole of the Besht's circle is charged with high spiritual tension. As was shown above, several of his associates were clearly endowed with pneumatic qualities like his and even attracted disciples of their own, although the definition of 'disciple' in this context is, of course, fluid: a person could regard himself as someone's disciple and at the same time be regarded as the teacher and leader of others.[23] Later hasidic tradition could hardly

[18] See *Shivḥei haBesht*: ed. Mintz, 134; ed. Horodecky, 89–90; *In Praise*, 202–3.

[19] *Shivḥei haBesht*, ed. Mintz, 66; ed. Horodecky, 61; *In Praise*, 62–3.

[20] *Shivḥei haBesht*, ed. Mintz, 68; ed. Horodecky, 63; *In Praise*, 66–7.

[21] On this, see below, pp. 86–8 and n. 25.

[22] *Matsref ha'avodah* [Zhitomir, 1865] (1st edn. Königsberg, 1858), 58. See also the corresponding passage in *Vikuḥa rabah* (Munkacz, 1894), 32*a*. On the connection between the two works and on their author, see Y. Mondshine, 'Hasefarim *Matsref ha'avodah* u*Vikuḥa rabah*', *Alei sefer*, 5 (1978), 165–75.

[23] This applies also to the circle of the disciples of the Maggid of Mezhirech. See below, s. 3.

ignore this fact; nor has it escaped the attention of modern scholars. Distinguishing 'primitive' hasidism (after the model of 'primitive Christianity') from, on the one hand, the exclusive circles of 'aristocratic' kabbalists which preceded it—whose members segregated themselves from the community at large—and, on the other hand, from the popular 'cult of zaddikism' into which it was soon to degenerate—a cult which elevated the zaddikim over the community at large—scholars concluded that 'primitive hasidism' brought about, if only briefly, something of a democratization of religious life, inviting the whole community to strive towards the highest spiritual and mystical goals which it set forth.[24] This, then, was taken as the truly vital, original, creative stage in the history of hasidism, an initial period of purity, before the novel egalitarian ideals of the founders were corrupted under the compulsion of reality. For once the common people adopted the 'spiritual' mannerisms of the holy men, they inevitably reduced them to no more than empty gestures. This in turn was seen as the factor which prompted the leadership to reassess its methods and goals, a process which culminated in the rise of the institution of zaddikism. Hasidism now drew a fundamental distinction between the spiritual ideals which the zaddik alone could realize and the completely different spiritual possibilities which were open to the ordinary hasid.

The picture of a spiritually ambitious, egalitarian, 'democratic' hasidism, however attractive to the modern eye, does not square with one solid historical fact to which we have already alluded: it was precisely in this initial period that hasidism formulated the sharp distinction between the 'men of matter' and the 'men of form', between 'the ordinary organs of the body of the people' and the 'spiritual men' who were 'its head'. How is it possible to reconcile an image of egalitarian spiritual comradeship such as is so commonly associated with early hasidism with an anthropological doctrine which divides mankind (or rather, the Jewish component of mankind) into two clear-cut groups: a small minority, purely spiritual in nature, on one side, and, on the other, the great majority, characterized by crude corporeality (the ideal of the bond between the two sections of the people which hasidism also set up for itself, far from obscuring this fundamental distinction, is actually based on it and takes it as its starting point).[25] If hasidism in its initial stages did indeed throw open the gates of spiritual and mystical religiosity equally to everyone, whom did R. Jacob Joseph have in mind when he introduced the concepts and coined the various phrases and terms which have ever since served the hasidic movement to distinguish between the two divisions of humanity which he defined? The only possible answer to this question seems to be that the Besht and the 'spiritual' members of his circle all regarded themselves as representatives of the section described as 'the head', the leaders. It was only within that circle, not outside it, that they called for fulfilment of such mystical ideals as the requirement of constant *devekut*, worship though corporeality, the elevation of straying thoughts, etc. The 'corporeal' common people were situated on the margins of the circle or outside it, and the call directed to them, from the outset, was completely different: the masses were instructed above all to cleave [*lidbok*] to the leaders of their generation but not to copy

[24] I dealt with this *in extenso* in my article 'God and the Zaddik as the Two Focal Points of Hasidic Worship', *History of Religions*, 18: 4 (1979), 305 ff. (repr. in Hundert (ed.), *Essential Papers*, 307 ff.).

[25] On the formulations of these teachings in the works of R. Jacob Joseph of Polonnoye, see G. Nigal, *Manhig ve'edah* (Jerusalem, 1962), 50–65; S. H. Dresner, *The Zaddik* (New York, 1960), 113–90.

them. Thus, on the subject of the ideal of worship through corporeality, R. Jacob Joseph writes as follows, pointing out that this is a tradition which 'I believe I heard from my teacher', the Besht:

And it is in that sense that we should understand 'And warm yourself by the fire [Hebrew *or*—'light'] of the wise',[26] that is to say, it is while the wise are in the superior spiritual state of *gadlut* [expanded consciousness] and occupied with the light [*or*] of Torah and prayer, when they are literally aflame with the light of fire, that you should warm yourself by their fire. But 'beware of their embers',[27] that is to say, when they are in the lesser state of *katnut* [diminished consciousness], when they have no light to kindle them with an inner fire, a condition to which we apply the word 'embers', [when they are] devoid of inner fire. The disciple wishes to learn from his master how he occupies himself with material things, but he does not know that the master is, at the same time, fulfilling [the ideal expressed by the verse] 'I have hidden Your words in my heart',[28] occupying himself with material things but with an inner spiritual purpose. Thus *all that the disciple manages to learn from* [*his master*] *is to occupy himself on the material level, and he will be punished* [*for this*] [the emphasis is mine—A. R.-A.], 'for their bite is the bite of a fox and their sting is the sting of a scorpion.'[29] That is to say, he [the master] . . . is bringing seven levels . . . closer to their [spiritual] root.[30] But the disciple knows nothing of this and thinks his master is simply occupied with material things. And these are the words of a wise man.[31]

The traditions that have come down to us from that circle of the founders of hasidism often stress that the call to fulfil the mystical ideals is limited to 'the men of the spirit'. Sometimes they make this explicit, as in the passage quoted above; sometimes they do not spell out the limitation but it is clear to the reader that they regard it as self-evident, or else it is slipped in here and there, in some of the parallel traditions which have been preserved.[32] It is true that at this stage of the development of the movement there was not yet a standard terminology by which to refer to the leaders, and they were variously called 'men of form', 'scholars', 'men of understanding', 'men of knowledge', 'heads of the generation', 'the zaddikim', 'those of Israel who are perfect in their faith', and so on, but the collective consciousness of leadership which was shared within the

[26] Avot 2: 10. [27] Ibid. [28] Ps. 119: 11. [29] Avot 2: 10.

[30] That is to say, while the zaddik is working on the material level, he is in reality occupied in perfecting the upper worlds: in a play on the Hebrew word for 'scorpion' (*akrav*), he is said to bring closer (*mekarev*, containing the last three letters of *akrav*) seven levels each one of which consists of ten—the first letter of *akrav* being the letter *ayin*, which in *gematriyah* has the value 70, i.e. 7 × 10—and thus he raises them to their spiritual root. See G. Nigal, *Torot Ba'al haToledot* (Jerusalem, 1974), 119.

[31] Jacob Joseph of Polonnoye, *Tsafenat pa'neaḥ* (Korets, 1782] (New York, 1954), 32*a*. Cf. also id., *Ben porat Yosef* (New York, 1954), 127*a*.

[32] I discussed this more fully in my article 'God and the Zaddik', 301–5. I tried there to look beyond the literal sense of what appears to be a conflicting directive which also occurs here and there in early hasidic literature. This is the appeal, expressly directed at everyone, to aspire to the highest degree of spiritual perfection, offering an assurance that this goal is within everyone's reach. I pointed out there that this appeal, whose ethical-didactic motives are self-evident, appears at times even in the teachings of R. Nahman of Bratslav, alongside his more characteristic teachings which are unquestionably 'zaddikist' inasmuch as they draw the sharpest possible distinction between the zaddik's religious norms and those which define the much more limited scope for spiritual action by the ordinary men. There can be no doubt that it was the latter that reflected his true position. One must, therefore, be extremely cautious in assessing the implications of these apparently egalitarian demands for radical spirituality, and not attach to them any programmatic significance beyond the purpose of not discouraging the public in their aspiration to realize their (inherently limited) spiritual potential to the full. Ibid. 303–5.

circle is clear beyond all doubt, and, as we have seen, it is not focused at this stage on the figure of a single leader, not even on that of the Besht.[33]

[33] Weiss, in his article 'Reshit tsemiḥatah shel haderekh haḥasidit', 84–5, dealt with various expressions which alternate in parallel formulations of the earliest teachings relating to the status of the leaders. He pointed out that some of them, though certainly not most, spoke of 'the great man of the generation' (*gedol hador*) or 'the zaddik' in the singular. Weiss considered the possibility that these formulations reflect a tendency to attribute supreme leadership to one personality in the group comprising 'the great men of the generation' (*gedolei hador*), and he tried to demonstrate a connection between this tendency—if indeed its existence could be proved—and the Besht. But Weiss himself recognized the limitations of this approach, for often the singular appears in one text and the plural in the parallel version of the same teaching. Occasionally it appears that it is the framework of midrashic associations interspersed with biblical verses that dictates the random choice between singular and plural. Weiss's general conclusion is correct: 'By the very nature of the traditions it is clear that we must not attempt to draw too many fine distinctions from the language used, and it is impossible to subject the wording of these oral traditions to the sort of textual analysis which is customary in the interpretation of written speculative works' (ibid. 87). It may be that we should adopt the same attitude towards R. Jacob Joseph of Polonnoye's statement quoted in Ettinger's 'The Hasidic Movement', 130: 'And so, too, we should interpret the other plagues, up to the plagues of *arbeh* [locusts], the Targum of which is *gova* [locust] and also *bor* [Hebrew for 'pit'; the Aramaic *guba*, a pit, has the same consonants as *gova*], for it is a plural, as it is written: "I will multiply [*arbeh*, same spelling as for 'locust'] your seed etc." (Gen. 16: 10; 22: 17) and the fact that there is a plurality of leaders [*manhigim*] is so that there should not be only one leader [*dabar*] for the generation but rather the contrary, that they should all be heads and leaders, for I have heard that that was the blessing bestowed by Elijah on a certain town, namely that they should all be leaders, etc., and then a change came about from a single *dabar* to a *dever* [pestilence, the fifth plague], Heaven forbid, or to hail [the seventh plague, *barad*, the same three consonants], and through this "it covered the eye of the earth" [a literal reading of Exod. 10: 5]. He who was the eye of the earth was, as it were, the eyes of the congregation, for he was fitted to watch over the earth, [but] when these many people were created leaders the result was that they "covered the eye of the earth" and he could not see the earth so as to watch over them, as I have written on the verse "And the eyes of Israel were dim with age, and he could not see" (Gen. 48: 10) etc. And also what is meant by "and they [the locusts] shall eat what is left to you after the hail" (Exod. 10: 5) is that when there was one leader [*dabar*] for a generation there was blessing, but when a change came and many leaders [*manhigim*] were created, *dabar* became *barad*, hail, which ruins what is left. This is easy to understand' (Jacob Joseph of Polonnoye, *Toledot Ya'akov Yosef* [Korets, 1780] (Jerusalem, 1966), on 'Bo' [Exod. 10 ff.], 39*c–d*). On the face of it R. Jacob Joseph is here arguing for leadership by a single person (presumably the Besht) and attacking the multiplicity of leaders in his generation. And indeed, Ettinger suggested that in what R. Jacob Joseph says we can perhaps detect an echo of some criticism of the Besht by members of his own circle, a criticism which R. Jacob Joseph is seeking to rebut. In fact, however, this passage, which appears in the middle of a long sermon interspersed with scriptural quotations, need not be understood as a piece of polemic, especially as on the next page of the same sermon R. Jacob Joseph again speaks of 'the eyes of the congregation'—its leaders—in the plural as a desirable group, as he does elsewhere in his writings, e.g. *Toledot Ya'akov Yosef*, 'Vayetse' [Gen. 28: 10 ff.], 22*d*. And further on in the same sermon, on 'Bo' (43*b*), R. Jacob Joseph makes the following recommendation: 'And that is how "Be a tail to lions" (Avot 4: 15) should be understood: like a tail hanging behind him, so you should follow a lion, that is, righteous men [*anashim tsadikim*]' and a few lines further: ' "Why is the land ruined" etc., "Because they have forsaken My law which I set before them" (Jer. 9: 12), that is to say, they have forsaken the exalted spiritual qualities of the men of the Torah who are before them.' Here he actually expounds a singular noun ('My law', 'lion') by a plural equivalent ('men of the Torah', 'righteous men'). If he had wanted to emphasize the oneness of 'the zaddik of the generation', he could easily have kept to the singular with which the verse supplied him. Furthermore, there is not necessarily any contradiction between the view of a society divided into two groups, spiritual leaders and the worldly masses, and the view that in every generation one zaddik appears who is the head of them all and is spiritually superior to them all. His superiority need not find expression in supreme leadership within a hierarchical system. See Weiss, 'Reshit tsemiḥatah shel haderekh haḥasidit', 85. And compare with the explicit formulation of the problem in the foreword to Hielman, *Beit rabbi*, 14–15: 'Now it is true that in every generation there is certainly a particular zaddik who is called the zaddik of the generation. And this is the secret of the division between the hasidim, that one journeys to one zaddik and another to another zaddik (each according to the root of his soul) and each

Shivḥei haBesht ('The praises of the Besht'), a hagiography dedicated to the personality of the Besht, is also, in some measure, a hagiography of R. Gershon of Kutow, R. Jacob Joseph of Polonnoye, R. Aryeh Leib the Mokhiaḥ of Polonnoye, R. Dov Ber of Mezhirech, R. Phinehas of Korets, and all the other extraordinary figures who populate its pages. Although overshadowed by the Besht, they clearly belong to his superior category of humanity. The qualitative difference between him and them is insignificant when compared to the qualitative difference between the Besht and his circle, taken as one category, and the category comprising 'the common people', 'the men of matter', whose presence in *Shivḥei haBesht*, however dimly perceived, is not to be overlooked. True, *Shivḥei haBesht* is not concerned to portray the personalities of these 'common people' in any detail. Rarely even named, they serve only as a background, a narrative means of enhancing the spiritual quality and supernatural powers of the heroes. But they perform an important function, in that the Besht and his associates can only operate through them or on their behalf.[34] This tendency to highlight the individual personalities of the heroes while letting speak only from the shadows the ordinary mortals who witness and benefit from their actions is natural to the hagiographic genre, but it should not conceal from us that all those others who are obscure as individuals have a collective 'otherness' perceived with great clarity. The picture of society in the early days of hasidism as it emerges from *Shivḥei haBesht* is, then, that of a group of spiritual teachers who maintain a certain level of communication among themselves while at the same time maintaining an altogether different level of communication with a wider public among whom they operate but from whom they are conscious of being utterly different in every aspect of their spiritual constitution[35]—a picture which is wholly compatible with the anthropological doctrine of R. Jacob Joseph of Polonnoye.

If we seek to uncover the historical reality which underlies R. Jacob Joseph's observations concerning the 'body' of 'the common people', and to relate his speculative teachings to some concrete state of society in his day, *Shivḥei haBesht* supplies the answer in stories about the tax farmers, tradespeople, *ḥeder* teachers, and ritual slaughterers, men and women from all walks of life, who, lacking all 'spirituality' of their own, were passive witnesses of the wonderful deeds performed by the Besht and

one thinks that the zaddik to whom he journeys is the particular zaddik of the generation, but should we therefore speak ill, Heaven forbid, of the other zaddikim of the generation.' See also below, s. 7.

[34] These people are the 'tax farmer' (*arendator*) of *Shivḥei haBesht* (ed. Mintz, 54–5; *In Praise*, 35–8); 'a certain great merchant' and his son (ed. Mintz, 60; *In Praise*, 48); 'the wealthy man, Aizik' and his sick daughter (ed. Mintz, 73; *In Praise*, 77); 'two litigants' (ed. Mintz, 78; *In Praise*, 88); the 'treasurer' (*gabai*) (ed. Mintz, 79; *In Praise*, 90), 'a *shoḥet* who was very frivolous and a drunkard' (ed. Mintz, 79; *In Praise*, 90), and many others throughout the book. On the relationship between the spiritual leader and his congregation in this initial period, as distinct from later developments, see I. Etkes, 'Hasidism as a Movement: The First Stage', in B. Safran (ed.), *Hasidism: Continuity or Innovation?* (Cambridge, Mass., 1988), 1–26.

[35] Consciousness of this gap of course engendered the distinctly hasidic methods of bridging it: the doctrine of the descent of the zaddik in its hasidic versions, the doctrine of the leader as a 'channel' or intermediary between upper and lower worlds, etc. Were it not for this, it would be hard to explain the enormous success of hasidism, whose leaders stemmed from élitist circles but which nevertheless attracted to itself great numbers of 'simple' people, as it defined them, who found in it the opportunity to lead a vital and rich religious life. It is important to remember, however, that what was in question was the throwing of a bridge over the gap and not the closing of the gap.

his colleagues and came under the influence of their powers. And if a parallel is to be drawn between the fully developed hasidic community of recent generations, with the zaddik at its head, and any organizational structure in the first generation of hasidism, the lines will not run from the latter-day zaddik to the Besht and from the Besht's circle of associates and disciples to the latter-day hasidic community, as has generally been assumed in the historiography both within the hasidic movement and in the scholarly literature outside it; rather, the parallel lines will run from the latter-day zaddik to the entire circle of the Besht and his associates, and from the latter-day hasidic community to the wider public within which the Besht's circle operated.

The clarification of these issues has a direct bearing on the question which formed the starting point of the present discussion, namely whether leadership of the hasidic movement in the time of the Besht was in fact centralized. There is no doubt that the Besht's circle of associates and colleagues was influenced by his teachings,[36] and it is reasonable to assume that, in his time, he was regarded as the most prominent personality in that circle. From this point of view, it is understandable and legitimate that he should have been perpetuated in the collective memory of the movement as the chief or only leader of his day. But from an organizational point of view, it is quite clear that he did not act as the supreme leader in any hierarchic framework. Rather, he belonged to a whole network of charismatic personalities who were accepted by the wider community as teachers and spiritual leaders, and who, indeed, saw themselves in that light. Hasidism in its early stages did not create any centralized organizational framework, and its leadership structure in the generation of its founders was no less fragmented than it is generally taken to have been in later generations. The chain of events immediately after the death of the Besht emphasizes the absence of any centralized framework of leadership. If the Besht had, indeed, served in his lifetime as the supreme leader of the whole movement in the same way as every zaddik in succeeding generations was to act as sole leader of his own congregation of hasidim, we would expect an immediate successor to have been found, acceptable to the majority if not to all of the hasidim (although the appointment of such a successor might have followed a short contest for the position by a number of candidates from among his sons or his disciples). For were it not so, the movement as such would have broken up and disappeared from the arena of history, as did many hasidic congregations whose distinctive identity was weakened to the point of extinction after the death of their founder, in the absence of an 'heir' to succeed him. True, it is generally assumed that the Maggid of Mezhirech inherited the leadership in precisely this way, either on the strength of an explicit nomination by the

[36] e.g. it is told of R. Nahman of Horodenka that he said: 'When I was a great hasid I went every day to a cold *mikveh* . . . Despite this I could not rid myself of wayward thoughts, until I turned to the wisdom of the Besht' (*Shivḥei haBesht,* ed. Horodecky, 82; ed. Mintz, 112; *In Praise*, 156). And according to the traditions relating to R. Phinehas of Korets, R. Phinehas himself testified that 'from the day that I was with the Besht, God helped me toward the truth. And I walk in the path of King David, may he rest in peace. And similarly: 'Since the time when people began to follow the way of the Baal Shem Tov, many customs instituted by R. Judah the Hasid have been abrogated' (see 'R. Pinḥas of Korzec' in Heschel, *The Circle*, 10–14). And if this is true of R. Nahman of Horodenka and even more so of R. Phinehas of Korets, both of whom preserved a certain distance in their relations with the Besht, maintained their own circles of hasidim, and did not fear to differ from the Besht's opinions at times, it is certainly true of people who were beyond doubt disciples of the Besht, for example R. Jacob Joseph of Polonnoye, who consistently calls him 'my teacher' and acts as a mouthpiece for his teachings.

Besht before he died or through being 'elected' to office by the other disciples of the Besht, because, so the argument goes, the natural candidate, R. Zevi, the son of the Besht, was either unfit for leadership or unwilling to accept it.[37] However, the evidence for all this is meagre and problematical: the Maggid of Mezhirech was certainly not the natural candidate for the succession, since he came to hasidism only a short time before the Besht died.[38] As was demonstrated by Heschel, he was not acceptable to everyone; the majority of the disciples and associates of the Besht did not regard the Maggid as their leader and were not numbered among his disciples. But Heschel's suggestion, which was intended to resolve this question, is far from satisfactory:

The followers of the Besht, *who apparently were unaware that he had chosen R. Ber* [the emphasis is mine—A. R.-A.], refused to accept his authority. Only two or three of the youngest disciples attached themselves to him.[39]

It is hard to believe that the Besht's associates and disciples, who were his most intimate companions, would not have known of a decision so important for all of them as his nomination of the Maggid to be his successor. It is also hard to conceive of any reason why such a decision should have been kept intentionally secret, for by its very nature its sole purpose would have been to legitimize the succession by making it public. This question-mark over the circumstances of the transfer of the leadership from the Besht to the Maggid also gave rise to the conjecture that the Maggid was not recognized as leader of the movement until the year 1766, about six years after the death of the Besht, and that during those six years a strenuous contest for the leadership was waged between the Maggid of Mezhirech and R. Jacob Joseph of Polonnoye, and perhaps also R. Menahem Mendel of Peremyshlany.[40]

The notion of a long-drawn-out struggle for the succession to the leadership is unconvincing: if hasidism in the generation of the Besht had indeed crystallized round

[37] See e.g. Dubnow, *Toledot haḥasidut*, 69, 80; Horodecky, *Haḥasidut vehaḥasidim*, i. 80; D. Kahana, *Toledot hamekubalim hashabeta'im vehaḥasidim* (2 vols.; Tel Aviv, 1926–7), ii. 82.

[38] See n. 2 above and nn. 47 and 76 below. I shall deal with this fully elsewhere.

[39] Heschel, 'R. Pinḥas of Korzec', 16.

[40] See A. Rubinstein, 'Shevaḥ miShivḥei haBesht', *Tarbiz*, 35 (1966), 178–80. He relies mainly on the testimony of the mitnagged R. David of Makow: first, the remark in R. David's letter to R. Solomon Zalman Lipschitz of Nasielsk that 'only in 5526 [1776] did R. Berush [= Ber] become famous, and a number of rabbis and geonim journeyed to him' (ibid. 179 n. 23; and see also M. Wilensky, *Ḥasidim umitnaggedim* (2 vols.; Jerusalem, 1970), ii, 235); and secondly, the wording of R. David's will, from which it can be inferred that R. Levi Isaac of Berdichev entered into association with the Maggid of Mezhirech only in 1776 (Rubinstein, 'Shevaḥ'; Wilensky, *Ḥasidim umitnaggedim*, 244). In the opinion of Rubinstein, Menahem Mendel of Peremyshlany was one of the contenders for the succession in the years between the death of the Besht (1760) and the establishment of the leadership of the Maggid (1766). He infers this from the document which he published in which it is stated that R. Menahem Mendel 'journeyed to the Holy Land [in 1764—A. R.-A.] because people had begun to journey to see him for the purpose of engaging in business' (Rubinstein, 'Shevaḥ', 177, 191). Rubinstein offers the reasonable explanation that this sentence indicates that 'the author was referring to people who used to visit Mendel as a wonder-working zaddik for the sake of their business interests [but] R. Mendel turned his back on his visitors and journeyed to Erets Yisrael' ('Shevaḥ', 177). Y. Mondshine's criticisms of Rubinstein's conclusions ('Ha'omnam shevaḥ miShivḥei haBesht?', *Tarbiz*, 51 (1982), 673–7, replied to by Rubinstein, 'Shevaḥ', 677–80) do not affect the matter we are considering one way or the other unless we accept his hypothesis that the 'document' relating to R. Mendel's journey was a forgery and that its true author was Joseph Perl—a hypothesis which would deprive it of all historical value as evidence of the status of R. Menahem Mendel of Peremyshlany.

its 'zaddik' like a hasidic congregation of more recent times, it is hard to imagine that it could have survived as a movement for fully six years in the absence of the leader who was, after all, the source of its vitality and the focus for its distinctive identity; it would certainly have disintegrated or have split up, earlier rather than later, into separate and even mutually hostile congregations in the course of the protracted struggle between the rival claimants to the succession. Moreover, this hypothesis has no support in the sources. The facts and factors to which Heschel and Rubinstein drew attention are, indeed, correct and reasonable in themselves, but they do not necessarily combine to present us with a picture of a struggle for 'the crown of leadership' between the Maggid, R. Jacob Joseph, and R. Menahem Mendel of Peremyshlany. All that we know is: (*a*) that the Maggid of Mezhirech was accepted at some stage as the leader of a large circle of hasidim; (*b*) that R. Jacob Joseph of Polonnoye and R. Phinehas of Korets explicitly, and some of the other intimates of the Besht by implication (as we are prompted to conclude from the absence of their names from any list of the Maggid's disciples), did not accept the leadership of the Maggid and did not join his circle after the death of the Besht;[41] (*c*) that the Maggid of Mezhirech, and still more so some of his disciples, rejected the hasidic path taught by R. Phinehas of Korets;[42] (*d*) that R. Phinehas of Korets and R. Jacob Joseph of Polonnoye were on terms of affection and mutual respect;[43] (*e*) that R. Menahem Mendel of Peremyshlany, whether or not in accordance with his own wishes, was also accepted as spiritual leader by a section of the public until he left for Erets Yisrael in 1764.

If we do not start with the hypothesis of a struggle for the leadership which allegedly delayed the final decision for a full six years, the information in our possession does not in the least point to the creation of full-blown pressure groups fighting to advance R. Jacob Joseph, R. Phinehas of Korets, R. Menahem Menel of Peremyshlany, or anyone else to the position of supreme leader of hasidism, and the facts are open to a different interpretation. Heschel himself formulates his opinion cautiously and presents it only as a conjecture,[44] although it seems that both he and Dresner, who quotes him in full,[45] are convinced that it is correct. But this conjecture raises more problems than it solves: why did the majority of the Besht's disciples reject or ignore his nomination of the Maggid as his successor? Indeed, why did the Besht not choose a disciple who was of longer standing and closer to him, like R. Jacob Joseph of Polonnoye? And if, in fact, R. Jacob Joseph was considered unfit for leadership because of his difficult character,[46] just as R. Zevi, the son of the Besht, may have been considered unsuitable for high office (though it may be questioned whether such considerations would have been enough to oust a natural heir from his rightful position), why did the obvious talents of the Maggid of Mezhirech fail to earn him universal and immediate recognition?

The unlikely conjectures which have been offered in explanation of the allegedly irregular procedures following the death of the Besht stem from the anachronistic expectation that the leadership should have passed immediately and directly from the Besht to the Maggid of Mezhirech, just as it did eventually pass from father to son, son-in-law, or some other natural heir in the hasidic dynasties which developed later on. This expectation, which is common to both internal hasidic and critical scholarly

[41] Heschel, 'R. Pinḥas of Korzec', 16 ff.
[42] Ibid. 21 ff.
[43] Ibid. 17.
[44] Ibid. 16.
[45] See Dresner, *The Zaddik*, 60–2.
[46] Ibid. 61.

historiography, has grown out of the no less anachronistic assumption that the Besht acted as the sole central leader of an established community of 'his' hasidim. In fact the Besht was only one prominent personality among others in a circle of charismatics and pneumatics whose members all shared his supernatural qualities and his claims to spiritual leadership of the age, although it is quite likely that many of them drew their spiritual inspiration from him. We must therefore reject the conjectures outlined above; the facts in our possession will then fit without difficulty into an alternative reconstruction of the circumstances which followed the death of the Besht: the Maggid of Mezhirech did not 'inherit' the leadership of hasidism as a result of a secret or controversial 'nomination' by the Besht; nor was he 'elected' to office by a majority of the Baal Shem Tov's disciples as has generally been assumed either explicitly or implicitly despite the absence of any evidence for this in the sources.[47] His accession to power was

[47] The assumption that the Maggid was 'appointed' to the leadership by the Besht and even 'ordained' by him by the laying on of hands is based principally on the story of the commencement of the Maggid's association with the Besht, in the version given in *Shivḥei haBesht*, ed. Mintz, 75–6; ed. Horodecky, 70–2; *In Praise*, 81–4; ed. Mondshine 169–71; Yid. version, ch. 23, 11*a*–*b*; Ya'ari, 'Shetei mahadurot yesod', 405; and see e.g. Dresner, *The Zaddik*, 59–60, but it has no foundation in fact. The story in *Shivḥei haBesht* expressly concerns the Maggid's initiation into the circle of the Besht on the occasion of his first visit to him, and it is certainly not to be interpreted as describing a ceremony in which the succession to the leadership was bestowed on the chosen disciple. The exchange of blessings between them, too, and the laying of the hand upon his head, which is described at the end of the story, does not suggest ordination (*semikhah*) to the leadership. At most it can be understood as emphasizing the relations of equality between the Maggid and the Besht, with the object of providing *ex post facto* support for the position of the Maggid as leader after the death of the Besht (see also Dan, *Hasipur haḥasidi*, 128). It should be pointed out that in a second version of the story (Aaron of Opatow, *Keter shem tov* [Zholkva (Zolkiew), 1794–5] (Brooklyn, NY, 1972), part 2, s. 424, 124–5), the exchange of blessings does not appear at all. As for the suggestion that the other disciples of the Besht 'elected' the Maggid to the leadership (see e.g. Kahana, *Toledot hamekubalim*, ii. 82), that, too, has no support in the sources, for there is no trace at all in hasidism of any official electoral procedures such as were customary, for example, in the institutions of the *kahal*. Moreover, it is clear that the majority of the Besht's senior disciples had reservations as regards the Maggid's authority and did not accept his leadership. In the absence of clear evidence of the 'appointment', 'ordination', or 'election' of the Maggid to office by the Besht or any of the Besht's disciples, *Shivḥei haBesht* relies on the following tradition: 'I heard this from the rabbi, the hasid, R. Jeḥiel Michel of the holy community of Zloczow. When he visited here in the town of Linits for the wedding of his son, our teacher Ze'ev, he said that he was ordered from heaven to accept the Besht as his rabbi and to go and learn from him. They showed him the "streams of wisdom" which led to the Besht. When the Besht passed away he was ordered to accept the Great Maggid, Rabbi Dov, as his rabbi. They showed him that the same "streams of wisdom" that formerly ran to the Besht now led to the rabbi, the Maggid, God bless his memory' (*Shivḥei haBesht*, ed. Mintz, 126; ed. Horodecky, 72; *In Praise*, 185). The authority of the Maggid, according to this tradition, came direct from Heaven, and did not derive from the authority of his predecessor or the collective authority of the hasidim. This places it clearly within the definition of pure charismatic authority, and there is no doubt that the authority of the Maggid fell within that category just as had that of the Besht. It is interesting to note that apart from the stories of the Maggid's entry into association with the Besht, which were interpreted with excessive licence as referring to his 'ordination' to the leadership, the only documents in our possession indicating that the Besht expressly appointed the Maggid to succeed him as leader are the letters found in the Ḥerson *genizah*, which are universally regarded as forgeries. It seems that it was precisely the absence of early evidence of such an appointment that created the need to 'document' it in unambiguous fashion. In fact, the very existence of these letters in the Ḥerson *genizah* could serve as further proof of the weakness of the hasidic tradition regarding the appointment of the Maggid to office, for this *genizah* shows great sensitivity to the missing historical links in the sources and considerable concern to support later hasidic historiographic tradition. See C. E. Bichovsky, *Ginzei nistarot* (Jerusalem, 1924), 'Or Yisrael', 7, letter 21; 8, letter 23; 13, letter 46; 15, letter 52; 19, letter 61. See also *Hatamim*, i. 121 (no. 260). And cf. Rapoport-Albert, 'Hagiography', 131–7.

spontaneous, and it was based on his own charismatic personality, not on any formal, rational procedures. Indeed, such procedures had not yet crystallized in hasidism. It is very probable that not many people saw him as a leader in the period immediately following the death of the Besht, perhaps until 1776.[48] In other words, the status of the Maggid as the 'heir' of the Besht was not that of a direct, immediate, and formally instituted successor but of an 'heir' in the broadest sense of the word: he came to be regarded as the greatest hasidic leader of his time, just as the Besht had been regarded before him. The existence of an 'heir' in the latter sense would not, in principle, and (as we know) did not, in practice, necessitate the removal from the scene of other hasidic leaders who did not accept the authority of the Maggid, in just the same way as the activity of the Besht had not curbed the independent operations of his colleagues and their disciples in the preceding two decades.

This interpretation of the facts also relieves us of the need to cast R. Jacob Joseph in the unlikely role of an unsuccessful rival candidate for the leadership, when there is no evidence of any efforts by him in that direction, unless his well-known reservations with regard to the leadership of the Maggid were to be so construed.[49] That this is most unlikely becomes evident if we bear in mind that there were many internal controversies in the hasidic camp, and that the opposing parties entertained mutual reservations of various kinds in regard to worship, personal conduct, or distinct styles of communal leadership. These did not necessarily indicate the existence of a struggle for the 'crown' of supreme authority over the hasidic movement as a whole: indeed, in most cases they certainly did not. This is as true of the beginnings of hasidism as of its subsequent stages of development even up to the present day, when tensions and ideological or territorial disputes between the various hasidic courts have become commonplace, without ever turning upon the subject of rival claims to the supreme leadership of the entire movement, and without challenging the pluralistic principle which underlay the organizational structure of the movement from the start.[50]

One final point is worth noting in this connection: the Lithuanian *maggid* R. Israel Loebel, a zealous opponent of hasidism,[51] in his German tract on the hasidic 'sect' said: 'After the death of R. Israel Ba'al Shem, both the external and the internal government of the sect took on a new form. Instead of one supreme leader, many were chosen.'[52] Admittedly R. Israel Loebel's account, written at the end of the 1790s, is imprecise on the historical details of the beginnings of hasidism, and it is clear that his knowledge of

[48] This is asserted by R. David of Makow, and the remarks of A. Rubinstein on the interval between the death of the Besht and the leadership of the Maggid are reasonable in themselves, although the notion of struggles for the succession is essentially anachronistic (see above, pp. 90–1 and n. 40, and cf. n. 50 below).

[49] It certainly undermines the even weaker allegation that R. Menahem Mendel of Peremyshlany was a candidate for the *supreme* leadership (Rubinstein, 'Shevaḥ', 180). All that is known on this question from the document published by Rubinstein is that R. Menahem Mendel, like several other members of the Besht's circle, was accepted by the public as a spiritual leader in his own right, *alongside* the others and not necessarily as their head.

[50] On this, see also below, s. 7.

[51] See Dubnow, *Toledot haḥasidut*, 278–86; G. Scholem, 'Le'inyan R. Yisrael Leibl ufulmuso neged haḥasidut', *Zion*, 20 (1955), 153–62; Wilensky, *Ḥasidim umitnaggedim*, ii. 253–342.

[52] From Wilensky's Hebrew translation, *Ḥasidim umitnaggedim*, ii. 328.

the Besht is defective.[53] But he was a contemporary of many of the disciples of the Maggid of Mezhirech, and it is significant that he located the apparent decentralization of the hasidic leadership in the more distant past, after the death of the Besht, rather than associating the process with the situation he knew at first hand, following the death of the Maggid of Mezhirech. So far as he was aware, the hasidic movement had been governed by many leaders as far back as anyone could remember. It is not impossible that his picture of a fragmented leadership faithfully reflects the historical situation which existed in the 1760s and early 1770s—particularly as it was perceived in the strongholds of the mitnaggedim in Lithuania; for the few hasidic centres in mitnaggedic Lithuania, notably the one at Karlin, were as notorious as the hasidic centre at Mezhirech, and they were certainly regarded not as secondary branches but as important centres in their own right (see more on this below).

3. THE LEADERSHIP IN THE TIME OF THE MAGGID

The enormous influence of the Maggid of Mezhirech on his many disciples in the leadership of hasidism is so well documented as to be beyond dispute. It is precisely this that will throw into sharper relief the claim that the hasidic movement of his day was not centralized and did not produce any organizational framework for supreme leadership by the Maggid or anyone else.

The decisive influence of the Maggid is attested in hasidic literature both directly, in explicit acknowledgements, and indirectly, through the reflections of his views in the teachings of his disciples and their disciples. His influence, like that of the Besht, has become fixed in the historical memory of the movement. Hasidic historians present the Maggid as the second link in a chain of transmission of charismatic authority in hasidism which began with the Besht and continued through the Maggid to all the latter's disciples. Thus, instead of descending link by link from one generation to another, charismatic authority was seen as branching out in the third generation from the first two links, the Besht and the Maggid, into several ancillary chains of transmission. Aaron Walden, for example, author of *Shem hagedolim heḥadash*, described the ramification of charismatic authority after the Maggid of Mezhirech as follows: 'He drew living water from the well of that holy old man, the saintly, holy and awe-inspiring rabbi, the holy of holies, Israel Ba'al Shem Tov of Medzibezh, and gave all the holy and pure disciples to drink of it, and through them all the earth was illuminated.'[54]

The picture of a chain that was broken up, its first two links, the Besht and the Maggid, jointly connecting their numerous 'heirs' to the source of charismatic authority, naturally contributed to the assumption that in the generation of the Maggid's disciples there was a pronounced organizational shift from central leadership by a single

[53] e.g. he states that the Besht became famous in the years 1760–5, i.e. in the five years following the known date of his death. See ibid. 259, 326. Wilensky, the translator and editor of Israel Loebel's tract, comments here (ibid. 328 n. 12) that in fact, 'after the death of the Besht, R. Dov Ber, the Maggid of Mezhirech, became the leader of the sect, and only after his death, "instead of one supreme leader, many were chosen" '. Wilensky is 'correcting' Israel Loebel's 'mistake', offering us the conventional view of the matter, but see below.

[54] *Shem hagedolim heḥadash* (Warsaw, 1870), 11*a*, s. 24. And cf. *Seder hadorot heḥadash*, 16–17.

figure to a decentralized structure of leadership by many. However, this picture does not differentiate the strong personal and ideological connection which undoubtedly existed between the links from the loose organizational connection between them.

There is no doubt that the disciples of the Maggid of Mezhirech were fully conscious of their ties to their common master. Not only did many of them continue to regard him as their teacher, and to acknowledge this proudly on numerous occasions even long after they had begun to lead their own hasidic communities; in addition, the teachings of the Maggid certainly played a decisive part in the subsequent development of all the speculative doctrines of hasidism. Notably, at least one sharp ideological dispute between two hasidic leaders of the generation of the Maggid's disciples was perceived by the protagonists as primarily a clash between two conflicting interpretations of the original teaching of the Maggid. This was the dispute between R. Abraham of Kalisk and R. Shneur Zalman of Lyady, in which R. Levi Isaac of Berdichev was also involved, and which spilt over into the struggle for control of the funds raised for the hasidic community in Erets Yisrael.[55]

But the influence of the Maggid as a teacher was not such as to inhibit the existence of independent hasidic centres away from Mezhirech. New courts were set up, not only after 1772 but also during his lifetime and apparently on his initiative, in the years when, supposedly, he functioned as the sole leader of the whole hasidic movement and exercised central control.

Although the Maggid, as we have said, was not accepted by all the intimates of the Besht as the 'heir' to the leadership,[56] a whole generation of hasidic leaders had spent some time at his court and regarded him as their foremost teacher and master. At the same time, apart from those of the Besht's associates who never affiliated themselves to the Maggid and continued independently to maintain circles of their own followers, there were some disciples of the Maggid who established communities of hasidim during the lifetime of their teacher, and each of them was regarded in his own court as its sole leader. Thus R. Abraham of Kalisk, for example, in spite of his personal deference to his teacher the Maggid, was already heading his own congregation of hasidim in Belorussia in 1770, more than two years before the death of the Maggid, and from one document it appears that his leadership of the hasidim in Kalisk may have begun as early as 1768.[57]

[55] Hielman, *Beit rabbi*, 43*a–b*; D. Z. Hillman, *Igrot ba'al haTanya uvenei doro* (Jerusalem, 1953), 105 and 167–79. For a discussion of the dispute among the disciples of the Maggid over his spiritual legacy, see Elior, 'Viku'aḥ Minsk', 189–99; Gries, 'Mimitos le'etos', 126–32.

[56] See above, pp. 90 ff.

[57] See Rabinowitsch, *Lithuanian Hasidism*, 15. The year 5530 (1770) was apparently the year which saw the emergence of a fully-fledged congregation of R. Abraham's hasidim in Kalisk, as is shown by the designation 'Ḥasidei Talk' (T'L'K, numerical value 530: the year 5530 is expressed as T'L'K, omitting the thousands) which is embodied in the Yiddish saying '*Der Talk iz on a talk*' (The hasidism of Talk is without any order, i.e. is disordered). The name 'Talk' is mentioned in the letter of 1801 from R. Abraham of Kalisk to R. Shneur Zalman of Lyady, in which he complains that the associates of R. Shneur Zalman are persecuting him (Hillman, *Igrot ba'al haTanya*, s. 94, 156; and see Hillman's remarks on his p. 160, n. 4, where he quotes the Habad tradition on this matter in the name of the *admor* R. Joseph Isaac of Lubavitch. See also the comment by M. Wilensky, *Kiryat sefer*, 1 (1924–5), 240). This chronology accords well with the testimony of R. Shneur Zalman in his letter to R. Abraham of Kalisk. He tells there of the meeting of the disciples of the Maggid in Rovno in the summer of 1772, when the Maggid delivered his well-known rebuke to R. Abraham 'on his bad behaviour towards our colleagues in Russia' and he also reminds

So, too, in 1772, while the Maggid was still living, R. Menahem Mendel of Vitebsk became known as the leader of a community of hasidim in Minsk, and he acquired a reputation among the mitnaggedim for the attraction he held for hasidic pilgrims.[58] R. Aaron of Karlin, too, established a centre of hasidism, the first in Lithuania, during the lifetime of the Maggid.[59] In fact, although he is usually counted among the Maggid's disciples and 'heirs' as a member of the third generation, he could only have served as a hasidic leader while the Maggid was still alive: he himself died in Nisan 5532 (1772), a few months before the death of the Maggid in Kislev of the following year.[60] According to all the available evidence, the Lithuanian hasidic centre in Karlin was not regarded as a subsidiary of the 'headquarters' of the movement in Volhynia, even though R. Aaron was known as a disciple of the great Maggid.[61] To outside observers of hasidism during this period of expansion, the court at Karlin appeared as a centre in its own right. In the same period (that is, before 1772) the movement established a number of other centres in various regions, and all were known as places to which hasidim were drawn on pilgrimages to their leaders' courts. Solomon Maimon, for example, reports on that period:

> Therefore it naturally occurred that those who were attracted to this sect increased greatly in numbers in a short time. They used to go to K[arlin], M[ezhirech], and other holy places where the leaders, teachers and luminaries of this sect lived . . . to visit the exalted '*rebbes*' and to hear them expound the new doctrine.[62]

He mentions Mezhirech and Karlin in the same breath, along with other unnamed hasidic centres, without suggesting any hierarchical connection between them.[63]

R. Abraham that R. Menahem Mendel of Vitebsk, too, 'was angry with the Rabbi [addressing R. Abraham in the third person] and with his conduct and with his associates' (See Hillman, *Igrot ba'al haTanya*, s. 103, 175–6). Hence R. Abraham was already known in 1772 as head of his own congregation of hasidim, which he led in his own way.

[58] See Rabinowitsch, *Lithuanian Hasidism*, 25. And see also R. Shneur Zalman's letter to R. Abraham of Kalisk, in which he said of R. Menahem Mendel of Vitebsk that 'in the summer of 5532'—i.e. as early as 1772, at the time of the Rovno conference of the Maggid's disciples—'the late rabbi was well and living in the holy congregation of Minsk' (Hillman, *Igrot ba'al haTanya*, 175).

[59] Rabinowitsch, *Lithuanian Hasidism*, 8–22.

[60] Ibid. 17, 23.

[61] Solomon Maimon took the trouble, as we know, to travel from his native city in Lithuania to Mezhirech in order to see 'the superior B.' in person (see *The Autobiography of Solomon Maimon*, trans. J. Clark Murray (London, 1954), 175, repr. in Hundert (ed.), *Essential Papers*, 9). He refers to the Maggid as '*der hohe Obere B.*'—'the exalted leader B.' (a description which is somewhat blurred in the Eng. trans.: see *Salomon Maimons Lebensgeschichte* (Munich, 1911), 202. His use of this term confirms the widely accepted assumption that the Maggid of Mezhirech had indeed established a reputation for himself as the greatest of the hasidic leaders of his time. But we are not entitled to conclude from this that the Maggid served as the supreme leader of the whole hasidic movement, exercising control from the centre, any more than we are entitled to conclude, e.g., that the Gaon of Vilna served as 'Chief Rabbi' of Lithuania from the fact that he had earned the reputation of being the greatest rabbinic authority of his generation.

[62] Maimon, *Salomon Maimons Lebensgeschichte*, 135. The Eng. trans. (*Autobiography*, 167–8) omits the references to 'K' and 'M'.

[63] Solomon Maimon wrote this about twenty years after the event. The historical details in his testimony therefore call for meticulous scrutiny. But in this case critical examination only serves to confirm the reliability of his statement: he left Poland almost immediately after his visit to Mezhirech, severing all his connections with the Jewish community in that part of the world and with hasidism (his latest information on the movement relates to the rising tide of mitnaggedism in Lithuania, headed by the Gaon of Vilna. Maimon innocently believed that this meant the end for hasidism. Ibid. 179). For that very reason he pre-

A similar conclusion can be drawn from the anti-hasidic anthology *Zemir aritsim veḥarvot tsurim*: even before 1772 the hasidim were known collectively, at least in Lithuania, not only as 'Mezheritscher' but also as 'Karliner', and the two names were used indiscriminately.[64]

The following hasidic tale about R. Zusya of Hanipoli will illustrate the ambivalent status—disciple and teacher—of all the Maggid's disciples who led their own hasidic communities while their own master was still living. The tale points to a level of personal relationship on which the Maggid remained, and was known to be, the spiritual teacher and mentor of his distinguished disciple even after the latter had left his court and set up a hasidic community of his own; but at the same time the tale makes it quite clear that for the hasidim of the Maggid's disciple it was that disciple, and he alone, who was their spiritual teacher and mentor, and all access to the supreme authority of the great Maggid of Mezhirech was barred to them from the outset:

A man who lived in the same town as Rabbi Zusya saw that he was very poor. So each day he put twenty pennies into the little bag in which Zusya kept his phylacteries, so that he and his family might buy the necessaries of life. From that time on, the man grew richer and richer. The more he had, the more he gave Zusya, and the more he gave Zusya, the more he had.

But once he recalled that Zusya was the disciple of a great maggid, and it occurred to him that if what he gave the disciple was so lavishly rewarded, he might become even more prosperous if he made presents to the master himself. So he travelled to Mezritch and induced Rabbi Ber to accept a substantial gift from him. From this time on, his means shrank until he had lost all the profits he had made during the more fortunate period. He took his trouble to Rabbi Zusya, told him the whole story, and asked him what his present predicament was due to. For had not the rabbi himself told him that his master was immeasurably greater than he?

Zusya replied: 'Look! As long as you gave and did not bother to whom, whether to Zusya or another, God gave to you and did not bother to whom. But when you began to seek out especially noble and distinguished recipients, God did exactly the same.'[65]

This attempt by the hasid, once he had made his way in the world, to bypass the lesser authority of R. Zusya in order to affiliate himself directly to the supreme authority of the Maggid appears to reflect a hierarchical outlook which can be understood in terms of the social dynamics of personal success. However, whether the details of the story are historically accurate or not,[66] there is no doubt that it warned against any deviation from the norm which required of every hasid that he should be 'connected' to his own *rebbe* and no other. The story castigates in the strongest terms the ambition to establish direct links with a supreme authority at the centre. It undoubtedly reflects the

served the memory of the situation as it had been at the time of his last stay in the area, and there is no reason to suspect him of having drawn an anachronistic picture coloured by the situation as it existed at the time he was writing, when the hasidic movement had 'split' into many congregations, according to the prevailing view.

[64] See e.g. Wilensky, *Ḥasidim umitnaggedim*, i. 64, 274–7. On the extension of the name 'Karliner' or, in Hebrew, 'Karliniyyim' to hasidim in general, see also Abraham Baer Gottlober, *Zikhronot umasa'ot*, ed. R. Goldberg (2 vols.; Jerusalem, 1976), i. 142.

[65] M. Buber, *Tales of the Hasidim* (2 vols.; New York, 1972) i. 238–9, on the basis of *Siḥot yekarim* (Satu-Mare n.d.).

[66] Buber points out that in *Ohel Elimelekh* the role of R. Zusya in the story is mistakenly given to R. Elimelekh of Lyzhansk, R. Zusya's younger brother (M. Buber, *Or haganuz* (Tel Aviv, 1977), 480); and cf. Abraham H. S. B. Michelsohn, *Ohel Elimelekh* (Przemysl, 1910), s. 44, 13.

non-centralist organizational structure of the movement, even during the lifetime of the Maggid, a structure which permitted every leader to be in sole charge of his own hasidim without in the least calling into question the spiritual supremacy of the Maggid.

We see, then, that the conventional and convenient chronological division of the early Hasidic leadership into three discrete 'generations', namely those of the Besht, the Maggid, and the Maggid's disciples, is arbitrary and rather misleading. The 'generations' overlapped to a considerable extent, and it is certainly difficult to separate the 'generation' of the Maggid's disciples, which began while he was still living, from that of the Maggid himself, which only lasted between six and twelve years.

Moreover, it appears that no machinery for overall supervision of the movement was ever set up in the Mezhirech centre. To the best of our knowledge the Maggid's disciples who, at the end of their apprenticeship at his court, went back to their home towns or left for other places in order to establish and head hasidic communities of their own rarely visited him and did not maintain any links by regular correspondence with him.[67] Nor did any tradition develop of regular meetings of hasidic leaders in Mezhirech or general assemblies there of hasidim from all other hasidic communities.[68] The only event of this kind was the meeting of the disciples of the Maggid at his court in Rovno in the summer of 1772, a few months before his death. This meeting, which is mentioned in R. Shneur Zalman of Lyady's letter to R. Abraham of Kalisk,[69] was called in response to the first proclamation of the *ḥerem* (excommunication) against the hasidim which had been issued in Lithuania and Galicia earlier that year. It appears that the meeting was convened in order to enable the hasidic leaders to consult on the campaign of the mitnaggedim and co-ordinate their attitude to it. All those who attended were disciples and intimates of the Maggid, and all of them of course regarded him as their spiritual master, even though some had already begun to lead hasidic congregations of their own. According to R. Shneur Zalman, the Maggid rebuked R.

[67] It is, of course, possible that such letters were written but have not survived. At any rate the Ḥerson *genizah*, which applies the actual organization of the hasidic community at the end of the 19th and the beginning of the 20th cents. retrospectively to the relations between the Maggid and his disciples in the 1770s, is sensitive, in this instance also, to the dearth of historical material that would document the presumed state of affairs, and it 'supplies' a lively correspondence between the Maggid's disciples and their master. See Bichovsky, *Ginzei nistarot*, 'Or ne'erav', 1–7. A fuller collection of letters from the Ḥerson *genizah* was published in the Habad periodical *Hatamim*; see esp. i. 283–5, 326–32.

[68] See below, s. 6. The difficulties of communication and travel over long distances at the end of the 18th cent. are likely to have contributed to the weakening of personal contacts between the Maggid and his scattered disciples, but these factors were not decisive. Within the framework of a centralist organization such as was constituted by each separate hasidic court, the hasidim overcame these difficulties and preserved their personal links with their leader. Thus, for example, R. Menahem Mendel of Vitebsk and R. Abraham of Kalisk kept up a correspondence with their disciples in Belorussia until the end of their days. The disciples of R. Menahem Mendel of Vitebsk, who were not content with this link and looked round for a zaddik to whom they could have personal access—a vital ingredient of the system of relations between the zaddik and his hasidim—began travelling to Karlin, and later to Ludmir, both situated a long way away, in order to visit the court of R. Solomon of Karlin (see Hielman, *Beit rabbi*, 24, 128; Rabinowitsch, *Lithuanian Hasidism*, 26–7). When R. Israel of Ruzhin was imprisoned and subsequently banished from the Ukraine, his hasidim continued to make the long journey to his new court in Sadgora, in the Bukovina region, which at that time was on the other side of the border, under Austrian sovereignty (see R. Mahler, *Hasidism and the Jewish Enlightenment* (Philadelphia, 1985), 129–34; Gottlober, *Zikhronot umasa'ot*, i. 153, 190). See also below, pp. 104–9.

[69] See Hillman, *Igrot ba'al haTanya* 175. And cf. n. 57 above.

Abraham of Kalisk for his wildly ecstatic style of worship and for the contempt for scholars which he had instilled into his hasidim, and it seems that he charged him with causing the outbreak of the dispute with the mitnaggedim.[70] The relations between the Maggid and R. Abraham are described as extremely strained, to the point where R. Abraham was afraid to enter the city of Rovno. He presented himself before the Maggid only after R. Jeḥiel Michel of Zloczow and R. Menahem Mendel of Vitebsk had interceded on his behalf and to some extent allayed the Maggid's wrath.

R. Shneur Zalman's testimony presents R. Abraham of Kalisk clearly as a disciple who submitted to the authority of the Maggid even after leaving his court. But at the same time it reinforces the claim that by this time R. Abraham was already serving as the established leader of a group of like-minded people on whom his distinctive personality and teaching had left their mark. Clearly he had founded a type of hasidism which was quite distinct from the hasidism of others and which, in some measure, was even opposed to it.

However angry the Maggid was with R. Abraham of Kalisk, the only recourse open to him was to persuade R. Abraham to mend his ways, and his only weapon was the force of his own personality. He had no formal powers under which to dismiss the controversial leader from his office or ensure that he moderated his activity among his hasidim, as one might have expected to happen if the Maggid really stood at the head of a centralist hierarchical organization. If the whole hasidic movement had functioned at that time as the personal court of the Maggid of Mezhirech, as the hypothesis of a centralized leadership in his time would require us to believe, the situation of R. Abraham of Kalisk would have corresponded to that of a disciple who is a functionary of the court or the broader framework of the particular hasidic community: the court *gabai*, the head of the hasidic yeshivah in recent generations, or the town's rabbi who defers to the spiritual authority of 'his' *rebbe*, and other such emissaries of the zaddik, all of whom he can appoint or dismiss at will, and whose authority stems mainly from him. It is obvious that this was not the situation of R. Abraham: he was already in sole charge of a community of hasidim, which he led in his own way.

The meeting of the Maggid's disciples in Rovno, apparently the only one of its kind during the lifetime of R. Dov Ber, was no doubt called in response to the emergency created by the first clash with the mitnaggedim. On the face of it, it could be construed as a centralist initiative stemming from the organizational headquarters of the movement. But we must not forget that even many years after the death of the Maggid of Mezhirech, by which time all agree that the organization of the movement was fragmented, the leaders of hasidism would meet from time to time to discuss matters of joint concern or internal disputes. No one would think of ascribing to such meetings an intention to centralize the leadership or undermine the pluralistic principle under which each hasidic master was fully acknowledged as a leader of his own hasidic following.[71]

From another point of view, too, it is quite evident that we cannot base any reconstruction of the organization of hasidism in its early stages, and especially in the lifetime of the Maggid of Mezhirech, on the pattern of the particular hasidic court of the nineteenth century and its central dynastic leader: the Maggid's disciples founded their own courts while he was still living and did not need to compete with him, oppose him,

[70] But see Gries, 'Mimitos le'etos', 126 ff.

[71] See s. 6 below.

or sour their relations with him in order to declare their independence as leaders of their own hasidim. To the best of our knowledge there was no element of tension or controversy in their parting from the Maggid,[72] and they may well have had his blessing. By contrast, in the fully developed centralized organization of the particular hasidic court in the nineteenth century, this could not be tolerated. Since it was only possible to join the hasidic camp by personal affiliation—*hitkarevut*—with one of its leaders, the nineteenth-century hasidic courts necessarily continued to receive into their midst some disciples whose magnetic personalities and spiritual powers sooner or later bore witness to the fact that they, too, were natural leaders of men. By its nature, the institutionalized hasidic court could only contain one dominant charismatic personality of this sort. The presence of others in the capacity of disciples charged the atmosphere of the court with tension,[73] and was liable to result in open conflict with the reigning zaddik, or, after his death, with the dynastic heir to the leadership. These clashes could take an ideological form, and would eventually lead to the emergence of new courts whose distinct identity, at least to begin with, was based precisely on the difference, or even the hostility, between them and the courts from which they had seceded.[74]

We can therefore draw a distinction at two stages between the non-centralist organization of the entire hasidic movement in the generation of the Maggid, on the one hand, and on the other hand the centralist pattern of organization which became characteristic of each particular court in the course of the nineteenth century. (*a*) First

[72] R. Shneur Zalman of Lyady's letter shows that it was not the fact of R. Abraham of Kalisk's leadership that aroused the anger of the Maggid at the Rovno conference in 1772, but the particular manner of his leadership, which fanned the flames of the controversy with the mitnaggedim. The Maggid's displeasure does not indicate any intention to cast doubt on the legitimacy of R. Abraham's position as a zaddik in his own right.

[73] e.g., according to one tradition, even before the outbreak of the dispute between the Seer of Lublin and his great disciple, 'the Jew of Pshiskhah (Przysucha)', some of the Seer's disciples, and even his wife, used to peddle reports to him that 'the Jew' was planning to turn him out of his position and take his place. See Buber, *Tales of the Hasidim*, 226–7 (extracted from *Tiferet hayehudi*). Similarly R. Shneur Zalman is said to have foreseen the dispute that would erupt between his son and heir, R. Dober [Dov Ber], and his favourite disciple, R. Aaron Halevi of Starosielce, at a time when the pair were still very close friends. See Hielman, *Beit rabbi*, 94*a* n. a. And indeed, a few years before R. Shneur Zalman died, a 'calumny' and a 'grave accusation' concerning R. Aaron were brought to his notice, apparently by members of R. Shneur Zalman's own family circle, with the result that R. Aaron was forced to leave Lyady and return to his native city of Orsha, although he continued to visit his master's court in Lyady 'from time to time'. Hielman, *Beit rabbi*, 67*b*, 94*a*.

[74] The final rift between R. Jacob Isaac, 'the Jew of Pshiskhah', and the court of his master, R. Jacob Isaac Horowitz, the Seer of Lublin, will serve as an example of this. See A. Z. Aescoly, 'Haḥasidut bePolin', in I. Halpern (ed.), *Beit Yisrael bePolin*, (2 vols.; Jerusalem, 1948–53), ii. 99–100. And the beginning of the Seer of Lublin's career as a leader during the lifetime of his master, R. Elimelekh of Lyzhansk, was similarly charged with tension between the master and his departing disciple. See Rachel Elior, 'Between *Yesh* and *Ayin*: The Doctrine of the Zaddik in the Works of Jacob Isaac, the Seer of Lublin', in Ada Rapoport-Albert and S. J. Zipperstein (eds.), *Jewish History: Essays in Honor of Chimen Abramsky* (London, 1988), 396–7. The dispute between R. Aaron Halevi of Starosielce and the son of R. Shneur Zalman, Dov Ber, the 'Mitteler Rebbe', in the second generation of the Habad leadership, is in the same category. See Rachel Elior, 'Hamaḥaloket al moreshet Ḥabad', *Tarbiz*, 49 (1980), 166–8; id., *Torat ha'elohut bador hasheni shel ḥasidut ḥabad* (Jerusalem, 1982), 5–14; Naftali Loewenthal, *Communicating the Infinite: The Emergence of the Habad School* (Chicago, 1990), 100–38; Louis Jacobs, *Seeker of Unity: The Life and Works of Aaron of Starosselje* (London, 1966), 11–13.

there is the stage when the disciples begin to lead their own hasidic communities in the lifetime of their master: in the institutionalized centralist court this would generally be accompanied by a fierce dispute and rivalry over hasidim, whereas in the circle of the Maggid the rise of the disciples to leadership does not appear to have generated any tension of this sort. (*b*) The second stage is when the disciples claim the leadership after the death of their master: in the institutionalized centralist court, a quarrel would break out between the disciple who was gathering hasidim to himself and the 'natural' dynastic heir to the leadership. In the circle of the Maggid's disciples, on the other hand, no claim was ever laid by a 'natural' heir and there was no dispute among the disciples over the inheritance. Such a dispute could not have developed at this time, partly because R. Abraham 'The Angel', the Maggid's son, took no part in public life and did not aspire to leadership,[75] but mainly because at that stage in the organizational development of hasidism, when the role of the zaddik had not yet crystallized into institutional office within a clearly demarcated territory and a fixed pattern of obligations and privileges, there was no expectation that a direct successor would step into such a role.

4. THE STRUCTURE OF THE LEADERSHIP AFTER 1772

The Besht and the Maggid, then, both operated within the framework of a non-centralist leadership which found its natural continuation in the fragmented structure of the hasidic leadership after 1772. It was precisely the existence of such a loose framework of organization that prevented the occurrence of any acute crises of leadership after the death of the Besht in 1760 and again after the death of the Maggid in 1772. Although their deaths were undoubtedly felt as a great personal loss by their respective circles of associates, neither left a void in the hasidic leadership, for a network of leaders, each with his own followers, was operating while they were still alive. Phinehas of Korets, Nahman of Horodenka, Menahem Mendel of Peremyshlany, the Maggid of Mezhirech, and the other members of the Besht's circle, who by their nature fell into the category of charismatic 'men of spirit', ensured the continuity of the leadership without there being any need to fill the place of the Besht by the appointment of a direct successor. Similarly, the disciples of the Maggid of Mezhirech who were actively engaged in hasidic agitation during his lifetime did not cease their operations when he died, and those of them who began to lead hasidic communities in various places after his death did not 'inherit' his position in the dynastic sense of the word but became integrated into the existing network of leaders just as others had done while he was alive.

Although I have contended here that hasidism did not undergo a drastic organizational change with the alleged decentralization of 1772, and that its fragmented structure thereafter simply continued a situation which had existed even before the death of the Maggid of Mezhirech, it is not my purpose to suggest that the movement did not experience any organizational change during this period. On the contrary, there is no doubt that extensive changes did occur in the organization of hasidism at the end of the eighteenth century and during the first half of the nineteenth. The anachronistic view

[75] See n. 2 above.

of the structure of the movement in its early stages, which pictures a centralist leadership that broke up, does not exaggerate the extent of the change but offers a mistaken diagnosis of its nature. According to that view, the hasidic leadership at its beginnings was set up as a dynastic, centralist institution which somehow malfunctioned from the outset: as a result of chance circumstances when the founder of the movement died, and again at the death of his 'unnatural' heir in the 'second generation', there were no natural heirs to the leadership. In both cases, we are asked to believe, matters went awry and the 'natural' hereditary processes for the transfer of authority from generation to generation were abandoned in favour of improvised, and not altogether satisfactory, ad hoc solutions to the problem of succession; the failure of the initial pattern of a centralist dynastic succession is thus assumed to have led to the fundamental structural change which found expression in decentralization.[76] But this supposed sequence of frustrated natural expectations, procedural irregularities, and unorthodox solutions is highly improbable in a novel situation in which set expectations, regular procedures, and orthodox practice have not yet had time to emerge. The very fact that the supposedly dynastic pattern of succession evidently failed to secure the 'natural' continuity of the leadership in the generation of the founders should give us pause: why should this

[76] It is interesting to note that Habad historiography, which consistently applies the fully developed organizational frameworks of the Habad movement retrospectively to the initial stages of hasidism, ascribes a short period as *nasi* at the head of the movement, immediately following the death of their fathers, to each of the two sons with doubtful qualifications for the succession, R. Zevi, the son of the Besht, and R. Abraham, the son of the Maggid. Thus they are represented as having assured the institutional continuity of the hasidic leadership, though there is no evidence to back this in other sources. With regard to the period of about a year allegedly spent by R. Zevi as *nasi*, the *admor* Joseph Isaac writes as follows in his essay 'Avot haḥasidut': 'After the decease of our teacher the Besht, his son, the rabbi and zaddik R. Zevi, was chosen as *nasi* and leader. However, when the first year had gone by, the holy company could see that the son of their teacher and master was a weak man and the situation at that time required strength and power and a man who had the spirit to stand at the head of the leadership, and they were very worried. On the second day of the festival of Shavuot, which was a day after the first *Jahrzeit* of our teacher the Besht, the holy rabbi and zaddik R. Zevi was sitting at the head of the table dressed in the holy garments of his saintly father, our teacher the Besht, surrounded by all the holy company. When he had finished speaking words of Torah he rose to his full height and said: Today my saintly father came to me and told me that the retinue of Heaven and their servants, who were wont to accompany him, have today gone over to our holy and awe-inspiring teacher and master R. Baer the son of R. Abraham; "therefore, my son, hand over to him the office of *nasi* in the presence of all the holy company, and he will sit in my place at the head of the table and you, my son, will sit in his place; and know that you [the holy company] will be twice as successful through his spirit." And as he spoke he turned to the holy rabbi, R. Dober, to congratulate him and took off his coat and gave it to our holy master, R. Dober, and put on the holy R. Dober's coat and sat in his place. And forthwith the holy rabbi, R. Dober, sat down at the head of the table, and all the holy company rose to their feet to hear the words of Torah which the new *nasi* would utter' (*Hatamim*, i. part 2, 140–1). On R. Abraham 'the Angel's' position as head of the movement during the two years immediately following the death of the Maggid, the *admor* R. Joseph Isaac writes as follows in the letter he wrote to his daughter Mushka in 1935: 'After the decease of the Maggid of Mezhirech on 19 Kislev 5533, the holy company of disciples of the Maggid accepted the holy rabbi, the learned rabbi, the righteous rabbi, the holy Angel, R. Abraham, as their *rebbe* . . . [His] *nesi'ut*, to our sorrow, did not last long, it lasted about two years, and in 5535 [1775] the holy and righteous rabbi, the holy Angel, passed away.' (Raphael Nahman, *Shemu'ot vesipurim*, part 3, 10–11 (the letter is published in Heb. trans. alongside the original Yid.); and see also *Igrot kodesh*, 162–3). These accounts are based on the letters from the Ḥerson *genizah* (see the *admor* R. Joseph Isaac's explicit statement in his defence of the Ḥerson letters, *Hatamim*, i. part 1, 12. I have been unable to identify the Ḥerson letter in which the *admor* says the matter is 'fully' explained, but there are several letters in the collection printed in *Hatamim* which deal with the leadership of R. Abraham 'the Angel'. See e.g. *Hatamim*, ii. part 7, 664–6, ss. 247, 249, 255.)

pattern and no other have been adopted, in circumstances to which it was so blatantly unsuited—the absence of natural heirs on the first two occasions when the leadership of the hasidic movement had to be passed on? From what has been said in the preceding sections it will be clear that this, too, is an anachronism—the application of later circumstances to an earlier situation in which these circumstances did not obtain. There is no doubt that the hereditary principle of succession had not yet gained currency in the leadership of hasidism during the generation of the founders. In fact the decisive change in the organization of the movement did not take the form of an abrupt transition from a hereditary and centralist to a hereditary but decentralized leadership structure: rather it was a shift from a loose, informal leadership structure which was neither hereditary nor centralist to an established institution which remained non-centralist in its overall structure but whose very consolidation was owed, in large measure, precisely to the adoption of the hereditary principle of succession in each one of its proliferating centres. The new structure could thus generate a multiplicity of dynastic leaders, each exerting supreme authority from the centre at his court over his own community of followers, and each associated with his fellows within an overall framework which remained loosely knit, non-centralist, and capable of giving rise to further proliferation. The hereditary principle of succession became accepted gradually, and not everywhere, at the end of the eighteenth and the beginning of the nineteenth centuries. Since the hasidic leadership had first entered the arena as a group of 'spiritual' individuals distinguished by the gift of personal charisma, the hereditary principle, and indeed any alternative rational measure of suitability for high office, was inherently foreign to it at the start. Only in the course of the nineteenth century did the leadership crystallize into a network of dynasties which availed themselves of the hereditary principle as a matter of course for the purpose of transmitting authority from one generation to the next and preserving the distinct character and identity of each dynasty within hasidism. The result was a movement which can be characterized as combining two distinct, if not diametrically opposed, modes of operation: the overall structure had always been, and remained, loose, pluralistic, and non-centralist—an association of distinct groups, each headed independently by its own charismatic leader. But in each of the constituent groups within that structure there developed the tightly knit and highly centralized organization of the 'court', whose sole head now drew his authority not only from any personal charismatic gifts he might possess but also from the routine presumption of charisma inherited from his predecessors in office.[77]

There is no doubt that the lines along which the movement expanded during the first half of the nineteenth century were non-centralist. Considering the historical circumstances—the non-centralist traditional regime of the autonomous *kehalim*, the abolition of the central Council of Four Lands, and the disintegration of the kingdom of Poland—out of which hasidism grew and by which it was affected during the whole

[77] It is clear that not all 19th-cent. Hasidic congregations developed a centralist dynastic leadership. Where a centralist dynasty had not come into existence the congregation dispersed after the death of its founder or was split up among a number of successors until it lost its original identity. The only exception is the Bratslav congregation, which preserved its distinctiveness even without a dynasty of zaddikim, and crystallized its independent identity round the Messianic figure of the dead R. Nahman. The question of the dynasties in general, and the anomalous case of Bratslav in particular, are outside the scope of the present study, and will be considered elsewhere.

period of its growth,[78] this is not surprising, and indeed it is hard to imagine that any other modes of expansion were open to it. But it should not be concluded from this that the growth in numbers and the geographical expansion of the last decades of the eighteenth century had forced the movement into a drastic revision of its organization and led inevitably to the fragmentation of a leadership which had been centralist so long as its area of influence was small. On the contrary, the movement had its beginnings in a distinctly non-centralist organizational framework, and the course of its expansion merely enhanced and brought to the fore the pluralistic tendency which had been inherent in it from the start.

Nor is there any substance in the claim that the partitions of Poland in 1772, 1783, and 1795 cut off the 'headquarters' of the hasidic movement from its branches and made it impossible to continue the leadership in its original centralist form[79]—a claim which has contributed to the generally accepted view that three decisive factors had combined to bring about the decentralization of the leadership in 1772.[80] The fact that by pure chance the first partition of Poland, the outbreak of the controversy with the mitnaggedim, and the death of the Maggid of Mezhirech occurred in a single year has created the illusion of a significant combination of circumstances sufficient to explain what appeared to be an abrupt organizational change. But once this explanation is shown to be misplaced—it purports to explain a decentralization which neither took place nor could have done, since no central institution of hasidic leadership existed before 1772—the triad of 'factors' can be resolved into its separate and unrelated components, none of which could have changed the course of the organizational development of the hasidic movement in the aftermath of 1772.

The possibility that the death of the Maggid of Mezhirech without leaving a natural successor might have led to the fragmentation of the leadership was examined above (section 3) and rejected: the examination revealed that the movement was fragmented even during his lifetime, and that his death did not alter the leadership structure but rather exposed and highlighted its non-centralist character. The remaining two 'factors'—the partition of Poland and the controversy with the mitnaggedim—can similarly be shown to have had little effect on the structure of the hasidic leadership during this period. Indeed, it is remarkable how slight was the imprint of these dramatic events on the organization of the hasidic movement in the last decades of the eighteenth century. Both must be seen against the same background of overall disintegration and fragmentation from which hasidism itself had sprung, and both similarly reflect its inherent pluralistic tendency rather than determine or enhance it.

The impact of the partition of Poland on the structure of the movement was slight. The new political boundaries did not break the bonds between hasidic leaders and their followers, just as they did not halt the expansion of hasidism far beyond its areas of provenance.[81] In 1784, some seven years after settling in Erets Yisrael, R. Menahem

[78] See the opening pages of the present chapter, and n. 6 above.

[79] See Rubinstein, 'Perakim betoledot haḥasidut', 758, 764 (pp. 242, 245 in the 1977 repr.).

[80] See the beginning of the present chapter.

[81] On the spread of hasidism in spite of the new political borders and the changes of regime in the parts of Poland which were annexed to the various Powers, see Dubnow, *Toledot haḥasidut,* 175, 177. On the travels back and forth of scholars and rabbis and their activities in the areas which were cut off from each

Mendel of Vitebsk advised his hasidim in Belorussia not to appoint 'some righteous man over them from among the famous men, the great zaddikim, and bring him to the lands of Russia'.[82] From what he went on to say it is clear that he meant a zaddik from Poland, that is 'the lands of Volhynia and Lithuania',[83] which in 1784, in the period between the first and second partitions of Poland, were still within the kingdom of Poland, while Belorussia, where R. Menahem Mendel's hasidim lived, had been annexed to Russia in 1772. As we know, R. Menahem Mendel of Vitebsk and R. Abraham of Kalisk failed in their attempt to maintain their leadership of their hasidim in Belorussia through the sole medium of correspondence from overseas. Their 'orphaned' hasidim began to visit courts in Poland across the border,[84] or tried to import a zaddik from there to lead them in their own locality. True, most of them eventually took the advice of their leaders in Erets Yisrael and accepted local zaddikim, of whom the most important was R. Shneur Zalman of Lyady.[85] But it was not the new political boundary which restrained them but the instructions of their spiritual mentors and the tradition of their particular form of hasidism, which the leaders in Erets Yisrael wanted to preserve, as is clear from all their pastoral letters. The 'Polish' zaddik who was approached by the hasidim of Belorussia in spite of the political break created by the first partition of Poland was the Lithuanian R. Solomon of Karlin. He frequently visited his new hasidim across the border, and, as is evident from his letter to his followers in Shklov, he tried to retain their allegiance even after they had ceased to visit his court and begun to attach themselves to R. Shneur Zalman of Lyady.[86]

If the hasidic movement as a whole had functioned as a centralist organization during that period, the partitions of Poland would undoubtedly not have broken the link between the centre and its offshoots. After all, they did not disturb the contacts between the zaddik and his hasidim in those institutional frameworks in which centralist patterns of organization are known to have been established, namely in the growing numbers of particular 'courts' whose leaders had succeeded in maintaining their connection with their followers across political boundaries in spite of the vicissitudes of the time. Thus, for example, Gottlober describes the area of influence of Habad in the middle of the nineteenth century as follows: 'The Habad sect in general is prominent in Lithuania (and there are some of them in Moldavia and Wallachia, and a few in Volhynia under the rule of R. Menahem Mendel)'.[87] The leader referred to was the Tsemaḥ Tsedek, who led Habad from 1828 until his death in 1866.[88] In the middle of the nineteenth century Lithuania and Volhynia formed part of a single political unit within the Russian Empire, but the distant territories of Moldavia and Wallachia had passed through a long period of political instability before they were united to form the

other politically but retained a sense of their cultural unity until the middle of the 19th cent., see A. Shulvass, 'Hatorah velimudah bePolin veLita', in *Beit Yisrael bePolin*, ii. 26. See also Rabinowitsch, *Lithuanian Hasidism*, 23, 26.

82 Barnai, *Igrot hasidim*, 108.

83 Ibid.

84 Ibid. 92–3, 96, 166.

85 Ibid. 93; and see also E. Etkes, 'Aliyato shel R. Shne'ur Zalman miLiadi le'emdat manhigut', *Tarbiz*, 54 (1985), 429–39.

86 Hielman, *Beit rabbi* 128; Rabinowitsch, *Lithuanian Hasidism*, 26–7.

87 Gottlober, *Zikhronot umasa'ot*, i. 152.

88 It is evident from this that Gottlober wrote this part of his memoirs before 1866, the year in which the Tsemaḥ Tsedek died. This accords with the information on his p. 158, where he specifies the date of writing as 'in the year 5625 [1865], 22 Marheshvan'.

independent state of Romania in 1858. The frequent changes of boundaries did not put an end to the existence of the Habad enclave in Romania, nor did they weaken the bond between the Habad hasidim there and their *rebbe* in Belorussia. Similarly Gottlober reports on the movements of R. Israel of Ruzhin and his hasidim:

R. Israel of Ruzhin increased the glory of his household so greatly that the eyes of the Government were opened towards him [i.e. lived a life of such luxury that he attracted the attention of the government], and certain other occurrences also contributed to his downfall, and he was taken from there and imprisoned in a fortress for many days. And after he had been released he feared for his life lest he be taken prisoner again, and he fled to the land of Galicia and dwelt for some years in Sadgora which is in Bukovina. Thereupon his Hasidim in our country began to visit him there.[89]

R. Israel of Ruzhin, after his imprisonment in Kamenets Podolsk and Kiev, fled from Russia in 1838,[90] and settled in a district within the jurisdiction of the Austro-Hungarian Empire. This did not prevent his hasidim from continuing to make the journey to see him, and hasidim from Russia continued this tradition of crossing the Austrian border even after his death, when the leadership had passed to his sons. According to the hostile account of the maskil Gottlober, the motives for these frequent crossings of the frontier were not purely hasidic:

They arise and cross the border of the country to bring merchandise from a foreign land contrary to the King's laws, hoping thereby to amass wealth without much exertion and without work, to which they are unaccustomed (we have seen such and we know for a certainty that some of these people who call themselves hasidim travel to Galicia to their rebbe, one of the sons of R. Israel of Ruzhin, [R. Israel] who fled thither, and on their return they bring with them some of the merchandise of that country, and that is virtually all that they want, and their journey to the rebbe is only a pretext).[91]

It is clear, at any rate, that it was easy to cross the frontier, and the hasidim did so frequently. And just as the political borders in the nineteenth century did not prevent the passage of hasidim from Russian territory to their zaddikim in Galicia, so, too, they did not prevent the hasidim from bringing their 'obscurantist' hasidic books into the enlightened province of Galicia in spite of the vain attempts of the Austrian censorship—prompted by maskilim headed by Joseph Perl—to prohibit this.[92]

In parallel with the spread of hasidism across the changing political borders, mitnaggedism spread too: the frontiers presented no barrier to either. The first *ḥerem* of Vilna was declared about four months before the first partition of Poland,[93] and it is therefore not surprising that the proclamation issued by the Vilna Gaon[94] became known throughout Lithuania, Belorussia and Galicia, which still formed a single politi-

[89] Gottlober, *Zikhronot umasa'ot*, i. 190.

[90] On this episode, see Mahler, *Hasidism and the Jewish Enlightenment*, 99, 129–34. Here, too, the picture agrees with the time at which Gottlober was writing, the year 1865: R. Israel of Ruzhin died in 1851, and during the 1860s the leadership was in the hands of his sons.

[91] Gottlober, *Zikhronot umasa'ot*, i. 153.

[92] See Dubnow, *Toledot haḥasidut*, 200; Mahler, *Hasidism and the Jewish Enlightenment*, 105 ff.

[93] Dubnow, *Toledot haḥasidut*, 126.

[94] See E. Etkes, 'HaGera vereshit hahitnagedut laḥasidut', in *Transition and Change in Modern Jewish History: Essays Presented in Honour of Shmuel Ettinger* (Jerusalem, 1987) (Heb.), 439–58.

cal unit within Poland.[95] But the severance of Galicia and Belorussia from the other regions of Poland (especially Lithuania) in the summer of 1772 did not hamper the distribution of the documents of excommunication across the new boundaries, nor did it halt the first controversy or hold back the waves of controversy which followed; they, too, encompassed Austrian Galicia no less than Polish Lithuania and Russian Belorussia.[96]

The fact is that all the excommunications and accusations, the denunciations to the authorities, the dismissals from office, and even the full weight of personal authority exerted by the Gaon of Vilna did not avail the mitnaggedim in their attempt to stamp out the hasidic 'sect'. But their failure did not stem from the political dismemberment of the kingdom of Poland which took place during those years. The partitions of Poland could not sever the links between the Jewish units of population which had previously been Polish, and therefore it did not interfere with the activities of the mitnaggedim, any more than it did with the activities of the hasidim throughout the former territories of Poland. The failure of the mitnaggedim to eradicate hasidism was largely due precisely to the tradition of non-centralist communal organization from which both hasidism and mitnaggedism grew—the tradition of the autonomous *kehilot*, each of which had been self-governing for centuries, and whose centralized institutions had gradually degenerated until they were finally abolished in 1764.[97] The traditionally non-centralist character of Jewish self-government in Poland was reinforced rather than undermined by the political disintegration of the Polish kingdom. This served the interests of hasidism well but worked against the interests of the mitnaggedim. The pluralistic pattern of communal organization provided the hasidic movement with a mode of growth and expansion which was natural and extremely convenient for it.[98] On the other hand, the efforts of the mitnaggedim to ban the hasidim and excommunicate them were frustrated time and again precisely because of the absence of any centralist organizational framework through which the anti-hasidic measures could be implemented effectively in all the diverse and widely spread communities in which the 'heresy' had taken root. The Gaon of Vilna could not secure the excommunication of the hasidim in all the *kehilot* of Poland or even in all those of Lithuania. In fact, he himself, having no official position in the *kahal* of Vilna, could only operate behind the scenes, spurring on his intimates and urging the official leadership to take action against the hasidim in their city. As for the other *kehilot*, he could only exert influence on them unofficially; no machinery was available to him by which to force his will on the Jewish community as a whole.[99] The mitnaggedim themselves were well aware of

[95] On the diffusion of the decrees of *ḥerem* from Vilna during the first dispute, see Dubnow, *Toledot haḥasidut*, 107–37; Wilensky, *Ḥasidim umitnaggedim*, *passim*.

[96] See Wilensky, *Ḥasidim umitnaggedim*; and also Dubnow, *Toledot haḥasidut*, 138–69, 242–89. The third dispute, which broke out in 1796, was the only one to occur after the reunification of Lithuania and Belorussia as part of the Russian Empire, in the Third Partition of Poland in 1795. But Galicia, which was no less active (see ibid. 283–6, on the activity of the *maggid* Israel Loebel the Lithuanian in Galicia) remained under the rule of the Austrian Empire.

[97] See n. 6 above.

[98] See pp. 101–4 above.

[99] On the position of the Gaon of Vilna and his influence on various communities in the campaign against hasidism, see Etkes, 'Hahitnagedut laḥasidut'; H. H. Ben-Sasson, 'Ishiyuto shel Hagra vehashpa'ato hahistorit', *Zion*, 31 (1966), 39–86, 197–216.

this limitation. The proclamation of the *ḥerem* by the *kahal* of Brody against the hasidic sect on 20 Sivan 5532 (1772) states:

Although our *kehillah* has no power to bind other honourable *kehillot* to undertake an investigation likewise and issue their own *ḥerem* in that regard, and we can only address a request to them for the sake of the glory of the Lord, blessed be He, the Holy One of Israel, all *kehillot* should be jealous for the Lord of Hosts; they and we are all children of one Father, children of the living God. And seeing that our *kehillah* is the largest community, the best Jewish city in the land . . . we have found ourselves obliged to take our place among those who arouse and penetrate the innermost feelings of all our brethren the house of Israel. And we shall send this proclamation to all the borders of Israel.[100]

The recognition of the difficulty is accompanied by a nostalgic reference to the centralist institution of the Council of Four Lands, which had dealt more efficiently with the heretics of its day:

Some years ago there were such wicked men in the world; there were also, at that time, the wisest men of their generations, leaders of the Four Lands, who pursued them and made their infamous conduct widely known, until they had been got rid of, but today the mitre has been removed and the crown taken away, the men of faith have perished and there is no-one to contend for us with evildoers.[101]

Of course, organizational structure was not the only factor responsible for the failure of the mitnaggedic campaign against hasidism. Other factors helped the hasidic movement to withstand the attempt of the mitnaggedim to eradicate it: on the one hand, its evident halakhic conservatism, which lessened the opposition to it, and on the other hand its gradual penetration of existing communal institutions without challenging them by a frontal assault—a method which facilitated the hasidic 'conquests' in eastern Europe.[102] Above all, the personal magnetism of the hasidic leaders and the new frameworks of religious life which they created were genuinely attractive and offered a viable alternative to the traditional values upheld by the mitnaggedim. However, the importance of the structural and organizational factor should not be underestimated.

[100] Wilensky, *Ḥasidim umitnaggedim*, i. 49. Cf. Dubnow, *Toledot haḥasidut*, 122.

[101] *Toledot haḥasidut*, 120; Wilensky, *Ḥasidim umitnaggedim*, i. 46. The 'wicked men' that the Council of Four Lands succeeded in getting rid of were no doubt the Sabbateans and the Frankists, but the statement exaggerates the power of that centralist institution to suppress and root out the heresy. Actually the communities did not 'get rid of' the Sabbateans and Frankists until these 'heretics' apostatized and so, by their own act, removed themselves from the Jewish fold. The pluralistic and non-centralist structure of the medieval Jewish communities in Europe, unlike the centralist and hierarchical structure of the medieval Church, was not conducive to the formation of heretical sects as such within the bounds of their own religion, precisely because there was no central apparatus for identifying and defining them as sects, or orchestrating a campaign against them in the way that the Church was able to campaign, successfully, against its own heretical sects. The structure of the autonomous *kehilot*, even within the framework of the central Councils, was flexible enough to prevent schismatic sectarianism: on the one hand, their pluralistic framework was able to assimilate local differences of custom and tradition and allow considerable scope for groups which would have broken out of a more homogeneous centralist structure; on the other hand, this fragmented framework deprived the communal organizations of the centralist power they would have required in order to eradicate 'sectarian' deviations. Moderate Sabbateanism, which did not follow the path of apostasy and did not break away from the Jewish community, was not suppressed or eradicated, even by 'the wisest men of their generations, the leaders of the Four Lands', as we might have deduced from the nostalgic tone of the proclamation.

[102] See I. Halpern, 'Ḥavurot letorah umitsvot vehatenu'ah haḥasidit behitpashetutah', in id., *Yehudim veyahadut bemizraḥ Eiropah* (Jerusalem, 1969), 313–32.

It appears, then, that the non-centralist, pluralistic structure which has become one of the hallmarks of the hasidic movement was not forced upon it at a certain moment, as a result of the events of 1772, by external factors such as the partitions of Poland or the controversy with the Lithuanian mitnaggedim, nor was it determined by a pure coincidence such as the absence of a natural successor to the Maggid of Mezhirech. This structure was dictated by the internal dynamic of the long-established tradition of non-centralist Jewish communal organization in eastern Europe, and it underlay the patterns of organization and expansion which were characteristic of hasidism from the outset. The events of 1772 simply exposed and reinforced this underlying structure, but they certainly did not divert the movement from a centralist organizational path into the multiple byways which came to typify it. The assumption that there was a centralist stage in the first two 'generations' of the leadership, until 1772, derives, as was shown above, from the anachronistic application of the nineteenth- and twentieth-century model of the individual hasidic court—a centrally led, dynastic institution—to a whole group of loosely associated circles which constituted the hasidic movement at its very beginnings, in the middle decades of the eighteenth century.

5. CENTRALIST TENDENCIES IN THE LEADERSHIP AFTER 1772?

If indeed the hasidic movement was never headed by a supreme central leader, even in the first two 'generations' of the founders, then it is important to examine carefully those apparently anomalous cases in subsequent generations, after the alleged decentralization of 1772, which have been taken by historians to represent a lingering presence of the original centralist tendency in the organization of the movement. These cases have been interpreted as expressions of longing, or even explicit demands, for the restoration of central authority to the descendants of the founders, and, in particular, to the line of the Besht. But since, as was argued above, neither the Maggid nor the Besht ever exercised exclusive central control, how are we to explain the apparent claims by the grandson of the Besht, R. Baruch of Medzibezh,[103] and even more so by his great-grandson, the one and only 'zaddik of the generation', R. Nahman of Bratslav, to the sole leadership of the movement on a hereditary and centralist basis?[104]

R. Baruch of Medzibezh, a son of the Besht's daughter, has often been portrayed by historians as 'an arrogant man, ambitious for authority, honour and riches', 'of limited intelligence and bad character', who wished 'to exploit the status of a grandson of the Besht . . . to lord it over the people and even over the Zaddikim of his generation'.[105] And in more restrained and objective terms:

[103] That is how his claims were interpreted by Dubnow (*Toledot haḥasidut*, 212–3), Horodecky (*Haḥasidut vehaḥasidim*, iii. 13); A. Kahana (*Sefer haḥasidut* (Warsaw, 1922), 317), and Ettinger ('The Hasidic Movement', 263, or 239 of the *Essential Papers* reprint).

[104] For this view of R. Nahman as laying claim to sole leadership, see Dubnow, *Toledot haḥasidut*, 295, 304; Ettinger, 'The Hasidic Movement', 264, or 240 of the *Essential Papers* reprint.

[105] Dubnow, *Toledot haḥasidut*, 208, 212–3; and cf. Kahana, *Sefer haḥasidut*, and Horodecky, *Haḥasidut vehaḥasidim*.

Rabbi Baruch saw himself as the man to continue the path of his grandfather the Besht. The Maggid of Mezhirech's disciples, who had established new Hasidic dynasties, refused to recognize R. Baruch of Medzibezh as supreme leader, and because of this grave disputes broke out between him and the Zaddikim of the generation.[106]

The view that R. Baruch of Medzibezh tried (and failed) to preserve in hasidism a tradition of centralist leadership as the hereditary prerogative of the line of the Besht is founded on a tendentious interpretation of evidence which itself is of very doubtful reliability. R. Baruch did not leave an extensive body of teachings or writings of his own, and all we have is a collection of statements by or about him which were published long after his death.[107] From the few items of evidence about him that remain, he appears as a zaddik relying on the merit of his grandfather the Besht, and it is very probable that he saw himself as his successor.[108] But his ambition to take the place of his grandfather in Medzibezh was not necessarily inspired by any aspiration to centralist leadership over the whole hasidic movement of his day. That interpretation of his ambition is conditioned by the view of the Besht himself as supreme leader, exercising control from the centre, but there is no compelling evidence for it whatsoever in the traditions relating to R. Baruch himself.[109] As soon as we drop the assumption that the Besht was a supreme overseer of the hasidism of his time, there cease to be grounds on which to ascribe to R. Baruch any centralist-monopolistic claim to the leadership of hasidism by right of hereditary entitlement. The provocative declarations he is alleged to have made, which have been represented in the scholarly literature as reflecting his desire to assume his grandfather's 'crown' as leader of all the zaddikim of hasidism, do not survive critical examination. Some of them have been taken out of context and interpreted without sufficient regard for their plain meaning, and others were set down by writers and compilers who lived scores of years after his time. They shared the anachronistic view of the leadership of the Besht, attributing to it, and therefore also to the leadership of his grandson, the exclusive centralist quality discussed above. Horodecky, for example, describes R. Baruch as follows: 'And in his great self-confidence . . . he waged his war with all the zaddikim, and was not ashamed even to pray: "*velehevei ana pakida bego tsadikaya*" '—which Horodecky translates as 'I desire to be an officer [in charge] of the Zaddikim.'[110] The book *Butsina dinehora* brought together the sayings of R. Baruch and his few teachings. This work, contrary to what was said by the publisher in the foreword, appears never to have existed as an original and complete manuscript but was compiled from a variety of sources, including, apparently, the works of others, shortly before its publication in 1880.[111] In the book, this

[106] Y. Alfasi, *Entsiklopediah lahasidut*, vol. *Ishim*—'Personalities' (Jerusalem, 1986), col. 375; and cf. Ettinger, 'The Hasidic Movement', 263, or 239 of the *Essential Papers* reprint.

[107] See below, and n. 111.

[108] See *Butsina dinehora* (Lemberg, 1884), 58, 59.

[109] See the letter from R. Baruch to R. Menahem Mendel of Vitebsk in which he describes the circumstances of his rise to leadership. It appears from this that, against his own inclinations, R. Baruch acceded to pressure from local people to become their 'head' and settled in Tulchin. It is clear that there was no question of centralist leadership extending beyond his own locality. The letter was published at the end of *Butsina dinehora*, 65. Cf. *Butsina dinehora hashalem* (Bilgoraj, n.d.), 10–11, s. 4, and the remarks by the editor, Reuben Margaliot, on p. 10, setting the letter in its context.

[110] Horodecky, *Haḥasidut vehaḥasidim*, iii. 13, relying on the collection of the sayings and teachings of R. Baruch in *Butsina dinehora*, and see below.

[111] See A. Schischa Halevi, 'Al hasefer *Butsina dinehora*', *Alei sefer*, 8 (1980), 155–7.

declaration by R. Baruch appears in a different context: 'Once he said "*ulemehevei ana pekuda bego tsadikei*—Master of the universe, may I be numbered among the Zaddikim.[112] I do not mean them, I mean with the holy rabbi R. Phinehas of Ostrog and with the holy rabbi of Polonnoye." '[113] Only in what follows there do we find the play upon words which allows *pekuda* to be understood as 'appointed over the zaddikim' and not simply as 'numbered with them'—a double meaning firmly embedded in the perception which all hasidim have of their zaddik: they laud his superiority over all other zaddikim without going so far as to deny the right of the others to independent authority over their own followers.[114]

It is clear, at any rate, that the friction between R. Baruch and a number of his contemporaries in the leadership arose from clashes over territory and from his fears of encroachment by others, not from any fundamental opposition by R. Baruch to the right of others to lead hasidim within their own borders.[115] A well-known tradition purports to record a pertinent exchange of words between R. Baruch and R. Shneur Zalman of Lyady on the occasion of R. Shneur Zalman's visit to R. Baruch. This tradition has been taken as reflecting a fundamental disagreement between them on the principle which should determine how the authority of the leader was to be transmitted, whether from father to son or from teacher to disciples.[116] However, not only is the tradition itself of doubtful reliability but even as it stands, if it is read carefully, it can hardly be construed as evidence for such a clash over two alternative principles of succession in the central leadership of hasidism. According to the tradition, 'Finally our rabbi [R. Baruch] became angry and said, "I am the grandson of the Besht and I should be shown respect." The rabbi [R. Shneur Zalman] answered: "I, too, am the grandson of the Besht, his spiritual grandson, for the great Maggid was an outstanding disciple of the Besht and I am a disciple of the Maggid." '[117] This conversation appears in the book *Butsina dinehora hashalem*, which was published, edited, collated from various sources and even, in part, composed by Rabbi Reuben Margaliot during the 1920s.[118] The book includes the whole of the 1880 edition of *Butsina dinehora*, the reliability of whose contents and even their connection with R. Baruch are in doubt, as has been indicated above.[119] To that material Rabbi Margaliot made numerous addi-

[112] See Zohar 2: 206*a*: '*velehevei ana avdakh pakida bego tsadikaya*' (may I, Your servant, be numbered among the zaddikim), and cf. Isaiah Tishby, *Mishnat hazohar* (1971), pub. in Eng. as *The Wisdom of the Zohar* (3 vols.; Oxford, 1989), iii. 1037. This quotation from the Zohar is very well known because it is incorporated in the order of service according to the Lurianic rite. It is recited when the Sefer Torah is taken out of the Ark for the Reading of the Law.

[113] *Butsina dinehora*, 49.

[114] Ibid.

[115] See the famous letter of R. Shneur Zalman of Lyady, written in 1810, on his quarrel with R. Baruch: 'And I asked him: "Then why are you angry with me?" And he replied: "Why did you come to our province?" [i.e. why have you invaded my territory?]'. Hillman, *Igrot ba'al haTanya*, 192, letter 113, and cf. S. B. Levine (ed.), *Igrot kodesh Admor haZaken, Admor ha'Emtsa'i, Admor haTsemah Tsedek*' (Brooklyn, NY, 1980), letter 60, 142.

[116] See Ettinger, 'The Hasidic Movement', 263, 239 of the *Essential Papers* reprint.

[117] *Butsina dinehora hashalem*, the part entitled 'Mekor barukh', s. 9, 24.

[118] The part entitled 'Mekor barukh' was published by Reuben Margaliot in Zamosc in 1931 as a separate pamphlet from the matrices of the Bilgoraj edition of *Butsina dinehora hashalem*, which had been published, without a date, a few years previously. I should like to thank Mr Avraham Schischa Halevi for his help in clarifying this point. See also Alfasi, *Entsiklopediah lahasidut*, vol. *Ishim*—'Personalities', cols. 377–8; S. H. Porush, *Entsiklopediah lahasidut*, vol. *Sefarim*—'Works' (Jerusalem, 1980), col. 416, no. 2; s. 9, col. 418, no. 7.

[119] See n. 111 above.

tions from later sources, some of which are even more questionable. Thus, for example, he drew heavily on the documents of the forged *Ḥerson genizah*.[120] Rabbi Margaliot appears to have extracted the conversation between R. Baruch and R. Shneur Zalman of Lyady from Michael Levi Rodkinson's hagiographical work on R. Shneur Zalman of Lyady entitled *Shivḥei haRav*,[121] and he inserted it as a direct continuation of an authentic letter he quoted in which R. Shneur Zalman reported his dispute with R. Baruch.[122] Thus was created the false impression that the account of the exchange of words between the biological grandson, R. Baruch, and the 'spiritual grandson', R. Shneur Zalman, was written by the founder of Habad himself in his letter. In fact, I have not found any reference to this matter in any source earlier than Rodkinson's book. It seems to be a piece of fictional writing by Rodkinson, inspired by the dynastic outlook which had become characteristic of Habad by the second half of the nineteenth century, when the group had developed a strong sense of its unique position in the history of the hasidic movement, claiming to be the one school which maintained an unbroken and exceptionally intimate connection with the Besht and the Maggid of Mezhirech, and thus preserving more authentically than any other school the original teaching of hasidism.[123] In any event, this sort of controversy over the 'legacy', of

[120] Pub. by C. E. Bichovsky in *Ginezei nistarot* (Jerusalem, 1924). See e.g. *Butsina dinehora hashalem*, 'Mekor barukh', 7, s. 1, which reproduces the text of 'a note from the members of the Besht's household' taken from *Ginzei nistarot*, 'Or Yisrael', 19, s. 60; 'Mekor barukh', 8, s. 2, reproducing the letter of R. Baruch's brother R. Ephraim of Sudylkow from *Ginzei nistarot*, 'Or Ne'erav', 14, s. 31; 'Mekor barukh', 20–1, s. 8, reproducing the letter from R. Baruch to R. Abraham of Kalisk from *Ginzei nistarot*, 'Or ne'erav', 10, s. 24; etc. And see the letter of R. Hayyim Issachar Gross of Munkachevo (Munkacz) 'Ḥayim uverakhah', printed at the end of *Butsina dinehora hashalem*, 88, ss. 4, 9, in which he criticizes Reuben Margaliot's use of the suspect Ḥerson letters.

[121] On Rodkinson, his works, and his 'conversion' to Haskalah see G. Nigal, *Hasiporet haḥasidit: Toledoteihah venose'eihah* (Jerusalem, 1981), 28–30; id., 'Perek betoledot hasipur haḥasidi', in *Sefer sipurei kedoshim*, ed. G. Nigal (Jerusalem, 1977), 87–109; and cf. Dan, *Hasipur haḥasidi*, 195 ff.

Michael Levi (Frumkin) Rodkinson's first work was published for the first time in 1864 (see Nigal, *Hasiporet haḥasidit*, 29). I had before me the Jerusalem edition [n.d.] in which the conversation in question appears on p. 33. The whole episode was reprinted by Rodkinson in his later book *Toledot amudei Ḥabad* (Königsberg, 1876), 81–2. Reuben Margaliot could have drawn the conversation directly from the works of Rodkinson, and also from Kahana's *Sefer haḥasidut*, which was published a few years before *Butsina dinehora hashalem* and which reproduced the whole conversation in the chapter headed 'Divrei agadah' on R. Shneur Zalman of Lyady, 217.

[122] On this letter see n. 115 above.

[123] It seems that Rodkinson both reflects and nourishes this self-awareness on the part of Habad. His stories, being among the first, and very few, on the history of Habad hasidism, contributed to the enrichment of Habad's sense of its position as the central stream and most authentic representative of hasidism. That is how modern Habad historiography, which stems from the sixth *admor*, R. Joseph Isaac Schneersohn (see nn. 2 and 76 above), came to accept the tradition that R. Shneur Zalman used to call the Besht *zeide*, as if the Besht were his grandfather. This tradition appears dozens of times in R. Joseph Isaac's writings, from which it has found its way into all the rich and varied Habad literature of the present day. For example, it is transmitted as follows by the *admor* Joseph Isaac in his memoirs: 'The old *admor*, R. Shneur Zalman, used to call the Besht "the grandfather". This was because he was the disciple of his disciple . . . R. Shneur Zalman regarded himself as the "grandson" of the Besht, and used to say: "R. Baruch (of Medzibezh) is the physical grandson of the Besht, whereas I am the spiritual grandson of the Besht" ' (*Sefer hazikhronot*, i. 37). Since this version does not appear anywhere in the published writings of the Rabbi of Lyady, not even in relation to his dispute with R. Baruch (n. 124 below), it is not impossible that the *admor* R. Joseph Isaac, like Reuben Margaliot in *Butsina dinehora hashalem*, drew upon Rodkinson's *Shivḥei harav* for the tradition of R. Shneur Zalman's spiritual descent from the Besht, as against R. Baruch's physical descent.

central leadership in hasidism is the fruit of the anachronistic imagination of recent generations, and has no basis in the historical reality of the early generations, in which R. Baruch and R. Shneur Zalman actually operated.[124]

As for R. Nahman of Bratslav's claim to the supreme leadership, R. Nahman indeed regarded himself, and was regarded by his followers, as 'the zaddik of the generation'. But his claim needs to be examined in its peculiar ideological context. R. Nahman's status as 'zaddik of the generation' or 'the true zaddik' was undoubtedly connected with his messianic view of himself. On this level the quality of his leadership was indeed seen as unique, in that it alone could trigger off the messianic advent by effecting the *tikun* of the entire generation—his own handful of hasidim, all the other zaddikim, 'and even the nations of the world'.[125] But these exaltations of R. Nahman's unique messianic mission were never meant to undermine the position of other zaddikim in the hasidic leadership of his generation. On the level of sober consciousness he recognized his overt position in the reality of pre-messianic existence as the obverse of his messianic status, which was to remain concealed for the time being. And so not only

Further testimony (dating, like *Shivḥei harav*, from the second half of the 19th cent.) to the consciousness in Habad of a special and intimate relationship with the founders of hasidism is furnished by another member of Habad, R. Jacob Kadaner, in his hagiographic anthology *Sipurim nora'im* (on this book, see Nigal, *Hasiporet haḥasidit*, 38. On the author and his other works, see Mondshine, 'Hasefarim', 165–75). In one of his stories about R. Shneur Zalman's time as a pupil in Mezhirech (*Sipurim nora'im* [Lemberg, 1875], pages unnumbered; pp. 59–61 according to my count), Kadaner eulogizes 'the holiness of the young R. Shneur Zalman', which the Maggid found it difficult to reveal to the other disciples when they wondered what sort of person he was. When the Maggid died, 'the disciples immersed his holy body in a *mikveh* of running water and drew lots to determine who should hold each limb, and it fell out that he [R. Shneur Zalman] should hold his head. And all the disciples were greatly moved by this and realized that he [the Maggid] had bequeathed the whole of his [wisdom in the] Torah to him [R. Shneur Zalman].' This story, too, is incorporated in the historical writings of the *admor* Joseph Isaac (see 'Avot haḥasidut', in which it is quoted as an oral tradition which passed from R. Shneur Zalman to his grandson, the Tsemaḥ Tsedek, and from him—presumably—through the generations of the Habad leadership to the *admor* Joseph Isaac himself. The *admor* makes no reference at all to the version published in Kadaner's book, which may have served him as a source, just as did Rodkinson's stories.

[124] Indeed, the genuine letter of R. Shneur Zalman (n. 115 above) on his quarrel with R. Baruch of Medzibezh itself demonstrates how foreign to R. Shneur Zalman's view of himself was the claim to be the 'spiritual grandson' of the Besht. On his connection with the founder of hasidism he writes in that letter: 'On the two occasions that I was in P-b [St Petersburg] it was for *his* [R. Baruch's] *grandfather* [the emphasis is mine—A. R.-A] the Besht, may he be remembered for life in the world to come, and I could have said "*His grandson* is very much alive, let him come and explain all the difficulties raised against him", and I did not say "Who am I that the teaching of the Besht should be sanctified by me.' (ibid.) It is, indeed, evident that these turns of phrase by R. Shneur Zalman could have engendered the claim on his behalf to the status of 'grandson' in the imagination of anyone brought up in a tradition that regarded R. Shneur Zalman as the principal bearer of the hasidic heritage (the tradition that there is an almost dynastic continuity in the hasidic leadership, which passed from the Besht to the Maggid of Mezhirech and from him to R. Shneur Zalman and, after him, to the other leaders of Habad. Cf. n. 184 below). However, it is also clear that it did not occur to the Rabbi of Lyady himself to use the term 'grandson' in anything other than its simple biological meaning. His reference to R. Baruch as a grandson is unambiguous, and however much he identifies with the teaching of the Besht, even to the extent of defending and 'sanctifying' it in the face of the attack by the mitnaggedim, he is entirely free of the proprietary attitude displayed by R. Baruch, to which he alludes with a certain measure of irony.

[125] See e.g. *Ḥayei Moharan*, part ii (*Shivḥei Moharan*), 'Gedulat hasagato', 9, ss. 8, 10, 11; and cf. ibid. part i, 'Nesi'ato le'Erets Yisrael', 65, s. 20. For a discussion of R. Nahman's messianic leadership, see e.g. Arthur Green, *Tormented Master: A Life of Rabbi Nahman of Bratslav* (University of Alabama Press, 1979), 116–23, 182–220.

did he accept as legitimate the existence of other zaddikim in the leadership but he also recognized the superior qualities of some of them (though he sharply criticized the way of life of others), and acknowledged their success compared to his own failure as a controversial leader whose hasidim were few and persecuted. R. Nathan Sternhartz, R. Nahman's literary secretary, offers this explanation of 'torah' no. 56 in *Likutei Moharan*, Part I,[126] which R. Nahman 'said' on Shavuot 5565 (1805):

And he then delivered [the] wonderful teaching on the verse 'And on the day of the first-fruits' [Num. 28: 26] [which is to be found in] section 56 [of *Likutei Moharan*, part I], beginning 'For in each member of Israel there is a quality of kingship'. After he had said this teaching, in which he discussed the quality of kingship which is in every Jew etc., and [distinguished between] 'revealed kingship' and 'concealed kingship' etc., and [spoke about] 'one man who has no revealed dominion, and yet in concealment' etc., he then said explicitly about himself: To you [my Hasidim] it seems that I have no dominion except over you. In truth I rule even over all the Zaddikim of the generation, but this is in concealment.[127]

A clear distinction must be drawn between R. Nahman's consciousness of 'concealed' or 'secret' kingship and his consciousness of 'revealed kingship.' 'In great concealment and secrecy he rules over the whole generation and even over every zaddik of the generation. For their souls are all under his dominion and kingship and all of them submit to him and are subjected to him.'[128] But this conception is far removed in its internal logic and origins from any concrete claim to the position of supreme central leader by right of direct descent from the Besht.[129] R. Nahman's messianic leadership 'in great secrecy' is a metaphysical and cosmic leadership, not a concrete organizational one, and what inspires it is his consciousness of his absolute and extraordinary uniqueness, not his dynastic connection with the line of the Besht. This 'concealed' leadership operates not only horizontally over all the zaddikim of his own generation but also vertically over all his predecessors in hasidism (including the Besht, the alleged source of his supreme authority) and even over the leaders who ruled in the distant past—all the distinguished personalities in the history of the nation who failed to bring the messianic project to fruition; he alone would fulfil it, either during his life or in the more distant future, after his death.[130] On this plane of consciousness he could claim that not only his colleagues, the zaddikim of his own generation, but also 'all the sages of Israel are as nothing compared to me'.[131] In this way he actually shook off the legacy of leadership of the Besht:

I have heard it reported in his name that he said 'The world thinks that it is because I am the [great-]grandson of the Besht that I have attained this eminence. Not so. Only through one

[126] *Sefer likutei Moharan* (New York, 1966), part i, *torah* 56, 150–6.

[127] *Ḥayei Moharan*, part i, 'Siḥot hashayakhim lehatorot', 15, s. 22.

[128] *Likutei Moharan*, 150.

[129] On this interpretation of R. Nahman's view of his leadership, see n. 104 above.

[130] See *Ḥayei Moharan*, part ii, 'Ma'alat torato usefarav hakedoshim', 26, s. 14; ibid. 29, s. 34; ibid., 'Gedulat hasagato', 16, s. 50; ibid., part i, 'Nesi'ato viyeshivato be'Uman', 90, s. 45.

[131] Ibid., part ii, 'Gedulat hasagato', 16, s. 50. R. Nahman here uses, word for word, the well-known statement by Ben Azzai (*Bekhorot* 58*a*), and hints that unlike Ben Azzai, who excepted 'this baldhead' (Rashi explains: R. Akiva) from the generality of the sages of Israel who were worthless compared to him, he, R. Nahman, could make no exception.

thing have I succeeded, and through it I have been able to ascend and achieve what I have.' And he repeated in Yiddish: 'With one thing I have succeeded.'[132]

Without denying the fact of his family connection with the Besht, R. Nahman stood the relationship between them on its head: rather than that he needed the Besht, the Besht needed him. He expressed himself to that effect while on his visit to Medzibezh before leaving for Erets Yisrael in 1798:

And when he came to Medzibezh to the house of his righteous father and mother, may their memory be for a blessing, and they rejoiced greatly at his coming, his mother said to him: 'My son, when will you go to your grandfather the Besht?' meaning, to his holy grave.[133] Our rabbi, may his memory be for a blessing, replied: 'If my grandfather wants to see me let him come here.'[134]

On the *madregah* (the spiritual rank) of the Besht, on the metaphysical source from which he drew his teaching, and on the efficacy of his advice to his hasidim, his esoteric writings and his power to effect the *tikun* of the world, R. Nahman repeatedly commented with condescension, expressed or implied.[135] In doing so he even incurred the wrath of his uncle, R. Baruch of Medzibezh, who took his remarks as a personal insult (rightly so, since R. Baruch's claim to the leadership rested on his descent from the Besht), and the incident was to mark the start of a lifelong quarrel between them. Thus, for example, R. Nahman declared to his uncle that he himself had overtaken the spiritual rank of the Besht when he was only 13 years old:

And our rabbi (may the memory of that righteous and holy man be for a blessing) came to the rabbi R. Baruch, and when our rabbi sat down next to him our rabbi sighed. And R. Baruch said to him 'Why are you sighing?' And our rabbi answered: 'Because I long to reach your *madregah*' [spiritual rank]. He then listed the *madregot* attained by various Zaddikim, and

[132] *Siḥot haRan* (in *Shivḥei haRan*) (Lemberg, 1901), 60*b*, s. 166; and cf. *Shivḥei haRan*, 6*b*, s. 25.

[133] As a child he had, in fact, frequently prayed at the grave of the Besht and felt the need to ask for his guidance. See below, p. 118.

[134] *Ḥayei Moharan*, 'Nesi'ato le'Erets Yisrael', 61, s. 1.

[135] On R. Nahman's sense of superiority to the Besht, in which there is an element of assertion of his independence and uniqueness as a hasidic leader—as it were, 'a new thing the like of which the world had never seen'—see *Siḥot haRan* 73b, s. 239; ibid., 'Seder hanesi'ah shelo le'Erets Yisrael', 7b, s.4; *Ḥayei Moharan*, part i, 'Nesi'ato le'Erets Yisrael', 63, s. 11; part ii, 'Ma'alot torato usefarav hakedoshim', 29, s. 34; Abraham Hazan of Tulchin, *Avaneihah barzel* (in the volume entitled *Sefer kokhvei or*), (Jerusalem, 1961), 17, s. 15. And cf. n. 132 above. Similarly R. Nahman contemptuously shrugged off the heritage of his maternal grandfather, R. Nahman of Horodenka (see *Siḥot haRan*, 68*b*, s. 210). Whether or not his rejection of his links with the latter grandfather was in the nature of a defence against allegations that he was tainted with Sabbateanism (see Weiss, 'Reshit tsemiḥatah shel haderekh haḥasidit', 89–90 n. 14; and cf. Y. Liebes, 'Hatikun hakelali shel R. Naḥman miBraslav veyaḥaso lashabeta'ut', *Zion*, 45 (1980), 226–7 n. 93), it is clear that his dissociation of himself from the legacy of his grandfather was bound up with R. Nahman's view of his own unique and wondrous quality and his superiority 'in secret' (*be'itkasya*) to the leaders of every generation, in the past, the present, and even the future. This feeling of superiority undoubtedly stands in complete contrast to the sense of the 'continual decline of the generations' (*holekh ufoḥet*) which is a universal perception, characteristic of Jewish tradition and Western culture in general. On the consciousness of 'continual decline' as the ideology which legitimized the promotion in hasidism of the tale and of mundane conversation to the highest level of the zaddik's spirituality, see M. Piekarz, *Ḥasidut Braslav* (Jerusalem, 1972), 102–4. On the tension between the sense of 'continual decline' and the sense of spiritual and prophetic innovation in hasidism, see L. Jacobs, 'Hasidism and the Dogma of the Decline of the Generations', below, Ch. 11.

finally mentioned the *madregah* of the Besht, may his memory be for a blessing, and our rabbi said that he had attained his *madregah* too, and had done so at the age of 13 (and then R. Baruch pushed him so that he almost fell from the upper room, until his mother, mistress Feiga, may her memory be for a blessing, came from the upper world and saved him from falling) and from that time the quarrel between them began.[136]

On the other hand, on the plane of consciousness of his 'revealed' existence, R. Nahman took for granted the presence on the scene of other zaddikim and did not in the least object to it. On this plane he held a sober view of himself as a man 'who has no dominion', who was 'poorer than all the great men: one has property, another has money, another owns towns, and I—I have nothing'.[137] His attitude to the zaddikim of his generation was very matter-of-fact. With some he clashed, others he despised, but for some he had great respect. He maintained working 'diplomatic' relations with other hasidic courts and took part in the internal politics of contemporary hasidism as a member of a pluralistic system of leadership which he regarded as valid in itself, despite his strong disagreement with some of its other members.

The list of zaddikim who met with R. Nahman's approval was headed by R. Levi Isaac of Berdichev, of whom he said, 'The rabbi of Berdichev is very great in my eyes,'[138] and he even called him 'unique in this generation'[139] and 'the glory of Israel'.[140] He praised his virtues so highly that his eulogy after R. Levi Isaac's death was taken as alluding to his own virtues.[141] He made the acquaintance of R. Abraham of Kalisk in Tiberias on the occasion of his visit to Erets Yisrael in 1798, and the two developed a friendship based on mutual respect.[142] He also made friends with R. Samson of Shepetovka in the course of the same visit, and even succeeded in establishing peace between him and R. Abraham of Kalisk.[143] On his return from Erets Yisrael he travelled to the court of R. Shneur Zalman of Lyady[144] 'and spoke much with him about the people of Erets Yisrael'.[145] It appears that he approached R. Shneur Zalman on behalf of R. Abraham of Kalisk and asked him not to hold up the funds raised for the hasidim of Erets Yisrael but to hand them over to R. Abraham's emissary.[146] To R. Shneur

[136] *Avaneihah barzel*, 17, s. 15.

[137] *Ḥayei Moharan*, part i, 'Nesi'ato le'Erets Yisrael', 65, s. 19; and cf. *Yemei Moharnat* (Bnei Brak, 1956), 46*b*.

[138] *Ḥayei Moharan*, part ii, 'Gedulat hasagato', 12, s. 30.

[139] Ibid., 'Avodat hashem', 65–6, s. 105.

[140] *Yemei Moharnat*, part i, 29*a*.

[141] See ibid. 30*b*, and cf. J. Weiss, *Meḥkarim bahasidut Braslav* (Jerusalem, 1974), 36–41.

[142] See *Shivḥei haRan*, 'Seder hanesi'ah shelo le'Erets Yisrael', 12*a*–13*b*, ss. 19–20; and also R. Abraham's letter to R. Nahman, *Ḥayei Moharan*, part i, 'Nesi'ato le'Erets Yisrael', 66.

[143] *Shivḥei haRan*, 'Seder hanesi'ah shelo le'Erets Yisrael', 13*b*, s. 20.

[144] According to R. Nathan's account (n. 145 below), R. Nahman went to 'the holy congregation of Lyady' to see R. Shneur Zalman 'immediately on his arrival from Erets Yisrael', i.e. in the summer of 5559 (1799), apparently after the release of R. Shneur Zalman in Kislev of that year from his first spell of imprisonment. At the time R. Shneur Zalman was still living in Liozno, for in his petition addressed to the Emperor in Aug. 1801 he still signs as 'the rabbi of Liozno' (see Dubnow, *Toledot haḥasidut*, 278), and it seems that he did not move to Lyady until after his return from St Petersburg for the second time, in 5562 (1802) (ibid. 332–3). R. Nathan Sternhartz recorded these events in *Ḥayei Moharan* many years after their occurrence, when R. Shneur Zalman had become known as 'the Rabbi of Lyady', and he was clearly mistaken in locating the rabbi's court at Lyady in 5559 (1799) instead of Liozno.

[145] *Ḥayei Moharan*, part i, 'Mekom yeshivato unesi'otav', 52–3, s. 10; and cf. *Avaneihah barzel*, 33–4, s. 46.

[146] See R. Abraham of Kalisk's letter to R. Nahman (n. 142 above).

Zalman himself R. Nahman's attitude was somewhat ambivalent: he was undoubtedly impressed by his large following. When R. Shneur Zalman visited him in Bratslav, on the way to his famous meeting with R. Baruch of Medzibezh:[147]

Our master, may the memory of that righteous and holy man be for a blessing, said to his people concerning the Rabbi [Shneur Zalman]: Show honour to 'a ruler of a thousand' [cf. Exod. 18: 21]. And our master asked the Rabbi: Is it true, as they say about you, that you have eighty thousand Hasidim? And the Rabbi said to him that he had Hasidim who were teachers and each one had a charity box for him, and since the youngsters gave charity for him they would presumably not be opposed to him.[148]

R. Nahman felt a sense of comradeship with R. Shneur Zalman on account of the situation in which they both found themselves, for both were involved in a bitter quarrel with R. Nahman's uncle, R. Baruch of Medzibezh. Two late traditions, apparently independent of each other, record R. Nahman's mocking humour at the expense of his uncle in conversation with R. Shneur Zalman of Lyady.[149] On the other hand, he did not accept the hasidic doctrine of R. Shneur Zalman and did not hesitate to make this plain in front of the Rabbi of Lyady's disciples.[150] Shortly after his return from Erets Yisrael R. Nahman also visited the courts of R. Mordecai of Nezkhis, R. Zevi Aryeh of Olyka and R. Aryeh Leib, the Zeide ('grandfather') of Shpola; at that time, before the outbreak of the controversy between them, R. Aryeh Leib regarded R. Nahman with great respect.[151] R. Nahman despised the popular zaddikism of these hasidic leaders, and emphasized the difference between their kind of leadership and his:

Could I not have been 'a famous one' and a leader of the kind called a *guter yid* [literally 'a good Jew'] to whom the hasidim journey and do not know for what purpose they journey. They come again and again without knowing why they have come. But I wanted nothing to do with any of that. I simply committed myself to this task in order to bring you back to a better way of life.[152]

[147] See pp. 109–13 above.

[148] *Avaneihah barzel*, 34, s. 46.

[149] See Gottlober, *Zikhronot umasa'ot*, i. 168; and cf. *Avaneihah barzel*, 34, s. 46.

[150] See *Avaneihah barzel*, 34, s. 46, and cf. *Ḥayei Moharan*, part i, 'Nesi'ato leErets Yisrael', 61–2, s. 4. It can hardly be supposed that R. Nahman was unaware of the fundamental difference between his own outlook on hasidism and that of R. Shneur Zalman as expressed in his published work, *Tanya*, a difference so pronounced that it provided hasidic scholarship with the typological distinction between the hasidism of 'faith' and 'contemplative' or 'mystical' hasidism. See Weiss, *Meḥkarim*, 87–95, Eng. version in Weiss, *Eastern European Jewish Mysticism*, 43–55.

[151] See *Ḥayei Moharan*, part i, 'Mekom yeshivato unesi'otav', 52–4, s. 10; and see the discussion of this point in Green, *Tormented Master*, 99–100.

[152] *Ḥayei Moharan*, part ii, 'Ma'alat hamitkarvim eilav', 22, s. 95; and cf. *Avaneihah barzel* 136, 8, s. 6; *Likutei Moharan*, part ii, *torah* 15, 46–7. In this *torah* R. Nahman distinguishes between 'those who falsely boast of great deeds and wonders, as if nothing is beyond their ability and everything is within their powers, and some of them are [the] leaders of the generation', and, on the other hand, 'true zaddikim, of great spiritual eminence, whose mouth is holy and its way is to utter great and wonderful things, and they can truly serve the Lord through anything in the world, through eating, drinking and other things' (p. 46). As R. Nahman often does in expressing himself on 'the true zaddikim', he slips from 'zaddikim' in the plural to 'zaddik' in the singular, and there is no doubt that in doing so he is alluding to his own pre-eminence as 'the zaddik of the generation'. But one should not underestimate the reality in R. Nahman's mind of 'the true zaddikim' as a whole group whose existence is clearly 'revealed' to the world, and which is distinct from the group of 'lying hypocrites who mimic [the true zaddikim] like an ape. The legitimate and 'revealed' status of the true zaddikim is as real to him as his own 'secret' status as zaddik of the generation. It is interesting to note that R. Nathan Sternhartz enumerates a long list of zaddikim which includes

It is clear, however, that he did not regard all the zaddikim of his generation in this light, and that his objection was not to the multiplicity of zaddikim in itself but to the type of leadership offered by a particular kind of zaddik: the miracle-workers, the men without learning, 'who have made gatherings to eat and drink the main feature of the worship of the Lord, blessed be He'.[153]

It is probable that, together with other factors, R. Nahman's hasidic lineage—his descent from the Besht—helped, from the start, to develop in him a sense of his unique and extraordinary qualities. As a child he often prayed at the grave of the Besht, 'asking his grandfather to help him to draw near to the Lord, blessed be He',[154] and in his first contacts with other zaddikim they all showed him great respect as 'the seed of the Besht'.[155] The value of lineage and ancestral merit was one of east European Jewry's most ancient Ashkenazi legacies,[156] and it is hard to imagine that R. Nahman's sense of his special mission was not fostered by his pedigree when he started out on the path of zaddikism. But once this sense of mission had crystallized, not only did it extend far beyond the hereditary link with the Besht but it actually led R. Nahman to reject that link, which did not accord with his conception of himself as a *ḥidush*—an extraordinary phenomenon the like of which the world had never seen.[157] R. Nahman saw himself as a unique messianic *ḥidush* whose dominion extended over all creation, and not as a supreme leader within the prosaic framework of a hierarchical organization, for which, as we have said, there was no precedent in the actual historical circumstances of his environment. By contrast, in his day-to-day activities as a zaddik, his position was simply that of a constituent part of the large network of hasidic leaders of his time. The particular messianic dimension of his leadership 'in concealment' found concrete historical expression not in opposition to the pluralistic principle which allowed all other zaddikim to lead their own followers, but in the rejection, within the Bratslav school itself, of the dynastic solution to the problem of preserving the distinctive identity of the school after the death of its founder. Most hasidic communities were beginning at that time to adopt the dynastic solution to this problem. In most cases it ensured their organizational continuity and maintained their original identity (and those hasidic communities that did not adopt this method disappeared from the scene with the death of their founders). Alone of all the hasidic circles and schools, the Bratslav community, which had been nurtured on the sense of R. Nahman's unique

almost indiscriminately all R. Nahman's predecessors in the hasidic movement as well as many of his contemporaries, for all of whom R. Nahman allegedly felt great respect and on whose holiness he lavished praise. This contrasts with his caustic and derisive comments (likewise recorded by R. Nathan), in various other contexts, on 'all the sages of Israel' in general and many of the hasidic leaders in particular. From the fact that the list even includes R. Nahman's uncle and adversary, 'the holy rabbi R. Baruch, of blessed memory', it is evident that it is an exercise in apologetics, serving, as it were, as a reply to claims that R. Nahman exalted himself above other people. Genuine praise, such as the expression of R. Nahman's regard for the eminence of R. Levi Isaac of Berdichev, appears in it alongside vague expressions of praise for all the great hasidic personages of the generation. See *Ḥayei Moharan*, part ii, 65–6, s. 105.

153 *Avaneihah barzel*, 8, s. 6.

154 *Shivḥei haRan*, 5*a*, s. 19; and see also ibid. s. 20.

155 See e.g. ibid., 'Seder hanesi'ah shelo le'Erets Yisrael', 12*b*, s. 19.

156 See A. Grossman, 'Yiḥus mishpaḥah umekomo baḥevrah hayehudit be'Ashkenaz hakedumah', in I. Etkes and Y. Salmon (eds.), *Perakim betoledot haḥevrah hayehudit biyemei habeinayimn uva'et haḥadashah, mukdashim leYa'akov Katz* (Jerusalem, 1980), 9–23.

157 See *Ḥayei Moharan*, part ii, 'Gedulat hasagato', 9, s. 7.

messianic role, was able to preserve its own cohesiveness and distinct identity, without anyone succeeding R. Nahman to the leadership, by regarding his death as a temporary stage of further 'concealment' in which he continued to have dominion over them, and by waiting patiently for the extension of his 'revealed' dominion in the messianic time to come.

6. CONFERENCES OF ZADDIKIM

Apart from the alleged claims of individuals to supreme leadership, which were discussed above and shown to have been misconstrued as such, it is important to examine yet another possible indication of the apparent survival of centralist traditions in the leadership of post-1772 hasidism from the days of its founders. I refer to the meetings of the hasidic leaders of one region or another which were convened from time to time for a variety of reasons and which could be construed as the remnants of an institution facilitating control from the centre, first established by the Maggid of Mezhirech.

The disciples of the Maggid appear to have come together only once, in Rovno, towards the end of their master's life, in the summer of 1772. This we gather from R. Shneur Zalman of Lyady's letter to R. Abraham of Kalisk written at the end of 1805 or in 1806.[158] The letter was intended, among other things, to remind R. Abraham, who was in dispute with R. Shneur Zalman, of the sins of his youth, when he incurred the wrath of the Maggid and had to ask the Rabbi of Lyady to intercede on his behalf.[159] Recently doubt has been cast on the reliability of the hasidic historiographical tradition and the sources on which it was based, starting with the letters of the hasidic leaders who emigrated to Erets Yisrael and their contemporaries, through the literature of the polemic between the hasidim and the mitnaggedim, to the early hagiographical tales of hasidism. It is claimed that all these bodies of literature emanated from the Habad school and all reflect the particularly biased perspective of Habad, in much the same way as does the internal historiography of Habad in the twentieth century.[160] It is, however, difficult to treat these diverse sources as a homogeneous literary tradition simply on the grounds of the Habad thread which runs through them all. Certainly they do not all display the tendentiousness by which Habad historiography has been marked in recent decades.[161]

[158] See Hillman, *Igrot ba'al haTanya*, *Igeret* 103, 175; and, on 177, Hillman's comment on the date when this was written. Cf. Levine, *Igrot kodesh*, *Igeret* 51, 125–6; and see the presumed date (Elul 5565 = 1805) given on 120.

[159] See p. 95 above and n. 57.

[160] See Z. Gries, 'Hasidism: The Present State of Research and Some Desirable Priorities', *Numen*, 34: 1 (1987), 101–3.

[161] On Habad historiography in the 20th cent., and especially on the writings of the *admor* Joseph Isaac, see nn. 2 and 76 above; and below, in the present section. But it is hard to accept the claim that *Shivḥei haBesht*, for example, reflects a distinctly Habad viewpoint, with the characteristic Habad tendency towards 'organization and propaganda' (see Gries 'Hasidism', 102–3), simply because the book was published by R. Israel Jaffe, who was one of the hasidim of R. Shneur Zalman of Lyady. R. Shneur Zalman and his family are not mentioned at all in the tales of *Shivḥei haBesht*, whereas the Habad historiography stemming from the *admor* Joseph Isaac Schneersohn places R. Shneur Zalman and his family at the centre of the hasidic movement from its very beginning in the time of the Besht, and even alleges the Belorussian town of Lubavitch to have been a secret centre of hasidism during the Besht's lifetime (see

Although all our information on the Rovno meeting of the Maggid's disciples in 1772 is derived from Habad sources, there is no good reason to suspect its reliability. The purpose of the meeting as recorded by R. Shneur Zalman in his letter, namely 'to take counsel' in response to the outbreak of the controversy with the mitnaggedim, seems entirely reasonable.

We have no knowledge of any other conferences or assemblies of the Maggid's disciples during his lifetime, or of any regular meetings of hasidic leaders after his death which might have been convened by one or other of them in order to determine the policy of the hasidic movement as a whole.[162] On the other hand, we know that hasidic leaders did occasionally come together under various circumstances to deal with topical issues and also to argue out disputes between opposing hasidic camps. However, none of these conferences placed any obligation on the participants, and no individual leader ever emerged as a sufficiently dominant figure to impose his authority on the others. It is quite clear that the organizational framework within which these meetings took place did not offer any machinery for the imposition of central control.

Conferences of this kind took place in Berdichev at the beginning of the first decade of the nineteenth century. Gottlober[163] reports on a meeting of communal leaders, most of them hasidic leaders, invited by R. Levi Isaac of Berdichev to his town 'to consult together and defend their lives' on account of 'a great calamity' and 'a day of darkness' the nature of which he does not specify. Dubnow[164] identified this calamity as the establishment, by order of Tsar Alexander I, of 'the Committee for the Amelioration of the Jews' in St Petersburg in 1802, a committee which, in December 1804, issued the notorious 'Statute Concerning the Organization of the Jews', excluding the Jews from their traditional rural occupations and expelling them from the villages and hamlets in a vast area in which they had long been resident.[165] Dubnow put forward the hypothesis that R. Levi Isaac of Berdichev called his fellow hasidic leaders together in his town in order to forestall this misfortune and plan joint action, and he therefore conjectured that the meeting was held in 1802 or 1803.[166] Israel Halpern, however, observed that the internal chronology of Gottlober's account was problematic and did not necessarily point to the date proposed by Dubnow.[167] It appears that Gottlober himself supposed

Sefer hazikhronot, part i, 28–36; Rapoport-Albert, 'Hagiography', 154). Similarly the orientation towards 'organization and propaganda' which is characteristic of Habad, and which, indeed, the *admor* Joseph Isaac adopted retrospectively in his reconstruction of the birth of hasidism (see nn. 2 and 75 above, and more below), is quite absent from *Shivḥei haBesht*. The tales in that work reflect a weak organizational framework and 'propaganda' activities which are merely incidental. As to the letters which passed between the leaders of Belorussian hasidism in Erets Yisrael and their hasidim, and which were likewise preserved and distributed by Habad, these, too, lack the tendentiousness typical of later Habad historiography: rather than claiming to present a picture of the contemporary state of hasidism as a whole in which Belorussian hasidism, and ultimately Habad hasidism, were shown serving as the headquarters of the movement and its most important centre, the letters actually document internal developments in Belorussia as such.

162 The writings of the *admor* Joseph Isaac Schneersohn are an exception. They tell of regular and fairly frequent meetings of the disciples of the Maggid, presided over by R. Shneur Zalman. On this, see below.

163 Gottlober, *Zikhronot umasa'ot*, i. 173–8.

164 Dubnow, *Toledot haḥasidut*, 310.

165 See also S. Dubnow, *History of the Jews in Russia and Poland* (3 vols.; Philadelphia, 1916–20), i. 335 ff.; J. D. Klier, *Russia Gathers her Jews* (Dekalb, Ill. 1986), 116–43.

166 And cf. the editor's note no. 103 in Gottlober, *Zikhronot umasa'ot*, 173.

167 'R. Levi Yitsḥak miBerdichev ugezerot hamalkhut beyamav', in Halpern, *Yehudim veyahadut*, 345–6.

the meeting to have taken place in 1809, though the accuracy of his memory at the time of writing may be questionable. Just as in the case of the Rovno meeting of the Maggid of Mezhirech's disciples in 1772—as reported in R. Shneur Zalman's letter[168]—so, too, on this occasion it appears that the leaders were called together in the first place in response to a grave external danger facing them all, but the meeting became the arena for an internal dispute: in Rovno the Maggid and some of his intimates fell out with R. Abraham of Kalisk, and in Berdichev some thirty years later R. Baruch of Medzibezh, the grandson of the Besht, was in dispute with R. Aryeh Leib, the Zeide of Shpola.

Another description of a conference of hasidic leaders in Berdichev during the same period appears in the biography of R. Nahman of Bratslav by his disciple, R. Nathan Sternhartz.[169] According to that account the conference of the zaddikim in Berdichev took place 'in the summer of 1802' on the occasion of the wedding of the son of one of the 'great men'. In spite of the obvious difference between Gottlober's account of the circumstances of the undated Berdichev conference and the report in *Ḥayei Moharan* on the meeting in the same town which was held in the summer of 1802, one detail is common to both accounts: on both occasions the hostility of the participants was focused on the figure of the Zeide of Shpola. He was insulted and publicly humiliated by R. Baruch of Medzibezh, according to Gottlober;[170] according to R. Nathan Sternhartz, the majority of those present in Berdichev came close to excommunicating him because of his intrigues against R. Nahman, and he was only saved by the intervention of R. Levi Isaac himself.[171] In Gottlober's account the precise date and circumstances are unclear; the Bratslav source is patently tendentious and polemical—it places the dispute between the Zeide of Shpola and R. Nahman at the centre of events and may well have neglected to report additional items of information which lie outside the immediate concern of the author. Dubnow's hypothesis that the Berdichev conference mentioned by Gottlober was held in 1802 or 1803 is not an easy one to maintain in the face of all the difficulties advanced against it by Halpern, but Halpern does not altogether reject it, and prefers to leave the matter open until such time as fresh evidence on the question may come to light.[172] Given all these uncertainties it is just possible that the 1802 conference in Berdichev reported in *Ḥayei Moharan* and the Berdichev conference reported by Gottlober and tentatively dated to 1802/3 are one and the same.[173]

Another meeting of a large number of hasidic leaders is known to us only from hagiographical sources,[174] but the facts are not in doubt. This meeting, too, took place on the occasion of a marriage in the house of a zaddik—the famous wedding of the grandson of the *rebbe* of Apta in Ustila (Uscilug). It, too, became the scene of a sharp dispute between the assembled guests. In the nature of things, the marriages of

[168] See n. 57 above.

[169] *Ḥayei Moharan*, 'Mekom yeshivato unesi'otav', 58, s. 19; and cf. *Pe'ulat hatsadik* (Jerusalem, 1981), 142, s. 379.

[170] Gottlober, *Zikhronot umasa'ot*, i. 177–8.

[171] See *Ḥayei Moharan*, 'Mekom yeshivato unesi'otav', 58, s. 19.

[172] Halpern, *Yehudim veyahadut*, 347.

[173] But cf. Green, *Tormented Master*, 110, 140. He takes the two accounts of a conference in Berdichev as relating to two separate events, and surmises that R. Nahman was not present at the conference described by Gottlober.

[174] See Buber, *Tales of the Hasidim*, ii. 258–9.

zaddikim and of their children provided opportunities for a number of hasidic leaders to meet in one court, especially as there was a great deal of intermarriage between the dynasties in the course of the nineteenth century. All our information on such meetings and conferences, far from reflecting the presence of a certain centralist, hierarchical mode of operation, actually emphasizes the degree of independence of each court, and, at times, the high level of tension and mutual hostility which characterized the relations between the courts even when their leaders came together under the roof of their host to discuss matters of common concern.

In contrast to all the sources mentioned above, there exists a single body of source material which attributes a distinctly centralist tendency to the hasidic leadership not only during the lifetime of the Besht and the Maggid of Mezhirech—as has been the general assumption—but even in the period following the death of the Maggid, in the 1770s and 1780s. These sources mention regular conventions of all the disciples of the Maggid, who place in charge over themselves a 'managing committee' and other centralist institutions, which 'oversee' the internal administration of the movement as well as the wider dissemination of its teachings. The sources in question are the internal historiography of Habad, of which the most systematic and prolific exponent was the *admor* Joseph Isaac Schneersohn.[175] In his historical writings the figure which stands out among the disciples of the Maggid as the leader who was chosen by his colleagues to 'oversee' the affairs of the movement is, of course, R. Shneur Zalman of Lyady.

Contrary to the picture which emerges from the evidence considered above of a leadership structure which was fragmented from the start, and contrary, too, to the view which has prevailed both in the scholarly literature and in later hasidic writings that the leadership was decentralized after 1772, the *admor* R. Joseph Isaac reconstructs the events which followed the death of the Maggid, and the outbreak of the controversy with the mitnaggedim, as follows:

> The situation at the time required that in charge of affairs there should be a man with the spirit to speak plainly to the opponents and not take fright at the noise of the excommunications and proclamations fired off by the opponents at the followers of Hasidism. Accordingly it was decided then to elect a management committee, with a general organizer—authorized by the holy Rabbi, R. Abraham[176] and the entire holy fraternity—having power and authority to act on his own responsibility and to give such instructions to all the centres as seemed to him necessary for the good of the cause. And the holy fraternity—in general session—elected our venerable and holy Old Rebbe [*der alte rebbe*][177] to be the general organizer with full authority, and they empowered him to organize the work of all the centres and the work of propaganda throughout the country, and also to visit from time to time the places of residence of the disciples of our teacher, may his soul rest in Eden.[178] For about three years—from 1773 to 1776—the Old Rebbe was engaged in various journeys to various places to examine the situation of the

[175] See n. 2 above and, in particular, Rapoport-Albert, 'Hagiography', 145–50.

[176] The reference is to the son of the Maggid, R. Abraham 'the Angel', who is presented as having inherited his father's position as supreme leader of the Hasidic movement (see nn. 2 and 76 above) but being incapable of actually exercising that function because of his temperamental preference for the reclusive life of the ascetic. This is why he had to delegate the practice of leadership to the various institutions and office-holders described in the remainder of the passage quoted.

[177] The reference is to R. Shneur Zalman.

[178] The Maggid of Mezhirech.

disciples of the Maggid and to see whether the work in the centres was in accordance with the arrangements prescribed by the management committee.[179]

This reconstruction is clearly anachronistic: the model of the centralized Habad court, and its characteristic concern with 'organization' and 'propaganda', which marked especially the difficult and heroic leadership of the author from the end of the 1920s until his death in 1950,[180] is applied retrospectively to the structure of the entire hasidic movement of the 1770s. The account is out of step with everything we know from other sources: there is no reference in the contemporary writings of members of 'the holy fraternity' themselves to any such centralized organizational activity on their part, nor to R. Shneur Zalman of Lyady's exalted position at the centre of affairs, particularly during this early period, at the beginning and in the middle of the 1770s. R. Shneur Zalman had not yet become leader of the hasidim of Belorussia at that time, and certainly did not attain this position before the departure for Erets Yisrael, in 1777, of R. Menahem Mendel of Vitebsk and R. Abraham of Kalisk—the two disciples of the Maggid of Mezhirech who led the hasidic communities of the region during the Maggid's lifetime. R. Shneur Zalman's rise to leadership was a long-drawn-out process, and it was not completed until the end of the 1780s, with the death of R. Menahem Mendel of Vitebsk in Erets Yisrael.[181] What is more, his leadership, even when established, did not extend over all the areas of influence of the Maggid's disciples throughout the crumbling kingdom of Poland, as would appear from the *admor*'s remarks quoted above. The Rabbi of Lyady served as leader of his hasidim in his own area, like the Maggid's other disciples and the other zaddikim in their own areas and for their own hasidim. The only centralized function which can be attributed to him—the collection of money on behalf of the hasidim in Erets Yisrael—was itself not exclusive to him, for he was never the sole 'authorized person' in charge of this task in all the areas of hasidism;[182] and in any event, there were those who objected to his having even this authority, and the matter became a bone of contention.[183]

In addition to ascribing to R. Shneur Zalman of Lyady the status of supreme leader

[179] The *admor* Joseph Isaac Schneersohn, 'Avot haḥasidut', i, part 2, ch. 10, 144.

[180] The *admor* Joseph Isaac led his hasidim in Russia during the period of oppression by the Soviet regime under Stalin. He was imprisoned, persecuted, and expelled on account of his covert activity aimed at preserving traditional Jewish religious life in Russia. He continued his activity even after he escaped to Latvia, then to Poland, and later, during the Second World War, to the USA. There he rehabilitated the Habad movement, establishing it on a new basis in a new world. All this is documented in his many writings, and especially in the twelve volumes of his letters, which have been published in New York in recent years. Basing himself on the *admor*'s own writings, R. Abraham H. Glitzenstein wrote a biography of the *admor*—*Sefer hatoledot Rabbi Yosef Yitsḥak Schneersohn miLubavitch: Admor Moharits* (4 parts in 3 vols; 1971–4). Parts iii (for the years 1921–8, spanning his activity up to the time he left Russia) and iv (1928–50, up to his death in New York) relate to the period with which we are concerned. In addition, the central part played by the *admor* Joseph Isaac, at considerable danger to himself, in the struggle to preserve Judaism in Russia during those years is documented in works quite independent of the official hagiographic literature of Habad. See e.g. A. A. Gershuni, *Yahadut beRusiah haSovietit: Lekorot redifot hadat* (Jerusalem, 1961), 156–207; J. Rothenberg, *The Jewish Religion in the Soviet Union* (New York, 1971), 161, 178.

[181] For a detailed reconstruction of this process, see Etkes, 'R. Shene'ur Zalman miLadi', 429–39.

[182] Ibid. 434.

[183] See Hielman, *Beit rabbi*, 81–90; A. J. Brawer, 'Al hamaḥaloket bein haRashaz miLiady veR. Avraham Hakohen miKalisk', *Kiryat sefer*, 1 (1924–5), 142–50, 226–38; Elior, 'Vikuaḥ Minsk', 198–9.

at this time—an heir, as it were, to the Maggid of Mezhirech's leadership,[184] the centralist nature of which is taken for granted—Habad tradition attributes to the hasidic leadership during those years a formal centralist structure which was expressed above all in regular and fairly frequent—almost annual—conventions of all the Maggid's disciples. In his 'historical' writings the *admor* R. Joseph Isaac claims that such conventions were held at least in 1773, 1776, 1777, 1779, and 1782.[185] According to him, they constituted the forum at which the policy of the hasidic movement as a whole was formulated, and the decisions of the leaders who attended were binding upon everyone. Thus, for example, it was decided at the meeting in 1776 that R. Menahem Mendel of Vitebsk should go to Erets Yisrael, and also that R. Shneur Zalman should be appointed to the positions of *nasi* (head) of the hasidim in Lithuania and 'general organizer' of the entire movement.[186] At the meeting in 1777 the 'fraternity' said farewell to R. Menahem Mendel, who was about to leave for Erets Yisrael; undertook to see to the maintenance of 'our masters who are journeying to the Holy Land, and their families'; acknowledged the principle that 'every member of the fraternity is head (*nasi*) in his place and in his district' (which is as much as to say that the phenomenon of decentralization was itself the result of a policy formulated in the upper echelon of the central leadership); fixed the limits of R. Shneur Zalman's authority in Lithuania and Belorussia; and also appointed him supreme head (*nesi hanesi'im*) in the matter of the collection of funds for Erets Yisrael, and general 'organizer' of the whole fraternity for a

[184] On the view of R. Shneur Zalman as the Maggid's successor to the central leadership of hasidism as a whole and as the most authentic representative of the hasidic path laid down by the founders of the movement, see e.g. the claim implicit in the dynastic chart, 'Shalshelet nesi'ei haḥasidut hakelalit unesi'ei ḥasidei Ḥabad', which is printed on the title-pages of many Habad books in recent years, in both Hebrew and English (e.g. all the biographies of the Habad leaders written by Abraham C. Glitzenstein). In the chart the Besht and the Maggid of Mezhirech are counted as the 'first generation' and 'second generation', R. Shneur Zalman is named immediately after them as the 'third generation', and after him come all his successors as leaders of Habad down to the last *admor*, who was the 'ninth generation' in the leadership of hasidism. See also above, p. 112 and n. 123. It is not only in Habad hasidism that there appears this tendency to credit the Besht and the Maggid of Mezhirech with the parentage of a particular hasidic dynasty whose founder is regarded as their sole or principal heir. Thus, for example, hagiographic tradition presents R. Elimelekh of Lyzhansk as a disciple who was chosen to succeed to the central position of his master, the Maggid of Mezhirech, as the leader of the whole hasidic movement. See *Ohel Elimelekh*, 49–50, s. 24. 'For after the decease of the rabbi, R. Ber of Mezhirech, may the memory of that righteous and holy man be for a blessing, all his associates came there to pay their last respects to him. Among them were the rabbi, R. Elimelekh and his brother, the rabbi R. Zusya of Hanipoli, may their merit protect us, who, too, had previously journeyed to the rabbi, R. Ber, may his merit protect us; and after the "holy ark" [coffin] of the rabbi, R. Ber, was buried, it was proposed in the course of discussion among his disciples that they should place themselves under the authority of a new master who would take the place of the rabbi, R. Ber, may his merit protect us. And they began to conduct inquiries as to whether there was such a man among them who would be worthy to take the place of the rabbi, R. Ber. And they all agreed to accept as their master the rabbi, R. Elimelekh of Lyzhansk. And forthwith they placed the crown of sovereignty on his head and all cried "Long live our *admor* the rabbi, R. Elimelekh" . . . and they said "Then blessed be the Lord who has not left us like sheep without a shepherd. For he is truly worthy to take the place of the rabbi, R. Ber, may his merit protect us."' A tradition of the Gur dynasty ascribed a similar status to the 'Seer' of Lublin. See Aescoly, 'Haḥasidut bePolin', 128. This proprietary sense with regard to the legacy of the Besht and the Maggid of Mezhirech as the central leaders of the whole of the hasidic movement descends also, via R. Elimelekh of Lyzhansk and the 'Seer' of Lublin, to R. Isaac Judah Jeḥiel Safrin of Komarno, and finds expression in his *Megilat setarim*, ed. N. Ben-Menahem (Jerusalem, 1944), 51.

[185] See 'Avot haḥasidut', part 2, chs. 10–11, 144; Elior, 'Vikuaḥ Minsk', 211, 214, 218, 219.

[186] 'Avot haḥasidut', part 2, chs. 10–11, 144.

period of five years.[187] The meetings were always held in the area where the Maggid of Mezhirech had lived, and the Rabbi of Lyady was repeatedly obliged to travel to 'Volhynia, the place which the holy fraternity fixed for their assembly'.[188] This reflects the assumption of the writer that the institution of the regular conventions of the Maggid's disciples began during the lifetime of their master, when they would doubtless have met in his court (even after they began to lead their own congregations of hasidim), in the same way as they had met once in Rovno in 1772, according to the famous letter of R. Shneur Zalman of Lyady. It is clear that the historic meeting in Rovno, which was apparently an ad hoc gathering to consider the unprecedented problem of the controversy with the mitnaggedim, served the *admor* R. Joseph Isaac as a peg on which to hang his reconstruction of events in the 1770s and 1780s from the Habad perspective. There is no mention of most of the details of his reconstruction in contemporary sources; and however much he may employ the professional mannerisms of the historian, his work both serves and reflects the internal needs of Habad more than it suggests any interest in the writing of history as such. The *admor* Joseph Isaac, who was not a professional historian but a leader of a large community in extremely difficult circumstances, subordinated the writing and documentation of history to the needs of the making of history, in which indeed he took an active part. Fuller consideration has been given elsewhere to his seemingly historiographic activity as part of the courageous enterprise of rehabilitating and consolidating the Habad movement in

187 'Vikuaḥ Minsk', 214–15. It is interesting to note that the *admor* Joseph Isaac does not mention R. Abraham of Kalisk in this connection, even though he was one of the leaders of Belorussian hasidism and a colleague of R. Menahem Mendel of Vitebsk, with whom he emigrated to Erets Yisrael. Surely, it might have been expected that, in the *admor*'s version of events, the disciples would decide on R. Abraham's departure also and would take leave of him, too, as they did with his travelling companion R. Menahem Mendel of Vitebsk. The *admor* Joseph Isaac's peculiar silence on all this may well be intended to serve as an implicit reminder of, in the first instance, the disapproval of R. Abraham by the Maggid and the rest of his disciples on account of his wild and disgraceful behaviour in 1772, which angered the Maggid and also, according to R. Shneur Zalman, aroused the wrath of the mitnaggedim (see n. 57 above, and n. 70, which draws attention to Z. Gries's reservations in this regard). But in addition, it constitutes an implicit condemnation by Habad of R. Abraham of Kalisk for his subsequent dispute with R. Shneur Zalman of Lyady (see n. 183 above). It is this above all that lies behind the silence of the *admor* Joseph Isaac on R. Abraham of Kalisk's role in the alleged events of 1777.

188 In this acknowledgement of the awkward distance between the historic geographical centre of the hasidic movement in Volhynia, where the Maggid of Mezhirech and many of his disciples lived, and the relatively isolated centre of Habad hasidism in Belorussia, we may detect a certain consciousness on the part of the *admor* Joseph Isaac, a consciousness to which he gives more explicit expression elsewhere, that 'Polish' hasidism, which he often contrasts with the hasidism of Habad, enjoys a certain emotional affinity with, and has some sort of historic 'proprietary' right over, the original founders of hasidism who all began their activities in Polish Podolia and Volhynia. See e.g. the *admor*'s long letter to his son-in-law Menahem Mendel, the last *admor* of Habad, sent to Berlin from Riga in 1932. The letter was first published in *Hatamim* and is now included in *Igrot-Kodesh . . . Morenu haRav Yosef Yitsḥak*., ii (New York, 1983), 371–7. The special affinity of 'Polish' hasidism to the Besht and the Maggid of Mezhirech requires an explanation from the Habad point of view, since it clashes with Habad's view of itself as the hasidic school with the strongest claim to be the legitimate and most authentic heir to the tradition of the founders of the movement. Notably, this sensitivity to the closer geographic, and, in some respects, temperamental ties between 'Polish' hasidism and the founders of the movement appears to have found its first expression in the period when Habad was uprooted from its historic centre in Belorussia and, under the leadership of the *admor* Joseph Isaac, was exposed for the first time to intensive contact with a large and vigorous Polish hasidic world in inter-war Warsaw. I intend to publish elsewhere a detailed study of this interesting chapter in the history of Habad.

conditions of crisis,[189] an enterprise which was inspired by his view that the 'travails' of the time heralded the coming of the messiah.

7. THE IDEOLOGICAL FRAMEWORK IN RELATION TO THE REALITIES OF ORGANIZATIONAL CHANGE

The hasidic movement, then, operated as a network of separate congregations of hasidim, each under the exclusive leadership and central control of its own charismatic leader, which, however, did not infringe on the no less exclusive and central authority of other zaddikim over their hasidim. This organizational structure found ideological expression in various formulations of the doctrine of the affinity of souls—souls which had their origin in the same 'root' or 'family' in Heaven. The doctrine, which sprang from medieval kabbalah,[190] reached its full development in the sixteenth-century kabbalah of Safed.[191] It provided hasidism with a means of explaining and legitimizing, in terms of well-known kabbalistic ideas, the novel leadership structure of the movement and the intricate relationships within it: each zaddik is capable of drawing to himself, reforming ('effecting the *tikun*' of), and elevating only the individual souls which belong to the root of his soul, and this leaves the field open for the activity of other zaddikim whose souls are derived from other roots. R. Elimelekh of Lyzhansk, for example, formulates the principle of the affinity between the roots of the souls of the zaddik and his particular hasidim as follows:

'If your brother becomes poor and sells [part] of his property' [Hebrew *umakhar me'aḥuzato*] etc. [Lev. 25: 25]. The meaning of '*umakhar*' is 'he sells himself'; *me'aḥuzato*, 'out of his property', is the upper world from which he was hewn, and which is his true possession. For example, we observe that a person who is not yet grown up is greatly attached to his father by bonds of love, but as he grows and his understanding in matters of corporeal, worldly affairs is strengthened, he gradually becomes detached from his father until he is entirely separated and he leaves his father and becomes like a different person. Similarly with the soul, when it first comes to this world it still has bonds with the upper world, for it was hewn from that world . . . but later, when a person has become part of the corporeality of this world . . . his mind separates itself from the service of the Creator . . . and he sells himself and is deprived of the Lord, blessed be He, [as is alluded to in the verse (Ps. 106: 43):] 'and they were brought low for their iniquity'. That is what is meant by *umakhar me'aḥuzato*; and what is its remedy? 'His kinsman who is nearest to him shall come and redeem what his brother has sold' [ibid.], and he, his kinsman, is the zaddik nearest to him in the Garden of Eden, their souls being attached to each other because they stem from the same root; 'and shall redeem what his brother has sold', i.e. he shall aid and assist him to separate himself from this lowly world and to attach himself to upper worlds. And that is the meaning of the verse 'Better is a neighbour who is near than a brother who is far off' (Prov. 27: 10), 'a neighbour who is near' refers to the affinity of souls; although in this world they appear to be distant from each other, nevertheless they are near to each other in the upper world, and that is better than 'a brother who is far off', someone who

189 Rapoport-Albert, 'Hagiography', 137 ff.

190 See G. Scholem, *The Mystical Shape of the Godhead* (New York, 1991), 215 ff., 223–6, 231–5.

191 Ibid. 223–5, 231 ff.; Bracha Sack, 'Sheloshet zemanei ge'ulah be'*Or yakar* leR. Moshe Cordovero', in Z. Baras (ed.), *Meshiḥiyut ve'eskhatologiah* (Jerusalem, 1984), 282; B. Sack, 'Ha'adam kemarah vera'ayon ha'arevut hahadadit', *Da'at*, 12 (1984), 37.

is a brother in this world but is distant from him in the upper world,[192] for such a brother can avail him nothing, whereas the zaddik who is with him in one and the same root, he is his true redeemer [*go'el*, which also means 'kinsman']. And that is the meaning of 'shall redeem what his brother has sold', see above.[193]

Such statements provide a theoretical basis for the demarcation of the 'territory' of each zaddik and for the exclusive links between him and his own hasidim. Thus it is related of a man who was a hasid of R. David of Lelov, one of the disciples of R. Elimelekh of Lyzhansk, but who decided to try out another *rebbe* by joining the ranks of Habad:

One day it occurred to him to journey to the holy Eminence, the author of the *Tanya* (may the memory of that righteous and holy man be for a blessing) in Liozna, and he did so, but when he arrived he could not go in to see him for eight days. On the eighth day the 'Tanya' himself came to him and greeted him and said to him 'Go to the rabbi, R. David of Lelov, for the root of your soul does not belong to me but to him.'[194]

On this R. Mordechai Brokman, compiler of the hagiographical anthology *Migdal David*, observes: 'It is well known that every soul is drawn to its root, for it goes to the zaddik together with whom it previously existed in the upper world, and as is mentioned in *No*[*am*] *E*[*limelekh*] on the verse "If your brother becomes poor", your brother from the upper world: see what is said there.'[195]

In its original kabbalistic context, the doctrine of the affinity between the roots of souls is linked with that of transmigration, the means by which souls return to their families, their tribes, or their roots in the upper world.[196] On the other hand, in the hasidic versions of the doctrine, transmigration is displaced from its central position and, instead, emphasis is placed on the ability of the zaddik to elevate the souls of his hasidim to their root through his *devekut*. While he is in the state of *devekut*, his soul

[192] On the idea, expressed by R. Hayyim Vital, that bonds of family kinship do not necessarily coincide with the bonds of affinity of the roots of souls, see e.g. *Sha'ar hamitsvot* (Tel Aviv, 1962), on 'Yitro', 33–5: 'But it has long been known that most children are not from one root, but one [stems] from Lovingkindness (the *sefirah* Ḥesed) and another from Might (the *sefirah* Din) and so on, and particularly is this so with regard to those who have undergone *gilgul* (transmigration of soul) for in most cases they have no connection with their ancestors, neither do they have any connection or affinity whatsoever with the souls of their fathers and mothers . . . and there is no connection between father and son or between the son and his father and mother and his older brother. Each one goes to his own root, but when their souls are all from one root, then kinsfolk are joined together as they were at first'. Cf. *Sha'ar hagilgulim* (Tel Aviv, 1963), 'Hakdamah' 10, 34; and see Scholem, *The Mystical Shape*, 235.

[193] Elimelekh of Lyzhansk, *No'am Elimelekh* [Lemberg, 1788], ed. G. Nigal (2 vols.; Jerusalem, 1978), vol. ii on 'Behar', 65*c* (p. 350); and cf. vol. i on 'Bo', 37*c* (p. 198); and see the editor's remarks in the introduction, p. 22. See also Rivka Schatz-Uffenheimer, 'Lemahuto shel hatsadik baḥasidut', *Molad*, 18: 144–5 (1960), 375.

[194] Mordechai Brokman, *Migdal David* (Piotrkow, 1930), repr. in *Sefarim kedoshim migedolei talmidei Ba'al Shem Tov hakadosh*, iii (Brooklyn, NY, 1981), 50. This motif also appears in the tale quoted by Buber in *Tales of the Hasidim*, ii. 108–10. According to this tale, which originated in the circle of R. Moses Leib of Sasow, R. Abraham Joshua Heshel of Apta (Opatow) became a disciple of R. Elimelekh of Lyzhansk on the instructions of R. Levi Isaac of Berdichev and R. Moses Leib of Sasow, who both recognized that he belonged to the root of R. Elimelekh's soul.

[195] *Migdal David*, 50. On *Migdal David* and its author, see Nigal, *Hasiporet haḥasidit*, 51–2. For the references in *No'am Elimelekh* see n. 193 above.

[196] See Scholem, *The Mystical Shape*, 218 ff.

becomes bound up with theirs, in exactly the same way that it becomes bound up with all the captive sparks in his immediate material environment—his food, his utensils, his animals—which also belong to the root of his soul and achieve their *tikun* through him.[197] On the evidence of the tales cited above about zaddikim who were able to tell that certain hasidim who sought to approach them actually 'belonged' to other zaddikim,[198] every zaddik can identify the original heavenly root of every soul, be it destined to be perfected by him or by one of his colleagues. This view springs from the belief that the zaddikim possess such exalted souls that they have already accomplished their own *tikun* and returned to their root; they descend to the world only in order to perfect and 'redeem' the lowly souls which are dependent on them. Underlying this view is the élitist consciousness shared by kabbalists of previous generations who saw themselves collectively as a vanguard, 'the exalted souls which were the first to ascend and have already been perfected, then they descend to guide and set straight those lowly souls in order that they [too] may be perfected'.[199]

The doctrine of the root-affinity between the souls of the hasidic leader and his followers not only enabled every zaddik to draw towards him only those hasidim whom he recognized as being from the root of his own soul and reject others with 'foreign' souls: it also explained and legitimized the search of every hasid for a leader who suited his own disposition; for 'the young people' (*benei hane'urim*)—the early recruits to hasidism during its first period of expansion—were apparently given to wandering from court to court before attaching themselves permanently to the 'right' master. We shall return to this below.

It follows, then, that the kabbalistic doctrine of the root-affinity between particular souls, which, in origin, was unquestionably deterministic, was transformed by early hasidism, in effect if not in fully articulated theory, into the doctrine of voluntary association between individuals: the approach to hasidism was a process of mutual choice between particular hasidim and particular zaddikim who knew each other personally. It is true that, on the face of it, the choice was not a free one but was simply a matter of identifying the primordial link between the roots of their souls, a link which had been established in the upper worlds during the initial stages of the Creation. Actually, however, as soon as this link was put to the test of immediate personal contact between the spiritual leader and the 'lowly souls' which were dependent on him, the deterministic element was displaced by the element of free will. In contrast to the kabbalistic élite who restored souls to their root by spiritual action which did not require personal contact with their individual embodiment, every hasidic zaddik restored the souls related to him to their root through direct contact with their owners, within the concrete social framework of his congregation.

The doctrine of the affinity between the root of every zaddik's soul and that of his particular hasidim is formulated in parallel in the teachings of several hasidic leaders at the end of the eighteenth and the beginning of the nineteenth centuries.[200] That was

[197] Scholem, *The Mystical Shape*, 241 ff. [198] See n. 194 above.

[199] *Sha'ar hagilgulim*, 'Hakdamah', 5, p. 24; and see Sack, 'Ha'adam', 43.

[200] In addition to the remarks of R. Elimelekh of Lyzhansk (pp. 126–7 above and n. 193), see e.g. *Likutei Moharan*, part ii, *torah* 1, 'Tike'u memshalah', s. 3: 'It is necessary to know the origin of all souls and the source of their vitality, whence each soul receives its vitality, and the most important thing is to know all the famous men of the generation, for if you cannot know and bind yourself individually to each

precisely the period in which the hasidic circles were emerging as fully institutionalized and distinct courts, each under an undoubtedly centralist leadership which was beginning, at least in some cases, to show a tendency towards dynasticism.[201] But in the selfsame period there also developed a sense of cohesion and interconnection which bound the various courts together within the framework of the whole of hasidism, now newly perceived as a coherent movement. For the 'primitive' hasidism of the 1750s and 1760s had neither felt itself to be a movement nor been looked upon as one, until it came up against mitnaggedism and learnt from its opponents to regard itself as a 'sect'.[202] At the outset it merely consisted of a cluster of charismatic individuals and 'holy fraternities' whose relationship to each other and to the wider public was unstructured, personal, and spontaneous.[203] Admittedly the Besht, R. Phinehas of Korets, R.

and every soul, you must bind yourself to all the famous men and leaders of the generation, for the souls are distributed among them; for every famous man and leader of the generation has a number of souls who belong to his allotted portion, and when you bind yourself to the famous men, you are bound together with all the individual souls of Israel.' Admittedly this statement is made from the peculiar viewpoint of R. Nahman—the messianic zaddik of the generation who aspires to form a bond, directly or indirectly, with the souls of all Israel—but it is clear that the doctrine of the special affinity between the sparks of every leader's soul and his 'private' hasidim underlies his view on the existence of a bond between the zaddik of the generation and every soul. Another formulation of the same doctrine appears in R. Kalonymus Kalman Epstein of Cracow's *Ma'or vashemesh* [Breslau, 1842] (Jerusalem, 1986), part ii, on 'Ḥukat', 59–60: 'And so, too, every zaddik has people who journey to him to join themselves to him, and they are branches of the root of his soul. And inasmuch as they affiliate with him he raises up their soul and binds it to their root above, for they are his sparks which must be raised up . . . The zaddik must take the greatest care to distance himself from those persons who are not of the root of his soul. That is to say, he must certainly love every Jew, but he must be careful not to weary himself to raise them [all] up and bind them to their root, for by doing so the zaddik could fall, Heaven forbid, below his [spiritual] level, and he must, therefore, greatly beware of them. The enlightened man will understand this.'

201 The dynastic solution to the problem of preserving the special identity of a hasidic community which had formed round a particular founder even after his death makes its first appearance in the hasidism of Chernobyl, where R. Mordecai succeeded to the leadership on the death of his father, R. Menahem Nahum, in 1798. In Karlin hasidism it was a disciple, R. Solomon, who first succeeded to the leadership of the community on the death of its founder, R. Aaron of Karlin, in 1772. After the death of R. Solomon in 1792, the leadership passed to the founder's grandson, R. Asher of Karlin-Stolin, and from him to his sons. In Habad hasidism R. Dov Ber succeeded to the leadership after the death of his father, R. Shneur Zalman of Lyady, in 1813. In Lyzhansk hasidism, when R. Elimelekh died in 1786, the leadership of his community was shared by his two sons, though they were not particularly successful in that role. In the hasidic community founded by R. Israel, the Maggid of Kozienice, who died in 1814, the Maggid was succeeded by his sons. In Lelov hasidism R. Moses inherited the leadership from his father, R. David, who died in 1813. See also Aescoly, 'Haḥasidut bePolin', 96. Cf. the genealogical chart of the leading hasidic dynasties in *Encyclopaedia Judaica* (Jerusalem, 1972), i. 160–7. For a discussion of the dynastic principle in the hasidic leadership in its sociological context, see S. Sharot, *Messianism, Mysticism and Magic: A Sociological Analysis of Jewish Religious Movements* (Chapel Hill, NC, 1982), the chapter on 'Hasidism and the Routinization of Charisma', 155–88.

202 See pp. 131–3 below.

203 Unlike the literature of the organized mitnaggedic campaigns against hasidism during the 1770s and 1780s, the earliest documents—for the most part hostile—on fraternities of hasidim in the time of the Besht still relate to the activity of individuals. See the remarks of R. Jacob of Satanov in *Mishmeret hakodesh* and R. Solomon of Chelm in *Mirkevet hamishneh*, both quoted by G. Scholem, 'Shetei ha'eduyot harishonot al ḥavurot ḥasidim vehaBesht', in Rubinstein, *Perakim betorat haḥasidut*, 198–240, although it is not clear whether they actually refer to the Besht and his circle. On this subject, see also H. Lieberman, 'Keitsad ḥokerim ḥasidut beYisrael', in id., *Ohel Raḥel* (3 vols.; New York, 1980–4), i. 12–49; G. Scholem, 'Hapulmus al haḥasidut umanhigeihah besefer *Nezed hadema*', *Zion*, 20 (1955), 73–81; Piekarz, *Biyemei tsemiḥat haḥasidut*, 131 ff.

Nahman of Kosov, R. Isaac of Drohobycz, R. Aryeh Leib the Mokhiaḥ of Polonnoye, R. Jacob Joseph of Polonnoye, the Maggid of Mezhirech, and other members of what the historians have termed 'the circle of the Besht' knew each other, spoke to each other, and influenced each other significantly, as is evident from the traditions quoted in their name and about them. But at the same time it is very doubtful whether they saw themselves as the standard-bearers of a newly established movement within a solid ideological and social framework such as might define, on the one hand, the exclusive zone of operations of each one among his own followers and, on the other, some common ideological platform and scope for action which distinguished them from the non-hasidic community.

It is not without significance that the theme of the exclusive nature of the bond between the soul of each zaddik and the souls of his particular hasidim is totally absent from R. Jacob Joseph's discussions of the root-affinity between the souls of the spiritual leaders and those of the common people; and his discussions may be taken as representative of the views prevalent within the early 'circle' of the Besht. As was noted by Weiss: 'In the generation of the "circle" the connecting line is generally drawn between Zaddikim and common people in the nation at large. The social collectivity to which the doctrine of leadership applies is not, as yet, the hasidic congregation specifically but the whole nation, the whole generation.'[204] R. Jacob Joseph puts the point as follows:

And afterwards, in speaking words of correction and rebuke to the inhabitants of his town, let him see to it that he first binds himself to Him, blessed be He, and then let him see to it that he attaches and binds himself to them by way of complete unity and incorporation with them, for the leaders of the generation and the members of his [*sic*] generation have one and the same root,[205] and if he does this, the Lord his God will be with him and he will ascend [literally 'he has ascended'] with them in order to attach them to Him, blessed be He.[206]

It is true that the leader's words of correction and rebuke are here directed to a more specific audience defined as 'the inhabitants of his town'; but the choice of this wording undoubtedly stems from the personal experience of the writer, who served for the greater part of his life as communal rabbi in various towns,[207] and 'the inhabitants of the town' were his natural professional environment. None the less, those who are linked with the leaders of the generation by the principle of the root-affinity of their souls are clearly all 'the members of his generation'—the whole of Jewry, without any distinction between the hasidim of one zaddik and another or between hasidim and non-hasidim. From this point of view the link between the hasidic leader and the community at this stage in the history of hasidism was the direct continuation of the

[204] Weiss, 'Reshit tsemiḥatah shel haderekh haḥasidit', 149.

[205] On the interchange of singular and plural in R. Jacob Joseph's references to the leaders of the generation, see n. 33 above.

[206] *Toledot Ya'akov Yosef*, on 'Mishpatim', 29*a*; and cf. ibid., on 'Ḥayei Sarah', 18*b*: 'for the Zaddik, after ascending to the upper world, descends again in order to raise up [other] levels in accordance with the mystical principle [which underlies the verse] "The righteous man falls seven times and rises again" [a literal rendering of Prov. 24: 16] . . . and this applies [to his activities] both in this world and in the world to come, for he returns [by means of *gilgul*] reincarnated in order to raise up the levels of the people who are his sparks and his branches, so that they may all achieve *tikun*'. Cf. also *Degel maḥaneh Efrayim* (Zhitomir, 1875), on 'Noaḥ', p. 6*a*.

[207] See Dubnow, *Toledot haḥasidut*, 93–6.

traditional link—close in the upper worlds but free from direct personal involvement—between the kabbalists and the souls of the generation. This is a far cry from the relationship of later hasidic leaders with their own clearly differentiated and personally affiliated hasidim. There is not a trace here of any sense of belonging to a sect or movement, either in the internal relations between individuals within the loosely knit network of 'leaders of the generation'—the circle of the Besht and his associates—or in their external relations with the wider public within which and for the benefit of which they worked. In fact the demarcation between 'exterior' and 'interior', that is, between non-hasidic and hasidic, at this stage was rather blurred: the operative distinction was between the anthropological category of the 'spiritual people'—those 'exalted men' who were 'leaders of the generation'—and the category of 'common people' to which the rest of Jewry belonged; and the two categories were called upon to bind themselves to each other in a bond of mutual dependence.

It was not until the 1770s and 1780s that hasidism first began to display some signs of a budding collective identity as a movement, and this precisely at the same time as each of the proliferating hasidic centres which constituted the movement was crystallizing its separate identity within it. These two processes, each accelerated by interaction with the other, can be understood as nothing other than manifestations of a new self-awareness which was aroused and sharpened by the external stimulus of the controversy with the mitnaggedim; for it was in the writings of the mitnaggedim that the hasidim and their leaders, their diverse prayer groups and fraternities, as well as various types of individuals who were sympathetic to them, were first treated as a coherent 'sect',[208] and it was in the proclamations of the *ḥerem* that all these varied expressions of the new spiritual and religious awakening were first lumped together. Thus, for example, the Vilna proclamation of 1781 excommunicates a whole range of 'deviant' groups and individuals who are identified with hasidism but who do not necessarily have any connection with each other:

> In regard to this the chiefs and princes of the holy congregation [of Vilna] have been aroused . . . and have renewed the great *ḥerem* . . . against the aforesaid sect in every place where there are groups of the aforesaid people and [those] who follow their practices, and also to individuals who follow their practices and customs in their homes and in secret; also the[ir] branches, and those who assist and advise them and protect them, and of course those who believe in them, [to those persons] all the aforesaid *ḥaramot* apply.[209]

Until the outbreak of the controversy with the mitnaggedim it was possible to sample the hasidic experience—to take the measure of its leaders, join its prayer groups, or adopt some of its customs—out of curiosity or a spirit of adventure, without being obliged to undergo a complete change of identity or a clear-cut transfer from one camp to another. In *Shivḥei haBesht* there are many descriptions of individuals joining the Besht and his circle, as well as of visits with a less clear motive by people who came on their own initiative, or were sent, to find out what sort of men the new leaders were and

[208] See e.g. Wilensky, *Ḥasidim umitnaggedim*, vol. i *passim*, e.g. 59, 62, 63, 67.

[209] Ibid. 104. And in this connection see Z. Gries, 'Sifrut hahanhagot haḥasidit', *Zion*, 46 (1981), 233, where he points out that the wide circulation of the booklets of *hanhagot* (rules of conduct) up to the year 1800 confirms the existence of a variegated pattern of affiliation with hasidism, comprising many different forms, and more or less intense shades of commitment.

test their powers. These descriptions contain no hint of any upset in the family life of the visitors or any break with their previous social environment.[210] On the contrary, it emerges from the story of how the Maggid of Mezhirech became a disciple of the Besht that 'his relatives pressed him to go to the Besht' in the hope that he would find a cure for his illness there;[211] and R. Abraham, the father of R. Phinehas of Korets, did not disown his son, and it seems that his relations with him remained extremely good in spite of the fact that he knew of his son's links with the Besht, and that R. Abraham considered the Besht 'insignificant'.[212] Similarly it appears from the autobiography of Solomon Maimon that his association with hasidism in the court of the Maggid of Mezhirech was not attended by any family crisis or by a break, recognized either by him or by those around him, with the pattern of his earlier life. When he made the acquaintance of a young man with leanings towards hasidism, who aroused his curiosity and fanned the flames of his spiritual and intellectual unrest, he got up and went to Mezhirech. Even his prolonged absence from home was nothing out of the ordinary for him, for in any event he had to live in other people's houses and away from his home town in the course of earning his living as a children's tutor.[213] And when he grew tired of Mezhirech hasidism he went back peacefully to his home. If any alarm or anger had been occasioned among the members of his household (especially his mother-in-law, whom he describes as a Xanthippe[214]) by the fact that he had been attracted to the new 'sect' of hasidism, we could have expected to find some reference to this in his book, for he has a great deal to say about dramatic domestic incidents, and says it very well. Actually he appears to have regarded his connection with hasidism at this stage as unremarkable and not involving him in any obligation. That, indeed, is how the matter was presented to him by the young man who first introduced him to hasidism: 'As far as the mode of admission was concerned . . . he assured me that that was the simplest thing in the world. Any man who felt a desire for perfection, but did not know how to

[210] *Shivḥei haBesht*: 75–6 (ed. Mintz), 70–2 (ed. Horodecky), 81–4 (*In Praise*) on the *hitkarevut* of the Maggid of Mezhirech); 66 (ed. Mintz), 60–1 (ed. Horodecky), and 61–3 (*In Praise*) on the *hitkarevut* of R. Jacob Joseph of Polonnoye; 58–9 (ed. Mintz), 54 (ed. Horodecky), and 45–6 (*In Praise*) on the *hitkarevut* of 'R. David the preacher of the holy congregation of Kolomyya'; 86–7 (ed. Mintz), 128–9 (ed. Horodecky), and 105–6 (*In Praise*) on two visits to take the measure of the Besht; 107–8 (ed. Mintz), 80–2 (ed. Horodecky), and 146–9 (*In Praise*) on the meeting between R. Abraham—the father of R. Phinehas of Korets—and the Besht, which took place in spite of R. Abraham's contempt for the Besht and his objection to the relations between the Besht and R. Phinehas; etc. *Shivḥei haBesht* does indeed report that R. Jacob Joseph was expelled from his position as rabbi of Sharigrad (Shargorod), apparently as early as 1748, because he had begun 'to consort with hasidim', and that he 'persisted in his righteous course' for a long time. However, at this time and in this environment the expulsion of rabbis from their posts was not a rare phenomenon (see e.g. S. Assaf, 'Lekorot harabanut', in id., *Be'oholei Ya'akov* (Jerusalem, 1943), 56–9), and the precise background to the expulsion from Shargorod is not known from any other source. *Shivḥei haBesht*, which was compiled many decades after the events described here and in full familiarity with the mitnaggedic controversy of the 1770s and 1780s, was quite capable of explaining the expulsion of R. Jacob Joseph as a self-evident consequence of his hasidism. In any event it is clear, even from what we are told, that the relations between R. Jacob Joseph and his congregation deteriorated gradually, and only culminated in his expulsion after some time. This was not an immediate reaction to his identification as a hasid.

[211] Ibid. ed. Mintz, 75; ed. Horodecky, 70; *In Praise*, 82.

[212] Ibid. ed. Mintz, 108; ed. Horodecky, 81; *In Praise*, 147.

[213] See Maimon, *Autobiography*, 175 (19 of the *Essential Papers* reprint), 89 (not reprinted).

[214] Ibid. 53 (not reprinted).

satisfy it . . . had nothing to do but apply to the superiors of the society, and automatically he became a member.'[215]

Unlike these contacts which were free of any hint of crisis, the act of conversion to hasidism in the period following the outbreak of the controversy with the mitnaggedim involved a transformation of consciousness which demanded the total isolation of the convert from his old environment and the adoption of a new identity. In the unique hasidic autobiography *Yemei Moharnat*, R. Nathan Sternhartz, R. Nahman of Bratslav's literary secretary, documents his conversion from mitnagged to hasid at the end of the 1790s, some twenty-five years after Solomon Maimon's visit to Mezhirech:

And at that time I was a great opponent [mitnagged] of the hasidim because my father-in-law strongly disagreed with them and spoke a great deal about them to me and his other sons-in-law and the members of his household and said that his whole intention in speaking to us was to distance us from them. Afterwards I left Sh"g [Shargorod] at Sukkot, at the beginning of 5556 [1796], and came to the holy congregation of Nemirov together with my wife and boarded at my late father's table, and I joined with my late friend to study during the winter. He had been brought up from childhood among the hasidim and had spent some time with a number of zaddikim, and he spoke with me a great deal, arguing that the hasidim were God-fearing and that their famous zaddikim were men of very great eminence and served the Lord, blessed be He, in truth (as indeed they do). And other people, too, argued with me about this but I nevertheless remained firm and determined in my opposition . . . and because of this, during the whole of the winter I spent in Nemirov, I was still opposed to them. Subsequently, as a result of my friend's and other people's continuing to press their arguments, I realized the truth and was privileged to be initiated into the belief in the sages. I agreed with the hasidim that it was good to associate with the famous zaddikim, the great men of the hasidim, because they are men of truth and the Lord is with them, and then, to some extent, the fear of Heaven was drawn down upon me and I changed for the better in regard to several matters known to me. But in spite of this I was still wandering aimlessly and did not know my right hand from my left, for I had no one to lead me properly, and it would take too long to tell everything that happened to me during that time.

In the year 5562 [1802] in the month of Ellul I was privileged to become a follower of the holy and awe-inspiring *admor*, the true teacher, Moharan [R. Nahman], may the memory of that righteous and holy man be for a blessing . . . and it is impossible to imagine how many obstacles and afflictions I endured in that year, namely 5562, for everyone was opposed to me, both my wife and my father, may his light shine, and all the members of his household and all the household of my late grandfather . . . and immediately, that winter, my father, may his light shine, drove me away from his table and I was obliged to eat in my grandfather's home and my wife ate with my father, may his light shine.[216]

Although both these autobiographical accounts were written many years after the events that they described,[217] the difference between them illustrates very well the

[215] Ibid. 173 (18 of the *Essential Papers* reprint).

[216] *Yemei Moharnat*, part i, 6*a*–7*b*.

[217] Solomon Maimon finished writing his autobiography in 1792, when he was almost 40 years old, whereas the episode of his affiliation with hasidism occurred during his youth, apparently at the end of the 1760s or the beginning of the 1770s, and in any event before the death of the Maggid of Mezhirech in 1772 (see Maimon, *Autobiography*, Heb. edn., *Ḥayei Shelomo Maimon* (Tel Aviv, 1942), the introd. by P. Lachower, 35, 48. *Yemei Moharnat* concludes with a description of the episode of R. Nathan's journey to Erets Yisrael in 1822. It appears to have been written over a period of many years (R. Nathan died in 1845). In it, dated diary entries are randomly interspersed with sections which are more in the nature of memoirs.

enormous change of consciousness which had occurred during the twenty-five years between Solomon Maimon's initiation into hasidism and that of R. Nathan Sternhartz. Solomon Maimon, at the very beginning of his book, defines himself as belonging to the well-to-do learned class, whose values he is still able to regard as an absolute and universal norm for the Jewish world. R. Nathan Sternhartz indicates that his identity at the outset was conditioned by his membership of the selfsame class. But he expresses this by defining himself as 'a great mitnagged'—a relative definition of an identity which has meaning only in reference, and by opposition, to a clearly defined alternative hasidic identity. It is true that in his general, preliminary remarks at the start of the chapter which he entitles 'On a Secret Society and Therefore a Long Chapter' Solomon Maimon refers to hasidism as 'a sect of my nation called the "New Hasidim" ',[218] and introduces it as a distinctive movement, but this does not square with the main substance of the chapter, where he describes the details of his affiliation to the hasidic fraternity at Mezhirech. The sectarian terminology of the introductory section apparently reflects his later sensitivity, at the time of writing in Berlin, to 'secret societies' (such as the Freemasons) which were then in vogue, and in the context of which he saw the rise of hasidism among the Jews.[219] In contrast to Solomon Maimon's free movement into hasidism and out again, which had no repercussions on his status in the society in which he had grown up, R. Nathan Sternhartz was ejected from his family circle and deprived of his status the moment they became aware of his conversion to hasidism. The breakdown of relations between them, which ultimately led to his financial ruin, is alluded to in brief comments scattered throughout the autobiography, and is documented in detail in the later literature of the Bratslav circle.[220]

The attempt of the mitnaggedim to exclude the various kinds of 'new hasidim' from the body of the Jewish community (the fact that in the end they failed is irrelevant for our present purpose) introduced into the hitherto holistic, integrative hasidic outlook a keen sense of the boundary between the world of hasidism 'within' and the hostile community 'without', thus generating the new consciousness of hasidism as a movement.[221] One of the first manifestations of this enhanced awareness was the meeting of the disciples of the Maggid of Mezhirech at Rovno in the summer of 1772, shortly before his death. They came together 'to take counsel' and to consider the threat from the mitnaggedim which faced them all.[222] No doubt the personal links between the assembled zaddikim, founded on their association with their common master, created a

[218] See e.g. Maimon, *Autobiography*, 166 (11 of the *Essential Papers* reprint).

[219] See e.g. ibid. 168 n. 1 (23 of the *Essential Papers* reprint); 184–5 (not reprinted), and p. 34 of Lachower's introd. to the Heb. edn.

[220] See e.g. *Avaneihah barzel*, 'Kokhevei or', 'Anshei Moharan', 9–11, 3 ff. See also Weiss, *Meḥkarim*, 66–77.

[221] See above, pp. 131–3. The arousal of this awareness completes the process the beginning of which was described by Katz, *Tradition and Crisis*, 239–40. According to Katz the 'dissociation' of the hasidim from the public at large was perceived as a sectarian and isolationist initiative which preceded and gave rise to mitnaggedism. But the isolationism of the hasidim in the period leading up to the campaign against them found expression only in the initiatives of individuals in various communities who adopted as hasidic certain norms which had been current in kabbalistic circles for generations. These norms did not stem from a coherent policy of any new 'movement' as such, and the relationship between the various individuals and circles adopting them was rather loose at that stage. See also above, pp. 80 ff.

[222] See above, n. 57, and cf. s. 6 above.

natural and convenient framework in which to consider their common predicament, and fostered their newly awakened sense of belonging collectively to a tangible organization. But this feeling was determined in the first instance by their new relationship to the outside world, a world which had now revealed itself as distinct from the world of hasidism 'within', and even hostile to it. This orientation was in marked contrast to the all-embracing view of the world held in the previous generation by the circle of the Besht, which had drawn no distinction whatsoever between 'without' and 'within', and whose field of vision still encompassed the nation or the 'generation' as a whole.

The awakening of this collective consciousness of belonging to one movement among the disciples of the Maggid of Mezhirech was in apparent conflict with the sense of the unique identity of each of the individual courts which developed simultaneously after the outbreak of the controversy with the mitnaggedim. The meeting at Rovno was not only the first collective initiative of hasidism as a movement. It was also the arena for the first internal struggle between different factions within it. The special identity of each faction was all the more keenly felt precisely as a result of their growing awareness that they shared a common destiny as a movement: for example, R. Abraham of Kalisk's style of hasidism was revealed at the meeting as distinctive and controversial enough to be regarded by the others as deviant, and it was denounced under the pressure of the collective interest in appeasing the mitnaggedim.[223] R. Abraham later levelled the same charge against his attackers, chief among them R. Shneur Zalman of Lyady.[224] Once the dynamic of delimitation of boundaries and the growing recognition of distinctive identity began to work, it operated not just on the conception of the world 'outside' as against the world 'within' hasidism but also on the sense of distinctive identity within hasidism itself. The crystallization of the disjointed world of hasidism as a clearly defined and coherent entity, under the pressure of the controversy from 'without', necessarily heightened the awareness of those 'within' that their world was a complex one, and it led to the conscious differentiation of its constituent parts from each other; for until the whole was recognized as such, its parts would be perceived as single items only randomly interconnected, so that there would be no need or reason to define them in relation to one another. This is precisely how the tensions between individual leaders in the generation of the Besht may be understood. They occurred during the period which preceded the consolidation of discrete hasidic fraternities into a cohesive movement in response to the campaign of the mitnaggedim. The antagonism between R. Nahman of Kosov and the Besht,[225] for example, or between R. Jacob Joseph and R. Phinehas of Korets on the one hand and the Maggid of Mezhirech on the other,[226] was not centred on a struggle for the legacy of the supposedly centralist leadership of the Besht, as has been suggested by historians,[227] and it certainly did not go beyond personal rivalry or disagreement between individuals with different religious temperaments. The tense relationships between them, where they occurred, were incidental and did not define their individual religious identities. By contrast, the internal divisions within hasidism which occurred later, such as the clashes between

[223] See above, n. 57, and s. 6.

[224] See n. 55 above, and cf. Gries, 'Mimitos le'etos', 126–32.

[225] See above, pp. 81–3, and n. 14.

[226] See above, p. 91, and nn. 42–3.

[227] See pp. 88–94 above.

R. Abraham of Kalisk and R. Shneur Zalman of Lyady,[228] between R. Nahman of Bratslav and his uncle R. Baruch, and between R. Nahman and his great enemy the Zeide of Shpola,[229] as well as many other disputes which took place in the period following 1772, were the products of a novel sense of mutual accountability within the movement as a whole. The component parts of the movement were now essentially related to one another, however tense this relation might be. These disputes were concerned with conflicting claims of authenticity and loyalty to a common spiritual legacy, and they were fought out on both the ideological and the organizational planes. On the ideological plane, the speculative doctrine of the Maggid of Mezhirech was the common legacy of all his disciples in the leadership of hasidism after 1772, and the disputes between them were perceived as turning upon the proper interpretation of his teachings.[230] The leaders of other hasidic factions, who had not served their apprenticeship at the court of the Maggid, developed not only a sense of their own interrelationship but also an affinity with the disciples of the Maggid through the connecting link of the Besht, who was seen as the mentor of the Maggid of Mezhirech and the teacher of them all.[231] On the organizational plane, the hasidic leaders of that generation disagreed over encroachments on each other's preserves concerning both their influence over hasidim and the joint collection of funds for the hasidic community in Erets Yisrael.[232]

The emergence of a distinctive identity in each one of the hasidic courts alongside the collective identity of the courts as a movement was clearly discernible by the end of the 1790s and the beginning of the nineteenth century. The process is reflected quite well in the account cited above of R. Nathan's conversion to hasidism. R. Nathan himself distinguishes two stages in his transition from mitnagged to hasid: in the first stage 'I was privileged to be initiated into the belief in the sages. I agreed with the hasidim that it was good to associate with the famous zaddikim, the great men of the hasidim . . . But in spite of this I was still wandering aimlessly and did not know my right hand from my left, for I had no one to lead me properly.'[233] In other words, in the first stage R. Nathan shook off his identity as a mitnagged and adopted a new but internally undifferentiated identity as a hasid. At that time, then—1796—it was possible to be identified as a hasid in one's relations with the world which lay outside hasidism (and to suffer all the consequences which that involved) without necessarily being identified in one's intra-hasidic relations as a committed follower of a particular zaddik. From 1796 until he associated himself with R. Nahman of Bratslav in Elul 5562 (1802), R. Nathan wandered from one hasidic court to another without finding a leader after his own heart. He himself does not detail the names of the zaddikim to whom he attached himself temporarily. There is no doubt that he regarded the whole of his life up to the time that he became a follower of R. Nahman—both his time as a mitnagged and his time as a hasid—as quite meaningless, and he devotes no more than one and a half pages to it, apart from some brief remarks scattered here and there in his autobiography. However, later Bratslav hasidism—which, as we know, preserved old traditions and (unlike R. Nathan) did not hesitate to disseminate them in print—elaborated R. Nathan's

[228] See above, p. 95, and nn. 55, 57.

[229] See end of n. 5 above, and cf. Green, *Tormented Master*, 94–134.

[230] See above, p. 95, and n. 55.

[231] See above, pp. 80–2, 94.

[232] See pp. 119–22 above.

[233] See p. 133 above.

summary account, out of admiration for him as a remarkable and saintly man, second only to R. Nahman himself. Bratslav tradition invests with meaning all the episodes of R. Nathan's life and records them as fully as possible. It thus enumerates 'R. Zusya, of blessed memory, and the righteous rabbi R. Levi Isaac of Berdichev, and the holy rabbi R. Baruch, of blessed memory, and the zaddik R. Gedaliah of Luniets [Linits], of blessed memory, and the righteous rabbi R. Shalom of Pohorbishch [Pogrebishchenski], of blessed memory, and other great men, may their memory be for a blessing',[234] as leaders whose courts were all visited by R. Nathan during those years. A parallel tradition adds to this list R. Phinehas of Korets, R. Jeḥiel Michel of Zloczow, and R. Mordecai of Kremenets.[235] Not until 1802, after six years of searching for someone 'to lead me properly', did R. Nathan have the good fortune 'to become a follower of the holy and awe-inspiring *admor*, the true teacher, Moharan, may the memory of that righteous and holy man be for a blessing'.[236] Only then, in the second stage of the process of his conversion to hasidism, did he adopt the specific hasidic identity of a Bratslav hasid.

It appears that this two-stage process was typical of the young recruits to hasidism during this period.[237] And it is no wonder that the hasidic adaptation of the kabbalistic doctrine which identified the root-affinity between the souls of particular zaddikim and particular hasidim was emerging precisely at that time, for this version of the doctrine reflected the process of mutual choice between zaddikim and hasidim and served it very well. However, once this doctrine had established itself in hasidism it never lost its hold, even when the circumstances which it had served and mirrored altered during the early decades of the nineteenth century with the evolution of the hasidic leadership into a hereditary institution.

The hereditary principle under which the leadership of hasidism began to be transmitted within dynasties from one generation to the next[238] was also applied at the level of the ordinary hasidim to their affiliation with a particular court and leader. This affiliation was now beginning to be transmitted from generation to generation as an established family tradition. It is not impossible that the dynastic pattern on which the hasidic courts were modelled at this stage, as well as the hereditary pattern of affiliation to particular courts, was the feudal pattern of relationships on the Polish–Russian estates, with their proprietors, the noblemen who inherited the estates from their forefathers, and their tenants, the peasants who had 'belonged' to the estates for generations.[239] The period in which R. Nathan Sternhartz's conversion to hasidism took place was characterized by the two-stage process in which a complete transformation of outlook, from mitnagged to hasid, was followed by the free choice of one zaddik out of many. But in the course of the nineteenth century, with the institutionalization of dynastic zaddikism and the stabilization, by heredity, of the community of followers within the framework of the court over a period of several generations, the hasidic

234 Abraham Hazan of Tulchin, *Sefer kokhevei or*, 9.

235 *Avaneihah barzel*, 4–6, ss. A–B.

236 See p. 133 above.

237 Weiss, *Meḥkarim*, 70–72.

238 See above, p. 129 and n. 201.

239 See above, p. 79 and n. 6. On the transformation of the spontaneous voluntary association between hasid and zaddik by a fixed hereditary link, see Rubinstein, *Perakim betoledot haḥasidut*, 765, 767, (246, 247). The matter has not been addressed by scholars, but the institutionalization of the hereditary principle in both zaddikism and hasidism should not be taken as self-explanatory.

identity of those who frequented each one of the courts became the product of a sense of continuity rather than severance and transformation of consciousness. The voluntary act of conversion by individuals was replaced by an inherited affiliation to hasidism of whole families and even whole populations in localities which had come to belong by tradition to the area of influence of a particular dynasty of leaders. Just as the leadership passed by inheritance, so, too, did the particular hasidic identity of the followers. At the same time, the collective hasidic identity, clearly differentiated from the non-hasidic or anti-hasidic world 'without', but undifferentiated by particular affiliations 'within' (as in the first stage of R. Nathan Sternhartz's conversion to hasidism before he became a follower specifically of R. Nahman of Bratslav), grew steadily less distinct. The particular, usually inherited, affiliation of the follower of a particular hasidic leader became the essential component of his identity as a hasid. From then on one could be born or become the hasid of a particular court but one could not be simply a hasid of no one in particular. That was the process which led to the virtual displacement of the old absolute meaning of the title 'hasid' by its new relative meaning.[240]

It appears that at this stage, when the place of the individual within hasidism had become a matter of inheritance rather than choice, the doctrine of the common roots of the soul which linked every zaddik exclusively with his own hasidim—a doctrine deterministic in its original kabbalistic form, but harnessed to the service of the novel principle of mutual choice in pre-dynastic hasidism—continued to confer legitimacy on the multiplicity of rival courts and their leaders in spite of the fact that the scope for free choice between hasidim and zaddikim had been restricted. Thus, for example, R. Hayyim Me'ir Hielman, author of the well-known history of Habad *Beit rabbi*, makes use of this doctrine in his protest about the internal rivalries and disputes among the diverse branches of the hasidic movement of his time. In the preface to his book he writes:

> And this is the secret of the division between hasidim, that one of them journeys to one zaddik and another journeys to a different zaddik (each according to the root of his soul) and each one thinks that the zaddik to whom he journeys is the only zaddik of the generation. But should we therefore speak ill, heaven forbid, of the other zaddikim of the generation . . . Let each one journey to the place to which his heart draws him, and let him drink living, flowing water from his well etc. And let him be bound to that place with cords of love, so that he may never be moved. And let him look with kindness and compassion on others and not set them at naught or interfere with their worship.[241]

Hielman here treats the link of each hasid with 'his' zaddik as a voluntary link 'to the place to which his heart draws him'. But in fact, when those words were written, at

[240] See A. Green, 'Typologies of Leadership and the Hasidic Zaddik', in id. (ed.), *Jewish Spirituality*, ii: *From the Sixteenth Century Revival to the Present* (New York, 1987), 153 n. 2. Green's observation that the term 'hasid' at first denoted affiliation only to the hasidic movement and not to a particular hasidic leader is perfectly compatible with, and may even be explained by, the suggestion that, at the end of the 18th cent. and the beginning of the 19th, it was still usual for youngsters joining the hasidic movement to wander from court to court and be known as 'hasidim' without associating themselves permanently with a particular hasidic master. Only when permanent affiliation with a particular master ceased to be a voluntary act by individuals who had reached the end of one stage of their spiritual journey, and became an established family tradition into which one was initiated at birth, could the term 'hasid' assume its later relative meaning of disciple or adherent *of* a particular hasidic leader.

[241] Hielman, *Beit rabbi*, 14–15.

the beginning of the twentieth century, the link with the zaddik was no longer open to the free choice of the hasid. In most cases his heart was drawn to none other than the court to which his parents and grandparents had been attached, and he inherited his connection from them.

At this stage, when the hereditary link between every zaddik and his hasidim had become stable enough to restrict their freedom of mutual choice, there was no longer any need to reinforce and legitimize the internally differentiated hasidic identity of each court by means of the doctrine of the exclusive affinity between the roots of the souls of each community of hasidim and their particular zaddik. This affinity was now taken for granted. The sentiment which was in fact undermined as a result of the processes of hereditary stabilization within each one of the courts was the sense of the collective identity and solidarity of the hasidim within the movement at large, and it was this sentiment that the author of *Beit rabbi* felt called upon to strengthen. By the beginning of the twentieth century, the sense of belonging to hasidism as a movement had given way to the more vital sense of belonging to a particular hasidic court. New political and ideological divides were now cutting across the hasidic camp, aligning some of its factions with non-hasidic forces in Orthodoxy, with which hasidism had become identified through the struggle against secularization and modernity. The boundary between the Orthodox world 'within' and the Orthodox world outside hasidism was becoming blurred once again, while the internal divisions between the hasidic courts were felt as acutely as ever. Yet the collective identity of hasidism as a movement could continue to draw strength from the very doctrine which in its time had supplied the kabbalistic basis for legitimizing the very opposite process of differentiating the individual courts from one another. *Beit rabbi* makes use of this doctrine to ease the growing tension between the hasidic factions of its day, each one of which tended to see itself and its leader as the only authentic embodiment of the hasidic teaching while questioning the authenticity and piety of the others. This is clearly the context in which to explain not only the tendency of each hasidic community to regard its leader as 'the only zaddik of the generation' and to 'speak ill, Heaven forbid, of the other zaddikim of the generation'. It is also quite clearly the context in which to place the tendency of several hasidic communities, chief among them Habad, to adopt the Besht and the Maggid of Mezhirech (who, from the outset, had constituted the basis of the collective identity of hasidism as a movement) as an integral part of their own particular history, and to appropriate them as an asset to which they claim exclusive title.[242]

In order to invoke the kabbalistic doctrine of the root-affinity between souls in support of the call to strengthen the collective hasidic identity, which was growing weaker, it was necessary to forgo one of the original components of the doctrine—the principle that 'most of the children are not from one root',[243] that is to say, that kinship between blood-relatives is unlikely to be matched by common association with one 'root' or one 'family' of souls. Once the association between a given zaddik and his

[242] See above, nn. 123, 127, 184.

[243] See n. 192 above; and this is how R. Elimelekh still conceived of this principle in the period of voluntary attachment and effective freedom of choice which operated between the zaddik and his hasidim. Cf. pp. 126–7 above.

followers had become hereditary and therefore not subject to choice, the doctrine of the root-affinity between the souls of the zaddik and his hasidim reverted to its deterministic origin—with the difference that the predetermined root-affinity now tended to overlap the hereditary family link, apparently as a self-evident truth which did not need to be pitted against the previous incarnations of the idea.

SEVEN

The Hasidic Managing Editor as an Agent of Culture

ZEEV GRIES

THE religious ideals and social institutions of the hasidic movement have aroused considerable scholarly interest as well as popular fascination. By contrast, the history of the hasidic book has attracted little attention. The reason for this seems obvious: while the study of the mystical doctrines of hasidism and their paradoxical, often controversial, expression in communal life tends to revolve round extraordinary personalities and dramatic events, the history of the publication and dissemination of hasidic texts inevitably features more pedestrian processes and relatively colourless personalities—the little-known scribes, copyists, editors, and printers who, for better or for worse, have determined the shape in which hasidic tradition has come down to us and dictated the course and pace of its transmission.[1] The present chapter is an attempt to redress the balance of hasidic scholarship by focusing on the history of hasidic books and on the individuals who saw them into print. In their humble way, they played a crucial part in the process of converting oral traditions to literary documents and thus of constructing not only the collective memory of the hasidic movement but also our own critical perception of its history.

Much of the vast literature of hasidism was derived from the verbal addresses—sermons or homiletic discourses in Yiddish—delivered by the leaders of the movement to the gatherings of their followers at their 'courts', usually for the third sabbath meal or on festival days.[2] The address of the hasidic leader would be committed to memory first and only later, once the holy day was over, would the 'court' scribe record it in writing. However good his memory, though, the scribe was unlikely to produce a verbatim record of the oral discourse since his written version was invariably not only a transcript but also a translation from Yiddish into Hebrew. Like all translations, it contained a certain element of interpretation while also elevating the popular idiom of the original to the more scholarly idiom of Hebrew—a feature which was inherent in the process of translation from Yiddish into Hebrew in general.[3] The outcome was rarely

[1] For a discussion of this state of affairs in hasidic scholarship see Z. Gries, 'Hasidism: The Present State of Research and Some Desirable Priorities', *Numen*, 34: 1 (1987), 97–108.

[2] See J. G. Weiss, 'A Circle of Pneumatics in Pre-Hasidism', *Journal of Jewish Studies*, 8 (1957), 199–213, repr. in id., *Studies in Eastern European Jewish Mysticism* (Oxford, 1985), 31–5; I. Tishby, *The Wisdom of the Zohar* (3 vols.; Oxford, 1989), iii. 1234–6, J. Gartner, 'Se'udah shelishit: Hebetim hilkhatiyim', *Sidra*, 6 (1990), 5–24.

[3] On the close relations between Yiddish and Hebrew ethical literature, and on the issue of translation in particular, see I. Zinberg, *Toledot sifrut Yisrael* (6 vols.; Tel Aviv, 1955–60), iv. 77–88 and the addi-

scrutinized, edited, or even approved by the 'author' (the hasidic master whose discourses were being transcribed and eventually published in this manner); he might have little interest in literary production or be too old and frail to be involved with it personally, or, indeed, his discourses might not be edited and prepared for publication until long after his death.

One important implication of all this is that the living oral traditions of hasidism must have played a more direct, immediate and significant part in determining the nature of the hasidic experience than did any of its written texts—a point which should be borne in mind and to which we shall return at the conclusion of the present chapter. Nevertheless, since the oral traditions of early hasidism are no longer retrievable in their original form, and since our only access to them is through the literary adaptations and translations in which they have been preserved, it is important to shed some light on the often obscure processes of their recension, publication, and dissemination by apparently minor figures whose agency was nevertheless indispensable—the hasidic managing editors.

That the task of the managing editor was fraught with difficulties is clear from such statements as the one which appears in the introduction to *Teshu'ot ḥen* by R. Gedaliah of Luniets. The editor of the book, Yehudah Leib b. Dov Ber of Luniets, apologizes to his readers as follows: 'If the reader should come across errors or find the text difficult to understand, this is the result of scribal incompetence and the problems which are often associated with translation from one language [Yiddish] into another [Hebrew].'[4] Such complaints about the poor quality of the manuscripts, the shortcomings of the scribes, and other aberrations of the texts are extremely common. In many cases the complaints are clearly intended on the one hand to silence any critics of the editorial work and on the other hand to draw attention to the ingenuity and excellence of its final product. This is particularly true of the publication of second or third editions of well-known hasidic books. The managing editor of such an edition would either claim to possess a better manuscript than was available to his predecessors, presumably one written by a more competent scribe, or else promote the superiority of his own editorial skills to those of rival editors. His reasons for doing so would be purely commercial—to capture a market for his new edition of the work.

Two examples of introductions to previously published hasidic works, written by managing editors eager to promote the virtues of their new editions, should suffice to illustrate this point. The first introduces the teachings of Abraham Joshua Heschel of Apta. When his grandson, Meshullam Zusya b. Isaac Meir of Zinkov, published his edition of the famous Zaddik of Apta's teachings in 1861 under the title *Ohev Yisrael*, he was well aware that the same teachings had already been published seven years earlier as *Torat emet* (Lemberg, 1854). He took it upon himself to explain to his readers that

> In Kolbishov [Kolbuszowa] there was only one person who wrote down [the teachings] with my grandfather's knowledge [*biyedi'at*—which does not necessarily imply consent or approval], and in the Holy Community of Jassy there was another man who wrote down a

tional remarks by M. Piekarz, ibid. 251–3; C. Shmeruk, *Sifrut Yidish bePolin* (Jerusalem, 1981), 43–63; C. Turniansky, *Sefer masah umerivah leRabbi Alexander beRabbi Yitsḥak Pfaffenhofen* (Jerusalem, 1985), 58–61.

[4] Gedaliah of Luniets, *Teshu'ot ḥen* [Berdichev, 1816] (Brooklyn, 1982), introd.

little. Towards the end of his [the Zaddik of Apta's] life his son, my father . . . Isaac Meir, of blessed memory, realized that there were too many copyists and that each one was acting on his own understanding. He was afraid that if they were to produce a false record [of the teachings] through error, people would attribute absurd statements to the great zaddik. For this reason he chose one man who was an erudite and sharp witted scholar and an excellent scribe. He appointed him to record the holy utterances of the zaddik. At the end of each sabbath or festival day he [the scribe] would show [his transcripts] to my holy grandfather, of blessed memory, and my grandfather would occasionally correct them as necessary or select from them what he saw fit.

R. Meshullam claims that, after the death of the Zaddik of Apta, when his son R. Isaac Meir (R. Meshullam's own father) succeeded him in office he tried in vain to publish the teachings of his father and finally, in the last two years of his life, he entrusted this task to his son. R. Meshullam reports:

My father ordered that I should take into my house a certain man who was extremely learned and God-fearing, of sufficient maturity and literary skill to put the manuscripts in order, each in its appropriate position. I assisted him in this work, and we consulted my father whenever we encountered a difficulty. My father would put it right from memory, since it is well known that he had been very close to his father and had spent most of his time by his side, day and night.

R. Meshullam concludes his introduction with the statement that he has bought the copyright to these manuscripts and that his is the only authorized version of the teachings. He points out that other manuscript versions had been offered to him by trustworthy men but that he had chosen to exclude them from his own edition in order not to adulterate with extraneous materials the version authorized by both his father and grandfather.

Now it is quite clear that R. Meshullam's edition contained no significant alterations or additions to the previously published teachings of the Zaddik of Apta,[5] and one can only conclude that he was prompted to describe the process of their transmission and recension in such detail simply in order to enhance the commercial value of his enterprise.[6] Nevertheless, while his claim to exclusive rights over the only authentic version of his grandfather's teachings need not be taken too seriously, his account does contain the valuable information that the Zaddik of Apta himself was indifferent to the quality of the transcripts of his teachings which were produced by various scribes and copyists, and that neither he nor his son, R. Meshullam's father, ever published any of these teachings themselves.

The second example is from another introduction to a famous hasidic work, similarly penned by a direct descendant of the 'author'. This is R. Shimshon Halevi Heller who

[5] This has already been observed by Alfasi. See I. Alfasi, *Bisdeh haḥasidut* (Tel Aviv, 1986), 532–4.

[6] The publication history of Zevi Hirsch of Nadworna's *Alfa beta* supplies further illustration of this point. The book had been available in print in several editions before it was published in Berdichev, in 1818, by David Aryeh, the author's son, who claimed in the introduction that all previous editions of the work were unreliable. On close inspection, however, the text of his Berdichev edition has proved to offer no significant improvements on any of the earlier editions. For more details on this case see Z. Gries, *Sifrut hahanhagot* (Jerusalem, 1989), 120–1, 288–9. For a similar claim by another author's son, Eleazar, the son of R. Elimelekh of Lyzhansk, who was critical of the earlier edition of his father's work, see his remarks in the opening lines of the Shklov, 1790 edition of *No'am Elimelekh*.

published an edition of *Yosher divrei emet* by R. Meshullam Phoebus Heller of Zbarazh in Munkacz (Munkachevo) in 1905. In the introduction he claimed that his edition was based on the only authorized version of the teachings and that it contained numerous additions, drawn from authentic 'holy manuscripts', to the previously published versions of the work. The approbation (*haskamah*) by R. Aaron Moses Taubes corroborates this claim:

The material [previously] published in the book *Likutim yekarim* in the name of the above-mentioned [R. Meshullam Phoebus Heller of Zbarazh] consists of short discourses which were transcribed by one of his disciples. He wrote them down to the best of his understanding, but anyone who has examined the remaining manuscripts [of the teachings] of the above mentioned . . . [R. Meshullam Phoebus] would sense and grasp with his own intelligence that the true spirit of these delightful discourses was quite different.

The previously published *Likutim yekarim* was, indeed, an anthology of hasidic traditions ascribed to and probably compiled by R. Meshullam Phoebus of Zbarazh.[7] But both R. Aaron Moses Taubes's approbation and R. Shimshon Halevi Heller's introduction to *Yosher divrei emet* are justified in claiming that the new edition of R. Meshullam Phoebus Heller's teachings contained a considerable amount of previously unpublished material which was not included in either *Likutim yekarim* or *Derekh emet*, the two earlier editions of the work.[8]

The false attribution of teachings to famous hasidic 'authors' was another problem about which the managing editors often complained. Elsewhere I have been able to demonstrate the false attribution of authorship in the literary traditions of both the Stolin and the Kozienice dynasties.[9] This was not at all uncommon, and the complaints of the managing editors on this score were fully justified. Authors and works were matched together arbitrarily, not only because of the generally corrupt state in which hasidic manuscripts were circulating but also because the original scribes and copyists often neglected to ascribe their transcripts of the teachings to any particular hasidic master. Presumably, in the initial stages the 'authorship' of any body of hasidic teachings was common knowledge within the court from which it had originated. But by the time the manuscript copies of the teachings were being edited for publication—often many years or even decades later—no one could be sure of the identity of the original 'author'.[10]

This was a characteristic feature of hasidic literature from the outset. As early as the beginning of the 1780s, a scribe had mixed up the discourses of the Maggid of Mezhirech with the sayings of the famous founder of hasidism, Israel Baal Shem Tov.[11] The popular hasidic book *Darkhei tsedek* was similarly the product of an attempt by the managing editor to abridge and combine the discourses of R. Jacob Joseph of

[7] See on this J. G. Weiss, 'The Kavvanoth of Prayer in Early Hasidism', *Journal of Jewish Studies*, 9 (1958), 163–92 repr. in id., *Eastern European Jewish Mysticism*, 122–4, n. 57.

[8] On the editorial problems connected with *Likutim yekarim* see Z. Gries, 'Arikhat tsava'at haRivash', *Kiryat sefer*, 52 (1977), 193–5.

[9] See Gries, *Sifrut hahanhagot*, 111–12, 130–2. For similar problems in the editions of both *Toledot Ya'akov Yosef* [Korets, 1780] and *Maggid devarav leYa'akov* [Korets, 1781], see the discussion below.

[10] See on this Gries, 'Hasidism' 104; 107 n. 11.

[11] See Gries, *Sifrut hahanhagot*, 174 and n. 95 on that page.

Polonnoye with those of the Maggid of Mezhirech.[12] This apparent lack of concern for the proper attribution of authorship was defended by the managing editors on the grounds that they were eager to publish the 'holy manuscripts' in the precise state in which they had been preserved. For this reason the books often contained whole sections of text which reproduced previously published materials without any acknowledgement or possibly even awareness of this fact.[13]

We do not as yet possess a complete literary history of hasidism. The development of the distinct literary genres in which the movement expressed itself in print—the homiletic (*derush*), the ethical conduct (*hanhagot*), the epistolary (*igerot*), and the hagiographical (*shevaḥim*), not to mention the large volume of halakhic writings produced mainly by nineteenth-century Polish hasidism—has not been documented systematically or placed in any historical context, whether Jewish or general European. In focusing on the activities of the hasidic managing editors who played a crucial part in the evolution of all these genres, the present discussion attempts to supply such a context in which hasidic literature may be evaluated in socio-historical terms.

Little is known about the managing editor of the early history of Jewish printing. He was first referred to as *magiha* (proof-reader) and eventually came to be known as the *mevi leveit hadefus* (literally: the one who brings [the manuscript] to the printing press), usually abbreviated to *malbihad*. Like his Gentile contemporary, the Jewish managing editor played a decisive role in the process of book production. He was often a member of the educated classes—sufficiently versed in the subject matter to be in a position to select the best manuscript version of each of the books he published. Indeed, we find Jewish rabbinical scholars as well as Christian priests involved in editorial work,[14] and the famous Antwerp publishing house of Plantin put out a collection of reference works for the use of proof-readers and editors.[15] One of the few personalities in the world of early Jewish publishing to have attracted some scholarly attention is Samuel Boehm, who was active, first in Italy and later in Poland, during the last quarter of the sixteenth century.[16] However, the scale of his operations has not been fully appreciated, and no attempt has been made to define his position and function, or indeed those of his fellow managing editors, in the history of Hebrew printing. He, and others like him, had set

[12] Ibid. 112–14.

[13] This was the case, for example, with the collection of 'conducts' (*hanhagot*) of Jacob Isaac, the Seer of Lublin, as published in his *Divrei emet*. See Gries, *Sifrut hahanhagot*, 128. Generally, the written or printed versions of oral teachings of the leaders were not regarded as authoritative 'sacred writings' in themselves, as will be shown below. In the light of this attitude, the managing editor's explanations in his introduction to *Divrei emet* are but a feeble excuse for his failure to edit the text he published.

[14] See P. H. Hirsch, *Printing, Selling and Reading, 1450–1550* (Wiesbaden, 1967; rev. edn., 1974), 47; E. Eisenstein, *The Printing Press as an Agent of Change* (New York, 1985), 55.

[15] See L. Voet, *The Golden Compasses: A History and Evaluation of the Publishing Activities of the Officina Plantiniana at Antwerp* (2 vols.; Amsterdam, 1969–72), i. 339; Eisenstein, *The Printing Press* 75.

[16] See F. H. Wettstein, 'Letoledot gedolei Yisrael', in *Sefer hayovel likhvod Naḥum Sokolov* (Warsaw, 1904), 280; I. Sonne, 'Expurgation of Hebrew Books: The Work of Jewish Scholars: A Contribution to the History of Censorship of Hebrew Books in Italy in the Sixteenth Century', *Bulletin of the New York Public Library*, 46 (1942), 1000–1; M. Benayahu, *Hadefus ha'ivri biKremona* (Jerusalem, 1971), 58–9; id., *Haskamah ureshut bidfusei Venetsiah* (Jerusalem, 1971), 198–200. Samuel Boehm and his involvement in Hebrew printing in Poland were the subject of an unpublished paper entitled 'The Early Printing of Hebrew Ethical Books in Poland' which I presented to the International Conference on Polish Jewry held in Jerusalem in the winter of 1988.

the standards and patterns of work for future generations of managing editors. They were scholars who had mastered rabbinic literature, skilful editors of texts, independently wealthy or else well connected and thus in a position to raise funds for the production of certain books, in partnership either with the printers or with the sponsors (who would be listed on the front page as 'the facilitators'—*hamishtadelim*). As for the hasidic managing editors of the late eighteenth to the twentieth centuries, practically no work has been done to identify them or to define their role in the context of the history of Jewish printing in general or in the history of hasidic book production in particular.

Among the hasidic managing editors one finds the dedicated disciples of famous hasidic masters, such as Solomon of Lutsk, who was a disciple of the Maggid of Mezhirech, or Nathan Sternhartz of Nemirov, who was a disciple of R. Nahman of Bratslav,[17] as well as the offspring of hasidic masters, such as Solomon of Ludmir, who saw to print the book *Or haganuz* which contained the teachings of his maternal grandfather R. Judah Loeb of Annopol. In this case, however, Solomon of Ludmir's share in the production of the book was limited, while the editorial work was carried out by one of the leading hasidic managing editors of his time, R. Moses Hacohen b. R. Isaiah, son-in-law of R. Issachar who was the grandson of the Maggid of Kozienice.[18] To this list should be added the colourful figure of Michael Levi (Frumkin) Rodkinson whose life story, including numerous romantic entanglements, a wide-ranging literary activity which encompassed the compilation of hasidic tales, active involvement in both the Hebrew and the Yiddish periodical presses, the translation of the Talmud into English, and much more besides, still awaits the comprehensive biography which it deserves.[19] Rodkinson introduced a certain element of Haskalah sensibility to his editorial work, and this was evident even in his hasidic publications. He was brought up in the hasidic environment of Habad and was a direct descendant of one of its most prominent figures, R. Aaron Halevi of Starosielce. His large output of hasidic hagiographical tales was thus the product not only of his intimate association with the hasidic world from which he had come—and especially the hasidic school of Habad, which was actively involved in the preservation of hasidic hagiography—but also of the Haskalah world which he entered, a world which displayed a marked interest in Jewish folk tradition and legend as a part of its mission to promote the national spirit of the Jewish people.[20]

[17] On Nathan Sternhartz's involvement in the publication of Nahman of Bratslav's works see J. G. Weiss, *Meḥkarim bahasidut Braslav*, ed. M. Piekarz (Jerusalem, 1974), 257–71, and esp. 275–7; Z. Gries, 'Kuntres hanhagot ne'elam leRabi Naḥman miBraslav?', *Kiryat sefer*, 53 (1978), 767–8.

[18] See the introd. to Judah Loeb of Annopol's *Or haganuz* (Lemberg, 1866). R. Moses Hacohen discussed his editorial difficulties at length in his introductions to two other hasidic books, *Divrei Shemuel* by Samuel Shmelke of Nikolsburg (Mikulov), published in Lemberg in 1862, and *Da'at Moshe* by R. Moses Eliakim Briah, published in Lemberg in 1879.

[19] See G. Kressel, *Leksikon hasifrut ha'ivrit badorot ha'aḥaronim* (2 vols.; Tel Aviv, 1967), ii. 838–9, and the bibliography there; J. Dan, *Hasipur haḥasidi* (Jerusalem, 1975), 195–220; G. Nigal, *Hasiporet haḥasidit: Toledoteihah venoseihah* (Jerusalem, 1981), 28–31; id., *Sipurei Michael Levi Rodkinson* (Jerusalem, 1989), 7–14.

[20] See Z. Gries, 'Der jüdische Hintergrund für Bubers Vorgehen bei seiner Gestaltung der chassidischen Erzählungen', in M. Buber, *Die Geschichten des Rabbi Nachman* (Heidelberg, 1989) (publ. in Heb. trans. as 'Hareka hayehudi life'ulato shel Buber be'itsuv hasipur haḥasidi', *Meḥkerei Yerushalayim befolklor yehudi*, 11–12 (1990), 46–56); id. *Sefer, sofer, vesipur bereshit haḥasidut* (Tel Aviv, 1992), 37–8; 48; 123–4 nn. 107–8; 127 nn. 8–10.

As I have pointed out elsewhere, the Habad school was distinguished by its historiographical concerns almost from the outset. It had adopted certain elements of Haskalah ideology and techniques for the purpose of recording its own history and the history of the hasidic movement as a whole.[21] In his literary activities and publication ventures,[22] Rodkinson exemplifies this mid-nineteenth-century interrelationship between hasidism and certain aspects of Haskalah. Both movements were engaged in intensive literary activity as a means of constructing community spirit.

Any definition of the function of the hasidic managing editor is bound to be somewhat fluid. At times his involvement in the production of books would be primarily financial. He would employ a printer in whose workshop a proof-reader would be employed who would be responsible for editing and proof-reading the text. Without performing the technical work himself, the managing editor might then act in a supervisory capacity and oversee the entire process of production, since the financial risk entailed in the venture would be entirely his own. He would usually be responsible for marketing the book in advance, and would attempt to establish the size of its potential market in order to determine the appropriate scale of investment. He would also deal with distribution, sometimes selling the books himself. At other times the managing editor would take on the responsibility of proof-reading himself. He would thus be involved personally, day by day, in every stage of the production and distribution of the books he managed. Both these patterns of involvement had been established long before the rise of hasidism, since the early days of Jewish printing.

The career of Solomon of Lutsk, who was a close disciple of the Maggid of Mezhirech, can best illustrate the full range of the managing editor's activities in the environment of early hasidism. He was not only an accomplished editor of texts but he also financed the publication of books in Korets,[23] worked in partnership as a printer in Poritsk,[24] and authored a homiletic work of his own. Although, through his involvement in all these aspects of Hebrew book publishing, he clearly enjoyed good access to the facility of print, he never published his own work, and it was not until long after his death that his *Divrat Shelomo* was published in Zolkiew (Zholkva) in 1848.[25] His apparent failure to see to the publication of his own writings reflected the common hasidic attitude to the printed book: early hasidism did not consider the book an important tool for the dissemination of hasidic ideas or the construction of a distinctive

[21] On the historiographical activities of the Habad school, see Gries, 'Hasidism', 101–3; A. Rapoport-Albert, 'Hagiography with Footnotes: Edifying Tales and the Writing of History in Hasidism', *History and Theory, Beiheft* 27, *Essays in Jewish Historiography* (1988), 119–59; id., 'Hasidism after 1772: Structural Continuity and Change', Ch. 6 above; I. Bartal, 'Shimon hakofer: Perek behistoriografiah ortodoksit', in I. Bartal, E. Mendelsohn, and C. Turniansky (eds.), *Keminhag Ashkenaz uPolin: Sefer yovel leChone Shmeruk* (Jerusalem, 1994), 243–68; Gries, *Sefer, sofer, vesipur*, 17; 33; 110 n. 1; 119 n. 84.

[22] See Nigal, *Sipurei Michael*, 13 n. 24.

[23] See A. Tauber, 'Defusei Korets' *Kiryat sefer*, 1 (1924–5), 303–4.

[24] See H. D. Friedberg, *Toledot hadefus ha'ivri bePolaniah* [Antwerp, 1932], 71–2 (2nd edn., Tel Aviv, 1950), 93). See also A. Ya'ari's review of this book in *Kiryat sefer*, 9 (1932–3), 438, as well as id., 'Likutim bibliografiyim 49: Hadefus ha'ivri bePoritsk', *Kiryat sefer*, 20 (1943–4), 110–15, and I. Rivkind, 'Letoledot hadefus ha'ivri bePolin', *Kiryat sefer*, 11 (1934–5), 394–5.

[25] *Divrat Shelomo* was published with an undated approbation by Jacob Isaac, the Seer of Lublin, and a letter by the author's son, acknowledging with thanks a generous donation which helped finance the publication of the book.

community ethos; both of these functions were performed primarily by the circulation of oral traditions.

The earliest information we possess about the activities of Solomon of Lutsk dates back to the late 1770s when, in partnership with a certain Simon b. Judah Loeb Ashkenazi —invariably referred to as an old man—he financed the publication of a number of kabbalistic and hasidic books at the famous printing press of Zevi Hirsch Margolis in Korets.[26] Margolis had begun his career as a printer in Novy Oleksiniec, with the publication of the first anthology of anti-hasidic proclamations, *Zemir aritsim veḥarevot tsurim* (Oleksiniec, 1772). He later moved to Korets and continued to be involved in printing there together with his son-in-law Samuel b. Issachar Ber Segal, who was eventually to become the most prominent Jewish printer in eastern Poland and Belorussia.[27]

Simon Ashkenazi and Solomon of Lutsk, in partnership or independently of one another, collaborated also with J. A. Krieger, the Gentile German printer who published numerous Jewish books in Poland during this period.[28] Another of Solomon's partners was his son-in-law, who became managing editor and joined his publishing enterprises in Korets,[29] eventually, together with a third partner—Elimelekh b. Jacob Lutsk—founding a Hebrew printing press in Poritsk in 1786.[30] When the third partner died in late 1788 or early 1789, Solomon's son-in-law opened his own printing presses in both Korets and Ostrog.[31]

The publications in which Solomon of Lutsk was involved as managing editor

[26] Regarding the kabbalistic books, see Zohar (Korets, 1778) and see Tauber's remarks in 'Defusei Korets', 303 no. 2, as well as I. Yudlov, *Ginzei Yisrael* (Jerusalem, 1985), no. 1070. See also *Sefer yetsirah* (Korets, 1779), and see Tauber's remarks in 'Defusei Korets', 303–4 no. 3; *Tikunei zohar* (Korets, 1780), and see Tauber's remarks, 'Defusei Korets', 304 no. 4.

Regarding the hasidic books, see Jacob Joseph of Polonnoye, *Toledot Ya'akov Yosef* (Korets, 1780) and Tauber's remarks, 'Defusei Korets', 304 no. 6; Dov Ber of Mezhirech, *Likutei amarim: Maggid devarav leYa'akov* (Korets, 1781) and Tauber's remarks, 'Defusei Korets', 304 no. 8. Tauber did not note Simon b. Judah Loeb Ashkenazi as Solomon of Lutsk's partner in the publication of *Likutei amarim* since his name did not appear on the title page, but Solomon referred to R. Simon as his partner in his first introduction to the book.

[27] See Gries, 'Kuntres hanhagot' 776–8, and the additional bibliography there.

[28] See Nathan Shapiro, *Maḥberet hakodesh* (Korets, 1783), which Solomon of Lutsk edited on his own, without the collaboration of his partner Simon Ashkenazi Cf. A. Tauber, 'Defusei Korets: Hemshekh', *Kiryat sefer*, 2 (1925–6), 64 no. 15. On the other hand, *Sefer hapeli'ah* (Korets, 1784) was published by Simon Ashkenazi without the collaboration of Solomon of Lutsk. Cf. Tauber, 'Defusei Korets: Hemshekh', 65 no. 23. The 2nd edn. of Dov Ber of Mezhirech's *Maggid devarav leYa'akov* (Korets, 1784) was published by both partners in collaboration. Cf. Tauber, 'Defusei Korets: Hemshekh', 66 no. 24. However, Hayyim Vital's *Ets Hayim* (Korets, 1784), was published, according to the approbation of R. Yitsḥak Isaac of Ostrog who was in Korets at the time of writing, by Simon Ashkenazi and his son-in-law, without the collaboration of Solomon of Lutsk. Cf. Tauber, 'Defusei Korets: Hemshekh', 218 no. 46. For the publication of Menahem Azariah Fano's *Kanfei yonah* (4 vols; Korets, 1786), Simon Ashkenazi had acquired a new partner, R. Eliezer Lieber. See Tauber, 'Defusei Korets: Hemshekh,' 218 no. 47.

[29] See Isaac Tyrnau, *Sefer minhagim* (Korets, 1781), which R. Abraham, Solomon of Lutsk's son-in-law, published in partnership with R. Gedaliah b. Eliakim, employing the services of the printers Zevi Hirsch Margolis and his son-in-law, Samuel b. Issachar Baer Segal. Cf. Tauber, 'Defusei Korets', 304 no. 8. R. Abraham also published Isaac Luria's *Sefer hakavonot* (Korets, 1784), acting as sole managing editor, in collaboration with the printer J. A. Krieger. On Krieger's activities see E. Ringelblum, 'Johann Anton Krieger der Nayhofer druker fun hebreishe sforim', *Yivo Bleter*, 7 (1934), 88–109.

[30] See Ya'ari, 'Likutim bibliografiyim' 102.

[31] See I. Ta-Shma, 'Hadefus ha'ivri be'Ostraha: Tikunim vehashlamot', *Alei sefer*, 6–7 (1979), 210.

include some which he edited himself and others for which he supplied the financial backing only. For example, together with his partner Simon Ashkenazi, and at the invitation of the author's son and son-in-law, he financed the publication of, but did not personally edit, R. Jacob Joseph of Polonnoye's *Toledot Ya'akov Yosef*. The author, who was an old man by that time, was either unable or unwilling to supervise the publication of the work himself. The book was published in Korets in 1780, and the Korets proof-reader who edited the text, Alexander Ziskind b. Mordecai of Zhitomir, appended to it a characteristic disclaimer to the effect that such errors as may have occurred in the text were the result not of his own incompetence but of the fact that the edition was based on a number of copies, made by various scribes, of the original autograph of R. Jacob Joseph of Polonnoye—a manuscript which he was not able to inspect himself. Indeed, as was observed by Piekarz, *Toledot Ya'akov Yosef* contains a considerable number of apparent inconsistencies: the same statement may be quoted in the name of one hasidic master on one occasion and in the name of another on another occasion.[32] It is not clear why R. Solomon of Lutsk, who was, after all, an accomplished editor himself (he produced a model edition of the Maggid of Mezhirech's *Maggid devarav leYa'akov*, as we shall see below), did not take personal charge of the editorial work on *Toledot Ya'akov Yosef*, to help the proof-reader out of his textual quandaries. He may have been excluded from such intimate involvement with the text by the author or his relatives, who might have wished to control the work themselves or to adhere as faithfully as possible to the original transcripts of R. Jacob Joseph's homilies, however crude their editorial state. But this explanation, which presupposes a reverential attitude to the precise written form in which the homilies were preserved, is incompatible with the common disregard within hasidism for the manner and shape in which the oral teachings of the masters were being committed to writing. This attitude had prevailed for the first eight decades of hasidic publication history, and it is not at all impossible that, rather than wishing to control the final recension of the text themselves or to preserve for posterity in print the most 'authentic' and comprehensive manuscript version of R. Jacob Joseph's teachings, in fact neither the author nor his relatives were particularly concerned with the state of the manuscripts on which the edition was based. Since these manuscript versions of the teachings were produced by more than one hand, and since they derived from R. Jacob Joseph's verbal addresses which had been delivered at different times and places over a period of many years, it was inevitable that they should contain some repetitions, inaccuracies, and erroneous attributions which the family simply did not identify as a problem requiring careful editorial attention.

This impression, that such indifference to the accuracy of written texts, which were derived from the oral teachings of the masters, was not at all uncommon in the hasidic camp, is strengthened by the fact that a similar situation obtained in the hasidic court of Kozienice, even though its early leaders were particularly noted for their interest in the dissemination of knowledge through print. R. Israel b. Shabbetai, the famous Maggid of Kozienice, is known to have initiated and sponsored the republication of the Maharal of Prague's works which had been out of print for over two centuries. He was

[32] See M. Piekarz, *Biyemei tsemiḥat haḥasidut: Megamot ra'ayoniot besifrei derush umusar* (Jerusalem, 1978), 20, 27, 29, 31.

also involved in the publication of various midrashic and halakhic works, for dozens of which he supplied his personal approbation (*haskamah*). Nevertheless, neither he nor his son Moses Eliakim Briah ever attempted to record their own hasidic teachings in book form or otherwise to disseminate them more widely through the services of the printing press.[33]

Solomon of Lutsk was faced with the problems arising from this attitude on more than one occasion. In 1701, in collaboration with his partner, he edited *Likutei amarim*—also titled *Maggid devarav leYa'akov*—by the Great Maggid of Mezhirech. In his first introduction to the book he drew attention to the editorial difficulties it presented. Like the editor of *Toledot Ya'akov Yosef*, he was forced to base the edition on a number of manuscript versions of the teachings which had been produced by various scribes or copyists at different times and places, without the benefit of comparison with the Maggid's own autograph version. He claimed that he would not have undertaken the task at all if not for the Maggid's personal encouragement. Since the Maggid of Mezhirech died in 1772 while the book was not published until 1781, it seems that the preparation of the manuscript for print was a complicated and lengthy task indeed. That Solomon of Lutsk carried it out with the utmost precision and care is borne out by the comparison of his edition with the various manuscript versions which were available to him. Time and again, when confronted by several alternative versions of the same text, he chose the one that offered the best reading and must have best preserved the original statements of the Maggid.

There was another reason for Solomon's initial reluctance to undertake the preparation of the Maggid's collection of teachings for publication. This, as he states in the same introduction, was related to the contents of the work rather than to the state of its manuscript versions. The Maggid's homilies contained interpretations of the highly esoteric Lurianic kabbalah. Unlike the works of Moses Cordovero, which guided their readers towards a sound understanding of the mystical doctrines of classical kabbalah, the teachings of Luria had been addressed to a select group of intimate disciples and were not intended for wider circulation. They were liable to be misunderstood, and Solomon of Lutsk was reluctant to make them accessible to an unqualified readership through the publication of the 'Lurianic' homilies of the Maggid of Mezhirech.

Whether it was on account of the engagingly lively address to the readers which it contained, or by reason of the high esteem in which Solomon of Lutsk himself was held, his introduction to *Maggid devarav leYa'akov* became the model for subsequent hasidic managing editors, who prefaced the books they published with similar explanatory remarks. They shared with the readers the difficulties they encountered in the preparation for publication of corrupt manuscript versions of teachings whose 'authors'—the hasidic masters in whose verbal addresses the written versions of the teachings had originated—were not themselves concerned to preserve them in a coherent and reliable form.[34]

In addition to his involvement with the publication of hasidic texts, Solomon of

[33] See Z. Gries, 'Rabbi Yisrael b. Shabbetai haMagid miKozienice uferushav lemasekhet avot', in R. Elior, I. Bartal, and C. Shmeruk (eds.), *Tsadikim ve'anshei ma'aseh* (Jerusalem, 1994), 127–65. See also the managing editor's introduction to Moses Eliakim Briah's *Da'at Moshe*.

[34] See e.g. the managing editors' introductions to Israel b. Shabbetai, the Maggid of Kozienice's *Avodat Yisrael* (Josefov, 1842), Jeḥiel Michel, the Maggid of Zloczow's *Mayim rabim* (Warsaw, 1899), and R. Menahem Mendel Hager of Kosov's *Ahavat shalom* (Lemberg, 1833).

Lutsk was intensely active in propagating the study of kabbalah through print. With his partner he published an edition of the Zohar (Korets, 1778), of the *Book of Creation* (*Sefer yetsirah*) with the commentary *Otsar adonai* (Korets, 1779) by the kabbalist Moses b. Jacob of Kiev, author of *Shoshan sodot*, and of the *Tikunei zohar* (Korets, 1780), as well as editing from manuscript and publishing on his own a work which he discovered in the library of the *beit midrash* of Mezhirech, *Maḥberet hakodesh* (Korets, 1783)—a collection of Lurianic customs compiled by the Polish kabbalist Nathan Shapiro as an addition to Hayyim Vital's *Peri ets ḥayyim*.

The scholars of the *beit midrash* of Mezhirech, who were the signatories to the letter of approbation introducing *Maḥberet hakodesh*, reported in it that they had encouraged and urged Solomon of Lutsk to undertake the publication of the work. This is further proof of Solomon's own reluctance to publish and thus publicize Lurianic (as opposed to classical) kabbalah. They referred also to the existence in their *beit midrash* of a collection of kabbalistic manuscripts assembled by one of their number, a certain R. Mordecai.

Solomon of Lutsk and the scholars of the *beit midrash* of Mezhirech were not alone in displaying such a keen interest in the publication of kabbalistic works during this period. R. Levi Isaac of Berdichev in his approbation of the book *Kanfei yonah* by the Lurianic kabbalist Menahem Azariah of Fano (Korets, 1786) refers to another managing editor, R. Eleazar Loeb, who made a point of searching out valuable old kabbalistic manuscripts in order to print them. All these isolated items of information combine to suggest that we still know very little about the channels through which kabbalistic works were distributed and studied during the final decades of the eighteenth century. What is clear, however, is that it was precisely during this period that the study of speculative Lurianic kabbalah was becoming a popular pursuit.[35]

The same approbation by the scholars of the *beit midrash* of Mezhirech provides an additional insight into the conditions in which the study of kabbalistic texts was facilitated: libraries such as the one situated in the *beit midrash* of the town of Mezhirech must have existed in many other Jewish communities. Their prevalence, scope, and contents have not been sufficiently studied, and their full history in the context of the intellectual and cultural life of eastern European Jewry is yet to be written. Notably, in a memorandum to the Austrian authorities dated 22 March 1838, the maskil Joseph Perl urged that the *batei midrash* libraries in the towns which contained large concentrations of hasidic inhabitants should be investigated in order to expose what he considered to be the 'subversive' religious activities of the hasidim.[36] It is not his polemical or political aims that concern us here but rather the importance he clearly ascribed to these libraries, which functioned as centres of intellectual life for the local Jewish intelligentsia. It would appear that, sometime in the course of the second half of the

[35] See Gries, *Sifrut hahanhagot*, 16–18, 42–5, 56–7, 81–6, 91. See also, and at length, M. Idel, 'One from a Town, Two from a Clan: The Question of the Diffusion of Lurianic Kabbalah and Sabbateanism: A Re-examination', *Jewish History*, 7 (1993), 79–104, id.; 'Perceptions of the Kabbalah in the Second Half of the Eighteenth Century', *Journal of Jewish Thought and Philosophy*, 1 (1991), 56–114; Z. Gries, 'Bein sifrut lehistoriah: hakdamot lediyun ve'iyun be*Shivḥei haBesht*', *Tura*, 3 (1994), 161–5.

[36] See S. Assaf, 'Sifriyot batei hamidrash', *Yad lakore*, 1: 7–9 (1946–7), 170–1, R. Mahler, *Haḥasidut vehahaskalah* (Merhavya, 1946), 168–71, 451–5, id., *Hasidism and the Jewish Enlightenment* (Philadelphia, 1985), 134–40; Z. Gries, 'Between History and Literature: The Case of Jewish Preaching', *Journal of Jewish Thought and Philosophy* 4: 1 (1994), 120.

eighteenth century, manuscripts and valuable books of kabbalah had found their way from the private collections of dedicated kabbalists to the local public libraries of eastern European *batei midrash*. This is not a mere shift of location but a sign of the very transformation of kabbalistic study during this period: kabbalistic works were now being diffused in much wider circles of eastern European readers. This process of diffusion was either initiated or stimulated by the activities of such industrious managing editors as Solomon of Lutsk, R. Eleazar Loeb, and others who clearly served as important agents of change in this respect.

As has already been observed by the late Haim Lieberman, Solomon of Lutsk was by no means concerned solely or even primarily with the publication of hasidic books. The printing press he founded with his partners in Poritsk did not publish a single hasidic book.[37] Moreover, the last of the books they did publish there was *Margaliot hatorah* (Poritsk, 1788) by Zevi Hirsch b. Samuel Zanvil Segal, a student of the most famous opponent of hasidism, the Gaon of Vilna.[38] This fact not only provides us with further evidence to the effect that the hasidic movement did not, at this stage, ascribe much value to the preservation and distribution in print of its orally transmitted teachings, but it also suggests that the gulf between the intellectual worlds of hasidim and mitnaggedim was not as wide as we might have imagined.[39]

Turning now to Solomon of Lutsk's other capacity, that of hasidic author, his book *Divrat Shelomo* provides valuable insights into his personal educational background and method of writing. The book is a homiletic commentary on the Torah, drawing on a variety of literary sources which are, as a rule, quoted from memory, without verification of the precise location and wording of the passages quoted. The sources from which the quotations are drawn represent the library of works with which, through regular study, Solomon was intimately acquainted: Gemara, Midrash *Rabbah*, standard Bible commentaries, for example, Rashi's, Nahmanides', and, though quoted less frequently, Jacob b. Asher's commentary on the Torah, as well as *Ma'asei adonai* by Eliezer Ashkenazi, the famous aggadic anthology *Tana devei Eliyahu*, and the Zohar, which is quoted, or rather paraphrased, on almost every page. That Solomon was quoting from memory without checking his sources becomes obvious when one encounters, for example, a reference to a 'Gemara' passage which is not to be found anywhere in the Gemara but only in Midrash *Bereshit rabbah*.[40] In this respect, as was

[37] See H. Lieberman, *Ohel Raḥel* (3 vols.; New York, 1980–4), iii. 59–60.

[38] Zevi Hirsch b. Samuel Zanvil Segal, *Margaliyot hatorah* (Poritsk, 1788), the approbations.

[39] Another indication of this is the fact that Hayyim of Volozhin, the famous disciple of the Gaon of Vilna, and the eminent hasidic leader Levi Isaac of Berdichev were able to give their approbations to the same books and have them published alongside each other. See on this Lieberman, *Ohel Raḥel*, i. 127–8; S. Stampfer, 'Rabi Hayyim miVolozhin vehaskamotav', *Alei sefer*, 4 (1977), 165–7; Z. Gries, 'Sifrut hahanhagot haḥasidit', *Zion*, 46 (1981), 230–3. In the light of this, Balaban's claim (M. Balaban, *Yidn in Poyln* (Vilna, 1930), 229–30) that, during the controversy between the hasidim and the mitnaggedim, both sides repeatedly attempted to use the weapon of censorship by the non-Jewish authorities against one another's literatures requires some modification: such attempts were only sporadic and local.

[40] Cf. Solomon of Lutsk, *Divrat Shelomo* (Zolkiew (Zholkva), 1848), on 'Ḥayei Sarah', 4*c* with *Bereshit rabbah*, 58:3. It is obvious that Solomon of Lutsk is quoting from *Bereshit rabbah* and not from the parallel passage in *Yalkut shim'oni* on 'Esther', 1045, since the *Yalkut* has a different reading here. For other casual, paraphrastic quotations from the Gemara cf. *Divrat Shelomo* on 'Bereshit', 3*c*, with the Babylonian Talmud, Ber. 5*a*; *Divrat Shelomo* on 'Vayetse', 10*b*, with Bab. Tal., Ḥul. 89*a*.

observed by Piekarz,[41] Solomon of Lutsk was following in the eastern European tradition of casual, often imprecise, references to sources quoted. A hasidic hagiographical tradition alludes to this habit while crediting the Sefardim with the discipline of weaving into their sermons well-informed and precise quotations. This is a tale, recorded in *Shivḥei haBesht*, about R. Gershon of Kutow, the brother-in-law of the Besht, who, when invited on one occasion to preach [to a largely Sefardi audience] in Jerusalem, where 'it is the custom of the preachers . . . to give exact quotes from the Gemara, the Midrash, or Bible, and they are shamed if they make any changes in the text', 'prepared himself for this sermon by rehearsing the text several times so that he could quote the words exactly', and 'did not sleep the whole night' until 'by dawn his throat was sore'.[42] This echo of the apparent difference between the Ashkenazi sermon and its Sefardi counterpart must be qualified by the evidence of the famous Sefardi scholar, traveller, and prolific author Hayyim Joseph David Azulai (the *Ḥida*), a contemporary of the hasidic protagonists of *Shivḥei haBesht*, who noted in his personal diary, *Ma'agal tov*, that local Sefardi preachers whom he encountered during his travels in Tunisia were similarly prone to quote their sources inaccurately from memory.[43]

Solomon of Lutsk was capable of attributing to *ḥazal* (the sages of late antiquity) a medieval phrase which he uses often: *kol ha'olamot kegarger ḥardal lefanav* ('all the worlds are as a grain of mustard to Him'),[44] a phrase which originates in Gabirol's *Keter malkhut* but which had almost certainly become familiar to Solomon and his readers through the popular hasidic book *Tsava'at haRibash*,[45] or the kabbalistic works *Reshit ḥokhmah* and *Shenei luḥot haberit*.[46] Such impressionistic attributions of medieval and even later phrases to the classical rabbinic idiom of *ḥazal* were not at all unusual. The famous medieval saying, originating in the Zohar, *hakol talui bemazal, afilu sefer torah shebaheikhal* ('Everything depends on fortune, even the scroll of the Law in the Holy Ark'),[47] was attributed to *ḥazal* by many authors, as was the hasidic saying which appears in *Shivḥei haBesht*: *kol hamesaper beshivḥei tsadikim ke'osek bema'aseh merkavah* ('He who tells stories in praise of the zaddikim is [considered] as though he was concentrating on the mystery of the divine Chariot') for which Scholem had found an earlier Sabbatean source, but which was attributed to *ḥazal* ('our sages') in a non-hasidic book published several years prior to the publication of *Shivḥei haBesht*.[48]

Solomon of Lutsk's *Divrat Shelomo* also contains quotations from Lurianic writings,[49]

[41] See Piekarz, *Biyemei tsemiḥat haḥasidut*, 13–14.

[42] Dov Ber b. Shmuel, *Shivḥei haBesht* [Kopys, 1814], ed. B. Mintz (Tel Aviv, 1961), 71; trans. D. Ben-Amos and J. R. Mintz as *In Praise of the Baal Shem Tov* (Bloomington, Ind., 1970), tale 55, 73.

[43] See Hayyim Joseph David Azulai, *Ma'agal tov*, ed. A. Freimann (Jerusalem, 1934), 57, 62–3.

[44] See *Divrat Shelomo* on 'Vayera', 4*c*; on 'Toledot', 5*c*; on 'Vayetse', 5*d*, and on 'Vayeshev', 9*c*, where the phrase is attributed to *ḥazal* ('our sages').

[45] See Solomon Ibn Gabirol, *Shirei hakodesh*, ed. D. Jarden (2 vols.; Jerusalem, 1971–3), i. 51. Cf. *Tsava'at haRibash* [n.p. (Ostrog?), 1793; Zolkiew, 1795], ed. J. I. Schochet (Brooklyn, NY, 1975), 6.

[46] See Elijah b. Moses De Vidas, *Reshit ḥokhmah* (Jerusalem, 1972), 216*c*; Isaiah b. Abraham Halevi Horowitz, *Shenei luḥot haberit* (Amsterdam, 1698), 48*a*.

[47] See Zohar, 3:154*a*.

[48] See *In Praise*, 1, 199, and cf. Z. Gries, review of M. Meged's *Ha'or haneḥshakh*, *Kiryat sefer*, 55 (1980), 376 n. 24; id., *Sifrut hahanhagot*, 141, n. 153.

[49] See e.g. *Divrat Shelomo* on 'Bereshit', 3*b*; on 'Noaḥ', 3*c*; on 'Lekh lekha', 3*d*–4*a*; on 'Ḥayei Sarah', 4*c*, 4*d*, 5*a*; on 'Vayetse', 5*d*; on 'Vayishlaḥ', 8*a*, 9*c*; on 'Vayeshev', 10*d*, and so on.

as well as quotations, or reports on teachings heard, from the Maggid of Mezhirech.[50] But the book is primarily a traditional homiletic commentary on Scripture; the concern to admonish the readers to adhere to the strictures of halakhah is secondary,[51] while the specifically hasidic approach to Scripture is even less prominent and lies outside the scope of the present discussion.

Solomon's career, especially his activities in the diverse capacities of managing editor, provides an insight into what must be acknowledged as a crucially important and yet relatively obscure aspect of the history of hasidism. Since hasidic lore was transmitted orally long before it was committed to writing, and since the oral traditions have come down to us largely through the mediation of such men as Solomon of Lutsk and his fellow managing editors, it is important to study their modes of operation in order to assess their reliability as transmitters of tradition, to gauge the extent to which they might have shaped the tradition themselves, and altogether to reconstruct the historical context in which the literature of hasidism came to represent a hasidic experience which was not essentially literary but rather a direct, immediate, personal experience of relationship with the hasidic leader and his community of followers. The very function of literature as a reflection of experience must be examined against the background of the growing body of recent research on the transition from oral to written tradition in various societies the world over.[52] The history of the hasidic book is the history of the transition from oral to written lore in hasidism. The relationship between the two, and the precise place, function, and weight ascribed to each one by the society which generated them, is an issue which still requires careful examination.

This is borne out by a remark made by S. Y. Agnon in his book of memoirs *Me'atsmi el atsmi*. Agnon notes that when he first met Martin Buber—the modern anthologizer of the hagiographical literature of hasidism—he was surprised to discover that the hasidic tales he had heard told in his youth in his home town in Galicia, tales which became familiar to him as a living oral tradition, had been available in print for decades and could be read in numerous volumes of which he, living at the heart of an eastern European hasidic milieu, was simply unaware. By contrast, the speculative, homiletic hasidic discourses which he discussed with Buber on the same occasion were known to him only from books,[53] even though, like the tales, they had originated in oral lore. Clearly, in Agnon's hasidic milieu, the homiletic discourses of the early hasidic masters had ceased to function as a living oral tradition while the tales retained this status long after they had become available in print.[54]

[50] See *Divrat Shelomo* on 'Noaḥ', 3*b*; on 'Ḥayei Sarah', 4*d*, 5*a*; on 'Vayeshev', 10*a–b*, and so on.

[51] See e.g. *Divrat Shelomo* on 'Lekh lekha', 4*a*, on the importance of strict observance of *halakhah*.

[52] Among the most important recent works on this subject are W. J. Ong, *Orality and Literacy: The Technologizing of the Word* (New York, 1987), and E. A. Havelock, *The Muse Learns to Write* (New Haven, 1986), with additional relevant bibliography. In addition, a new scholarly journal, *Oral Tradition*, was launched in 1986 and is entirely dedicated to publications in this field.

[53] See S. Y. Agnon, *Me'atsmi el atsmi* (Tel Aviv, 1976), 270–1.

[54] That the speculative teachings of the early masters of hasidism did circulate orally at one time is evident in Solomon Maimon's account of his encounter with a young hasid who recited for him hasidic interpretations of passages from biblical and rabbinic literature. See Solomon Maimon, *Salomon Maimons Lebensgeschichte* [Berlin, 1793] (Munich, 1911), publ. in Eng. as *The Autobiography of Solomon Maimon*, trans. J. Clark Murray (London, 1954), 173–5. Solomon Maimon's description of the hasidic sabbath in Mezhirech (ibid. 175–6) lends further support to the claim that it was the direct, live encounter between

There is no doubt that the transformation of Yiddish oral traditions into written, and ultimately published, Hebrew lore was not a random accident of history but a purposeful enterprise, inspired by the desire to preserve a body of traditions which were considered sacred and authoritative but which might not have survived otherwise. What is not entirely clear, however, is precisely who initiated this enterprise, and whose interests it was designed to serve. As we have seen, hasidic literature, whether in manuscript versions or in print, never became an indispensable part of the hasidic experience, either as an object of personal study at home or through any programme of instruction or study within the hasidic *beit midrash*. The majority of hasidic leaders and their communities of followers appear to have shown little interest in the preservation of the holy utterances of the masters in print. It would seem that without the initiative and efforts of the managing editors who published this lore, much of it would have been lost once it stopped being transmitted orally. From the middle of the nineteenth century on, managing editors, whether hasidic or not, appear to have been prompted by a new, romantic interest in the commemoration of the past, an enterprise which was believed by hasidim and maskilim alike to be capable of restoring the 'spirit' of the nation to great heights. This was reflected also in typographical advances: while the first generation of hasidic managing editors printed small editions, roughly produced, by the second half of the nineteenth century the printing presses of eastern Europe were producing larger and finer editions of hasidic works.[55]

All this is an area of investigation which has only just begun to unfold, and which should inform our understanding of an important chapter in the history of eastern European Jewry and hasidism.

the hasidic community and its leader that constituted the essential hasidic experience, not the literary activity of recording, and eventually reading, the 'holy utterances' of the zaddikim.

[55] The revival of Jewish printing in Poland in the second half of the 18th cent. produced a new class of agents of popular culture—the Jewish pedlars who distributed Hebrew and Yiddish chap-books and whose activities and impact still await the scholarly evaluation which they deserve. While the present paper has stressed the importance of direct experience and oral communication over and above the written word as the means by which hasidism propagated itself, it cannot be denied that the publication of hasidic works did contribute to the expansion of hasidism in its own way. This is evidenced by the publication in numerous editions of such popular hasidic books as *Tsava'at haRibash* and *Darkhei tsedek* during the final decade of the 18th cent. Nevertheless, the impact of these publications was limited by comparison with the impact of the printed word on contemporary European society, where it can be shown that the printing press stimulated revolutionary ideas and trends rather than merely reflecting them. For the impact of the printing press on the French Revolution, for example, see R. Darnton and D. Roche (eds.), *Revolution in Print: The Press in France, 1775–1800* (Berkeley, 1989).

PART III

THE SOCIAL FUNCTION OF MYSTICAL IDEALS IN HASIDISM

EIGHT

The Zaddik: The Interrelationship between Religious Doctrine and Social Organization

IMMANUEL ETKES

THE bulk of the scholarship concerned with the position of the leader in hasidism has been focused on the ideology (usually referred to as the doctrine) of zaddikism rather than on the social institution of the zaddik.[1] There are two principal reasons for this preference. First, for the past few decades, the academic study of hasidism has been dominated by the late Gershom Scholem and his students, all of whom have approached the subject primarily from the point of view of the history of ideas. Second, while the religious teaching of hasidism has been preserved in an abundance of primary literary sources, the documentary sources for the study of hasidism as a social movement have been scarce. It is therefore not surprising that much of the discussion on the doctrine of the zaddik has been conducted without reference to the socio-historical phenomenon of zaddikism. As a result, the relationship between doctrine and social institution has not been addressed in a systematic way. Scholars have tended to view the theory as a blueprint for social action—a programme by which the institution of the zaddik was ultimately shaped in reality.

In what follows I propose to examine the relationship between the theory and practice of zaddikism, in an attempt to answer the following questions. What was the relationship between the various conceptions of the leader and the new mode of communal leadership that emerged in hasidism? Did abstract speculation on the nature of leadership in fact nourish and inform it, or did it merely reflect the social practice of zaddikism? In other words, did the theory of zaddikism anticipate the operations of the early

[1] See e.g. G. Scholem, 'Hatsadik', in *Pirkei yesod behavanat hakabalah usemaleihah* (Jerusalem, 1976), 213–58, trans. as 'The Righteous One', in id., *The Mystical Shape of the Godhead* (New York, 1991), 88–139; J. Weiss, 'Reshit tsemiḥatah shel haderekh haḥasidit', *Zion*, 16 (1951), 46–105, repr. in A. Rubinstein (ed.), *Perakim betorat haḥasidut vetoledoteihah* (Jerusalem, 1977), 122–81; Rivka Schatz-Uffenheimer, 'Lemahuto shel hatsadik baḥasidut', *Molad*, 18: 144–5 (1960), 365–78; G. Nigal, *Manhig ve'edah* (Jerusalem, 1962); I. Tishby and J. Dan, 'Torat haḥasidut vesifrutah', in *Hebrew Encyclopedia*, xvii (1965), 779–84, repr. as a pamphlet by Academon, Jerusalem, and in Rubinstein (ed.), *Perakim betorat haḥasidut*, 250–312; A. Rapoport-Albert, 'God and the Zaddik as the Two Focal Points of Hasidic Worship', *History of Religions*, 18: 4 (1979), 296–325, repr. in G. D. Hundert (ed.), *Essential Papers on Hasidism* (New York, 1991), 299–329; A. Green, 'Typologies of Leadership and the Hasidic Zaddiq', in id. (ed.), *Jewish Spirituality*, ii: *From the Sixteenth Century Revival to the Present* (New York, 1987), 127–56; Samuel H. Dresner, *The Zaddik* (New York, 1960).

hasidic masters as leaders of their communities, or did it emerge only in retrospect, to invest with legitimacy and authority a social institution that already existed in practice?

The initial stage in the development of hasidism was clearly marked by the personality and leadership of Israel Baal Shem Tov. Contrary to the commonly held view of the Besht, he never attempted to establish a broadly based, popular movement. His activities as a kabbalist who was prepared to share with others the lesson of his personal experience in the service of God were confined to a small circle of individuals who had identified themselves as hasidim even before they met him. In fact, the Besht and his circle may be described as the kernel from which hasidism as a movement was to grow in the course of time. The questions why and how it developed from an esoteric phenomenon into a mass movement are too complex to be addressed fully within the scope of the present discussion, but it seems to me that at least one aspect of the issue is particularly pertinent here. I refer to the new style of leadership which was embodied in the personality of the Besht.[2]

The Besht was a guide in the service of God to the immediate circle of his associates by personal example, individual instruction, and the formulation of his ideas in succinct statements or brief homilies. However, he considered himself to be responsible also for the welfare of the community as a whole. His activities in the public domain may be viewed as the expression of his concern for communal needs, both in the religious and ethical spheres and in concrete, material affairs. Thus he undertook, on the one hand, to supervise the work of ritual slaughterers in order to secure the ritual purity of the meat, and on the other hand to warn a certain community of the imminent danger of a blood libel. In addition, he took it upon himself to intervene in the supernal worlds in order to abrogate harsh decrees against the Jewish people. What all these activities had in common was the sense that they were facilitated by the unusual spiritual powers of the Besht. Indeed, he is said to have acknowledged that these powers had been granted precisely in order that he should employ them for the good of the community. This belief constitutes a novel perception of leadership: unlike the earlier kabbalistic hasidim, who withdrew from society in order to achieve their own spiritual perfection, the Besht was a mystic who, while transmitting a particular religious message to his own circle of fellow mystics, assumed also the responsibility for the well-being of the wider community, both spiritually and in worldly affairs. This was accomplished, as we have seen, by means of the supernatural powers which had been granted to him for this purpose.

How did the Besht and his circle define the function of the zaddik? Did they create a fully-fledged ideology of leadership? Joseph Weiss answered this question in the affirmative. In his seminal essay 'The Beginnings of Hasidism' he identified in the sources an 'early doctrine of the leader' which could be contrasted with later hasidic conceptions of the zaddik.[3] Weiss located the main difference between the early and the later doctrine in the absence from the former of any notion of the leader's responsibility for the material welfare of the community. This early view of the leader was expressed, according to Weiss, in the teachings of the Besht and a handful of contemporary

[2] See I. Etkes, 'Hasidism as a Movement: The First Stage', in B. Safran (ed.), *Hasidism: Continuity or Innovation?* (Cambridge, Mass., 1988), 1–26.

[3] 'Reshit tsemiḥatah shel haderekh haḥasidit.'

preachers. They never formulated their ideas in writing; rather, their views have come down to us via the literary works of R. Jacob Joseph of Polonnoye. Weiss found the similarity between the views of the Besht and those of his associates to be so great that he considered them an ideologically coherent circle. However, a critical examination of both his sources and his analysis leaves considerable room for doubt on this point: while he rightly perceived a certain affinity between the ideas of the Besht and those of the preachers cited in the works of R. Jacob Joseph of Polonnoye, Weiss overlooked a number of crucial differences between them. Moreover, his use of the phrase 'the early doctrine of the leader' seems to imply a coherent set of ideas that reflect the existence in practice of a fixed pattern of leadership at this stage; but is there any evidence for this in reality?

It would be useful at this point to review briefly both the similarities and the differences between the Besht and his associates on the subject of leadership. The Besht and the preachers cited by R. Jacob Joseph of Polonnoye shared the view that the individuals that make up the Jewish people constitute a single organic entity—a view which was based on kabbalistic concepts relating to the metaphysical connections that link all the souls of Israel to one another.[4] As a consequence of this organic coherence, sins committed by the worst offenders affect the moral standing of the entire body of the nation, including its most righteous and eminent leaders. The message implicit in this concept and the images which express it are unequivocal: the spiritual élite cannot disengage itself from the masses and is responsible for their moral welfare.

The Besht and his associates similarly share the perception of the individual who has achieved the highest spiritual level, the person able to forge a mystical connection with the divine realm, as a link between ordinary folk and the supernal worlds. This idea shows the mystical orientation of the entire circle: they share a common spiritual platform with the Besht, even if they do not quite match his own achievements in this sphere.

The main difference, on the other hand, between the Besht and his companions is that, unlike him, they define leadership from the narrow perspective of their own profession: as preachers they are dedicated to the moral correction of the public by means of the only instrument at their disposal—the sabbath sermon in the synagogue. This explains their constant concern that the preacher must not content himself with mere verbal chastisement, since the public may pay no heed to his bitter words of rebuke. Instead they suggest that, prior to the sermon, the preacher should connect himself mystically both to his audience and to God. In this way he would make sure that, while delivering his sermon, he has improved their moral condition or brought them nearer to God, regardless of their own intentions.[5] An occupational risk that troubles the preachers and shapes their perception of leadership is the likelihood of their own spiritual and moral decline through their constant proximity to sinners. They deal with this problem by presenting the spiritual decline of the preacher as a necessary evil, but warn that he must take all appropriate precautions.[6]

[4] Texts which reflect the position of the circle on this issue are cited by Weiss, ibid. 82–3. For the Besht's view of the organic unity of the Jewish people see Jacob Joseph of Polonnoye, *Ketonet pasim* (Lemberg, 1866), 13*b*.

[5] See e.g. Jacob Joseph of Polonnoye, *Toledot Ya'akov Yosef* [Korets, 1780] (Jerusalem, 1966), 59*a*.

[6] See id., *Ketonet pasim*, 22*a*.

By contrast, the Besht can improve the community's moral standing without resort to sermons. Instead he employs a variety of theurgic practices which do not necessitate direct contact with the public and do not depend on public willingness to cooperate. He says: 'the head of the generation can raise the [mundane] words and stories of the people of his generation, to connect the material with the spiritual.'[7] There is no reference here to the moral chastisement of sinners but rather to the endeavour to sanctify the mundane experience of the common people by connecting it to the supernal worlds. And when the Besht spoke of the head of the generation, he was clearly referring to himself.

Even with regard to the correction of sinners, the Besht recommends indirect action. He believes that the transgressions of the commonest people are bound to cast doubts on the leaders as well, but his solution to this problem is simple: if the heads of the generation repent, this will automatically improve the sinners' moral condition.[8] This is why the Besht does not concern himself with the problem that so troubled the preachers of his generation—the moral decline or 'descent' of the preacher that results from his contacts with sinners.

These differences between the Besht's perception of the leader and that of the preachers in whose environment he operated clearly point to the existence of two distinct models of leadership. Despite their peculiarly mystical orientation, the preachers quoted by R. Jacob Joseph of Polonnoye did not essentially differ from all other preachers in seeing their goal as the ethical and religious correction of the public by the traditional means of direct verbal rebuke. The Besht, on the other hand, acted as a mystic who had been granted extraordinary spiritual powers in order to employ them for the good of the community. The distinction between these two conceptions of leadership is of great significance, since the new institution of the zaddik in hasidism can be shown to have combined the two models into one.

In the light of all this, it is difficult to accept Weiss's contention that the ideas of the Besht and those of 'his' circle of preachers constituted a single system of thought that generated the 'early doctrine of the leader' in hasidism. Rather, these ideas represent two quite distinct conceptions of leadership. To integrate them into one within a single literary framework was R. Jacob Joseph of Polonnoye's decision, and it reflected his own interest in both strands of thought rather than any inherent or historical affinity between them.

The questions why R. Jacob Joseph saw fit to integrate these ideas in his writings and how much he contributed to them himself are discussed below. For the time being, let us turn to the next stage in the development of hasidism: the period in which R. Dov Ber, the Maggid of Mezhirech, became the dominant figure in the leadership of the movement. It is important to bear in mind that only at this stage can one begin to speak of hasidism as a movement, since it is only at this stage that a campaign is launched to recruit converts to the new teaching by means of emissaries sent out from Mezhirech and Karlin. Notably, even at this stage, the hasidic propaganda emanating from Mezhirech is not directed to the masses but to the scholarly classes. Moreover, it is only

[7] Aaron of Opatow, *Keter shem tov* [2 vols.; Zholkva (Zolkiew), 1794–5; 1 vol.; Korets, 1797] (Bnei Brak, 1957), 7.

[8] See Jacob Joseph of Polonnoye, *Toledot,* 70*a*.

at this stage, under the leadership of the Maggid of Mezhirech, that the institution of the 'court' is established, to become one of the hallmarks of hasidism as a movement.

The function of the sermon as an expression of communal leadership in the court of the Maggid of Mezhirech is highly significant, and this is documented in the autobiography of Solomon Maimon.[9] From Maimon's account it emerges quite clearly that the sermon that the Maggid delivered to a group of followers gathered at his court was the climax of his visit to Mezhirech. The Maggid had earlier asked each of the assembled guests to recite a biblical verse of his choice. He then astounded his audience by weaving together discrete verses, totally unrelated to one another, into a coherent sermon in which all these random elements had been integrated. But even more impressive was the discovery by each of the guests that the sermon contained some message which related personally to him. In this way the Maggid displayed his ability to uncover the secret thoughts of all the guests assembled at his court.

The Maggid of Mezhirech was a hasidic leader who combined the two earlier models of communal leadership: that of the Baal Shem Tov-type mystic and that of the mystically oriented preacher. As a mystic, he followed the example of the Besht in exploring the way, and guiding a group of select disciples, to the ultimate goal of *devekut*.[10] Like the Besht, he believed that the mystic must not turn his back on society but should assume responsibility for both the religious and the material well-being of the community. But unlike the Besht, the Maggid clearly adopted the sermon as his main instrument of public leadership; all subsequent leaders of hasidism were to follow him in this respect.

The assimilation of the preacher-type leadership model into the new mode of leadership that was emerging in hasidism is evident not only in the virtually universal resort by the early hasidic masters to the traditional medium of the sermon; it can also be detected in (and may even explain) the very endeavour to disseminate the teachings of hasidism more widely. After all, the preacher's concern had always been the religious condition of the community as a whole rather than of any particular class or section within it. That the traditional role of the preacher was being subsumed under the new function of the leader in hasidism is an observation that goes beyond the subtleties of typological analysis; it explains the robust historical fact that wherever hasidism was most widespread and influential the traditional institution of the preacher simply disappeared, while in those parts of eastern Europe where the spread of hasidism was arrested, traditional preachers continued to operate as in past generations.

The Maggid of Mezhirech, a prolific and original thinker, scarcely touched on the subject of the leader in his teachings. It was R. Jacob Joseph of Polonnoye who first articulated the theory of leadership in hasidism.[11] His writings represent in the first instance an elaboration of the motifs that feature in the discourses of the Besht and the preachers of his generation. He repeats, for example, in various forms, the idea that the

[9] Solomon Maimon, *The Autobiography of Solomon Maimon*, trans. J. Clark Murray (London, 1954), 173–6.

[10] For the status and significance of *devekut* in hasidism see, G. Scholem, '*Devekut*, or Communion with God', *Review of Religion*, 14 (1949–50), 115–39, repr. in id., *The Messianic Idea in Judaism* (New York, 1971), 203–27.

[11] R. Jacob Joseph's view of the zaddik was discussed extensively by both Dresner, *The Zaddik* and Nigal, *Manhig ve'edah*. See also G. Nigal, *Torot ba'al haToledot* (Jerusalem, 1974).

entire Jewish people comprises a single organic entity that links the masses to the spiritual élite, an idea from which follows the obligation of the élite towards the public. Similarly, R. Jacob Joseph deals repeatedly with the risk to the moral integrity of the leader that arises from his exposure to direct contact with the public—the issue to which the scholarly literature usually refers as the 'descent of the zaddik'. His critique of the traditional leadership, especially of preachers,[12] occupies a place of prime importance in his works. Time and again he accuses the preachers of failing to exert any influence on the public since they exclude themselves from the call to repent and improve.[13]

The novel component of R. Jacob Joseph's teaching on leadership is his expansion of a certain idea that he ascribes to the Besht and his associate preachers. The Besht had argued that the spiritual leader was capable of linking the mundane experience of the masses to the supernal worlds; the preachers had envisaged their own ability to refine the mundane experience of the masses as the product of the mystical connection that linked together their own consciousness, the consciousness of the masses, and the divine consciousness itself. According to both views, the responsibility for forging these mystical connections and links rests entirely with the spiritual leadership; the masses are mere passive beneficiaries. R. Jacob Joseph, on the other hand, shifts the responsibility to the masses: the ordinary Jew is called to adhere to the spiritual leader in order to be connected to the divine realm.[14] The novelty here is not in the notion of the spiritual leader as a bridge to the supernal worlds, but rather in the very expectation that the ordinary person should actively aspire to commune with God, for surely mystical communion with God had always been regarded as the prerogative of a small minority of spiritually gifted men. This ideological turning-point reflects the novel mode of operation in society adopted by a previously reclusive class of mystics—the endeavours of hasidic propagandists and emissaries to reach out to a larger section of the public. As a result of the fresh encounter between this public and the hasidic élite, the gap was fully exposed between the exclusive religious ideals of the élite and the impoverished spirituality of the masses. It was this gap that R. Jacob Joseph's new type of leader was aiming to bridge.

R. Jacob Joseph's teaching on leaders and leadership has been labelled his 'doctrine of the zaddik', supplying a hasidic answer to contemporary problems. But is it a 'doctrine of leadership' in the full sense of the term? How does it relate to the emergence of the institution of the zaddik in practice?

It would seem to me naïve to assume that R. Jacob Joseph's reflections on the subject of leadership could have shaped the pattern of leadership in practice as it was evolving under the guidance of the Maggid of Mezhirech. The Maggid was acting independently, by personal inspiration from the Besht as well as through the force of his own charismatic personality. Moreover, R. Jacob Joseph's ideas need not be seen as reflecting the existence in practice of a particular institution of leadership, nor do they amount to a coherent programme for the establishment of such an institution in hasidism. It is altogether doubtful whether the term 'doctrine' could be applied to his

[12] See Nigal, *Torot ba'al haToledot*, 71–92; M. Piekarz, *Biyemei tsemiḥat haḥasidut: Megamot ra'ayoniyot besifrei derush umusar* (Jerusalem, 1978), 96–172.

[13] See e.g. Jacob Joseph of Polonnoye, *Toledot*, 90*b*.

[14] See ibid., on 'Naso', 120*d*–121*a*.

abstract ruminations; they are better viewed as a literary reflection of new developments in the practical application of hasidic ideals in society. His critique of the traditional leadership; his appeal to the leaders to mend their ways; the various expressions he gives to the idea of the organic unity of the people; his deliberations on the issue of preserving the moral integrity of the leaders—all these reflect the increasing involvement of the hasidic élite in communal leadership and public affairs during the 1760s. R. Jacob Joseph's reflections are compatible with this trend and express it fully, but they neither shape it nor provide its theoretical underpinnings.

The term 'doctrine' applies fully only to the theory of zaddikism that emerged during the next stage in the development of the hasidic movement, the stage which is often designated 'the generation of the disciples of the Maggid of Mezhirech'. By this stage, hasidism was expanding so widely that, for the first time in its history, it became a truly popular movement. It was at this stage that hasidic writings concerned primarily with the issue of leadership began to proliferate, attempting to formulate what we may now call the proper doctrine of the zaddik in hasidism. The best example of this is to be found in the teachings of R. Elimelekh of Lyzhansk.[15]

R. Elimelekh's reflections on the subject of leadership may be distinguished from those of his predecessors by a number of features that render them, and others like them, a fully-fledged theory of zaddikism:

1. He is the first to be consistent in referring to the hasidic leader by the title 'zaddik'. By contrast, R. Jacob Joseph had used it casually, alongside a variety of other designations. This terminological shift is the clear expression of social change: affiliation to hasidism is no longer the prerogative of the élite; the hasidic leader—a mystic who embodies the traditionally exclusive values of hasidic piety—now attracts a popular following of people who identify with these values, and who become identified as 'hasidim'. The term 'hasid' begins to apply to the ordinary person who 'adheres' to a hasidic leader;[16] it no longer distinguishes the spiritual élite from the masses. By virtue of being free from any specific institutional connotations, the alternative term 'zaddik' is appropriated at this point by the élite as the standard Hebrew designation of the leader and to distinguish him from his followers—the hasidim. As Scholem has observed,[17] the term zaddik was particularly well suited for this purpose: in kabbalistic literature it had always symbolized that aspect of the Godhead (*sefirah*) that discharged the flow of divine energy (*shefa*) to the lower worlds in order to sustain them—a function that the leaders of hasidism, in taking upon themselves the responsibility for the material welfare of the community, were regarded as obliged to fulfil.

2. Unlike R. Jacob Joseph of Polonnoye, in whose writings the spiritual leadership is often discussed in the plural, R. Elimelekh consistently refers to 'the zaddik' in the singular. Once again, there is no doubt that the terminological shift, which may be described as the individualization of zaddikism, reflects a decisive move towards the establishment of the hasidic leadership as a social institution.

[15] For the most extensive and exhaustive discussion of R. Elimelekh's doctrine of the zaddik see Elimelekh of Lyzhansk, *No'am Elimelekh*, ed. G. Nigal (2 vols.; Jerusalem, 1978), i. 19–123.

[16] See *Igeret hakodesh*, ibid. ii. 496.

[17] See Scholem, 'Hatsadik'.

3. R. Elimelekh's teaching on leadership, and that of others among his contemporaries, constitutes an attempt to set out systematically a comprehensive network of mutual obligations between the zaddik and his followers. This theoretical scheme appears to match and parallel the effective pattern of leadership in hasidism at the time.

4. A certain tendency, first noted in the works of R. Jacob Joseph of Polonnoye, is developed in the teachings of R. Elimelekh of Lyzhansk and becomes very clearly pronounced. This is the appeal to the ordinary Jew to attach himself to the zaddik. The appeal is invested with greater urgency and force by the assertion that the ordinary Jew is altogether incapable of fulfilling his duty in the service of God without resorting to the assistance of the zaddik.

5. The precise nature of the obligation by which the hasidic community is bound to the zaddik becomes a central issue in the teachings of R. Elimelekh and his contemporaries. This clearly indicates where these teachings are directed. While the notions of leadership associated with the Besht and the preachers of his generation, including R. Jacob Joseph of Polonnoye, were addressed primarily to their own class—the spiritual and religious élite—and may be seen as a collective exercise in self-scrutiny, R. Elimelekh of Lyzhansk and the hasidic leaders who followed him addressed their message primarily to their 'flock'.

How can one account for the emergence of this doctrine of the leader, and what was its function?

There seems little doubt that the doctrine did not serve as a programme by which the institution of the zaddik was to be set up and operate in practice. The sermons in which it was articulated all date from the period by which the institution of the zaddik had become well established. Both the contents of these sermons and the audience at whom they were targeted suggest that their principal function was to place the existing practice of zaddikism on a sound theoretical basis. The leaders of hasidism were well aware that their mode of communal leadership was radically novel. The need to legitimize this novelty by anchoring it in a theoretical framework which would draw its phraseology and symbolism from tradition became more acute during the 1770s and 1780s, as a result both of the increasing involvement of hasidism in public affairs and of the fierce opposition to it by the Gaon of Vilna and the traditional establishment.

The need felt at this time by a number of hasidic leaders to base their authority on an explicitly formulated doctrine of zaddikism is better understood if we bear in mind that the distinctive mode of leadership that became characteristic of the zaddik in hasidism was an amalgamation of two earlier modes, the mystic's and the preacher's. The preacher's authority was derived from the ethical norms that he set his public, and it depended on the willingness of the public to comply; the authority of the mystic—the Besht, for example—was derived from his supernatural powers to exert an influence on both the upper and the lower worlds for the sake of the entire community, whether or not it was willing to cooperate. The hasidic zaddik resembled the preacher in addressing his followers directly and appealing for their cooperation. But this appeal was now based on his personal charismatic powers, which required no theoretical re-inforcement so long as they were demonstrated and acknowledged spontaneously through his direct contact with the public. It was from these powers that the Besht and the Maggid of Mezhirech had derived their authority. Only in the generation of the Maggid's disciples, through the institutionalization of the leader's charismatic authority and the growing range of his influence on public affairs, was it first felt necessary to supply a theoretical foundation for his relationship with the community, and the doctrine of the zaddik assumed its fully articulated literary form. The supernatural powers claimed by the leaders, and the network of mutual obligations between them and their followers, were now couched in metaphysical terms, invested with the authority of divinely ordained universal law.

In conclusion, it seems to me that the novel hasidic institution of the zaddik did not arise from any ready-made doctrine or theory of leadership. The doctrine reflected a new mode of communal leadership, one for which it was to supply a retrospective theoretical legitimization, and developed together with it. Yet, it is not impossible that the kabbalistic symbols that supplied this theoretical legitimization had shaped the consciousness and self-perception of the early hasidic masters from the start. This possibility is yet to be explored as a topic for discussion in its own right.

NINE

The Paradigms of *Yesh* and *Ayin* in Hasidic Thought

RACHEL ELIOR

THE social manifestations of late hasidism—its successes as a popular movement, the new patterns of communal organization that it created, as well as the overtly messianic orientation adopted by some hasidic circles in recent times—have all distracted scholarly attention from the early conceptual foundation of the hasidic experience.

Hasidism is a complex phenomenon, marked by extraordinary literary diversity, a wide variety of social expressions, and a history which spans two and a half centuries. It does not lend itself to general characterization or definition. Nevertheless, certain shared conceptual patterns can be shown to have served as a premiss underlying diverse strands of hasidic thought.

The present discussion focuses on the final decades of the eighteenth century. This was a period of rapid expansion for hasidism, with hasidic leaders reaching out to a wider audience not least through the publication and dissemination of the earliest formulations of hasidic ideas in writing.

At the core of hasidic thought lies the idea of the dual nature of reality. The two contradictory aspects of all existence are bound to one another dialectically.[1] This duality applies to all dimensions of reality and mirrors the perception of the deity as a dialectic unity of oppositions.

The deity is perceived as a dialectic process of reversible and variable opposites. This unity of opposites is expressed in pairs of contradictory concepts: 'expansion and limitation', 'emanation and withdrawal', 'revelation and concealment', 'creation and annihilation', 'unity and differentiation', 'being and non-being', '*yesh* and *ayin*'.[2] All these concepts clearly derive from the kabbalistic heritage of hasidism.[3] But while the kabbalistic interest in dialectic opposites relates only to the heavenly realm, the new

[1] The two aspects of reality are referred to by a variety of designations: *yesh* and *ayin, hitpashetut* and *histalekut*, matter and form, the active and the passive, etc. See Dov Ber of Mezhirech, *Maggid devarav le Ya'akov*, critical edn. by R. Schatz-Uffenheimer (Jerusalem, 1976), 108: 'It is well known that everything has both matter and form'; see also ibid. 150. See further Solomon of Lutsk, *Divrat Shelomo* (Jerusalem, 1972), 60–3.

[2] S. B. Levine (ed.), *Igrot kodesh Admor hazaken, Admor ha'emtsa'i, Admor haTsemaḥ Tsedek* (Brooklyn, NY, 1980), 173: 'It is well known that every holy thing consists of both facets'; see also *Maggid devarav leYa'akov*, s. 124.

[3] G. Scholem, *Major Trends in Jewish Mysticism* (New York, 1964), 23, 217–24, 261–3.

hasidic concern encompasses all aspects of reality. The principles of *yesh* and *ayin* are thus projected in hasidism from the domain of the Godhead onto the domain of religious awareness and divine service.[4]

The concern with these dialectical processes has found diverse expression and emphasis in hasidism. The Maggid of Mezhirech, for example, was concerned primarily with the mutual transformations of the two poles.[5] Bratslav hasidism expressed the tragic dimension of the paradox.[6] Habad is more concerned with the dialectical movement between *yesh* and *ayin*.[7] Polish hasidism has highlighted the embodiment of the opposites in the figure of the zaddik.[8] Whether the emphasis was placed on the Cordoverian tension between revelation and concealment or on the Lurianic dichotomy of transcendence and immanence,[9] many hasidic authors have grappled with the ambivalence of the divine dialectics, and most have had to address the complex contradiction between *yesh* and *ayin*.

The hasidic concern with these concepts was expressed in traditional kabbalistic terms. This is evident, for example, in R. Nahman of Bratslav's Lurianically inspired account of Creation:

> When God, blessed be He, wanted to create the world, there was no space in which to create it, for everywhere there was infinite God. Therefore, God withdrew His light to the sides, and by means of this withdrawal, the empty space was created . . . This *tsimtsum* of the empty space cannot be understood or grasped until the messianic future, for two contradictory statements must be made about it—it is being (*yesh*) and it is non-being (*ayin*).[10]

In this and the many similar statements which occur throughout the literature of hasidism, the deity is presented as possessed of two opposite but interrelated aspects.

[4] See H. Zeitlin, *Befardes haḥasidut* (Tel Aviv, 1965), 11–25. Zeitlin noted the centrality of the concepts of *yesh* and *ayin* in hasidic thought. See also Menahem Mendel of Vitebsk, *Peri ha'arets* [Kopys, 1814] (Jerusalem, 1974), 57. See further A. Green, 'Neo-Hasidism and our Theological Struggle', *Ra'ayonot*, 4: 3 (1984), 13: 'This primal pair, the potential and the actual, or non-being and being, is the essential dyad of Hasidic Mysticism. The realization of their oneness, the realization that *yesh* is *ayin* and *ayin* is *yesh* is the essential goal of mystical awareness.'

[5] See *Maggid devarav leYa'akov*, 19, 24, 38, 83–6, 91, 94, 124, 134, and the comments of R. Schatz-Uffenheimer ad loc. See also Meshullam Phoebus Heller of Zbarazh, *Yosher divrei emet* (New York, 1974), 14*b*–15*b*; Menahem Mendel of Vitebsk, *Peri ha'arets*, 51–2, 72.

[6] See J. G. Weiss, *Meḥkarim bahasidut Braslav* (Jerusalem, 1974), 121–5.

[7] See R. Shneur Zalman of Lyady, *Torah or* [Kopys, 1836; Zhitomir, 1862] (Brooklyn, NY, 1984), on 'Bereshit', 5a; on 'Va'era', 57a; id., *Likutei amarim: Tanya* [Slavuta, 1796; Vilna, 1900], bilingual edn., trans. N. Mindel, N. Mangel, Z. Posner, and J. I. Schochet (London, 1973), 'Sha'ar hayiḥud', ch. 3, 78*a*; ch. 4, 79*a*–*b*; 'Igeret hakodesh', 129*a*–*b*. See also R. Elior, *Torat ha'elohut bador hasheni shel ḥasidut Ḥabad* (Jerusalem, 1982), 125–30, and also index entries on *ayin* and *yesh*; id., 'HaBaD: The Contemplative Ascent to God', in A. Green (ed.), *Jewish Spirituality*, ii: *From the Sixteenth Century Revival to the Present* (New York, 1987), 157–205.

[8] See R. Elior, 'Between *Yesh* and *Ayin*: The Doctrine of the Zaddik in the Works of Jacob Isaac, the Seer of Lublin', in A. Rapoport-Albert and S. J. Zipperstein (eds.), *Jewish History: Essays in Honor of Chimen Abramsky* (London, 1988), 393–455.

[9] On the question of the relationship between kabbalah and hasidism see A. Green, 'Hasidism: Discovery and Retreat', in P. Berger (ed.), *The Other Side of God: A Polarity in World Religions* (New York, 1981), 110–13; R. Elior, 'Hazikah shebein kabalah laḥasidut: Retsifut utemurah', *The Proceedings of the Ninth World Congress of Jewish Studies* (Jerusalem, 1986), 107–14.

[10] See Nahman of Bratslav, *Likutei Moharan* [2 vols.; Ostrog, 1808; Mogilev, 1811] (1 vol.; Jerusalem, 1969), part 1, *torah* 64, start of s. 1. This subject has been discussed extensively by a number of Bratslav scholars; see below, n. 24.

The first is limitless 'thought', boundless expansion or 'infinity', which is beyond human comprehension; it is the ultimate unity and formlessness of God, the expansive principle, usually referred to as *ayin*.[11] The second aspect is the divine principle of form and limit; it suggests differentiation, contraction, and withdrawal within the divinity. This includes material creation and is referred to as *yesh* or *tsimtsum*.[12]

These two aspects precondition and complement each other: the perceptible attributes of the material *yesh* are rooted in the imperceptible divine *ayin* from which they derive their very existence and sustenance.[13] Similarly, the divine *ayin* cannot manifest itself or be perceived without being limited or concealed in the material *yesh*.[14] R. Levi Isaac of Berdichev expressed this idea as the principle whereby all things exist in two dimensions, one perceptible, within nature, and the other concealed, beyond nature. He stated: '*Ayin* is the way in which all things are maintained beyond nature, and *yesh* is the way that nature is . . . since the imperceptible is implied in *ayin* and the perceptible is implied in *yesh*.'[15]

These two dimensions, which are inherent in the nature of the divine, operate as a dynamic unity of opposites. On the one hand, the divine process unfolds through concealment and disguise from the state of unity, expansion, and abstraction towards differentiation, contraction, and the creation of the mundane; in other words, *ayin* is transformed through concealment into *yesh*. On the other hand, the process is reversed to convert *yesh* into *ayin*, to return to a state of unity and simplicity through the annihilation of differentiation and complexity, of material existence and mundane reality.[16] In the words of R. Shneur Zalman of Lyady: 'The purpose of the creation of the worlds from *ayin* into *yesh* is to reverse them from *yesh* into *ayin*.'[17]

The polarity of *yesh* and *ayin* is known from earlier kabbalistic sources, but only in hasidic thought is it deployed as a conceptual framework for the interpretation of every aspect of reality. This occurs in conjunction with the formulation of another principle, whereby every manifestation of reality which is finite and apparent is a concealment of that which is infinite and real. In other words, every apparent *yesh* contains a concealed *ayin*, and thus all things embody the two opposite poles of existence simultaneously. Consequently, all reality may be understood as an infinite divine essence enveloped within a finite, concrete 'garment'. In the words of R. Menahem Mendel of Vitebsk: 'It is known to those who believe in the divine vitality and the holy sparks that all things

[11] For the historical context of the development of the concept of *ayin* see Scholem, *Major Trends*, 25, 217, 221; see also D. C. Matt, 'Ayin: The Concept of Nothingness in Mystical Judaism', *Tikkun*' 3: 3 (1988), 43–7; Y. Liebes, 'Rabbi Solomon Ibn Gabirol's Use of the *Sefer Yetsirah* and a Commentary on the Poem "I Love Thee" '(Heb.), *Jerusalem Studies in Jewish Thought*, 6: 3–4 (1987), 80–4. On the concept of *ayin* in hasidic literature see R. Schatz-Uffenheimer, *Haḥasidut kemistikah* (Jerusalem, 1968), 22–31, 45; Elior, *Torat ha'elohut*, 48–51 and index entries on *ayin*.

[12] See Shneur Zalman, *Tanya*, 129*a*–130*b*; Menahem Mendel of Vitebsk, *Peri ha'arets*, on 'Vayigash', 31; on 'Tetsaveh', 57; *Divrat Shelomo*, on 'Va'era', 63; R. Hayyim Haikel b. Samuel of Amdur, *Ḥayim vaḥesed* [Warsaw, 1891] (Jerusalem, 1975), 84, 88.

[13] See *Maggid devarav le Ya'akov*, 101. See also Shneur Zalman, *Tanya*, 26*a*; 'Sha'ar hayiḥud', 86*a*–*b*; Menahem Mendel of Vitebsk, *Peri ha'arets*, 44, 48.

[14] Menahem Mendel of Vitebsk, *Peri ha'arets*, 54–5.

[15] *Kedushat Levi* [Slavuta, 1798] (Jerusalem, 1958; Brooklyn, NY, 1978), 1.

[16] See Elior, 'HaBaD: The Contemplative Ascent', 168–9.

[17] *Torah or*, on 'Vayetse', 22b.

material and all thought, words, and expressions derive from God who dwells within them in reality . . . and without His presence, nothing can exist.'[18] The same idea is expressed in the common hasidic dictum: 'One should think at all times that all things of this world are filled with the divine expansion.'[19]

In hasidic thought there is no infinite, spiritual reality other than that which is concealed within a finite, concrete manifestation. Conversely, there is no finite, concrete reality other than that which is nurtured and sustained by the infinite, spiritual source of all existence.

The perception of the infinite divine substance as being the vital force which sustains all finite reality, and the depiction of the mundane world as a veil which obscures the infinitely expanding vitality of the divine—these are the principles underlying the hasidic doctrine of immanence.[20] However, it should be noted that the doctrine of immanence itself is deduced from the principle of the dynamic unity of opposites within the Godhead, the world, and man. In hasidic thought everything simultaneously incorporates both *yesh* and *ayin, ratso vashov*, ascent and descent, apparent limitation and infinite expansion in reality. Since there can be no revelation of the spiritual vitality of the divine except by means of concealment, the material cannot exist except inasmuch as it is being sustained and nurtured by its spiritual source.

These two poles of the divine force are equally valued, since both dictate the dialectic rhythm of the flow of divine energy. However, once projected onto human reality and religious experience, they are ascribed somewhat different values.

The substantial duality of the divine expressed in the dynamic polarity of expansion and withdrawal, annihilation and creation, *ratso vashov*, is altered in human perception to become an apparently static polarity of 'inwardness' and 'outwardness', holiness and evil (*kedushah* and *kelipah*), spirituality and materiality, all of which amount to a reality perceived as devoid of divine presence alternating with an attainable reality, saturated with the divine presence. The 'inwardness' relates to immanence—the sense of immediate divine presence, while the 'outwardness' expresses the sense of transcendence—the withdrawal and unattainability of God.[21]

This paradox is articulated clearly in the introduction to R. Solomon of Lutsk's *Divrat Shelomo*: 'In all things there is divine vitality . . . However, it is . . . veiled and materialized within the husks of corporeality, and it is called *sitra aḥra*.'[22]

The conflict between the immanentist perception of divine omnipresence and the common human experience of a world devoid of God determines the paradoxical

[18] *Peri ha'arets*, 68. See also Solomon of Lutsk, *Divrat Shelomo*, 2, 47: 'Even those who appear utterly mundane . . . all are spirituality and the illumination of His divine light.' Concerning the ambivalence of appearance, see R. Schatz-Uffenheimer, *Haḥasidut kemistikah*, 156.

[19] Solomon of Lutsk, *Divrat Shelomo*, part 2, p. 45; See also *Tsava'at haRibash* [n.p. (Ostrog?), 1793; Zolkiew, 1795], ed. J. I. Schochet (Brooklyn, NY, 1975), 26, s. 84.

[20] On the hasidic theory of divine immanence see Solomon Schechter, *Studies in Judaism* (3 vols.; Philadelphia, 1896–1924), i. 19–21; Scholem, *Major Trends*, 336–47; I. Tishby and J. Dan, 'Torat haḥasidut vesifrutah', *Hebrew Encyclopaedia*, xvii (1965), 769–821 (repr. as a pamphlet by Academon, Jerusalem, and in A. Rubinstein (ed.), *Perakim betorat haḥasidut vetoledoteihah* (Jerusalem, 1977), 250–312); Elior, 'Hazikah', 108–10.

[21] See Elior, 'HaBaD: The Contemplative Ascent', 170.

[22] *Divrat Shelomo*, on 'Lekh lekha', 4; on 'Mikets' 24. For the distinction between 'inwardness' and 'outwardness' see *Maggid devarav leYa'akov*, 29, 45; *Torah or*, 102*a*.

nature of the hasidic consciousness. Awareness of this conflict demands constant attention to the relationship between *yesh* and *ayin*, between the apparent withdrawal and actual flow of divine abundance, in defiance of the evidence of sensual experience.[23]

R. Nahman of Bratslav states the problem succinctly in his discussion of the conflict between the 'empty space'—reality devoid of God—and the sense of divine omnipresence:

Now, without this empty space there could be no world, as there would be no room for creation at all. This *tsimtsum* of the empty space cannot be understood or grasped until the messianic future, for two contradictory statements must be made about it, it is being (*yesh*) and it is non-being (*ayin*). For the empty space comes about through *tsimtsum*, through God's withdrawal of Himself from there. There is, as it were, no God there. For if this were not so, there would be no *tsimtsum*, all would be infinite God and there would be no place for the creation of the world at all. But in truth, God must be there as well—for there is nothing at all without His life in it. And that is why the empty space will not be understood until the messianic future.[24]

The ontological principles of expansion and withdrawal in kabbalah are turned in hasidic thought into the paradox of immanence and transcendence as the two conflicting modes of human perception. Immanence—reality saturated with divinity—is alien to human sensory perception; transcendence, understood as withdrawal and abandonment—reality devoid of God—is all that man can experience. Human experience is confined to the realm of the mundane *yesh*.[25]

In confronting this paradox, the hasidic masters employed the concepts of 'inwardness' and 'outwardness' to express the dual nature of all existence. Outwardness—the *yesh*—refers to material reality and corresponds to sensory experience, also known as the 'Eyes of Flesh'. Inwardness—the *ayin*—refers to the absolute reality of the divine presence and corresponds to spiritual, contemplative, or mystical insight, also known as the 'Eyes of the Mind'.[26]

To be a hasid is to confront these two dimensions of being and to understand that the contradiction between them is only apparent. Since the principles of *yesh* and *ayin* are reversible in the divine realm, inasmuch as *ayin* becomes *yesh* and *yesh* becomes *ayin*, human consciousness should follow the same course and convert the apparent 'outwardness'—reality devoid of divinity—into 'inwardness'—a world saturated with the flow of divine abundance.[27] 'Inwardness' is the object of contemplation, mystical communion, and spiritual exaltation,[28] while 'outwardness' is addressed with equanimity, through the

[23] Meshullam Phœbus Heller of Zbarazh, *Yosher divrei emet*, 19, end of s. 23: 'For this person, the whole world is filled with His glory . . . for those who do not fall into this category, God forbid, the world is seen as being empty and devoid of His divine presence.'

[24] *Likutei Moharan*, part 1, *torah* 64, s. 1. For an analysis of this passage see Weiss, *Meḥkarim*, 123–4; A. Green, *Tormented Master: A Life of Rabbi Nahman of Bratslav* (University of Alabama Press, 1979), app. A; A. Rapoport-Albert, 'God and the Zaddik as the Two Focal Points of Hasidic Worship', *History of Religions*, 18: 4 (1979), 323–5.

[25] See Weiss, *Meḥkarim*, 123–7; Tishby and Dan, 'Hasidut', 779; Elior, 'Hazikah', 112.

[26] See *Maggid devarav le Ya'akov*, 124. On the 'Eyes of the Flesh' see Levine, *Igrot kodesh*, 229; Shneur Zalman, *Tanya*, part 2, ch. 3.

[27] Menahem Mendel of Vitebsk, *Peri ha'arets*, 45; *Maggid devarav leYa'akov*, 124; cf. Hayyim Haikel of Amdur, *Ḥayim vaḥesed*, 17.

[28] For these concepts in hasidic thought see M. Buber, *Befardes haḥasidut* (Tel Aviv, 1945); Tishby and Dan, 'Hasidut', 803; Schatz-Uffenheimer, *Haḥasidut kemistikah*, index, s.v. *hitbonenut*, *devekut*, *hitlahavut*; Elior, *Torat ha'elohut*, index, s.v. *hitbonenut* and *hasagah*.

annihilation of material existence, the nullification of the *yesh*.[29] The hasidic attitude to 'outwardness' has been stated in unequivocal terms: 'One must pay no attention to corporeality but only to "inwardness".'[30] 'One should not observe worldly matters or consider them at all in order to separate oneself from profane worldliness.'[31] 'One should consider oneself as not being, meaning that one should think oneself not of this world.'[32]

The relationship to 'inwardness' or *ayin* has been stated equally clearly: 'It should always be maintained in thought and emotion, and truly grasped by the mind, that one's eyes are perceiving nothing other than the revelation of the deity.'[33] 'The purpose of Torah, wisdom, thought, speech, and action is to attain *ayin* and non-being, to achieve self-abnegation.'[34]

Hasidic writings are replete with statements of this kind negating human sensory experience and denying the reality of independent existence outside God. Corporeality must be perceived as a manifestation of divine substance or it is said to lack autonomous existence and is considered an illusion, a misrepresentation of reality, a lie, defilement, or void. R. Shneur Zalman of Lyady argued: 'Even if we perceive the world as "being", it is an absolute lie.'[35]

Hasidic literature severely rebukes all those who take the world to be a one-dimensional, independent material entity. It invites them to focus their attention on the hidden divine dimension of material reality, the expansion which exists beyond withdrawal, and to transform *yesh* into *ayin*.[36]

The transformative principles which govern the divine processes are thus applied to human thought: the material may be transformed into the spiritual, the evil 'husks' into holiness, and the energy of the *sitra aḥra* into divine vitality, since all these contradictory possibilities are inherent in their nature.[37] The Maggid of Mezhirech claims: 'The purpose of creating man is for him to elevate the worlds to their root, that is, he restores them to a state of non-being (*ayin*).'[38]

And R. Menahem Mendel of Vitebsk states: 'The sole purpose of human existence and the aim of man's creation is to elevate all things from down below upward, to subject outwardness to inwardness, to discover His divinity, blessed be He, in all things, and there is no place devoid of Him.'[39]

Hasidic endeavour is directed to this end: the conscious passage from an inherently

[29] For the concept of *hishtavut* see below, n. 43; for *bitul hayesh* see J. Weiss, '*Via Passiva* in Early Hasidism', *Journal of Jewish Studies*, ii (1960), 137–55, repr. in id., *Studies in Eastern European Jewish Mysticism* (Oxford, 1985), 69–94; Elior, *Torat ha'elohut*, 178–243.

[30] Menahem Mendel of Vitebsk, *Peri ha'arets*, Letters, p. 6.

[31] Hayyim Haikel of Amdur, *Ḥayim vaḥesed*, 60, s. 122; cf. *Tsava'at haRibash*, 2, s. 5.

[32] *Tsava'at haRibash*, 9, s. 53.

[33] Shneur Zalman, *Torah or*, on 'Mishpatim', 79*a*.

[34] Menahem Mendel of Vitebsk, *Peri ha'arets*, letter of Abraham Hacohen of Kalisk (seventh letter, unpaginated).

[35] Shneur Zalman, *Torah or*, on 'Ki Tisa', 86*b*; Solomon of Lutsk, *Divrat Shelomo*, on 'Vayishlaḥ', 20; Dov Ber of Mezhirech, *Maggid devarav leYa'akov*, 80. See also Hayyim Haikel of Amdur, *Ḥayim vakḥesed*, 21: 'Because this world is a lie, extremely loathsome, and it is as nothing.'

[36] See Green, 'Hasidism: Discovery and Retreat', 114; cf. Dov Ber of Mezhirech, *Maggid devarav leYa'akov*, 153, end of s. 87; Hayyim Haikel of Amdur, *Ḥayim vakḥesed*, 63, 138.

[37] See Menahem Mendel of Vitebsk, *Peri ha'arets*, on 'Koraḥ', 92; Solomon of Lutsk, *Divrat Shelomo*, on 'Shemot', 54.

[38] *Maggid devarav leYa'akov*, 109. s. 66.

[39] *Peri ha'arets*, on 'Vayigash', 35.

limited experience of the *yesh* into the ultimate realization of *ayin*. Hasidic worship is a call to unveil the spiritual root of all concrete things and to engage in the transformative process that unites the finite and the infinite. Thus, 'inwardness' is to be sought within 'outwardness', the divine soul beyond the animal soul, *ayin*—the unlimited flow of divine spirit—beyond *ani*—the sense of self or the restrictive material configuration of *ayin*, expansion beyond withdrawal, and the divine beyond the human.[40] This is also the main object of hasidic contemplation, which seeks to penetrate through apparent reality into its true essence, to attain the spiritual consciousness that 'the *ayin* is the essence and the *yesh* is inferior'.[41]

This transformation of human awareness is known as *bitul hayesh, hafshatat hagashmiyut, berur, hitbonenut, ha'atakah*, or *hazazah*, and it requires a conscious rejection of material reality.[42] Thus, the hasidic ethos is based on indifference to mundane existence and earthly concerns, a state which conditions the conversion of sensory perception into the illuminated consciousness of the *ayin*.[43] R. Solomon of Lutsk describes this process as follows:

> As a person acquires illuminated consciousness and comes to possess 'Eyes of the Mind', even if the visible spark which is perceived through the 'Eyes of Flesh' is very small, when one strips the spark of its enveloping corporeality one must imagine that it is nothing other than divine vitality drawn from its supernal root; then, surely, its light and vitality are infinitely magnified since, by virtue of its spirituality and vital force, one cleaves to the source and beholds the divine root and origin of all things.[44]

Materiality and empirical reality are viewed as devoid of all validity, lacking substance and meaning, since the unattainable *ayin* has become the only meaningful dimension of being. This reversal of the laws governing human perception is the core of the matter. However, ecstatic transformation or illuminated perception is not easily achieved, and the great difficulties which it presents are often recounted in hasidic writings.

The hasidic masters were fully aware of the disparity between their perception of the universe as God-filled and the human experience of God's transcendence and inaccessibility.[45] They explained this disparity as arising from the fact that the human

[40] See Elior, *Torat ha'elohut*, 121–243; Weiss, *Eastern European Jewish Mysticism*, 47–83, 142–54.

[41] Shneur Zalman, *Torah or*, on 'Vayehi', 102*a*.

[42] For a hasidic formulation of this idea, see S. B. Levine (ed.), *Igrot kodesh: Kuntres miluim* (Brooklyn, NY, 1981), 11 ff.: 'The essence of divine worship is to divest oneself of human sensual perception in order to perceive the true and unconcealed reality . . . Believe me, in truth, since this is the beginning of all worship, to be removed and to transcend one's place . . . the essence is contemplation . . . the main thing is to nullify one's place.' Cf. Menahem Mendel of Vitebsk, *Peri ha'arets*, 9: 'When one becomes accustomed to contemplating God in such a manner, one may transcend nature'; cf. pp. 75–6; Meshullam Phoebus Heller, *Yosher divrei emet*, 9, 12; Dov Ber of Mezhirech, *Maggid devarav leYa'akov*, 186; Shneur Zalman, *Tanya*, ch. 33, 41*b*; ch. 50, 70*b*.

[43] On 'indifference' or 'equanimity' (*hishtavut*) see Scholem, *Major Trends*, 96–7, 372; Schatz-Uffenheimer, *Haḥasidut kemistikah*, 104: Matt, '*Ayin*', 46–7; cf. Hayyim Haikel of Amdur, *Ḥayim vaḥesed*, 2, 96–7; *Tsava'at haRibash*, ss. 2, 4, 6, 10.

[44] *Maggid devarav leYa'akov*, introd. p. 6.

[45] Menahem Mendel, *Peri ha'arets*, Letters, 9; on 'Va'yetse', 21; cf. Shneur Zalman, *Tanya*, ch. 17, 22*b*: 'With the above in mind, one can understand the scriptural text, "But the thing is very nigh unto thee." At first glance, the statement that "the thing is very nigh unto thee . . . in thy heart" seems to be contrary to our experience. For it is not a "very nigh thing" to change one's heart from mundane desires to a sincere love of God."' Cf. the references cited above in n. 24.

senses can perceive only the material reality of *yesh* but cannot respond to the challenge of detecting its hidden divinity in *ayin*. Therefore, the thrust of all their endeavours was to clarify and define the true relationship between *yesh* and *ayin*.

Many hasidic works are concerned with the denial of sensual experience, the renunciation of any consciousness of autonomous existence, and the invalidation of corporeality in order to acquire the 'Eyes of the Mind' with which to grasp the dual nature of reality.

An anonymous letter of Habad provenance reflects an acute awareness of the disparity between, on the one hand, the hasidic axiom whereby a spiritual truth lies beyond every sensory 'illusion', and, on the other hand, the reality of the material world as it is encountered in daily life:

> Truly, the essence of perception is in the knowledge which unites the mind and the heart within the sense of *ayin* . . . since truly all things are but naught and nothing . . . But on account of our worldly habit of seeing only coarse materiality, and our inability to observe anything other than the material aspect of those things which conceal and disguise and deny the truth, on account of the concealment of the divine we imagine [the material aspect] to have substance. . . .
>
> The essence of divine worship is to divest oneself of human sensual perception in order to perceive the true, unconcealed reality . . . that is, to accustom oneself to the contemplation of the enlivening spirituality . . . And the main attainment is [to grasp] that all reality and its diverse manifestations is *ayin*. This is the starting point of divine worship, but alas, what can I do on your behalf? I cannot show you how to perceive the *ayin* . . . and believe me, the starting point of divine worship is to be removed from and to transcend one's place. But alas, what can I do? You are not accustomed to beholding the heavens but only the earth below . . . while the main point is to abnegate the self.[46]

It is evident that the author of the letter was fully aware of the difficulty of teaching his followers how to see with the 'Eyes of the Mind': 'Truly you are *not* accustomed to this kind of perception but only to human perception which grasps by means of the profane material senses.'[47]

The hasidic leadership encountered great difficulties in its attempt to transmit to a wider public this peculiar understanding of the relationship between *ayin* and *yesh* as developed by the early founders of hasidism who were, after all, endowed with special spiritual insight.[48] One cannot compare the ecstatic atmosphere which marks the circle of the Baal Shem Tov or the profound mystical orientation of the school of the Maggid with the popular spirituality of the masses who would later affiliate themselves with the flourishing hasidic community.[49] The new recruits were neither mystics nor pneumatics. They were perplexed by the notion of divine omnipresence and the requirement to perceive the *ayin* through the *yesh*.

[46] The letter was published from manuscript in Levine, *Igrot kodesh, Kuntres miluim*, 10–12, and ascribed to R. Shneur Zalman of Lyady on the basis of a number of manuscript traditions. However, the same letter is ascribed to R. Aaron Halevi of Starosielce in *Avodat halevi* [2 vols.; Lemberg, 1848–62 (i); 1866 (ii)] (Jerusalem, 1972), part 3, 97*b*, Cf. *He'arot uve'urim*, i (Brooklyn, NY, 1983), on 'Bo', 21, s. 6.

[47] Levine, *Igrot kodesh*, *Kuntres miluim*, 10.

[48] This is evident from such deliberations as are introduced by phrases like: 'And if you ask what is the way by which to attain the *ayin* . . .' (e.g. Levine, *Igrot kodesh*, 11).

[49] On the profound mystical orientation of the school of the Maggid see the description in Solomon Maimon, *The Autobiography of Solomon Maimon*, trans. J. Clark Murray (London, 1954), 166–79.

Hasidic works dating from this period of expansion contain many expressions of doubt as to the feasibility of transmitting the denial of sensory experience in favour of a mystical, contemplative spiritualization of reality.[50] The pastoral letters of the leaders to their newly formed communities, the introductions to their books, and other literary sources all testify to these doubts regarding the spiritual capabilities of the masses.[51]

It seems that neither by correspondence nor by direct instruction, neither by literary tracts and treatises nor by extensive discussion in homiletic works setting out the demands of hasidic worship, could the hasidic leaders allay these doubts or resolve the difficulties experienced by those who sought the *ayin* and encountered only the *yesh*.

The only solution to the problem so tragically expressed by the exclamation 'what can I do on your behalf? I cannot show you how to perceive the *ayin*' was to present the zaddik himself as proof that the divine is present in material reality.[52] The zaddik embodies the duality which underlies the whole of hasidic thought; he expresses the unity of *yesh* and *ayin* and mirrors the divine unity of opposites.[53]

R. Solomon of Lutsk defined the zaddik as follows:

He is known as zaddik, through whom the divine bounty and vitality are drawn down, and he concentrates the glory of God, blessed be He, in this world; through him, God's divinity will be revealed in this world. In other words, through the zaddik, it becomes known that God is immanent throughout the world . . . In principle, the zaddik must know and reveal all this, namely that God animates and creates all things so that His kingdom and dominion will be revealed in this world.[54]

The ability to reveal God's immanence despite the veils of corporeality and the limitation of sensory perception, to demonstrate the divine presence by means of signs

[50] On stages in the process of communicating these hasidic ideals see T. Loewenthal, 'Early Hasidic Teachings: Esoteric Mysticism or a Medium of Communal Leadership?', *Journal of Jewish Studies*, 37 (1986), 58–66; I. Etkes, 'Darko shel R. Shne'ur Zalman miLiadi kemanhig shel ḥasidim', *Zion*, 50 (1986), 321–2, 332–3. For an acknowledgement of the difficulties see Levine, *Igrot kodesh*, 116–262, 263; cf. Meshullam Phoebus Heller, *Yosher divrei emet*, 20: 'the divestment of corporeality . . . is not clearly understood by everybody.'

[51] A number of letters as well as the introductions to the *Tract on Ecstasy* and the *Tract on Contemplation* by Dov Ber, the Mitteler Rebbe, attest to this confusion. See R. Elior, 'Hamaḥaloket al moreshet Ḥabad', *Tarbiz*, 49 (1980), 166–86; the literature of the Habad circle is replete with discussions of this topic, but there is little doubt that the problem was shared by all the hasidic circles that attempted to transmit the mystical ideals of hasidism to a large following.

[52] The literature on the concept of the zaddik is extensive. See Scholem, *Major Trends*, 337–47; id., 'Hatsadik', in *Pirkei yesod behavanat hakabalah usemaleihah* (Jerusalem, 1976), 213–58, pub. in Eng. as 'The Righteous One', in id., *The Mystical Shape of the Godhead* (New York, 1991), 88–139; S. Dresner, *The Zaddik* (New York, 1960), 113–222; J. Weiss, 'Reshit tsemiḥatah shel haderekh haḥasidit', *Zion*, 16 (1951), 365–78, repr. in Rubinstein (ed.), *Perakim betorat haḥasidut*, 122–81; Rapoport-Albert, 'God and the Zaddik', 296–325; A. Green, 'The Zaddiq as *Axis Mundi* in Later Judaism', *Journal of the American Academy of Religion*, 45 (1977), 327–47; Tishby and Dan, 'Hasidut', 779–83; S. Ettinger, 'The Hasidic Movement: Reality and Ideals', in H. H. Ben-Sasson and S. Ettinger (eds.), *Jewish Society through the Ages* (New York, 1971), 251–66, orig. pub. in *Cahiers d'histoire mondiale: Journal of World History*, 11: 1–2 (1968), 251–66, repr. in G. D. Hundert (ed.), *Essential Papers on Hasidism* (New York, 1991), 226–43; Elior, 'Between *Yesh* and *Ayin*'.

[53] See the interesting statement by R. Hayyim Haikel of Amdur: 'It should be well known to you that the zaddik is beyond the nature of the world' (*Ḥayim vaḥesed*, 16); cf. Elior, 'Between *Yesh* and *Ayin*', 414–24.

[54] See *Divrat Shelomo*, 'Mikets', 33; cf. *Peri ha'arets*, on 'Lekh lekha', 4; *Hayim vaḥesed*, 'Vayeshev', 25.

and miracles, defies all the conflicting evidence to the effect that reality is seemingly devoid of God.[55] As the introduction to *Maggid devarav leYa'akov* states explicitly: 'I wrote all this in order that all should know that even in this bitter exile, in this defiled country, God has not abandoned us!'[56]

Similar ideas can be found in other hasidic books which emphasize the proximity of God and His immediate presence in defiance of mundane experience and the contrasting argument for His transcendence.[57] Countering the overwhelming sense of abandonment, of the 'empty space' and the 'withdrawal' of God from a world perceived as irredeemably material, the zaddik affirms while at the same time embodying the principle of God's omnipresence. He thereby opens up the possibility of perceiving *ayin* through *yesh*.

The zaddik demonstrates the immediacy of the divine presence by working miracles and by similar displays of divine inspiration.[58] By these means he transforms the transcendent divinity into an immanent one, attesting through his own existence to the existence of a divine reality beyond the experience of the senses.[59]

The zaddik is thus described as *mishkan ha'edut*—the 'abode' or 'tabernacle' of testimony: 'The Abode of Testimony also means that God abides amongst us, and because of this one may perform miracles and wonders for the sake of Israel. This is a testimony to the inspiration of the divine presence dwelling within us, that He is responding to our summons.'[60]

Clearly, the argument for divine immanence is not readily acceptable. The assimilation into one's inner consciousness of the principle of divine immanence is very difficult, since it cannot be facilitated by the sensual experience of the 'Eyes of the Flesh', nor is it capable of being immediately perceived by the 'Eyes of the Mind'. The validity of this perception requires demonstration. The zaddik fulfils this requirement by his very being. He is a living testimony of the immediate presence and inspiration of the divine, challenging the validity of any other view of reality.[61]

However, this is but one aspect of the zaddik's complex task of reflecting the polarity of the twofold divine process. In contrast to the two distinct modes of divine being,

[55] It is this sensibility that underlies the sharp attack on those who interpret the idea of 'withdrawal' literally (*tsimtsum kifshuto*), such as that expressed by R. Shneur Zalman in *Tanya*: 'In the light of what has been said above, it is possible to understand the error of some, scholars in their own eyes, may God forgive them, who erred and misinterpreted in the course of their studies of the writings of the Ari . . . and understood the doctrine of *tsimtsum* which is mentioned therein, literally, that the Holy One, blessed be He, removed Himself and His essence, God forbid, from this world.' *Tanya*, 'Sha'ar hayiḥud veha'emunah', 83*a*. Cf. Elior, *Torat ha'elohut*, 62–5.

[56] See *Maggid devarav leYa'akov*, introd. 3.

[57] Note the introd. to *Shivḥei haBesht* by Dov Ber of Linits (Luniets), who explained the need to tell the 'praises' of the zaddikim by the need to demonstrate the immanence of God. See Dov Ber b. Shmuel, *Shivḥei haBesht* [Kopys, 1814], pub. in Eng. as *In Praise of the Baal Shem Tov*, trans. D. Ben-Amos and J. R. Mintz (Bloomington, Ind., 1970) 3–6.

[58] See Jacob Isaac of Lublin, *Zikaron zot* [Warsaw, 1869] (Munkacz, 1942), 150: 'And the miracles and wonders are only from Him, blessed be He, without magic or sorcery.' See also ibid. 46, 139; cf. id., *Zot Zikaron* [Lemberg, 1851] (Munkacz, 1942), 192; Elior, 'Between *Yesh* and *Ayin*', 408–14.

[59] See Hayyim Haikel, *Ḥayim vaḥesed*, on 'Va'era', 34: 'When God sends us miracles and wonders, we can by this power overcome nature, in order that we should know that God is the ruler of everything in the world.' Cf. Jacob Isaac of Lublin, *Zikaron zot*, on 'Pekudei', 73, 139; *Zot zikaron*, 192.

[60] *Zikaron zot*, on 'Pekudei', 73; cf. Elior, 'Between *Yesh* and *Ayin*' 412–4.

[61] See n. 58 above.

expansion and withdrawal, the zaddik embodies simultaneously both withdrawal from and expansion into the world.[62] These opposite states mirror his own transcendent as well as immanent aspects. For the zaddik yearns to ascend to the upper worlds while at the same time seeking to plunge into the corporeal world below in order to release the divine influx which sustains it. The dialectic of withdrawal to a state of transcendence and return to a state of immanence is transformed in the zaddik into the abandonment of worldly concerns in order to cleave to the upper worlds, and the expansion into material reality in order to release the flow of divine bounty to the world.

Hasidic literature defines the transcendent aspect of the zaddik in such formulas as: 'One who is not of this world', or 'the zaddik is he whose principal abode is on your Holy Mountain', and he is likened to a 'castle floating in the clouds, like one who has abandoned corporeal and material existence'.[63] The immanence of the zaddik is expressed in such terms as: 'He is obliged to draw into this world the bounty of children, health, and sustenance', or 'he must be actively involved in material reality, within the congregation and the community'.[64]

The zaddik manifests the paradoxical unity of spiritual 'elevation' and corporeal 'descent'; he embodies the ambivalence of *yesh* and *ayin* as two reversible points on a continuum of both earthly and heavenly realities. In the zaddik, the opposite states of *yesh* and *ayin* in the divine are transformed into ambivalent states which are prerequisites for each other: *ayin*, the source of all substance in the divine, acquires the additional meanings of abnegation, humility and self-annihilation in its human manifestation in the zaddik; *yesh*, the emanated substance and vitality of the divine, acquires also the meanings of material bounty, corporeality, and worldliness when applied to the zaddik.[65]

The zaddik thus embodies all four aspects of *ayin* and *yesh* and the constant movement between them. The human *ayin*, nothingness, is expressed as his self-annihilation, submissiveness, and humility,[66] while the divine *ayin* is expressed as his spiritual elevation or mystical contemplation in a state of communion with the omnipresent divine being.[67] Likewise, the material *yesh* is expressed in terms of his concern for 'children, health, and sustenance'—the material well-being of the community[68]—while the divine *yesh* is expressed when he attracts the heavenly flow and performs miracles.[69]

[62] On the zaddik as both a heavenly and an earthly being see Green, 'The Zaddiq', 341–2.

[63] Jacob Isaac of Lublin, *Zikaron zot*, on 'Lekh lekha', 9; cf. Hayyim Haikel, *Ḥayim vaḥesed*, 97.

[64] Jacob Isaac of Lublin, *Zikaron zot*, on 'Lekh lekha', 9; cf. 13, 39, 104, 190; id., *Zot zikaron*, 191, 203–4. For the significance of the activity of the zaddik in the community see Ettinger, 'The Hasidic Movement'.

[65] On the mystical and ethical dimensions of *ayin* see Scholem, 'Hatsadik', 252–3, and 133–4 of 'The Righteous One'; cf. Tishby and Dan, 'Ḥasidut', 808. On the two aspects of *yesh* see Elior, *Torat ha'elohut*, 43–51, index s.v. *yesh*.

[66] See Dov Ber of Mezhirech, *Maggid devarav leYa'akov*, 85; cf. Jacob Isaac of Lublin, *Zot zikaron*, 6, and see below, n. 74.

[67] Cf. the common hasidic saying: 'It is well known that God emanated the worlds and created *yesh* out of *ayin* (something out of nothing) in order that the zaddik should transform the *yesh* to *ayin*' (Menahem Mendel of Vitebsk, *Peri ha'arets*, 156).

[68] Cf. Elior, 'Between *Yesh* and *Ayin*', 425–41.

[69] Thus e.g. R. Solomon of Lutsk: 'The zaddik always yearns to cleave to God, and by his cleaving, God's divinity and His vitality are drawn down to all the worlds and especially to the nation of Israel' (*Divrat Shelomo*, on 'Shemot', 54); cf. *Zot zikaron*, 181.

R. Jacob Isaac, the Seer of Lublin, states in this connection: 'The principal trait of the zaddik is that he is submissive in his mind and acknowledges his deficiencies. Through his own humility, he stirs the world of *ayin* to sustain the world [by way of] *yesh* out of *ayin*, as in the beginning, when the world was created [by way of] *yesh* out of *ayin*.'[70]

Meekness, humility, and submissiveness are the outward manifestations of the process of transforming the *ani* (self) into *ayin* (nothingness).[71] Similarly, ecstatic illumination, divine revelation (*torah min hashamayim*), miracles, and wonders are the outward manifestations of the transformation of the divine nothingness into *yesh*.[72]

The zaddik must negate his earthly existence for the sake of his union with the divine *ayin*. Only by means of his self-abnegation may he attain the consciousness of divine omnipresence which preconditions his access to the divine vitality of *ayin*.[73] As R. Ephraim of Sudylkow states in his *Degel maḥaneh Efrayim*: 'By means of the attribute of humility which the zaddik must possess, he causes the holy presence to rest upon him, as it is said in Isaiah (57: 15) "I dwell . . . with him also that is of a contrite and humble spirit." '[74] Or in the words of the Seer of Lublin: 'He who perceives himself as naught is able to draw down things which are dependent upon the divine flow, [namely] children, health, and sustenance.'[75]

The alteration of the material *yesh* into *ayin* within the consciousness of the zaddik is a prerequisite for the transformation of the divine *ayin* into material *yesh*. This manifests itself as the flow of material bounty to the world whenever the divine presence rests upon the zaddik. The zaddik who has abnegated his earthly self and who has achieved the 'divestment of corporeality' by turning his *ani* (self) into *ayin* (nothingness) has become a receptacle for the divine *ayin*, the bounty which flows through him to the entire world.[76] By these means he accomplishes the twofold task which begins with the transformation of his material being into divine nothingness and is completed with the conversion of the divine *ayin* into material *yesh*. Alongside the commitment to divest himself of corporeality, the discharge of material bounty becomes the religious duty of the zaddik. He alone must unite the opposites of *yesh* and *ayin*.

In conclusion it may be said that the elaboration of the kabbalistic concepts of *yesh* and *ayin* in hasidic thought reflects a distinctly hasidic world-view and provides a key to the understanding and general characterization of the hasidic phenomenon.

The close relations between the dialectic of *yesh* and *ayin* in hasidic doctrine and its novel expression in the concrete reality of hasidic worship, as well as in the emergence of the social institution of the zaddik who embodies it, exemplify the way in which theological paradigms can provide the framework for social action.

[70] Jacob Isaac of Lublin, *Divrei emet* (Munkacz, 1942), 16; cf. id., *Zot zikaron*, 44: 'For the one who is contrite in his own eyes, the divine flow always comes'; cf. Meshullam Phoebus Heller, *Yosher divrei emet*, 20; Dov Ber of Mezhirech, *Maggid devarav leYa'akov*, 230.

[71] See Schatz-Uffenheimer, *Haḥasidut kemistikah*, 22–31, 113–14.

[72] See Elior, 'Between *Yesh* and *Ayin*', 411–14.

[73] See Schatz-Uffenheimer, *Haḥasidut kemistikah*, 81.

[74] *Degel maḥaneh Efrayim* [1808] (Jerusalem, 1963), 'Noaḥ', 10; cf. Tishby and Dan, 'Hasidut', 808.

[75] *Zot zikaron*, 167; cf. *Zikaron zot*, 9, and Dov Ber of Mezhirech, *Maggid devarav leYa'akov*, 85.

[76] See Scholem, 'Hatsadik', 252–3, and 133–4 of 'The Righteous One'; cf. Weiss, '*Via Passiva*', 69–94. On the function of this perception in hasidism see Schatz-Uffenheimer, *Haḥasidut kemistikah*, 111–13.

TEN

Walking as a Sacred Duty: Theological Transformation of Social Reality in Early Hasidism

ELLIOT R. WOLFSON

I

One of the central images in both the homiletic and folkloristic traditions in hasidic literature is that of the itinerant. The importance of this image for the social history of early hasidism has been well documented in several major studies with special reference to the role played by wandering preachers (*mokhiḥim* and *maggidim*) and exorcists (*ba'alei shem*) in the formation of pietistic circles in eighteenth-century Ukraine.[1] What has been less carefully studied, however, is the theological significance that this image assumed in subsequent hasidic thought.[2] Even a cursory glance at the sources from the second and third generations of the hasidic movement would indicate the extent to which this literature is characterized by an impressive preponderance of imagery having to do with walking, taking a journey,[3] and the like—images, that is, derived from the

[1] See B. Dinur, *Bemifneh hadorot* (Jerusalem, 1955), 134–47; J. Weiss, 'Reshit tsemiḥatah shel haderekh haḥasidit', *Zion*, 16 (1951), 46–105, repr. in A. Rubinstein (ed.), *Perakim betorat haḥasidut vetoledoteihah* (Jerusalem, 1977), 122–81; id., *Studies in Eastern European Jewish Mysticism* (Oxford, 1985), 3–42. For a criticism of Weiss's views, see S. Ettinger, 'The Hasidic Movement: Reality and Ideals', in H. H. Ben-Sasson and S. Ettinger (eds.), *Jewish Society through the Ages* (New York, 1971), 251–66; orig. pub. in *Cahiers d'histoire mondiale: Journal of World History* 11: 1–2 (1968), 25–66, repr. in G. D. Hundert (ed.), *Essential Papers on Hasidism* (New York, 1991), 226–43. See also S. Ettinger, 'The Crystallization of the Hasidic Movement: The Maggid of Mezhirech and his Disciples', in H. H. Ben-Sasson (ed.), *A History of the Jewish People* (London, 1976), 770. And cf. M. Piekarz, *Biyemei tsemiḥat haḥasidut: Megamot ra'ayoniyot besifrei derush umusar* (Jerusalem, 1978), 22, 96–8, 136–7, 206–7. For a reformulation of Weiss's position, see S. Sharot, *Messianism, Mysticism and Magic: A Sociological Analysis of Jewish Religious Movements* (Chapel Hill, NC, 1982), 149.

[2] Weiss touches upon this aspect of the phenomenon from the perspective of the shift from the itinerant leader to the settled zaddik who typically held court; see 'Reshit tsemiḥatah shel haderekh haḥasidit', 103–5 and *Eastern European Jewish Mysticism*, 17–22. Despite the usefulness of some of his remarks he is still more concerned with the implications of this shift for the social history of the hasidic movement rather than with the intrinsic theological significance of the itinerant image. The spiritualization of the physical journey is a much older motif in Jewish sources. Thus, see e.g. the passage of Saadya Gaon on the benefit of journeys, printed in *Commentary on Genesis*, ed. M. Zucker (New York, 1984), 431–5 (my thanks to Dr Zeev Gries for calling my attention to this reference). Cf. Baḥya b. Asher, *Rabbenu Baḥya: Be'ur al hatorah*, ed. C. Chavel (3 vols.; Jerusalem, 1981), on Gen. 13: 17.

[3] It should be noted that in hasidic sources the words for travel or journey and walking are used interchangeably, a fact that reflects two of the basic meanings of the root *halakh*, to walk from one place to

itinerant lifestyle. It is the aim of this chapter to fill that scholarly gap by presenting some crucial aspects of the itinerant motif as it is developed in early hasidism.

At the outset let me note that two distinct typologies can be distinguished, although only the latter is rooted in teachings ascribed to the Besht. The first involves the use of the walking motif as a symbol for the spiritual progression through various grades, culminating ultimately in a state of *devekut*, cleaving or attachment to God. This usage is found in a wide range of authors including two of the most prominent followers of the Besht, Jacob Joseph of Polonnoye (d. 1782)[4] and Dov Ber, the Maggid of Mezhirech

another or to travel by means of some vehicle. Hence, in my treatment of the motif of walking, *halikhah*, I also discuss passages dealing with travel, *nesi'ah*. See e.g. Jacob Joseph of Polonnoye, *Ketonet pasim* [Lemberg, 1866] ed. G. Nigal (Jerusalem, 1985), 75, where *halakh* is used synonymously with *nasa*. See also p. 243. A notable exception to this is the famous chorus to a song of one of the hasidim of Menahem Mendel of Kotsk: 'To Kotsk one does not travel (*furt men nisht*). To Kotsk one may only walk (*geyt men*) . . . To Kotsk one must walk as does a pilgrim (*darf men oyleh regel zeyn*).' Cf. Arthur Green, 'The Zaddiq as *Axis Mundi* in Later Judaism', *Journal of the American Academy of Religion*, 45 (1977), 329–30. In this case walking as a sacred pilgrimage (*aliyat regel*) to see the *rebbe* in his court is distinguished from everyday mundane travel. The concern, then, is not with *halikhah* in the narrow sense of physical walking, but with the broader sense of travelling or journeying. Nevertheless, as will be seen in the course of this analysis, the essential component of movement by foot remains a critical part of the use of *halikhah* in the hasidic sources.

4 That the act of walking was used as a metaphor for the spiritual quest in Jacob Joseph's thought can be adduced from several contexts in his literary corpus. In particular, he contrasted *halikhah*, going, with *bi'ah*, arriving: the one who considers that he is on the way is really at the goal whereas the one who thinks he has arrived is not only still on the way but on the wrong way. In several places he attributes the distinction to the Baal Shem Tov based on an interpretation of Ps. 126: 6: one who constantly journeys for the sake of divine worship and does not consider that he has reached the end of his journey in the end will produce seed, whereas one who is convinced that he has reached that destination and considers that he has already come to where he has to be, begins with joy but in the end will prove to be infertile. Cf. Jacob Joseph of Polonnoye, *Ben porat Yosef* [Korets, 1781] (Brooklyn, NY, 1976), 32*d*; id., *Toledot Ya'akov Yosef* [Korets, 1780] (Jerusalem, 1966), 194*d*. A similar interpretation of Ps. 126: 6, without however being attributed to the Besht, is to be found in Dov Ber of Mezhirech, *Or torah* [Korets, 1804] (Brooklyn, NY, 1972), 72*b*–*c*. Cf. Meir Margulies, *Sod yakhin uvo'az* (Ostrog, 1794), 4*a*–*b*. See also the collection of sayings of the Maggid edited by Meshullam Phoebus Heller (on this attribution, cf. Weiss, *Eastern European Jewish Mysticism*, 122–3 n. 57), *Likutim yekarim* [Lemberg, 1792], ed. Abraham Isaac Kahan (Jerusalem, 1974), 14, cited as well in *Sefer Ba'al Shem Tov*, ed. Simon Menahem Mendel of Govartchov (2 vols.; Lodz, 1938), ii. 34*a*. See also the interpretation of Baruch of Medzibezh, *Butsina dinehora hashalem* [Bilgoraj, n.d.] (Jerusalem, 1985), 74. It is significant that Jacob Joseph connects the Besht's teaching about *bi'ah* in the sense of reaching one's destination with the mishnaic ruling (cf. Kid. 1: 1) about *bi'ah* in the sense of one's conjugal obligation. Walking in the spiritual plane thus parallels sexual intercourse in the physical. Cf. *Ketonet pasim*, 192, and see discussion below in the last section of this paper. In other contexts Jacob Joseph distinguishes at least three senses of walking or to go on the way: (a) to cleave to God even when involved in corporeal matters (*avodah begashmiyut*), (b) to progress from grade to grade, and (c) to descend from the higher level of spiritual consciousness in order to help others. See *Ketonet pasim*, 141. Concerning the first meaning, see also *Ben porat Yosef*, 48*c*; *Toledot*, 6*c* '"And Jacob lifted up his feet" (Gen. 29: 1), that is to say he lifted up his grade, which is to say himself, to cleave by means of his walking to God (*ledabek bahalikhato bidevekut kono*.)' Cf. the interpretation of this verse in Dov Ber of Mezhirech, *Or torah*, 9*d* and in Menahem Nahum of Chernobyl, *Me'or einayim* (Brooklyn, NY, 1984), 23*b*. With respect to the second meaning Jacob Joseph distinguishes man from the angels: the former is in the category of *holekh*, one who goes from grade to grade, ever-changing like a wheel, while the latter are in the category of *omed*, standing in one permanent condition; cf. *Toledot*, 37*a* and see *Me 'or einayim*, 34*d*–35*a*; *Butsina dinehora*, 73. Shneur Zalman of Lyady often distinguishes between the status of the angels as *omedim* and that of the Jewish souls when they descend to this world as *mehalkhim*. See Shneur Zalman of Lyady, *Likutei amarim: Tanya* [Slavuta, 1796; Vilna, 1900] bilingual edn., trans. N. Mindel, N. Mangel, Z. Posner, and J. I. Schochet (London, 1973), 76*a*; id., *Torah or* [Kopys, 1836; Zhitomir, 1862] (Brooklyn, NY, 1984), 30*a*; id.,

(1704–72),[5] as well as many of the latter's disciples.[6] One can indeed distinguish between at least two models of cleaving to God in hasidic sources: (*a*) a vertical one, which entails the metaphor of ascent and descent, and (*b*) a horizontal one, which entails the metaphor of traversing from place to place. Hasidic writers used both models to delineate the individual's intimate relationship with God; it cannot be said, there-

Likutei torah [Zhitomir, 1848] (Brooklyn, 1984), on 'Vayikra', 45*a*, 'Bamidbar', 38*b*, 64*c*; id., *Ma'amrei admor hazaken al parshiyot hatorah vehamo'adim* (2 vols.; Brooklyn, NY, 1982–3), ii. 729. (The characterization of the angels as beings who stand is made already in classical rabbinic sources and is often repeated in kabbalistic texts; cf. J. Ber. 1: 1; Ber. 10*b*; Hag. 15*b*; Zohar, 2: 241*b*, 3: 260*a*; Elliot R. Wolfson, *The Book of the Pomegranate: Moses de Leon's Sefer Ha-Rimmon* (Atlanta, 1988), 80 (Heb. section). Concerning the last meaning, see below, n. 46. See also *Toledot*, 194*d*; Nahman of Bratslav, *Likutei Moharan* [2 vols.; Ostrog, 1808, Magilev, 1811] (1 vol.; Bnei Brak, 1972), part 1, *torah* 20, ss. 7 ff.; *Shivḥei haRan* (Brooklyn, NY, 1972), 'Seder hanesi'ah shelo le'Erets Yisrael', s. 33, and cf. Y. Liebes, 'Hatikun hakelali shel R. Naḥman miBraslav veyaḥaso lashabeta'ut', *Zion*, 45 (1980), 210.

[5] Cf. Dov Ber of Mezhirech *Maggid devarav leYa'akov* [Korets, 1784], ed. R. Schatz-Uffenheimer (Jerusalem, 1976), 261: 'If your soul inquires how one can raise in his thought everything so that it will be mitigated in its source . . . If one wants to ascend when he stands on the lower level, he cannot reach and attain the higher level except as he traverses from level to level. If, however, he is standing on the higher [level] he can ascend from below in one moment.' See n. 9.

[6] Cf. *Me'or einayim*, 17*d*, 23*b*, 29*d*. And see Asher Zevi of Ostrog (d. 1817), *Ma'ayan haḥokhmah* [Korets, 1817] (Jerusalem, 1971), 11*b*: 'A person must contemplate and know that it is impossible to raise the gradations when he is standing in one place. Rather [this can be accomplished] when he is going (*holekh*) from gradation to gradation.' Cf. Abraham Hayyim of Zloczew (1750–1816), *Oraḥ laḥayim*, repr. in *Sefarim kedoshim migelodei talmidei Ba'al Shem Tov* (35 + 3 vols., Brooklyn, NY, 1981–6), xxii. 47: 'When the zaddik worships God, blessed be He, he is called "the one who is walking" (*holekh*), for he goes from gradation to gradation. But Abraham was sitting and he did not walk. Even so [it is written] "the Lord appeared to him" for God, blessed be He, appeared to Abraham in order to arouse him . . . he was in the aspect of sitting but not that of walking.' See also Shneur Zalman of Lyady, *Ma'amrei Admor haZaken* 5564 [1803–4] (Brooklyn, NY 1980), 111–12, who distinguishes, on the basis of Ps. 126: 6 (see above, n. 4), between two kinds of *halikhah*: the first is that which characterizes the one who, like Abraham, goes from one level of comprehension to a higher one by means of love, whereas the second, the level of Jacob or the attribute of mercy, comprises traversing in the way of crying (*halikhah shebaderekh bekhiyah*). The second way is marked by the awareness of one's lowly state which only increases the more one ascends. For a different distinction between two types of walking (*hilukh*), see Shneur Zalman, *Torah or*, 112*a*. And see *Likutei torah* on 'Vayikra', 48*a*: 'the aspect of walking (*halikhah*) is the aspect of love, to be contained in unity (*ulehitkalel be'eḥad*) . . . for the essence of the walking (*hahalikhah*) is [for the person] to contain his soul in the one, to cleave to Him.' The image of *hitkalelut* and its relation to the ideal of *devekut* in the thought of Shneur Zalman has been recently discussed by M. Idel, 'Universalization and Integration: Two Conceptions of Mystical Union in Jewish Mysticism', in M. Idel and B. McGinn (eds.), *Mystical Union and the Monotheistic Faith* (New York, 1989), 27–58. See also *Likutei torah* on 'Bamidbar', 20*b*: 'The angels are called those who stand (*omedim*) . . . And the matter is that "there is no standing but silence" [cf. Sotah, 39*a*], and the explanation of silence is the negation of the essence from everything (*bitul ha'atsmut mikol vakhol*), i. e., the negation of the will (*bitul haratson*) . . . And the reason this aspect is called standing (*amidah*) is because when the person has love and cleaves to God, this aspect is called walking (*mehalekh*) . . . but before he can attain the level of walking (*hilukh*) and this love, he must first have the aspect of standing.' Shneur Zalman goes on to contrast this type of walking with God that leads to *devekut* with the walking of the evil inclination. On the concept of *bitul* in Habad philosophy, see R. Elior, *Torat ha'elohut bador hasheni shel ḥasidut Ḥabad* (Jerusalem, 1982), 178–243, and the shorter English summary in id., 'HaBaD: The Contemplative Ascent to God', in A. Green (ed.), *Jewish Spirituality*, ii: *From the Sixteenth Century Revival to the Present* (New York, 1987), 81–98. On *halikhah* (or *hilukh*) as a metaphor for the process of love leading to a state of *devekut*, see also *Likutei torah* on 'Devarim', 19*d*; on 'Shir hashirim', 25*d*. And cf. *Ma'amrei Admor haZaken al parshiyot hatorah vehamo'adim*, ii. 729–30, where Shneur Zalman explains that the status of man in his descent to the world as 'one who walks', as opposed to his status before descent as 'one who stands', involves a 'spiritual walking from comprehension to comprehension' (*halikhah ruḥanit mehasagah lehasagah*) rather than a 'physical walking' (*halikhah gash-*

fore, as it has been recently argued, that one took precedence over the other.[7] Hence, the image of the itinerant was upheld as a model for the mystic path. It is true, however, that some hasidic writers viewed the itinerant lifestyle as a distraction and obstacle for the zaddik, drawing him away from a state of cleaving to God through contemplative prayer and Torah study.[8] Yet there is an abundance of textual evidence which demonstrates conclusively that the early writers saw no conflict between walking and the spiritual state leading to *devekut*. On the contrary, the proper worship of God was said to be realized even as one physically walked about and was engaged in social commerce.[9] As such, *halikhah*, walking, became a popular metaphor for following the spiritual path.

The second typology, which is traceable to the Besht himself, or so one may gather from the hasidic sources, is decidedly soteriological in its orientation:[10] it emphasizes two acts whose redemptive nature, from the kabbalistic perspective, is beyond question,

mit). See also Dov Ber Shneuri of Lubavitch (the Mitteler Rebbe), *Sha'ar ha'emunah*, vol. 1 of *Ner mitsvah vetorah or* [Kopys, 1820] (2 vols; Brooklyn, NY, 1974), i. 105*b*: 'the aspect of negation (*bitul*) and containment (*hitkalelut*) of the lower in the upper, for example, [to ascend] from [the world of] doing (*asiyah*) to [the world of] formation (*yetsirah*), and from [the world of] formation (*yetsirah*) to [the world of] creation (*beri'ah*) etc., [a process] which is called walking (*hilukh*), like one who goes by foot (*keholekh baregel*), for he progresses and ascends from below to above, from what is low to what is high'. Cf. Dov Ber Shneuri of Lubavitch, *Ma'amrei Admor ha'Emtsa'i* (10 vols.; Brooklyn, NY, 1985–9), on 'Vayikra', ii. 753. On two types of *hilukh* as the worship of God, *panim* and *aḥor*, in Habad philosophy, see also Menahem Mendel (the Tsemaḥ Tsedek), *Or hatorah: Bereshit–Devarim* (24 vols.; 1950–74), xiv. 640–1; xvi. 476–7. A glance at the frequent appearance of this term in Menahem Mendel's corpus demonstrates how central a motif it is in Habad thinking. See *Sefer halikutim: Tsemaḥ Tsedek* (26 vols.; Brooklyn, NY, 1977–83), vol. xviii, s.v. 'halikhah', 158–77. A detailed study of this image in Habad would no doubt prove instructive. See also Margulies, *Sod yakhin uvo'az*, 3*b*, where the term *mehalkhim* is used in reference to those who perform the commandments for they go from level to level; and cf 4*a*, where the term *holekh* is applied specifically to the zaddik.

[7] See M. Verman, 'Aliyah and Yeridah: Journeys of the Besht and R. Nachman to Israel', in D. Blumenthal (ed.), *Approaches to Judaism in Medieval Times* (Atlanta, 1988), iii. 159–71. Though I have availed myself of Verman's terminology, I cannot agree with his conclusion: 'Moreover, although it is in the nature of a journey for space to be traversed horizontally, traveling from point A to point B, the Hasidim, in their commitment to devekut, were much more concerned with their vertical state of being, i.e. their relationship to God.' In fact, hasidic texts abound with images of the horizontal type that depict the relationship of man to God. See, in particular, Kalonymus Kalman of Cracow (d. 1823), *Ma'or vashemesh* [Breslau, 1842] (Brooklyn, NY, 1985), 46*a*: 'By means of this the zaddik should decide if the way before him is the right one: if in the way that he goes the zaddik does not cease from cleaving to God, then he knows that this way before him is the right one. However, if he sees that the cleaving [to God] has ceased for him, then he should stand still and go no more on that way.' See nn. 4 and 6.

[8] See the exemplary passages from *Likutim yekarim; Zot zikaron* of Jacob Isaac Horowitz, the Seer of Lublin (1745–1815); and *Or hame'ir* of Ze'ev Wolf of Zhitomir, cited by Weiss, 'Reshit tsemiḥatah shel haderekh haḥasidit', 104–5; *Eastern European Jewish Mysticism*, 20–1.

[9] See e.g. the words of the Maggid in *Or torah*, 67*a–b*, on Ps. 16: 8: 'Sometimes a person moves about (*holekh*) and speaks with people, and as a result he cannot study; yet he must cleave to God, blessed be He, and unify the unifications. Similarly when a person travels in the way (*holekh baderekh*) and he cannot pray or study as is his wont, he must worship [God] in other manners, and he should not worry about this. For God wants the person to worship Him in all manners . . . Therefore the opportunity arose for him to travel in the way or to speak with people so that he would worship Him in an alternative manner.' Hasidic masters linked their ideal of communion (*devekut*) as a constant being-with-God even in a social context to the view of Nahmanides as expressed in his commentary to Deut. 11: 22; see G. Scholem, *The Messianic Idea in Judaism* (New York, 1971), 204–5. See below, nn. 27 and 44.

[10] I am employing the word soteriological to encompass both individual and communal redemption, the latter of course being closely associated with messianism. Although some of the early hasidic masters do differentiate between individual redemption and that of the nation at large, in the terminology of Jacob Joseph, *ge'ulah peratit* and *ge'ulah kelalit* (see e.g. *Toledot*, 198*a*), I do not think that the two aspects are

namely the liberation of the sparks of light trapped in the demonic shells and the unification of the masculine and feminine aspects of the divine. These two themes were already prominently connected in Lurianic mythology, but hasidim combined the Lurianic ideas with still older kabbalistic themes and symbols. It should be noted further that hasidic ideas in this regard share some phenomenological similarities with Sabbatean circles, but I would argue that the similarities stem from the common literary sources of Lurianic kabbalah rather than any direct borrowing. In discussions on the possible messianic and Sabbatean elements in hasidism this crucial dimension has been hitherto ignored.

It is this latter typology that is the subject of my analysis. I shall limit my discussion to the treatment of this motif in three authors: Jacob Joseph of Polonnoye, Menahem Naḥum of Chernobyl (1730–97), and Moses Hayyim Ephraim of Sudylkow (*c.*1737–1800).

II

Viewing the act of walking or migration in a soteriological context is not an innovation of the Besht or any of his immediate disciples. Indeed, already in the writings of Moses Cordovero (1522–70) the peregrinations of the kabbalists were understood as a means to provide some form of temporary dwelling for the Shekhinah in her exilic state. Cordovero effectively inverted the Zoharic teaching—which, incidentally, provides the mystical backdrop for the narrative of the Zohar—that the Shekhinah accompanies the righteous in all their wanderings in exile.[11] Paradoxically, according to Cordovero, by means of the *gerushin*—the forced 'banishments' or 'exile wanderings' from place to place—the kabbalists were elevated above their own state of exile, for in return for lending support to the weakened Shekhinah they received mystical illumination in the form of innovative scriptural interpretations.[12]

ever to be viewed as absolutely separate as they are not separate in the Lurianic writings. That is to say, then, that individual redemption is part of the national (and cosmic) redemptive process. In light of this I cannot agree with Scholem's statements in *The Messianic Idea*, 195–201, to the effect that hasidism removed the 'acute Messianic tension' from the Lurianic doctrine of uplifting the sparks, for while the 'school of Lurianism made every Jew a protagonist in the great Messianic struggle [and] did not allegorize Messianism into a state of personal life . . . Hasidism in its most vigorous stages took precisely this step. The one and unique great act of final redemption . . . was thrown out, i.e., was removed from the sphere of man's immediate responsibility and thrown back into God's inscrutable councils.' My reasons for disagreeing with Scholem, however, differ from the classical rebuttal of I. Tishby, 'Hara'ayon hameshiḥi vehamegamot hameshiḥiyot bitsemiḥat haḥasidut', *Zion*, 32 (1967), 1–45. It strikes me that there is an implicit messianic spirit in hasidic doctrine, and it was precisely this factor that instilled—and continues to instil—in the hearts and minds of the pious an intense religious fervour. The whole question of messianism in hasidism, I believe, should be re-examined from a phenomenological as opposed to a historical point of view, i.e. it should not be judged solely from the point of view of its rejection or assimilation of Sabbateanism. See below, n. 63. On the implicit messianic dimension of Beshtian hasidism, connected especially with the social need to communicate esoteric truths, see now N. Loewenthal, *Communicating the Infinite: The Emergence of the Habad School* (Chicago, 1990), 6–14.

[11] See e.g. Zohar 1: 49*b* (and cf. *Ketonet pasim*, 195), 68*b*–69*a*, 189*a*; 2: 163*b*. The Zoharic idea, of course, has its source in the older aggadic motif of the exile of the Shekhinah. Cf. I. Tishby, *Mishnat hazohar* (2 vols.; Jerusalem, 1971), i. 229–31, pub. in Eng. as *The Wisdom of the Zohar* (3 vols.; Oxford, 1989), ii. 382–7.

[12] See R. J. Zwi Werblowsky, *Joseph Karo: Lawyer and Mystic* (Philadelphia, 1977), 51–4; B. Sack, 'Galut Yisrael vegalut haShekhinah be *Or yakar* leR. Moshe Cordovero', *Meḥkerei Yerushalayim bemaḥshevet Yisrael*, 4 (1982), 176–8.

Closer to home for the circle of the Besht is the idea expressed in the eighteenth century homiletic work *Sha'ar hamelekh (*1762, 1774) of Mordecai b. Samuel, regarding the itinerant preachers, the 'feet of the Shekhinah',[13] whose journeys from town to town symbolized the exile of the Shekhinah.[14] These preachers were forced by poverty to wander about in order to earn a living, but on a more profound level through their journeying they not only sought to turn the masses to repentance but also accompanied the Shekhinah in her homeless state. Hence, they were called the 'camp of the Shekhinah',[15] for they join the Shekhinah as she wanders from her place. . . and they are the messengers of God (*sheluḥei deraḥmana*)'.[16] The socio-economic status of the preachers is thus transformed in light of the theological belief concerning the exile of the Shekhinah.

It is within this latter framework that the hasidic idea of *halikhah* must be evaluated. The significance that the itinerant life assumed for the hasidim is evident not only from the legendary tales about the Besht—including his own journeys and the journeys of others coming to see him[17]—but also from comments on the nature of travel attributed directly to him by some of his disciples. I begin with the writings of Jacob Joseph, which are widely acknowledged to be the richest treasure trove of the Besht's teachings.

Jacob Joseph reports that the Besht taught that by means of one's journeying from

[13] The image is talmudic in origin; cf. Ber. 43*b*; Ḥag. 16*a*; Kid. 31*a*. For an early mystical use of this expression, see P. Schäfer (ed.), *Synopse zur Hekhalot-Literatur* (Tübingen, 1981), ss. 441, 745–6, pp. 185, 270. Cf. *Toledot*, 130*d*, where Israel is identified as the 'feet of the Shekhinah' (*raglin dishekhinta*) for 'just as feet lead a person according to his desire and will so [they] raise prayer to the place which She loves'. An earlier source for this usage is found in *Tikunei zohar*, ed. R. Margaliot (Jerusalem, 1948), *Tikun* 18: 35*a*.

[14] Cf. M. Piekarz, 'Hara'ayon hameshiḥi biyemei tsemiḥat haḥasidut', in *Hara'ayon hameshiḥi beYisrael: Yom iyun leregel melot shemonim shanah leGershom Scholem* (Jerusalem, 1982), 237–52. See Dinur, *Bemifneh hadorot*, 81 n. 733, who already noted the relationship of this text to hasidic sources with respect to the question of specific religious customs.

[15] Cf. Pes. 68*a*; Zev. 116*b*; see also Yoma, 3*b*; Sanh. 91*b*.

[16] *Sha'ar hamelekh* (Zolkiew, 1774), part 2, 3: 5, 95*d*. In the Talmud the priests are referred to as *sheluḥei deraḥmana*; see Yoma, 19*a*; Kid. 23*b*. Jacob Joseph refers to the zaddikim as the *sheluḥei dematronita*; see, e.g. *Toledot*, 32*d*, 38*c* (in the name of Besht), 137*c*; *Ben porat Yosef*, 55*b*. See also Moses Hayyim Ephraim of Sudylkow, *Degel maḥaneh Efrayim* [1808] (Brooklyn, NY, 1984), on 'Beḥukotai', 55*a*.

[17] According to an account in the anthology *Keter shem tov*, compiled by R. Aaron of Opatow and published in Zolkiew, 1794–5 (concerning this book see G. Nigal, 'Makor rishoni lesifrut hasipurim haḥasidit: Al sefer *Keter shem tov* umekorotav', *Sinai*, 79 (1976), 132–46), the Maggid of Mezhirech set out on a journey to visit the Besht in order to test his learning. Upon arriving at the Besht's dwelling the Maggid expected to hear words of Torah. Instead, in their first meeting the Besht reportedly told him various anecdotes about travel. The editor adds at this point that in all of these tales there was contained 'great and wondrous wisdom (*ḥokhmah rabah venifla'ah*) for the one who understands'. See *Keter shem tov* (Brooklyn, NY, 1972), part 2, 62*b*–63*a*, s. 424, also cited in *Sefer Ba'al Shem Tov*, i. 12, sec. 8. See A. Ya'ari, 'Shetei mahadurot yesod shel *Shivḥei haBesht*', *Kiryat sefer*, 39 (1964), 403–7. Concerning this tale, see also G. Nigal, *Hasiporet haḥasidit: Toledoteihah venos'eihah* (Jerusalem, 1981), 21–2. There is no exact parallel to this tale about the Maggid's first meeting with the Besht in the Heb. edn. of *Shivḥei haBesht* but there is one in the Yid. version, ch. 23; see Nigal, *Hasiporet haḥasidit*, 91 n. 58*a*. On the other hand, as Nigal notes, p. 21, there is a parallel between this tale and another in *Keter shem tov*, 21*b*–22*a*, concerning a sage who doubted the Besht's talmudic learning. To this later tale there is a parallel in *Shivḥei haBesht*, ed. B. Mintz (Jerusalem, 1969), 97.

place to place one uplifts the fallen sparks of one's soul-root[18] and restores them to their proper source.[19] He thus writes in his *Ketonet pasim*:

I have written elsewhere the explanation of the passage in Ḥullin (91*b*): 'The ground on which you [Jacob] are lying I will assign to you (Gen. 28: 13),' what is the significance of this comment? R. Isaac said: 'this teaches that the Holy One, blessed be He, folded all of the land of Israel and placed it under him [i.e. Jacob].' I have heard in the name of my teacher [i.e. the Besht] that travelling from place to place is [for the sake of] purifying the sparks. Jacob, under whom [God] folded all the land of Israel, did not have to travel, but he was able to purify the sparks in his place by means of the study of Torah.[20]

Reflecting on a parallel passage to the above citation in Jacob Joseph's *Ben porat Yosef*, Joseph Weiss wrote that

Besht's theory of the sparks belonging to one person and yet scattered should be understood as conditioned by his own situation, and indeed it precisely reflects the predicament of the peddler in magical amulets and charms who wanders through the Jewish settlements of Eastern Europe, but dreams in Lurianic terms of the possibility of earning a living in a way that would allow him to gather up the sparks of his soul in one place without having to move from village to village. However, this dream of an ideal sedentary existence could not sufficiently be fulfilled in his own lifetime.[21]

Weiss therefore sees in this teaching attributed to the Besht the beginnings of the shift from the itinerant *ba'al shem* to the settled zaddik who holds court and thus earns his

[18] In the Lurianic scheme one can already speak of two kinds of sparks: the sparks of Shekhinah and those of the soul of primal Adam. It is, moreover, the task of man to seek out the sparks of his soul-root so that he may uplift them and restore them to their source. The hasidic teaching added a personal and unique dimension to this idea by stressing that there are sparks in the cosmos that belong exclusively to an individual. See Scholem, *The Messianic Idea*, 186–92; Louis Jacobs, 'The Uplifting of the Sparks in Later Jewish Mysticism', in A. Green, *Jewish Spirituality*, ii: *From the Sixteenth Century Revival to the Present* (New York, 1987), 117.

[19] Cf. Menahem Mendel of Peremyshlany, *Darkhei yesharim* [Zhitomir, 1805], in *Torat haḥasidim harishonim* (Bnei Brak, 1981), 274 '"The steps of a man are made firm by the Lord" (Ps. 37: 23): Each and every step that a person takes is through [divine] providence so that he will gather the sparks of his soul from there where they are scattered; the sparks wait and anticipate his coming so that they will be joined with him [as they are] the sparks of his soul." See also Aaron Roth, *Shulḥan hatahor* [Satu-Mare (Satmar), 1933] (Jerusalem, 1989), 127*b*: 'Our teacher, the Besht, may his merit protect us, revealed that sometimes a person must travel a long distance and he thinks that he travels for business, but the intended purpose [of the journey] is that there is [in that place] a spark which he must elevate . . . and every holy spark must necessarily be uplifted by that very person, for it is a portion of his soul, and it cannot be uplifted by anyone else.' Cf. Scholem, *The Messianic Idea*, 191. This theoretical position underlies a theme repeated constantly in hasidic tales concerning a master who is propelled by an uncontrollable force to journey to distant places in order to perform a seemingly menial task that, in fact, has the power to liberate sparks of his soul-root. See Jacobs, 'The Uplifting of the Sparks', 117

[20] *Ketonet pasim*, 75. For an entirely different explanation of Jacob's journey from Be'er Sheva to Haran, which represents the departure from a state of *devekut*, see *Toledot*, 6*a*. See also *Me'or einayim*, 18*d*, 20*b*. In contrast to the interpretation of the Besht, the *rebbe* from Chernobyl interprets the talmudic dictum that God folded all of Israel under Jacob not to mean that Jacob could perform his duties without travelling but rather that wherever Jacob went the aspect of holiness emanating from the Land of Israel went with him. For other interpretations of this verse that emphasize a departure, see also Jacob Isaac of Lublin, *Zikaron zot* [Warsaw, 1869] (Munkacz, 1942), 19; id., *Divrei emet* [Zolkiew, 1830–1] (Munkacz, 1942), 28, 30; Hayyim b. Leibush Halberstam of Zanz, *Divrei Ḥayim* [Munkacz, 1877] (Jerusalem, 1988), part 1, 9*a*.

[21] Weiss, *Eastern European Jewish Mysticism*, 20.

living in a way that allows him to gather the sparks in one place. In fact, however, it can be shown from a careful analysis of all the relevant texts in Jacob Joseph's corpus that this was not the intent of the Besht's teaching, or at least the teaching he reports in the name of the Besht. Rather, the contrast is between one who is compelled to go out to earn a living and one who is worthy to study Torah in a more or less stable position.[22] Hence, in the passage from *Ketonet pasim* cited above, Jacob's study of Torah in one fixed place is contrasted with the individual who must move from place to place, although both have the same goal in mind, namely, purification of the fallen sparks. Support for my interpretation may be gathered from Jacob Joseph's own complicated exegesis of Song of Songs 6: 1–3 in the continuation of this passage:

'Whither has your beloved gone, O fairest of women' (Song 6: 1)—this refers to the sage who is called beloved . . . 'Whither has your beloved gone', to seek a livelihood for his household. Could the Holy One, blessed be He, not have provided for them in their place? . . . But [as the next verse says] 'My beloved has gone down to his garden' (ibid. 2), i.e., the place wherein my sparks were sown. The meaning of the word 'his garden' is that in that place the holy sparks have fallen . . . Therefore he has 'to browse in many gardens' i.e., in every place where he is, and 'to pick lilies,' my sparks. This is not the case for [the one thus described] 'I am my beloved's and my beloved is mine; he browses among the lilies' (ibid. 3), i.e., one who cleaves (*medabek*) to the Torah which is called 'my beloved' (*dodi*) and then the Torah is [in a state of] 'my beloved is mine.' For I am one who 'browses among the lilies' as is proper in his place, and I do not have to travel hither and thither.[23]

Jacob Joseph thus distinguishes clearly between two classes of men. On the one hand we have the sage who must travel from place to place to earn a living. To the question of why God cannot provide sustenance for the sage (a position indeed taken by several hasidim)[24] he answers that there is a deeper, mystical meaning to the journeying of the sage: to purify the fallen sparks of his soul-root and restore them to their source. There is, however, a higher level: that of Jacob—he who studies Torah in his fixed place and thereby purifies the fallen sparks. The interesting shift in pronouns from the third to first person may indicate that Jacob Joseph identified with the biblical Jacob in this regard.

In a subsequent passage in the same work, Jacob Joseph returns to the teaching of the Besht and further elaborates on his own distinction between two models of spiritual restoration (*tikun*):

The matter of a person's travelling from this place to that place for the sake of a livelihood or the like is due to the fact that in the place [to which he goes] are found his sparks and he must release them from there and purify them. Thus we can understand why [Jacob] did not have to

[22] It should be noted that, even in those contexts where Jacob Joseph speaks in general terms about man's *halikhah*, upon examination it becomes clear that he is really speaking about the élite segment of the population, the 'men of form' or 'spirit', the zaddikim, and not the masses, the 'men of matter' or 'body'. This phenomenon in the writings of Jacob Joseph, with special reference to the idea of *devekut*, has already been noted by A. Rapoport-Albert, 'God and the Zaddik as the Two Focal Points of Hasidic Worship', *History of Religions*, 18: 4 (1979), 306–9, repr. in G. D. Hundert (ed.), *Essential Papers on Hasidism* (NewYork, 1991), 299–329. On the doctrine of matter and form in Jacob Joseph, see Weiss, 'Reshit tsemiḥatah shel haderekh haḥasidit', 51 n. 13; S. Dresner, *The Zaddik* (New York, 1960), 136–7.

[23] *Ketonet pasim*, 75–6.

[24] See Dinur, *Bemifneh hadorot*, 106 n. 613; Ettinger, 'The Hasidic Movement', 255.

travel from place to place in order to purify his sparks for all the land of Israel was contained under him and he purified his sparks in his place . . . just as there is an aspect of restoration (*tikun*) by means of action (*hama'aseh*) for the masses so there is such an aspect [of *tikun*] in the diligent study of Torah (*be'esek hatorah*) of the sage . . . Jacob is himself the aspect of Torah . . . and therefore Jacob was able to purify [the sparks] in his place just as another person accomplishes this by going out to action (*lelekh bema'aseh*).[25]

There are thus two levels of *tikun*, both understood in terms of the traditional Lurianic conception of uplifting the sparks. There is the level achieved by one who is involved with wordly pursuits, the man of action for whom even mundane journeys have a spiritual value. Such a man must travel from place to place in order to earn a living, but in truth his journeys have a profound mystical significance for the place to where he journeys contains sparks of his soul-root that must be redeemed.[26] On the other hand there is the level achieved by one who is deeply engaged in the study of Torah, who performs the *tikun* by staying in one fixed place. While Jacob is a paradigmatic example of the latter, Abraham is prototypical of the former as he is commanded, 'Rise up and walk about the land' (Gen. 13: 17), that is, 'he had to walk about the land from place to place in order to purify the sparks'. Although Jacob Joseph begins by saying that only Jacob was on the level of purifying the sparks by staying in one place, in a subsequent passage he notes that Moses, who is identified with the 'good' and the Torah, 'was able to purify [the sparks] in his place by means of diligent study of Torah (*esek hatorah*), and he took the good from the bad, but he did not have to be driven from place to place'.[27] Moses, therefore, is on the same level as Jacob, a theme that can be traced back to classical kabbalistic sources, most importantly the Zohar.[28]

In still another passage from his *Ben porat Yosef*, to which I alluded above, Jacob Joseph mentions the Besht's teaching and equates the status of Jacob with that of Noah:

I have heard in the name of my teacher an explanation of [the passage in] the tractate Ḥullin: [God] folded all of the land of Israel under Jacob . . . he did not have to travel from place to place to purify his sparks for he could purify them in his place . . . And according to this the verse, 'But Noah found favour with the Lord' (Gen. 6: 8) can be understood . . . Noah was in his place and purified his sparks according to the mystery of 'he was a righteous man, blameless in his age' (Gen. 6: 9), i.e. to purify the sparks of the generation. For 'Noah walked with God' (ibid.), i.e. he meditated on Torah and the worship of God all day, and by means of this he purified [the sparks] in his place.[29]

Here again we find Jacob Joseph elaborating on the Besht's teaching by drawing a comparison between Jacob and Noah. Just as Jacob was able to liberate the sparks while

[25] *Ketonet pasim*, 242–3.

[26] Cf. Levi Isaac of Berdichev, *Kedushat Levi* [Slavuta, 1798] (Brooklyn, NY, 1978), 5*a*, and the passage from Uri Feivel of Dubnekow, *Or haḥokhmah*, cited in *Sefer Ba'al Shem Tov*, 1: 110*b*.

[27] *Ketonet pasim*, 244. Elsewhere in Jacob Joseph's writings Moses is depicted as the zaddik who was able to achieve *devekut* even when he was amongst others and involved in physical matters. See *Ketonet pasim*, 53–4, 246, 276; Jacob Joseph, *Tsafenat pa'neaḥ* [Korets, 1782] (New York, 1954), 95*b*. Jacob Joseph also attributes this interpretation of Moses' status to Menahem b. Aaron ibn Zeraḥ's *Tseidah laderekh* (Ferrara, 1554). See below, n. 44.

[28] See e.g. Zohar 1: 21*b*.

[29] *Ben porat Yosef*, 18*b*, 20*a*. The passage is partially translated and discussed by Weiss, *Eastern European Jewish Mysticism*, 19–20. See also G. Nigal, *Torot ba'al haToledot* (Jerusalem, 1974), 16–17.

staying in one place, so too was Noah, who was described in Scripture by the expression 'Noah walked with God.' The essence of walking, from the pietistic perspective, is therefore to purify the holy sparks and release them from their carnal bondage. Noah, paradoxically, accomplished this by staying in one place.[30]

The above passage in which Jacob Joseph extols the virtue of Noah as one who could gather all the divine sparks by standing still contrasts sharply with another interpretation he offers of the verse 'Noah walked with God.' A comparison of the two interpretations highlights a basic tension in Jacob Joseph's writings, most recently discussed by Ya'akov Hisdai, between the clashing ideals of separatism or spiritual élitism and communal responsibility.[31] The text from *Ben porat Yosef* is based on a passage in the *Shenei luḥot haberit* of Isaiah Horowitz (1565–1630)[32] which, in turn, is based on a passage in the *Sefer ḥaredim* of Eleazar Azikri (1533–1600).[33] Jacob Joseph writes:

Noah secluded himself (*mitboded*) with God and did not admonish the people of his generation. Therefore [it is written] 'he was a righteous man, blameless in his age' (Gen. 6: 9). That

[30] Interesting in this regard is Jacob Joseph's interpretation of another passage in tractate Ḥul. (110*b*). 'Whoever lives inside the land of Israel is like one who has a God but whoever lives outside of Israel is like one who has no God': 'I have heard from my teacher that a person is entirely in the place where his mind is concentrated (cf. *Toledot*, 20*a*). If he lives outside the Land of Israel and constantly thinks about and desires the Land of Israel he is like one who has no God etc. But in truth he has one because his mind is constantly on Israel unlike the one who is in Israel who sets up his livelihood in the Diaspora. Such a person's mind is constantly on the Diaspora to bring sustenance for his household. He is like one who has [a God] but in truth he has none because his mind is outside the Land of Israel' (*Ben porat Yosef*, 77*b*). See Dinur, *Bemifneh hadorot*, 194, who discussed the passage from Jacob Joseph in connection with a passage from *Shivḥei haBesht*, 68, concerning Jacob Joseph's desire to go up to Palestine. The Besht reportedly told him: 'Do not go . . . this should be as a sign in your hand: whenever the desire to travel to the holy land falls upon you, know the truth that there are judgements [hanging] upon the city . . . Satan interferes with you so that you will not pray on behalf of the city. Therefore when the desire for Palestine falls upon you, pray on behalf of the city [where you are].'

[31] Y. Hisdai, 'The Emergence of Hasidim and Mitnaggedim in the Light of the Homiletical Literature' (Heb.) (Ph.D. dissertation. Hebrew University, 1984), 147–62. As Hisdai notes, this tension can be traced to the teachings of the pre-Beshtian zaddikim and hasidim. Hisdai has further argued, on the basis of a key passage in the *Toledot*, 124*a*, that Jacob Joseph's dismissal from his post as rabbi in Shargorod was connected with this very problem, i.e. the community decided that Jacob Joseph had neglected his social responsibilities by adopting the ascetic practices of the hasidim and by separating himself with respect to matters concerning prayer and the ritual slaughter of animals. Hisdai is of the opinion that for Jacob Joseph the ultimate perfection indeed consists of worshipping God and not serving human society. For a discussion of the two typologies of *devekut* in hasidic sources, contemplation that is beyond this world and contemplation within this world, see Weiss, 'Reshit tsemiḥatah shel haderekh haḥasidit', 60–9.

[32] Isaiah b. Abraham Halevi Horowitz, *Shenei luḥot haberit* [Amsterdam, 1648] (2 vols.; Warsaw, 1862), 'Sha'ar ha'otiyot', i. 52*b*. On the influence of the Shelah on both the ethical-homiletic and hasidic literature, see Piekarz, *Biyemei tsemiḥat haḥasidut*, 209–18. The contrast between Abraham's righteousness and that of Noah has a long tradition in Jewish sources; see in particular the comment of Rashi on Gen. 6: 9, 'Noah walked with God.' See also Moses Alshekh, *Torat Moshe* (Amsterdam, 1777), 15*c*. And cf. Ephraim Solomon b. Aaron of Leczyca (Luntshits), *Olelot Efrayim* [Lublin, 1590] (Jerusalem, 1989), s. 118, 157–9, who distinguishes, on the basis of biblical terminology, three types of *halikhah* in relation to God: (*a*) walking behind God, which characterizes the people of Israel after they received the Torah at Sinai, being compared to a servant of a king who is completely trustworthy because he has been tested and signed a contract; (*b*) walking in front of God, which characterizes Abraham, who was like the servant that was tested but had not yet signed a contract: and (*c*) walking with, i.e. alongside, God, which characterizes Noah, one of 'little faith', who is comparable to the servant who cannot at all be trusted because he has neither been tested nor signed a contract.

[33] *Sefer ḥaredim* [Venice, 1601] (Jerusalem, 1980), ch. 66, 262; trans. in Werblowsky, *Joseph Karo*, 60.

is, the people of his age considered him righteous for he walked with God; had he admonished his generation, however, he would not have been considered righteous.[34]

One cannot fail to note the irony in Jacob Joseph's statement that, in the eyes of the community, one who isolates himself and devotes all his energies to perfecting his own spiritual state is considered righteous, whereas one who shows an interest in reproving others and leading them to repentance is not. In fact, the latter, and not the former, is the true zaddik.[35] This, of course, reflects the typology developed in many of the hasidic texts, based in turn on earlier homiletic and ethical literature, which distinguishes two kinds of zaddikim: one who is only concerned for himself, and one who is concerned for himself and others.[36] That Noah's walking with God involved the former state, according to Jacob Joseph, is evident from various other comments he makes in connection to this verse. 'This is the meaning of "Noah walked with God", in every place where he went he would go "with God" for he constantly clove his thought to God.'[37] Walking with God thus entailed *devekut*, cleaving to God, attained by means of *hitbodedut*, a term which connotes both a state of mental concentration and social isolation.[38] Indeed, in one sermon Jacob Joseph interprets Noah's being locked in the ark not as a reward for his righteous behaviour but rather as a punishment for secluding himself in the worship of God in houses of study and prayer while ignoring the plight of his generation.[39]

The righteousness of Noah is elsewhere contrasted with that of Abraham.[40] While the former was content with perfecting his own lot—thus he is described as walking 'with God'—the latter sought to go out to perfect the status of others—thus he walked 'before God'. For Jacob Joseph, therefore, the communion with God achieved through *hitbodedut* serves only as a preliminary stage, preparing the zaddik for his ultimate task. Indeed, on occasion Jacob Joseph attributes this perfection to Noah: 'It says that [Noah was] "a righteous man, he was blameless in his age", i.e. also when he went out into the city amongst the people of his age he was a righteous man, to fulfil [the verse] "I am ever mindful of the Lord's presence" (Ps. 16: 8) . . . And this caused that at first he "walked with God", i.e. he secluded himself (*shehitboded*) so that he would bind himself and cleave to God, blessed be He, before he went out into the city.'[41] The ideal,

34 *Ben porat Yosef*, 22*a*.

35 Cf. Dresner, *The Zaddik*, 151–172.

36 See A. Green, 'Typologies of Leadership and the Hasidic Zaddiq', in *Jewish Spirituality*, ii. 135–6. For the earlier sources of these types, see Piekarz, *Biyemei tsemiḥat haḥasidut*, 107. On the two types of zaddik in the writings of Elimelekh of Lyzhansk, see R. Schatz-Uffenheimer, 'Lemahuto shel hatsadik baḥasidut', *Molad*, 18: 144–5 (1960), 370–1. For a similar doctrine in the teaching of the Maggid of Kozienice, see Sara Steinfeld, 'The Hassidic Teachings of Rabbi Israel, the Maggid of Koznitz' (thesis, Jewish Theological Seminary, 1981), 99–141. It is essential to note that the social function of the zaddik to pursue the wicked at all costs in order to bring them back to divine worship is emphasized already in Zohar 2: 128*b*. This text serves as an important basis for Jacob Joseph; see *Toledot*, 61*d*, 139*c*; *Ben porat Yosef*, 33*a*, 33*d*. See also Nigal, *Torot ba'al haToledot*, 14 n. 18.

37 *Ben porat Yosef*, 22*a*; cf. *Tsafenat pa'neaḥ*, 95*b*.

38 For a study on the concept of *hitbodedut* in the history of kabbalah, particularly as it took shape in the school of Abraham Abulafia, see M. Idel, 'Hahitbodedut kerikuz bakabalah ha'ekstatit vegilguleihah', *Da'at*, 14 (1985), 35–82; and id., *Studies in Ecstatic Kabbalah* (Albany, NY, 1988), 103–69.

39 *Toledot*, 14*b*. On Jacob Joseph's use of Noah as a symbol for the secluded leader, see Dresner, *The Zaddik*, 104–7.

40 See Dresner, *The Zaddik*, 151–4, and references given there on 283–4 nn. 15–25.

41 *Ben porat Yosef*, 22*b*.

then, is that of the zaddik who first achieves communion with God in isolation and then goes out to help others in their spiritual quest.[42] Whether or not Noah achieved this state (and there is some confusion in Jacob Joseph on this matter), from other contexts it is clear that Jacob Joseph thought that Noah fell short of the ideal of the zaddik, linked by hasidic writers to the Besht himself,[43] whose cleaving to God was not disrupted by social discourse. One of the basic hasidic principles—attributed to the Besht, but formulated succinctly by Jacob Joseph—is that there are two types of *devekut*: one that is realized in a state of isolation from others (*hitbodedut*), mostly through the devotional acts of study and prayer; and one that is realized in a state of community, even through physical acts such as eating, drinking, and the like. While Noah represented the former type, Moses is the model of the second.[44] Following the teaching attributed to both the Besht and R. Nahman of Kosov,[45] Jacob Joseph thus maintained that the true zaddik is not only one who enters the social arena after a state of *devekut*, but one who can maintain that state of religious intensity and devotion in that context. The act of communion with God that is realized within the framework of social relations is referred to on occasion as *halikhah*:

By means of this one can understand [the statement], 'R. Yose ben Qisma said, "one day I was going in the way",'[46] i.e. I was once in the capacity of one who goes, which is the opposite of *bi'ah*, i.e. one occupied with corporeal matters. In any event, my thought cleaved to God . . . *Halikhah* applies to one who goes from grade to grade, the opposite of angels who are called standing on one level, and the goal of the upper level is to cleave one's thought to God. He was going in this grade [of *devekut*] even when he went in the way amidst the level of the masses.[47]

From still other passages in Jacob Joseph's writings it is clear that the purpose of the zaddik's journey is not to improve his own situation by gathering the sparks of his soul-root, but rather to elevate others to a higher level of spiritual fulfilment. *Halikhah* thus means descending from one's grade in order to rebuke and instruct others, to lead them to repent:

With this one can understand [the words of] R. Yose ben Qisma: 'one time I was going in the way', for *halikhah* means when one descends from his grade, the opposite of *bi'ah*. This is the

42 See *Ketonet passim*, 10, and references given there in n. 101. Cf. Dresner, *The Zaddik*, 271 n. 25.

43 Cf. A. Rubinstein, 'Al rabo shel haBesht ve'al haketavim shemehem lamad haBesht', *Tarbiz*, 48 (1978–9), 151.

44 *Tsafenat pa'neaḥ*, 95*b*. Cf. ibid. 24*c*, and *Ketonet pasim* 53, 206, 249. Mention should be made of the statement in *Shivḥei haBesht*, 98, to the effect that the Besht could not talk to people on account of his *devekut*. It was the Besht's celestial teacher, Ahijah the Shilonite (see below, n. 79), who taught him the proper wisdom, consisting in part in the recitation of verses from psalms, by which he could communicate with people and still remain in a state of pietistic devotion. Cf. Rubinstein, 'Al rabo shel haBesht', 150–2. The distinction in Jacob Joseph's writings between two types of *devekut* is based in several cases on Nahmanides' commentary to Deut. 11: 22; see above, n. 9. He also mentions in this context Menahem b. Zeraḥ's *Tseidah laderekh*; see above, n. 27. In other places, e.g. *Tsafenat pa'neaḥ*, 29*a*, Jacob Joseph distinguishes in another way between two types of *devekut*, that of the *talmid ḥakham* who cleaves directly to God and that of the masses who cleave to God by means of cleaving to the *talmid ḥakham*. In *Tsafenat pa'neaḥ*, 95*a–b*, he brings together the two distinctions.

45 Cf. Weiss, 'Reshit tsemiḥatah shel haderekh haḥasidit', 60–1.

46 Avot 6: 9.

47 *Ketonet pasim*, 194. On the contrast between *halikhah* and *bi'ah* in Jacob Joseph, see above, n. 4.

meaning of 'I was going in the way,' he knew the aspect of his grade from which he descended which is called 'going in the way' (*mehalekh baderekh*).[48]

It seems that R. Yose said, 'I went in the way,' in order to instruct sinners in the way, to rebuke them . . . This is the description 'walking' (*mehalekh*), i.e. to descend from his level. I conducted myself in this way, I would give rebuke to others; this is the meaning of walking in the way (*mehalekh baderekh*).[49]

In this case too the task of *halikhah* is to uplift the sparks, for Jacob Joseph, following the teaching attributed to the Besht,[50] includes under the rubric of *ha'ala'at hanitsotsot* the imperative to attend to the religious and moral welfare of the community. It is in this sense, furthermore, that one can speak of a 'social transformation' of the Lurianic idea in early hasidism, a phenomenon well attested in the scholarly literature.[51] Indeed, according to one passage, the zaddik who ascends upward must return and descend 'to raise the level of the masses who are his sparks(!) and his branches that they all should be rectified'.[52] *Halikhah* is therefore equated with *yeridah*, for both are understood in terms of the need for the zaddik to redeem the fallen sparks.[53]

This is the meaning of 'Go forth (*lekh lekha*) from your native land and from your father's house' (Gen. 12: 1)—after you set yourself at a distance from matter [the masses] to make yourself into form [the élite] . . . then you are far from evil and strange thoughts called 'your father's house' . . . And after you are removed from the corporeality of matter . . . then you attain the level that is known, called 'the seeing of the supernal land,' i.e. cleaving to God, blessed be He. This [cleaving] is called ascent (*aliyah*), for one goes from one grade to the upper grade until one returns to the earth in his death, which is called descent from the level of man to the level of inanimate object.[54] It is all for the sake of purifying the holy sparks from the depth of the shells which are below.[55]

That purification of the sparks spoken of here refers to the elevation of the masses can be seen from the following passage:

This is the import of the verse, 'who will give purity from impurity' (Job 14: 4), for the zaddik is called pure, but on occasion some impurity is found in him so that he may join the impure to

[48] *Ketonet pasim*, 213.

[49] *Tsafenat pa'neaḥ*, 20*d*.

[50] Cf. ibid. 60*a*; see Weiss, 'Reshit tsemiḥatah shel haderekh haḥasidit', 64 n. 61. The same idea is attributed by Jacob Joseph to Menahem Mendel of Bar. See I. Tishby and J. Dan, 'Torat haḥasidut vesifrutah', in A. Rubinstein, *Perakim betorat haḥasidut vetoledoteihah* (Jerusalem, 1977), 250–312.

[51] Cf. Weiss, 'Reshit tsemiḥatah shel haderekh haḥasidit', 69 ff.; Piekarz, *Biyemei tsemiḥat haḥasidut*, 86, 206, 253, 258–9, 302.

[52] *Toledot*, 18*c–d*. Mention should be made of the fact that, according to Shneur Zalman of Lyady, foreign thoughts lifted up by the zaddik are in truth the evil thoughts of others; see *Tanya*, 35*a*.

[53] Cf. *Ben porat Yosef*, 54*d*, where there is an attempt to synthesize the two meanings. Cf. Isaac Judah Jeḥiel Safrin of Komarno, *Netiv mitsvoteikha* [Lemberg, 1858] (Jerusalem, 1983), 18. The correlation of *yeridah* and *halikhah* from a different perspective is assumed in the thought of Shneur Zalman of Lyady as well inasmuch as he claims that the Jewish soul is transformed from the status of standing to that of walking in its descent from the heavenly realms to this world; see references given above, n. 6. On the double meaning of *yeridah* as a descent from a state of *devekut* and as the acceptance of social obligation, see Scholem, *The Messianic Idea*, 219–22.

[54] On death as a symbol for the departure of a zaddik from a state of *devekut*, see e.g. *Toledot*, 6*a*, 34*a*. Elsewhere Jacob Joseph calls the wicked 'dead'; see *Toledot*, 11*b*, 197*b*, and Weiss, 'Reshit tsemiḥatah shel haderekh haḥasidit', 63 n. 57.

[55] *Toledot*, 137*b*. Cf. 6*b*, 99*a*, 136*a*.

elevate them to [a state of] purity . . . According to this we can explain the words, 'Go forth (*lekh lekha*)' (Gen. 12: 1) . . . The meaning of 'go' (*lekh*) is to be explained by the expression 'Go (*lekhi*) and diminish youself.'[56] The word 'yourself' (*lekha*) means for your good and your enjoyment, for by means of this [going] 'I will make you a great nation', for you will join them to release them.[57]

There is thus a perfect parallel in Jacob Joseph's writings between walking (*halikhah*) and descent (*yeridah*), on the one hand, and uplifting the sparks of one's soul and elevating the masses, on the other. '"Jacob lifted up his feet" (Gen. 49: 1) . . . he departed from the physical to the spiritual . . .[58] In another place I have written. "Go and diminish yourself so there will be rule by day and night",' i.e. so that you may join the masses in order to raise them up . . . Accordingly, one can understand Jacob's going down to Egypt, i.e. to the physical in order to purify the sparks, to join the masses.[59]

It seems to me that one can therefore distinguish between two approaches in the writings of Jacob Joseph. One—which he attributes to the Besht—employs the Lurianic term to describe both one who studies Torah in a fixed place and one who journeys about, presumably on any type of business trip; the other applies this same terminology to characterize the religious leader who must descend in order to admonish the masses. From the relevant sources I think it can be said, moreover, that it was Jacob Joseph who translated the Beshtian teaching concerning *halikhah* from the individualistic mode to one of great social and ethical consequence. What is essential to both, however, is the soteriological aspect expressed in Lurianic terminology. Although several scholars, most notably, Benzion Dinur and Isaiah Tishby,[60] have duly noted the messianic dimensions in Jacob Joseph, there has been no appreciation of the unique redemptive aspect of *halikhah* as it relates to the task of the zaddik who descends to the level of the masses. That Jacob Joseph in general understood the lifting up of the sparks in its original Lurianic sense as part of an eschatological *tikun* on a cosmic level, and not simply in a 'strictly personal sphere',[61] is beyond question.[62] That the messianic implication applies specifically to the case I am examining is also abundantly clear from the fact that discussions about the Besht's teaching are accompanied by a citation of a critical text from *Peri ets ḥayim* that deals with the messianic task of redeeming the sparks.[63]

There is, in particular, one telling passage in the *Toledot Ya'akov Yosef* which, in my view, must be examined in the context of the theme that I am discussing: 'It is

[56] According to the legend of the diminished moon in Ḥul. 60*b*.

[57] *Toledot*, 34*a*. Cf. 16*b*, 54*a*.

[58] Cf. the Maggid's interpretation of this verse in *Or torah*, 14*d*: '"Jacob lifted up his feet and came to the land of the Easterners" (Gen. 29: 1). That is . . . he went out from his earthliness (*shehalakh me'artsiyut shelo*), i.e. his corporeality (*hagashmiyut shelo*), to the worship of God, blessed be He, a portion of divinity (*ḥelek elohut*).'

[59] *Ben porat Yosef*, 80*a–b*.

[60] Dinur, *Bemifneh hadorot*, 181–8. Tishby, 'Hara'ayon hameshiḥi', 33.

[61] Cf. Scholem. *The Messianic Idea*, 191. See following note.

[62] See *Toledot*, 135*b*, 144*c*, and elsewhere. In light of these passages I cannot agree with Scholem's assessment of the lack of an 'acute Messianism' in the writings of Jacob Joseph (see *The Messianic Idea*, 184). Moreover I find Scholem's general characterization lacking; see p. 185: 'Hasidism, without changing the outward façade of Lurianic teaching and terminology, introduced such subtle but effective changes as would eliminate the Messianic meaning of the central doctrine of tikkun or at least defer it to a remote stage where it became again a matter of utopianism without immediate impact.' See above, n. 10.

[63] Hayyim Vital, *Peri ets ḥayim* [Korets, 1782] (Jerusalem, 1980). 'Sha'ar keriat shema', ch. 3, 164–5.

written in the writings of the Ari[64] with respect to the purification of the sparks until the [time of the] "footprints of the messiah" (*ikvot meshiḥa*), for in each generation one limb from the configuration (*partsuf*) of the whole world is purified, until the end, the time of the messiah, when the limb of the feet [will be purified], for it is the heels of the messiah (*ikvot meshiḥa*), when "the feet will reach the feet" (*dematu raglin beraglin*).'[65] Jacob Joseph further contends that his is the time of the 'footprints of the messiah', for in his generation these souls of the feet are to be redeemed.[66] Without entering into a long discussion on the Lurianic theme briefly alluded to in Jacob Joseph's citation, suffice it to say that the Lurianic kabbalists understood the 'footsteps of the messiah' in one of two ways: in some texts this period was described as the time when the sparks of the souls entrapped in the feet of *adam beliya'al* (the demonic being) in the world of Asiyah were to be redeemed, when, paraphrasing the Zoharic passage, 'the feet will reach the feet'.[67] Alternatively, *ikvot meshiḥa* was explained as a time when the sparks in the shells lodged in the feet of Adam Kadmon situated in the world of Asiyah would be redeemed.[68] The version of this motif offered by Jacob Joseph inclines more towards the latter model.[69]

It is pertinent to recall that, in a relatively early hasidic commentary on Ps. 107 (ascribed erroneously by some later authorities to the Besht himself), the language of Lurianic kabbalah is utilized but approximating the first model that I delineated: 'This is the secret of the exile of Shekhinah [when She descends to the demonic shells] all six days of the week, and this is the secret of the "footsteps of messiah" (*ikvot meshiḥa*), for when She finishes gathering those souls that are in the heels of that impure one [i.e. *adam beliya'al* who is the "end of the impure body" (*sof haguf hatame*) then messiah

[64] I have yet to locate an exact source in the Lurianic corpus, but the critical passage characterizing the messianic period as a time of purification of the feet is found in several places. See e.g. Hayyim Vital, *Sha'ar hagilgulim* (Jerusalem, 1912), s. 15, 16*b*. See also reference given in the preceding note. In fact, it is probable that the text cited by Jacob Joseph is not an exact source at all, but is rather a paraphrase of some Lurianic passage, blended together with Jacob Joseph's own ideas. On this phenomenon in Jacob Joseph's writings, see Scholem, *The Messianic Idea*, 188. On the Zoharic expression *dematu raglin beraglin* according to the messianic interpretation proffered by Lurianic kabbalists, see also Hayim Hakohen of Aleppo, *Tur bareket* (Amsterdam, 1654), 3*d*, and Isaac Judah Jeḥiel Safrin of Komarno, *Zohar ḥai* (Przemysl, 1878), 274*b*.

[65] *Toledot*, 123*c*.

[66] Ibid. 123*d*. Cf. 189*d*, where the feet are used as a metaphor for the exile of the soul (*galut neshamah*).

[67] See Zohar 2: 258*a*. The same Zoharic text is cited by Vital (see references in n. 65) as well as Nathan of Gaza (see below, n. 78).

[68] See I. Tishby, *Torat hara vehakelipah bekabalat haAri* (Jerusalem, 1942), 134–5.

[69] Cf. *Ben porat Yosef*, 33*d*: 'Bathe your feet, to remove the pollution from the two pillars of truth [i.e. Netsaḥ and Hod, see below, n. 122], for this is faith. And this is the secret of washing the feet on Sabbath eve to remove the shell and the pollution from the feet of Adam of [the world of] Asiyah, as it is explained in the writings of the Ari.' Cf. *Peri ets ḥayim*, 'Sha'ar hashabbat', ch. 3, 384. See also *Ketonet pasim*, 319, where the zaddik is said to descend from the head, the 'aspect of king', to the feet, 'the place of dominion of the shells'. And cf. *Toledot*, 189*b*, where the exile of the soul is described as extending to the feet. See also Nathan Sternhartz of Nemirov, *Likutei Halakhot* [8 vols.; Zolkiew (Zhalkva), 1846?–Lemberg, 1861] (Jerusalem, 1970), *Oraḥ ḥayim*, iii, 'Hilkhot ḥanukah', 2: 6, 243*d*, where the rabbinic ruling that Hanukah candles are lit until there is no one walking about in the market place, *ad shetikhleh regel min hashuk* ('Masekhet soferim', 20: 2; Shab. 21*b*), is interpreted as follows: 'That is, to elevate all the lower levels, which are the feet of holiness (*raglei hakedushah*) clothed and bound to the outer places [i.e., demonic forces] which are the aspect of the market place (*shuk*) . . . The lighting of the candle of Hanukah is to elevate the holiness from the [demonic] other side.'

will come.'[70] The centrality of this belief in hasidic circles is well attested from various sources. While Tishby did not discuss the passage from the hasidic commentary of Ps. 107 cited above, or that of the *Toledot*, he did note that Aaron b. Mosel Halevi of Starosielce reported that his teacher, Shneur Zalman of Lyady, received from his teacher, Dov Ber of Mezhirech, who received from his teacher, the Besht, that they were living in the time of *ikvot meshiḥa*.[71] Indeed, Shneur Zalman says on several occasions that his generation was that of the 'footsteps of the messiah'.[72]

In this connection mention should also be made of the version of the narrative concerning the Besht's attempted journey to the Holy Land reported by Isaac Judah Jeḥiel Safrin of Komarno.[73] According to this version, the Besht, who is described as the soul (*nefesh*) of David in [the world] of Atsilut desired to join together with Hayyim ibn Attar, whose soul (*neshamah*) is described as deriving from the spirit (*ruaḥ*) of David in [the world of] Atsilut, so that 'the true redemption (*hage'ulah ha'amitit*) would occur'.[74] The Besht reportedly asked R. Hayyim, through Gershon of Kutow, his brother-in-law, if the time were propitious for him to travel to Jerusalem to see him face to face. R. Hayyim responded that the Besht should write and tell him whether or not, when he beheld the 'image of his form' (*tselem demut tavnito*) in the upper worlds, he saw 'all his limbs and his image'. I assume that this refers to the divine image and form of the messiah in the celestial realm.[75] The Besht responded that he did not see the heels of this form. R. Hayyim then replied that he should not bother going to the Land of Israel for his efforts would prove to be futile, but the Besht did not receive this response and decided to undertake the journey. After spending some time in Istanbul,[76] where he performed 'great and wondrous' things, he was forced to flee. He suffered much sorrow

[70] Published by R. Schatz-Uffenheimer, 'Perusho shel haBesht lemizmor 107', *Tarbiz*, 42 (1972–3), 168; pub. as 'The Ba'al Shem Tov's Commentary to Psalm 107: Myth and Ritual of the Descent to She'ol', in R. Schatz-Uffenheimer, *Hasidism as Mysticism: Quietistic Elements in Eighteenth Century Hasidic Thought* (Princeton, 1993), 342–82. Schatz-Uffenheimer accepted the attribution of the text to the Besht as authentic. See, however, Scholem, *The Messianic Idea*, 189, who suggests that the commentary was written by Menahem Mendel of Bar in 1760, a view discussed and rejected by Schatz-Uffenheimer, 'Perusho shel haBesht', 161–2.

[71] Tishby, 'Hara'ayon hameshiḥi', 39.

[72] For references, see ibid. 38, nn. 169–70. See also Shneur Zalman of Lyady, *Ma'amrei Admor haZaken: 5565* [1804–5], vols. i and ii (Brooklyn, NY, 1980–1), i. 410; and id., *Ma'amrei Admor haZaken: 5566* [1805–6] (Brooklyn, NY, 1979), 278. See also Dov Ber Shneuri, *Ner mitsvah vetorah or*, part 1, 101*b*, 104*a*. And cf. Menahem Mendel (the Tsemaḥ Tsedek), *Or hatorah*, xiv. 1: 650, where the *ikvot meshiḥa* is characterized as a time of *halikhah* by the *ba'al teshuvah* who purifies the sparks in the feet primarily by means of charity. See p. 208, and *Or hatorah* (Brooklyn, NY, 1985), xxv. 986.

[73] *Netiv mitsvotekha*, 7–8. This version of the legend concerning the Besht's attempted journey to Palestine was discussed by B. Drobitscher, 'Shalosh nusḥa'ot linesi'at zekeni haBesht le'Erets Yisrael', *Yeda am*, 6 (1960), 44.

[74] According to another version of the legend, discussed by Drobitscher, 'Shalosh nusḥa'ot' 41, the meeting of the Besht and Hayyim ibn Attar was to result in the redemption due to the fact that the soul of the Besht was from the messiah of David and the soul of ibn Attar from the messiah of Ephraim.

[75] The Besht's confronting the soul of the messiah in his celestial abode in a direct visual experience is a motif known from other hasidic sources, including the Besht's own letter to Gershon of Kutow, first published by Jacob Joseph at the end of *Ben porat Yosef*, 128*a*. For the various versions of this letter, see Y. Mondshine, *Shivḥei haBesht: Ketav yad* (Jerusalem, 1982), 234. See also *Shivḥei haBesht*, ed. Mintz, 64.

[76] The Yid. version of *Shivḥei haBesht* likewise relates that the Besht stayed in Istanbul on his way to the Land of Israel. See Ya'ari, 'Shetei mahadurot yesod', 559–61. One tale in the Heb. version of *Shivḥei*

and pain on the continuation of his journey including shipwreck and the near-drowning of his daughter Edel in the sea, until at last his celestial teacher Ahijah, the prophet of Shiloh,[77] came to save him, bringing him back to Istanbul from where he returned to his home. The critical point for my purposes is the connection made between the act of journeying to the Land of Israel and the 'heels' of the divine image. Clearly, the implication here is that the Besht's not beholding the heels of the divine figure was a sign that he was not yet ready to undertake this journey; the detail of the heels, I suggest, should be interpreted in light of the standard Lurianic symbolism of the *ikvot meshiḥa*. Had the Besht seen the full figure—including, most importantly, the heels—then he would have been ready to undertake the journey, for this would have been a sign that the time of the final rectification was at hand.

Although this relatively late embellishment of the tale reveals a marked tendency to 'neutralize' the messianic impulse, inasmuch as it understands the Besht's failed journey in terms of the traditional notion of 'pressing for the end'—hastening messianic redemption before its time—it nevertheless demonstrates how crucial the Lurianic notion of *ikvot meshiḥa* was in early hasidic circles. There can be no question, moreover, that some of the early hasidim maintained the belief that they were living close to the messianic era, the *ikvot meshiḥa*, in which time the final *tikun* was to be realized before the advent of the messiah. Mention should also be made of the fact that the same Lurianic ideas served as an important source for the development of the Sabbatean theology of Nathan of Gaza concerning the task of the messiah to redeem the sparks lodged in the feet, for this very place was the root of his soul.[78] One should not, of course, rule out a priori a Sabbatean connection in the case of the hasidic authors, but it does seem to me more likely that we are dealing with two distinct interpretative traditions coming out of one source. In any event, what is critical from my vantage point is Jacob Joseph's particular usage of this Lurianic tradition. This may be gathered from other contexts where the masses of people are identified as the 'feet' of the configuration of the world; the zaddikim by contrast are the 'eyes of the congregation' or the head of the cosmic figure.[79] By means of this symbolism one can understand Jacob Joseph's interpretation of the Lurianic concept of the *ikvot meshiḥa* referring to the laity who need to be redeemed at this historical juncture. Thus he states explicitly in one place: 'This is the [meaning of the] verse, "holding on to the heel of Esau" (Gen. 25: 26), which refers to the masses of people who are called heel

haBesht mentions the Besht's being in Istanbul, without however any connection to his journey to Israel. See *Shivḥei haBesht*, 151. According to Ya'ari, this is one of several examples which show that the editors of the Hebrew version of *Shivḥei haBesht* wanted to obscure the details connected to the Besht's aborted effort to reach Palestine. There is no parallel to this tale in the edn. published by Mondshine (see previous note).

[77] On this figure as the Besht's teacher, see *Toledot*, 156*a*. See also the allusion to the Besht's teacher in his letter to Gershon of Kutow, published in *Ben porat Yosef*, 128*a*. There are several allusions to Ahijah the Shilonite as well in the standard version of *Shivḥei haBesht*, ed. Mintz, 64, 90, 98, 102. Concerning this tradition, see Rubinstein, 'Al rabo shel haBesht'. See also L. Ginzberg, *The Legends of the Jews* (7 vols.; Philadelphia, 1968), vi. 305 n. 5; G. Nigal, 'Moro verabo shel R. Yisrael Ba'al Shem Tov', *Sinai*, 71 (1972), 150–9; A Chitrik, 'Al pegishat haBesht im Aḥiyah Hashiloni', *Sinai*, 73 (1973), 189–90.

[78] See G. Scholem, *Sabbatai Sevi: The Mystical Messiah*, trans. R. J. Z. Werblowsky (Princeton, 1973), 303, and references given in n. 279 ad loc.

[79] Cf. *Toledot*, 22*d*, 130*c*.

(*akev*) according to the secret of the footsteps of the Messiah (*ikvot meshiḥa*).[80] It follows, therefore, that the *tikun* of the feet in the period right before the advent of the messiah consists of the perfection of the masses by the élite, the hasidic leadership. This is made clear in a comment near the end of the introduction to the *Toledot* '"Jacob lifted his feet" (Gen. 49: 1). He lifted up the lower level called "his feet", to the higher level . . . he lifted up the men of matter called "his feet" to the upper form.'[81] In another passage he puts the matter as follows:

There is a spiritual characteristic [literally, aspect, *beḥinah*] of he who after his ascent returns and descends in order to raise the level of the lower ones, in the mystery of 'I have bathed my feet, was I to soil them again?' (S. of S. 5: 3). And this is the secret of 'running and returning' (Ezek. 1: 14), and it is called [the state of] smallness (*katnut*) and [the state of] greatness (*gadlut*). In each descent there must be a warning regarding how to return and to ascend, so one does not, God forfend, remain [in the lower state] as I have heard from my teacher that there are some who have remained.[82]

III

It must be acknowledged, however, that Jacob Joseph does not connect the Lurianic tradition concerning the *tikun* of the feet in the *ikvot meshiḥa* with the Beshtian teaching concerning the *berur nitsotsot* by means of one's journeying. Interestingly enough, however, in a comment of a disciple of the Maggid of Mezhirech, Menahem Nahum of Chernobyl (1730–97), who, according to tradition, also had personal contact with the Besht, the two motifs are indeed brought together:

The sages, blessed be their memory, said: 'Receiving guests is greater than receiving the face of the Shekhinah'.[83] This is the explanation of, 'The guest by his feet does not come' (Isa. 41: 3)[84] . . . for the guest does not come for his own sake but he is the messenger of God (*sheluḥa*

[80] Ibid. 30*a*.

[81] Ibid. 6*c*. Cf. *Ben porat Yosef*, 54*d*. And see the similar interpretation of Jacob Isaac of Lublin, *Divrei emet*, 33: '"Jacob lifted up his feet" (Gen. 29: 1). The essence of Jacob's activity was for the sake of the children of Israel. And it says in the Zohar that he left all the blessings and removed them until the end of the exile (*sof hagalut*), as is known. The [period of the] footsteps of Messiah (*ikvot meshiḥa*) is called the end of exile. And this is [the meaning of] "Jacob lifted up his feet etc."'

[82] *Toledot*, 17*b* (cf. Isaac Judah Jeḥiel Safrin of Komarno, *Ḥamishah ḥumshei torah*, i: *Heikhal haberakhah*, on Gen. (Lemberg, 1869), 181). Cf. Scholem, *The Messianic Idea*, 198, who takes the statement concerning those who have descended without returning as an apparent reference to Sabbateans. See also *Toledot*, 18*d*. For a similar concern in the hasidic commentary on Ps. 107 attributed to the Besht, cf. Schatz-Uffenheimer, 'Perusho shel haBesht', 179. It must be pointed out that within the Lurianic corpus there is expressed concern as well with those who ritually re-enact a descent to the demonic shells during the prayer of *nefilat apayim*, i.e. there are some souls who cannot ascend from this descent and they thus remain trapped in the demonic realm. Cf. Hayyim Vital, *Sha'ar hakavanot* (Jerusalem, 1963), 47*b*; *Peri ets ḥayim*, 'Sha'ar nefilat apayim', ch. 2, 295. It is not, however, clear that the reference to the Besht's warning in the *Toledot* about those who do not ascend is addressing the same phenomenon.

[83] Shab. 127*a*. Cf. *Toledot*, 201*b*, where Jacob Joseph briefly alludes to an interpretation of this talmudic passage which he heard from the Besht.

[84] I have rendered the text in accordance with the meaning as assumed by Menahem Nahum. The literal rendering according to the new JPS translation is: 'No shackle (*oraḥ*, derived from Old Aramaic root *orḥ*) is placed on his feet.'

derahmana)[85] to raise the sparks that belong to his soul, and he is obligated to raise them. This is [the meaning of] 'the son of David [i.e. the messiah] will not come until there are no more souls in the body.' The Ari, blessed be his memory, explained that there is a body of *adam beliya'al* etc. and each Jew must raise the souls from *adam beliya'al*. Therefore a person must go to the place where the sparks are so that he may raise them. This is what the Besht, blessed be his memory, said [with respect to the verse] 'The steps of a man are decided by the Lord, when He delights in his way' (Ps. 37: 23).[86] The verse is redundant, 'the steps of man' and 'his way.' The sages, blessed be their memory, said: 'The steps of a man are decided by the Lord,' for God leads a man to a certain place by means of that desirable thing which is in that place. Yet, 'He delights in his way' for God wants to repair (*letaken*) the person there by raising the holy sparks that are there. Then there is unity between the two names, YHVH and Adonai.[87]

Here we see quite unambiguously that the Besht's teaching regarding the mystical intent of journeying was understood in the context of the Lurianic idea of raising the sparks entrapped in the demonic realm, a theme that is repeated on several occasions in the *Me'or einayim*. The Besht, as understood by both Jacob Joseph and Menahem Nahum, was not speaking merely about individual salvation. Rather, the concern was with cosmic rectification that begins on the individual level.[88] Menahem Nahum adds one new element, the well-known kabbalistic tradition of two divine names symbolizing the masculine and feminine aspects of the sefirotic realm. Elevation of the sparks accomplished by means of one's going to the proper place results in the unity of these two names, the sign of the ultimate redemption.[89] In this regard too, the *rebbe* of Chernobyl was closely following Lurianic kabbalah, according to which the liberation of the sparks from the shells was intended to assist in the face-to-face reunification of

[85] See above, n. 16.

[86] Cf. Ze'ev Wolf of Zhitomir, *Or hame'ir* [Korets, 1798] (Lemberg, 1871), 96*a–c*, who cites a similar interpretation of Ps. 37: 23 in the name of the Besht. The passage is partially translated and discussed in Weiss, *Eastern European Jewish Mysticism*, 21–2. See also Moses Shoham b. Dan of Dolina, *Divrei Moshe* (Zolkiew, 1865), 14*c*.

[87] *Me'or einayim*, 42*b–c*.

[88] Cf. *Toledot*, 198*a*; and see Scholem, *The Messianic Idea*, 195–6.

[89] A similar connection between liberating the sparks and unifying the two names is found in a passage attributed to Jacob Joseph in Gedaliah of Linits (Luniets), *Teshu'ot hen* [Berdichev, 1816] (Brooklyn, NY, 1982), 21*b*. It is also to be found in Elimelekh of Lyzhansk, *No'am Elimelekh* [Lemberg, 1788] ed. G. Nigal (2 vols.; Jerusalem, 1978), ii. 617, with specific reference to food (the numerical value of *ma'akhal*, food, equalling 91, the same numerical value as the two divine names). Cf. Jacobs, 'The Uplifting of the Sparks', 120–1; id., 'Eating as an Act of Worship in Hasidic Thought', in S. Stein and P. Loewe (eds.), *Studies in Jewish Religious and Intellectual History Presented to Alexander Altmann on the Occasion of his Seventieth Birthday* (University of Alabama Press, 1979), 165–6 n. 23. See, however, *Igeret hakodesh* of Shneur Zalman of Lyady, *Likutei amarim: Tanya*, 145*a*, where the two tasks are held in distinction, for the acts of unification are said to follow the completion of the purification of the sparks. The centrality of the male–female unification in the hasidic notion of messianic redemption can be seen in the following comment recorded by Jacob Joseph in *Toledot*, 38*d*: 'I have heard in the name of my teacher [the Besht] what was said to him from heaven concerning the reason for the delay in the coming of the Messiah, for [the Jews] do not prolong the "great love" (Ahavah Rabah) [i.e. the prayer recited before the Shema], the secret of the kisses prior to the unification (*zivug*) which are intended to arouse her desire [i.e. the desire of Shekhinah] so that she will produce seed first and give birth to a male which is [the attribute of] mercy.' Presumably, with the proper unification the messiah's coming would no longer be delayed. The mystical understanding of messianic redemption in terms of *hieros gamos* is a theme that can be traced to earlier kabbalistic sources, most significantly the Zohar. See esp. Y. Liebes, 'Hamashiah shel haZohar', in *Hara'ayon hameshihi beYisrael: Yom iyun leregel melot shemonim shanah le Gershom Scholem* (Jerusalem, 1982), 198–203.

Ze'eir Anpin and Nukba, the lower two *partsufim*, although he used the more traditional Zoharic terminology of the Holy One, blessed be He, and the Shekhinah.

In the case of the Besht's grandson, Moses Hayyim Ephraim of Sudylkow (1748–1800), one likewise finds the two soteriological explanations of walking or taking a journey as lifting the sparks or unifying the masculine and feminine aspects of God. In the first instance, Moses Hayyim cites an interpretation of Ps. 37: 23 in the name of his teachers similar to the one cited in the name of the Besht by Menahem Nahum of Chernobyl. Like the latter, Moses Hayyim emphasizes that a person thinks he goes to a particular place to attain something he desires, but in truth that person is led to that place by God so that he may raise 'the holy sparks that have fallen and are sunk within the depths of the shells'. In particular, Moses Hayyim applies the Besht's teaching to the zaddik 'who is like the wise Master, blessed by He, who sends the will (*ratson*) to a zaddik to go in this way, and by means of his holy thoughts and his holy worship he raises the holy sparks to their source and origin'.[90]

The redemptive aspect of the journey is affirmed in another comment in *Degel maḥaneh Efrayim*, but in that context the aim that is portrayed is not to redeem the sparks entrapped in the demonic realm but to unify the masculine and feminine aspects of God. Moses Hayyim reports that he has heard in the name of the Besht that the forty-two journeys of the Israelites in the desert 'are to [be found] in every person from the day of his birth until he returns to his world [at death]'. Each individual's birth is connected to the exodus from Egypt, and the subsequent stages of life are journeys that lead from place to place until one comes to the 'supernal world of life', that is, the Shekhinah.[91] Moses wrote down the journeyings of Israel so that 'a person may know the way in which he should go'. Moses knew the purpose of these excursions—'to effect the unifications [of the divine names] in each and every place according to its spiritual character' (*leyaḥed yiḥudim bekhol makom umakom lefi beḥinato*)—whereas the rest of Israel did not know the inner purpose of their journeys. 'Moses knew the content of the inner intent of God in each and every journey, and all the unifications that were done in each and every place (*vekhol hayiḥudim shena'asu bekhol makom umakom*). And this is the meaning of *al pi* [i.e. in the verse "Moses recorded the starting points of their various marches as directed by the Lord," *al pi* YHVH (Num. 33: 2)], the numerical value of [the word] *pi* is ninety-one [i.e.] including the word itself (*im hakolel*),[92] and this [represents] the unity of YHVH and Adonai [i.e. 26 + 65].'[93] The purpose of the journey is thus to unify the two names which, as we have seen, symbolize the masculine and feminine potencies of the divine. By means of the movement of one's feet, therefore, sexual unification on high is enhanced.

That walking serves as a metaphor for sexual activity, which itself represents the supreme mode of *tikun* on the spiritual plane—an idea well rooted in the kabbalistic sources—can be seen clearly from a tradition recorded in Jacob Joseph as well, explaining why the ritualistic aspect of Torah is called *halakhah*. According to Jacob Joseph, this is to be explained in one of two ways: the word *halakhah* is related, on the one

[90] *Degel maḥaneh Efrayim*, 66*a*.

[91] Ibid. 65*b–c*.

[92] That is, the consonants of the word *pi* equal ninety; to get the sum ninety-one the word itself, which counts as one, must be added.

[93] *Degel maḥaneh Efrayim*, 65*d*.

hand, to *halikhah*, walking or going,[94] and on the other, to *hakalah*, the bride.[95] These two explanations correspond in turn to two modes of study. The prior stage of *halikhah* means that one 'progresses and ascends from grade to grade', that is, from the level of study for an ulterior motive to study for its own sake, *torah lishmah*.[96] When one attains this latter level, then one studies—literally—for the sake of the name, *lishmah*,[97] that is, for the sake of the Shekhinah; this is alluded to as well in the fact that the expression *hakalah*, the bride, comprises the same Hebrew letters as the word *halakhah*. More specifically, Jacob Joseph employs an older Zoharic idea to the effect that the particular halakhic rulings regarding what is permissible and forbidden are akin to embellishments of the bride (*kishuta dekhalah*).[98] *Halikhah* is thus the adornment of the *kalah* through the means of *halakhah*. By contrast, study of Torah for its own sake, without any immediate practical implications, results in the unification of the individual with the 'denuded' Torah. In Jacob Joseph's own words:

[94] On the possible etymology of *halakhah* from the root *hlkh*, see A. Even-Shoshan, *Hamilon heḥadash* (3 vols.; Jerusalem, 1969), i. 271, s.v. 'halakhah'. The rabbis exploited this etymological connection; see references below, n. 99. The connection between *halikhah* and *halakhah* is also implicit in Shneur Zalman's assertion that by means of the fulfilment of the commandments the soul of the Jew attains the level of *halikhah* in this world; see *Likutei torah*, on 'Bamidbar', 38*d*. See also 64*c–d*, and see above, n. 4. And cf. Shneur Zalman, *Ma'amrei Admor haZaken al parshiyot hatorah vehamo'adim*, ii. 603, where the aspect of Torah is described as a process of *hilukh* from above to below and, conversely, the aspect of *mitsvot* (i.e. *halakhah*) is described as the process of *hilukh* from below to above. Cf. Menahem Mendel (the Tsemaḥ Tsedek), *Or hatorah*, xvi. 638, 650–1.

[95] Cf. *Toledot*, 169*a*; *Ketonet pasim*, 8. As Nigal points out (*Ketonet pasim*, n. 76), a possible source for Jacob Joseph's identification of *halakhah* as *hakalah* may have been the *Peri ets ḥayim*; see 'Sha'ar hanhagat halimud', 353. On this correspondence in the writings of Vital, cf. L. Fine, 'The Study of Torah as a Rite of Theurgical Contemplation in Lurianic Kabbalah', in D. Blumenthal (ed.), *Approaches to Judaism in Medieval Times* (Atlanta, 1988), iii. 38. Cf. the wording of the following kabbalistic prayer to be uttered before learning *halakhah* found in Nathan Nata Hannover, *Sha'arei Tsion* [Prague, 1662] (Jerusalem, 1980), 601: 'Behold I am learning *halakhah* which is the letters *hé kalah*, in order to adorn (*lekashet*) the name Adonai [i.e. the Shekhinah] which is the supernal *hé-kalah*, with twenty-four adornments of the bride (*kishutei kalah*) to join her with her husband [i.e. Tiferet]. The connection between Shekhinah and *halakhah* was made, however, at a much earlier period. See e.g. Zohar 3: 20*a* (*Ra'aya mehemna*). According to one tradition, Shekhinah is called *halakhah* before She receives the divine influx from the masculine potency, whereas She is called *kabalah* after she has received it. See *Tikunei zohar*, 21, 58*a*; Joseph of Hamadan, *Sefer tashak*, critical text edn. with introd. by J. Zwelling (Ph.D. dissertation, Brandeis University, 1975), 11–12; and cf. JTSA MS Mic. 1804, fo. 61*a*. See also Moses Cordovero, *Pardes rimonim* [Cracow, 1592] (Jerusalem, 1962), gate 23, s.v. 'halakhah', 14*a*. 'This [word] refers to Shekhinah . . . And this is [the meaning of the expression] *halakhah leMosheh miSinai*, for it is the bride of Moses (*kalat mosheh*).'

[96] For a discussion of the hasidic meaning of the traditional expression 'Torah for its own sake', see Weiss, *Eastern European Jewish Mysticism*, 56–68; Scholem, *The Messianic Idea*, 212–13.

[97] In this context Jacob Joseph employs the older kabbalistic interpretation of *torah lishmah*, i.e. the theurgical meaning of Torah study as a means to enhance the Shekhinah rather than the novel hasidic doctrine 'Torah for the sake of the letter.' See also *Ben porat Yosef*, 33*a*, where *torah lishmah* is similarly explained as Torah for the sake of the letter *hé*, *leshem hé*, i.e. for the sake of the Shekhinah. An attempt to synthesize the older kabbalistic notion of *torah lishmah* as *leshem hé* and the hasidic idea of *leshem ha'otiyot* can be found in Isaac Judah Jeḥiel Safrin's *Heikhal haberakhah*, 5: 206.

[98] See *Zohar ḥadash*, ed. R. Margaliot (Jerusalem, 1978), 64*a*. And cf. Tishby, *Mishnat hazohar*, ii. 375. The source for the Zoharic view may have been *Sefer habahir*, ed. R. Margaliot (Jerusalem, 1978), s. 196, where in the context of discussing the theurgical significance of Torah study as a means to unite the upper Torah and the Holy One, blessed be He, the former is described parabolically as the bride who is adorned and crowned. Cf. Isaac of Acre, *Sefer me'irat einayim lerabi Yitsḥak demin Ako*, ed. A. Goldreich (Jerusalem, 1981), 61–2. See also *Tikunei zohar*, 21, 46*a*, where halakhic decisions (*pesakot*) are described as the 'garments of the Matrona' (*levushin dematronita*). Cf. *Toledot*, 140*d*, 190*a*.

This is the meaning [of the rabbinic dictum] 'Do not read *halikhah* but rather *halakhah*'[99] for it is the bride (*hakalah*). The bride [Shekhinah] should not remain embellished, but rather he [the earthly zaddik] should go from this grade [i.e. studying for the sake of another end] to the higher grade, which is the unification without garment or adornment, but only the cleaving of his inner essence to the inner essence of the Torah.[100]

Alternatively expressed, the primary mode of study consists of adorning the bride with jewels and garments by means of a detailed analysis of the rules and regulations of normative Jewish practice. Beyond this stage, however, is that in which the adornments are removed, when the Torah stands, as it were, 'naked without garment'.[101] In such a state the individual cleaves to and is united with the letters of the Torah.[102] In any event, from this intriguing web of word-plays, one sees that for Jacob Joseph the word *halikhah* is related to *halakhah* which, understood in kabbalistic terms, refers to the arousal of the union of the masculine and feminine aspects of God. As Jacob Joseph puts it in another context:

By this you can understand the talmudic statement, '[Since the Temple was destroyed] the Holy One, blessed be He, has only four cubits of *halakhah* in His world.'[103] That is, there is no unity (*yiḥud*) between the Holy One, blessed be He, and His Shekhinah, who is called 'His world', except by means of the four cubits of *halakhah*, in which the persons of knowledge [i.e. the spiritual élite] are engaged. And there is an advantage for the one so engaged, for light and pleasure proceed from the darkness of the people of the world [i.e. the masses], and there is unity between the Holy One, blessed be He, and His Shekhinah.[104]

In still other contexts in Jacob Joseph's corpus, it can be shown that walking serves as a metaphor for sexual activity. Thus, commenting on the talmudic interpretation that God came to visit Abraham on the third day after his circumcision,[105] Jacob Joseph distinguishes between three aspects of circumcision. The first aspect is that of sitting (*yoshev*), that is, 'the one who does evil',[106] the second that of standing (*omed*),[107]

[99] Cf. Meg. 28*a*; Nidd. 73*a*. [100] *Toledot*, 131*b*. [101] Cf. Job 24: 7, 10.

[102] *Toledot*, 132*b*. Underlying this notion is a decidedly feminine conception of the Torah, a theme that is well rooted in older aggadic and kabbalistic sources. See E. R. Wolfson, 'Female Imaging of the Torah: From Literary Metaphor to Religious Symbol', in J. Neusner, E. Frerichs, and N. Sarna (eds.), *From Ancient Israel to Modern Judaism: Intellect in Quest of Understanding: Essays in Honor of Marvin Fox* (4 vols.; Atlanta, 1989), ii. 271–307, esp. 302–3.

[103] Ber. 8*a*. [104] *Tsafenat pa'neaḥ*, 34*c*. [105] BM, 86*b*.

[106] Cf. Shneur Zalman, *Torah or*, 27*a*, where the word *vayeshev*, to sit, is interpreted as a 'lowering and descent from the place of one's standing'.

[107] Elsewhere Jacob Joseph identifies the angel as one who stands (*omed*) in contrast to man who traverses various levels; see above, n. 4. In still other places he characterizes the zaddik as the one who stands; cf. *Ben porat Yosef*, 31*a*: 'There is a difference between sitting (*yeshivah*) in the world-of-the-feminine (*bealma denukba*) and standing (*amidah*) in the masculine (*bidekhura*). And the righteous one (zaddik), in contrast to the wicked, is called the one who is standing (*omed*).' And cf. *Toledot*, 28*a–b*: 'Jacob, who is called Tiferet, is the masculine world that is [in the position of] standing, and he wanted to join the feminine world [Shekhinah] which is [in the position of] sitting, by means of Yesod which is called peace and tranquillity.' See also the citation from Abraham Hayyim of Zloczow above, n. 10. Jacob Joseph is here drawing upon an older kabbalistic motif expressed in the Zohar. The world-of-the-feminine is a standard Zoharic symbol for the tenth gradation, Shekhinah, whereas the world-of-the-masculine, or the shorthand masculine, symbolizes the ninth gradation, Yesod, or Binah, the third emanation or the totality of the upper *sefirot*. For references, see G. Scholem, 'Hitpateḥut torat ha'olamot bekabalat harishonim', *Tarbiz*, 3 (1932), 66–7. Moreover, already in the Zohar these two divine emanations are correlated with the activities of sitting and standing: sitting with the feminine and standing with the masculine.

that is 'the one who does not do evil but needs instruction (*musar*)' about doing good; and the third that of walking (*holekh*), that is, 'the one who goes from gradation to gradation'.[108] Jacob Joseph goes on to identify these three aspects with the three men who came to Abraham (see Gen. 18: 2), who in turn symbolize the three lines in the divine realm: the left, right, and middle. The aspect of sitting, *yeshivah*, corresponds to the left, that of standing, *amidah*, to the right, and walking, *halikhah*, to the middle. Although it is not stated explicitly in this context, according to the standard kabbalistic symbolism adopted by the hasidim, the gradation of the zaddik is in the middle. For Jacob Joseph, therefore, the act of walking is applicable to the divine gradation Yesod which corresponds to the zaddik below. That walking most appropriately characterizes the zaddik, who is the mundane correlate of the supernal grade that is in the position of the *membrum virile*, signifies that walking is, in fact, to be understood as a euphemism for the sexual act.[109] That is to say, just as the divine zaddik serves as a conduit connecting the Holy One, blessed be He, and the Shekhinah, so by means of walking the earthly zaddik unites with the feminine Presence.

Underlying the above conception is the identification of the feet as a phallic symbol.[110] While this euphemistic use is of hoary antiquity, attested in the Bible[111] and

[108] *Ben porat Yosef*, 34*a*. See above, nn. 7–10. The source for the expression, 'to go from gradation to gradation' may have been the interpretation of Gen. 12: 9 in Zohar 1: 80*a*.

[109] Cf. *Toledot*, 67*a*, where the mystical significance of walking around the pulpit (*lehakif behilukh et hateivah*) with the *lulav* is to 'draw down two aspects in Ze'eir Anpin to Malkhut', i.e. to create an overflow from the masculine to the feminine. To be sure, this is based on earlier kabbalistic explanations of this ritual, especially in the Lurianic corpus. Cf. Hayyim Vital, *Sha'ar hakavanot*, 104*d*, 105*c*; *Peri ets ḥayim*, 'Sha'ar lulav', ch. 3, 63*o*; *Tur bareket*, s. 660, 403*a*; *Ḥemdat yamim* [3 vols.; Smyrna, 1791–2] (4 vols.; Jerusalem, 1970), iv. 82*d*–83*a*. The implication of the hasidic understanding of walking is made explicit by Shneur Zalman, *Likutei torah*, 'Bamidbar', 24*b*: 'Walking (*halikhah*) denotes the unification (*kinui el hazivug*), for one walks by way of the Yesod of Nukba in the foot that is blessed (*regel mevorekhet*) which is Yesod.' On the foot as a phallic symbol, see following note. And cf. Menahem Mendel, *Or hatorah*, xiv. 651, where the aspect of *amidah* is applied to a state of limitation (i.e. the feminine attribute of *din*) in which the 'soul is confined in a vessel', whereas the aspect of *hilukh* is applied to a state of expansion (i.e. the masculine attribute of *ḥesed*) wherein the 'light emanates and is revealed without concealment'. See *Or hatorah*, xiv. 680.

[110] I have treated some of the relevant sources for this symbolic usage in Jewish mystical texts in my study 'Images of God's Feet: Some Observations on the Divine Body in Judaism', in Howard Eilberg-Schwartz (ed.), *People of the Body: Jews and Judaism from an Embodied Perspective* (Albany, NY, 1992), 143–82. For a discussion of this theme in non-Jewish sources, cf. Siegman Schultze-Galléra, *Fuss- und Schusymbolik und -Erotik* (Leipzig, 1909). A particularly interesting example from hasidic literature is found in *Ma'or vashemesh*, 46*d*. '[Joseph] said to them, "You are spies, you have come to see the land in its nakedness" (Gen. 42: 9) . . . This alludes to the essence of the rectification of the covenant (*ikar tikun haberit*) [i.e. sins connected to the phallus], and especially in these generations, for no man can escape it. The rectification of the matter is through one's joining oneself to the zaddik, for the zaddik is called All (*kol*) . . . And this is [the import of] what Joseph said to them, "You are spies." [The term] spies (*meragelim*) is from the word feet (*raglayim*), for this refers to the rectification of the covenant (*tikun haberit*). "You have come to see the land in its nakedness" . . . you want to rectify the nakedness of the land, i.e. the sin of the feet.' See also the commentary on Ps. 107 attributed to the Besht, ed. Schatz-Uffenheimer, 165, where the zaddik is described as causing the sparks trapped in the demonic shells to walk (*leholikh*) on Friday evening for they did not have the power to walk by themselves during the week. In this case walking obviously has soteriological significance that is connected to the unification of masculine and feminine. That the zaddik is empowered to cause these sparks to walk is related to his position corresponding to the divine phallus. Thus see on the same page the explanation of the term *vayadrikhem*, 'he led them' (Ps. 107: 6): 'this corresponds to Yesod for it guides (*molikh*) the seminal drop to Malkhut.'

[111] Cf. Judg. 3: 24; 1 Sam. 24: 3; Ruth 3: 4, 7–8, 14.

the Talmud,[112] the specific understanding of walking as a sexual act of union is to be found in the sixteenth-century kabbalists Moses Cordovero and Abraham Galante.[113] It is not unlikely that from these sources this motif passed into the hands of the hasidic writers. It is of interest to note here that it is precisely this dynamic that underlies one of the better known, but not fully understood, hasidic legends concerning Enoch the cobbler. Gershom Scholem has shown that the literary origin of this legend is to be found in the *Me'irat einayim* of the thirteenth–fourteenth-century kabbalist Isaac of Acre, who himself attributes the legend to R. Judah Hadarshan Ashkenazi.[114] According to the text of R. Isaac, Enoch was a cobbler and 'with each and every stitch that he made with his awl in the leather he would bless God with a complete heart and with perfect intention, and thereby cause the blessing to flow upon the emanated Metatron'.[115] The precise point of the legend is to explain the ancient mystical tradition concerning the ascension of Enoch and his transformation into the angelic Metatron; however, as may be gathered from the full context of R. Isaac's text, the transformation is here understood as Enoch's becoming one with the Shekhinah, also referred to as the upper Metatron. Scholem rightly sees in this story an example of the 'sacral transformation of the purely profane', for even the mundane act of cobbling has cosmic ramifications. The theurgical element of this legend, with its implicit sexual nuance, proved to be highly influential in subsequent kabbalistic literature. An especially telling reworking of this legend can be found in the following text of Cordovero:

By means of his activity man becomes a chariot for one of the *sefirot*. And thus it is with respect to Enoch–Metatron. They said that he merited this gradation for he was a cobbler, and in each and every stitch that he made with his awl he would bless for the sake of divine need (*letsorekh gavoha*) . . . for he unified Malkhut, who is called shoe (*na'al*), with Tiferet, by means of all his channels. And to this the stitchings allude. Thus it was appropriate for [Enoch] to be a chariot for Malkhut.[116]

Although Cordovero's version is clearly based on that of Isaac of Acre, and the theurgical dimension of the latter is preserved in the former, Cordovero has significantly elaborated upon the sexual implications of the whole legend. That is to say, by means of the

[112] Cf. Ber. 23*a*. The thematic connection between the phallus and the feet can be traced to *Sefer yetsirah*, 6: 4 where the covenant of circumcision is said to be set between the ten toes of the feet. For a particularly interesting development of this motif in hasidic thought, see the words of Phinehas of Korets cited in *Likutei R. Hai Ga'on im perush Ner Yisrael* [Lemberg, 1800] (Warsaw, 1840), 50*b*–51*a*.

[113] B. Sack, 'Al perushav shel R. Avraham Galante: Kamah he'arot al zikatam lekhitvei rabotav', *Misgav Yerushalayim Studies in Jewish Literature* (Jerusalem, 1987), 78. See also the euphemistic use of the word *metayelin* (literally, they walked about) for sexual activity in Isaiah Horowitz, *Shenei luḥot haberit*, Torah shebikhtav, on 'Vayeshev', ii. 30*a*. For discussion of this passage see now M. Idel, *Golem: Jewish Magical and Mystical Traditions on the Artificial Anthropoid* (Albany, NY, 1990), 236. A sexual connotation for the word *tiyul* is evident already in *Sefer habahir*, s. 62 (see also s. 92, where the word *halakh* assumes sexual meaning); and cf. Zohar 1: 60*b*.

[114] Cf. G. Scholem, *On the Kabbalah and its Symbolism* (London, 1965), 132; id., *Major Trends in Jewish Mysticism* (New York, 1954), 365 n. 101. Concerning this legend, see also Martin Buber, *The Origin and Meaning of Hasidism* (New York, 1960), 126.

[115] Isaac of Acre, *Sefer me'irat einayim*, 47.

[116] Moses Cordovero, *Pardes rimonim*, gate 22, ch. 4, 108*b*. Cf. gate 16, ch. 4, 79*a*. For additional sources in later kabbalistic literature where this motif occurs, see R. Margaliot, *Malakhei elyon* (Jerusalem, 1945), 76 n. 10.

stitching the cobbler works upon the Shekhinah, symbolized by the shoe,[117] and thereby unifies the feminine and masculine potencies of God, Shekhinah (or Malkhut) and Tiferet. The cobbler therefore stands in the position of the zaddik or Yesod, the conduit that connects the masculine and feminine.[118] As such, Enoch properly merited to be unified with the Shekhinah, for through his activity he united the Shekhinah with the masculine aspect of the divine.

In hasidic circles the sexual import of the legend was highlighted as well. To substantiate this claim one would do well to recall the interpretation that this legend receives in a host of passages in Jacob Joseph's writings. As a representative example I cite one such passage:

I heard from my teacher [the Besht] an explanation of the verse, 'Whatever it is in your power to do, do with all your might' (Eccles. 9: 10). Enoch–Metatron unified with every stitch the Holy One, blessed be He, and the Shekhinah . . . and he thus bound together the physical action of the lower world by means of thought, which is 'your power', to the upper spiritual world. With this he fulfilled [the verse] 'in all your ways', i.e. of a physical nature, 'know Him', i.e. unify the *hé* [corresponding to the Shekhinah] to the *vav* [the Holy One, blessed be He].[119]

Through his stitching, therefore, the legendary Enoch–Metatron was able to unite the Holy One, blessed be He, and the Shekhinah, heaven and earth, the physical and spiritual, action and thought.[120] Just as the *sefirah* of Yesod above serves to unite the *vav* and *hé* of the Tetragrammaton, the feminine and masculine, so Enoch below. Each stitch that the cobbler makes assists in this unification. That Enoch is indeed in the position of Yesod is brought out even more clearly in the following passage in *Keter shem tov* which, so far as I can tell, blends together various passages in Jacob Joseph's writings:

'Whatever it is in your power to do, do with all your might' (Eccles. 9: 10). This means to unite the action with the power of thought. And this is the meaning of the words 'do with all your might' which refers to the gradation of Enoch-Metatron, for he united the Holy One, blessed be He, with each stitch. And this was the level of Moses or master, may peace be upon

[117] To be sure, this symbolism is expressed in earlier kabbalistic sources. See, e.g. *Zohar ḥadash*, 72*d*; *Tikunei zohar*, 21, 60*b*. See also the tradition included in Eleazar of Worms, *Sefer haḥokhmah*, MS Oxford 1812, 63*a*, where the glory revealed to Moses, the luminous speculum (*ispaklariyah metsuḥtsaḥat*), is identified as both God's crown and His shoe (*pazmekei*). In other contexts the shoe is associated with the masculine principle, Yesod, see Zohar 3: 148*a*, 180*a*; *Zohar ḥadash* 88*b* (*Midrash hane'elam*); Wolfson (ed.), *The Book of the Pomegranate*, 253 (Heb. section); Moses de Leon, *Shushan edut*, ed. G. Scholem, *Kovets al yad*, NS 8 (1975), 359 n. 237; id., *Sefer hamishkal*, ed. J. Wijnhoven (Ph.D. thesis, Brandeis University, 1964), 145–6; Horowitz, *Shenei luḥot haberit*, Torah shebikhtav, on 'Vayeshev', ii: 28*d*–29 *a*. On the specific connection between feet and the Shekhinah see Nahmanides on Exod. 28: 2 (ed. Chavel, 1: 471–2); Zohar 1: 112*b*; Joseph of Hamadan, *Sefer Tashak*, ed. Zwelling, 11–12; Cordovero, *Pardes rimonim*, 23, s.v. 'raglayim': '*Malkhut* is called feet in the mystery of the lowest aspect [of the divine realm] that is clothed with the shell. This is the esoteric meaning of the verse, "I have bathed my feet, was I to soil them again?" (S. of S. 5: 3). This refers to the dissemination of the sparks that are clothed in the shells.' In this context it should also be noted that hasidic writers identified the feet with the divine attribute of Faith. See e.g. *Toledot*, 44*a*; Menahem Mendel of Vitebsk, *Peri ha'arets*, repr. in *Sefarim kedoshim mitalmidei Ba'al Shem Tov* (35 + 3 vols.; Brooklyn, NY, 1981–6), xviii (1984), 25*a*.

[118] Cf. Hayyim Vital, *Sha'ar ma'amrei Rashbi* (Jerusalem, 1898), 3*d*.

[119] *Tsafenat pa'neaḥ*, 118*c*. Cf. *Toledot*, 163*c*, 17*b*, 29*b*, 167*b*, and elsewhere; *Ketonet pasim*, 54.

[120] Ibid. Cf. Safrin, 'Heikhal haberakhah', 1: 181.

him, 'But you remain standing here with me etc.' (Deut. 5: 28). 'Jacob lifted up his feet' (Gen. 29: 1). That is, by means of faith he lifted the feet of Malkhut 'whose feet go down to death' (Prov. 5: 5) and binds her with the pillars of truth (*samkhei keshot*) of Ze'eir Anpin.[121]

According to this passage, then, the level of Enoch–Metatron is the same as that of Moses and Jacob. That is to say, the act of stitching is further understood from the acts of standing upright (attributed to Moses) and lifting up one's feet to resume a journey (attributed to Jacob). Moreover, all three activities point to the *tikun* of the Shekhinah or the unification of the feminine and masculine potencies within the divine. This is expressed at the end of the passage in the technical language of the kabbalah: Jacob bound the feminine Malkhut to the pillars of truth, that is Netsaḥ and Hod[122] of the masculine Ze'eir Anpin, the central *sefirah* of Tiferet. The acts of standing on one's feet and lifting one's feet have the same symbolic valence as Enoch's cobbling. All of these actions characterize the zaddik, and their common denominator is clearly the use of one's feet. It seems fairly obvious, moreover, that all such activity with one's feet is to be taken as a euphemism for sexual action (a usage well attested in earlier kabbalistic literature), for the zaddik not only enhances the unification of male and female aspects within God, but he is himself united with the feminine Shekhinah.[123] The *tikun* performed by Moses, who stood up erectly; by Jacob, who commenced his walking; and by Enoch, who stitched together shoes is the unification of the feminine and masculine within the divine, the Holy One, blessed be He, and the Shekhinah.

It is of interest to note, finally, that the use of feet as a euphemism for sexual activity underlies the hasidic teaching concerning dance. Thus, in one place Jacob Joseph reports the following teaching that he heard from the Besht: 'dance (*harikud*) is for the sake of elevating the sparks and raising the lower gradation to the higher one.[124] From the fuller context, an explication of the talmudic dictum 'how does one dance [that is, what must one say] before the bride',[125] it can be shown that the purpose of dance as construed in the Beshtian teaching is to elevate the Shekhinah from Her exilic state so that She will become a 'bride' wedded to Her masculine consort. This sexually nuanced conception of dancing underlies a passage in *Shivḥei haBesht* concerning the poor man, the Besht's daughter Edel, and the birth of Baruch of Tulchin:

Once on Simḥat Torah the members of the holy group, the disciples of the Besht, were dancing joyfully in a circle and the Shekhinah was in flames about them.[126] During the dance the shoe of one of the lesser members of the group was torn. He was a poor man and it angered

[121] *Keter shem tov*, 4*b*. Cf. *Ben porat Yosef*, 56*a*, 80*a*, 116*a–b*; *Toledot*, 47*a*; *Ketonet pasim*, 319.

[122] Cf. *Toledot*, 170 *a*; *Ben porat Yosef*, 17*a*, 33*d*, 56*a*, 116*a–b*.

[123] See, e.g. *Toledot*, 16*d*, 32*c*, 66*c*, 138*b*; *Ben porat Yosef*, 33*a*; *Tsafenat pa'neaḥ*, 92*c*.

[124] *Tsafenat pa'neaḥ*, 46*a*, cited as well in *Keter shem tov*, 23. See below, n. 128. On dancing as expression of ecstatic joy, see Dov Ber Shneuri, 'Sha'ar ha'emunah', 106*a*.

[125] Ketubot 16*b*.

[126] For an alternative expression of the same theme in another passage, see *Shivḥei haBesht*, 75 (ed. Mondshine, 94). See also reference in n. 128 to the development of this motif in Nahman of Bratslav. On a state of illumination created by dancing on Simḥat Torah, see the letter of R. Hayyim ibn Attar cited in A. Ya'ari, *Igrot Erets Yisrael* (Jerusalem, 1950), 269. On the hasidic motif of dancing with the Shekhinah on Simḥat Torah, see also Sholom Aleichem, *Ḥayei adam*, trans. J. Berkovitz (New York, 1920), ii. 89; pub. in Eng. in *From the Fair: The Autobiography of Sholom Aleichem*, trans. and ed. C. Leviant (New York, 1985), 131–2.

him that he was prevented from dancing with his friends and from rejoicing in the festivity of the *mitsvah*. The Besht's daughter, the pious Edel . . . said to the disciple: 'If you promise me that I will give birth to a baby boy this year, I will give you good shoes immediately.' She could say this because she had shoes in the store. He promised her that she certainly would have a baby boy. And so it was that the rabbi, our rabbi and teacher, Barukh of the holy community of Tulchin, was born to her.[127]

In this passage it is clear that the act of dancing expresses an intimate relationship between the individual hasid and the Shekhinah.[128] That this activity, moreover, symbolizes the act of union between the hasid and the Shekhinah may be gathered from the otherwise mundane account of the poor man's ceasing to dance on account of his torn shoe. Admittedly, this is an innocuous detail that, prima facie, would hardly excite one's interest. Yet it is precisely such a detail that contains, from the hasidic point of view, deep metaphysical and spiritual significance. The wearing of the shoe in this case, as in the other instances that I have mentioned above, is the symbolic enactment of the unification of the masculine individual and the feminine aspect of God. When the shoe is torn, the unification is severed, and the individual can no longer dance. The Besht's

[127] Dov Ber b. Shmuel, *Shivḥei haBesht*, 144. I have utilized the English translation of D. Ben-Amos and J. Mintz, *In Praise Of the Baal Shem Tov* (New York, 1984), 223–4. There is no parallel to this tale in the manuscript version of *Shivḥei haBesht* published by Mondshine.

[128] For the sexual implication of the traditional circular dance on Simḥat Torah, see *Ma'or vashemesh*, on 'Beshalaḥ', 119*a*. The hasidic idea is based, of course, on earlier kabbalistic writings, especially those betraying a Lurianic influence, which likewise explain the *hakafot* on Simḥat Torah in a decidedly sexual manner, i.e. the circular dancing around the pulpit—which symbolizes the Presence—creates an influx from the masculine to the feminine. See e.g. *Sha'ar hakavanot*, 104*a*; *Tur bareket*, 41*a–b*; see also Issachar Berish, *Sefer malbush leshabat veyom tov* (Bilgoraj, 1937), 64*d*. The use of feet as an euphemism for sexual activity, in my opinion, also underlies R. Nahman of Bratslav's teaching concerning the centrality of dance in religious worship. See, in particular, *Likutei Moharan*, part 1, *torah* 10, s. 6 'This is the aspect of dancing and clapping of the hands, for dancing and clapping of the hands are derived from the aspect of the spirit in the heart . . . This is the aspect of "his heart lifted his feet", i.e., by means of the spirit in the heart the dancing is derived. That is, by means of zaddik (!), who is the aspect of the spirit, the pride is annulled, as is written, "Let not the foot of the arrogant tread on me" (Ps. 36: 12). And the worship of idols was nullified, as it is written, "bathe your feet" (Gen. 18: 4), this refers to idol worship. When the feet are raised by means of the dancing—the aspect of his heart lifted his feet—the pride, i.e. idol worship, is nullified and the judgments are mitigated . . . And then the feet are in the aspect of "the feet of his pious" (1 Sam. 2: 9) . . . Then is established [the verse] "My feet are on level ground" (Ps. 26: 12), which is the aspect of faith. For heresy is the aspect of feet that have strayed, as Asaf says, "My feet had almost strayed" (ibid. 73: 2) . . . "My feet are on level ground" instructs about faith, and then is established, "His hands were steady" (Exod. 17: 12).' The messianic implication of dancing in Nahman's teaching may be alluded to in the characterization of the seventh beggar in the tale 'The Seven Beggars' as one without feet. This beggar, unlike the previous six, never arrives at the wedding to demonstrate that his seeming imperfection is in reality a perfection. One may conjecture, however, that the seventh beggar represents the ultimate rectification (*tikun*) and hence the coming of the messiah. The messianic character of this tale was perceived by the traditional editors of the *Sipurei ma'asiyot* who added the following postscript: 'The end of the story, i.e. what occurred on the seventh day concerning the beggar without feet, as well as the end of the first part of the story concerning the king, we have not merited to hear . . . We will not hear it until the messiah comes.' On the messianic implication of this tale, especially its end, see J. Dan, *Hasipur haḥasidi* (Jerusalem 1975), 169; Y. Liebes, 'Hatikun hakelali', 207 n. 22, and 237. The possible connection of Nahman's teaching about feet from *Likutei Moharan* that I cited above and the tale about the seventh beggar without feet has been noted by Martin Mantel, 'Rabbi Nachman of Bratzlav's Tales: A Critical Translation from the Yiddish with Annotations and Commentary', (Ph.D. thesis, Princeton University, 1975), ii. 238–9 n. 25. See, however, p. 239 n. 26, where Mantel rejects the soteriological reading of 'The Seven Beggars'.

daughter Edel is willing to rectify the situation by supplying the man with new shoes—which, as we are told, she readily has in her possession—but only in exchange for a blessing that she will give birth to a male child. The blessing is thus a perfect reflection of the act that Edel performed for the man—that is, just as she supplied him with new shoes, to enable him to continue dancing and thereby to unite the masculine and feminine, so would she be blessed with a child, the ultimate fruit of sexual unification.

From the various texts that I have examined it has thus become clear that in early hasidism the physical act of travel or walking was understood not only in a restorative sense (as the Besht taught) but in a generative sense as well. That is, the double task of the zaddik in his moving about from place to place is to redeem the fallen sparks and to assist in the unification of the male and female aspects of God. The two acts are not really distinct, for unification is brought about through liberation of the sparks. In addition, the soteriological implications of both these actions for the early hasidic authors must be acknowledged. In his capacity as one who walks or journeys, man assists in the redemption on both an individual and cosmic level.[129]

[129] A convergence of the themes that I have analysed in this paper, the messianic and sexual implications of walking, is evident in a striking manner in the following passage from Israel Dov Ber of Weledniki, *She'erit Yisrael* (Zhitomir, 1868), sermon 9, 13*c*: 'Jacob is the aspect of the light of Messiah . . . for with Jacob the spirit of Messiah began to shine . . . By means of the aspect of Jacob the blemish of the All [the *sefirah* of Yesod which corresponds to the phallus] was rectified . . . This is [alluded to in the name] Jacob [Ya'akov]: *yod akev*, the perfection of the aspect of the heels [*akevim*] i.e. the aspect of the "feet which go down to death" (Prov. 5: 5). And this is [the meaning of] "Jacob lifted up his feet" (Gen. 29: 1), i.e. the aspect of the blemish of *yesod* . . . and it thus became easy [*kal*] to walk, i.e. the aspect of 130 [130 = *kl*, the same consonants of the word *kal*] in which Adam separated [from Eve] and gave birth to [evil spirits and demons in the world] (cf. Er. 18*b*; Zohar 1: 19*b*, 55*a*; 2 231*b*; 3: 76*b*). By means of the aspect of Jacob there was an uplifting of these 130 years.' According to this text, Jacob is identified as a messianic figure who specifically rectifies the blemish of Yesod which corresponds to the phallus, i.e. sexual sin. Furthermore, the whole process is related to the feet or the heels. Hence, it is clear that feet symbolize the phallus and the aspect of walking is the perfection of the sexual offence brought about through the feet.

ELEVEN

Hasidism and the Dogma of the Decline of the Generations

LOUIS JACOBS

FROM the very beginnings of hasidism enormous claims were made by the hasidim on behalf of the great masters, the zaddikim, who were seen as spiritual supermen endowed with the holy spirit, possessing a degree of sanctity unparalleled in many an age and with the power to work extraordinary miracles. The Baal Shem Tov came to be seen as a unique personality who came into the world to teach a new 'way' that amounted to a new revelation of God's truth. (Whether this 'way' is really original is beside the point since the hasidim themselves certainly saw it as such.) Even the *torot* of the later zaddikim were seen as fresh revelations hitherto undisclosed. These claims, as opponents of the movement were not slow to point out, were in flat contradiction to what had become virtually a dogma long before the rise of hasidism: that each successive generation after the revelation at Sinai exhibits further decline. This idea, implied in a number of rabbinic texts, was known to the hasidim, as it was to most learned Jews, but the problem became especially acute once the talmudic rabbis came to be viewed as infallible teachers who constituted the final court of appeal for all matters concerning the Jewish religion.

One of the rabbinic texts (Ber. 20*a*) refers specifically to miracle-working:

> R. Papa asked Abbaye: 'Why is it that miracles were performed for those of former generations but no miracles are performed for us? It cannot be because they were superior in their studies since in the days of R. Judah all their efforts were concentrated on *Nezikin*, whereas we study all the six orders . . . And yet when R. Judah drew off a single shoe the rains would come whereas we torment ourselves and cry out loudly and not the slightest notice is taken of us.' Abbaye replied: 'The former generations were ready to sacrifice themselves for the sanctification of the divine name whereas we are not ready to sacrifice ourselves for the sanctification of the divine name.'

The passage concludes with a story illustrating the readiness for self-sacrifice on the part of a saint belonging to an earlier generation.

In this passage the power to work miracles through prayer is made to depend on readiness to sacrifice oneself for the sake of God, it being implied that the talmudic giants, Abbaye and R. Papa, were incapable of this degree of selflessness and hence miracles could not be performed for them. Since Abbaye and R. Papa said this about themselves and their contemporaries, it would seem to follow that it applied *a fortiori* to post-talmudic teachers, and yet the hasidim repeatedly made the claim that the zaddikim could work miracles by the power of their prayers.

Interestingly enough, the decline in the generations is not applied to learning. It is acknowledged that Abbaye and R. Papa are superior in learning to R. Judah. But that is because R. Judah was an *amora*. In another passage (Er. 53*a*) the learning of the *amora'im* is compared adversely to that of the *tanna'im*

R. Johanan said: 'The heart of the earlier ones was open like the entrance to the Outer Hall of the Temple while the heart of the later ones was open only like the entrance to the Inner hall (which was smaller). But as for us the opening is no bigger than the eye of a fine needle' . . . Abayye said: 'We are like a peg in a wall with regard to *gemara*'. Rava said: 'We are like a finger in wax with regard to *sevara*'. R. Ashi said: 'We are like a finger in a pit with regard to forgetfulness'.

However, the passage usually quoted for the doctrine of the progressive decline of the generations is one in which the doctrine is presented in the starkest terms (Shab. 112*b*): 'R. Zera said that Rava bar Zamina said: "If the early ones were like angels then we are like human beings, but if the early ones were like human beings then we are like donkeys; not like the donkey of R. Hanina b. Dosa or the donkey of R. Pinhas b. Yair but like ordinary donkeys." '[1]

The medieval Jewish teachers, refusing to allow themselves to become completely stultified by the dogma of inferiority *vis-à-vis* the talmudic sages, adopted various ploys in defence of their capacity for original thought. The best known of these is to use the famous illustration, going back to John of Salisbury, of the pygmy standing on the shoulders of a giant. Later teachers are, indeed, mere spiritual pygmies in relation to the giants of the past, especially to the talmudic rabbis, but they have the shoulders of the ancients upon which to stand and can therefore possess vistas quite impossible for them had they stood only on their own two feet. Now that they do have the shoulders of the ancients upon which to stand they can, on occasion, see further than the ancients themselves.[2]

For Maimonides the ancient teachers of the Talmud could possess less knowledge of such matters as astronomy than the Gentile scholars of his day possessed.[3] For the Geonim, the talmudic rabbis only had the medical knowledge of their day, so that cures found in the Talmud should not be relied on unless contemporary doctors concur.[4] For all that, very few Jews in the early eighteenth century were prepared to compromise in any way on the view that the talmudic rabbis were infallible in all matters. This was the

[1] For the donkey of R. Phinehas see Ḥul. 7*a*–*b*; for the donkey of R. Hanina b. Dosa see *Avot deRabbi Natan*, ed. S. Schechter [1887] (New York, 1967), ch. 8, 38. Both R. Phinehas and R. Hanina are renowned in the rabbinic literature as saints and are often used as rabbinic models for the hasidic zaddik. In the Ḥul. narrative R. Phinehas (who is described in the narrative as a 'zaddik') has the miraculous power to cause a river to part and his efforts are compared to those of Moses at the Sea of Reeds: The Zoharic statement (Zohar 3: 2*a*) on the difference with regard to mystical knowledge between the earlier and later generations is obviously an amplification of the talmudic statement.

[2] For the literature on the pygmy and the giant motif in Jewish thought see Jacob Haberman, *Maimonides and Aquinas* (New York 1979), 203–5.

[3] *Guide*, iii. 14–end.

[4] See the Geonic comments on Git. 68f. quoted in B. M. Lewin, *Otsar hage'onim* (13 vols.; Haifa–Jerusalem, 1928–62), vol. on *Gittin* (1941), 152f.

problem hasidism had to face. Repeatedly one finds in the mitnaggedic polemics the taunt that the hasidim make claims for their zaddikim quite impossible for those in 'our orphaned generations'.[5]

Moreover, the pygmy on the shoulders of the giant idea could not be used as a defence by the hasidim since that would imply something far less than complete originality on the part of the Baal Shem Tov and his 'way',[6] and, in any event, such an idea could not apply to the alleged power to work miracles. The *torot* of the zaddikim could also not be defended in this way since, it was believed, these were in the nature of fresh divine communications, 'the Shekhinah speaking out of the throat of the zaddik'.[7]

In a sense, the kabbalists had to face the same problem. But the Zohar was believed to be the work of R. Simeon b. Yoḥai, himself a *tanna* and hence one of the ancients. The problem did, however, arise for the post-zoharic kabbalists, that is, those who lived after the Zohar had been 'revealed'. The usual device adopted by the kabbalists was to claim that the mysteries were revealed by Elijah, the link with Moses,[8] so that the 'new' teachings were really the old ones 'received' anew, as the name 'kabbalah' implies. For all that, some kabbalists did admit the possibility of entirely new revelations in spite of the doctrine of spiritual decline. Thus in the work *Berit menuḥah*, attributed to Abraham of Granada,[9] it is suggested that the doctrine of spiritual decline does not apply to the very latest mystics. This is because there are cycles in mystical power, just as there are cycles in nature. Just as in the revolution of the great sphere the planets eventually come round full circle, so it is with regard to mystical illumination. Only those mystics who came in between the ancients and contemporaries are inferior because in their day the cycle was in mid-course. 'Nowadays' the cycle has begun again

[5] See Mordecai Wilensky, *Ḥasidim umitnaggedim* (2 vols.; Jerusalem, 1970), index, s.v. *mofetim*, and esp. the polemics of Israel Loebel, *Sefer vikuaḥ* [Warsaw, 1798], repr. in Wilensky, *Ḥasidim umitnaggedim*, ii. 320–2. Even if it be admitted, says this author, that the hasidic zaddikim do perform miracles they do so by means of the black art (*kishuf*) as did (in veiled reference) Jesus, Muhammad, and Shabbetai Zevi!

[6] In every version of hasidism, the Baal Shem Tov's complete originality is stressed. See e.g. the well-known observation of the Baal Shem Tov's grandson Moses Hayyim Ephraim of Sudylkow in his *Degel maḥaneh Efrayim* [1808] (Jerusalem, 1963), on Exod. 14: 8, 100–1. The *Targum* renders *beyad ramah* as *beresh gelei*. The children of Israel 'go out' of the Exile through the revelation of the Zohar—*beresh* stands for R. Shimon ben Yohai, *gelei* stands for the new 'revelation'. The word *beresh* also stands for R. Israel Baal Shem. The maskilim poured scorn on the hasidic glorification of the Baal Shem Tov; see e.g. Joseph Perl, *Megaleh temirin* (Vienna, 1819), 1, who quotes in this connection the famous sying: 'The word of the Lord was with the Baal Shem and whatsoever he decreed came to pass. He was unique. Of the earlier ones none arose like unto him and after him who can arise upon earth.' Perl quotes this derogatorily as the introduction to the Kopys edn. of *Shivḥei haBesht* but the source is, in fact, *Peri ha'arets* of R. Menahem Mendel of Vitebsk [Kopys, 1814] (Jerusalem, 1965), 60, and the startling saying should be seen in context. A follower had asked R. Menahem Mendel to pray for him that he should be blessed with a child. In his humility, Menahem Mendel observes that he cannot compare in any way with the Baal Shem Tov and *in this* the Baal Shem Tov was unique. However, it is not only Perl who takes the saying out of context but all the subsequent hasidic hagiographers who quote the saying.

[7] See Rivka Schatz-Uffenheimer, *Haḥasidut kemistikah* (Jerusalem, 1968), 108, 118–19.

[8] See Gershom G. Scholem, *On the Kabbalah and its Symbolism* (London, 1965), 19–21, on *gilui Eliyahu* as a device used by the mystics to justify their originality while preserving their links with the Jewish tradition.

[9] Abraham of Granada, *Berit menuḥah* [Amsterdam, 1648] (Warsaw, 1864), 24*a*. Cf. Zohar 1: 118*a* 'The Holy One, blessed be He, does not desire that so much be revealed to the world, but when the days of the Messiah are near at hand, even children will discover the secrets of wisdom.'

so that it is even possible for a contemporary to have greater illuminations than those teachers who lived in an earlier period but after the cycle had begun.

An early hasidic reply is to be found in the letter by Eleazar, son of R. Elimelekh of Lyzhansk.[10] Eleazar published his father's work *No'am Elimelekh* a year after his father's death. Eleazar's letter in defence of the zaddikim is appended to the work. Eleazar remarks that even the opponents of hasidism admit that the saints of old were gifted with the holy spirit and were able to perform miracles but they argue that such things are impossible for those who live in later generations. This, says Eleazar, is because saints are rarely acknowledged as such by their contemporaries. Even so elevated a holy man as the Ari was the object of criticism in his day, whereas now all acknowledge his great sanctity. This is the meaning of the saying, 'the righteous are greater when dead than in their lifetime' (Ḥul. 7*b*). Evidently, a man can only be acknowledged as a saint when he has died. The accolade is only awarded posthumously, the 'canonization' process, so to speak, can only be initiated after the candidate's death. (Needless to say, Eleazar would not have used such an illustration, though the comparison with the procedures of the Catholic Church is not without its own interest.)

In the name of R. Elimelekh it is even said that 'nowadays' it is far easier to attain to the holy spirit than in former times. This is because the Shekhinah, now in exile, is very near. R. Elimelekh quotes the parable given by the Maggid of Rovno (i.e., the Maggid of Mezhirech, residing at that time in Rovno).[11] When the king is in his palace he will only leave it to stay for a time in a splendid mansion where full regal honours can be paid to him. But when the king is on a journey he is prepared to enter the most humble of dwellings provided it is clean and he is offered hospitality.

R. Phinehas of Korets appears to be grappling with our problem. R. Phinehas is reported to have said that Abraham Ibn Ezra is not to be blamed for his rationalism in daring to criticize such ancient teachers as Kalir, held to be a *tanna*.[12] The *tanna'im*, who lived soon after the destruction of the Temple, were still able to avail themselves of the tremendous illuminations that proceeded from the holy place, even though these illuminations had begun to wane in their day. The medieval teachers like Ibn Ezra could not avail themselves of the Temple illuminations because in their day these had waned completely. But contemporary zaddikim, though even more distant from the Temple period, are very close to the dawning light of the Messianic Age. Distant in time and hence 'late' in relation to the illuminations of the past, they are very near and hence 'early' to the even greater illuminations of the future. One would have to be blind, remarks R. Phinehas, not to see now the dawning light of the messiah.

These ideas became current in hasidic circles. The reputed teachings of the hasidic master Uri of Strelisk (d. 1826) were published under the title of *Imrei kodesh*.[13] Here the editor's introduction deals with our problem. We are not supplied with the editor's name but, since he remarks that it is over 130 years since Uri died, it is obvious that he

[10] *No'am Elimelekh* [Lemberg, 1788], ed. G. Nigal (2 vols.; Jerusalem, 1978), ii. 593–602.

[11] Ibid. i. 109–10, on Gen. 37: 1. As Nigal notes, the parable is found in the writings of the Maggid, *Maggid devarav le Ya'akov* [Korets, 1784], ed. Rivka Schatz-Uffenheimer (Jerusalem, 1976), no. 49, p. 70.

[12] *Midrash Pinḥas*, [Warsaw, 1876]. Repr. in *Sefarim kedoshim migedolei talmidei Ba'al Shem Tov* (35 + 3 vols.; Brooklyn, NY, 1981–6), i, no. 7, p. 82.

[13] *Or olam: Sefer imrei kodesh hashalem* (Jerusalem, 1961), ch. 1 (no pagination, but at beginning of the work).

is writing around 1956. It is, consequently, a little dubious to use what he says for our purpose. Yet it is not irrelevant for the consideration of how our problem is treated in the hasidic tradition. After referring to the talmudic passages about the decline of the generations, this author quotes the passage from the *Berit menuḥah* (he italicizes the words 'the later sages *are greater than the earlier ones*') and the passage from Phinehas of Korets. He concludes:

Since this is so it is no cause for surprise that we see, after the darkness which prevailed in the middle ages, when the light was concealed and every vision blocked, all generations become progressively weaker, that the Lord should have illumined our way, that a star should have arisen in Jacob whose light has extended over all the earth, namely, Israel's illumination and holy one, the Baal Shem Tov, may his merits shield us. He is the man, the great lion of the supernal forest. He ascended the heights to become the disciple of Ahijah the Shilonite who had heard the Torah from Moses our teacher himself, on whom be peace. After all these generations the wheel has come full circle so that they are able to draw down the holy spirit from the Source and the word of the Lord has been spread abroad.[14]

Similarly relying on hasidic traditions are the remarks of Israel Berger in the introduction of his *Eser orot*, a collection of tales of the zaddikim including many miracle tales.[15] Fully aware of opposition even on the part of faithful Jews to the cult of the zaddik, Berger feels obliged to deal with four objections to the institutions: (*a*) Where do we find in the classical sources of Judaism that the saints can change the laws of nature in such radical ways as the zaddikim are said to be able to do? (*b*) Even if such things were possible for the ancients, how can they be possible nowadays, in view of the talmudic statements about the decline of the generations? (*c*) What basis is there for the strange methods of biblical exegesis employed by the zaddikim? (*d*) How can the zaddikim enjoy supernatural powers since some of them are unlearned in the Talmud and the Codes?

Berger's replies to questions (*c*) and (*d*), interesting in themselves, are not strictly relevant to our inquiry. In reply to the first objection, Berger has no difficulty in

[14] The reference to Ahijah as the mystical mentor of the Baal Shem Tov occurs in the first hasidic work to be printed, Jacob Joseph of Polonnoye, *Toledot Ya'akov Yosef* [Korets, 1780] (Jerusalem, 1966). The *Toledot* (on 'Balak', 156*a*) observes: 'Ahijah received (*kibel*) from Moses our Teacher and he was one of those who came out of Egypt and afterwards from the Court of David and he was the mentor of Elijah and of my master.' This is obviously based on the chain of tradition as portrayed in the introd. to M. Maimonides, *Mishneh torah*, but Maimonides only uses the term *kibel* when speaking of Ahijah receiving from David. In relation to Ahijah and Moses he uses the term *shama*, 'he heard it'. Possibly, R. Jacob Joseph was quoting from memory. In any event the purpose is clear. The Baal Shem Tov's teacher Ahijah is the link, skipping the generations of the usual chain of tradition, with Moses. Louis Ginzberg's suggestion (*Jewish Encyclopedia* (12 vols.; New York, 1901–6), ii. 383–6, s.v. 'Ba'al Shem Tov, Israel B. Eliezer') that Ahijah features as the mentor of the Baal Shem Tov because the prophet, at the bidding of God, brought about the breach between the Davidic line and Jeroboam, as the Baal Shem Tov broke with the rabbinic tradition, is extremely unlikely. The hasidim would never have implied that the Baal Shem Tov can be compared to Jeroboam.

[15] I. Berger, *Eser orot* [Piotrkow, 1907] (Warsaw, 1913), 4–15. Berger's remarks are quoted verbatim in Zevi Moskovitch, *Ma'aseh Neḥemiah* (Jerusalem, 1956), s. 13, 27–31. Cf. the opening passage in R. Shneur Zalman of Lyady, *Likutei amarim: Tanya* [Slavuta, 1796; Vilna, 1900], bilingual edn. trans. N. Mindel, N. Mangel, Z. Posner, and J. I. Schochet (London, 1973), 5*a*–*b* on the statement by Rabbah in the Talmud (Ber. 61*b*) that he was only an average man (*beinoni*), not even a zaddik. The *Tanya* solves the problem by elevating the *beinoni* to an extraordinary stage of spiritual attainment.

adducing a list of miracle tales in the Talmud and other sources where the laws of nature are set at naught by the powers of the saint. In reply to the second question, that is, to our problem, Berger advances the following arguments, obviously relying on what his predecessors have said.

First, he argues, the *amora'im* who spoke of the decline of the generations were not making any kind of categorical statement but were only thinking, in their humility, of themselves. All they were saying was that they themselves were inferior to the ancients, not that there is a dogma that all generations are necessarily inferior to early ones. Second, even if their statements applied to their whole generation, there could still be exceptions. Third, Berger quotes Abraham of Granada. Once the wheel has come full circle there is a fresh outburst of spiritual power. Fourth, in an age of spiritual darkness God sends down to earth a lofty soul that has previously been on earth in the time of the ancients. Thus the souls of the zaddikim do not belong to the generations in decline but to the generations in which they lived in their previous incarnation.

In every reformist or revisionist movement there is bound to be tension between the need for continuity and the need for originality, between the claims of the past and those of the present and future, between what the founding fathers said when they were alive and what it is imagined they would say were they to come back to earth to face the new situation. For hasidism the tensions were aggravated by the doctrine of the decline of the generations. In their attempted solutions they, too, tried to have their cake and eat it. All the attempted solutions are really an attempt to abolish the time sequence altogether. But then, on the hasidic view, the zaddikim can reach the world that is beyond time. In such a world it is not impossible to have one's cake and eat it.

TWELVE

Personal Redemption in Hasidism

MORRIS M. FAIERSTEIN

HASIDISM has been a bifurcated movement from its inception. It was both a popular movement centred around the charismatic figure of the zaddik who reached down to all strata of the community to elevate them spiritually, and at the same time a continuation of the kabbalistic tradition for a spiritual élite.[1] The question of messianism or redemption is one area where the distinctions between the popular and élitist aspects of hasidism can be clearly discerned. Though messianism in hasidism has been discussed at length,[2] there is very little discussion of personal redemption, a theme closely related to the élitist aspect of hasidism.[3]

Personal redemption is relevant to a small spiritual élite who attempt to attain this state in their personal lives without regard to the redemptive state of the world as a whole. This concept is found in the writings of R. Jacob Joseph of Polonnoye who attributes it to the Baal Shem Tov. The Maggid of Mezhirech relates it to his doctrine of *unio mystica*. His disciples moved away from this concept as the idea of the popular zaddik grew in prominence. Personal redemption again became a central concern with the rejection of popular zaddikism by the Przysucha–Kotsk school. It reached its fullest development in the writings of R. Mordecai Joseph of Izbica who made it the cornerstone of his teachings.

Gedaliah Nigal has recently called attention to the importance of personal redemp-

[1] Recent studies which emphasize the élitist aspect of hasidism include M. Piekarz's major work *Biyemei tsemiḥat Haḥasidut: Megamot ra'ayoniyot besifrei derush umusar* (Jerusalem, 1978); S. Ettinger, 'The Hasidic Movement: Reality and Ideals', in H. H. Ben-Sasson and S. Ettinger (eds.), *Jewish Society through the Ages* (New York, 1971), 251–66, orig. pub. in *Cahiers d'histoire mondiale: Journal of World History*, 11: 1–2 1968), 251–66; repr. in G. D. Hundert (ed.), *Essential Papers on Hasidism* (New York, 1991), 226–43; I. Etkes, 'Hasidism as a Movement: The First Stage', in B. Safran (ed.), *Hasidism: Continuity or Innovation?* (Cambridge, Mass., 1988), 1–26.

[2] The major studies of messianism in hasidism are G. Scholem, 'The Neutralization of the Messianic Element in Early Hasidism', *Journal of Jewish Studies*, 20 (1969), 25–55, repr. in id., *The Messianic Idea in Judaism* (London, 1971), 176–202; I. Tishby, 'Hara'ayon hameshiḥi vehamegamot hameshiḥiyot bitsemiḥat haḥasidut', *Zion*, 32 (1967), 1–45; M. Piekarz, 'Hara'ayon hameshiḥi biyemei tsemiḥat haḥasidut', in *Hara'ayon hameshiḥi beYisrael: Yom iyun leregel melot shemonim shanah leGershom Scholem* (Jersualem, 1982), 237–53. See also M. Faierstein, 'Gershom Scholem and Hasidism' *Journal of Jewish Studies*, 38 (1987), 230–3, and Jacob Joseph of Polonnoye, *Tsafenat pa'neaḥ* [Korets, 1782], ed. G. Nigal (Jerusalem, 1989), introd. 39 n. 1.

[3] Earlier discussions of personal redemption include R. Schatz-Uffenheimer, 'Self-Redemption in Hasidic Thought', in R. J. Z. Werblowsky and C. J. Bleeker (eds.), *Types of Redemption* (Leiden, 1970), 207–12; M. Faierstein, *All Is in the Hands of Heaven: The Teachings of Rabbi Mordecai Joseph of Izbica* (New York, 1989), ch. 4.

tion in the writings of R. Jacob Joseph of Polonnoye.[4] Redemption, like many other concepts in R. Jacob Joseph's teachings, operates on three levels, *olam* (the sefirotic world), *shanah* (the physical world), and *nefesh* (the individual).[5] The three levels of exile and redemption are those of the Shekhinah, the Jewish people, and the individual soul. The individual soul is in the exile of the evil inclination (*yetser hara*) and spiritual darkness. Since this was the first exile, it is also the first redemption that must be prayed for. It is only after attaining the personal redemption of the soul that one can aspire to the other levels of redemption. It would seem to be related to the zaddik's self-preparation for his task of spiritually raising his followers. One must redeem oneself before attempting to redeem others. Personal redemption is intimately related to the major themes in R. Jacob Joseph's thought and can only be properly understood in the context of a comprehensive study of his writings.[6]

Personal redemption was an integral part of the Maggid of Mezhirech's teachings. As R. Schatz has observed: 'The theoretical formulation of individualistic mysticism, with its emphasis on personal self-redemption, was the achievement of this master.'[7] Many of the Maggid's disciples, notably R. Elimelekh of Lyzhansk, moved away from his élitist individualistic mysticism and gave a new centrality to the concept of zaddik, a concept virtually absent from the Maggid's own teachings.[8] As a result, the idea of personal redemption disappears from their teachings and is replaced by redemption through adherence to the zaddik. The zaddik becomes the intermediary through whom all spiritual and physical needs are met.[9] This doctrine reached its apogee in the teachings of R. Elimelekh's disciple, the Seer of Lublin.[10]

The departure of the Jew of Przysucha from the Seer's court and his establishment of his own school restored personal redemption to a place of prominence in hasidism. The Yehudi rejected the role of the zaddik as intermediary, which was the hallmark of 'popular zaddikism'. He removed the task of attaining spiritual perfection from the shoulders of the zaddik and returned it to the individual hasid. The individual was now responsible for his own spiritual perfection. The zaddik's role was that of spiritual guide or facilitator who can show the way and keep the individual from straying too far from the spiritual path, but who ultimately cannot attain vicarious spiritual perfection

[4] *Tsafenat pa'neaḥ*, introd. 39–50.

[5] Ibid. 14–21.

[6] Specific studies of aspects of R. Jacob Joseph's thought include S. Dresner, *The Zaddik* (New York, 1960) and G. Nigal, *Manhig ve'edah* (Jerusalem, 1962). Both focus on the concept of the zaddik, but do not deal with R. Jacob Joseph's thought as a whole.

[7] Schatz-Uffenheimer, 'Self-Redemption', 209.

[8] The doctrine of the zaddik does not play a significant role in the teachings of the Maggid. As A. Rapoport-Albert has stated, 'The difference between his religious temperament and that of R. Jacob Joseph of Polonnoye entirely accounts for his complete lack of interest in the structure of society or the responsibility toward the community of spiritually gifted men'. ('God and the Zaddik as the Two Focal Points of Hasidic Worship', *History of Religions*, 18 (1979); repr. in Hundert (ed.), *Essential Papers*, 319).

[9] Two important studies on the zaddik as intermediary are Rapoport-Albert, 'God and the Zaddik' and A. Green, 'The Zaddik as *Axis Mundi* in Later Judaism', *Journal of the American Academy of Religion*, 44 (1977), 327–47.

[10] For the Seer's doctrine of the zaddik see R. Elior, 'Between *Yesh* and *Ayin*: The Doctrine of the Zaddik in the Works of Jacob Isaac, the Seer of Lublin', in A. Rapoport-Albert and S. J. Zipperstein (eds.), *Jewish History: Essays in Honor of Chimen Abramsky* (London, 1988), 393–455.

from him.[11] The Yehudi also rejected the role of the zaddik as miracle-worker, a role which was central to 'popular zaddikism'. He is reported as saying: 'It is no trick to be a miracle-worker. Any Jew who has attained a level of spirituality can overturn heaven and earth. But to be a Jew [a *yid*] is difficult.[12]

The Yehudi's successor, R. Simḥah Bunem of Przysucha, continued the emphasis on the self-perfection of the individual and the role of the zaddik as spiritual guide.[13] R. Simḥah Bunem taught that 'every Jew who sets out to worship God should dig a well in his own essence by means of which he will be able to cleave to his creator.'[14] His goal was to mould an individual who would seek to know himself without illusions and find his own unique path to God. If one knew where to look, it was possible to find one's spiritual path without travelling to a zaddik or even associating with other hasidim.[15]

The Przysucha school did not develop a specific spiritual path, but reverted to the pre-hasidic rabbinic spirituality which emphasized the study of Talmud and other classics of Jewish thought. In many respects the zaddik reverted to being a scholar or *rosh yeshivah*. Both the Yehudi and R. Simḥah Bunem considered it their responsibility to give regular lectures on talmudic problems (*shiurim*). It is also noteworthy that Maimonides' *Guide for the Perplexed* and the writings of R. Judah Loewe, the Maharal of Prague, held an honoured place in the Przysucha curriculum.[16]

R. Menahem Mendel of Kotsk, R. Simḥah Bunem's successor, developed the ideas of his teachers in a new and more radical direction. R. Menahem Mendel elevated the concept of individual perfection and redemption to new heights. In Przysucha, the search for individual redemption was somewhat tempered by one's normal social and familial obligations. For R. Menahem Mendel, the striving for spiritual freedom and individual redemption was the only thing of consequence. A. J. Heschel has observed that

> The most profound aspect of the Kotsker *rebbe's* path was a striving for spiritual freedom. Spiritual freedom means: flattering no one, neither oneself nor the world; not being subservient to anyone: neither to the self nor to society.[17]

The quest for spiritual freedom manifested itself in Kotsk in a form of stoicism which disdained all expressions of vanity and disregarded social niceties.[18] R. Menahem Mendel is reported to have said, 'A hasid rejects the world and he who rejects the

[11] Z. M. Rabinowicz, *Rabbi Ya'akov Yitsḥak miPeshisḥah: HaYehudi haKadosh* (Piotrkow, 1932), 93–4.

[12] Ibid. 82.

[13] On R. Simḥah Bunem's concept of the zaddik see Z. M. Rabinowicz, *Rabbi Simḥah Bunem miPeshisḥah* (Tel Aviv, 1944), 76–82.

[14] Simhah Bunem of Przysucha, *Kol simḥah* (Breslau, 1859), on 'Toledot', 14*a*.

[15] The parable of R. Isaac, son of R. Yekel of Cracow, was told by R. Simḥah Bunem to illustrate this point. The parable is translated in full in the appendix. It is found in I. Berger, *Simḥat Yisrael* (Piotrkow, 1910), 49. A paraphrased version of this parable is also found in M. Buber, *Tales of the Hasidim* (2 vols.; New York, 1972), ii. 245–6.

[16] Rabinowicz, *Rabbi Simḥah Bunem*, 47. For R. Judah Loewe's influence on the Przysucha–Kotsk school see Byron L. Sherwin, *Mystical Theology and Social Dissent: The Life and Works of Judah Loewe of Prague* (London, 1982), 51–5. On Maimonides' influence see J. Dienstag, 'Ha*Moreh nevukhim* ve*Sefer hamada* besifrut haḥasidut', in *Sefer yovel likhvod harav Dr Avraham Weiss* (New York, 1964), 323.

[17] A. J. Heschel, *Kotsk: In Gerangel far Emesdikeit* (2 vols.; Tel Aviv, 1973), ii. 523.

[18] For numerous examples of this see R. Mahler, *Hasidism and the Jewish Enlightenment* (Philadelphia, 1985), 283–9.

world is a hasid.'[19] This was coupled with a form of asceticism that did not glorify abstinence but merely disregarded the physical needs of the body. Like everything else, asceticism could also be a trap. As R. Samuel of Sochaczew put it, 'It is easier to endure all sorts of ascetic practice and torments than it is to endure the yoke of Heaven.[20] Completely accepting the 'yoke of Heaven' was the only true goal of the hasid. If one has achieved this, then one has everything that is important. When R. Menahem Mendel was once asked to pray for a hasid who had become impoverished, he responded: 'If that man is indeed a Hasid, then he lacks for nothing.'[21]

In Kotsk, the struggle was never-ending. To attain spiritual perfection in this world is virtually impossible. There are always traps and snares lying in wait for the unwary spiritual seeker. 'Working on oneself', striving to divest oneself of personal desires and vanity, was a lifelong process. It was a vain illusion even to think that perfection was an attainable goal for the hasid. All that R. Menahem Mendel held out to his disciples was the struggle to achieve it.[22]

In Przysucha and Kotsk, each hasid strove to find the impediments that held him back from spiritual perfection and to overcome them. The methods used in this process varied widely. For some it meant total immersion in talmudic study. For others, the means was engaging in outrageous behaviour in order to destroy one's ego. The latter was especially favoured in Kotsk. The greatest sin for a Kotsker hasid was to appear to be pious or to give others the impression that one was a spiritual seeker. This attitude is summarized in the saying:

> What is the difference between the *hasidim* of Kotsk and other *hasidim*? The latter perform the commandments openly but commit transgressions in secret, while the *hasidim* of Kotsk commit transgressions openly and perform the commandments secretly.[23]

For some Kotsker hasidim defeating the ego, which was meant to be a means, had become an end. There is an impression of much spiritual thrashing about which did not lead to a specific goal. The dominant mood in Kotsk was chaos. This situation intensified as R. Menahem Mendel gradually withdrew from active leadership, isolating himself in his room and denying access to all but a few close disciples.

R. Menahem Mendel had never intended to lead a mass movement. His desire was to lead a small group of élite disciples who would stand on the rooftops and attain the spiritual level of the prophets.[24] In such a small élite group each disciple could be led to a spiritual path that was custom tailored to his own needs. However, in a large group it was impossible for the *rebbe* to give each disciple the close personal supervision necessary to keep the hasid from falling into traps along the spiritual path. In effect, what was needed was a spiritual road map to help the hasid find his own way, with some

[19] Ibid. 284. One must be very careful in claiming that statements attributed to R. Menahem Mendel of Kotsk are his *ipsissima verba*: see J. Levinger, 'Imrot otentiyot shel haRabbi miKotsk', *Tarbiz*, 55 (1986), 109–35. However, one can get a sense of the Kotsker *Weltanschauung* from the weight of the accumulated material. The statements cited here are meant merely as reflections of the Kotsker ideology. The same caveat should be made about the statements attributed to the Holy Jew and R. Simḥah Bunem of Przysucha.

[20] Mahler, *Hasidism and Jewish Enlightenment*, 284.

[21] Menaham Mendel of Kotsk, *Emet ve'emunah*, ed. Israel Jacob Araten (Jerusalem, 1948), para. 731.

[22] Heschel, *Kotsk*, i. 111–14.

[23] Mahler, *Hasidism and the Jewish Enlightenment*, 292.

[24] Y. K. K. Rokotz, *Si'aḥ sarfei kodesh* (Jerusalem, n.d.), i. 27, para. 134.

guidance and supervision by the *rebbe*. Such a spiritual road map was described by R. Mordecai Joseph of Izbica.[25]

R. Mordecai Joseph, one of R. Menahem Mendel's oldest friends and closest disciples, left Kotsk in the autumn of 1839 in the wake of a major clash with R. Menahem Mendel.[26] After his departure from Kotsk and settlement in Izbica, R. Mordecai Joseph developed a new and unique theology. An important part of this theology was a new interpretation of the concept of individual redemption that played such a central role in Przysucha and Kotsk. R. Mordecai Joseph builds on this concept, arguing that it is attainable in this world, at least for a small élite. In addition and more importantly, he lays out a specific path to achieve this goal.

R. Mordecai Joseph builds his theology of individual redemption on the concepts of *ḥisaron*, *mitsvah peratit*, and *berur*. Hasidism had already shifted the emphasis from the cosmos to the individual. The Lurianic process of *tikun* and lifting up the sparks had been personalized and 'psychologized' through the reinterpretation of the concept of *devekut*.[27] Very early in the history of hasidism questions had arisen about *devekut* and *tikun*. Were they open to everyone or was it only within the province of the zaddik to be able to attain the state of *devekut*?[28] Gradually, it became the exclusive prerogative of the zaddik. One of his central tasks was to help his followers lift up the sparks, which they could not elevate without his mediation.[29]

R. Mordecai Joseph, following the traditions of the Przysucha–Kotsk school, de-emphasizes the central role of the zaddik in the process and brings it back to the spiritual life of the individual. A probable basis for this concept is the kabbalistic idea that each person has a unique understanding of the Torah. This is expressed in the Lurianic literature in the following way:

> Consequently, there are 600,000 aspects and meanings in the Torah. According to each one of these ways of explaining the Torah, the root of a soul has been fashioned in Israel. In the Messianic age, every single man in Israel will read the Torah in accordance with the meaning peculiar to his root. And thus also is the Torah understood in Paradise.[30]

R. Mordecai Joseph's innovation is that he is not prepared to wait for the eschaton to discover this unique interpretation. He feels it is the will of God that some people seek and find their unique root in the present pre-eschatological period.

R. Mordecai Joseph substitutes the concepts of defect (*ḥisaron*) and clarification

[25] The pioneering studies of R. Mordecai Joseph's thought are two articles by Joseph G. Weiss, 'Torat hedeterminism hadati leR. Mordecai Yosef Leiner meIzbica', in *Sefer yovel leYitsḥak Baer* (Jerusalem, 1961), 447–53; 'Eine spätjüdischer Utopie religiöser Freiheit', *Eranos Jahrbuch*, 32 (Zurich, 1964), 235–80, pub. in Eng. as 'A Late Jewish Utopia of Religious Freedom', in id., *Studies in Eastern European Jewish Mysticism* (Oxford, 1985), 209–48; Rivka Schatz-Uffenheimer, 'Autonomiah shel haru'aḥ vetorat Mosheh', *Molad*, 1: 183–4 (1963), 554–61. A more recent study is Faierstein, *In the Hands of Heaven*.

[26] The reasons for R. Mordecai Joseph's departure from Kotsk are complex. For an analysis of the relationship between R. Menahem Mendel and R. Mordecai Joseph see Faierstein, *In the Hands of Heaven*, chs. 2, 5, 6.

[27] The classic study of this concept is G. Scholem, 'Devekut, or Communion with God', *Review of Religion*, 14 (1949–50), 115–39; repr. in id., *The Messianic Idea*, 203–26.

[28] See Scholem, 'Neutralization of the Messianic Element', 191–2.

[29] This concept is discussed at length in Dresner, *The Zaddik*, 148–221.

[30] Quoted in G. Scholem, 'The Meaning of the Torah in Jewish Mysticism', in id., *On the Kabbalah and its Symbolism* (London, 1965), 65.

(*berur*) for the Lurianic ones of *shevirat hakelim* and *tikun*. He teaches that each individual acquires his defect at birth.[31] Every person, beginning with Adam, has been born with a specific defect. The process of redemption for each one lies in recognizing and appropriately rectifying that defect. Adam's defect, for example, was related to God's command not to eat of the tree of knowledge. Adam was aware of his defect. It was only the taunting of the serpent that caused him to eat the forbidden fruit. The serpent was punished because of the embarrassment it caused Adam by pointing out his defect.[32] In this way, R. Mordecai Joseph explains the serpent's role and subsequent punishment in the biblical story. He also makes an important psychological point, namely, that it is often easier to recognize another's defect than one's own. It is not helpful to one who has a blind spot in his defect to be taunted or embarrassed with this knowledge. It is necessary to have God's help in reaching awareness of one's defect. A person remains unaware of his defect until God is ready to show it to him. Only at that point will the person recognize that all of his deficiencies derive from his one defect. At the same time, God gives him the ability to plead and pray to Him for help in repairing his defect.[33]

To have a 'defect' is a universal predicament, but each person has his own particular defect. Once the person has recognized the defect, he must concentrate on those aspects of the Torah which deal with his defect until he has resolved the issues involved.[34] The good that is inherent in the person will not come to the fore until he has properly dealt with his defect, and will be efficacious only when he has clarified it.[35]

Awareness of the defect leads one to the fear of God (*yirat hashem*) which takes two forms, fear of YHVH and fear of Elohim.[36] Fear of Elohim denotes the mode of *avodah* the person adopts in the process of resolving his defect. During this period, the person must restrict himself and be punctilious in his observance of the commandments. When a person has satisfactorily repaired his defect he is theoretically no longer bound by the restrictions of the commandments. He now serves God from fear of YHVH. However, since not all people are equal, many of the individual's fellows may not yet have attained the resolution of their defects. Therefore, he must continue to observe the commandments as an act of compassion and behavioural solidarity with them. He should not separate himself from the community by exempting himself from the duty to observe, even though, now that his defect has been corrected, the commandments, at least technically, are no longer incumbent on him or really efficacious.[37]

Just as each person has a unique defect (*ḥisaron*), so too each person must follow a unique path to the clarification (*berur*) of his defect.[38] This path leads through one of the 613 commandments. It is through the performance of this one commandment that the person attains his personal redemption. The particular commandment that is

[31] Mordecai Joseph of Izbica, *Mei hashilo'aḥ* (2 vols. in 1; Brooklyn, NY, 1973; i, repr. of Vienna, 1860 edn.; ii, repr. of Lublin, 1922 edn.), i,'Bereshit', 4*a*–*b*; i, 'Vayetse' 12*b*; i, 'Koraḥ', 51*a*–*b*; i, 'Vayelekh', 64*b*–65*a*.

[32] Ibid. i, 'Bereshit', 4*a*–*b*.

[33] Ibid. ii, 'Shemot', 12*a*.

[34] Ibid. i, 'Ha'azinu', 65*b*.

[35] Ibid., 'Vayetse', 12*b*; i, 'Yitro', 26*a*.

[36] In kabbalistic symbolism, YHVH denotes the aspect of divinity derived from the side of Ḥesed (mercy), while 'Elohim' denotes the aspect of divinity derived from the side of Din (stern judgment).

[37] *Mei hashilo'aḥ*, i, 'Vayera', 9*a*; i, 'Mishpatim', 23*a*, 27*a*.

[38] For *berur* and its uses in the Lurianic corpus see A. Slotki, *Yad Eliyahu* (Jerusalem, 1963), 83–5.

appropriate for a specific person need not be one of the central commandments or one of the more difficult ones to perform. It can be any one of the 613 commandments of the Torah. When a person has determined which commandment is at the root of his soul, he must fulfil the precepts of that commandment even to the point of sacrificing his life for it. R. Mordecai Joseph is careful to demand this total devotion only in cases where it is certain that the particular commandment is at the root of one's soul. In all other cases he accepts the standard theological position whereby martyrdom is restricted to those cases in which one is compelled to violate the prohibitions on idolatry, murder, or illicit sexual relations.[39]

R. Mordecai Joseph cites two biblical examples of this principle, Mordecai and Daniel. In the Book of Esther, Mordecai refuses to bow down to Haman, thereby endangering his own life (Esther 3: 2–5). Similarly, Daniel disobeys the edict of Darius and continues to pray, putting his life at risk (Dan. 6: 5–18). In neither case was the commandment in question one of the three for which one is required to suffer martyrdom. These commandments were, however, at the root of the souls of Mordecai and Daniel. Therefore the two could not transgress them under any circumstances.[40]

R. Mordecai Joseph provides guidelines for the individual on how to identify his particular *mitsvah*. He suggests:

> 'O Lord, You have taught me from my youth and until now I proclaim your wondrous deed. Even in old age, O Lord, do not forsake me.' (Ps. 71: 17–18.) A person needs to examine and understand [himself] from his youth, before his inclinations forcefully overwhelm him. He needs to understand to which pleasures he is strongly attracted and which are far from his heart. From this [knowledge] he will have the insight [to know] what God has prepared for him, to test him so that he can clarify for himself (*yevarer*) what he has to overcome and [which commandment] to observe. For God has apportioned to each person a unique [commandment] with which to clarify himself. The person must achieve certainty with regard to the [commandment] relevant to him. He can contemplate this primarily in his youth, for when his inclinations overpower him many things will be indicated and he will not understand which is central to him. 'Lord You have taught me from my youth.' That is, a person can contemplate and attain this [understanding] from his youth. 'Even in old age, O Lord, do not forsake me.'[41]

Though the task of finding the particular *mitsvah* through which he can achieve the state of *berur* is an active one, the process of clarification is essentially passive. Man's task is to make himself a suitable vehicle for the reception of God's will. He is not an active partner with God in this process, a view which is in opposition to traditional kabbalistic and hasidic thought. R. Mordecai Joseph's explanation of the Shema, the central statement of Jewish belief, summarizes his approach to the process of *berur*. He writes:

> 'Hear O Israel, the Lord our God, etc.' (Deut. 6: 4), 'And you shall love the Lord your God, etc.' (Deut. 6: 5). 'When you shall come, etc.' (Deut. 6: 10.). This sequence of five verses [adumbrates] the five [steps] that a person should follow in the process of *berur* [clarification]. 'Hear O Israel', that is, the person should see that everything is from the hand of God and He

[39] *Mei hashilo'aḥ*, i, 'Va'etḥanan', 57*b*–58*a*; i, 'Ki tetse', 62*a*. The *locus classicus* in the Talmud concerning martyrdom is Sanh. 74*a*. See also M. Maimonides, *Mishneh torah: Yesodei hatorah*, 5: 3.

[40] *Mei hashilo'aḥ*, i, 'Va'etḥanan', 58*b*.

[41] Ibid. i, 'Likutim miketubim', 4*a*.

is one. 'And you shall love', that is, the person should be able to leave the pleasures of this world because of [his] love of God. 'When you shall come', that is, service [of God]. The person must serve the Lord with his whole soul, as it is written, 'You shall serve me' (Deut. 6: 13). Even if a person shall have everything good, as it is written, 'Houses full of good things' (Deut. 6: 11), he should not forget to serve God. 'You shall not try the Lord' (Deut. 6: 16); thus, after the person has clarified himself with these three clarifications, when the Holy One gives him goods in abundance, he should not be fearful or in doubt that this is not for his benefit.[42]

In this passage, R. Mordecai Joseph has touched on some of the central components of the process of clarification. The first aspect is the recognition and acceptance of God's total providence: that all is in the hands of Heaven. The second aspect is separating oneself from the desires of the world. For R. Mordecai Joseph, the negation of worldly desires is the basic prerequisite for the ability to discern the divine will. Desires and needs of the physcial world are veils which mask the true will of God. Attachment to the slightest need or desire will prevent the lifting of the veil which obscures the divine light.[43] Through the process of separation from earthly desires, the person makes room in his heart and consciousness for the reception of the divine will.[44]

Both the physical and the spiritual aspects of the person are involved. They are inseparable. R. Mordecai Joseph uses the analogy of the eyes and the soul as an illustration. The soul sees by means of the eyes and decides what is good on the basis of the data it receives. If the eyes have the slightest desire for the delights of the world, they are no longer auxiliaries of the soul but constitute independent entities. The result is that the soul is no longer able to distinguish the good from the bad and the person loses sight of the true will of God.[45]

In a rare departure from purely theoretical discussions, R. Mordecai Joseph describes a method for attaining the state of clarification (*berur*). He writes:

'And Israel said, it is enough, my son Joseph is still alive, I will go and see him before, etc.' (Gen. 45: 28). We find [the following comment] in the Talmud:

R. Levi b. Hama says in the name of R. Simeon b. Lakish: A man should always incite the good impulse to fight against the evil impulse. For it is written, 'Tremble and sin not' (Ps. 4: 5).[46] If he subdues it, well and good. If not, let him study Torah. For it is written, 'Commune with your heart'. If he subdues it, well and good. If not, let him recite the Shema. For it is written, 'Upon your bed'. If he subdues it, well and good. If not, let him remind himself of the day of death. For it is written, 'And be still, Selah.' (Ber. 5*a*)

R. Mordecai Joseph comments:

R. Levi b. Hama uses the phrase 'always incite' because 'always' contains all things that happen to a person. One must always discern and clarify whether something comes from God. Even matters of great significance can, Heaven forbid, contain a blemish or residue from another source. When a joyful matter comes to a person, even more clarification is necessary. Therefore, four levels of advice are offered to help the person to arrive at the depths of truth and come to a decision. Afterwards, when he has clarified with certainty that it is from God, he can

[42] Ibid. i, 'Va'etḥanan', 57*b*.
[43] Ibid. i, 'Kedoshim', 38*a*.
[44] Ibid. i, 'Vayikra', 32*b*.
[45] Ibid. i, 'Tetsaveh', 29*b*.
[46] All other quotations in these passages are from this verse.

allow himself to be expansive and know that it is a *mitsvah* or the joy of a *mitsvah*.[47] These four clarifications spoken of in the Talmud refer to a situation where some matter of this world that needs clarification is imposed on the person.

R. Mordecai Joseph then suggests that to incite one's good inclination means that one should interrupt one's indulgence by reminding oneself that this pleasure is not eternal since we only have a limited lifespan: of what value is that which may last seventy or eighty years at most? If one is still troubled by one's evil inclination and has not succeeded in overcoming it, one should proceed to the second step, which is the study of Torah:

> The teachings of the Torah help a person extricate himself from indulging in pleasures. 'But when the evil inclination is dominant, nobody remembers the good inclination.[48] This is why God made the Torah variegated. In truth, the person who is immersed in desire cannot extricate himself. At that point it will not help him to remember that it is forbidden. The prohibition does not have the power to separate the person from evil when the evil inclination is dominant. There the person is advised to remember that he can find this same good in the Torah, in holiness.

If the study of Torah does not overcome his inclination, the next step is to read the Shema. This will remind him of his special relationship with God and that God's actions are always for our ultimate benefit:

> If he is successful, it is good. If not, he should remember the day of death . . . he should imagine that now is the time of his death and in that situation there will be no place for physical pleasure. If, after all this, the delight of joy still remains in his heart, then it is evidence that it comes from God and will be eternal.[49]

Each person in completing the four steps sequentially sorts and sifts his motivation and determines whether it is truly the will of God that he partake of earthly delights or positive experiences. By attaining inner detachment, by being 'clarified' (one who has undergone *berur*), one truly discerns the will of God.

Through his reinterpretation of *ḥisaron* and *berur* R. Mordecai Joseph has combined the individualization and 'psychologization' of *devekut* with the intense individualism of Przysucha–Kotsk. Building on these concepts, R. Mordecai Joseph has taken a quantum leap and added a significant new dimension. He has taken the radical step of laying out a specific path to be followed in the quest for individual redemption. Hedging his path with warnings and cautions does little to mitigate his radicalism. Though it can be argued that he is taking the ideas of his teachers to their logical conclusion, he has nonetheless stepped over a boundary. He has put into writing ideas which were transmitted only orally in previous generations. R. Gershon Henoch of Radzyn, R. Mordecai Joseph's grandson and the editor of his writings, places R. Mordecai Joseph's theological radicalism in the context of the messianic expectations for the year 5600 (1840).[50]

[47] The term that is translated as 'to be expansive', *hitpashet*, normally has an antinomian connotation in R. Mordecai Joseph's writings. [48] Ned. 32 *b*. [49] *Mei hashilo'aḥ*, i, 'Vayigash', 16*b*–17*a*.

[50] R. Gershon Henoch gives his explanation of Izbica radicalism and its relation to messianic expectation in 1840 in his introduction to Jacob b. Mordecai Joseph Leiner of Izbica, *Beit Ya'akov* [Warsaw, 1890] (New York, 1978), i. introd. 7*a*–11*b*. For messianic expectation in 1840, see Aryeh Morgenstern, 'Tsipiyot meshiḥiyot likrat shenat haTar [1840]', in Z. Baras (ed.), *Meshiḥiyut ve'eskhatologiah* (Jerusalem, 1983), 343–64.

While this interpretation accounts for R. Gershon Henoch's own activities, including the 'rediscovery' of the *tekhelet* and his authorship of the *Sidrei tohorot*, it is not a satisfactory explanation for R. Mordecai Joseph's motivation.[51] Messianism, in the conventional sense, plays no role in the *Mei hashilo'aḥ*.

Though it is clear that R. Mordecai Joseph's emphasis on personal redemption and the broad outlines of his teachings are based on the ideas of the Przysucha–Kotsk school and the hasidic reinterpretation of *devekut*, the specific sources of many of his teachings and the role of personal redemption in the literature of hasidism need further study.

APPENDIX

My dear friend the sage and Hasid of Płonsk sent me a story that he heard from the holy R. Ḥanokh Henoch of Alexander, of blessed memory, who told it in the name of his teacher, the holy R. Bunem, of blessed memory. He said that every young man who comes to the zaddik for the first time to join the hasidic community needs to know the story of R. Isaac the son of R. Yekel of Cracow who built the synagogue in Cracow called the *shul* of R. Isaac the son of R. Yekel.

R. Isaac the son of R. Yekel dreamed a number of times that he should travel to Prague. There, close to the royal palace, under a bridge, he should dig in the ground and he would find a great treasure and become rich. He travelled to Prague. When he arrived, he went to the bridge that was near the royal palace. However, there were soldiers who stood guard there, day and night. He was afraid to dig in the ground to search for the treasure. He walked back and forth near the bridge all day, absorbed in his thoughts, in great despair. He had worked hard to come such a long way and now to return home with nothing. In the evening, he went to the inn to rest. On the second day and again on the third day, he returned in the morning and walked around all day. Towards evening he returned to the nearby inn. The commander of the royal guard, seeing a Jew walking around the bridge every day downcast, his appearance like a pauper enveloped in trouble and worry, called him over and gently asked him: What are you looking for and for whom are you waiting for so many days in this place? He told him the whole story, how he dreamed for several nights consecutively that a great treasure was buried here. He had come to Prague for this reason with great effort and difficulty. The officer laughed out loud and said to him: Was it worthwhile to travel such a long distance because of a dream? Who believes in dreams? I was told in a dream that I would travel to the city of Cracow. There is someone there by the name of Isaac the son of Yekel. If I dig under the oven in the house of the Jew Isaac the son of Yekel, I will find a great treasure. Should I put my trust in worthless dreams and travel to Cracow because of them? You did a foolish thing in coming here. When R. Isaac the son of R. Yekel heard the officer's story, he understood that the primary reason for his coming here was to hear these words. He now knew that the treasure was not found here, but in his own house. He had to dig and search in his house and the treasure would be found there. He returned home. He searched and found the treasure under

[51] See Weiss, 'A Late Utopia of Religious Freedom', 220–2.

the oven and became wealthy. He built the synagogue known as R. Isaac the son of R. Yekel's *shul.*

This is what every young man needs to know. Through coming to the zaddik and *rebbe* it will become known to him that the treasure is not to be sought near the *rebbe* but in his own house. When he returns home, he should dig and search to the extent of his ability. 'Seek and you shall find' (Meg. 6*b*) 'The thing is very close to you, in your mouth and in your heart, to observe it' (Deut. 30: 14). Very close, indeed. Understand. The words of a kabbalistic scholar. (Berger, *Simḥat Yisrael*, 49.)

THIRTEEN

Hasidism as a Socio-religious Movement on the Evidence of *Devekut*

MENDEL PIEKARZ

> The pleasure experienced by the man who is perfect in his study of the Torah and in his prayer consists in this, that he joins himself (*medabek et atsmo*) to the sacred letters, which are living spiritual creatures, holy souls—for [Job 19: 36] 'in my flesh I shall see my [*sic*] God'. As in the case of a live male member in coition, which is the greatest of all pleasures, so it is that the perfect man who has pleasure in his Torah study is described as being live, which is not the case where he has no such pleasure, for then he wields a dead, completely lifeless member; even if he has fear of Heaven, he must also have within him love and pleasure.'[1]

> If a person does not feel sweet pleasure in his worship, his acts are worthless; nevertheless, since the Lord does not deprive anyone of his recompense, He compensates him for his trouble and effort, but the act itself finds no favour at all with Him.[2]

> Nor should it be said that a person ought to savour and enjoy his worship; on the contrary, if his desire is to enjoy his worship, his service [of Heaven] has an attachment to this world, which is a world of falsehood, and everything he lays hold of is likewise false.[3]

> If, in the arbitrary exercise of his own judgement, he follows a good path . . . and applies his intellect to distinguish between evil and good . . . his thought is a contradiction of all the intentions of the Torah, for the essence of the Torah is that it imposes on man a command which he is compelled to obey . . . for it is impossible for a man, by his own efforts, to withstand the evil inclination, since the life of the flesh demands the satisfaction of its desire . . . it is only by wholly submitting to the Torah and the commandments, and fulfilling it all for the very reason that he is commanded to do so, that he can withstand the evil inclinations.[4]

THE first of the above four short extracts, which are merely specimens drawn from an extensive collection of material on this subject, comes from the works of R. Jacob Joseph of Polonnoye, a disciple of the Baal Shem Tov and the first man to expound hasidism in writing. The second is by R. David Solomon Eybeschuetz, rabbi of several communities in Galicia and a noted preacher, who lived in the second to the third generation of hasidism and who, towards the end of his life, settled in Erets Yisrael and

[1] Jacob Joseph of Polonnoye, *Toledot Ya'akov Yosef* [Korets, 1780], 102*d*.

[2] David Solomon Eybeschuetz, *Arvei naḥal* [2 vols.; Sudylkow, 1825–6] (Josefov, 1868), i. 109*d*.

[3] David Zevi of Neustadt, *Ḥemdat David* (Bilgoraj, 1930), 3*c–d*.

[4] David Bornstein of Sochaczew, *Ne'ot hadeshe*, ed. Aaron Israel Bornstein (2 vols.; Tel Aviv, 1974–8), ii. 358–9; spoken in 1938.

died there in 1813. The third extract is from remarks attributed to R. David Zevi Taub of Neustadt, one of the disciples of R. Menahem Mendel of Kotsk and son of the *admor* R. Ezekiel Taub of Kazimierz; he died in 1883. The author of the last extract was R. David Bornstein of Sochaczew, who died in the Warsaw ghetto in 1942.

To those who are familiar with hasidic literature it will be apparent that, whereas the first two passages exemplify a view entirely typical of the first generations of hasidic teachers—the importance attached to personal religious experience—the last two, both spoken with polemical fervour, could easily be taken to be accusations levelled by the mitnaggedim against hasidism. Thus the question must inevitably be asked: what are the bonds that have held together such disparate expressions of hasidism and assured its continuity as a movement, from the middle of the eighteenth century in eastern Europe to the present day in Israel and the USA?

Anyone acquainted with the diversity of spiritual temperament and orientation in the hasidic leadership during more than two and a half centuries of social, political and technological upheaval will find it hard to conceive of hasidism as a single religious ideology. Not only does an ideological gap divide the spiritual world of the early masters from that of the last hasidic leaders in eastern Europe, but even in the early period of hasidic growth and expansion there was a wide range of ill-assorted and even contradictory opinions and beliefs within hasidism. On the other hand, in the social sphere there is no difficulty in finding a common denominator that has linked all the separate factions of hasidism to one another across vast divides of time, space, and ideology; for the writings of the early teachers no less than those of the last contain the one element which establishes hasidism as a coherent movement despite its tendency to ramify and subdivide: namely, the social institution of zaddikism.[5]

It is true that, from the very beginning, the kabbalistic orientation of all the hasidic leaders lent a certain ideological coherence to the movement. This orientation is well attested in their writings, their mode of expression, and their customs, as well as in their consciousness of themselves as heirs to the tradition of Lurianic kabbalah (or as its reinterpreters). Moreover, we have evidence that several of their contemporaries regarded the founders of hasidism as kabbalists,[6] and among the array of prominent figures in the history of hasidism we find personalities who were wholly immersed in the world of kabbalah. For example, the writings of R. Dov Ber of Mezhirech leave us in no doubt that he was a mystic. However, the fact that his disciples responded to his mystical teaching by establishing such social institutions as the courts and dynasties of zaddikim calls for explanation. Historically speaking, what is important is not the zaddik as a mystic (whether in reality, in his own view of himself, or in the image which his contemporaries have formed of him); rather, it is the zaddik as a focal point for a

[5] While Bratslav hasidism—a small but very influential movement—has survived since 1810 without a living zaddik, it must be remembered that after the death of R. Nahman a number of influential Bratslav hasidim, substitutes for him in some respects, applied themselves to organizing the Bratslav fraternities in distinctive social patterns. However, because of the absence of a central court ruled by an *admor*, there has recently been a usurpation of authority within the Bratslav ranks. See my paper 'Hamifneh betoledoteihah shel hameshiḥiyut haḥasidit haBraslavit', in Z. Baras (ed.), *Mesiḥiyut ve'eskhatologiah* (Jerusalem, 1983), 325–42.

[6] See e.g. Shraga Feivel b. R. Moses Segal, *Safah berurah* (Zolkiew, 1778), 12, 1*d*; 15, 1*a*–*b*. See also Aaron Kregluszker, *Leḥem terumah* (Fürth, 1781), 4*a*, 25*d*.

new socio-religious grouping and as head of an eparchy which extends its domination over communities and communal office-holders, establishing itself in the public consciousness as an integral element of normative Judaism and Jewish society.

Certainly no one disputes the social character of hasidism, and the late Gershom Scholem not only placed much emphasis on the social aspects of its religious doctrine but even thought that there was something to be said in favour of the attempts by some scholars to deny the mystical character of hasidism. Fundamentally, however, Scholem perceived hasidism as the latest phase in the Jewish mystical tradition, and he regarded Lurianic kabbalah, Sabbateanism, and hasidism as three stages of the same process.[7] The problem of the relationship between the mystical element in hasidism and its social character was seen by Scholem as the problem of the popularization of kabbalistic thought or the problem of the social function of mystical ideas.[8] This question preoccupied Scholem, and in the Hebrew version of his essay on *devekut* he stated: 'The mystical movement in Judaism passed through two stages: one, basically theosophical in nature, which found its expression in the Kabbalah, and one which was anthropocentric . . . This stage was realized in hasidism.'[9] To the question 'Is there a central point on which hasidism is focused and from which its special attitude can be developed?' Scholem replied: 'I think there can be little doubt that there is indeed such a focal point the discussion of which will take us right into the heart of the problem. This is the doctrine of *devekut*.'[10] Starting from the proposition that 'the hasidic movement sought especially to explain the concepts of kabbalah to mortal men in terms of moral values', Scholem discusses the changes and transformations undergone by *devekut*.[11] He states:

> It is not so much the meaning of *devekut* that has changed in hasidism as its place, and this is a most significant change indeed. The novel element is the radical character given to *devekut* by this change. Hasidic *devekut* is no longer an extreme ideal, to be realized by some rare and sublime spirits at the end of the path. It is no longer the last rung in the ladder of ascent, as in kabbalism, but the first. Everything begins with man's decision to cleave to God. *Devekut* is a starting point and not the end. Everyone is able to realize it instantaneously. All he has to do is to take his monotheistic faith seriously.[12]

The scholars who were swayed by Scholem's brilliant and inspired essays did not pay regard to his declaration that

> since the hasidim drew much more on these [*musar* books—moralizing tracts of the preceding century] than on the metaphysical and theosophical literature of kabbalism, analysis of hasidic doctrines cannot afford to pass them by. Unfortunately no serious attempt has yet been made to establish the true relation between the traditional and the novel elements in hasidic thought . . . *In the absence of a competent scholarly work on the question one is reduced to dangerous generalizations from more or less vague impressions and occasional intuitive glimpses of the situation.*[13]

[7] Gershom Scholem, *Major Trends in Jewish Mysticism* (New York, 1954), 327.

[8] Ibid.; id., 'Mysticism and Society', *Diogenes*, 58 (1967).

[9] Id., 'Devekut, or Communion with God', *Review of Religion*, 14 (1949–50), 115–39, repr. in id., *The Messianic Idea in Judaism* (New York, 1971), 203–27, but the statement quoted occurs only in the Heb. version of the essay. 'Devekut o hitkasherut intimit im Elohim bereshit haḥasidut: Halakhah uma'aseh', in id., *Devarim bego* (Tel Aviv, 1975), 325.

[10] Ibid. (Eng. version), 203.

[11] Ibid. (Heb. version only), 325.

[12] Ibid. (Eng. version), 308.

[13] *Major Trends*, 340.

In considering these remarks one must bear in mind that the homiletic and moralistic literature contemporaneous with the rise of hasidism does not consist of obscure documents unknown to the reading public but includes the literary products of eminent personalities like the heads of the Brody *kloiz*, rabbis, and preachers of stature. But these men inspired a succession of epigones—individuals of lesser distinction who desired not only to be reckoned among the authors of learned works but also to use their works as a means of securing the patronage of the rich. These books can provide an insight into the *Zeitgeist* at the time when hasidism first emerged and was beginning to spread, and they throw fresh light on the teachings of the early masters of hasidism. The historical importance of these derivative homiletic and moralistic *musar* works is illustrated by the facts (*a*) that the first hasidic literary document to appear in print was published in one of them about two years before the publication of the first hasidic book, *Toledot Ya'akov Yosef*, and (*b*) that distinctly hasidic teachings were printed in a collection of homilies by an impoverished Lithuanian preacher a year after the appearance of the *Toledot*.[14]

Moreover, close scrutiny of the *musar* books dating from the early days of hasidic expansion will show that they are intimately related to the classical *musar* books, and especially to the *Shenei luḥot haberit* by R. Isaiah Horowitz, who is known by the acronym derived from this title as 'the holy Shelah'—a massive work of encyclopedic scope in which kabbalah, halakhah, ethics, religious custom (*minhag*), and important historical information are intermingled. The attentive reader of these books will find that sayings and maxims attributed by the early hasidic teachers to the Baal Shem Tov or to other founding fathers of the hasidic movement—sayings which had been regarded by scholars as crucial to the understanding of the nature of hasidism—actually originated with authors who preceded or were contemporary with the beginning of hasidism but had no connection whatsoever with the new movement. And as indicated above, the radical aim of achieving inner spirituality and personal religious experience was itself conceived by pietists and before the advent of Sabbateanism and propagated in their writings. The same is true of *devekut* in the writings of R. Jacob Joseph of Polonnoye, which left their mark on the formulations of the doctrine of the zaddik throughout the literature of hasidism; all that was *novel* in his treatment of this subject—was its appropriation as one of the foundations of the hasidic doctrine of leadership.

Scholem said that the history of religious ideas could not explain hasidism without comparing its early teachings with homiletic and *musar* works. We may assume, therefore, that if he had managed to carry out a systematic study of these works, they would have shaken his conviction that the Sabbatean heresy (refined, in his opinion, by the removal of its antinomian sting) had left its imprint on the early masters of hasidism.[15] Such a study of homiletic and *musar* books from the early days of hasidism, and particularly of works which preceded Sabbateanism, demonstrates that the early hasidic teachers did not initiate but merely continued the aspiration to set religious life on the

[14] See M. Piekarz, *Biyemei tsemiḥat haḥasidut: Megamot ra'ayoniyot besifrei derush umusar* (Jerusalem, 1978), 316–76.

[15] See Scholem, 'Devekut', 221 of Eng. version; id., 'Hatsadik', in *Pirkei yesod behavanat hakabalah usemaleihah* (Jerusalem, 1976), 213–58, pub. in Eng. as 'The Righteous One', in id., *The Mystical Shape of the Godhead* (New York, 1991), 124–6.

basis of inner spiritual values and personal religious experience. They are careful not to undermine the normative foundations of the Jewish religion which rest upon the notion of ultimate divine control, even if occasionally they did disturb the balance between this principle and such scope as it allows for human free will.

More important, the first leaders of hasidism inherited from pre-Sabbatean homiletic and *musar* literature not only the tendency to base religious life on inner spirituality but also the main ingredients of the hasidic doctrine of the zaddik. But these early hasidic teachers turned that tendency—which was expressed in a variety of ways, not all of them falling into a single pattern—into the ideology of an essentially social movement. Without wishing to underestimate the importance of the ideological factor in hasidism, I must again stress that what was decisive for the spiritual orientation of the movement was not the mosaic of mystical ideas inherited from past generations of kabbalists (which was occasionally reduced to empty rhetoric, void of its original content, and there were even important hasidic leaders in later generations who were altogether critical of the study of kabbalah); rather, it was the endeavour to realize the aim of inner spirituality through a new socio-religious movement whose ideology was influenced to some extent by kabbalistic ideas.

Before considering *devekut*, we must note the literary characteristics of hasidic writings. These include association of disparate ideas for homiletic purposes, disregard for precision of language and expression, resort to unbridled hyperbole, careless attribution of quotations, and lack of concern for their accuracy (even though misquotation does not always testify to conscious misrepresentation or tendentiousness). Above all, it must be remembered that hasidic discourses are not philosophical or theological treatises, and the teachers of hasidism were not bothered by the internal inconsistencies or even contradictions with which their discourses could be faulted. These characteristics are especially prominent with regard to the concept of *devekut*, which was never defined clearly either in hasidic literature or in earlier kabbalistic *musar* works. In both bodies of literature it is hard to distinguish the exact meanings of the term. Sometimes it is identical with *kavanot* in general; sometimes, in the sense of 'cleaving to God', it is presented as a state of mind without any specific content; sometimes it is a personal experience of God or His attributes which goes beyond what is ordinarily enjoined by religion; sometimes it is just another name for piety or devout faith. To this should be added the undeniable fact that in Yiddish, the language spoken by the teachers of hasidism, the corresponding term *dreykes* has several meanings, for example, feeling or emotion, outpouring of the soul, devotion, inner arousal, a bond, and so forth. Thus it is hardly surprising that the term *devekut* is often used indiscriminately, sometimes twice in the same passage, in two different senses.

Moreover, if the meaning of *devekut* is, as defined by Scholem, 'a close and most intimate communion with God', there are descriptions of such communion throughout the literature of hasidism which do not make use of this term. And in the works of R. Jacob Joseph of Polonnoye there are many statements relating to 'cleaving to God' through the medium of 'scholars'—zaddikim who 'cleave to God'—in which *devekut* is interchangeable with other terms such as 'holiness' as in his comment on Lev. 9: 1 and 9: 2. Basing himself on the premiss that the commandment 'You shall be holy, for I the Lord your God am holy' applies only to 'men of distinction who are able . . . to be a chariot for supreme holiness so as to resemble their Creator', because 'the common people are not in this category', R. Jacob Joseph asks: 'And how could it be said regarding the whole congregation of Israel "You shall be holy, for I am holy"?' His answer to this rhetorical question is that the command to be holy is identical with the command 'and to Him you shall cleave (*uvo tidbak*)' (Deut. 10: 20), for, according to rabbinic interpretation (Ket. 111*b*), cleaving to a Torah scholar is 'as if he were joined (*davuk*) to Him, blessed be He, and that is how the verse "Speak to all the congregation of the children of Israel" is to be understood. That is to say, they are all at unity with the Torah scholars through Da'at [the mediating kabbalistic *sefirah* ('knowledge')] which unites them, and thus you will all be holy through the scholars who cleave to His holiness, for "I am holy" and you cleave to them; this is easy to understand.'[16] Thus it is not surprising that hasidic leaders in later generations in Poland, for example, expressed an élitist conception of *devekut* without using the term at all, as will be shown below.

It appears, however, that among the welter of meanings conveyed by *devekut* two main categories can be distinguished: a mystical one, which itself embraces various nuances, and another, without any mystical content, which simply implies piety and the like.[17] Indeed, as Scholem observed, 'the term has not always a mystical connotation and it is not always easy to determine what is meant by it. Sometimes it only means concentration of mind by uniting all its powers on one focal point, sometimes it means even less; merely acknowledgment of God's unity.'[18] However, Scholem goes on to say: 'This latter meaning, however, is more or less restricted to non-mystical literature, where it is frequently found, whereas hasidic literature uses the term in the same special sense given to it by the kabbalists.'[19] This could be contradicted by evidence from the hasidic sources, as in the following example—one of many—in which R. Ephraim of Sudylkow quotes his grandfather the Baal Shem Tov:

As I heard my revered grandfather explain . . . on the verse 'Happy is the man unto whom the Lord imputeth not iniquity' [Ps. 32: 2]—that is to say, such a man's thoughts are constantly in a state of *devekut* to the Lord, blessed be He, and therefore if he were to fail for a single moment to keep the Lord in his thoughts it would be imputed to him as iniquity and sin. And that is what is meant by the text [the natural phrasing being ignored for homiletic effect]: '*Ashrei adam*—blessed is the man; *lo yaḥshov haShem*—if he were not to think of the Lord; *lo avon*—it would be iniquity on his part', and that is a sign that he cleaves constantly, in his thoughts, to the Lord, blessed be He, and therefore 'happy is he'.[20]

[16] Jacob Joseph of Polonnoye, *Ketonet pasim* [Lemberg, 1866] (NewYork, 1954), 17*c*.

[17] See Piekarz, *Biyemei tsemiḥat haḥasidut*, index, s.v. 'devekut'.

[18] Scholem, 'Devekut' (Eng. version), 214. On the difficulties presented by the subject of *devekut* in the Zohar, see also e.g. Isaiah Tishby, *Mishnat hazohar* (2 vols; Jerusalem, 1971), ii. 301–6, pub. in Eng. as *The Wisdom of the Zohar*, trans. D. Goldstein (3 vols.; Oxford, 1989), iii. 994–8.

[19] Scholem, 'Devekut' (Eng. version), 214.

[20] Moses Hayyim Ephraim of Sudylkow, *Degel maḥaneh Efrayim* [1808] (Szinervavalja, 1942), on 'Vayikra', 54*b*. Cf. ibid., on 'Balak,' the passage beginning '*Veyesh od bazeh derekh penimit*', where R. Ephraim makes use of the Besht's classic comment on Ps. 32: 2, describing the exalted state of constant communion with God as mere 'fear and humility' in the face of God, without once resorting to the term *devekut* itself: 'As my revered grandfather said . . . on the verse "Happy is the man unto whom the Lord imputeth not iniquity", "man" (*adam*) signifies one who has attained an exalted level, living in accordance with the verse "I have set the Lord always before me" [Ps. 16: 8], and when, at times, his thoughts are

We often find *devekut* used to mean nothing more than a social bond. When R. Jacob Joseph protests against the religious and moral decline of contemporary rabbis, he contrasts their behaviour with the religious and social way of life of the rabbis and scholars who were the founders of hasidism, men made in the image of 'the rabbis of old', who 'always cleaved to Him, blessed be He, in Torah and prayer', but who deliberately descended from their *devekut* from time to time and, as he expressed it, 'put off the holy garments of *devekut*' in order to associate with the common people and raise them up from their lowly condition. This descent is variously described in the writings of R. Jacob Joseph: in the example I quoted he represents it as consisting in the adoption of seductive rhetorical devices at the beginning of the sermon in order to capture the attention of the audience for its main theme, the religious and moral rebuke. 'But in our times', complains R. Jacob Joseph derisively, 'there has not been any need for all this, for in any event they have *devekut* with the common people and associate with them'.[21] Undoubtedly *devekut* in this ironical context means nothing more than a link between two parties equal in their inferior moral status; but even when R. Jacob Joseph said that rabbis in olden times cleaved to God, it was not necessarily the mystical meaning of *devekut* that he had in mind. This is even more clearly the case when he says, 'for the Lord, blessed be He, first warned the common people that they should support the Torah scholar [i.e. the zaddik] with their worldly wealth so that he should be free to live in seclusion and sanctity . . . and you, too, the scholars, should similarly cleave to (*lehidabek im*) the common people'.[22] However, in what R. Jacob Joseph says here, as elsewhere in his writings, we have indirect evidence of a growing concern for socio-religious issues at some stage in hasidism's development into a movement with a new leadership. Its novelty does not reside in the 'most significant change' seen by Scholem, namely a radical shift of *devekut* which brought it down from its supreme position on the last rung of the ladder of religious ascent to the level of a religious value equally accessible to all. Scholem's observation in this case is not consistent with the doctrine of the zaddik as formulated in the works of the early hasidic masters, for it is clear that the essential ingredient of that doctrine is its socio-religious élitism.

Nothing throws the socio-religious élitism in hasidism into sharper relief than the treatment of *devekut*. This is exemplified by the subdivision of the concept into 'first-class' *devekut* for zaddikim and 'second-class' for the common people: 'As I have written elsewhere, there are two categories of *devekut* (*a*) the scholar [i.e. the zaddik] is joined (*davuk*) to Him, blessed be He, and that is what is meant by the verse "and to Him you shall cleave" [Deut. 10: 20]. Category (*b*): the common people who are joined to the scholar, when it is as if they were joined to Him, blessed be He.'[23] R. Jacob Joseph's

diverted for a moment from the Lord, blessed be He, it is imputed as iniquity to him because he turned his thoughts away from *the fear of the Lord*, as in Rashi's comment on this verse: "I have always set the fear of Him before my face" [more accurately: 'In all my actions I have set the fear of Him before my eyes'], and as is explained at the beginning of the *Shulḥan arukh, Oraḥ ḥayim* " 'I have set the Lord always before me'—this is a great principle in the Torah", etc. All the more so when the Holy One, blessed be He, whose glory fills the whole earth [Isa. 6: 3], stands at his side and he sees Him and is immediately overtaken by *fear and humility*.' (Emphasis mine—M.P.)

[21] Jacob Joseph of Polonnoye, *Ben porat Yosef* [Korets, 1781; Piotrkow, 1884] (Brooklyn, NY, 1976), 96*c*.

[22] Id., *Tsafenat pa'neaḥ* [Korets, 1782; Piotrkow, 1884] (New York, 1954), 96*c*.

[23] Ibid. 29*a*.

category (*b*) signifies recognition of the authority of the zaddik and the duty of providing material support for him. Although *devekut* was not associated with zaddikism to begin with, the two became integrated during the formative stages of the institution of the zaddik, and it was not for nothing that R. Jacob Joseph's remarks on category (*b*) *devekut* were accompanied by a fervent polemical criticism of the common people (a term in which he included householders and communal leaders) who refused to recognize the special authority of new leaders.

We possess literary evidence that proves conclusively that R. Jacob Joseph was indeed the spokesman for a new socio-religious movement in the early stages of its consolidation. The document in question is a sermon in *Toledot Ya'akov Yosef* (123*b*–128*c*), which I summarized at the end of my book *Biyemei tsemiḥat haḥasidut*.[24] Here it will suffice to note that the sermon deals with the expulsion of R. Jacob Joseph from Shargorod, where he had been serving as head of the rabbinical court. Simon Dubnow supposes this to have taken place in 1748.[25] It was occasioned by the self-segregation of 'hasidim', 'the unblemished ones of the generation', 'the eminent men of Israel', from the congregation, participating neither in its prayer nor in its foods, and setting up a 'house of study'-cum-synagogue of their own.

Whatever *devekut* may have meant in the writings of R. Jacob Joseph of Polonnoye, R. Dov Ber the Maggid of Mezhirech, R. Elimelekh of Lyzhansk, and others, it was, for them, the prerogative of 'men of form' and not 'men of matter' (to use R. Jacob Joseph's terminology), men of 'substance' (*atsmut*) and not men of 'instruments' (*kelim*); men 'of exceeding understanding' or 'enlightened men'[26] (and similarly in the writings of the Maggid of Mezhirech)—men whose lives are conducted on a supernatural level. In the characteristic words of R. Jacob Joseph of Polonnoye—'man must sanctify his whole being . . . but that is for exalted persons . . . while the common people are not in this category'.[27] 'This commandment—"and to Him you shall cleave"—is not within the capacity of everyone to fulfil, nor can every Torah scholar fulfil it, but only exceptional individuals.'[28] 'Certainly the highest of all the commandments . . . is "and to Him you shall cleave" . . . however, this is not possible for everyone.'[29]

Even if we were to find textual support for Scholem's unequivocal statement that in hasidism the concept of *devekut* underwent a decisive change and came to represent a value equally accessible to everyone, we should be obliged to argue that R. Joseph Tsarfati's work *Yad Yosef*—first printed in Venice in 1616 during the lifetime of its author—anticipated hasidism in clear terms, and that R. Isaiah Horowitz's book *Shenei luḥot haberit* did so by implication. And should it be argued that *devekut* became a value equally accessible to everyone by virtue of the fact that the founders of hasidism demanded of the common people that they practise *devekut* class (*b*), that is, cleaving to the zaddik, this, too, was anticipated (by the Maharal of Prague) albeit, as we shall see below, in different historical circumstances and not in the name of a socio-religious movement.

[24] Piekarz, *Biyemei tsemiḥat haḥasidut*, 390–2.

[25] Simon Dubnow, *Toledot haḥasidut* [Tel Aviv, 1930–1] (Tel Aviv, 1960), 94.

[26] Ze'ev Wolf of Zhitomir, *Or hame'ir* [Korets, 1798] (New York, 1954), 293*d*–294*a*.

[27] *Ketonet pasim*, 17*c*. [28] *Tsafenat pa'neaḥ*, 95*a*. [29] *Toledot*, 72*c*.

Let us turn first to *Yad Yosef*, one of R. Jacob Joseph's declared sources.[30] The passage which is important for our purpose reads as follows:

Now it is true that the greatest perfection and happiness that the soul can attain is *devekut* with God, blessed be He, for it is the height of perfection for the part to adhere to (*lehidabek im*) the whole . . . and this *devekut*, in the opinion of the philosophers, is not attainable by the generality of the people but only by the perfect individual, and even the individual cannot attain this *devekut* except after death . . . and it was to exclude an opinion such as theirs that our master Moses, peace be unto him, said [Deut. 4: 4]: 'and you that cleave [not 'you that did cleave'—M.P.] to the Lord your God, all of you, even today while you are alive' . . . for even though they occupy themselves with material things and not with the Torah and have nothing but faith, that is enough to achieve *devekut* . . . and it is enough for the common people to believe in God, blessed be He, and His Torah for them to achieve *devekut*.[31]

Here it should be pointed out that the writings of the predecessors of the hasidim also often contain contradictory statements, as *Yad Yosef* itself will demonstrate. The extract reproduced below also reveals a disregard for precision of language, for the author of these sermons does not distinguish between the expressions '*devekut* with God' and '*devekut* with the Divine Presence' (the Shekhinah). Now R. Joseph Tsarfati is quoted without reservation by R. Jacob Joseph of Polonnoye, who gives the page reference, though he is not punctilious about textual accuracy. The actual words of R. Joseph Tsarfati are as follows:

The true good is none other than *devekut* with God, blessed be He, and, as it is written, 'it is good for me to draw near to God' [Ps. 73: 28], and *devekut* with the Divine Presence cannot be attained except through the humbling of man's material self and of his evil inclination, and the evil inclination cannot be humbled except through affliction, since without affliction 'Yeshurun waxed fat and kicked' [Deut. 32: 15].[32]

Not only did R. Jacob Joseph quote this extract without any qualification, but there are muffled echoes of it elsewhere in his writings, as for example:

Remove from a man pride and lust; then he will easily be able to cleave to Him, blessed be He . . . for his cleaving to eternal life is 'with unleavened bread', that is to say, through being deprived of the pleasures of this world, pride and lust, as is implied by 'unleavened bread', and that is not possible except by adding 'and bitter herbs' [Num. 9: 11], which are affliction. Only then will he become accustomed to separation from corporeality and be able to cleave to spiritual life'.[33]

Clearly these expressions do not accord with the great principle popular with the teachers of hasidism and inherited by them from their predecessors, a principle generally enunciated in the terms of Prov. 3:6—'In all your ways acknowledge Him'—which is taken as meaning also in business transactions, eating and drinking, and sexual intercourse. But no one versed in hasidic literature will be surprised by this contradiction,

[30] See Gedaliah Nigal, 'Al mekorot hadevekut besifrut reshit haḥasidut', *Kiryat sefer*, 46 (1971), 343–8.

[31] Joseph b. Hayyim Tsarfati, *Yad Yosef* [Venice, 1617]; (Amsterdam, 1700), 225*a*–*b*.

[32] Ibid. 197*a* (quoted in *Toledot Ya'akov Yosef*, 33*c*).

[33] *Toledot*, 45*b*. And see also e.g. 135*b*. For a selection of the writings of R. Jacob Joseph of Polonnoye on *devekut* in its mystical sense see R. Nahman Goldstein of Tcherin (Chigirin), *Leshon ḥasidim* [Lemberg, 1876] (facsimile, Israel, n.d.), 'Devekut veyiḥudim'; see also, by the same editor, an anthology of the writings of hasidic teachers entitled *Derekh ḥasidim* [Lemberg, 1876] (facsimile, Israel, n.d.), 'Devekut veyiḥudim'.

for the spiritual and intellectual make-up of the early hasidic masters must be inferred from their innovations, which were mainly in the realm of concrete social matters, rather than from ideas that originated with their predecessors. If we look for a feature common to *Yad Yosef* and the writings of the first teachers of hasidism, we shall find it in their declarations that *devekut* with God is 'the acme (*takhlit*) of all perfection', that 'the true good is none other than *devekut* with God, blessed be He' (*Yad Yosef*); that 'the supreme goal (*takhlit*) is that man should cleave to Him, blessed be He' (*Ketonet pasim*, 10*a*, and in very many other places); and so, too, R. Moses of Dolina: 'It is well known that the essence of the perfection of the zaddik is that he should always cleave in his thoughts to Him, blessed be He' (*Divrei Mosheh*, 9*c*). And there are many such examples, too numerous to quote.

It would seem that nothing serves so well as *Shenei luḥot haberit* to confirm that statement I have quoted from Scholem that in the absence of a comparative study of homiletic and moralistic literature 'one is reduced to dangerous generalizations from more or less vague impressions', and so forth. This is because that work had a powerful influence on kabbalists, pietists and preachers, among them the founders of hasidism—a point I have dealt with elsewhere.[34] In the opinion of Scholem, 'this idea of *devekut* as the ultimate fulfilment of the mystic's path permeates the theosophical and ethical literature of the kabbalists.[35] Isaiah Horowitz connects the state of *ḥasidut* with that of *devekut*.'[36] Scholem quotes as evidence the words of the Shelah: 'Who is a hasid? He who shows piety towards (*mitḥased im*) his Maker. He pleases his Creator and his whole purpose is *devekut* to Him, blessed be He, for the sake of His great name, and he becomes a chariot for Him [a vehicle for expressing His will].' It must be admitted that, if it is hard to establish the exact meanings of the concept of *devekut* in homiletic and *musar* literature generally, it is much harder in the case of the Shelah, for the example quoted by Scholem is no more than a drop in the ocean. But since the book is of crucial importance for our purpose, we must attempt to consider the principal levels of meaning of *devekut* which may be discerned in it. It appears to me that, not counting the mystical cleaving to God by Israel as a nation through the mystical Torah whose mystical letters correspond to the souls of Israel,[37] there are three levels of meaning which differ from each other in regard to the nature of *devekut*, the way in which it is achieved, and the sort of persons who achieve it:

1. *Mystical* devekut *which involves leading a solitary existence, cut off from the life of the community*. This is a spiritual level attained only by an exalted few. The *Shelah* illustrates this in explaining the fact that Scripture in several places calls Moses the servant of the Lord and does not refer to him as a son:

This is certainly true of the great majority of people . . . Truly, among the spiritually exalted (*benei aliyah*) the rank of servant is regarded as superior . . . spiritually exalted men are few,

[34] The late H. H. Ben-Sasson, who was not an authority on hasidism, was nevertheless right in saying, 'It appears that he (the Shelah) had a strong influence on Beshtian hasidism (*Ha'entsiklopediah ha'ivrit, s.v.* 'Isaiah ben Abraham Halevi Horowitz the Holy Shelah)', xii. 946).

[35] Scholem, 'Devekut' (Eng. version), 206.

[36] Isaiah b. Abraham Halevi Horowitz, *Shenei luḥot haberit (Shelah)* [Amsterdam, 1648] (2 vols.; Warsaw, 1862), 152*a*.

[37] Ibid. 154*a*.

and through their inner love they enter into fear of Heaven, which is deep within and confers on them the quality of the Hasid 'who acts piously towards (*mitḥased im*) his Maker' . . . and his whole purpose is to achieve attachment to Him (*hadevekut bo*), blessed be He . . . and all his service is service of the King . . . and it is in this sense that Moses is called the servant of the Lord . . . and Moses includes them all.[38]

Another important and concrete illustration of the use of *devekut* in the sense of close contact with God can be found in the *Shelah*, although it is not original to him, as I mistakenly thought.[39] but was derived from R. Eleazar Azikri's *Sefer ḥaredim*. I shall not reproduce here the whole Azikri quotation given in the *Shelah*, but it is important to point out that one maxim it included occurs in a manuscript recension of teachings attributed to R. Dov Ber of Mezhirech where it is erroneously said to derive not only from the *Shelah* but also from *Ḥovot halevavot* 'And as was written by the author of *Ḥovot halevavot* and the holy *Shelah* "*Devekut* is seven times better than study".'[40]

2. *Mystical* devekut *as a platform for social action.* Because it is the duty of every man 'to resemble Him, blessed be He . . . in so far as that is possible', it follows that, just as God is hidden from us in all that concerns His essence but He reveals Himself through His actions, 'so, too, must a man's essential nature remain hidden', that is, he must live apart, isolating himself 'from everyone; let him only be alone with his Maker . . . and then it will be well with him in all that concerns his essence, for he will be attached to his Maker (*davuk bekono*) and will be revealed through his actions, by doing good . . . for example, by going among the many and among individuals to teach them Torah and reprove them'.[41] *Devekut*, which is a spiritual path for the individual to follow, is also a stimulus for socio-religious action—the spiritual and religious uplifting of one's fellow-men. In fact, the early hasidic masters argue that the man who resembles his Maker is a zaddik not only for himself but for others also; by virtue of the *devekut* to God which he has attained, he goes forth among his fellow-men on a holy mission.

The great similarity between the views of the Shelah and those of the early teachers of hasidism emerges even more clearly where R. Isaiah Horowitz draws a distinction between Noah and Abraham: Noah, of whom it was said (Gen. 6: 9) 'Noah walked with God', 'that is to say, in isolated places where only the Lord, blessed be He, was present, because his *devekut* to God was too weak to withstand the damaging influence of his wicked generation; and Abraham, who by virtue of his strong *devekut* to God did not fear to walk among men in order to correct them'.[42] This distinction is one of the most important motifs of the hasidic typology of zaddikism, and a popular theme throughout the homiletic literature of the time. It contrasts the zaddik who devotes himself entirely to perfecting his own spiritual and religious condition with the zaddik whose *devekut* to God is bound up with social action.[43]

[38] Ibid. 51*a–b*. And see also 106*a*.

[39] Piekarz, *Biyemei tsemiḥat haḥasidut*, n. 166. I was mistaken in claiming there that the relevant statement could be found only in the *Shelah* and not in Azikri's work.

[40] See Rivka Schatz-Uffenheimer, *Haḥasidut kemistikah* (Jerusalem, 1968), 161–2, and Piekarz, *Biyemei tsemiḥat haḥasidut*, 355–6 (but see n. 39 above).

[41] Horowitz, *Shenei luḥot haberit*, 381*a*. [42] Ibid, 72*a*, 209*b*. [43] See e.g. *Tsafenat pa'neaḥ*, 95*b*.

3. Devekut *which is reverential in character.* It signifies purity of thought and intention, faithfulness to God's commandments and principles, and the endeavour to model oneself on His attributes and cleave to what is eternal rather than transient. It is required of every Jew not only while he is occupied in prayer and study—'of both exoteric and esoteric teachings, according to the extent of his understanding'—but also while he is engaged in the daily activities essential for his physical existence, when 'let him cleave to the Lord, blessed be He, in his thoughts; let him not depart from this *devekut* for an instant'.[44] Elsewhere R. Isaiah Horowitz prescribes *devekut* at all times even for the ordinary person. In the kabbalistic terminology which was to be adopted by the founders of hasidism, this would be *devekut* while in the lesser spiritual state of *katnut:*

When he is carrying on business, let him think: I am engaged in this transaction and I will hope in the Lord, blessed be He, [that He may grant] that I profit by it, for it is He, blessed be He, who is the Giver, and thus I shall be performing a *mitsvah:* I shall be supporting myself and my wife and children so that they may live to serve the Lord, blessed be He, and I shall give money to charity and to the Talmud Torah and so on. And so, too, when he eats or goes to bed he should direct his mind to this so that his body may be strong in order to occupy himself with the Torah and to do *mitsvot* and so on . . . with the result that all the days of his life he will always be attached to (*davuk be-*) the Lord, blessed be He, if he follows this path, and then he will have earned eternal *devekut* to Him, blessed be he.[45]

Undoubtedly there is an ideological connection between these instructions and the opposition of the Shelah to asceticism, as expressed, for example, in the following: 'It is well known that people are divided on how best to serve the Lord, blessed be He; some mortify themselves and are unwilling to enjoy bodily pleasures and utterly abstain from them, and this is not the right way, for it is not what the Creator, blessed be He, intends.'[46] This accords very well with the instructions of the Shelah to serve God in all one's actions:

The principle thus derived that all your actions should be for the sake of Heaven does not apply only to the action of fulfilling the Torah and the commandments so that every such action should be for the sake of Heaven . . . but also to secular activity, that is, in one's business affairs, in eating and drinking and sexual intercourse and many other such matters; all should be for the sake of Heaven—secular actions performed in complete holiness, with the result that all a person's actions, throughout his life, will be for the sake of Heaven.[47]

And it is worth quoting briefly from another statement on the same subject:

The principle thus derived is as I explained in relation to rejoicing on a festival; everything leads to one conclusion, which is that one should celebrate the festival by rejoicing . . . with both body and soul . . . and when we perform the *mitsvah* in this manner, the soul enjoys great pleasure, and at the same time even bodily pleasures such as eating and drinking and so on all become spiritual and are transformed into the service of the Lord.[48]

It may have been under the influence of the Shelah that R. Moses Hayyim Luzzatto said: 'When a man sanctifies himself with the holiness of his Creator, even his bodily

[44] Horowitz, *Shenei luḥot haberit*, 104*a*; see also 290*b* and 2*b*.
[45] Ibid. 370*a*.
[46] Ibid. 246*a*, and see also 247*a*–*b*.
[47] Ibid. 57*a*; see also 60*a*.
[48] Ibid. 246*b*.

actions are transformed into things of veritable holiness'.[49] And perhaps there is a connection between the words of the Shelah and the play upon words by R. Jacob Joseph, who says, among other things:

'And I will give you your rains (*gishmeikhem*) in their season [Lev. 26: 4]'—this is in the sense indicated by 'the vitality [Ezek. 1: 14, reading *haḥayut*, 'the vitality', instead of *haḥayot*, 'the living creatures'] ran and returned' . . . that is to say, your corporeality (*gashmiyut*), your eating, drinking, sexual intercourse and concern with your livelihood will take place in their season, that is to say, at a time when it is necessary to draw back from the service of the Lord, as indicated by 'running and returning', and then the corporeal (*hagashmi*), too, will acquire spiritual vitality (*ḥayut haruḥant*).[50]

Here it should be emphasized that for the Shelah as for R. Joseph Tsarfati, and as was the accepted view among the teachers of hasidism, *devekut* was central to religious life. We find an illustration of this in the words of the Shelah: 'All our study of the Torah and all our deeds, the fulfilment of positive and negative precepts and all the holiness with which we sanctify ourselves, all of this is so that we may be worthy to attain His *devekut*, blessed be His name.'[51] The verse beginning 'But you that did cleave' (Deut. 4: 4) 'includes all the Torah study and all the deeds of man, his ways and his conduct, in all of which he must be in a state of *devekut* with the Lord, blessed be He, all for His name's sake'.[52]

There is, therefore, no difference in principle between the senses in which the term *devekut* is used in the *Shelah* and in the teachings of the founders of hasidism, other than the concrete social aim of the latter. This is expressed, for example, in R. Jacob Joseph of Polonnoye's declaration (to which there is no parallel in the *Shelah*) that 'there are two kinds of *devekut*, which is the purpose to which the whole of the Torah is directed': (*a*) *devekut* to God 'if the person is one of those of Israel who are perfect in their faith'; (*b*) *devekut* to Torah scholars (*Tsafenat pa'neaḥ*, 95*a*), that is, to the zaddikim. The practical implication is that those who are fit only for the second type of *devekut* should join the hasidic fraternities and provide for the maintenance of the zaddik so as to free him to devote himself to his social and religious mission.

It must be admitted that references to both types of *devekut* are also to be found in the writings of the Maharal of Prague. But before we consider him I shall try to present a picture of hasidism as a socio-religious movement rather than as a link in the chain of the history of Jewish mysticism. This I shall do by reference to R. Jacob Joseph's use of the talmudic story (in Ta'an. 22*a*) in praise of two jesters who used to go into the market to cheer up sad people and make peace between those who had quarrelled. Scholem stated that 'the Baal-Shem-Tov was very fond of this story, and it does, indeed, have a true Hasidic ring to it', and he also found in it a reflection of the social significance of *devekut* in hasidism.[53] He appears to have overlooked the fact that the same note was struck many years before the Baal Shem Tov by R. Elijah de Vidas in his great work *Reshit ḥokhmah*, according to which the man who is 'a lover of God' and 'pious' (*ḥasid*)

[49] Moses Hayyim Luzzatto, *Mesilat yesharim* [Amsterdam, 1740], pub. in bilingual edn. as *Mesillat Yesharim: The Path of the Just*, trans. S. Silverstein (Jerusalem, 1966), ch. 26.

[50] *Ketonet pasim*, 17*b*.

[51] Horowitz, *Shenei luḥot haberit*, 70*b*.

[52] Ibid. 370*a*.

[53] Scholem, 'The Righteous One', 128–9; id., 'Mysticism and Society', 17–18.

is he who has attained these three qualities: 'trust', 'faith', and 'joy' (cf. Avot, 6: 1). R. Elijah de Vidas illustrates the social advantage in the quality of joy by the same talmudic story of the two jesters who cheered up sad people and, 'when they saw two people quarrelling, would crack jokes until they made peace between them'.[54] The same story is also quoted by R. Elijah Hakohen of Smyrna in his *Shevet musar* (ch. 14). It is, indeed, frequently referred to by R. Jacob Joseph with an attribution to the Baal Shem Tov, but with one essential difference: he uses it to illustrate the ideology of the newly emerging hasidic leadership in their approach to society. And it is not without significance that, in many places in the writings of R. Jacob Joseph, the story of the two jesters (*terei badoḥei*) is closely associated with a number of motifs which are central to the ideology of zaddikism: witness, for example, its use in his exegesis of Num. 27: 16–17, 'Let the Lord, the God of the spirits of all flesh, appoint a man over the congregation who shall go out before them and go in before them, who shall lead them out and bring them in; that the congregation of the Lord may not be as sheep which have no shepherd'. On this R. Jacob Joseph says, 'As I have written in the name of my teacher . . . let the Lord appoint a man who shall lead them out and bring them in, for the leader of his generation will be able to raise up all the [mundane] utterances and stories of his generation in order to link the corporeal with the spiritual, as, for example, the two jesters, etc.'[55] Here, then, the reference is to a 'leader of his generation' who comes forward to guide his flock in all their movements. R. Jacob Joseph's interest in the concrete social application of the story of the jesters will be very plain to us if we remember that although (like the Baal Shem Tov, it seems) he was moved to follow R. Elijah de Vidas in using it—without mentioning R. Elijah, it is true—he was not drawn into following R. Elijah's interpretation of the story as an act of kindness by two pious men.[56] Textual proof that R. Jacob Joseph was familiar with that interpretation is provided by one of his homilies:

He who would lead the congregation for the sake of Heaven, directing the people aright in matters material and spiritual, not only by deed and word, rebuke and moral teaching, but also in thought, let him first bind himself to Him, blessed be He, and after that let him attend to binding himself to his generation and raising them up and seeing that they cleave to Him, blessed be He. Provided that they, in turn, cleave to the leaders of their generation, and then the leaders of the generation will be able to take them by the hand and raise them up etc. That being so, it has been well explained that everyone who believes in the shepherd of Israel [is as if he believed in the One who spoke and the world came into existence],[57] and this belief consists in loving him and cleaving to him (*ledabek et atsmo bo*); and see what is written in *Reshit ḥokhmah*, 'Sha'ar ha'ahavah', ch. 12.[58]

The question here is no longer one of a pious man impelled by his inner spirit to do good to people in the streets of the city: the kind of man R. Jacob Joseph is concerned

[54] Elijah b. Moses de Vidas, *Reshit ḥokhmah* [Venice, 1579], 'Sha'ar ha'ahavah', ch. 12.

[55] *Ben porat Yosef*, 16*a*.

[56] On traces of R. Elijah de Vidas's *Reshit ḥokhmah* in the works of R. Jacob Joseph see Nigal, 'Al mekorot'; M. Pechter, 'Ikvot hashpa'ato shel sefer *Reshit ḥokhmah* le R. Eliyahu de Vidas bekhitvei R. Ya'akov Yosef miPolonoyeh', in J. Dan and J. Hacker (eds.), *Studies in Jewish Mysticism, Philosophy and Ethical Literature Presented to Isaiah Tishby* (Heb.) (Jerusalem, 1986), 569–91.

[57] Mekh. on 'Beshalaḥ', 31.

[58] *Toledot Ya'akov Yosef*, 171*b*.

with is a public figure, one who leads the community 'for the sake of Heaven' (in contrast to communal leaders acting for their own benefit), who achieves intimate contact with God, and whose spirit, by virtue of this contact, joins with the spirit of his contemporaries in order to raise them up. This, however, is on condition that his contemporaries do his bidding and acknowledge his metaphysical authority to lead the community. As is characteristic of R. Jacob Joseph's writings, that which is obscure in one place is clarified in another. Thus we learn from other references that one of the bases of the doctrine of leadership 'for the sake of Heaven' is the concept of the Jewish people as a mystical organism whose various parts are interconnected and influence each other. The zaddikim, the common people, and the wicked are all organs of a single body, though some of them are whole and sound and others defective and diseased. As in a natural organism in which the important organs, the head and the heart, must oversee the proper functioning of the lesser organs, so the zaddik has a special responsibility towards the common people and the wicked in the holy body called Israel. Just as the lesser organs in the human body, such as the feet, have an influence on the supreme organ, the head, so, too, the spiritual state of the common people influences the condition of their spiritual leaders. When the feet are sunk in a deep pit, the head is necessarily there with them. Hence the similes and parables of moralists and philosophers, rabbis, kabbalists, pietists, and preachers, among them the early hasidic masters, aimed at illustrating in concrete terms the socio-religious mission of the preacher who is stirred from within to arise and fulminate against the misdeeds of the generation. Among these similes and parables is one motif from the Zohar which praises the zaddik who takes the wicked man by the hand and leads him to repentance. There is, for example, an allusion to this in the statement of R. Jacob Joseph quoted above that the common people must do the bidding of the 'leaders of the generation' and that these leaders must 'take them by the hand and raise them up'.[59] It should be emphasized that the use of this motif is not confined to the founders of hasidism, for the principle of mutual responsibility is the basis of the mission of the preacher.[60] But the first teachers of hasidism used this motif from the Zohar to reinforce the ideological foundations of the new socio-religious movement. The reference, then, is to positive action, a descent to the level of the common people, even though this involves wallowing in mire and the danger of sinking in it. From this point of view it is appropriate to quote here the following passage from R. Jacob Joseph's *Tsafenat pa'neaḥ*:

And with regard to what I have written elsewhere on 'and to Him you shall cleave' and its exposition by our sages of blessed memory, who said 'Is it possible' etc. 'but rather, cleave to a Torah scholar' etc., the difficulty presented itself: how could they reject the plain meaning of the text in favour of this homiletic exposition? And I wrote that if a man attaches himself to a scholar who is attached to Him (*davuk bo*), blessed be He, that man, too, becomes actually attached to Him, blessed be He . . . and it seems that this is what is meant by what is written in the Zohar: 'the righteous man is he who takes the wicked by the hand'.[61] And I heard from the rabbi, the *maggid* Moharam [i.e. 'our teacher and master, Rabbi M.'—R. Menahem Mendel of

[59] Ibid.

[60] See Piekarz, *Biyemei tsemiḥat haḥasidut*, 101–11.

[61] Zohar, 2: 128*b* 'Come and see, he who takes the wicked by the hand and tries to persuade him to abandon his evil ways, he ascends three times.' See on this Piekarz, *Biyemei tsemiḥat haḥasidut*, 111–12 n. 59.

Bar] that he who rebukes the public with words of moral reproof must not rely on words alone, for if his hearer does not heed him he has achieved nothing, but he must take positive action to join himself to him and raise him up. And that is what is meant by 'the righteous man is he who takes the wicked by the hand' etc . . . If only we would understand what is meant by 'the righteous man is he who takes the wicked by the hand' etc., for the zaddik must sometimes clothe himself in the garment of the wicked for the sake of Heaven.[62]

The significance of *devekut* here, then, is none other than as one of the important elements in the doctrine of the zaddik. Its connection with that doctrine is not always obvious in the works in question, but the point of *devekut* in the passage quoted and in others like it lies in its furnishing an ideological basis for the doctrine. For while *devekut*, for the zaddik, means existence on an exalted spiritual level, his descent, which sometimes involves his 'clothing himself in the garment of the wicked for the sake of Heaven', is in essence (if we discard the literary motifs from the Zohar and Lurianic kabbalah) purely socio-religious. Certainly the first teachers of hasidism were fascinated by the forms this descent could take and by the dangers inherent in it. References to exemplary actions by the patriarchs and the great national figures are scattered in abundance throughout their works with the object of legitimizing the idea of descent. Sometimes it is described as a voluntary action, as the deliberate adoption of unworthy or even reprehensible measures for a holy purpose, the restoration of the entire nation to religious and moral health; sometimes it is represented as a forced descent—that is to say, a fall from the supreme height because the sins of the generation have harmed its leaders. But three elements are always at the heart of this descent: the leadership, the leaders, and the led. The doctrine of the descent of the zaddik is therefore the doctrine of hasidic leadership. Those who try to account for the remarkable ability of hasidism to survive through the changing circumstances of the times will find one of the answers in this doctrine. It has served as an ideological basis for the resort to worldly organization and political measures by the leaders of the movement in their efforts to strengthen the ties that have bound it together and to adapt to the vicissitudes of history.

It is in that spirit that we must understand the homily by R. Jacob Joseph on Exod. 27: 20, 'And you shall command the children of Israel that they bring to you pure beaten olive oil', in which he brings in the story of the two jesters and the principle of mutual responsibility of the zaddik and the common people. It reads as follows:

For man was created of matter and form to the end that he might subdue the matter to the form . . . and this applies to the world in general, that he should get the wicked to mend their ways . . . and when the common people ascend one degree, the leader of the generation, too, ascends . . . and vice versa . . . but in order to get the common people to mend their ways, he must associate with them . . . and that is how 'and you shall command' (*ve'atah tetsaveh*) is to be understood. That is to say, if you enter into association (*tsavta vehithabrut*) with the children of Israel in order to raise them up so that they mend their ways, great good will come to you too from this, 'and they will bring olive oil to you', that is, they will draw down the flow of divine bounty (for which 'oil' is another name) for you, too . . . I should add that I heard an explanation given in the name of my teacher concerning the reference in the Talmud to those two jesters who had earned a place in the world to come . . . The meaning of the story was that

[62] *Tsafenat pa'neaḥ*, 117*d*–118*a*.

the whole concern of these two was to associate with everyone and achieve the unification of the Holy One, blessed be He, and His Shekhinah, in every detail of the works of man . . . but they could not effect this unification and associate with anyone who was in sorrow, Heaven forfend. Therefore they would cheer him up with their talk until he was happy, and then they could bring him to associate with them in cleaving to Him, blessed by He, etc. This is the great principle which you should understand.[63]

The writings of R. Jacob Joseph were a sort of repository in which notes and homilies were piled up as opportunity offers, so it is no wonder that from time to time the reader comes across a new layer of motifs. This is evident in the following, which reproduces the Baal Shem Tov's interpretation of the story of the two jesters and adds another characteristic motif of the doctrine of the zaddik:

And it appears to me, with regard to the commandment in the Torah [Deut. 10: 20] 'and to Him you shall cleave', which our sages, of blessed memory, explained [in Ket. 111*b*] as meaning 'cleave to a Torah scholar' etc. . . . that if one is attached to a scholar who attaches himself to Him blessed be He, it follows as a matter of course that such a person joins in the scholar's attachment to Him, blessed be He. And that is the meaning of the story of those two jesters who, if people were sad and could not join with them, would make them laugh, because through mirth they became joined with them (*nidbeku imahem*), and then they joined (*ḥiberu*) them to Him, blessed be He. And let it be understood that this is a degree of virtue above all others, for all the commandments have no other purpose than to bring us to cleave to Him, blessed be He, and if a person does not know how to proceed in order to achieve *devekut* to Him, blessed be He, the Torah has fitly commanded: cleave to a scholar, and through him you, too, will ascend . . . for he is a pathway (*shevil*) and channel for the transmission of the divine bounty, and, as our sages of blessed memory said, 'the whole world is nourished through the pathway of [*bishevil*, literally 'for the sake of'] My son Hanina' etc. [Ber. 17*b*] . . . but there is a curtain which divides him off from the *devekut* of the scholar because of his spiritual coarseness.[64]

This interpretation of the rabbinic saying 'The whole world is nourished for the sake of My son Hanina, and a kab of carobs suffices My son Hanina from one sabbath eve to the next', in which the zaddik is represented as a 'pathway and channel' through which the flow of divine bounty is transmitted to the world, occurs very frequently in the writings of R. Jacob Joseph, sometimes with an attribution to the Baal Shem Tov and sometimes without.[65] However, the Baal Shem Tov is not its author: it originates in the Shelah (if, indeed, the Shelah was not anticipated by someone else), where some of the main outlines of the figure of the zaddik in hasidism are sharply delineated: 'For R. Hanina was the greatest zaddik of his generation, the single pillar on which the world stands [a reference to the *sefirah* Yesod (= foundation)]; hence the saying '*bishevil* [for the sake of] My son Hanina', in which the meaning of *bishevil* is a pathway and channel.'[66] The Shelah goes on to speak of Joseph the righteous, the *sefirah* Yesod, a channel through which divine bounty flows to the world. It need hardly be said that the author of the Shelah was not operating in a vacuum, and what he says here may well be a variation on the following exegesis by his predecessor, R. Joseph Tsarfati, in his *Yad Yosef*, which was first printed in 1616 during the lifetime of its author:

[63] *Toledot Ya'akov Yosef*, 64*b*.
[64] Ibid. 120*d*.
[65] See Piekarz, *Biyemei tsemiḥat haḥasidut*, 16–17.
[66] Horowitz, *Shenei luḥot haberit*, 19*b*.

It is well known that the zaddik is the foundation and pillar of the world, as it is written [Prov. 10: 25]: 'but the zaddik is the foundation of the world' [*olam* is here understood as 'the world' rather than as 'for ever', 'eternal', 'everlasting', which is the more common translation] and he supports the world as a foundation supports a house. And there is no question that he is worthy and able to draw down the divine bounty and goodness to himself, but he also serves as a channel to draw down bounty and goodness upon all his generation; and as was said by our sages, of blessed memory, 'the whole world is nourished for the sake of My son Hanina, and a kab of carobs suffices My son Hanina from one sabbath eve to the next', their meaning being that because (*bishevil*) he contents himself with what is essential, which is a great virtue, therefore (*bishevil zeh*) all the world is nourished through the pathway of (*bishevil*) My son Hanina.[67]

We should not overlook the fact that this exegesis by Tsarfati—like other statements of his, as we have seen above—was present in R. Jacob Joseph's mind, for he quotes it:

For it says in the Talmud, 'A divine voice went forth, saying "The whole world is nourished for the sake of My son Hanina, and a kab of carobs suffices My son Hanina from one sabbath even to the next."' See *Ber.*, ch. 2. And the problem is well known: why does the Talmud add 'and a kab of carobs suffices My son Hanina' etc. And I have seen in *Yad Yosef* that this additional statement provides the reason why the whole world is nourished for the sake of [or 'through the path of'] My son Hanina; it is because a kab of carobs suffices My son Hanina etc. that this merit suffices for the whole world to be nourished, etc. See what is said there.[68]

R. Jacob Joseph goes on to quote the Baal Shem Tov as follows:

'for My son Hanina has made a path and a channel to draw down the divine bounty into the world. And that is why it says "All the world is nourished *bishevil* My son Hanina"' . . . But it seems to me that he did not merely make a path and channel etc. but was himself called a path and channel through which the flow of bounty passed.[69]

As well as in *Yad Yosef*, these sentiments are expressed—though not as a gloss on the text from *Berakhot* discussed above—in another work which was very popular with kabbalists, pietists and preachers, namely *Ḥesed le'Avraham*, by R. Abraham Azulai (1570–1643): 'For the zaddikim are our benefactors, for they are a way and a channel through which the waters of the divine flow are brought down to cultivate the fruit of our material and spiritual success.'[70]

Clearly, then, the glosses of the Baal Shem Tov and R. Jacob Joseph of Polonnoye on the voice from Heaven which praised R. Hanina are not original in substance. It is the use made of them which is novel: the homiletic tradition on the passage is invoked in order to provide literary and ideological support for a new type of leadership and a new socio-religious movement. This is evident in the statements made by R. Jacob Joseph of Polonnoye when the new movement was beginning to take shape. Somewhat later, the passage was put to the same purpose by others, for example R. Isaac of Radziwillow (1741–1825), the son of R. Jeḥiel Michel of Zloczow and son-in-law of R. Moses Shoham of Dolina. His remarks on this accord well with the views prevalent in the hasidic movement of his time:

67 *Yad Yosef*, 12*c*. 68 *Ben porat Yosef*, 80*d*. 69 Ibid.

70 Abraham b. Mordecai Azulai, *Ḥesed le'Avraham* [Amsterdam, 1685] (Lemberg, 1863; Jerusalem, 1968), *ma'ayan* 4, *nahar* 57.

My brethren, the holy Torah is His very essence, and through the Torah and the zaddikim of the generation we actually cleave to Him, blessed be He; and as it is written [Ḥag. 12*b*], 'there is one pillar in the world and Zaddik is his name'. It is on the zaddik that the world depends for its existence; on account of [the constraints of the divine property of] Judgment, the world cannot receive the flow of divine bounty [directly] from the Upper Pool, but [only] through the zaddik, who is the channel which receives it and bestows it on the world, as it is written [Ber. 17*b*]: 'the whole world is only nourished through the channel of My son Hanina'. Now in truth the zaddik despises material things, but it is [only] the zaddik, who does all the [material] things that we do, namely eating and drinking and sexual intercourse, while he is attached to the true Ein Sof in the purity of his thoughts and binds all these [material] things to the Source, only he receives and bestows . . . therefore the zaddik must enjoy the things of this world, and everything he does is in holiness and purity . . . for this reason Scripture says [Gen. 6: 21]. 'And you', the zaddik, 'take for yourself some of every sort of food', that is, of all the things of this world.[71]

As far back as the second or third generation of hasidism we find the second part of the pronouncement from Heaven being questioned: R. Hanina, 'by his prayer, always created a path by which to bring down the divine flow; how did the flow pass from him to others without his receiving anything?' The man who posed this question, R. David Solomon Eybeschuetz, supplied an answer that need not concern us here but he did not seek to depart from the literal meaning of the text.[72] On the other hand, many of the hasidic leaders of later generations enthusiastically accepted the first half of the statement but entirely discarded the evident meaning of the second half by a well-known homiletic device which exploited the absence of punctuation in ancient texts. They stood the content of this half on its head, and, with it, the meaning of the divine pronouncement as a whole. They read the sentence not as a statement, which is its natural interpretation, but as a rhetorical question: ' "The whole world is nourished for the sake of my son Hanina, and should a kab of carobs suffice for my son R. Hanina from one sabbath eve to the next?" On the contrary, the zaddikim "must enjoy the pleasures of this world . . . so that they may be able to draw down the divine bounty . . . for those of little understanding also"; they must fufil the commandment "thou shalt love thy neighbour as thyself" [Lev. 19: 18] even in relation to ordinary people of little understanding . . . and then they will be able to accomplish the service of Heaven to perfection'. This interpretation was put forward by the *admor* of Biala, R. Isaac Jacob (d. 1905), who was a member of the Przysucha dynasty; he ascribed it to 'a certain zaddik' but did not name him.[73] It is possible that he was alluding to a report quoted in

[71] *Or Yitsḥak* (Jerusalem, 1961), 21. Cf. *Atsei Levanon al hatorah*, by 'R. Joseph David Rubin *khoneh poh kehilat Szczerzec . . . ben morenu haRav Eleazar shelita miSasov*' (Lvov, 1928), 11: 'I heard this from my grandfather . . . of Sasov and later saw it in a certain book in the name of the zaddik . . . of Ruzhin . . . [In] the statement in the Gemara "The whole world is nourished *bishevil* My son Hanina and a kab of carobs suffices My son Hanina . . ." etc., "*bishevil*" has the sense of "a path" . . . meaning that Hanina established such a path by which to lead a frugal life, restricting himself to a kab of carobs, and so the flow of divine bounty which he brought down to the world was similarly restricted. And therefore Noah, who was the zaddik of his generation and controlled the flow of divine bounty to the world, was told: "And as for you, take yourself some of every food that is eaten", in other words, conduct yourself in an expansive way, not restricting yourself, and this will give you strength to release the flow of divine bounty over the whole world, likewise, in an expansive way.'

[72] *Arvei naḥal*, ii., 61*b*–*c*, on 'Beha'alotekha'.

[73] Isaac Jacob, *Yishrei lev* (Lublin, 1906), 15d–16a.

Divrei Me'ir, by R. Meir of Peremyshlany (d. 1850)—a disciple of R. Jacob Isaac, the Seer of Lublin—to the effect that 'villainous students' (*parkhevate*) jeered at the zaddikim, falsely alleging that they took the 'voice from Heaven' quoted above to be complaining about the householders 'who do not look after the zaddik of the generation, for the whole world is nourished for his sake, and in the end, his own sustenance is meagre, and is a kab of carobs enough for him?!' The rabbi of Lublin capped their taunt: 'We know, do we not, that the divine voice can only be heard by the zaddik, whereas the [householders] cannot hear it; what, then, is the point of this complaint by the divine voice?' From this he deduced that the actual complaint of the divine voice was that the zaddikim did not open up a broad road for the flow of material bounty from Heaven but a narrow path, corresponding to the extreme humility of R. Hanina, who was content with a kab of carobs. And certainly the zaddikim did heed the complaint of the divine voice. Here R. Me'ir of Peremyshlany added his own interpretation—one which, as we have seen, had already been propounded by R. Joseph Tsarfati—namely, that the world was nourished solely through the merit of the zaddik who was faithful to the principle of humility characteristic of R. Hanina, 'who led a most frugal life and was content with little and for whom a kab of carobs sufficed'.[74]

There seems good justification for reading this as a protest against the trend among hasidic leaders illustrated by the statements of the rabbi of Lublin, and even more clearly by those of R. Israel of Ruzhin (1796–1850), such as the following:

'All the world is nourished *bishevil* My son Hanina and a kab of carobs suffices for him.' *Shevil* means restriction, meagreness. And what our sages meant is this: Why is the whole world nourished *bishevil*, that is to say, meagrely? Because a kab of carobs suffices for My son Hanina. It follows that the zaddik of the generation must behave as befits a rich man in order to draw down the divine bounty to the world; and if 'My son Hanina'—the zaddik of his generation—behaves as a poor man, he does not draw down the divine bounty, and so the world, too, is poor.[75]

As has been mentioned, the Maharal of Prague is another important source for the hasidic concept of *devekut*. In seeking to raise the status of the Jewish spiritual leadership and demanding unconditional obedience to the rabbis and Torah scholars who were its authorized representatives, the Maharal was pursuing an aim which had features in common with the new social objectives pursued by R. Jacob Joseph of Polonnoye. It is true that R. Jacob Joseph makes no reference to the Maharal in this connection, but the spirit of his words pervades the writings of hasidic teachers from the end of the eighteenth century onwards. I am referring here to the statement of the Maharal in *Be'er hagolah*:

But those who are closely attached to a Torah scholar are regarded in the same light as the scholar, for what is joined to a thing is as if it were the thing itself. Man, for example, is so called on account of the rational soul within him . . . and certainly that name applies to his body also, because all the organs are joined to the rational soul and they are collectively called man. So it is, too, when a man has an attachment to the intellect, that is, to the Torah scholar; when he has such an attachment he is classed with the scholar. That is why the Talmud says

[74] Meir b. Aaron Leib of Peremyshlany, *Divrei Me'ir* (Bartfeld [Bardejov], 1901), 23*a*–*c*.
[75] Israel of Ruzhin, *Keneset Yisrael* [Warsaw, 1906] (Bnei Brak, n.d.), 25.

[Ket. 111*b*]: '"to love the Lord your God etc. and to cleave to Him": is it possible to cleave to the Shekhinah, seeing that He is a devouring fire?' But rather, he who cleaves to a Torah scholar is as if he cleaved to the Shekhinah. This is because the Torah scholar has *devekut* to the Shekhinah by reason of the divine intellect with which he is endowed. And therefore a person who cleaves to a Torah scholar who has *devekut* to the Shekhinah has, likewise, *devekut* to the Shekhinah even though he himself is not a scholar at all.[76]

These remarks by the Maharal stem from his distinctly élitist view of the status of Torah scholars and rabbis, a view that recognizes the divine source of their authority and hence the reward for blind obedience to their instructions. He sees such scholars as a vital element in the scheme of God's laws for the world.[77] In his comments on this verse he declares it to be an absolute duty to obey Torah sages even if 'they say that something the Torah allows you to do is forbidden', and vice versa.[78] And he spells this out:

For the Torah scholar is like the Torah itself and resembles it completely, and this is undoubtedly why the Torah says you shall not turn aside to the right or the left from all that they instruct you, for the sages are the very Torah, and just as the Lord, blessed be He, by His decree gave the Torah to Israel, so, too, did He give us the sages, and they, too, are the very Torah.[79]

Echoes of the Maharal's words can be traced in the teachings of *admorim* and hasidic writers from the second and third generations of hasidism onwards.[80] Although R. Jacob Joseph does not quote them, one of his homilies is very reminiscent of the Maharal's remarks, and the points of similarity between them acquired greater social importance in recent generations, as the hasidic leadership engaged in the battle against modernizing tendencies. The homily in question, from *Toledot Ya'akov Yosef*, 72*c*, may be summarized as follows: (*a*) The greatest of all the *mitsvot* is 'and to Him you shall cleave' (Deut. 10: 20); but (*b*) *devekut* to God is beyond the reach of the common people. For this reason our sages said (*c*) '"Cleave to a Torah scholar", for he is attached (*davuk*) to the Lord, blessed be He, and through him you, too, will be able to cleave to Him, blessed be He.' R. Jacob Joseph amplifies this elsewhere: 'And as for the commandment which embodies the whole of the Torah—"and to Him you shall cleave"—our sages explained it as meaning "cleave to a Torah scholar" in matters both material and spiritual, because through having many people to help him and cleave to him he will be free to live apart and cleave to Him, blessed be He, and become a throne for His *devekut*.'[81] The kind of *devekut* enjoined in (*c*) means acknowledgement of the spiritual supremacy of the zaddik. Supporting him materially and socially arouses opposition, R. Jacob Joseph informs us, because *devekut* is 'an extraordinary level of

[76] Judah Loew b. Bezalel (the Maharal) of Prague, *Be'er hagolah* [Prague, 1598], repr. in *Kol sifrei Maharal miPrag* (12 vols.; New York, 1969), iv, the seventh *be'er*, 142. Cf. also the sermons of the Maharal of Prague; ibid. 38.

[77] Ibid., the first *be'er*, 16.

[78] Judah Loew b. Bezalel, *Gur Aryeh* [Prague, 1578] (5 vols.; Bnei Brak, 1972), v, on 'Shofetim', dictum beginning '*afilu omer al yamin*'.

[79] Judah Loew b. Bezalel (the Maharal) of Prague, *Netivot olam* [Prague, 1595–6], repr. in *Kol sifrei Maharal miPrag*, vii–viii, 'Netiv hatorah', ch. 11.

[80] See M. Piekarz, *Ḥasidut Polin: Megamot ra'ayoniyot bein shetei hamilḥamot uvigezeirot* 1940–1945 (Jerusalem, 1990).

[81] *Tsafenat pa'neaḥ*, 96*a*.

exaltation, the greatest of all, and therefore the evil inclination brings accusations against Torah scholars, raising questions and doubts about them in order to prevent people from cleaving to a scholar who is attached to Him, blessed be He'. What he says elsewhere shows that he is referring here to the refusal of the common people to recognize the superior spiritual level of the zaddik, with whom they claim equal rank, '"people and priest alike" [Isa. 24: 2], equating the great with the small, and regarding it as appropriate that the zaddikim should associate with them'.[82] R. Jacob Joseph therefore avails himself of the scriptural verse whose exegesis has been a bone of contention for many generations, namely Deut. 17: 11: '"You shall not turn aside from what they tell you, either to the right or to the left", which our sages interpreted [Rashi on this verse, quoting *Sifrei*] as meaning even if they say that right is left etc. This applies only to a judge in your own times etc. [this last statement being added] to remove all doubt.'

These remarks by R. Jacob Joseph still fall short of demanding the absolute and unconditional obedience to the instructions of Torah sages which was called for by the Maharal and even more emphatically, in recent times, by many *admorim* who claim that as the authorized representatives of the Torah they have the right to decide all questions arising in day-to-day life of the Jewish community.[83] However, there is no doubt that the ground for zaddikism in its recent manifestations was prepared not only by the élitist outlook of the early hasidic masters (one of the ways in which they most clearly expressed it being their statements about *devekut* to God) but also over a period of centuries by scholars like the Maharal of Prague and the Shelah. After all, R. Nahman of Bratslav, that author of the most extreme expressions of zaddikism, was fully in line with the general standpoint of hasidism when he demanded complete self-abasement before the zaddik and unthinking obedience to his every word:

The fundamental principle on which everything depends is that you must bind yourself to the zaddik of the generation and accept his verdict on every matter, whether large or small, without turning (Heaven forfend) either right or left from what he instructs you, as was said by our rabbis, of blessed memory [in their comments on Deut. 17: 11, see above], 'even if he tells you that right is left' etc. You must cast away all your learning and put aside your understanding as if you had no intellect (*sekhel*) other than that which you receive from the zaddik of the generation and the rabbi of the generation. And for so long as a person still has any intellect of his own he is not in a state of perfection and is not bound to the zaddik'.[84]

There is undoubtedly a link between this statement and R. Nahman's argument in the following passages:

Do not question the fact that the zaddik benefits from others in order to conduct his household with wealth and honour . . . Do not question it, for everything which brings pleasure and comfort to the zaddik enlarges his soul, and then a house of rest is provided for the Shekhinah of the Holy One, blessed be He, and therefore one should not come empty-handed.[85]

For fear and love cannot be attained except through the zaddikim of the generation, for it is the zaddik who reveals fear and love.[86]

[82] *Tsafenat pa'neaḥ*, 96*b*.

[83] Piekarz, *Ḥasidut Polin*, ch. 3.

[84] Nahman of Bratslav, *Likutei Moharan* [2 vols.: Ostrog, 1808; Mogilev, 1811] (1 vol.; Jerusalem, 1969), part 1, *torah* 123.

[85] *Sefer hamidot* [Mogilev, 1811] (New York, 1948), s.v. 'Zaddik', s.20.

[86] *Likutei Moharan*, part 1, *torah* 17, sec. 1.

R. Nahman's uncle, R. Baruch of Medzibezh (1756–1810), expresses himself in a similar vein, saying, for example, that 'the deeds of the zaddikim, the holy ones of the Supreme Being', cannot be imitated by others. Others enjoy the pleasures of this world, 'and they eat and drink and do not pray much, and most of their talk is of worldly affairs'. The zaddik 'is holy and pure from childhood onwards, and because of this he is able, even by such slight service, to bind his thoughts to the Lord, blessed be He'.[87]

The statements of R. Nahman of Bratslav and R. Baruch of Medzibezh on the nature of the affiliation to the zaddik show no evidence of having been influenced by the Maharal of Prague, but in the works of many hasidic leaders from the nineteenth century onwards there are clear traces of his doctrine on *devekut* to Torah scholars and the duty of unquestioning obedience to their instructions, though of course in different historical circumstances.

In spite of the romantic tradition that the leaders of Przysucha hasidism were responsible for a revolt against the vulgarization of zaddikism, an important and apparently reliable tradition has been preserved which points in a completely different direction. It is quoted by R. Simḥah Bunem of Przysucha, who reports his master, R. Jacob Isaac, 'the holy Jew', as praising people of little worth who attach themselves to the zaddik, and as justifying his praise by analogy with the statement in Kel. 12: 2 'What is joined to what is pure (*tahor*) is itself pure.' To R. Simḥah Bunem's question 'How can so small a matter enable a person to rise to the exalted level of the zaddik who abstains from the pleasures of this world?' R. Jacob Isaac replied, 'This is because it is harder to attach oneself to a zaddik than to be a zaddik oneself.'[88]

As a matter of fact, some hasidic leaders extended the basic tenet of *devekut* to the zaddik so far as to declare that it had the power to purify a man steeped in villainy. One of those who advanced this opinion was R. Samuel Shemariah, rabbi of Ostrowiec (d. 1847), a disciple of several *admorim*, among them R. Jacob Isaac of Przysucha. According to a statement attributed to him, a man sunk in the depths of sin and held fast in the grip of the evil inclination could be elevated to the level of the zaddik, that is, to metaphysical heights beyond the concepts of sin and punishment, provided that he attached himself to the zaddik and gave him material support:

> For even the wicked man, if he attaches himself to the zaddikim, may be redeemed, even though the evil inclination has mastery over him . . . at any rate [the judgement on him] will be mitigated through the pious deeds of the zaddikim in their mutual association.[89]

> For the zaddik can annul the judgements of Heaven, even on a man who has sinned, if that man is attached to the zaddik, who stands on a lofty height in an upper world, because through *devekut* to the zaddik he, too, is drawn up to that eminence, sometimes by making a charitable gift to the zaddik, and sometimes by showing remorse before the zaddik so that he excites compassion and [the zaddik] draws him up to his world, where sin holds no sway.[90]

Similar remarks were made by R. Solomon Rabinowitz of Radomsk (1803–6), a disciple of Polish *admorim* who were not members of the dynasties of Przysucha or Kotsk. The following is from his comments on Lev. 6: 11 (6: 19 in the English versions):

87 *Butsina dinehora* [Lemberg, 1879, 1884] (New York, 1956), [12].
88 Piekarz, *Ḥasidut Polin*, ch. 7.
89 *Zikhron Shemu'el* (2 vols.; Warsaw, 1908–Bardejov, 1925), ii, on the Torah, 34*c*, 45*c*.
90 Ibid. 56*b*.

'Every male among the children of Aaron may eat of it . . . whatever touches it shall be holy': for the Torah here indicates how great is the merit of adhering (*dibuk*) to scholars and the zaddikim of the generation. Everyone who shelters in their shadow and sits amid the dust of their feet, even though he is below the proper degree of merit, will be raised up if he is joined to what is pure and will be elevated through the zaddik, because everything that is joined to what is pure is itself pure.

He reinforces this statement by reference to Zev. 9: 5. According to this Mishnah horns and hoofs (the parts of an animal of least worth) must go up to the altar if they are still attached to the animal but not if they have been severed. This, he says, 'is an allusion to what I have said above; if people are joined to the zaddik they will go up with him even though they themselves are of low degree'.[91] Statements by the Maharal of Prague are frequently echoed in the homilies of the *admor* of Radomsk. For example: 'It has long been well known that ever since the Lord created the world and the fullness thereof . . . He has consigned to the care of the zaddikim all aspects of the nature and conduct of this world and all the forces of the host of Heaven above so that all of them are required to obey the zaddikim who are in this world.[92] Because his authority is conferred by the Creator, belief in the supernatural power of the zaddik is a fundamental element of Judaism and anyone who denies it 'is no Jew',[93] His authority extends over all spheres of life: 'All the ways of the world must be [governed] by the zaddik.'

Certain other aspects of *devekut* in homiletic and moralistic works, including those of the early hasidic masters, are dealt with in my book *Biyemei tsemiḥat haḥasidut* and in some of my essays, and I shall not cover the same ground here.

I have argued here that hasidism should not be seen as a stage in the history of Jewish mysticism, nor as an anthropocentric trend in the mystical tradition of Judaism, but rather as a socio-religious movement with an ideology rooted in the kabbalah, and more particularly in the homiletic and *musar* books permeated by kabbalistic ideas. Clearly, if this contention is correct, some change of direction is called for in scholarly research into hasidism.

[91] Solomon Rabinowitz of Radomsk, *Tiferet Shelomo* (2 vols.; Warsaw, 1867, Piotrkow, 1890), ii: *al hatorah*, on 'Tsav', 152–3; cf. ibid. on 'Pinḥas', 209–10.

[92] Ibid. i: *al hazemanim vehamo'adim*, on 'Rimzei Pesaḥ', 124*c–d*.

[93] Ibid. 133*a*.

PART IV

DISTINCTIVE OUTLOOKS AND SCHOOLS OF THOUGHT WITHIN HASIDISM

FOURTEEN

The Influence of *Reshit ḥokhmah* on the Teachings of the Maggid of Mezhirech

BRACHA SACK

IN his *Major Trends in Jewish Mysticism* G. Scholem wrote: 'What has really become important in Hasidism [is] the mysticism of personal life . . . Hasidism is practical mysticism at its highest. Almost all the Kabbalistic ideas are now placed in relation to values peculiar to the individual life . . . Particular emphasis is laid on ideas and concepts concerning the relation of the Individual to God.'[1] In this context I shall here consider the hasidic conception of man and of divine service. I shall show that in both areas the ideas of R. Dov Ber, the Maggid of Mezhirech, are clearly related to those expressed by the sixteenth-century Safed kabbalist Elijah de Vidas in his book *Reshit ḥokhmah*.[2]

The relationship between hasidism and the ethical literature of the Safed kabbalists has attracted significant scholarly attention; I. Tishby, J. Dan, M. Pechter, and G. Nigal have all noted the popularity of *Reshit ḥokhmah* and its impact on hasidic thought.[3] It seems clear that although kabbalistic ideas reached hasidism from a wide variety of literary sources, *Reshit ḥokhmah* was among the most important. Undoubtedly, both the anthropocentric tendency of hasidic teaching and its special concern with the individual soul can be traced back to *Reshit ḥokhmah*. Most strikingly, there is a particularly close affinity between *Reshit ḥokhmah* and the teachings of the Maggid of

I should like to thank Prof. Daniel Boyarin for his help in translating the quotations from the primary sources.

[1] G. G. Scholem, *Major Trends in Jewish Mysticism* (New York, 1954), 341.

[2] All references are to Dov Ber of Mezhirech, *Maggid devarav le Ya'akov*, ed. R. Schatz-Uffenheimer (Jerusalem, 1976), and to Elijah de Vidas, *Reshit ḥokhmah hashalem*, ed. H. J. Valdman (3 vols.; Jerusalem, 1984).

[3] I. Tishby and J. Dan, 'Torat haḥasidut vesifrutah', *Hebrew Encyclopaedia*, xvii (1965), 770, repr. as a pamphlet by Academon, Jerusalem, and in A. Rubinstein, *Perakim betorat haḥasidut vetoledoteihah* (Jerusalem, 1977), 250–312; M. Pechter, 'Sefer *Reshit ḥokhmah* leRabi Eliyahu de Vidas vekitsurav', *Kiryat sefer*, 47 (1972), 686–710; id., 'Ikvot hashpa'ato shel sefer *Reshit Ḥokhmah* le R. Eliyahu de Vidas bekhitvei R. Ya'akov Yosef miPolonoyeh', in J. Dan and J. Hacker (eds.), *Studies in Jewish Mysticism, Philosophy and Ethical Literature Presented to Isaiah Tishby* (Heb.) (Jerusalem, 1986), 569–91; G. Nigal, 'Al mekorot hadevekut besifrut reshit haḥasidut', *Kiryat sefer*, 46 (1971), 345–6; M. Piekarz, *Biyemei tsemiḥat haḥasidut: Megamot ra'ayoniyot besifrei derush umusar* (Jerusalem, 1978), 102 n. 20; M. Idel, *Kabbalah: New Perspectives* (New Haven, 1988), 49–51, 62–7.

Mezhirech. I shall therefore attempt to demonstrate the influence of the book on the Maggid's principal teachings, specifically with regard to the inner purification of man and his service of God.

At the beginning of *Maggid devarav le Ya'akov*, the verse 'the King is held captive in the tresses' (S. of S. 7: 6) is interpreted as referring to the 'tresses' of the human mind. In doing so, the Maggid draws on the discussion in *Tikunei zohar* (*tikun* 6) concerning the mystical significance of the phylacteries of the head;[4] the author of *Tikunei zohar* uses the verse to highlight the close relationship between God and Israel, a relationship which he holds to be symbolized by the phylacteries.[5] The Maggid also draws on the classical rabbinic concept of *tsimtsum*, the contraction of Shekhinah (the divine presence) between the two staves of the Ark.[6] For the Maggid, the strength of the individual's power of perception governs the extent to which the Shekhinah dwells in his intellect and 'the King is held captive' therein:

And this is the meaning of 'The eyes of God are on the righteous' [Ps. 34: 16]: it is comparable to a son who acts childishly; he [thereby] draws the intellect of his father into his childish act [he lowers his father's intellect to his own level]. So do the righteous make God, as it were, resemble their own intellect, so that He, may He be blessed, will think what they think. If they think with love, they bring God to the world of love, as it is written in the Zohar: 'the King is held captive in the tresses'—in the veins of the brain. And this is the meaning of the contraction of the Shekhinah between the 'staves of the Ark'.[7]

The same use of sources and the same combination of motifs can be found in *Reshit ḥokhmah*:

When one thinks that God, King of the World, dwells in the veins of the brain and is held captive within man who was created from a stinking drop, this is similar to God's contraction of His Shekhinah between the staves of the Ark, even though 'the Heavens and the Upper Heavens cannot contain Him' [2 Chr. 6: 18], and therefore it is appropriate that one should attach one's soul, which dwells in the brain, to the love of Him, may He be blessed, a love which dwells in His brain.[8]

According to both *Reshit ḥokhmah* and the Maggid, communion between man and God is made possible because the soul is a divine spark emanating from the Godhead itself, and because God's fatherly love penetrates and dwells in the human intellect. Man must purify his thoughts so as to prepare a fitting dwelling for the divine holiness:

The dwelling of the Shekhinah is in the pure soul, and this is [the meaning of] 'And they shall make me a temple and I will dwell among them' [Exod. 25: 8]. Scripture does not say 'in it', but 'among them', meaning within them, and this is one aspect of the creation of man by the soul that is a part of God above and by God who attaches Himself to man in order to save Him. And when he calls Him, He will answer . . . when man contemplates this matter, his soul becomes kindled with love, and he says in his heart: am I truly worthy, man made of clay, dust

[4] *Tikunei zohar*, ed. R. Margaliot (Jerusalem, 1948), 21*b*.

[5] I. Tishby, *Mishnat hazohar* (2 vols.; Jerusalem, 1961), ii. 439, pub. in Eng. as *The Wisdom of the Zohar* (3 vols.; Oxford, 1989).

[6] Midrash *Tanḥuma* on 'Vayakhel', 7; cf. E. E. Urbach, *The Sages: Their Concepts and Beliefs* (Jerusalem, 1979), 47–8.

[7] *Maggid devarav le Ya'akov*, 11–12.

[8] *Reshit ḥokhmah*, 'The Gate of Holiness', 6. 72.

and ashes, that God whom the upper Heavens cannot contain should be willing to dwell with me? And what am I that the Mighty King should come to dwell in my house? It is appropriate for me to prepare a pleasant dwelling for Him so that He will come to dwell with me.[9]

The Maggid and de Vidas likewise describe in the same manner the thoughts of a person who prepares himself to pray to God. Both believe that if he removes all evil thoughts from his heart, God will be compelled to draw near to him:

Grasp Him that He will attach Himself to you. And how may you grasp Him? By means of Torah and commandments and the purification of thought; then He is *forced* as it were, to come to dwell with you, for you grasp Him powerfully, and you prepare for Him a lovely bed and a lovely dwelling, perfumed with a variety of perfumes. The 'Friend' finds there pleasure for His spirit (*naḥat ruaḥ*), and it is certain that there He will stay.[10]

By virtue of His fatherly love, God is willing to radiate His light without limit; it is the recipients who set the limits, contracting the light to fit their own limited capacity. To explain this idea, the Maggid uses the same parables as de Vidas—the parable of the father and the son, and the parable of 'the cow desiring to suckle more than the calf wishes to suck' (Pes. 112*a*).[11] In fact, the idea goes back to de Vidas's teacher, R. Moses Cordovero, who states in his *Shi'ur komah* that in order to reach the righteous, God contracts his intellect to match their intellectual capacity.[12] However, according to the Maggid: 'Like the son whose childish acts bring the intellect of his father down to his own level . . . so the righteous cause God to think what they think.'[13] Indeed, this new and succinct expression of the idea points clearly to the peculiar direction of the Maggid's thought: the contraction is a form of human cognition which compels God to manifest Himself in accordance with the rules governing the human intellect.

Kabbalistic texts often refer to the first *sefirah*, Keter, as Ayin (nothingness). In his *Tomer Deborah*, Cordovero instructs the individual to emulate the qualities of Keter, to 'turn his mind to nothing but thoughts of Torah' and the greatness of God: 'no foreign or vain things should be allowed to intercept these thoughts'. Cordovero adds that the 'main thing' the individual should grasp is humility, and that 'the main point in humility is that one should consider oneself as naught', in the same way as Keter 'regards itself as naught when compared to its emanator'.[14] In *Reshit ḥokhmah* de Vidas uses Cordovero's ideas to show how communion with God may be achieved. In this connection he expresses his own ideas concerning humility and the 'broken heart': man is

[9] Ibid., 'The Gate of Love', 6. 19. On the concept of the soul as a divine spark in kabbalah, see L. Jacobs, 'The Doctrine of the "Divine Spark" in Man in Jewish Sources', in R. Loewe (ed.), *Studies in Rationalism, Judaism, and Universalism in Memory of Leon Roth* (New York, 1966), 87–114. The instruction to prepare a proper dwelling also contains an echo of *Tikunei zohar, tikun* 6. But in *Maggid devarav le Ya'akov* as in *Reshit ḥokhmah*, the meaning of this preparation is the removal of evil thoughts. See *Reshit ḥokhmah*, 'The Gate of Holiness', 7. 103; 'The Gate of Love', 11. 160.

[10] *Reshit ḥokhmah*, 'The Gate of Love', 6. 18. On the idea of the removal of evil thoughts, see e.g. Piekarz, *Biyemei tsemiḥat haḥasidut*, 271.

[11] *Reshit ḥokhmah*, 'The Gate of Love', 6. 9; *Maggid devarav le Ya'akov*, 37–8, 144, 204, 212.

[12] See my article 'The Theory of Tsimtsum of R. Moses Cordovero' (Heb.), *Tarbiz*, 58 (1989), 207–37.

[13] *Maggid devarav le Ya'akov*, 11.

[14] M. Cordovero, *Tomer Deborah*, trans. as 'The Palm Tree of Deborah' by R. Ben-Zion Boxer, in *An Anthology of Jewish Mysticism* (New York, 1981), ch. 2, 36–46.

instructed to emulate Keter by following the *via passiva* which will enable him to gain holiness and to become indifferent to abuse, but at the same time to maintain some degree of activity by performing good deeds at all times, and even while being abused:

Man lowers his head in the presence of one who is greater than him, and so does the attribute Keter lower itself before the Cause of Causes and is called nothingness, since it considers itself as nothing when compared to the Emanator. And it (Keter) lowers its head in order to watch over and to emanate onto the lower worlds, which all incline to suckle from this attribute. Therefore, it is fitting for man to think himself as nothing before His greatness, may He be blessed, which has no end or limit.[15]

In one passage in *Maggid devarav le Ya'akov* the Maggid refers in similar terms to the individual who has attained the quality of humility and who regards himself as naught so that God contracts His Shekhinah [to dwell] upon him: 'God is proud of the Jew who maintains the quality of humility and makes himself small like a child or a youth . . . And if he makes himself small and thinks of himself as nothing, then God contracts His Shekhinah and dwells upon him.'[16] This passage contains the motifs encountered in *Reshit ḥokhmah* in connection with the concept of Ayin: *imitatio dei*, the thirteen qualities of mercy and the thirteen *tikunim*, humility, and man's obligation to regard himself as naught in order to make the Shekhinah dwell upon him or in him (although, as J. G. Weiss has remarked, the Maggid refers to Ḥokhmah not Keter as Ayin, since it is 'the matrix of all subsequent emanations in the Intelligible Universe').[17]

The notion of the contraction of Shekhinah within the individual leads the Maggid to a related idea which he expresses through the phrase 'the Shekhinah spoke from his throat'.[18] According to de Vidas, the individual—whose soul is a divine spark—needs the help of God when he begins to pray. For this reason the Prayer (the Amidah)

[15] *Reshit ḥokhmah*, 'The Gate of Humility', 1. 15, and see the rest of the chapter as well as 'The Gate of Holiness', 7. 110. On the idea of the broken heart, see Tishby, *Mishnat hazohar*, ii. 583, 673, 693–4. On the concept of *via passiva*, see J. Weiss, '*Via Passiva* in Early Hasidism', *Journal of Jewish Studies*, 11 (1960), 137–55, repr. in id., *Studies in Eastern European Jewish Mysticism* (Oxford, 1985), 69–94. On the kabbalistic idea of change, see e.g. E. Gottlieb, *Meḥkarim besifrut hakabalah* (Tel Aviv, 1976), 231–47, esp. 238 n. 14.

[16] *Maggid devarav le Ya'akov*, 296–7. For an extensive discussion of the issue of Ayin see R. Schatz-Uffenheimer, *Haḥasidut kemistikah* (Jerusalem, 1968), 22–31; D. C. Matt, 'Ayin: The Concept of Nothingness in Jewish Mysticism', in R. K. C. Forman (ed.) *The Problem of Pure Consciousness* (New York and Oxford, 1990), 121–59.

[17] *Maggid devarav le Ya'akov*, 296–7; *Reshit ḥokhmah*, 'The Gate of Humility', 1; cf. J. G. Weiss, 'The Great Maggid's Theory of Contemplative Magic', *Hebrew Union College Annual*, 31 (1960), 140, and generally on Ayin, 137–47; A. Green, 'Hasidism: Discovery and Retreat', in P. Berger (ed.), *The Other Side of God: A Polarity in World Religions* (New York, 1981), 112. On the idea of *imitatio dei* see e.g. A. Marmorstein, 'Imitation of God in the Haggada', in id., *Studies in Jewish Theology* (Oxford, 1950), 106–21; A. Altmann, 'Homo Imago Dei in Jewish and Christian Theology', *Journal of Religion*, 48 (1968), 235–59; S. T. Katz, 'Models, Modeling and Mystical Training', *Religion*, 12 (1982), 247–75. On this idea in *Tomer Deborah*, see J. Dan, *Sifrut hamusar vehaderush* (Jerusalem, 1975), 213. On the thirteen *tikunim* (reparations), see Y. Liebes, 'Hamashiaḥ shel haZohar', in *Hara'ayon hameshiḥi be Yisrael: Yom iyun leregel melot shemonim shanah leGershom Scholem* (Jerusalem, 1982), 175–91. On this theme in *Reshit ḥokhmah*, see M. Pechter, 'Homiletical and Ethical Literature of Safed in the Sixteenth Century' (Heb.) (Ph.D. thesis, Hebrew University of Jerusalem, 1976), 377–8. On humility in *Reshit ḥokhmah*, see Pechter, 'Homiletical and Ethical Literature', 375–8, 435–43.

[18] See M. Idel, 'Abraham Abulafia's Works and Doctrine,' (Heb.) (Ph.D. thesis, Hebrew University of Jerusalem, 1976), 299 and 340, nn. 36 and 37.

begins with the verse, 'O Lord, open thou my lips' (Ps. 51: 17); without divine help and without God's will the movement of the lips in prayer would be impossible:

Behold it is known that the soul is a part of Him, blessed be He, as Scripture says, 'His people is a part of Him [literally 'His people in His inheritance'; Deut. 32: 9]. And it says, 'And He breathed into their nostrils the breath of life' [Gen. 2: 7]. Anyone who breathes, breathes of his essence. Now the faculty of speech in man is derived from his soul, and God can take away his soul in an instant, as Scripture says: 'He will gather to Himself His spirit and His soul, and all flesh shall perish together' [Job 34: 14–15] . . . and therefore [David] said, 'O Lord open thou my lips' [Ps. 51: 17], for I am not able to open my lips to speak, except by His power, may He be blessed, which draws into man the life of the soul in order that he may speak.[19]

I believe that this discussion by de Vidas could have served as the source from which the Maggid extracted the main components of his own idea: 'The Shekhinah contracts itself, as it were, and dwells in his speech, in his mouth . . . He shall only think that he is a part of God above, and he will pray for what is lacking in this part.[20]

From Cordovero, de Vidas had learnt that, in the material world, man must worship God 'in thought, speech, and deed'.[21] Cordovero offers two explanations for this concept. In his *Tomer Deborah*, the 'deed' is accomplished by entering the synagogue and bowing before His Holy Temple; the 'speech' is accomplished by reciting in so doing the verse: 'But as for me, in the abundance of Thy loving kindness will I come into thy house . . . (Ps. 5: 8); and the 'thought' is accomplished by having in mind the *sefirot* that are alluded to in entering the synagogue and reciting the verse.[22] But in his commentary on the Zohar Cordovero offers another interpretation and it is this interpretation that found its way into *Reshit ḥokhmah*.[23] In this view, 'thought' is not directed to any specific *sefirah* but is a general 'intention' to achieve 'the unification of one's Maker' (*yiḥud kono*), and 'speech' is represented by recitation of the formula 'for the sake of the unification of God and His Shekhinah':

And therefore, man's deeds must be for the sake of Heaven; in thought [means that] he should direct his thoughts at [the time of] the deed to the unification of his Maker, as is known. As for speech, he should utter with his mouth [the phrase]: 'for the sake of the unification of God and His Shekhinah', while his deed should aim to be untainted, since thought and speech alone will not profit him, for if the vessel is unsightly He will not dwell in it. Therefore, when he builds a house [for God], his thoughts should be set on the worship of his Maker and his

[19] *Reshit ḥokhmah*, 'Totse'ot ḥayim', 178. On the concept of the origin of the soul in kabbalah, see M. Hallamish, 'On the Origin of a Proverb in Kabbalistic Literature' (Heb.), *Bar-Ilan*, 13 (Ramat Gan, 1970), 211–28. On the concept of prayer in Cordovero's writings see my article 'R. Moshe Cordovero's Theory of Prayer' (Heb.), *Da'at*, 9 (1982), 5–12. On the five vowels of the prayer in earlier kabbalistic literature, see M. Idel, *The Mystical Experience in Abraham Abulafia* (Albany, NY, 1988), 62–3 and 69 n. 59.

[20] *Maggid devarav le Ya'akov*, 183.

[21] On the importance of thought, speech, and deed in Persian religion see G. Scholem, 'The Paradisic Garb of Souls and the Origin of the Concept of Ḥaluka de-Rabbanan' (Heb.), *Tarbiz*, 24 (1955), 302–4.

[22] Cordovero, *Tomer Deborah*, ch. 10, 77–80.

[23] See G. Scholem, 'Hashekhinah', in *Pirkei yesod behavanat hakabalah usemaleihah* (Jerusalem, 1976), 303 n. 93, pub. in Engl. as 'The Feminine Element of Divinity', in id., *The Mystical Shape of the Godhead* (New York, 1991), 192 n. 100. (The passage in *Reshit ḥokhmah* is derived from Cordovero's *Zohar im perush Or Yakar* (22 vols.; Jerusalem, 1962–92), xvii. 23–4, on Zohar *Shir hashirim*). Also published in R. Margaliot, *Malakhei elyon* (Jerusalem, 1945), app., 65–6.

speech should be for the sake of Heaven, God and His Shekhinah, and so with his deed. Then righteousness shall dwell in and evil will depart from there.[24]

De Vidas regards thought, speech, and deed as the sources of the three levels of the soul, *neshamah, ruaḥ*, and *nefesh*, which emanate from the world of Atsilut and are connected with the other three worlds (Beri'ah, Yetsirah, Asiyah). He compares thought, speech, and deed to these worlds and regards them as three degrees of holiness.[25] He claims that only one who maintains full integrity of 'deed, speech and thought' can achieve full *devekut*.[26]

Once again, the same motifs are also to be found in *Maggid devarav le Ya'akov*. The Maggid similarly refers to them as distinct layers of Torah, stressing the importance of the deed and establishing the comparability of thought, speech, and deed with the kabbalistic 'worlds':

A commandment must be carried out in deed, thought, speech, and with pleasure (which means that one must bring oneself to a state of great *devekut*, until one reaches the state of pleasure) . . . The deed is in our hands, for while we are actually performing the commandment, we are uniting the act of the commandment, which is the world as Asiyah, with the speech and thought [of the commandment] which are the worlds of Yetsirah and Beri'ah.[27]

In referring to the pleasure of *devekut* that may be gained by serving God in deed, speech and thought, the Maggid may be echoing the image of ascending a ladder which occurs also in *Reshit ḥokhmah*. Both Cordovero and de Vidas had taught that every deed, however mundane (as, for example, the building of a house), should be accompanied by the recitation of the formula 'for the sake of the *yiḥud* (unification)', and the concentration of one's mind upon this act of unification.[28] In this way they connected the idea to the doctrine of serving God through material acts.[29]

The Maggid endorsed the tradition of reciting the unification formula with every deed.[30] His model was the patriarch Enoch, who was portrayed in a tale of the medieval Ashkenazi hasidim as a cobbler.[31] According to the Maggid, Enoch recited this formula with every stitch of his awl. In this way he expressed the idea that worship is accomplished not only by studying Torah and performing commandments but also by

[24] *Reshit ḥokhmah*, 'The Gate of Holiness', 16. 31.

[25] Ibid. 4. 11.

[26] Ibid. 4. 43. On the motif of the ladder in both philosophy and kabbalah see A. Altmann, 'The Ladder of Ascension', in id., *Studies in Religious Philosophy and Mysticism* (New York, 1969), 41–72. On the concept of *devekut* in *Reshit ḥokhmah*, see M. Pechter, 'The Concept of Devekut in the Homiletical Ethical Writings of Sixteenth Century Safed', in I. Twersky (ed.), *Studies in Medieval Jewish History and Literature* (2 vols.; Cambridge, Mass., 1979–84), ii. 171–230. For *devekut* in hasidism, see G. Scholem, 'Devekut, or Communion with God', *Review of Religion*, 14 (1949–50), 115–39, repr. in id., *The Messianic Idea in Judaism* (New York, 1971), 203–27. Cf. Tishby, *Mishnat hazohar*, ii. 289–90; Idel, *Kabbalah*, 35–73.

[27] *Maggid devarav le Ya'akov*, 236.

[28] See n. 23, above.

[29] On this doctrine see e.g. R. Schatz-Uffenheimer, 'Contemplative Prayer in Hasidism', in E. E. Urbach, R. J. Z. Werblowsky, and C. Wirszubski (eds.), *Studies in Mysticism and Religion Presented to Gershom G. Scholem* (Jerusalem, 1967), 210; I. Tishby, 'The Influence of R. Moses Hayyim Luzzatto on Hasidic Teaching' (Heb.), *Zion*, 43 (1978), 207–10.

[30] *Maggid devarav le Ya'akov*, 164.

[31] G. Scholem, 'Tradition and New Creation in the Ritual of the Kabbalists', in id., *On the Kabbalah and its Symbolism* (London, 1965), 132. This is mentioned by Cordovero in his commentary on Zohar 2: 216*b*: *Zohar im perush Or Yakar*, xi. 103.

worldly actions.[32] In the section of *Reshit ḥokhmah* entitled 'The Gate of Holiness', the Maggid could have found numerous references to the concept of worship through such corporeal acts, including the main points of his own teaching on the subject, as follows:[33]

1. Every act can be sanctified ('In all thy ways acknowledge Him'—Prov. 3: 6).[34]
2. By meditation, one can penetrate the material shell and pierce through to the mystical significance of existence.[35]
3. While performing mundane acts, one can detach oneself from the profane world and focus one's mind upon the One who gives life to all existence in all the worlds.[36]

These findings would seem amply to confirm the importance of *Reshit ḥokhmah* as a source for some of the central teachings of *Maggid devarav le Ya'akov*.

[32] *Maggid devarav le Ya'akov*, 164.
[33] All are conveniently grouped together in 'The Gate of Holiness'.
[34] *Reshit ḥokhmah*, 'The Gate of Holiness', 15. 88.
[35] Ibid. 15. 97.
[36] Ibid. 16. 10.

FIFTEEN

Torah lishmah as a Central Concept in the *Degel maḥaneh Efrayim* of Moses Hayyim Ephraim of Sudylkow

ROLAND GOETSCHEL

R. Moses Hayyim Ephraim of Sudylkow is one of the most important figures in the second generation of the hasidic movement. This is due in part to his family connections: he was the son of the Baal Shem Tov's daughter Edel, the brother of Baruch Jeḥiel of Medzibezh, and the uncle of Nahman of Bratslav.[1] But an even more important factor in accounting for his status is the numerous passages in his collected teachings, the *Degel maḥaneh Efrayim*, where he reports statements in the name of such hasidic luminaries as the Baal Shem Tov, R. Jacob Joseph of Polonnoye. R. Nahman of Horodenka, and the Maggid of Mezhirech making him one of the most valuable sources of information on the hasidic doctrine at its earliest stages of development.[2] The *Degel maḥaneh Efrayim* is also important for another reason, in that it provides an insight into R. Moses Hayyim Ephraim's own method of integrating into his sermons the main themes of hasidic revivalism.

1. THE SIGNIFICANCE OF *TORAH LISHMAH* IN THE CONTROVERSY BETWEEN HASIDIM AND MITNAGGEDIM

The meaning of *torah lishmah* (study of Torah 'for its own sake'—without ulterior motives) occupies a place of prime importance in R. Moses Hayyim Ephraim's work. This can be understood in the context of the hasidic–mitnaggedic polemic of his time: one of the most bitterly contested points was the significance of the study of Torah, and the discussion of this controversy revolved critically around the concepts of *torah lishmah* and *torah shelo lishmah*.[3]

R. Moses Hayyim Ephraim of Sudylkow states his position in a homily on the

[1] See S. Dubnow, *Geschichte des Chassidismus* (2 vols.; Berlin, 1931), 60–5. See also Nathan Sternhartz, *Shivḥei haRan* (Jerusalem, 1979), 5, s. 3.

[2] All references to *Degel maḥaneh Efrayim* are to the Jerusalem, 1963, edn. There are more than eighty citations of the Baal Shem Tov, more than thirty of R. Jacob Joseph of Polonnoye, six of R. Nahman of Horodenka.

[3] See the references in M. Wilensky, *Ḥasidim umitnaggedim* (2 vols.; Jerusalem, 1970), ii, index, 370, s.v. 'Bitul torah velomedeiha'.

conflict between Sarah and Hagar in Gen. 16 that starts at Gen. 16: 2, 'Go in unto my maid; it may be that I may obtain children by her.' Following R. Nahman of Horodenka, he interprets the conflict as an allegory addressing the question of how one is to proceed in the study of Torah and in divine worship.[4] 'Maid' refers to the individual who studies or worships *shelo lishmah* (with ulterior motives); 'it may be that I may obtain children by her' comes to mean that even if he studies *shelo lishmah*, his study may prove to be productive. Sarah, who represents the Shekhinah, says: 'it is possible that if in the beginning he learns from ulterior motives, he may come to learn for its own sake' (*mitokh shelo lishmah yavo lishmah*).[5]

R. Moses Hayyim Ephraim of Sudylkow elaborates on this further. The 'maid', he says, represents study *shelo lishmah* for material gain. Study *lishmah*, on the other hand, he who studies for truth, in fulfilment of God's will, is represented by the 'son'. These two modalities may be subject to gradation by levels of intensity and purity, but ultimately, the 'maid', whose entire endeavour is directed towards the wages which she expects to earn from her 'master', may be contrasted with the 'mistress' or 'queen'. Through her worship *lishmah* the latter proclaims the kingship of the Holy One, Blessed be He, and his Shekhinah in all the worlds, effecting the manifestation of His glory and kingship in each dominion and the submission of the forces of evil, the *kelipot*.

The authentic study of *torah lishmah* is understood not as a purely intellectual activity but as a theurgic and cosmological practice aimed at inducing the full revelation of the Godhead and the submission of evil to the domain of sanctity. Accordingly, what R. Nahman of Horodenka meant was that *torah shelo lishmah* can be a preparation for *torah lishmah*, and this appears to have been the opinion of the Baal Shem Tov as well.[6] But there are those people, continues R. Moses Hayyim Ephraim—and here he launches his attack on the mitnaggedim—who begin to study *shelo lishmah* and go on in this way all through life. They do not endeavour to achieve the true and ultimate aim of study. Moreover, when they attain positions of power, they come to despise the zaddikim, who study little but with proper 'intent'. They say ' "Our hand is triumphant"[7] because they have filled their bellies with much study.' The division between the two camps is clearly delineated: on the one hand, there are the mitnaggedim who are proud of their scholarship; and, on the other hand, the zaddikim who study less but with proper, heartfelt intent. The 'maid' of whom the Torah says (Gen. 16: 4): 'and when she saw that she had conceived, her mistress was despised in her eyes', this 'maid' is analogous to the scholars who, because they have studied for so long, have come to despise and hate the zaddikim. The zaddikim, in turn, are identified with the 'mistress'. They study little, but *bekhavanah deliba lishmah*.

To all external appearances, there is virtually no difference between the people who study *lishmah* and those who study *shelo lishmah*, in much the same way as it is only one small dot, a mere *dagesh*, that makes up all the difference between leaven (*ḥamets*) and unleavened bread (*matsah*). This single dot stands for the 'truth of the heart' (*amitat halev*).[8] Sarah's initial statement, 'I have given my maid into thy bosom' (Gen. 16: 5), may be understood as describing a device adopted in fulfilment of a larger goal. The

[4] *Degel maḥaneh Efrayim*, on 'Lekh lekha', 16*a*.
[5] See Pes. 50*b*.
[6] *Degel maḥaneh Efrayim*, on 'Lekh lekha', 16*b*.
[7] See Deut. 32: 27.
[8] *Degel maḥaneh Efrayim*, on 'Lekh lekha', 17*a*.

consequence of this action, however, comes as a surprise to her: 'I was despised in her eyes'—the zaddikim who cleave to truth, to the modality of the Shekhinah as represented here by Sarah the mistress, are despised and hated by the 'maid'. Sarah in turn humiliates the maid. In other words, the Shekhinah humiliates and humbles the scholar who follows the modality of the 'maid' (Gen. 16: 6): 'She fled from her', that is, from the Shekhinah and the Torah, meaning that the scholar who follows the modality of the 'maid' is cut off from the Torah altogether and forgets what he has studied. R. Moses Hayyim Ephraim adds: 'I have heard many reports of such people who forgot all that they had studied in an altogether fruitless manner.'[9]

Praise for those who study in the hasidic way follows directly on this critique of the mitnaggedim. With regard to the hasidim, 'King David has said (Ps. 15: 4): "He honours them who fear the Lord."' These are the people who study little, but *bekhavanah lishmah*; they will grow and bear fruit. In addition, there are also those scholars who repent with all their heart and soul. To them the Torah says (Gen. 16: 9): 'Return to thy mistress and submit thyself to her hands.' This refers to attaching oneself to *torah lishmah*, following the modality of the 'mistress', without any concern for profit. R. Moses Hayyim Ephraim adds:

> He has great regard for the zaddikim who study little but with proper intent (*bekhavanah*); for it is better to study little with proper intent than to study much without intent. This is the meaning of 'submit thyself to her hands,' he should humble himself before the zaddikim. Then the angel will say to him (Gen. 16: 10): '*I will multiply thy seed exceedingly*'—this is the fruit produced by truthful study, *torat emet*, when one has gone beyond the study *shelo lishmah*.

This is a good illustration of the hasidic stance *vis-à-vis* the mitnageddim. The author concludes with the hope that the time will come when the latter will acknowledge the authority of the zaddikim and the essential superiority of *torah lishmah*.[10]

2. *TORAH LISHMAH* AS A VEHICLE FOR *DEVEKUT*

R. Moses Hayyim Ephraim extracts the same meaning from the incident in Gen. 38 involving Judah and Tamar. Tamar symbolizes Torah. The lust that she arouses in Judah is thus a lust for study, so that he begins to expound both *peshat* and *derush*, albeit *shelo lishmah*, 'for through the work done for a selfish purpose he will arrive at work for its own sake'. It is this manner of studying that is indicated by the words (Gen. 38: 14): ' "and she sat in an open place (*befetaḥ einayim*)". This means that at the beginning of his study (*bapetiḥah*), the Torah inspires him with mere lust, but he may eventually arrive at study *lishmah*. So long as he was studying *shelo lishmah* "he thought her to be a harlot" (Gen. 38: 15).' To such a scholar the Torah appears initially as mere narrative (*sipurei ma'asiyot*). He thinks that it contains no *penimiyut*, no inner meaning beyond the surface meaning of the narrative accounts. But once he decides to adopt the right manner of studying, he turns for help to those who know the inner meaning of Torah. ' "Then he asked the men of that place (*anshei mekomah*)" (Gen. 38: 21). This refers

9 *Degel maḥaneh Efrayim*, on 'Lekh lekha', 17*a*.
10 The same motif recurs ibid., on 'Vayishlaḥ', 51*a*, and on 'Mishpatim', 115*b*.

to the zaddikim and the sages who cleave to God (*hadevekim lamakom*) by means of study (*be'inyan hatorah*). They will say to him: "There was no harlot in this place" (ibid). The Torah is no harlot who arouses mere lust and in whom there is no inner depth of beauty. The essence of study is to cleave to the inner beauty and light of the Torah (*ledabek bapenimiyut uve'or hatorah*).[11] Here again, we are reminded of the distinction between the two modes of study, of the need to adhere to the zaddik, and, above all, of the identification of *torah lishmah* with *devekut*.

R. Moses Hayyim Ephraim returns to the same topic in his discussion of the typographically incongruous small letter *alef* at the end of the word *vayikra* ('and [the Lord] called') in Lev. 1: 1. He ascribes the following statement to R. Jacob Joseph of Polonnoye: 'People say: *halomedim lernen yo und di ḥasidim lernen nit* (the scholars learn and the hasidim do not).' To this expression of popular opinion the answer must be: the more that scholars study, the higher their opinion of themselves. They think that they have already studied all that is necessary. By contrast, the more that hasidim study, the humbler they become. Their sole intention is to learn how to be low and humble. It is to this that the small *alef* of *vayikra* alludes.[12] We see here how the author subverts the anti-hasidic argument of the mitnaggedim. Their apparent virtue, scholarship, is exposed as a source of unwarranted pride and self-preoccupation, while the hasidim's lack of scholarship is presented as cause for humility. The terms *yo* and *nit* clearly allude to the hasidic dialectic of *yesh* and *ayin*.

It is clear from all this that *torah lishmah* is first and foremost a spiritual attitude. This is confirmed by R. Moses Hayyim Ephraim's comment on the encounter of Jacob and Rachel at the well (Gen. 29), which according to him demonstrates the true nature of *torah lishmah*. He derives this from Avot 6: 1 where those who study *torah lishmah* are likened to a water-source ('like a never failing fountain and like a river that flows on with ever sustained vigour'), which he sees as comparable to the well of the Genesis narrative. The main point of *torah lishmah* is to study with fear and love—*bideḥilu ureḥimu* in the language of the Zohar. Indeed, the Zohar on Num. 21: 18 identifies the 'princes' (*nedivei ha'am*) who 'dug the well' with the Patriarchs.[13] The well stands for Torah. He who studies with the virtues of the Patriarchs—*ḥesed, gevurah,* and *tiferet,* or *ahavah*, *yir'ah* and *yir'ah dekelulah*—is able to raise up all the lower levels of existence which are clothed in the *kelipot*. This applies to Jacob, of whom it was said: '*vayisa Ya'akov raglav*' (Gen. 29: 1; literally, 'Jacob lifted his feet'), that is to say, he raised all the lower levels—the modalities of 'the heels' (*akevim*).

In the following commentary on this story, R. Moses Hayyim Ephraim explains how this may be achieved:

'And he looked, and behold a well in the field'. This is the Torah of running water. 'And lo, there were three flocks of sheep lying by it.' These are the Patriarchs, because it is impossible to go to the well without the virtues of the three Patriarchs. 'For out of that well they watered

[11] Ibid., on 'Vayeshev', 56*a–b*. The name Tamar is equivalent to Torah by its numerical value of 640 which corresponds to 613, the number of *mitsvot*, together with the 22 letters of the alphabet and including the 'doubles'.

[12] Ibid., on 'Vayikra', 149*b*. See also 145*b*, where, in connection with Exod. 36: 7, the author recalls the motif of *ḥasidim rishonim* mentioned in Ber. 32*b*.

[13] See Zohar 3: 62*a*, 103*a*, 286*a*.

the flocks.' This means that the shepherd of each generation waters Israel who is called the flock: all these shepherds water their generations with the Torah and *musar*—ethical directives—which they draw from that well. 'And a great stone was upon the well's mouth.' The well's mouth is understood as referring to the zaddik, while the large stone is compared to a barrier that separates the well's mouth from the flock, or the zaddik and the 'water' of Torah and *musar* from the people of Israel who need to imbibe it for their sustenance, because of the shortcoming of the recipients (*meḥamat ḥesron hamekabel*). But there is a way out of this situation, which depends primarily on their own initiative: 'and thither were all the flocks gathered'—when all of Israel gather together and are desirous of the Torah and *musar* which flow from the lips of the zaddik. Then 'Jacob went near and rolled the stone from the well's mouth': at such times the screen which separates them from the flow of Torah and *musar* is removed. However, there are occasions when the zaddik recognizes some special and urgent need (*tsorekh sha'ah*) to effect *tikun* on the Shekhinah, identified here with Torah and *musar*. On these occasions he rolls the stone from the well's mouth at his own initiative—he delivers words of Torah and *musar* in order to unite the Holy One, blessed be He, with the Shekhinah. 'Now when Jacob saw Rachel'—this is his recognition of the special need of the Shekhinah. But the action required to fulfil this need, as Rashi suggests in his comment on the verse, calls for superior strength of which not everyone is capable.[14]

This interpretation of the encounter between Jacob and Rachel at the well touches on three major hasidic themes: (*a*) The study of *torah lishmah* requires not only intellectual but also intense emotional application through fear and love. (*b*) Study of *torah lishmah* can raise up and free the divine sparks from their confinement in the realm of the *kelipot*. (*c*) The zaddik is the 'shepherd' of the generation. He can 'water the flock'—teach Torah and *musar*—only when the people are gathered around the 'well' of Torah, eager to 'drink'. But in special circumstances, when the situation calls for unusual measures, the zaddik must take the initiative and act independently of the 'flock', in response to the urgent need of the Shekhinah. There is no doubt that our author is referring to the circumstances of his own generation: the leaders must assume their responsibility and 'roll away the stone', that is, they must initiate the removal of the barrier that separates Israel from Torah.

3. THE POWER OF MEDITATING ON THE LETTERS

For the method to which the zaddik resorts we can look to R. Moses Hayyim Ephraim's comment on Exod. 25: 7: 'Onyx stones (*avnei shoham*) and 'stones to be set' (*avnei milu'im*), in the ephod and in the breastplate.' The two categories of stones allude to two modes of study. There is study of Torah by way of reading the letters which make up the words as they are, in order to understand the text rationally. This is the usual mode of study. But there is also another way of studying—'with heart-felt intent (*bekhavanah deliba*)' and 'with holy and pure thoughts (*bemaḥshavot kedoshot utehorot*).' In the *Sefer yetsirah* words are referred to as 'stones'.[15] Similarly here, 'onyx stones' are the words understood literally, studied 'as they are' (*keshehem*). But he who utters the

[14] *Degel maḥaneh Efrayim*, on 'Vayetse', 43*a*–44*a*. Similar interpretations of the passage in Avot 6: 1 also occur ibid., in 'Ki tisa', 135*b*; 'Beḥukotai', 189*a*; 'Devarim', 226*a*; Likutim, 272*a*–*b*.

[15] See *Sefer yetsirah*, 4: 12.

words with heart-felt intent and draws out the holy and pure intentions which are contained in them is at the level of 'stones to be set', for he 'sets into' or 'fills' (*memale*) the words with numerous letters. Thousands of letters may be discerned in one verse if the intentions of the words are uttered as numerous permutations of letters.[16] As R. Moses Hayyim Ephraim remarks in connection with Gen. 6: 16, playing on the double meaning of the word *teivah* as both 'ark' and 'word', each component letter or word embraces higher realities: 'For in every word there are worlds, souls and divinity.'[17]

This exegesis of the two categories of stones makes it clear that study with 'heart-felt intent' is equivalent to the theory of the contemplation of letters which is associated with the Baal Shem Tov and some of his disciples: rather than following the plain meaning of the text, whereby each letter has the value of one sign only, a contemplative technique is preferred which generates a multiplicity of signs and values. This is echoed in the quotation from *Sefer yetsirah* which points to the possibility of deconstructing and reconstructing the words constituting each verse so that, as R. Moses Hayyim Ephraim proclaims, 'thousands of letters may be discerned in one verse'. As the late Joseph Weiss noted, he goes so far as to personify the letters, stating in the name of the Baal Shem Tov that one has 'to ask of the letters' (*levakesh min ha'otiyot*), namely, one must address the divine light (*or ha'elohut*) which is contained in them.[18]

This capacity for permutating the letters is rooted in human nature. We learn this from R. Nahman of Horodenka, who said: 'Each man has the twenty-two letters of the alphabet for himself.'[19] R. Moses Hayyim Ephraim connects this with the statement in *Sefer yetsirah* (3: 6): 'God made the letter *alef* king over the air and He crowned it, and combined them with one another, and He sealed with them ether in the universe, moisture in the year, body in the person'. As a result of the presence within him of the twenty-two letters of the alphabet, man has the ability, once he has reached the age of 13—the age when he is capable of physical procreation—to procreate spiritually too. In the same year he attains both physical and mental maturity (*kelal da'at ukhlal haneshamah*); he acquires the ability to form holy and pure combinations, to unite and permutate the twenty-two letters of the alphabet by the light of his soul. The brighter the light of his soul and the more intense his cleaving to God, the greater the number of permutations and unifications he can perform. R. Moses Hayyim Ephraim then develops the analogy between physical and spiritual procreation: 'On the physical plane, the more a person makes use of his member the greater his lust to use it again, on account of the pleasure he experiences in the act; similarly on the spiritual plane, the more one unites the letters by the power of the light of one's soul, the greater one's desire to perform such hierogamies (*zivugim kedoshim*) by means of the twenty-two letters of the alphabet. Thus one would train oneself to operate in the mode of the 'orchard'

16 *Degel maḥaneh Efrayim*, on 'Terumah', 121*b*–122*a*.

17 Ibid., on 'Noaḥ', 9*b*, and on 'Yitro', 112*b*. Cf. the letter written by the Baal Shem Tov to his brother-in-law, published at the end of R. Jacob Joseph of Polonnoye, *Ben porat Yosef* [Korets, 1781] (Brooklyn, NY, 1976), 127*b*–128*b*, and also Aaron of Opatow, *Keter shem tov* [2 vols.; Zolkiew, 1794–5; 1 vol.; Korets, 1797] (Jerusalem, 1975), 48*b*–48*c*.

18 See J. Weiss, 'Talmud torah leshitat R. Yisrael Besht', in *Sefer hayovel tiferet yisrael likhvod R. Israel Brodie* (London, 1967), 151–69, esp. 167–8, and cf. L. Jacobs, *Hasidic Prayer* (London, 1972), 70–81.

19 *Degel maḥaneh Efrayim*, on 'Ekev', 238*b*.

(*pardes*) by means of the Torah—the 248 positive and 365 negative commandments. But when a person fails to operate in this mode, the twenty-two letters of the alphabet do not illuminate his soul and he cannot permutate, combine, or unify them at all. Sometimes, Heaven forbid, the evil inclination prevails. Then the good permutations are reversed, the power of Torah is annulled, and with it the power of all the worlds connected with it. It follows that the destiny of all the worlds which have their root in the Torah is placed in the hands of man'.[20]

4. THE SPECIAL POWER OF THE ZADDIK TO MANIPULATE LETTERS

The ontological grounds for this function of the letters are clearly laid in the explanation elsewhere in R. Moses Hayyim Ephraim's book, whereby the letters are holy and serve as instruments of creation. All man's actions are expressed in the letters. When he does evil, he damages them by forming evil combinations and draws them down toward the abyss of the *kelipot*.

However, when zaddikim are present in the world, they can purify the letters and restore their sanctity not only by means of uttering words of Torah or prayer with love and fear, but also through 'worship in corporeality' (*avodah begashmiyut*), words spoken in mundane conversation (*besipurei ma'asiyot*) while they operate in the profane sphere (*bedivrei gashmiyut*). As the Baal Shem Tov taught, fallen men may be raised even by means of profane tales. R. Moses Hayyim Ephraim adds to this that, as in the case of rolling the stone off the well's mouth, not everyone is capable of achieving such feats, for 'not everyone who goes up will ascend'.[21] Only the charismatic man may purify the worlds and letters of which mere tales or profane conversations are made. He alone can raise them from the realm of the base and turbid to a state of great luminosity. Such a man 'merits many things' (*zokheh lidevarim rabim*). This is understood as 'he purifies (*mezakekh*) . . . many words' (*diburim rabim*).[22]

We can deduce from this that R. Moses Hayyim Ephraim restricts the practice of *torah lishmah* to a small élite, even though he acknowledges that every individual contains within himself the twenty-two letters of the alphabet. This is evident in his resort to the distinction between 'men of form' and 'men of matter' (*anshei tsurah* and *anshei ḥomer*), a distinction which was first formulated in hasidism by R. Jacob Joseph of Polonnoye.[23]

On two occasions R. Moses stresses that Adam's sin caused a break, a *shevirah*, as a result of which Creation fell into the abyss of the *kelipot*, so that good and evil were confused. It became necessary for man to engage in the thirty-nine material occupations listed in the Mishnah in order to sustain life on earth. But the scholar (*talmid*

[20] *Degel maḥaneh Efrayim*, on 'Ekev', 238*a*–239*a*.

[21] Ber. 2: 8. My analysis confirms the views of A. Rapoport-Albert and T. Loewenthal on *devekut* as the prerogative of the zaddik, not of every hasid. See A. Rapoport-Albert, 'God and the Zaddik as the Two Focal Points of Hasidic Worship', *History of Religions*, 18: 4 (1979), 296–325, and T. Loewenthal, 'Early Hasidic Teachings: Esoteric Mysticism or a Medium of Communal Leadership?', *Journal of Jewish Studies*, 37 (1986), 58–75.

[22] *Degel maḥaneh Efrayim* on 'Ki tisa', 135*b*.

[23] Ibid., on 'Tsav', 153*a*–157*a*.

ḥakham) who applies himself to the study of Torah need not engage in any of the material occupations, for the study of Torah alone sustains him.[24] For him, every day is like *Shabbat*. If he studies Torah for its own sake, it is as if he has engaged in all the thirty-nine occupations, for in applying himself to Torah he elevates all the holy sparks. And further: all work accomplished by others in the material world is elevated through his holy utterances. By cleaving to Torah and to God, he injects vitality (*ḥiyut*) into the Torah itself.[25]

Zaddikim may exercise their power to combine the letters again and again, as we read:

> The principle of the matter is that the letters come out of the mouth of the Holy One, blessed be He, in order to govern the world. And when the letters come out into the world, they are combined according to [the deeds of] the recipients (*lefi hamekabelim*), for good or for its opposite, Heaven forbid! But when there is a zaddik in the world who is wise and who knows the letters as they first came out of the mouth of God, although they now appear in an unfavourable combination, he can reverse them by means of his study and prayer, so that he turns *met* (dead) to *tam* (perfect) or *nega* (disease) into *oneg* (pleasure).[26] This is what the Baal Shem Tov once did when the community of Zaslaw was threatened by danger.[27]

The intervention of the Baal Shem Tov on that occasion must be considered a model for the function of zaddikim in general. They transform unfavourable combinations of letters, distortions which result from human misconduct and which affect mankind adversely, into the favourable permutations which had originally emanated from the Godhead.

5. THE REDEMPTIVE POWER OF THE LETTERS

R. Moses Hayyim Ephraim establishes a connection between the theurgy of the letters and the concept of redemption with reference to Ruth 4: 7: 'Now this was the manner in former times in Israel concerning redeeming and concerning changing.' His comment on this passage synthesizes many of the important motifs that are current throughout his homilies. He asserts that whenever man eats, carries out business transactions, enters into profane conversation, or tells profane tales, he must remember that all his activities are manifestations of holy letters, emanating from the upper worlds. They are rooted in holiness, but when they come down into this world, they clothe themselves in

24 See Ketubot, 111*b* and *Tikunei zohar*, ed. R. Margaliot (Jerusalem, 1948), 'Hakdamah', 12*a*, and Tikun 19, 38*b*.

25 *Degel maḥaneh Efrayim*, on 'Toledot', 39*a*, and 'Ki tisa', 133*a*.

26 Ibid., on 'Emor', 180*a*–181*b*. See *Sefer yetsirah*, ii. 1. One older source for this theme may be found, as was suggested to me by M. Idel, in the foreword to *Or haḥamah*, 4 vols. [Prezemysl, 1896–8] (Bnei Brak, 1973), i. 1*c*, where R. Abraham Azulai speaks of the elevation of the letters uttered by man to their root as a means of inducing a state of *devekut* between man and God. R. Abraham Galante in his comment on Zohar 1: 67*b* (*Or haḥamah*, i. 62*d*) speaks of the creation of man by means of the twenty-two letters of the alphabet and of reversing the combinations of letters. Cf. G. Scholem, *On the Kabbalah and its Symbolism* (London, 1965), 196 n. 1.

27 See Dov Ber b. Shmuel of Linits (Luniets), *Shivḥei haBesht* [Kopys, 1814], pub. in Eng. as *In Praise of the Baal Shem Tov*, trans. D. Ben-Amos and J. R. Mintz (Bloomington, Ind., 1970), 78–80.

materiality. This way of thinking is in fact shared by several other figures in the early generations of the hasidic movement.[28]

The *Degel maḥaneh Efrayim* argues that all such profane activities must be carried out with 'intellect, insight and fear of Heaven' (*sekhel, da'at veyirat shamayim*) in order to reunite them with their divine roots. This is a common enough motif, but here it acquires new emphasis through the suggestion that man redeems his profane activities from *temurah* (a term which means 'exchange' but is used in some kabbalistic sources to signify the realm of evil paralleling and constantly threatening to invade the divine realm). In other words, when he illuminates the obscure material substance of his activities, man restores them from darkness to light, from servitude to redemption (*mishi'abud lige'ulah*). The messianic motif intermingles with the Platonic one. R. Moses Hayyim Ephraim expounds the expression 'former times' (*lefanim*) from the verse in Ruth in the same manner, as referring to the return of a union 'face to face' (*panim el apnim*) between God and man, and he speaks of the children of Israel as those who realize this union through their good deeds and through their Torah and its constituent letters. But this redemption remains an individual one, as we can see from the example which he supplies concerning the individual who suffers and conceals his pain, or consults the holy letters concerning it. In doing so, he illuminates the letters he is addressing and they are redeemed from their material obscurity, thereby redeeming him from his pain. Lev. 25: 24 is interpreted in the same way: '"And in all the land (*erets*) of your possession, you shall grant a redemption for the land." This means that in all material realities (*artsiyut o inyenei gashmiyut*) you shall grant a redemption for the land, as it were, to redeem the letters from the abyss. Now it is known that the Shekhinah is called "land" (*erets*), and so she is redeemed by the same act, for he (the one who grants a redemption) and she (the Shekhinah) are one (*da veda eḥad hu*). In illuminating the letters of his pain, he illuminates the Shekhinah, because his pain and that of the Shekhinah are one, so to speak.'[29] It is evident from all this that the mystical union obtained by means of meditating on the letters is the redemption both of the individual and of the Shekhinah. But even if R. Moses Hayyim Ephraim is not ignorant of the notion of collective redemption, for him the concepts of *galut* and *ge'ulah* are subjective states, and he quotes the Baal Shem Tov to this effect: 'Each man must redeem himself.'[30]

In conclusion, it can be said that the problematics of *torah lishmah* are central to the work of R. Moses Hayyim Ephraim of Sudylkow. This prominent theme comprises, in the first instance, the polemic with the mitnaggedim, in which he overturns their argumentation and invites them to recognize the authority of the zaddikim. To do so, he points to the integrative power of the study of *torah lishmah*, not only as an intellectual activity, but also as an activity which has consequences on both ethical and cosmic planes. It is expected of the zaddik that he should engage in *torah lishmah* even if this presents a certain danger to his personal integrity.

[28] See K. E. Grözinger, 'Neoplatonisches Denken in Hasidut und Kabbala', *Frankfurter judaistische Beiträge*, 11 (1983), 57–89.

[29] *Degel maḥaneh Efrayim*, on 'Behar', 184*a*–*b*.

[30] Ibid., on 'Balak', 214*a*: '*kol adam ḥayav lige'ol atsmo*'. On *galut* and *geulah* see ibid., on 'Vayetse', 42*a*–*b*.

The medium of study *lishmah* is the twenty-two letters of the Hebrew alphabet. These letters represent the divine origin of reality; they are also the ultimate manifestation of Torah, and the substance of human nature. This triple function of the letters gives the zaddik, and only the zaddik, the ability to perform *tserufim* and *zivugim* which affect the sphere of holiness while at the same time transforming the material world and enabling him to intervene in its affairs. He does this by illuminating the material expression of the letters with divine light and raising them to their spiritual source. The same technique enables each individual to redeem himself. The idea has a certain affinity with Abraham Abulafia's notion of the power of *tserufim*, and a concrete link could, perhaps, be established between the two kabbalists through the book *Berit menuḥah*, a work which R. Moses Hayyim Ephraim quotes several times.[31] But unlike Abulafia, he does not conceive of himself as the hero of a messianic venture. In his case, as with other figures in the hasidic leadership of that generation, the neutralization of the messianic idea is clearly in evidence.

[31] Ibid., on 'Bereshit', 6*a*; on 'Va'era', 89*a*.

SIXTEEN

The Teachings of R. Menahem Mendel of Vitebsk

MOSHE HALLAMISH

THE BESHT seems to have spread the message of hasidism while travelling through towns and villages and in the course of such activities as healing the sick.[1] It was only under the leadership of R. Dov Ber, 'the Great Maggid' of Mezhirech, that the institution of zaddikism was properly established, with the zaddik now staying at home and a community gathering round him.[2] Among the many disciples who came together in the school of the Maggid, there may have been circles of more restricted membership which were formed by people drawn to each other by spiritual and personal affinity. Undoubtedly one of the most important personalities among them was R. Menahem Mendel b. Moses of Vitebsk.[3] It will be recalled that in the Vilna *ḥerem* of 8 Iyar 5532 (1772), R. Menahem Mendel alone is mentioned as an example of a person who 'had the reputation of being one of the greatest among their company, the companies of evil'.[4] Equally, when the hasidim sought to send a representative to R. Elijah, the Gaon of Vilna, to explain the doctrine of hasidism and to prevent a further outbreak of opposition to the new movement, they turned to R. Menahem Mendel to fulfil this mission. Tactically this may have been somewhat imprudent, even if R. Menahem Mendel was accompanied by so great a Torah scholar as R. Shneur Zalman of Lyady, for, as we have seen, it was R. Menahem Mendel who was the target for the attacks; nevertheless, the nomination itself shows clearly what an important position he occupied in the nascent world of hasidism. Around him there gathered a group who were at once his close associates and his disciples, although they were people of varying stature and abilities.

This is an expanded version of a paper presented at the Tenth World Congress of Jewish Studies which took place in Jerusalem in the summer of 1989.

[1] See G. Scholem, 'Demuto hahistorit shel R. Yisrael Ba'al Shem Tov', *Molad*, 18 (1960); repr. in id., *Devarim bego* (Tel Aviv, 1975), 287–324; I. Tishby and J. Dan, 'Torat haḥasidut vesifrutah', *Hebrew* Encyclopaedia, xvii (1965), 769–821, repr. as a pamphlet by Academon, Jerusalem, and in A. Rubinstein (ed.), *Perakim betorat haḥasidut vetoledoteihah* (Jerusalem, 1977), 250–312.

[2] See Joseph Weiss, 'Reshit tsemiḥatah shel haderekh haḥasidit', *Zion*, 16 (1951), 103–5, repr. in Rubinstein (ed.), *Perakim betorat haḥasidut*, 179–81.

[3] Hasidim tell of the involvement of the Besht in the birth of Menahem Mendel of Vitebsk. See *Sefer ha'otsar misipurei tsadikim* (Warsaw, 1937), tale no. 13. Hasidic legend also tells of R. Menahem Mendel's visit to the home of the Besht.

[4] See M. Wilensky, *Ḥasidim umitnaggedim* (2 vols.; Jerusalem, 1970), i. 43; see also 28, 64–5.

R. Shneur Zalman of Lyady came to the Maggid of Mezhirech as a young man of 25. R. Menahem Mendel was some fifteen or twenty years his senior. There is no doubt that what brought them together was not merely their common geographical origin but their spiritual affinity.[5] It appears that R. Menahem Mendel attracted people of a particular type, and in one of his letters he refers to the great influence he had in the provinces of Volhynia, where he acquired a considerable following although he lived in that region for only a short time.[6] For his part, he testifies in a letter written in 5541 (1781): 'not a day has gone by on which I have not remembered them kindly, one and all. And through His compassion, blessed be His name, I will never forget them, Amen.'[7] Less than four years later he was to write to his hasidim in Belorussia (using the formal plural to refer to himself):

Our soul longs earnestly for those who are lodged in the recesses of our heart, our bowels yearn for them when we remember all the days we spent with them . . . the friends all over Russia who were close to our heart, who were wholehearted in their fear of Heaven, each one according to his attainments and his endeavours in serving Him, blessed be His name.[8]

While living in Tiberias, R. Menahem Mendel married into a distinguished Sefardi family.[9] We possess a letter written during the period of his residence in Tiberias by R. Solomon Zalman Hakohen Vilner on 27 Shevat 5546 (1786), in which he describes R. Menahem Mendel's sermons:

He reveals secrets and mysteries on Shabbat after Shabbat which the tongue would weary to recite and the heart to think. Even if one did not understand these things, for they are ancient . . . he displays different aspects of everything and strips them bare to their core, one layer after another, far beyond every jot and tittle—to the point of Infinity, blessed be He, as it were, and I can write no more about this, for I am not clever enough.[10]

There is also a eulogy by R. Moses Galante, one of the scholars of Damascus, written shortly after R. Menahem Mendel's death, which emphasizes, among other things, his unique qualities, his greatness, and his contemplative kabbalistic prayer.[11]

[5] And it was not without reason that the hasidim sent R. Shneur Zalman with R. Menahem Mendel on the mission to the Gaon of Vilna.

[6] See *Likutei amarim* [Lemberg, 1911], ii, letter 18, 25*a*. All references below to the letters of R. Menahem Mendel are to this collection while all references to the homilies in *Peri ha'arets* [Kopys, 1814] are by name of Torah portion alone. I do not burden the reader with references to the parallel versions unless there is some special reason to do so. See n. 21 below for the various editions of R. Menahem Mendel's works.

[7] *Likutei amarim*, letter 1, 4*b*.

[8] Ibid., letter 4, 6*a*.

[9] 'And one of the distinguished and important members of the Sefardic community, an in-law of the learned scholar in Tiberias, arranged a marriage between his daughter and R. Moses, the charming and amiable son of the late R. Menahem Mendel may his soul rest in Eden. And he gave him a dowry of 800 "lions".' See the section 'Nefesh Menahem: Toledot maran harav R. Menahem Mendel miVitebsk', printed at the head of *Likutei amarim*, i. 11*b*, 23.

[10] Ibid., letter 16, 21*b*.

[11] See M. Benayahu, 'Pinkasim bikhtav-yad leḤakham miDamesek', *Kiryat sefer*, 35 (1960), 526. Incidentally, letter 27 in Shneur Zalman of Lyady, *Igeret hakodesh* [Shklov, 1814], repr. in *Likutei amarim: Tanya*, bilingual edn., trans. N. Mindel, N. Mangel, Z. Posner, and J. I. Schochet (London, 1973), iv, is a letter of condolence from R. Shneur Zalman to the inhabitants of the Holy Land on the death of R. Menahem Mendel.

We may add here some further remarks on his character. In one of his first letters from Erets Yisrael Menahem Mendel expressed himself thus: 'I, too, greatly desired to perform *yiḥud* and achieve unity.'[12] For our purpose it is important to note that if this is not mere rhetoric, it is evidence that R. Menahem Mendel was imbued with a profound belief in the unity of God and in the need to bring about such unity in the world by raising up holy sparks and by the annulment of the *kelipot* (forces of evil) which would follow of itself. This, in turn, must find expression in the unity of mankind, in pursuit of which it was necessary to bring about the reconciliation of the mitnaggedim to hasidism and to establish peace with them. Indeed, in another letter he calls on people 'not to scoff at those who abandon the Torah'. He approves (on the basis of a pronouncement by the sages) the condemnation of anything which is actually evil, but forbids it to be cursed. The reason he gives is interesting: we are all called children of God, even the sinner, and when you curse him, you are looking upon yourself as distanced from him and separating yourself from the community at large. In doing so 'you become a cause of decline and degradation'.[13]

Another characteristic of Menahem Mendel is his modesty. He frequently signs his letters 'The truly humble'. He also speaks a great deal about humility as opposed to self-aggrandizement.[14] However, it appears that the latter is not merely a seemly moral attribute but something that is woven into the fabric of his speculative doctrine. 'The essence of the matter is the attachment [*hitkasherut*] of the humble man to the Supreme Will through humility and reverence, and from it he arrives at contemplation and study through [the application of] intellect and wisdom, to introduce these into every *mitsvah* with which he occupies himself.'[15] The explanation is, apparently, that only through humility and self-annulment is it possible to attach oneself to the Godhead.

To conclude this brief description, a further interesting point may be observed. In a letter to his hasidim written exactly a year before his death, R. Menahem Mendel testifies to his telepathic, or telecommunicative, ability:

My dear ones, my friends, my brethren . . . have you not known, have you not heard, has not the saying of our Sages been told you from the beginning [see Isa. 40: 21]. More than the calf desires to suck, the cow desires to give suck, and all my desire and the yearning of my love towards each one of you is many thousands of times greater than yours towards me, and each one is engraved on the tablet of my heart, as a sign upon my hand, and as a memorial between my eyes, directed always towards the Lord, as if their likeness stands before me so that I may recognize their appearance while their hearts, their nature and quality and the sum total of all their concerns stand revealed. And let not any newcomer entertain the thought that perhaps I am unaware of matters concerning them, the manner in which they conduct their religious life and their [spiritual] wisdom, the path which they tread and the deeds which they perform. For how should a thing be known which I have never seen, how can I explain this wonder. Behold, they know not, neither do they understand, they walk in darkness [Ps. 82: 5], but it is God's

[12] Wilensky, *Ḥasidim umitnaggedim*, i. 91; and on the date of the letter, 90, n. 1.

[13] *Likutei amarim*, letter 4, 8*a*.

[14] e.g. ibid., letters 3, 6*a* and 4, 7*b*–8*a*.

[15] *Peri ets* [Zhitomir, 1874] (Cracow, 1937), end of section on 'Noaḥ'. The humility of R. Menahem Mendel is also attested by R. Jacob Joseph of Polonnoye, according to the tale by M. L. Rodkinson, *Adat tsadikim* [Lemberg, 1864] 16*b* (not paginated in the original), repr. in G. Nigal (ed.), *Sipurei Michael Levi Rodkinson* (Jerusalem, 1988), 46–7.

truth that nothing concerning them is hidden from my eyes. I know every one of them from beginning to end. And I am not a prophet or a seer,[16] but it is in accordance with the Torah of truth and the design of the Lord that I should know all the people He has created [*anshei ma'asehu*—possibly a pun, referring also to the quality of *anshei ma'aseh*—men of righteous deeds—which characterizes those who had been converted to the 'fear of Heaven' by R. Menahem Mendel], since I have been favoured from the outset with the knowledge of the beginning of their fear of Heaven, knowledge derived from those long known to me in this respect. In this way I can tell the end of any matter in all its details precisely as it will present itself to the eye, and I will not err in my vision, with the help of the Lord . . .

You are my children just as if I had borne you; since you were initiated in the fear of Heaven by me, you will remain close to me. I shall never forget the times when you visited me, for through them you have given me life,[17] even into hoary-headed old age neither height nor breadth, neither horse nor chariot shall separate us from each other.[18]

This remarkable personal description shows that even while he was in Erets Yisrael, new hasidim joined his congregation in Belorussia, which is a fact of some significance.

The two colleagues mentioned, R. Shneur Zalman and R. Abraham of Kalisk, however close they were to R. Menahem Mendel, were different from each other. They both had strong personalities. For example, a man such as R. Abraham of Kalisk, who followed the controversial practice of *kolyen sich*, that is, turning somersaults in the street, and ignoring everyone who jeered at him, would certainly do so not merely out of a particular belief or a certain view of the world; the act itself demands an extraordinary temperament to stand up to such a situation. In my opinion, R. Abraham aspired more to centralist authority. Even the concept of *dibuk ḥaverim*, the cleaving together of friends,[19] seems to me to be connected with, and indeed to issue from, this aspiration to be able to stand at the head of a closed and close-knit group, directing it along a single path. R. Shneur Zalman, too, was a man of forceful personality, but he allowed every individual room to develop his own personality; his charisma was such that he could still unite them under his leadership.

Undoubtedly, during the time they spent together at the court of the Maggid, R. Menahem Mendel and R. Shneur Zalman would have discussed and clarified many issues. The close connection between them can be detected in expressions, turns of phrase, and terminology, although these were sometimes used to convey differing concepts.[20] As for their *Weltanschauung*, there were shared viewpoints as well as points of

[16] This expression, modelled on Scripture (cf. Amos 7: 14), also occurs in another letter. See David Zevi Hillman (ed.), *Igrot ba'al haTanya uvenei doro* (Jerusalem, 1953), 26.

[17] After Ps. 119: 93.

[18] *Likutei amarim*, letter 18, 24*b*–25*a* ff.

[19] See J. G. Weiss, 'R. Abraham Kalisker's Concept of Communion with G-d and Men', *Journal of Jewish Studies*, 6 (1955), 87–9, repr. in id., *Studies in Eastern European Jewish Mysticism* (Oxford, 1985), 155–69. And similarly Ze'ev Gries, 'Mimitos le'etos: Kavim lidmuto shel R. Avraham miKalisk', in the anthology *Umah vetoledoteihah* (2 vols.; Jerusalem, 1984), ii. 117–46. The psychological point discussed here briefly may explain the dual personality of R. Abraham of Kalisk, on which Gries commented, 'Mimitos le'etos', 126.

[20] E. Steinman, *Be'er haḥasidut* (10 vols.; Tel Aviv, 1951–62), ii. 39, goes too far when he declares that 'We find whole paragraphs almost word for word the same in the *Tanya* and in *Peri ha'arets*.' I regret to say that I have found no such paragraphs, but there are expressions, and subjects, which correspond closely. See e.g. '*betokpam ugevuratam*' ('by their power and might') in *Peri ha'arets* on 'Ki tavo', and

dispute. In general, R. Menahem Mendel was nearer in his ideas to his teacher the Maggid, whereas R. Shneur Zalman was influenced more by the world of kabbalah. It is proposed here to deal with a number of basic issues in R. Menahem Mendel's doctrine through a comparison with that of R. Shneur Zalman.[21]

frequently in the *Tanya*; '*ḥelek eloha mima'al mamash*' ('an actual part of God on high') in 'Vayeshev', and Shneur Zalman of Lyady, *Tanya*, ch. 2; for the evaluation of the body as flesh and not as the essence of man's being, see *Likutei amarim*, letter 4, 6*b* and *Tanya*, ch. 29, etc.—although the idea is very widespread in the literature of kabbalah; for the expression from *Tikunei hazohar* that fear and love are pinions on which to raise up thought see *Peri ha'arets* on 'Matot' and 'Masei', and *Tanya* ch. 41; for the explanation of the Tetragrammaton (*shem Havayah*) as *mehaveh hakol*, = 'bringing everything into being', transforming everything from Ayin to Yesh, see *Peri ha'arets* on 'Koraḥ' and *Tanya*, 'Sha'ar hayiḥud veha'emunah', ch. 4, as well as other kabbalistic works such as those of the Shelah and Remak [R. Moses Cordovero]; for the notion that 'All apparent evils are from Him, blessed be He, [and] in truth they are kindnesses' see *Peri ha'arets* on 'Vayera' and *Igeret hakodesh*, s. 11, as well as the homilies of the Maggid of Mezhirech; for the negative assessment of Torah study otherwise than for its own sake, in the sense of 'for one's own benefit', see *Likutei amarim*, letter 3, 5*b*, and *Tanya*, ch. 39 and *passim*, but also in various other hasidic works. On the other hand, R. Menahem Mendel's use of certain other expressions is quite distinctive, such as the epithets 'He who fills all worlds' and 'He who encircles all worlds', which refer to divine immanence (as in the *ra'aya meheimna*). Compare *Likutei amarim*, letter 9, 15*a*, with R. Shneur Zalman, who, following the Ari, draws an essential distinction: R. Menahem Mendel emphasizes the greatness of the Creator precisely on the evidence of the constant and natural guidance of the world (see *Peri ha'arets*, on 'Bo'), whereas for R. Shneur Zalman the miracle is revealed only by concealment (R. Shneur Zalman of Lyady, *Seder tefilot mikol hashanah im perush hamilot* [Zhitomir, 1863] (Brooklyn, NY, 1965), 44*b*); in R. Menahem Mendel's view (and that of the school of the Maggid) it is Keter which stands at the head of the *sefirot*, whereas for R. Shneur Zalman it is Ḥokhmah; for R. Menahem Mendel, Da'at is not an attribute in its own right (see *Peri ha'arets* on 'Matot' and 'Masei' and similarly *Peri ets* on 'Matot'), but for R. Shneur Zalman, Da'at is the third *sefirah* (*passim*). On the subject of Keter and Da'at, see also M. Hallamish, 'Mishnato ha'iyunit shel Rabbi Shne'ur Zalman miLiadi: Mekorotav bakabalah veyaḥaso lereshit haḥasidut' (Ph.D. thesis, Hebrew University of Jerusalem, 1976), 84, 217; and cf. below, nn. 22, 52, 57, 105, 106. Finally, it is worth mentioning that in several cases R. Menahem Mendel himself uses kabbalistic terms but gives them a new connotation: e.g. 'Shekhinah' is a name applied to the divine manifestation which is below Ḥokhmah; 'zaddik' can be 'He who has nothing of his own', which is generally a name for Malkhut, but for R. Menahem Mendel it is important to refer to the zaddik in this way in order to point out that it is his function to destroy corporeality and reduce it to nothing so as to raise everything up to its root (see *Peri ha'arets* on 'Lekh lekha').

[21] For the purpose of compiling an account of the doctrine of R. Menahem Mendel the following sources are available: *Peri ha'arets* (Kopys, 1814; Mogilev, 1818; n.p., n.d., but clearly later than 1818; Zhitomir, 1849; n.p. [Kónigsberg], 1857, Lemberg, 1862; Zhitomir, 1867; Warsaw, 1879, and Jerusalem, 1965 and subsequently). *Peri ets* (Zhitomir, 1874; Cracow, 1937). *Ets peri* (Safed, n.d. (the approbation is dated 1873, in fact a reversal of the title of *Peri ets*, apparently a copy from a corrupt MS) Zhitomir, 1874; Lvov, 1880). Important material is contained in letters from Erets Yisrael. Some of them are printed at the end of *Peri ha'arets* (except for the edition of unidentified date and place and those of Mogilev and Lemberg). Further letters were printed in *Likutei amarim* (see n. 6 above). Some were reprinted by Israel Halpern, *Ha'aliyot harishonot shel haḥasidim le'Erets Yisrael* (Tel Aviv, 1947); Hillman, *Igrot Ba'al haTanya*); Jacob Barnai, *Igrot ḥasidim meErets Yisrael* (Jerusalem, 1980). These books also note additional bibliographical sources.

Other discourses on doctrinal matters appear in *Likutei amarim*, i, and also in *Igeret hakodesh*, at the beginning of which there are several such passages. This has been reprinted many times (perhaps because of its brevity): 1799, 1800, 1810, 1840, etc. See also the 'testament' printed at the head of *Likutei amarim*, ii; and *Mikhtavim kedoshim mehaBesht vetalmidav*, ed. J. Margulies and A. H. Bierbrauer (Czernowitz, 1921), 15–16.

It must be borne in mind, however, that, according to the testimony of the publisher on the title-page, even *Peri ha'arets*, which is regarded as R. Menahem Mendel's principal work, was printed from material discovered by R. Eleazer Susman of Tiberias and arranged in the order of the sabbath sermons. The publisher adds that at the beginning, material has been added from the writings of R. Abraham 'the Angel',

The world was created through the free and 'simple' (not complex) will of the Ein Sof. This implies also the principle of man's free will. Since *hitpashetut* (egression) cannot be infinite, there is a second stage in which *tsimtsum* (contraction) occurs, and this is followed by a further series of *tsimtsumim* the purpose of which is to obscure the divine light. If this were not so, nothing could exist but the Ein Sof. Thus R. Menahem Mendel follows in the footsteps of the Maggid in his account of the doctrine of *tsimtsum*, whereas R. Shneur Zalman is more firmly grounded in the traditional world of kabbalah, and subjects such as *tsimtsum*, whether taken literally or merely figuratively, as well as other theological questions, are considered by him with meticulous attention. Thus, for the Maggid and R. Menahem Mendel *tsimtsum* is not a primary act which took place within the Ein Sof; it is not a first stage as in Lurianic kabbalah, but occurs in the *sefirah* Ḥokhmah, after the 'egression', and it means the concealment of the Ayin in order to render possible the revelation of the material world. Hence the saying that *olam*, the world, is derived from *he'alem*, to be hidden.[22] It is interesting that R. Shneur Zalman too explains *tsimtsum* in this way.[23]

Every descent of light to a lower stage increases the number of *tsimtsumim*, but the main point is that there is here a revelation of the divine from within the Ayin—the *sefirah* Keter (crown) which makes immanence possible.[24] For this reason, the Shekhinah, too, is explained not necessarily as the tenth *sefirah* but literally: the Godhead residing (*shokhenet*) in the world. In this connection the verses 'the whole earth is full of His glory' (Isa. 6: 3) and 'You preserve [or 'give life to'] them all' (Neh. 9: 6) are frequently quoted. This immanence is sometimes also called *galut shekhinah*, the exile of the divine presence,[25] without any reference to the kabbalistic meaning of sins and the war

comprising 'Bereshit' as far as the *kavanah* ('intention') of the *mikveh*, where it is stated: 'Here end the holy words of the aforesaid. our master and teacher Rabbi Abraham, which we found' (3*b*). However, in the body of the text there is no indication of where R. Abraham's remarks begin. That problem can be solved by consulting Abraham b. Alexander Katz of Kalisk, *Ḥesed le'Avraham* [Czernowitz, 1851], (Jerusalem, 1954), where, indeed, all the sermons appear, from the beginning of Genesis onward. But 'the intention of the *mikveh*' is not there. The whole question of the attribution of hasidic discourses to various sages, sometimes correctly and sometimes not, needs more rigorous examination than it has yet received, and it is doubtful whether we shall get to the bottom of the matter. By way of example in the present context, I would point out that the preface to *Ḥesed le'Avraham* appears not to have been printed in full, since MS New Haven 72 has a continuation. In any event, I have used all the material as published in *Peri ha'arets*, including the beginning, since it accords with the doctrines of R. Menahem Mendel as they appear in the rest of the book.

It should be pointed out further that some of the homilies are incomplete. See e.g. *Peri ha'arets*, on 'Vayetse', at the end.

A further problem is the language used at the beginning of 'Vayeshev': 'the rabbi began [*pataḥ harav*] . . . and the rabbi explained by another matter'. What is the reason for this choice of words? If the reference was to R. Menahem Mendel, it is interesting to note the application to him of the title 'rabbi'.

22 I have been told several times by Habad hasidim that this flash of linguistic inspiration originated with R. Shneur Zalman. It should be pointed out, however, that it is quoted in Aaron of Opatow, *Keter shem tov* (2 vols.; Zholkva (Zolkiew), 1794–95), in the name of the Besht. It is also mentioned in *Peri ha'arets* on 'Mishpatim'; and in the same period in R. Nahum of Chernobyl's *Me'or Einayim* ('Yismakh Lev'), at the head of Tractate *Beitzah*; and frequently in R. Shneur Zalman's writings.

23 See Hallamish, 'Mishnato ha'iyunit', 95–104.

24 It is apparently for this reason that R. Menahem Mendel writes, in *Peri ha'arets* at the start of 'Bereshit', of the *emanation* of the worlds and the *creation* of Yesh from Ayin.

25 *Peri ha'arets*, 'Sabbath falling during Passover' (after 'Vayikra'); *Likutei amarim*, letter 4, 6*b*, etc.

against evil: the concealment of the Godhead for the purpose of its revelation in the world is itself exile. That is a given situation of the very nature of immanence itself. Consequently the concept of *le'okama shekhinta me'afra* (to raise up the divine presence from the earth), which is referred to in R. Menahem Mendel's letters, for example, in connection with the giving of charity to the poor of Erets Yisrael, is explained as *hafshatat halevushim*—stripping off the outer coverings: 'to strip off all the ways of corporeality, which is "earth", and to raise them up to the place of the [divine] Will',[26] such as devoting the money of the corporeal world to the holy purpose of charity for those in need, those who are broken vessels. And thus the giver, too, 'is raised up together with it to the Ein Sof', although it is important that his intention should be to do the will of God and have no thought of 'reward and personal advantage'.[27] Man's duty is to discover the divinity concealed in those very things which are furthest removed from the source, to see the true light in everything, to elevate the divine vitality to its origin and root, to nullify and become null. 'And man's function above all is to bring forth the precious from the vile [Jer. 15: 19] . . . in whatever he turns to he will succeed and in all his ways he will know what it is that the Lord caused to happen to him and why, and who created these things—the Lord, of course, who brings all things into existence and endows them with life, who surrounds them and fills them', and so on.[28] When man, contemplating God, sees Him in the state of greatest *tsimtsum* and concealment, that is itself the greatest revelation of the Shekhinah. For this reason, anyone who does not see that the perpetuation of the natural order is due to divine providence and thinks that it occurs by chance is nothing but a fool. The true service of Heaven consists in recognizing also 'the nature and habitual state and continuous management of everything, and in truth it is I, even I, Ein Sof blessed be He, but this, however, is in concealment'. Man must match the 'returning' to the 'running' (*shov* and *ratso*—see Ezek. 1: 14), both of which serve to veil the celestial 'creatures'—the standard kabbalistic symbol of divine vitality and energy.[29] In other words, the function of the animal body and soul is to serve the rational, contemplative soul, and if a man follows his animal soul, that is to say if his vision remains limited by the horizons of the material world, he is 'an animal in human form'.[30] However, 'man was created for no other reason than to raise everything up from a lower to a higher level, and to subordinate the outward to the inner reality by discovering His divinity, blessed be He, in everything, there being no place where He is not'.[31]

A person who has attained this condition is, indeed, already in a state of *devekut*, and therefore it is only a man of irreproachable character, a zaddik, who can fulfil this function.[32] In this context we find the expression '*devekut* to the Shekhinah', again without any connection with the Shekhinah as female but in the sense of the divine immanence which pervades and fills all worlds. This sort of *devekut*, it is true, represents a stage which is low in the process of the ascent to *devekut* in the highest sense, but in the process of stripping off the outer coverings it is possible to become absorbed into the Ein Sof. It should be noted that, in these descriptions, the chain of the *sefirot* is not

[26] *Likutei amarim*, letter 4, 6*b*–7*a*.
[27] Ibid. 7*a*.
[28] *Peri ha'arets*, on 'Koraḥ'.
[29] Ibid., on 'Bo'.
[30] Ibid., on 'Behar'.
[31] Ibid., on 'Vayigash'.
[32] Ibid., on 'Bereshit', etc.

mentioned; as if its sole purpose were to serve as the contraction (*tsimtsum*) of the light of the Ein Sof descending from Ayin to Yesh. However, on the way upward again, the climb is really rapid.

Devekut is not a state of spontaneous illumination but is attained stage by stage. First comes fear. R. Abraham of Kalisk placed the utmost emphasis on the fear of punishment; he wrote in the name of his master R. Menahem Mendel:

> The beginning of worship every day is one of the aspects of the fear of punishment. And this [fear] is very necessary. That is where you begin, and once you see that you have attained the utmost fear of punishment, you ascend from that to fear of God's eminence (*romemut*) and to true love. And anyone who discards the fear of punishment will inevitably fall into the pit of destruction.[33]

However, this fear denotes distance, a condition which is opposed to *devekut*. Therefore a higher stage is constituted by the fear of God's eminence, or the fear of shame before the One who is the absolute master and ruler of the very essence and root of all worlds. It is true that even in this state a certain distance remains, but there is nevertheless a greater affinity and the gap is anyway narrowed. The next stage is a fear which is above all the varieties of love and beyond all the attributes, 'and that is when you clothe yourself in the Shekhinah and apply yourself wholly to serving as a chariot for Him, blessed be He . . . for they [who act thus] annul themselves and are absorbed into the channels of divine flow, and in that case fear is perfect *devekut*, for one becomes a part of the Ein Sof'.[34] That is to say, self-annulment and, correspondingly, clothing oneself in the Shekhinah or inclusion in the Ein Sof is perfect *devekut*.[35]

Coupled with the references to fear, references to faith frequently occur. 'Let him first accept the yoke of the kingdom of Heaven, which is fear and faith, as is well known. And then let him accept the yoke of the commandments and the yoke of the Torah', and this 'will teach him attachment to the Lord (*hitkasherut*) and love of Him and cleaving to His attributes', while at the same time overcoming the evil inclination; 'which would not be the case if he did not give first place to fear and faith in the Lord and the Torah . . . All the Torah and the commandments would be of no avail, and he would remain as grossly material a person as ever.'[36] R. Menahem Mendel returns repeatedly to the concept of faith. He sees the absence of faith as the cause of the Exile.[37] Faith is what leads to *devekut*, through the development of the personal attributes. In this arrangement the intellect has no place, and this is no accident. 'Certainly all one's [intellectual] attainments are quite without value and devoid of any *devekut* whatsoever. Let him live in his faith, to cleave to Him, blessed be He . . . for this faith emanates *from none other than Him Himself, blessed be He*.'[38] Here the intellect

[33] *Likutei amarim*, letter 38, 42*a*.

[34] *Peri ha'arets*, on 'Ekev'.

[35] I would not conclude from this sentence, in the context in which it appears, that we have here an actual reference to *unio mystica*, as was alleged by Moshe Idel, *Kabbalah: New Perspectives* (New Haven, 1988), 308. (Incidentally, there is an error in the page reference there because of incorrect pagination. '24*b*' should read '32*b*'.) However, other sources will be quoted below which clearly refer to the experience of *unio mystica*.

[36] *Peri ha'arets* on 'Devarim'. With regard to fear and faith, cf. also the letter of R. Abraham of Kalisk written in 1797, *Likutei amarim*, letter 38, 41a.

[37] *Peri ha'arets*, on 'Vayigash'.

[38] Ibid., on 'Lekh lekha', at the end. For the evaluation of the intellect see more below, p. 280.

is set in opposition to faith, for two reasons which are really one and the same: (*a*) the direct source of faith is the divinity, while the intellect is human—an argument which is of fundamental importance to the mystics; (*b*) therefore active faith has positive consequences, whereas the exercise of the intellect does not lead to religious achievements. Even the patriarch Abraham 'did not rely on his intellectual grasp' and overcame his doubts only through the power of faith.[39] And if that was true of Abraham, how much more must it apply to ordinary men. 'When a person falls, Heaven forbid, into opposition to Him, blessed be He, on rational grounds, what mainly helps him and enables him to ascend is simple faith, without any reasons or reasoning at all, for it [faith] can rend mountains and break rocks into pieces [Kgs. 19: 11]. If he is of stone, he is softened by the power of faith, and without it there is no cure or remedy for him; he cannot gain strength by the exercise of reason or intellect'.[40] The fact that the intellect is a human faculty carries with it its own limitation. The intellect sees multiplicity and restriction where faith points to wholeness and inner unity.[41] It needs to be added that multiplicity is a characteristic feature of the *sitra aḥra*, the forces of evil. That is how we should interpret the statement: 'The greatest knowledge of all is not to know.' That is to say, 'Whatever one succeeds in comprehending of the Divinity is itself a limitation . . . except only by faith, which is infinitely higher than the intellect can reach.'[42] The best example for R. Menahem Mendel is the contrast between Noah and Abraham. The faith of the righteous Noah was not founded on any process of reason: he overcame troublesome questions through his perfect faith in the Creator.[43] Abraham, on the other hand, recognized his Creator when he was 3 years old, according to Midrash; that is, he had a highly developed intellectual consciousness, and in the end, in spite of this, he realized the limitations of the intellect in the endeavour to reach the Ein Sof. And then he returned to faith—'And he believed in the Lord' (Gen. 15: 6). Emphasis is therefore laid on the verse 'And the righteous shall live by his faith' (Hab. 2: 4). At any rate it appears that R. Menahem Mendel did not totally deny the achievements of the intellect, on the grounds that Abraham himself made use of it, but he points out its limitations.[44] He explicitly states: 'The essence of the service of Heaven and of attachment (*hitkasherut*) to Him, blessed be He, is to attain the true *devekut* which is reached *after* all that the intellect can succeed in understanding.' However, in what he goes on to say there are indications that he rejects the intellect and holds it in open contempt: 'After all his intellectual and speculative endeavours to grasp *devekut*, let him believe with true faith, because of his own humility, that he must regard himself as dust and ashes, and then certainly all his intellectual attainments will be seen to be worthless.'[45]

The great importance that R. Menahem Mendel attached to faith can be seen in the astounding example (admittedly linked to the interpretation of scriptural verses) which he adduced in order to explain in concrete terms the difference between a person who

[39] *Likutei amarim*, letter 6, 11*b*. Cf. *Peri ha'arets*, on 'Vayera'.

[40] *Likutei amarim*, letter 11*a*. Cf. *Peri ha'arets*, on 'Vayera', at the beginning.

[41] *Likutei amarim*, letter 18, 24*a* (written in 1787).

[42] Ibid. Cf. also the letter of R. Abraham of Kalisk, ibid., letter 38, 41*a*.

[43] According to R. Menahem Mendel, this is why the reasons for the commandments were not explained in the Torah, for 'what is important above all is to cleave to what is beyond one's understanding' (*Peri ha'arets* on 'Tetsaveh'). Cf. also Rivka Schatz-Uffenheimer, *Haḥasidut kemistikah* (Jerusalem, 1968), 57.

[44] Cf. Tishby and Dan, 'Ḥasidut', 812.

[45] *Peri ha'arets*, on 'Lekh lekha'.

fulfils the Torah and the commandments spontaneously and one who fulfils them after faith is implanted in him. Torah not preceded by fear and faith is valueless, like consorting with a prostitute in order to satisfy a momentary appetite, in contrast to regular marital intercourse.[46] In other words, faith has a kind of settling and stabilizing power.

It should be pointed out that for R. Shneur Zalman, in contrast to R. Menahem Mendel, faith is a *fundamental* attribute presumed to exist in all Jews as a matter of course, since belief is inherent in them, and at *this* level faith exists without any special cause. But by passing through and beyond a stage of profound rational speculation, one reaches the highest stage of faith and *devekut*.[47]

Devekut appears on various levels in R. Menahem Mendel's writings. Its importance can be judged from one sentence: 'That from occupying oneself with the Torah and the commandments one arrives at perfect *devekut*. For the Torah is a spice (*tavlin*)[!]'[48] A spice or condiment can indeed impart flavour, but the essential is *devekut*.

R. Menahem Mendel frequently couples faith with *devekut*, just as, indeed, there similarly occurs in one place in *Maggid devarav leYa'akov* the explicit statement that 'faith is *devekut*'.[49] In other words, *devekut* is faith without the application of reason. Man cannot attain any element of divinity, but he can perceive the unity and interconnection of everything with the immanence of God in our world. By the very fact that he recognizes and believes in the constant presence of God, he achieves *devekut*. 'But *devekut* in Him [cleaving to Him] is by faith alone, unaccompanied by any reasons of love, affection or desire.'[50] In one place he quotes the rabbinic saying 'Let man always first offer (*yesader*) praise to God and then pray' [Ber. 32*a*], and he explains that it is not a question of the arrangement (*seder*) of times based on a hierarchic concern to show due honour—that is, first to adopt a proper attitude to the Holy One, blessed be He, and then to ask for the fulfilment of one's needs—but first to meditate on the immanent totality of the Divinity, and this would of itself lead him to prayer, which is to say, to *devekut*.[51] Man reaches *devekut* through the world, through corporality. In this sense, 'the great delight' is that 'he was distant and has drawn near'.[52] And that is the meaning of the terse statement: 'It is the Shekhinah that is called prayer, which consists in truly cleaving to (*devekut be-*) the Supreme Will through faith without any reason.'[53] That is to say, prayer seeks the Divine Presence because man's contemplation is directed towards the manifestations of the Divinity in the world, without any need for rational processes of thought: it is enough to have faith in this axiom, which, of itself, leads to '*truly* cleaving to the Supreme Will'. Other passages, too, demonstrate that no distinction is drawn between 'a man's business and his speech, his [observance of the] commandments, his [study of] the Torah and his prayer'.[54]

46 Ibid., on 'Matot' and 'Mas'ei', second sermon.

47 See Hallamish, 'Mishnato ha'iyunit', 200–8, where the point is treated more extensively.

48 *Peri ha'arets*, on 'Devarim', at the end.

49 See I. Tishby, *Mishnat hazohar* (2 vols.; Jerusalem, 1971); trans. as *The Wisdom of the Zohar* (3 vols.; Oxford, 1989), iii. 1015 n. 446.

50 *Peri ha'arets*, on 'Lekh lekha'.

51 Ibid., on 'Bo'. For a similar idea cf. *Keter shem tov* [Korets, 1797] 12*b*.

52 Ibid., on 'Koraḥ', where, incidentally, this path to *devekut* is called *ahavah mesuteret*—concealed love. The term is interpreted variously in the literature, e.g. by the Shelah, R. Shneur Zalman, and others.

53 *Peri ha'arets*, on 'Lekh lekha'.

54 Ibid., 'Sabbath falling during Passover', at the end.

There are, however, passages emphasizing that *devekut* is attained through 'holiness which is not the observance of the commandments or the study of the Torah or prayer'.[55] It seems that the intention here is to stress that this attainment is possible only through religious action and not through contact with corporeal and material things. Similarly in another passage: '*Mitsvah* means *tsavta*—togetherness—which is true *devekut* even in the lowest and most earthly of the low, a pleasant savour to the Lord who spoke and whose will was done. And that is the greatest joy before Him, blessed be He, and there are no bounds to the joy of the worldly ones [through observance of the commandments], exceeding that of all the spiritual beings.'[56]

A higher level of *devekut* finds expression in his statement that entry into the religious world demands the absolute abandonment of everything that went before, since attachment to any particular thing of itself demands severance from the past. In other words, one must abandon the material world in order to be able to realize *devekut*. For since Torah and the fulfilment of the commandments 'are, in a literal sense, Divinity', and since 'man is literally part of God on high', it follows that 'when a man immerses himself and all his thoughts in them with all his heart and soul and might, with desire and longing and *devekut*', and, as stated, this path exists, empathically, only '*when a man enters with his whole self* into some holy matter, some *mitsvah* or Torah and prayer, with such complete *devekut* that he divests himself of his previous attachment to material things and no longer notices them at all . . . he now clothes himself in a holy spirit. And when he clothes himself in the words (*teivot*) of the Torah and prayer, the scriptural verse [Gen. 7: 1] applies to him: "Go into the ark (*teivah*), you and all your family", for he enters into it with his whole self . . .[57] The annulment of the remnants of his previous feelings constitutes complete unity with Him, blessed be He . . . he enters into communion with Him, blessed be He, with nothing intervening between them' 'and experiences something of the taste of the world to come'.[58] Without doubt he thus attains a superlatively high degree of spiritual elevation.

It may sometimes occur that a man reaches a stage of ecstasy, and this precisely when he is turning from his past in penitence: that is to say, when he considers his sins and grieves ('out of his great bitterness') that he has allowed the vitality of holiness to enter into the *kelipah*, the husk of evil, he reaches a state in which his bitterness is so great that 'a fire not fanned [by man] [Job 20: 26] takes hold of him, to which he cannot respond in any words but only by an inarticulate groan . . . and he simply cries out to the Lord, and God answers him by a voice [Exod. 19: 19], for thereby the letters are

[55] *Peri ha'arets*, on 'Vayeshev', sabbath preceding Ḥanukah.

[56] Ibid., on 'Re'eh'. See also 'Yitro'; *Peri ets*, on 'Beshalaḥ'. This idea serves R. Menahem Mendel to explain why the pious look forward to the resurrection of the dead, for they desire to be in their bodies 'out of the greatness of the joy of bodily service of the Creator, blessed be His name' (ibid., on 'Re'eh'). A similar view was expressed by R. Shneur Zalman of Lyady in *Likutei torah* [Zhitomir, 1848] (Brooklyn, NY, 1984) on 'Behar', 42*b*. And the same reason is advanced to explain why a repentant sinner is greater than a zaddik, for he has already used his physical attributes for material purposes, and he now elevates them by his service of Heaven (*Peri ha'arets* on 'Ki tetse').

[57] This exegesis of the verse is apparently that of the Maggid. Cf. the opening of *Likutim yekarim* [Lemberg, 1792], ed. Abraham Isaac Kahan (Jerusalem, 1974); *Tsava'at haRibash* [n.p. (Ostrog?), 1793; Zolkiew, 1795], ed. J. I. Schochet (Brooklyn, NY, 1975), 8.

[58] See n. 55 above. On *devekut* which demands the abandonment of everything corporeal, including family ties, cf. *Tanya*, ch. 49, 137.

raised above evil.'[59] What is described here is a condition so exalted as to be beyond the possibility of utterance in words, and which can be expressed only in an ecstatic mystical experience. Another matter connected with this is the *simḥah shel mitsvah* (joy of fulfilling a religious precept), to which R. Menahem Mendel returns.[60]

Devekut at its highest level is sometimes formulated in very strong terms. For example, 'The path of *devekut* consists in the annihilation of self, which is perfect unity [in a bond] of love which is as strong as death [S. of S. 8: 6] and which makes parting difficult.'[61] Or 'to bind them and unify them with Him so that they become one in perfect *devekut*'.[62] And spelt out in detail: 'The meaning of *devekut* is that there should be nothing intervening, then it is possible to achieve *devekut*. Like the comparison drawn by the Baal Shem Tov, that it is impossible to solder two pieces of silver together unless one scrapes down to the actual silver at the point where the join is to be made; then it holds well . . . It is necessary to scrape one's personality so that no tarnish remains on it, nor any separating covering, but only the essential personality; then *devekut* becomes possible.'[63] It would seem unnecessary to add to formulations expressed in such clear terms, but it is further stated that the basis of *devekut* is that 'since man is an actual part of God on high, he should be able to join himself in perfect unity to Him, blessed be He, without any intervening barrier or separating curtain'.[64] This same starting point, of the return of the branch to its root, of the cleaving of the part to the perfect whole, also appears in another homily, and entitles us to conclude that there is nothing casual in this entire approach:

for when he concerns himself with the root of their [the worlds'] creation and touches it, all the branches are moved by the root, and when man is included in them because he resembles an angel [!] . . . and then he delivers his soul to be united with the Shekhinah (*moser nafsho bashekhinah*), then he climbs upward *through* the worlds and *together with* all the worlds, ever upward by means of the *mitsvot* . . . until his soul succeeds in divesting itself of concrete attributes, namely love, fear, etc., in order that he should cleave to their root and touch it directly, without any intervening barrier.

This mystical and ecstatic description of 'cleaving to their root directly without any intervening barrier' is referred to further on as 'a marvellous and impenetrable secret, which cannot be revealed because it is disclosed to none but oneself'.[65] There is no doubt that in these descriptions R. Menahem Mendel rose to an extremely high mystical level for which it is not easy to find parallels. A similar statement, however, is made by R. Shneur Zalman:

And it is in the nature of a merging of the Jewish people *into the Source that hewed them out*, with a unification so perfect that they are regarded as actually one body, etc. For example, when one joins two different things together with glue, the advantage of glueing them together is that they become so closely united as to be regarded as a single body . . . and it is as if he were actually glued to the Lord, etc., and through the strength of this adhesion he could never be separated . . . *and although he concerns himself with business affairs all day long* and is in close

[59] *Peri ha'arets*, on 'Va'etḥanan'. Incidentally, the expression 'to cry out to the Lord' used by R. Menahem Mendel is apparently not lightly chosen. Cf. M. Hallamish, *Nativ laTanya* (Tel Aviv, 1987), 250 and n. 22.

[60] *Peri ha'arets*, on 'Ki tetse', 'Ki tavo', etc.

[61] Ibid., on Shabbat Naḥamu.

[62] *Peri ets*, on 'Noaḥ'.

[63] *Peri ha'arets*, on 'Ki tisa'.

[64] Ibid., on 'Vayeshev', sabbath preceding Ḥanukah.

[65] *Peri ets*, on 'Ki tetse'.

proximity to the influence of the 'external' [evil] forces of the desire for alien [material] things, this will not in the least break his unity with the Lord, because he has been united to Him through prayer and joined with Him in a union so close as to be inseparable for ever etc. And that is what is meant by 'And to Him you shall cleave' [Deut. 13: 5], i.e. *in true devekut* so as to become literally one.[66]

Particularly in the remarkable latter description, the word *devekut* is given its simplest meaning, derived from *davak*, to stick. But the power of the description is obvious in both cases, and it seems to me that herein lies the secret of the close bond between these two outstanding men. In any event, we have here clear evidence to counter Gershom Scholem's assumption that the concept of *unio mystica* does not exist in Jewish thought.

We need, however, to set the matter in proper perspective. The late Professor Rivka Schatz-Uffenheimer defined R. Menahem Mendel's doctrine as consisting '*entirely* [the emphasis is mine—M.H.] of extreme spiritualism while deliberately preaching the daily fulfilment of the commandments'.[67] In my opinion, the matter needs to be seen in a somewhat different light, or at least certain additional points need to be mentioned in order to complete the picture.

Two contrasting strata may be distinguished in R. Menahem Mendel's doctrine. The first is that of simple faith, without any reason or logical explanation (i.e. without any *sevara*). The justification for this is that in an intellectual argument it is always possible to advance a counter-argument,[68] and no clear-cut decision can be reached. This is also made clear in another passage in which R. Menahem Mendel puts forward the principle of *zeh le'umat zeh*, the existence of opposites, which is a central principle of Creation. Man therefore encounters things which are 'upside down'.[69] The mind confines man within the limits of his intellectual grasp, that is to say, still in this world, where dualism and lack of clarity are part of the normal order. As against this, if a man rises beyond the world to the realm of the Ein Sof he discovers there that in the Source everything is one, without any alteration or substitution, and that that is the true creative principle which endows everything with life. This insight can be attained only by means of faith, which is firmly anchored in the true reality of things and which alone can define them. It goes without saying that to achieve this a man must be active in his religious life. The fulfilment of practical *mitsvot* is a vital stage. Moreover, it generates social uniformity.

Contrasting with the stratum of simple faith there is the spiritual level. This is not a matter for simple folk, but a personal path appropriate solely for the elect, a path that cannot even be explained to others. However, this contrast is the very soul of hasidism, a movement within which simple folk and people of exalted spirit are closely associated. The factor common to all of them is their final goal; where they differ is in the means of attaining that goal, and the means, of itself, confers a certain distinctive quality on the goal.

The contrast referred to may be observed in another area: the difference between

66 Preface to the prayer book, headword 'aḥarei hashem', 26. And see similar remarks in Shneur Zalman of Lyady, *Ma'amrei Admor haZaken 5562* [1801–2] (2 vols.; Brooklyn, NY, 1964–81), 58.

67 Schatz-Uffenheimer, *Haḥasidut kemistikah*, 64.

68 *Likutei amarim*, letter 6, 11*a*. See above, n. 38.

69 *Peri ha'arets*, on 'Lekh lekha'. There is no need to interpret this word as meaning 'paradoxical', as Schatz-Uffenheimer does: *Haḥasidut kemistikah*, 58.

the fear of punishment and the fear of God's majesty. In a homily on the Torah portion 'Balak' (Num. 22–5), R. Menahem Mendel lets slip almost casually the observation that the fear of punishment is universal, necessary even to 'the great and the zaddikim'. On the other hand, the fear of God's majesty is personal, 'and therefore it is impossible for any man to attune his deeds and thoughts and ways to the ways of some zaddik in order to be like him, because sometimes the ethical norms and conduct of that zaddik will be of no use to him. And even for one man it is impossible to be the same in his own eyes and [unchanging in] his ways and ethical standards day by day; everything depends on the time.'[70]

To return to our main topic: in a letter written in 1784, R. Menahem Mendel says:

As soon as he rises in the morning, a man ought to be ready to serve his Creator, and to give first place to the soul. For it is the soul that is the principal thing and not the material being, which perishes and is lost. And to be in as spiritual a state as possible, that is the great principle, and therefore one should not act or calculate one's actions with a view to the world to come. For whatever he achieves in this world while he is still in his body is corporeal. And even if he takes care, in his endeavour to attain the world to come, to refrain from any kind of worldly action, by whatever means he attains his goal it will still be corporeal, since he has attained it while still inhabiting his body.[71]

That, then, is the fundamental aim: 'to give first place to the soul', to aspire to spiritualization through renunciation of the thoughts and possessions of this world.[72] And if a person follows this path, he perceives no distinction between 'the affairs of this world and the performance of the commandments', for

such is the way of all *devekut* and union with God's holiness, blessed be He and his Shekhinah, in the affairs of this world or the performance of the commandments and the Torah; it is to cleave [to Him] in perfect *devekut* and to continue to clothe oneself in that same holy vitality that resides in one's business affairs, one's speech, one's fulfilment of the commandments, one's study of the Torah, and one's prayer. It is that which cleanses the bodily organs and all material substance, releasing them from the power of evil (*kelipot*). For when he admits the Lord, blessed be He, into himself, there all the doers of evil are scattered [Ps. 92: 10].[73]

When one reaches 'the root of the whole Torah and the commandments, which is . . . simple unity and Ein Sof, when he stands there, the wings of all the commandments and statutes droop limply, and all are nullified, for that condition is the nullification of the evil inclination.'[74] True, Adam required only one commandment—*devekut*—and Abraham only love, but 'because of the inadequacy of the human mind everyone [else] needs . . . all the commandments of the Torah and the fences round it, which are combinations of principles of conduct and counsels for cleaving to the Creator, blessed be He'.[75] Even one who is spiritual on the most exalted level fulfils *mitsvot*, but he does so naturally, as a matter which has no heteronomous significance but springs autonomously from the depths of his heart.[76]

[70] Cf. also *Peri ha'arets*, on 'Matot' and 'Mas'ei'.

[71] *Likutei amarim*, letter 4, 6*b*.

[72] Cf. Schatz-Uffenheimer, *Haḥasidut kemistikah*, 33, 42, and elsewhere.

[73] *Peri ha'arets*, 'Sabbath falling during Passover', at the end.

[74] Ibid., on 'Toledot'.

[75] *Likutei amarim*, letter 18, 24*b*.

[76] *Peri ha'arets*, on 'Toledot'.

The clearest description of this spiritual state occurs in a homily in which R. Menahem Mendel mentions

> the ancients who did not know whether it was night or day or how many days it was since they had entered into that state of wisdom which consisted in casting off everything corporeal . . . The man who applies himself and his vitality entirely and solely to speculative wisdom and contemplation of the greatness of the Creator, may His name be blessed, and leaves behind all corporeality and all the various worlds and attributes until he has ascended to the greatness of intensive contemplation of divine wisdom with all his strength and vitality and with his whole self . . . such a man is called *a godly man* . . . to sum up, that he himself should be as if he did not exist, abandoning both his body and his soul, in some manner to be blotted out of this world and the world to come for the sake of the sanctification of His name, blessed be He, and in any event that he should not be drawn by his desires in any direction save only towards Him, blessed be His name, through the intensity of his contemplation of the greatness of the Creator . . . *for what does it matter to him how or what he is and in what manner he exists, or whether he was never created or whether he was created and perished* . . . for his individuality has already been altogether annihilated through his contemplation of the greatness of the Creator, blessed be His name. And all his desire and his longing are only that His name, blessed be He, should be magnified and sanctified and that His divinity should be revealed. Now *certainly a wise man such as this will be detached from everything*, for he has no desire for anything, 'and the Lord alone will be exalted on that day' [Isa. 2: 11].[77]

So hyperbolic a description ranks R. Menahem Mendel with the Quietists.

There is, however, another side to the coin. Certainly it would be a noble thing for a man to start his day with worship of the Creator, to persevere in his worship to the point of perfect *devekut*, and to strive to attain such lofty pinnacles. But life is complex, and man is put to a severe test every day in contending with material and corporeal things. Moreover, R. Menahem Mendel says explicitly that it is impossible to practise complete abstinence from everything corporeal, since Scripture says 'and live by them' (Lev. 18: 5). But the reason he goes on to give is much more 'convincing': we are not commanded to be angels! 'If indeed one were, of a certainty, pure and holy—one would be like the ministering angels. Nevertheless the Torah was *not* given to the ministering angels.'[78] That, he says, is why the practical commandments were given, for 'matter can be purified by nothing but [the fulfilment of] *practical* commandments'.[79] That, too, was the purpose of the practical instructions concerning 'worship through corporeality', the battle against 'straying thoughts' (*mahshavot zarot*), and so on. 'In sum,' says R. Menahem Mendel, 'without contemplation and the attainment of *devekut*, the fulfilment of commandment[s] is itself corporeal, and conversely, without the commandment[s] which are a corporeal matter, contemplation and the attainment of *devekut* do not bring a man into communion with the Creator.'[80] In this way, it appears, the emphasis on spirituality is softened. It is not clear whether the remarks are addressed to all who seek to share this experience, to inform them that no one is entitled to forgo corporeal matters and religious worship,[81] or whether the intention is to distinguish between different types of people: there are some who can ascend by purely

[77] *Peri ets*, on 'Kedoshim'; italics mine.
[78] *Peri ha'arets*, on 'Re'eh'.
[79] Ibid., on 'Naso'.
[80] *Peri ets*, on 'Noaḥ', at the end.
[81] And see the treatment *in extenso* in Schatz-Uffenheimer, *Haḥasidut kemistikah*, ch. 5.

spiritual endeavour, while others must always couple spirituality with practical endeavour, in order to ascend.

This leads to a consideration of the opposite aspect, that of the material world. Professor Schatz-Uffenheimer was indeed right in saying that R. Menahem Mendel showed 'no enthusiasm for worship through corporality',[82] but nevertheless he did express himself explicitly in its favour. Two points of view must be distinguished. The first concentrates attention on the central cosmic principle that the Divinity lies concealed in everything. Therefore, when a person *chances to encounter* some object of love, he should not love its material aspect but should realize that it is 'its inner vitality' which inspires him with love for material substance; 'therefore he should cleave in his love to the inner vitality in that thing',[83] That, then, is the way to bring the divine element to the surface, as explained above. But there is another point of view which places not the Divinity but man at the centre. For example, R. Menahem Mendel speaks of physical pleasure 'which is to serve a bodily requirement and fulfil a commandment'. And then the Holy One, blessed be He, pays regard to the intention of the doer, and therefore the blessing pronounced by the doer is not 'on the corporeal act' but on the fulfilment of the commandment, 'which is in the nature of "In all your ways acknowledge Him" [Prov. 3: 6]'.[84] The very link with 'In all your ways' shows that it is possible to strip *every action* of its corporeal covering and to intend by it or by means of it the performance of a spiritual act 'which is in the nature of "In all your ways acknowledge Him" so as to act in all corporeal matters with *devekut* and attachment to the Shekhinah'.[85] As a corollary of this approach, 'if a man regards himself during his meal as consuming food given to him from the house of the King, the Holy One, blessed be He, and he eats and drinks and beholds God, drawing near to Him by means of the meal . . . the vitality he acquires in eating is increased, and this vitality itself has reached the level of "this is the law for man" [2 Sam. 7: 19], and by everything that he does subsequently for the sake of Heaven, the vitality, too, is exalted.'[86] Moreover, it is possible that he will come to acquire the supernatural power of control over matter, and then he will even be able to bring about supernatural changes in the physical world.[87]

It is true that this approach is accompanied by the risk that a man may become immersed in material things and externalities and will not rise to become exalted. Fundamentally, to be sure, 'our teaching [*toratenu*] is one of truth and faithfulness, that man is certainly forbidden to expose himself to temptation, to immerse himself in straying thoughts in order to raise them up, Heaven forbid, for who knows if he will be as strong as a lion and rise up or whether he will descend ever lower and not be equal to the test.'[88] And from the injunction against immersing oneself in straying thoughts, it follows all the more clearly that 'it is not the intention, nor is man commanded, Heaven forbid, to transgress—may that be far from us—in order to arouse his ardour';[89]

[82] Ibid. 61.
[83] *Igeret hakodesh*, 1*b*, headwords '*vezehu bekhol derakheikha da'ehu*'. And cf. *Likutei amarim*, letter 9, 15*a*.
[84] *Peri ha'arets*, on 'Re'eh'.
[85] Ibid., 'Sabbath falling during Passover'.
[86] Ibid., on 'Vayigash', second sermon.
[87] *Likutei amarim*, letter 9, 15*a*.
[88] See n. 86 above; and also Tishby and Dan, 'Ḥasidut', 787.
[89] *Peri ha'arets*, on 'Ki tisa'.

unless, that is, 'he unintentionally finds himself confronted by the test, when certainly it is sent by the Lord to test him, and he must exert all his strength and devotion to prevail over it'.[90] That is to say, he is not to content himself with rejecting the straying thought, but must elevate it—unless it is to be feared that he will be unable to direct his mind to performing the action for the sake of its merit but will act for his own benefit, for then it would be better 'not to use it [the extraneous thought, the *kelipah*] at all'.[91] But 'when a man genuinely draws near to God in his innermost heart . . . [and] straying thoughts or attributes are awakened in him, since their desire is to be raised up, for behold, there is a place prepared beside them [an echo of Exod. 33: 21—'behold, there is a place beside Me'], to raise them up through repentance so that he becomes ready to serve in the Sanctuary',[92] then undoubtedly the obligation is imposed on him to bring them to repentance.

This point of view is also evident in another place, where R. Menahem Mendel 'resolves' an alleged contradiction between two scriptural verses. Ps. 33: 18 says: 'Behold, the eye of the Lord is upon them that fear him,' 'eye' being in the singular, whereas Ps. 34: 16 says: 'the eyes [plural] of the Lord are upon the righteous.' Consequently R. Menahem Mendel distinguishes between the God-fearing man and the zaddik. The God-fearing man is afraid of war against the evil inclination, and therefore rejects the evil inclination outright. He serves the Lord only with his good inclination, and hence 'eye' is written in the singular. By contrast, the zaddik brings both inclinations, the good and the evil, into equal partnership and 'binds together all the worlds, from the lesser spiritual levels (*katnut*) to the greater (*gadlut*) and to simple unity . . . and he does not reject *katnut*'. It is the latter person, of course, who is the better of the two (for which reason 'eyes' is written in the plural).[93] This viewpoint is similar to that expressed by R. Shneur Zalman in chs. 27–8 of the *Tanya*: the average man must reject temptation, and is advised against doing otherwise, because 'a man who wallows in the dust with what is vile becomes vile himself'. But the zaddik is at the level of converting evil to good; he is allowed, or even obliged, to concern himself also with deviant thoughts, and thereby to elevate them too (though these are the thoughts of others, since the zaddik himself, *ipso facto*, no longer entertains evil thoughts, according to the view of R. Shneur Zalman).

R. Menahem Mendel's doctrine of the zaddik contains some of the distinctive ingredients of hasidism. For example, from a personal point of view, 'sometimes a certain descent from the level of their thoughts is brought about in the zaddikim, but the truth is that this descent is only for the sake of further ascent'. This topic appears in hasidism in various contexts, but in the present context the matter is not elaborated. And from the social point of view R. Menahem Mendel establishes an important point: the zaddik, who is also called *ha'adam hakasher*, the man of unblemished character, is the socio-religious centre, like the Temple. 'To sum up, in the case of each and every

[90] n. 86 above. In principle, this is also the approach expounded in *Tsava'at haRibash*, where we read: 'If he has *suddenly* looked upon a beautiful woman', and not that one should deliberately seek out such temptation. The text goes on to explain that one should immediately begin to think of the source of her beauty and see the divine vitality etc., similarly to the sentiments we shall find expressed in the immediately following passage. See *Tsava'at HaRibash*, 23; Dov Ber of Mezhirech, *Or torah* (Jerusalem, 1968), on 'Tehilim', 105*b*.

[91] *Peri ha'arets*, on 'Bo'.

[92] n. 86 above.

[93] *Peri ha'arets*, on 'Vayeshev', at the end.

zaddik, everything that he encounters must pass through his thoughts until it reaches the place of his spiritual elevation. And even if a person claiming to be a Hasid says that he has already annulled all his feelings and desires, a fool does not realize that if he has not got them in one respect he has them in others.'[94]

Sometimes the figure of the zaddik appears cosmic in scale, 'binding together all the worlds from *katnut* to *gadlut*',[95] or, 'a zaddik . . . binds together all the worlds from the supreme root to the lowest depths, and through them [the zaddikim] all the worlds are conducted'.[96] But the most striking statement made about the zaddik is that it is within his power to bring about changes in the processes of nature and perform miracles and wonders. It is true that we also find similar remarks in R. Joseph Gikatilla's *Sha'arei orah*, but there the reference is to 'proper prayer', by means of which treasuries on high are opened up, 'and nothing can stand before him'.[97] It appears, therefore, that the passage refers solely to prayer. The subject of the 'change' (*hishtanut*) effected by the zaddik sometimes appears in *Maggid devarav le Ya'akov*, too.[98] But in R. Menahem Mendel's writings the idea is repeated in striking fashion. It is the zaddik who leads all things to the Source, and at the starting point it is possible to begin a new order of life. This even takes place 'of itself', without any additional preparation.[99] So great is the power of the zaddik that he is called '*ba'alah dematronit*, husband (or master) of the "matron"—Shekhinah or Malkhut—for he is master of the conduct of all the worlds' of which she is in charge, according to the kabbalistic scheme, and it is within his power 'to effect any change, miracles and wonders'.[100] He gives more light to the world than the sun at noon, and he is called the *memalé makom*,[101] the deputy—literally one who fills the place—of the Ein Sof. What is meant by this designation is a person who makes it possible for God—who is *mekomo shel olam*, the place of the world, according to the Midrash (and is also known as Hamakom, 'the Place')—literally to fill all the earth with His glory (as in Isa. 6: 3). A man who comes to recognize this is called *ḥakham*, wise—not, however, in the intellectual sense, but in the sense that he is

[94] Ibid., on 'Matot' and 'Mas'ei'.

[95] n. 93 above. And cf. Dov Ber of Mezhirech, *Maggid devarav le Ya'akov*, ed. R. Schatz-Uffenheimer (Jerusalem, 1976), 41*b*.

[96] *Peri ha'arets*, on 'Ekev', at the end. Cf. *Maggid devarav le Ya'akov*, 275: 'The intellect of the Zaddik encompasses the entire universe.'

[97] To quote him more fully: 'Proper prayer which gathers strength and ascends from *sefirah* to *sefirah* until it reaches the Will, which adheres to the *sefirah* Keter . . . and when the prayer reaches the place of the Will, all the gates above and below are opened before him and there is none there to hinder or obstruct his petition, for he is in the world of compassion [*raḥamim*]. And then all his needs and requests will be fulfilled, and nothing can stand in his way, for he draws [power] from the place of the Will, and can perform new signs and wonders as if the world were only then being created' (Joseph Gikatilla, *Sha'arei orah* (Warsaw, 1883), 'Sha'ar no. 9', 95*a*). And see also Ephraim Gottlieb, *Meḥkarim besifrut hakabalah* (Tel Aviv, 1976), 36.

[98] See e.g. *Maggid devarav le Ya'akov*, 220: 'that the Zaddik can effect a change whenever he wishes'. Similarly ibid. 23: 'If the Zaddik attaches himself to the primordial Will, he will be able to draw change[s] from there [if] he wishes to perform a miracle.'

[99] See *Peri ha'arets*, on 'Vayigash', headwords 'kelala demilta'.

[100] Ibid., on 'Ekev'. Generally, in kabbalah, *matronita* is a name for the *sefirah* Shekhinah, and her husband is, of course, Tiferet. But R. Menahem Mendel is faithful to his doctrine: the Shekhinah for him denotes the divine immanence in the world. It follows that the husband of the Shekhinah is he who has the power to introduce and determine changes in the order of the world.

[101] *Peri ha'arets*, on 'Bo' (twice).

identified with the *sefirah* Ḥokhmah, which derives from Ayin–Keter, from which the spread of immanence begins.[102]

The position of the zaddik in his *devekut* is not one of absolute self-annulment but, on the contrary, one of positive emulation of the Holy One, blessed be He, in that he becomes a source of the flow of divine bounty to all the worlds, and even to the *kelipot*, the forces of evil, for Scripture says 'and You give life to them all' (Neh. 9: 6; the versions translate 'You preserve them all'). For all the righteous deeds of the zaddikim, their chief desire is to cleave to the Lord, for the characteristic of the zaddik is *hitkasherut*, attachment to Him.[103]

R. Shneur Zalman's image of the zaddik is very different. He sees the zaddik's activity as essentially introspective—the conversion of the evil within him to holiness—whereas R. Menahem Mendel sees the zaddik's activity as directed towards the world. Even so, R. Shneur Zalman also speaks of the zaddik as elevating stray thoughts that are not his own but those of the members of his congregation, which is somewhat akin to R. Menahem Mendel's view that it is the duty of the zaddik to raise up his followers. The resemblance extends to a further point which it is surprising to encounter in R. Menahem Mendel. It is surprising, in the light of what has been said above, that when R. Menahem Mendel was asked by one of his disciples to bless him with a child, he answered sharply:

> I am overcome with shame, for am I in the place of God? [Gen. 30: 2] The word of God was indeed in the hand of the Baal Shem [Tov] and what he decreed would come to pass. He was unique, and among the ancients there arose none like him, and after he has returned to the dust who will arise? Although some of the great men among the zaddikim of our generation are talkers and make such announcements as they do, I do not regard myself thus.[104]

It may be that his remarks reflect opposition to the 'practical zaddikism' which existed in his time,[105] and the fact that unworthy men represented themselves as wonder-workers. His objection would then have been on practical grounds, although in principle his attitude to this question was extremely positive, as I have argued. R. Shneur Zalman, too, was opposed to 'practical zaddikism' and did not allow his hasidim to speak to him in private except on subjects connected with guidance on divine worship.[106]

R. Menahem Mendel's description of evil reveals a distinctly monistic viewpoint. Evil springs from the divine source, and stress is repeatedly laid on the verses 'and You give life to them all' (Neh. 9: 6) and 'His kingdom rules over all' (Ps. 103: 19).[107] But evil exists only in the sense that there should be something to nullify or elevate. R. Menahem Mendel also uses the parable of the harlot, that is to say, the evil inclination was sent into the world in order that man should not submit to its temptations.[108] He sometimes makes use of the philosophical rule that 'nature abhors a vacuum'—there is no empty space in the world—to teach that there will always be either impurity or holiness.[109]

[102] *Peri ets*, on 'Kedoshim'. [103] *Peri ha'arets*, on 'Va'etḥanan'. [104] *Likutei amarim*, letter 7, 13*a*.

[105] Cf. a similar appreciation with regard to R. Shneur Zalman in Hallamish, 'Mishnato ha'iyunit', 362–3.

[106] See M. Hallamish, 'Yaḥasei tsadik ve'edah bemishnat R. Sh. Z.', *Ḥevrah vehistoriah* (Jerusalem, 1980), 79–92.

[107] e.g. *Peri ha'arets* on 'Matot' and 'Mas'ei'. [108] *Likutei amarim*, letter 4, 7*a*.

[109] *Peri ha'arets*, on 'Sabbath falling during Passover'; and on 'Aḥarei mot'.

Where holiness is absent, evil will automatically have a hold. We therefore do not have to make any great effort in order for evil to exist. By contrast, man needs devotion and self-sacrifice in order to draw down holiness upon himself.[110] According to the order of events as seen by R. Menahem Mendel evil does not take hold until it is necessary to fight against it. It is true that he once makes allegorical use of the olive, pointing out that its skin must be broken in order for oil to be extracted from it.[111] But in general, or by the very fact of seeing the divine root of all things, it follows *automatically* that 'all the doers of iniquity are scattered' (Ps. 92: 10).[112] R. Shneur Zalman, on the other hand, maintains that evil does not exist in the metaphysical sense, but that on the cosmic and human plane evil is engaged in a mighty struggle against good. The whole of R. Shneur Zalman's basic typology of humanity—the zaddik, the wicked, and the average man—is set in the context of the power of evil and the need to subdue it.

The motives for R. Menahem Mendel's immigration to Erets Yisrael at the head of a congregation of hasidim—an immigration regarded by scholars as important and successful—have recently become the subject of scholarly debate. The main opinions are that the immigration was motivated by disappointment at the failure of the mission to the Vilna Gaon or by messianic beliefs. Let us therefore observe that in the extant homilies and letters of R. Menahem Mendel there is relatively little speculative material connected with the subject of redemption or with that of Erets Yisrael. There may be some who will take R. Menahem Mendel's relative silence on these questions as a possible pointer towards his messianic orientation, but, in my opinion, the evidence is far from compelling.[113]

[110] Ibid., on 'Va'ethanan'.

[111] Ibid., on 'Noah', at the end.

[112] See e.g. ibid. 'Sabbath falling during Passover', at the end; on 'Naso'; on 'Ki tetse', etc.

[113] On these issues in the writings of R. Menahem Mendel of Vitebsk and R. Shneur Zalman of Lyady, see my forthcoming paper, 'Hasidism and Erets Yisrael—Two Models', to be published by the Ben-Zvi Institute, Jerusalem, in a volume dedicated to the conception of Erets Yisrael in the modern era.

SEVENTEEN

Habad Approaches to Contemplative Prayer, 1790–1920

NAFTALI LOEWENTHAL

I. INTRODUCTION

MOST schools of early hasidism paid special attention to prayer.[1] A distinctive feature of the Habad branch is the endeavour to popularize a contemplative approach.[2] Tracts on contemplation were compiled by R. Shneur Zalman (1745–1812), the founder of this school, his son R. Dov Ber (1773–1827), known as the Mitteler Rebbe, the latter's rival, R. Aaron of Starosielce (1766–1828), and also later leaders.[3]

This chapter explores the dialectic implicit in popularizing a contemplative approach to prayer. A system of contemplation suitable for an élite group of men of stature may well need modification before it can be applied by a wider echelon of society. In fact, it would seem that R. Dov Ber felt that his initial guidance on the contemplative process was being misinterpreted; people were reaching too high. In consequence, he felt compelled to restrain the majority of his followers from the intense mode of contemplation that he had originally advocated in his works.

Later leaders of Habad continued the attempt to introduce deep and lengthy contemplation to the members of the fraternity. This was achieved with a surprising degree of success by R. Shalom Dovber (1860–1920), known as the Rashab, of the fifth

[1] Prominent studies on this topic include G. Scholem, 'Devekut, or Communion with God', *Review of Religion*, 14 (1949–50), 115–39, repr. in id., *The Messianic Idea in Judaism* (New York, 1971); J. G. Weiss, 'The Kavvanoth of Prayer in Early Hasidism', *Journal of Jewish Studies*, 9 (1958); and 'Petitionary Prayer in Early Hasidism', *Hebrew Union College Annual*, 31, both repr. in id., *Studies in East European Jewish Mysticism* (Oxford, 1985), 95–130; R. Schatz-Uffenheimer, 'Contemplative Prayer in Hasidism', in E. E. Urbach, R. J. Z. Werblowsky, and C. Wirszubski (eds.), *Studies in Mysticism and Religion Presented to Gershom G. Scholem* (Jerusalem, 1964); id., *Haḥasidut kemistikah* (Jerusalem, 1968), pub. in Eng. as *Hasidism as Mysticism* (Princeton, 1993); L. Jacobs, *Hasidic Prayer* (London, 1972).

[2] This was an aspect of the Habad endeavour to popularize the esoteric dimension of hasidism throughout the hasidic fraternity, which was opposed by R. Abraham of Kalisk. This conflict divided the hasidic movement. See my *Communicating the Infinite: The Emergence of the Habad School* (Chicago, 1990).

[3] A considerable number of works have been produced dealing with the first two generations of Habad. (For a bibliography of recent studies, see my 'Self-Sacrifice of the Zaddik in the Teachings of R. Dov Ber', in A. Rapoport-Albert and S. J. Zipperstein (eds.), *Jewish History: Essays in Honor of Chimen Abramsky* (London, 1988), n. 7). However, very little scholarly attention has been paid to the later generations. An exception is Ada Rapoport-Albert, 'Polish Hasidism in the Habad Perspective: The Admor Yosef Yitzḥak Schneersohn in Otwock and Warsaw' (forthcoming).

generation of Habad leaders.[4] At the beginning of the twentieth century he taught the art of intense contemplation to the youthful pupils in his Tomekhei Temimim yeshivah,[5] and one is left with the impression that the Habad contemplative ideal was realized to a greater extent around 1914 than a century earlier.

This phenomenon seems to defy the principle of *yeridat hadorot* (decline through the generations) that is assumed by scholars and—perhaps to an even greater extent—by hasidim themselves.[6] As I shall try to show, however, it is in fact the product of this very concept, together with some other relevant factors. Perhaps surprisingly, we shall find that in some ways the more institutionalized social structure of the twentieth century aided rather than hindered the quest for the spiritual.

2. R. SHNEUR ZALMAN'S SYSTEM

The basis of the Habad contemplative approach is found in R. Shneur Zalman's tract *Gate of Unity and Faith*, printed in 1796 as the second section of *Tanya*.[7] This work elaborates the idea that all existence is nothing but an expression of the Infinite, the Ein Sof, and that therefore the Infinite is the only true reality. This perspective, piercing the veil of existence, is called the Higher Unity. A further contemplative step, perhaps more difficult, that is proposed there is to appreciate the Lower Unity, that our

[4] R. Shalom Dovber was the son of R. Shmuel (1834–82) ('Maharash'), who was hasidic leader in Lubavitch after the demise of his father R. Menahem Mendel (1789–1866), known as the Tsemaḥ Tsedek. The latter was both the son-in-law of R. Dov Ber and a grandson of R. Shneur Zalman. R. Shalom Dovber's life is described in a number of Habad publications, in particular A. H. Glitzenstein, *Sefer hatoledot Rabbi Shalom Dovber: Admor Rashab* (Kfar Habad, 1972); S. A. Heilprin, *Sefer hatse'etsa'im* (Jerusalem, 1980), 179–95.

[5] This yeshivah was founded in Lubavitch in 1897. See the Habad publications by A. H. Glitzenstein, *Tomekhei temimim* (Brooklyn, NY, 1969), which includes letters and other documents, and R. Kahn, *Lubavitch vehayaleihah* (Kfar Habad, 1983).

[6] This concept is basic to the talmudic approach to Judaism, and is expressed in sayings such as 'if the *rishonim* (earlier scholars) were angels, we are men; if the *rishonim* were men, we are like donkeys (Shab. 112*b*). In Habad, the idea of the greatness of the earlier generations compared with the present is prominent in the teachings of the *admor* R. Joseph Isaac. However, inherent in hasidism is also the claim that the contemporary zaddik manifests the most exalted religious ideals. See L. Jacobs, 'Hasidism and the Dogma of the Decline of the Generations', in this volume.

[7] For a bibliography of this work by R. Shneur Zalman see Y. Mondshine, *Torat ḥabad: Bibliografiah: Likutei amarim—Sefer hatanya* (Kfar Habad, 1981). It was first published with the title *Likutei amarim* (Slavuta, 1796); the title *Tanya* was used in the second edition (Zolkiew, 1799). The standard edition is that of Vilna, 1900. My references will be to a reprint of this (Brooklyn, NY, 1984). The original manuscript version, which was distributed among R. Shneur Zalman's followers for several years before the work was printed in Slavuta, 1796, has been published as Shneur Zalman of Lyady, *Likutei amarim: Mahadura kama (mikitvei yad)*, ed. S. B. Levine (Brooklyn, NY, 1982). An annotated translation of the second section, 'Sha'ar hayiḥud veha'emunah', by R. Nisen Mangel, was published in Brooklyn in 1965 and is included in the Soncino edition of *Likutei amarim: Tanya* (London, 1973). For a Yid. trans., by R. Y. Weinberg, with extensive commentary, see *Shi'urim besefer haTanya* (4 vols.; Brooklyn, NY, 1980–6), iii. Other commentaries on this section of *Tanya* include those of R. Hillel Halevi of Parichi, a prominent disciple of R. Shneur Zalman, and later R. Dov Ber: his commentary on the introd. (*Ḥinukh katan*) is in his *Pelaḥ harimon* [3 vols.; Vilna, 1847] (Brooklyn, NY, 1954–7), i. 294–304; and that on the main body of the work is entitled 'Sha'ar hayiḥud' and is printed in Dov Ber Shneuri of Lubavitch, *Likutei be'urim* (Warsaw, 1868). See also Y. Korf, *Likutei be'urim besefer haTanya* (2 vols.; Brooklyn, NY, 1968–73), i. 319–71, and A. Steinsaltz, *Be'ur lesha'ar hayiḥud veha'emunah* (Jerusalem, 1987).

material world is to be perceived not as a concealing veil but as a direct manifestation of the Divine.[8]

The tract states that these two contemplative perspectives are expressed in the esoteric interpretation of the first two utterances of the Shema.[9] During the morning service, the disciple of R. Shneur Zalman was expected to contemplate these and similar ideas. It is reasonable to assume that contemplative themes of this kind did actually fill the head of the typical Habad follower in the 1790s and later as, robed in his *talit* and *tefilin*, he recited the morning prayers in the synagogue.

An impression of what the early Habad morning *minyan* was like is provided by R. Shneur Zalman's letters.[10] Before the prayers, which were held early in the morning, no talking was permitted.[11] Everyone would begin praying together, taking an hour, or an hour and a half, to cover the main section of the morning service. The first part of the liturgy was recited aloud in unison,[12] and was seen as an opportunity ıor contemplative preparation for the Shema, the ecstatic declaration of the 'Higher Unity'—that All is G-d—and the profound realization of the 'Lower Unity', that G-d is All. There was an intense emotional mood, described as 'great love', or 'outpouring of the soul', which culminated in a feeling of self-sacrifice and self-abandon as the congregation embarked on the silent Amidah.[13] The first section of *Tanya*, entitled *Likutei amarim*, as well as discourses which were studied in manuscript, provided further contemplative material which was employed to arouse these intense feelings.[14]

This method of prayer was designed for the hasid. R. Shneur Zalman was very concerned to make clear in his *Likutei amarim* that the highly mystical teachings of the Baal Shem Tov and the Maggid on 'raising foreign thoughts to their root' were only for the zaddik, the hasidic leader, not for the hasidic follower.[15] An essential element in the

[8] An introductory paragraph at the beginning of the version printed in 1796 (and subsequently) quotes Zohar I: 18*b*, where the terms 'Higher Unity' and 'Lower Unity' are employed with reference to the Shema (*Tanya*, 66*b*). The earlier manuscript versions omit this passage and lack a long section, spanning chs. 6–7, in which this concept is elaborated. The manuscript version of this tract therefore emphasizes chiefly the 'Higher Unity' mode of contemplation, reaching towards the perception of the dissolution of all existence: there is naught but the Divine. See *Mahadura kama*, 457, and 465 n. 1. The printed text, presented to a wider public, makes more prominent the contemplative 'return' to the world, described as the 'Lower Unity'.

[9] These comprise Deut. 6: 4 and the phrase *barukh shem kevod malkhuto le'olam va'ed* (Pes. 56*a*). See also previous note.

[10] See I. Etkes, 'Darko shel R. Shne'ur Zalman miLiadi kemanhig shel hasidim', *Zion*, 50 (1986), 347–9.

[11] See *Takanot liozna*, ordinances instituted by R. Shneur Zalman *c.*1800, in D. Z. Hillman (ed.), *Igrot ba'al haTanya uvenei doro* (Jerusalem, 1953), 58; S. B. Levine (ed.), *Igrot kodesh Admor haZaken*, *Admor ha'Emtsa'i*, *Admor haTsemaḥ Tsedek* (Brooklyn, NY, 1980), no. 42, 103.

[12] Levine, *Igrot kodesh*, nos. 8, 82, 84; see the letters collected in *Tanya*, 103*a*, 162*b*–163*a*.

[13] Ibid. 102*b*; cf. *Igrot kodesh*, no. 80, 173–4, and the related material on 462: a record by R. Israel Jaffe of an interview (*yeḥidut*) with R. Shneur Zalman.

[14] See *Tanya*, i, chs. 42–50.

[15] Cf. *Tanya*, i, ch. 35, 35*a*. R. Shneur Zalman's teachings on 'foreign thoughts' have been discussed in S. Dubnow, *Toledot haḥasidut* [Tel Aviv, 1930–1] (Tel Aviv, 1960), 239; J. G. Weiss, 'Reshit tsemiḥatah shel haderekh haḥasidit', *Zion*, 16 (1951), 103; Rivka Schatz-Uffenheimer, 'Antispiritualizm baḥasidut', *Molad*, 20: 171–2 (1962), p. 522; I. Tishby and Y. Dan, 'Torat haḥasidut vesifrutah', *Hebrew Encyclopaedia*, xvii (1965), 769–821, repr. as a pamphlet by Academon, Jerusalem and in A. Rubinstein, (ed.), *Perakim betorat haḥasidut vetoledoteihah* (Jerusalem, 1977), 275; Jacobs, *Hasidic Prayer*, 112–17; Moshe Hallamish, 'Mishnato ha'iyunit shel R. Shne'ur Zalman miLi'adi: Mekorotav bakabalah veyaḥaso lereshit haḥasidut' (Ph.D. thesis, Hebrew University of Jerusalem, 1976), 301–4.

contemplative technique taught by R. Shneur Zalman was, therefore, that one should 'know one's place',[16] and not 'be a fool', by attempting to overreach oneself in one's efforts in mystical prayer.[17]

R. Shneur Zalman insisted that the leader of the prayers and the core members of the congregation should proceed at a slow, meditative pace. He made allowances for those who did not have time for contemplation during the week, and permitted those individuals who had to hurry off to work to pray more quickly, but it was they who were out of step, not the contemplatives. On the sabbath, however, all his followers were expected to recite their prayers slowly and to utilize the Habad teachings for contemplation.[18]

An interesting problem was that of the people who wanted to engage in such lengthy contemplation that they would effectively end up praying by themselves. In general R. Shneur Zalman did not permit this, although he made some exceptions to this rule, presumably for the sake of men of unusual spiritual stature.[19]

These firm instructions concerning prayer were backed by a strict disciplinary system. This atmosphere of control was an important element in the process seeking the awakening of the spiritual power of the hasid. R. Shneur Zalman wrote in *Likutei amarim* that 'the beginning of service, its basis and root' is the arousal of an intense sense of personal discipline, termed *kabalat ol malkhut shamayim*, the acceptance of the yoke of the kingship of heaven. It is the feeling of tension which this engenders, 'as if one were standing before a king', which should fill one's being while one prepares for the morning prayers.[20] Thus, the mystical aspect of the Habad contemplative system was complemented by discipline and control. This can be seen in action in the second generation of the movement, after R. Shneur Zalman's death in 1812.

3. R. AARON HALEVI'S APPROACH

While the mainstream of Habad followed R. Shneur Zalman's eldest son, R. Dov Ber of Lubavitch, there was a considerable faction which took as their hasidic leader R. Shneur Zalman's leading disciple, R. Aaron Halevi Horowitz, who moved to Starosielce.[21] R. Aaron wrote pastoral letters on the subject of prayer, and later published two volumes of teachings which provide guidance on contemplation and ecstasy.[22] His *Gates of Unity and Faith*, a subtle elaboration of his teacher's contemplation tract, continues the quest for the 'Higher Unity'. As earlier writers have shown, for R. Aaron the goal of the contemplative system was emotion and ecstasy: he saw no purpose in contemplation without this inner emotional response.[23] This quest for emotion meant that R. Aaron's system led beyond the limited confines of the organized

16 *Tanya*, i, ch. 27, 34*a*. 17 Ibid., ch. 28, 35*a*. 18 Ibid. iv, ch. 1, 103*a*.

19 Cf. *Takanot liozna*, in Hillman, *Igrot ba'al haTanya*, 58; Levine, *Igrot kodesh*, 104.

20 *Tanya*, i, ch. 41, 56*a*–*b*.

21 Concerning R. Aaron see L. Jacobs, *Seeker of Unity: The Life and Works of Aaron of Starosselje* (London, 1966); Rachel Elior, *Torat ha'elokut bador hasheni shel ḥasidut ḥabad* (Jerusalem, 1982).

22 Aaron Halevi of Starosielce, *Sha'arei hayiḥud veha'emunah* [Shklov, 1820] (Jerusalem, 1970); id., *Sha'arei avodah* [Shklov, 1821] (Jerusalem, 1970); the letters are at the end of his *Avodat halevi* [2 vols.; Lemberg, 1842–62 (i); 1866 (ii)] (Jerusalem, 1972), i.

23 See Elior, *Torat ha'elokut*, 324.

synagogue service, even if the latter took an hour and a half as R. Shneur Zalman had stipulated.[24]

It is likely that R. Aaron was one of the people permitted by R. Shneur Zalman to pray at length separately from the congregation. R. Aaron permits this practice in a general directive to his followers, expressed in a pastoral letter.[25] However, this is not without an important measure of control. The instruction in the letter is that although one is praying at one's own pace, and one's prayer is going to continue long after the service has ended, one should still start the morning prayer together with the congregation. Through this, said R. Aaron, one has the spiritual benefit of praying in unison with others, for 'in holy matters the main thing is the beginning'.[26]

R. Aaron's teachings, with their strong emphasis on the need to attain heartfelt enthusiasm and intense religious emotion, suggest that his system of contemplation produced lengthy, ecstatic prayer in which each word was savoured as an ongoing expression of dissolution in the Divine. He expected all his followers to engage in the mode of lengthy prayer which in the time of R. Shneur Zalman had been permitted only to the rare individual. It is noteworthy that R. Aaron's letter quoted above is headed *ketav yad lehakelal* ('general pastoral letter'): it was addressed to everyone, not just to a unique pneumatic personality.

To what extent this demand for ecstasy was met by R. Aaron's followers is not known for certain. In one letter he accuses them of being 'asleep', on account of their lack of enthusiasm in prayer;[27] but this may well be an expression of the attempt to stir them to seek even greater heights. The followers of R. Aaron were a self-selected group who all shared the belief that emotional enthusiasm in prayer was the goal of spiritual striving. It is likely, therefore, that they themselves were able to experience this—especially since, in striking contrast to R. Dov Ber, R. Aaron tolerated self-conscious or even contrived varieties of emotion.[28]

While R. Aaron guided his followers to lengthy, private prayer which continued far beyond the synagogue service, it is noteworthy that, in his system, the contemplation *before* the prayer was relatively brief: the Starosielce hasid could begin his prayers at the same time as the rest of the congregation in the synagogue, just as had been the case during R. Shneur Zalman's lifetime. In this respect the early contemplative teachings of R. Dov Ber, the leader of the mainstream of the Habad fraternity, were quite different. Two tracts, circulated in manuscript form among his hasidim in 1814, present an interesting intensification of the contemplative process.[29]

24 *Tanya*, iv, ch. 1, 103*a*.

25 *Avodat halevi*, i, 'Likutim', 18*c* ff. Cf. also 20*c*–*d*.

26 Ibid. 20*c*.

27 Ibid. 3*a*.

28 Jacobs, *Seeker of Unity*, 86, 128; Elior, *Torat ha'elokut*, 308–9. The latter claims that, in R. Aaron's view, there is no real distinction between 'external' emotion and that which is divine. Hence all emotional enthusiasm 'is no illusion, it is all true'.

29 These are Dov Ber Shneuri of Lubavitch (the Mitteler Rebbe), *Kuntres hahitpa'alut*, which was first printed in the late 1830s, or even in the 1840s, and *Kuntres hahitbonenut*, also called *Sha'ar hayiḥud*. This was first published as the second part of *Ner mitsvah vetorah or* [Kopys, 1820] (Brooklyn, NY, 1974). Concerning the printing history of the first of these works, and the fact that it originally appeared much earlier in manuscript form, see Rachel Elior, '"Kuntres hahitpa'alut" le R. Dov Ber Shne'orson', *Kiryat sefer*, 54 (1979), 386. A note on this article, by S. B. Levine, *Kiryat sefer*, 54 (1979), 829–30, suggests that both works originally appeared in manuscript form in 1814. See also L. Jacobs's trans. of *Kuntres hahitpa'alut*, entitled *Tract on Ecstasy* (London, 1963), 28.

4. R. DOV BER'S METHOD

The inner effect of the mode of contemplation taught by R. Dov Ber is expressed in the first of these, known as *Tract on Ecstasy*.[30] This work provides an analysis of different levels of enthusiasm and ecstasy which might be achieved in prayer and, as has long been noted, presents a strongly critical approach to the question of authenticity and spontaneity of religious emotion. Spurious emotion is condemned as vain illusion. Instead of achieving a *derher*, meaning an intimation of the Divine, the intended effect of the contemplative process, the person who indulges in spurious enthusiasm merely *derhert zikh*, he reaches an 'intimation' of his own self: rather than serving G-d through his emotion, 'he serves himself'.[31]

A further aspect of this tract, which is not so obvious, is that it leads the reader to the realization that the highest level of attainment is *beyond* emotion. Although R. Dov Ber describes levels of genuine heartfelt ecstasy, he also makes clear that the ultimate achievement is not this, but rather 'utter *bitul*', self-nullification, based on the intellectualist contemplation of the hasidic teachings.

Bitul is a term which denotes 'nullification' in the halakhic sense (as with the nullification of leaven before Passover).[32] In this context, however, it means nullification of the self. It is an emotionless state, in which there is no self-awareness. The mind is focused on a stream of imagery, culled from kabbalah, which for R. Dov Ber and the élite of his followers functioned as a gateway to the mystical radiance of the Infinite, the Ein Sof. The effect of this radiance is to engender intense feelings of love of the Divine, which are genuine and also valuable. But, says R. Dov Ber, once the contemplative gives way to this emotion, however sincere it may be, the gateway to the divine radiance closes. Instead of the Infinite, one is left with one's own self: 'there is someone who loves',[33] and the quality of *nishtkayt*, being nothing, of 'utter *bitul*', is lost. The paradigm of *bitul* was R. Dov Ber himself, who could stand immobile for hours, silent, beyond the world.[34]

This emphasis on *bitul* rather than emotion was not entirely new. There are teachings by R. Shneur Zalman, dating from the latter period of his life, in which we find the idea that emotionless self-abnegation represents the higher attainment.[35] R. Aaron too subscribed to this idea in theory, but claimed that *bitul* was suitable only for the giants of the past.[36] Hence it had no place in his system. After R. Dov Ber became

30 All references are to the edition published with the title *Likutei be'urim* (Warsaw, 1868), and to Jacobs's trans. (see previous note).

31 *Likutei be'urim*, 8*a*–*b*; *Tract on Ecstasy*, 67–8.

32 'Nullification' of all leaven in one's possession on the eve of Passover. See Pes. 6*b*; Yad. *Hil. ḥamets umatsah* 3: 7.

33 *Likutei be'urim*, 52*a*; *Tract on Ecstasy*, 128.

34 H. M. Hielman, the Kopys follower who wrote chronicles of Habad history, is probably recording a reliable tradition when he writes of R. Dov Ber: 'His prayer was silent without any movement or stirring of any limb at all. Within him he was burning like a burning flame but it was not revealed externally at all' (*Beit rabbi* [Berdichev, 1903] (Tel Aviv, n.d.), 184). He adds that R. Dov Ber's son-in-law, the Tsemah Tsedek, said of his father-in-law: 'His prayer had a cerebral quality of . . . *bitul* which is beyond enthusiasm, totally pure' (ibid. n. 3). See also Loewenthal, 'Self-sacrifice of the Zaddik', 472ff.

35 See *Torah or* [Kopys, 1836] (Brooklyn, NY, 1984) (a collection of discourses by R. Shneur Zalman), 44*a*: '*bitul* is on a higher level than emotion'.

36 See R. Aaron's *Sha'arei avodah*, 'Hakdamah', 12*b* (considering the title-page as fo. 1); 'Sha'ar yiḥud haneshamot', 39*b*–40*a*.

leader, the men of stature among his followers sought to follow the path of *bitul*, and so, probably, did others—but not necessarily with his approval, as we shall see.

R. Dov Ber's contemplative method, which he intended to be utilized whether one's goal was *bitul* or some lower level of attainment, is described in the second of his works to be issued in manuscript in 1814: *Tract on Contemplation*.[37] In this R. Dov Ber defines two modes of contemplation: 'in general', and 'in detail'.[38] The 'general' mode is familiar from earlier Habad teachings. By contrast, the 'detailed' mode of contemplation is defined as 'contemplating each world, each created thing, on each of the different levels of the order of the downchaining of worlds'.[39] R. Dov Ber describes the step-by-step progress of this form of contemplation, beginning on the lowest level of the Lurianic world-order, and ascending level by level, through each of the *sefirot* in each of the four worlds described in kabbalah. A higher form of the same kind of contemplation starts in the realm of Atsilut—the highest 'world'—and ascends to the most exalted reaches of the Lurianic spiritual cosmology. Material for this highly intellectualist style of contemplation is provided by the remainder of the book, in more than forty chapters. These present the total schema of the kabbalistic cosmos, with strong emphasis on discovering the reality of this through introspective investigation of the parallel structure of the microcosm: the psychological make-up of humanity. Through this process one comes to appreciate the *hitkalelut*, the integration and unification of all.[40]

R. Dov Ber believed that through this 'detailed' form of contemplation, necessarily a lengthy process, the person would attain a far greater degree of spiritual union with the Divine. The 'general' method was easier, and more suitable for a beginner, but he considered it also more likely to lead to self-deception, with merely a superficial level of attainment.[41]

The style of contemplation implied by the detailed method was one of lengthy thought *before* the prayers. The élite of R. Dov Ber's followers would thus become absorbed in the boundless stream of kabbalistic imagery, and then, in a state of suspension of selfhood, utter *bitul*, would begin to pray. Those who could not reach 'utter *bitul*' would eventually give way to a flush of emotion. Habad hasidim today describe the followers of R. Dov Ber as struggling with great effort to hold back their welling emotion in order to maintain the exalted state of *bitul*. In the light of the relevant texts, such anecdotes may be rooted in fact.

We now have to consider the problems inherent in a system of contemplation in which self-abnegation is the ultimate ideal but is not suitable for all. Could the average follower of R. Dov Ber correctly recognize his place in the system? Or did he aim too high, and therefore need corrective guidance and discipline?

5. THE NEED FOR GUIDANCE

Letters by R. Dov Ber, also dating from around 1814, indicate that he was concerned about this very question. He criticizes the local leaders of the hasidic communities for

[37] See n. 29 above. An account of this tract is given by L. Jacobs in his *Hasidic Prayer*, 84–91, and by Rachel Elior in *Torat ha'elokut*, 315 ff.

[38] *Sha'ar hayiḥud*, ch. 4, 4*b*. See Jacobs, *Hasidic Prayer*, 87; Elior, *Torat ha'elokut*, 317.

[39] *Sha'ar hayiḥud*, 4*b*.

[40] The appreciation of *hitkalelut* is the central goal of this contemplative system; see *Sha'ar hayiḥud* chs. 10, 15, 21, 31, 36, 43, 53. See also Jacobs, *Hasidic Prayer*, 91, and Elior, *Torat ha'elokut*, 316.

[41] *Sha'ar hayiḥud*, 4*b*–5*a*.

presenting too coarse a representation of the Habad path, taking the concept of *bitul* to an extreme. 'They completely forbid enthusiasm', he complains. He pours scorn on those who try to rid themselves of emotion, who mock emotional expression by others, and who themselves—though clearly unsuited for it—are so eager to adopt the silent, emotionless mode of prayer that 'they sit silently thinking and fall asleep'.[42]

In fact, R. Dov Ber compiled his *Tract on Ecstasy* in order to provide guidance in this matter. Its presentation of a typology of the variety of different levels of attainment was intended to help the hasid recognize his own position and strive to achieve fulfilment on that level.[43] While the man of stature should strive for the highest level, *bitul*, R. Dov Ber expected the majority of his followers to understand that they should be striving for a lower level of attainment, such as genuine heartfelt emotion, or, lower still, simple *kabalat ol*, acceptance of the yoke of heaven. He was critical of those who overreached themselves. During the ensuing years of his leadership, we see further examples of guidance of his followers in application of the contemplative technique.

One problem was the relationship between the 'detailed' mode of contemplation and the text of the daily prayers. After spending, say, two hours conceptually entering the Lurianic spiritual cosmology, while the sense of union with G-d expressed by the Shema is heightened, the contemplative may well wonder about the relevance of the words of the Psalms and other liturgical compositions in the morning service.[44]

Thus R. Dov Ber writes in the introduction to the *Prayer Book* published in 1816: 'I know the pain of all those who seek to come close to the Divine in prayer. They are unable to connect the thoughts in their mind . . . their contemplation . . . with the words they are uttering with their mouths . . . They are not connected.'[45] The solution, states R. Dov Ber, is provided by the *Prayer Book*, which includes an extensive commentary on the prayers, explaining the wording—and the relevant Lurianic *kavanot*—in terms of the detailed spiritual cosmology found in *Tract on Contemplation*. By means of the teachings in the *Prayer Book*, the contemplative could follow a natural movement from the detailed contemplation before prayer to the awareness of the Divine during the prayer; one becomes an extension of the other.[46] This, at least, was the ideal. But

[42] *Likutei be'urim*, 1*b*: *Tract on Ecstasy*, 179. This letter is referred to in R. Dov Ber's introd. to *Kuntres hahitpa'alut* as 'my earlier letter' (*Likutei be'urim*, 4*a*; *Tract on Ecstasy*, 57). See n. 29 above for Levine's comments on the dating of this text.

[43] This view of R. Dov Ber's aim differs from that suggested by Rachel Elior in *Torat ha'elokut*, 296. She sees R. Dov Ber as demanding one specific style of service, while R. Aaron gave more freedom to the individual. It seems from the sources that the contrary is true: R. Aaron's insistent demand was for overt emotional enthusiasm. R. Dov Ber presented a typology of different varieties of inner 'movement' (*hitpa'alut*) so that each individual could find his level.

[44] The Talmud describes the practice of 'pausing', presumably in a contemplative mood, for an hour before reciting the Shema and the Amidah (Ber. 32*b*). The section in the liturgy of the morning service entitled *pesukei dezimrah* ('verses of praise'), consisting largely of Psalms, seems intended to provide textual substance for this preparatory period. The Habad method of meditation on kabbalistic themes was not thought of as a substitute for this earlier popular contemplative system but as absorbing and complementing it. This is typical of the conservative nature of the hasidic movement, balancing its radical aspects. See Schatz-Uffenheimer, *Haḥasidut kemistikah, passim*.

[45] 'Hakdamat vehaskamat . . . Dov Ber', in id., *Seder tefilot mikol hashanah* [Kopys, 1816] (Brooklyn, NY, 1965).

[46] The *Seder tefilot mikol hashanah* was first printed in Kopys, 1816, then in Berdichev, 1818. A third edition was published in Kopys, in 1823 (cf. Mondshine, *Torat ḥabad*, ii. 55–7). The text of the prayers is that of the Lurianic prayer book edited by R. Shneur Zalman and published in Shklov, 1803. Cf. ibid., and A. M. Habermann, 'Sha'arei ḥabad', in the Schocken Festschrift *Alei ayin: Minḥat devarim liShelomo*

was it achieved by the mass of the fraternity? The answer is provided by a pastoral letter written by R. Dov Ber in the early 1820s, demanding an abrupt change of style from his followers.

The background to this is the fact that in 1820 *Tract on Contemplation*, which previously had been available only in manuscript form, was printed.[47] It is likely that, as a result, a larger proportion of the scholars in the Habad fraternity were tempted to try to follow the intensive system of contemplation it expounds, with the attendant risk of reaching for too high a spiritual level: inert, utter *bitul*, transcending all emotion, instead of a more accessible variety of enthusiasm. R. Dov Ber issued his pastoral letter two or three years later.[48] In it he instructed the young full-time scholars among his followers that their mode of contemplation must change. It is this group who in his opinion were most likely to take the contemplative path too far. While conceding that their achievement in the area of lengthy contemplation was genuine, he saw a problem with the prayer service that followed:

> Although they are genuinely . . . inspired by [the hasidic teachings], this is only temporary, and they are too lenient with regard to effort . . . during their prayer. As everyone can see, even he who has thorough knowledge of hasidic teachings prays very briefly. If they would apply more effort . . . they would certainly spend longer in prayer—at least two hours.[49]

The implication is that, after the lengthy contemplation before prayer, these young scholars had exhausted their spiritual effort and could not carry through the same mood employing the teachings in the *Prayer Book*. R. Dov Ber therefore demanded a complete change in their approach. Instead of aiming for lengthy contemplation followed by lengthy prayer, they should divide their activities in two. On the one hand, they should study hasidic teachings 'every morning and evening', at which time the individual should use 'all his power' to consider their significance. This would provide a contemplative resource which should be applied during the second stage: the time of prayer. It is noteworthy that R. Dov Ber stresses that this should be 'specifically with heartfelt emotional enthusiasm', *hitpa'alut bemurgash belev basar davka*.[50] In other words, misguided attempts to achieve *bitul* should be abandoned.

Salman Schocken (Jerusalem, 1948–52), nos. 135–6. This text is accompanied by two kinds of commentary: (*a*) a detailed tract expounding, in the Habad style, almost line by line, the section of the prayers entitled *pesukei dezimrah*, generally with some reference to the relevant Lurianic *kavanot*: see (in the modern edn.) 39*b*ff., 178*a*ff.; (*b*) lengthy discourses explaining the inner meaning of *tsitsit*, *tefilin*, the Shema, and so on. The *Seder tefilot* also includes numerous halakhic notes and passages by R. Shneur Zalman which had appeared earlier in his own edition of the prayer book.

[47] Cf. n. 29 above.

[48] The letter was first printed as the introd. to the Warsaw, 1886 edition of the *Seder tefilot mikol hashanah* and is included in C. E. Bichovsky and H. M. Hielman (eds.), *Me'ah she'arim* [Berdichev, 1913] (Kfar Habad, 1967; Brooklyn, NY, 1975), 11*a*. Several manuscripts of this letter are extant, one of which bears a colophon with the date 1823. It is now printed in Levine, *Igrot kodesh*, 262–8; See also 494. There is repeated reference to '*all* the books [of Habad teachings] which have been printed' (my italics). Since, from 1816, roughly one book a year was published, this would suggest a date for the letter not earlier than 1820. In fact, the content of the letter suggests that it was written some time after the publication of *Sha'ar hayiḥud* in 1820. Internal evidence indicates it was written before 1826 when *Torat ḥayim* was printed. The latter work comprises teachings on the weekly scriptural reading; the letter advocates study of such teachings 'in manuscript' (Levine, *Igrot kodesh*, 265).

[49] Levine, *Igrot kodesh*, 263.

[50] Ibid. 267.

R. Dov Ber further insisted that the daily prayers of the full-time scholars should be recited aloud in a quorum together, although he did permit a minority of men of stature to pray in silence.[51] Still concerned at the disparity between the wording and the contemplative stream of thought, he demanded attention to the simple meaning of the text, *perush hamilot*, and insisted that contemplation during the prayer should be limited to the significance of the Shema.[52] That all this was a conscious change is evident from the letter: 'Behold my demand and request . . . is that you should obey my trustworthy counsel and change the mode of your service.'[53]

This directive by R. Dov Ber is a striking expression of the dialectic implicit in the process of communication of esoteric teachings. The Habad hasidic school, as a number of others, though a large group scattered in widespread communities, retained certain characteristics of the small mystic circle such as that of the Ari in sixteenth-century Safed. The guide to the esoteric path gives careful instruction to his followers, encouraging them while also restraining them, according to their respective abilities.

In R. Dov Ber's view, the intense, highly mystical technique advocated in his early tracts could be applied directly only by a small, élite group of men of stature: personalities like R. Hillel of Parichi (1795–1864), who wrote a commentary to *Tract on Ecstasy*.[54] As the Habad fraternity expanded and more young scholars sought to follow the contemplative path, he felt it necessary to institute controls in order to avoid the misinterpretations which, from the very beginning of his leadership, had caused him anxiety. He therefore now made it unambiguously clear that the earlier teachings on *bitul* were restricted to a small group of men of stature. Perhaps it is for this reason that *Tract on Ecstasy*, which expounds the path of esoteric *bitul*, was never printed in R. Dov Ber's lifetime. As Rachel Elior has shown, the first printed edition was not made available till some ten or twenty years after his death.[55]

[51] Ibid. [52] Ibid. 266. [53] Ibid.

[54] Published in *Likutei be'urim*. It is noteworthy that a manuscript discourse by R. Hillel discusses two different modes of contemplation before prayer. The first, cited in the name of R. Dov Ber, is 'to contemplate the *seder hahishtalshelut* (Lurianic world-system) in detail' leading to a sense of the *bitul* of all levels before the Divine. After this one prays, thinking of the hasidic explanation of the text of the prayers. Then, says R. Hillel, 'the meaning of the words will not contradict the general *kavanah* of prayer: [dedication] to Him alone. (And this was an answer to the question about the connection between the [Lurianic] *kavanah* of the words, such as *barukh she'amar* is *reisha delo ityeda*, and the [goal of] abnegation before G-d.)' This clearly is a description of the mode of contemplation and prayer counselled by R. Dov Ber *c.*1816. But then R. Hillel describes a second method, cited in the name of R. Menahem Mendel, the Tsemaḥ Tsedek: 'However, there is another, higher path which is needed particularly by lower souls [i.e. people on a lower spiritual level], and this is what I heard from *admor shelita* [i.e. the Tsemaḥ Tsedek], to think through a teaching from the hasidic writings, in the order [in which it was written], and it seems that he too was referring to the time before the prayer; and at the time of prayer to think [simply] the meaning of the words. But the thinking about the hasidic teaching, which he did before the prayer, adds power and strength to his soul till he is able to feel the life-force of the words of the prayer'—(MSS of the Jewish National and University Library of Jerusalem, 3504, 3547. I am grateful to Mr Y. Mondshine for bringing this to my attention and making it available to me.)

The second mode of contemplation seems to be a further development of the path taught in R. Dov Ber's letter of *c.*1823. In fact it is basically identical to the normative style of study-contemplation and prayer found in Habad synagogues and yeshivot today.

[55] See n. 29 above.

6. INTO THE TWENTIETH CENTURY

In later generations of Habad we might well expect the total disappearance of R. Dov Ber's 'detailed' mode of contemplation. This would be consistent with the concept of *yeridat hadorot* and the general suspicion among scholars that during the nineteenth century the hasidic movement in general consolidated its social structure but weakened its links with its mystical origins.

It is therefore interesting to discover that the 'detailed' mode of contemplation is found in full force almost a century later. R. Dov Ber's great-grandson, R. Shalom Dober ('Rashab'), founded his Tomekhei Temimim yeshivah in the townlet of Lubavitch in 1897.[56] A striking feature of this yeshivah was that, alongside Talmud, hasidic teachings were part of the daily curriculum. Further, an intense mode of contemplation was imparted to the youthful students through tracts written by the Rashab in order to provide guidance for the pupils at the yeshivah. Originally these texts were studied in manuscript, then in mimeographed form. Only years later were they printed.[57]

The first such work, *Tract on Prayer* (*Kuntres hatefilah*), was first distributed at the end of 1899. It represents an interesting application and development of the contemplative guidance of R. Dov Ber. The first chapter speaks of the ideal of *bitul* as a state in which the person achieves total abnegation of self, a state in which 'all feelings disappear' and the contemplative is in a state of 'expiration', 'like a stone'.[58] However, having defined this exalted level of attainment, the remainder of the tract describes more accessible categories of heartfelt enthusiasm and emotion. The path of utter *bitul* is there, but it is for the rare élite. An eyewitness account describes the style of prayer of a young student named Nissan Nemirov (*c.*1908–84), who was later to become famous as a hasidic luminary in his own right. Around 1917 he was studying in the Habad yeshivah in Kremenchug. According to this account, special permission was given to him to come late to the Talmud class, for he 'would pray for four hours, standing by the wall like a stick'.[59] A small proportion of the students in Tomekhei Temimim attained this level. Most, however, were seeking not *bitul*, but heartfelt emotion, as is made clear by the *Tract on Prayer*.

The Rashab emphasizes that the correct path of contemplation is the 'detailed method', taught by R. Dov Ber.[60] Only this leads to genuine *hitpa'alut*, emotion and ecstasy. However, in order to avoid the superficiality of which the earlier *Tract on Ecstasy* warns, the Rashab suggests also the technique proposed in R. Dov Ber's letter of 1823: lengthy contemplative thought about the hasidic teachings, *not* related to

[56] See n. 5 above.

[57] *Kuntres hatefilah*, distributed at the end of 1899, was first printed in Vilna in 1924. I shall quote the Brooklyn, 1956 edition. It is pub. in Eng. as *Tract on Prayer*, trans. Y. A. Danziger (Brooklyn, NY, 1992). Another work by Rashab, *Kuntres ets haḥayim* ('Tract on the Tree of Life'), first distributed in 1904, emphasizes the importance of study of hasidic teachings and specifies their role in the daily programme of study in the yeshivah; it was first printed in Brooklyn in 1946. A third tract, *Kuntres ha'avodah* ('Tract on Service'), a full and profound manual for the contemplative, appeared in 1910; this too was first printed in Brooklyn in 1946.

[58] *Kuntres hatefilah*, ch. 1.

[59] Oral communication from R. Yankel Gurkow (*c.*1906–93), collected in an interview in 1988.

[60] *Kuntres hatefilah*, ch. 2. The 'detailed method' of contemplation is also strongly recommended in the Rashab's later tract, *Kuntres ha'avodah*. See the Brooklyn, 1978 edn., ch. 6, 36–45. R. Dov Ber's *Sha'ar hayiḥud* is cited on 39.

prayer, but at other times. Thus, says the Rashab, the student 'should make a time to engage in deep, solitary thought about a concept of hasidic teaching for one or two hours'. Through this he will learn how to contemplate at length before and during prayer, 'and also go beyond the conceptual structure of the hasidic ideas, reaching to the divine radiance within'.[61]

As preparation for the morning service in the synagogue, the tract recommends contemplating in the detailed method for 'an hour or more' before the prayers.[62] Through this, cerebral ecstasy will flow to the heart without being forced: the emotion will flow of its own accord.[63] This will also have the eventual effect of transforming the inner life of the person in ethical terms: his animal emotions will become devoted to the Divine.[64]

Together with this encouragement to embark on the 'detailed' style of contemplation there was also an emphasis on personal discipline. The tract states that each person who seeks to follow the contemplative path must accept close personal guidance. The young student is warned not to attempt long, detailed contemplation too soon. He should study together with older scholars, and 'submit' to their instructions.[65] The author continues with strong emphasis on the virtue of *kabalat ol*, 'acceptance of the yoke' or in other words submission.[66] A second work, *Tract on Service*, distributed in 1910, elaborates on this, and describes the contemplative as living in a constant state of 'tension' of inner control (*shtendig farkvetsht*).[67]

This control, I suggest, is a key aspect of the contemplative process: through self-mastery and humble submission to guidance the individual was able to 'find his place' in the contemplative system. In the new Tomekhei Temimim yeshivah, a high level of personal supervision and guidance of the would-be contemplative was possible. Thus the discipline which had been characteristic of Habad from the time of R. Shneur Zalman, and which manifests the 'mystic circle' dimension of hasidism, was an important complement to the aim to achieve radiant intimations of the Divine in contemplative prayer.

We also find that the problems which had agitated R. Dov Ber were now viewed somewhat differently. A hasid is said to have asked the Rashab about connecting the theme of the contemplation with the actual words of the daily prayers. The Rashab answered that the text of the daily prayers includes all the varieties of radiance which might shine to a person while praying.[68] In other words, the Hebrew text transcends its literal meaning and includes the 'radiance' of the stream of contemplation.

On the problem of the contemplative expending all his spiritual energy before he actually begins praying, a later Habad answer was: 'What does it matter to you if you pray before the prayers?'[69] In other words, the process of contemplation is itself valid as divine service. None the less, one should try as much as one can to say the words with full intensity. Hence there is the concept of 'praying with a *knaitsh* (a folded page)

[61] *Kuntres hatefilah*, ch. 6. [62] Ibid., ch. 4. [63] Ibid., ch. 5.
[64] Ibid., chs. 5, 8. [65] Ibid., ch. 14. [66] Ibid., ch. 15.
[67] *Kuntres ha'avodah*, 13.
[68] Recounted by A. Chitrik in *Reshimot devarim* (2 vols.; Brooklyn, NY, 1981–5), i. 160.
[69] Recounted by S. Y. Zevin in *Sipurei ḥasidim*, 'Torah' (Tel Aviv, 1955), 454. The statement is attributed to R. Hillel of Parichi. In fact it is consistent with the second mode of contemplation described in the discourse of R. Hillel discussed in n. 54 above.

in the prayer book': each day, the hasid would make a fold at the page he reached with the full force of contemplative thought. Beyond that point he would complete the prayers in the normal way. The next day, he would try to improve his performance, and sustain the contemplative mood for longer, making a new fold further on in the prayer book.[70]

These points give the impression that early in the twentieth century there was a more relaxed attitude to spiritual attainment compared with a hundred years previously. It can be suggested that this was due to *yeridat hadorot*, the descent of the generations. Since people were considered to be on a lower level, less could be demanded of them. Thus instead of the punctilious perfectionism of R. Dov Ber, there was a wish to extend the ethos of deep contemplation and ecstasy to an entire generation of Habad scholars. This gave them a powerful ideal which was to help them maintain their spiritual balance in the contemporary atmosphere of widespread defection from traditional Judaism.[71] Their belief in the Torah was not based solely on faith, nor even on intellect, the hallmark of Habad: it had a personal experiential dimension as well. The need for this in the context also of the modern West was expressed by a later Habad leader, R. Joseph Isaac Schneersohn:

> The beginning of the fall, G-d forbid, is lack of *avodat hatefilah* (contemplative prayer). Everything becomes dry and cold, even habitual *mitzvot* become difficult. One hurries, one loses the *geshmak* ('delight') in Torah. The air thickens. Obviously, one is then quite unable to have any good effect on other people.[72]

R. Dov Ber's letter of around 1823 had reined in the majority of the hasidim, due to a feeling that they had not 'recognized their place': they were reaching too high in the world of the spirit. Three generations later, at the beginning of our century, the *Tract on Prayer* and other teachings on highly intensive contemplation express the Rashab's conviction of the need for deep spirituality in the contemporary Jewish world and also indicate his confidence in the inner discipline of his followers.

[70] Oral communication from R. Yankel Gurkow.

[71] See David E. Fishman, 'Preserving Tradition in the Land of Revolution: The Religious Leadership of Soviet Jewry, 1917–1930', in J. Wertheimer (ed.), *The Uses of Tradition: Jewish Continuity in the Modern Era* (New York, 1992), 85–118.

[72] *Hayom yom* (Brooklyn, NY, 1942), entry for 23 Iyar. This is a collection of aphorisms and passages from the writings of R. Joseph Isaac Schneersohn, arranged in the form of a calendar, edited by his future successor, R. M. M. Schneerson. This passage links the ideal of contemplative prayer with the religious activist aspect of modern Habad—the goal of having a 'good effect on other people'.

EIGHTEEN

The Fluidity of Categories in Hasidism: *Averah lishmah* in the Teachings of R. Zevi Elimelekh of Dynow

YEHOSHUA MONDSHINE

IT was the misfortune of R. Zevi Elimelekh Shapira of Dynow (1783–1841) that most of his life was lived in the nineteenth century, and for this reason scholars have deemed him and his teaching unworthy of serious consideration. Fortunately for us, intellectual fashions have changed in recent years, and many have come to recognize that even in the nineteenth century the sap of hasidism was by no means exhausted. Hasidic thought continued to develop and to diversify into streams of ever-increasing breadth and depth, with no evidence of the degeneration which its detractors in the not so distant past have claimed to perceive.

The editors of the *Hebrew Encyclopaedia* have seen fit to devote to the Rabbi of Dynow and his writings no more than eighteen lines, and the modern *Encyclopedia Judaica* less than a column. I myself do not propose to dwell in detail on his biography; in brief: he did not belong to a rabbinical dynasty; his principal teachers were Menahem Mendel of Rymanow and Jacob Isaac, the Seer of Lublin, and after them the Maggid of Kozienice and the Rabbi of Opatow (Apta). He had close links also with certain outstanding disciples of the Seer of Lublin, prominent among these being R. Naphtali of Ropczyce and R. Zevi Hirsch of Zhidachov.

The Rabbi of Dynow was one of the few whose teaching gained acceptance among all hasidic circles, and his book *Benei Yisakhar* is reckoned one of the classics of hasidism. Since 1846 it has been printed at least twenty-one times (an average of one edition per seven years), while the *Toledot Ya'akov Yosef*, which is of equivalent scope, has appeared since 1780 in sixteen editions, one for every thirteen years. And *Benei Yisakhar* is only one of a dozen major works composed by the Rabbi of Dynow.

In the course of editing the book *Sur mera va'aseh tov* by the Rabbi of Zhidachov, with commentary by the Rabbi of Dynow,[1] I had occasion to study his other works, and

[1] The book was first published (in Lemberg, *c.*1832) under the title *Hakdamah vederekh le'ets haḥayim*, without the Rabbi of Dynow's commentary. In 1840 it was published again, this time with the commentary, and since then it has been known by the title of *Sur mera va'aseh tov*. The early editions contained no more than half the commentary. It was published in full for the first time in the Munkachevo (Munkacz) edition of 1901. This edition contained the approbation of R. Zevi Hirsch of Munkacz who stated as follows: 'I have heard, and it is the generally accepted view, that the publisher of the first edition deliberately left out much of the material . . . I have recently had occasion to inspect . . . the holograph . . . of Rabbi Zevi Elimelekh of Dynow . . . I was alarmed to discover that the printed edition is very defective . . . To

through these I became aware of the concept of 'sin for the sake of Heaven' (*averah lishmah*) which is the focal point of the present discussion.

In broad terms, there are two types of 'sin for the sake of Heaven', one intended for zaddikim only, the other for ordinary people. The first type solves a problem which faces the zaddik: his usual concern is with *mitsvot* which by their nature draw down the benign forces of heavenly deliverance and grace on the world; but how is he to deal with cases in which it is his duty to bring down divine retribution on the heads of the enemies of Israel? In such cases he is called upon to commit a sin—albeit for the sake of Heaven—an act which by its nature brings judgements and accusations into being. However, the fact that it is done 'for the sake of Heaven' and with pure intention ensures that the retribution is directed towards the dire oppressors of Israel.

Thus he explains the deeds of Jael wife of Heber the Kenite, of Esther, and of Mordecai, who with his fast abrogated the commandment to celebrate the Passover festival; and thus also the sins ostensibly committed by the Holy One, blessed be He, when He descended into the defilement of Egypt, to smite their firstborn and to deliver Israel.[2]

When these statements are woven into verses of the Torah they gain additional sharpness: the verse (Deut. 11: 28) 'If ye will not obey the commandments of the Lord your God, but turn aside out of the way which I command you,' he interprets as if meaning, 'that which I command you is to turn aside out of the way and not to obey the commandments of the Lord your God'.

Similarly the verse (Deut. 12: 4) 'Ye shall not do so unto the Lord your God' takes on the meaning: 'the "not"—the thing that is forbidden—you shall do unto the Lord your God, when you have occasion to do so in good intention and for the sake of Heaven, which is sin for the sake of Heaven'.

The verse (Deut. 18: 14) 'For these nations . . . hearkened unto observers of times and unto diviners' is explained as meaning that the nations in their desire to defeat their enemies need recourse to augurers and diviners, but 'as for thee, the Lord thy God hath not suffered thee so to do'; to the Jew the Lord has given different counsel, and 'not so'—negative and affirmative combined—points to a sin that becomes a 'temporary' *mitsvah*. Thus the verse (Deut. 26: 13) 'I have *not* trangressed thy commandment' takes on the meaning: 'I have trangressed the *not*, but this was your commandment, for the sake of Heaven.'

It should be noted that the Rabbi of Dynow presents this idea several times as a 'tradition handed down by holy men', but on one occasion he states explicitly that the originator of the tradition is a certain zaddik, Solomon of N. (the place name, which

leave out such important material! Virtually every paragraph is defective.' My own attempts to uncover the reason for these editorial deletions have yielded no factor common to all the omitted passages other than their sheer length. It seems, therefore, that those parts of R. Zevi Elimelekh's commentary which were simply too long to be set on the same page as the main text by the Rabbi of Zhidachov were abridged or left out altogether. All references are to the Munkacz 1901 edn. [Louis Jacobs's translation—*Turn Aside from Evil and Do Good* (London, 1995)—was not available when this chapter was written.]

[2] For this type of 'sin for the sake of Heaven', and for an exposition of the biblical references listed above, see R. Zevi Elimelekh of Dynow, *Benei Yisakhar* (Munkacz, 1940), on 'Nisan', 52*b*, 56*d*; on 'Kislev-Tevet', 56*a*; id., *Agra dekhalah* [Lemberg, 1868] (Przemysl, 1910), on 'Bereshit', 8*a*, 55*b*; on 'Beha'alotekha', 52*c*–*d*; on 'Re'eh', 95*d*; on 'Shofetim', 99*d*, 100*c*; on 'Ki tavo', 106*a*.

can at best be transliterated as Nasheplits, is evidently corrupt beyond recognition), whom I have not been able to identify;[3] and once he implies that this was also the opinion of the Seer of Lublin.[4] But his own opinion is that it is not necessary to follow this course, since it is possible to achieve the same results by means of *repentance out of love* (as opposed to *repentance out of fear*) which transforms wickedness into merit, so that one's 'former sins' become the means for the salvation of Israel.[5]

Although this type of 'sin for the sake of Heaven' is more commonly found in his writings (in nine out of the sixteen discourses dealing with the subject), we shall, however, give more attention to the second type, which is the important one for our purposes.

One of the early followers of the Habad school defined the mitnagged as a 'portrait', a likeness with form and beauty, painted with pleasing colours.[6] 'He did not mean to emphasize the lack of spiritual life in this image, but rather to draw attention to the fact that it is a fixed image which undergoes no changes, or in his own words: 'it is the same yesterday, today and tomorrow, unlike the hasid who is "in" today and "out" tomorrow.'

The mitnaggedim find no fault in a life devoid of upheavals which is conducted *according* to the Torah, as may be seen from the statements of R. Joseph Soloveichik in his treatise *Ish hahalakhah* and from similar remarks of Professor Isaiah Leibowitz. This quality also characterizes the works *Yesod veshoresh ha'avodah* by R. Alexander Ziskind of Grodno and *Nefesh haḥayim* by R. Hayyim of Volozhin.

It is indeed true that the halakhah can be a powerful instrument in guiding the life of the individual down to its most minor details. Using a modern analogy, one can envisage a computer operating a halakhic programme which will guide the individual from birth to death, resolve all his doubts, and bring him to the life of the next world clean of all trace of sin and laden with Torah and *mitsvot*.[7]

However, this is not the case with the hasid. At every moment of his life he deliberates over every action or omission, and the halakhah is powerless to guide him. In addition to all other considerations he must also take account of 'the Will of God', a will that is not written in the Torah, since it changes according to time and place and to the spiritual

[3] *Agra dekhalah*, on 'Bereshit', 55*b*.

[4] Ibid., on 'Re'eh', 95*d*.

[5] Ibid., on 'Beha'alotekha'; on 'Re'eh'.

[6] This was R. Ze'ev Vilnekes. About him see H. M. Hielman, *Beit rabbi* [Berdichev, 1903] (Tel Aviv, n.d.), 151.

[7] It is true that the halakhah too, leaves the individual some scope for inner doubt and deliberation, as is evident, for example, in the call to consider the risk that to observe a particular *mitsvah* strictly may raise the question of spiritual ostentation by creating the impression of the presumption to be more observant than others (*ḥaishinan leyohara*). But the halakhah acknowledges such scruples only when they arise from the genuine endeavour to be most meticulous in the observance of *mitsvot*, not where their very observance is in question. Moreover, it points to the way out of such quandaries by prescribing ready-made rules of conduct rather than leaving the individual to make his own choices. Maimonides displays an analogous preference for prescription in the realm of halakhah. He admits that, in certain cases, the rabbinical judge was permitted to follow what he perceived to be the spirit rather than the letter of the law. However, since one could no longer rely on the personal integrity or insight of the judges, it was decided to refrain from ruling on the basis of anything other than what the law defined as conclusive evidence (see Moses Maimonides, *Mishneh torah*, 'Hilkhot Sanhedrin', ch. 24, 1–2). Similarly, those hasidic leaders who did not practise (or had reservations about, or even objected outright to) the 'deviations' described below, did so on the grounds that people whose moral integrity or insight were questionable might 'take the law into their own hands' and abuse it.

condition of the individual at any particular time. One might say that the hasid seeks to obey not the *letter* of the law, but the *spirit* of the law and the *intention* of the legislator.[8]

The range of considerations to be weighed up changed with the emergence of the new hasidic system of values, a system which was quite unlike that of the halakhah. In hasidism the 'concealment of good deeds' became an important value (see below), as did the well-known hasidic dictum:[9] 'Grief (*atsvut*) is not a sin, but it does more harm than the vilest of sins. Taking a ritual bath is not a *mitsvah*, but it exalts the soul more than do all the *mitsvot*.' Inevitably, this change in values brought about changes in halakhic practice. Flight from grief sometimes led to the relaxation of halakhic strictures, while ritual bathing could take place even at times and in situations in which the halakhah does not fully permit it.

To return to the teaching of the Rabbi of Dynow in this matter: in one of his comments on the book *Sur mera* (note 36), he criticizes at some length the followers of hasidism who relax certain halakhic prohibitions in order to conceal their own piety from the public eye. But at the same time he expresses the opinion that, when acting in public, it is advisable for the hasid to abandon the rigour of pious strictures so that he will not appear to be claiming the status of spiritual eminence; and on the other hand, he advises, the hasid should avoid excessive abstinence even in his home, adding that there are no absolute, universal guidelines to be offered; in the words of Zevi Elimelekh: 'It is impossible to spell out such profoundly personal matters, because they belong to the category of those things which are dependent on the individual, according to the particular circumstances of time and place.' These are precisely the things that cannot be programmed into the halakhic computer.

Continuing in the same vein, the Rabbi of Dynow draws attention (ibid.) to an anecdote in the Gemara,[10] a story told by the *tanna* R. Meir: 'When I came to R. Ishmael he said to me, my son, what is your work? I told him, I am a scribe. He said to me, my son, take great care in your work, which is divine work, lest you omit one letter or add one letter, and thus destroy the whole world.' The plain meaning of the story is to point out the great responsibility entrusted to those who copy sacred texts, but the Rabbi of Dynow interprets it as alluding to another meaning. He explains that R. Ishmael addressed his question specifically to R. Meir,[11] of whom it was said that his colleagues

[8] This may well be what R. Menahem Mendel of Kotsk had in mind when he said that the mitnagged fears the *Shulḥan arukh* (the law) while the hasid fears God (the legislator) (quoted in *Lahavot kodesh* (Jerusalem, 1980), 130, from Y. K. K. Rokotz, *Si'aḥ sarfei kodesh* (Lodz, 1928–1931)). [The tendency to give preference to what one perceives intuitively to be the will of God over the strict letter of the law, usually in the direction of greater strictness rather than leniency, is not unique to Beshtian hasidism. For an instructive parallel in medieval Ashkenazi pietism see H. Soloveitchik, 'Three Themes in the *Sefer hasidim*', *AJS Review*, 1 (1976), 311–57; cf. also G. Scholem, 'Three Types of Jewish Piety', *Eranos Jahrbuch*, 38 (1969), 331–48. Ed.] An interesting parallel may be drawn also with the 'vitalist' philosophical insights of Henri Bergson (1859–1941, a descendant of some of the intimate associates of the Przysucha and Kotsk dynasties). These include his dynamic conceptions of 'duration' and 'movement', the vital impulse and the notion of continuous regeneration and development, the constant clash between life and inertia, the central role of intuition by which man grasps the essence of reality, as well as his exposure as ridiculous of human conduct that is mechanical, rigid, or mimetic.

[9] This is usually ascribed to R. Aaron ('The Great') of Karlin, in whose name the entire discussion appears in Israel of Ruzhin, *Keneset Yisrael* (Warsaw, 1906), 145. However, the editor of *Si'aḥ sarfei kodesh* (115) claims the author to have been R. Ḥanokh of Aleksandrow.

[10] Eruvin, 13*a*.

[11] Ibid. 13*b*.

could never fully understand him, 'since his way and his conduct in matters of holiness and divine service were variable according to time and place'. Therefore R. Ishmael asked him to clarify the meaning of his strange and variable behaviour. To this R. Meir replied, 'I am a scribe', and in the word 'scribe' (*lavlar*) are concealed the initial letters of the saying 'the Merciful One looks to the heart' (*rakhmana liba ba'ei*)—meaning that the divine service of the individual and his deeds depend on the heart, and naturally the heart changes according to the circumstances of time and place. On hearing this R. Ishmael said to him, 'Take great care in this divine work, lest you omit or add!' For in divine service such as this, where decision is left to the heart of the individual, 'great caution and prudence of mind are needed to weigh everything in the scales of righteousness, for what is done by one person on one occasion is called a *mitsvah* while at another time the opposite is the case. Everything depends on the circumstances of time and place, and this is what is meant by omission or addition. Understand the matter, for it is impossible to explain it in writing, and you must know it for yourself.'

R. Zevi Hirsch of Zhidachov expresses a similar opinion:

> It is necessary to be . . . taking off one form and putting on another, all for the service of God, blessed be He . . . according to the particular requirements of time and circumstance . . . and everything should be weighed and measured and aimed precisely at the target, not missing by so much as a hair's breadth, for even the breadth of a fine hair may amount, Heaven forbid, to deviation from the truth, and those who seek after the truth with all their heart and soul know that there is no measure to these subtle and spiritual things. Go forth and learn from ethical works and from the words of our sages, learn how the righteous were punished who had sinned [in departing from the truth] by no more than a hair's breadth.[12]

One can sense the danger lying in wait for the individual who directs his divine service according to the wayward dictates of his heart rather than the straight path of the halakhah.

These doubts and deliberations are stated more explicitly where the Rabbi of Dynow illustrates the subtle distinction between 'one Lord' (Deut. 6: 4) and 'another god' (Exod. 19: 14),[13] a distinction which manifests itself in the minute orthographic difference between the Hebrew words for 'one' (*eḥad*) and 'another' (*aḥer*) respectively. The difference consists of the stroke which distinguishes between the letters *resh* and *dalet*. These are the two 'great letters', written larger than the rest in these two verses in order

> to show that they are to be studied carefully to distinguish an act which constitutes a *mitsvah*, alluded to by the expression 'one Lord' and belonging to the mystery of divine unity, from an act which constitutes a sin, alluded to by the expression 'another god', for idolatry may be defined as anything that an individual does, even a *mitsvah*, if he does it not for the glory of the Lord but for some ulterior motive . . . and sometimes it is the opposite: sin for the sake of Heaven is the greatest good, and when a man refrains from committing such a sin which is for the sake of Heaven (when he has a Heaven-sent opportunity!) . . . this is not the proper way, for in truth sin for the sake of Heaven at the appropriate time is also the way of goodness and of divine unity.

[12] *Beit Yisrael* (Lemberg, 1865), 32–3.

[13] *Agra dekhalah*, on 'Bereshit', 36*c–d*; id., *Maggid ta'alumah* (Przemysl, 1876), 83*a*; *Benei Yisakhar*, on 'Adar', 90*c–d*.

However, the alternative to this treacherous course is no better; a man can walk confidently in the straight path of the halakhah, without any deviation, but according to the Rabbi of Dynow, this is not only a 'portrait', it is an 'image' and a monument for idolatry! Thus he writes:

We have a tradition handed down by righteous men, whereby no day is like another, and sometimes what is done one day is a *mitsvah* and the next day the same thing is a sin. And it is impossible to explain the matter; the wise man should understand it by himself. And no hour is like another, for every hour requires a different act of divine service, and the individual must take care that all his acts are for the sake of Heaven, according to what is *really* required at every hour for His service, may He be blessed. But there are people who have a fixed position on everything, and *thus* they will act throughout their lives and *thus* they will conduct themselves without budging from their habitual way. This is alluded to in the verse (Deut. 16: 22) 'Neither shalt thou set thee up any image', the word 'image' (*matsevah*) implying a 'position' (*matsav*) in which your divine service is fixed without ever changing, and if you perform your service always by one rule, this is referred to in the second half of the verse as that 'which the Lord thy God hateth'. Moreover, there is a traditional interpretation of the verse (Deut. 12: 4) 'Ye shall not do so unto the Lord your God,' whereby *so* equals *thus*, meaning: in exactly the same manner, the same conduct. All this lest today this conduct is good and tomorrow it is the opposite. You should understand this, for it is impossible to expound everything in writing, but he who understands will understand.[14]

The Rabbi of Dynow reiterates this view when he explains why the miracle of Abraham's deliverance from the fiery furnace[15] is not recounted in the Torah:

Who gave permission to Abraham to submit himself to the fiery furnace, seeing that a 'Noahite' is not commanded to make himself a martyr, and he is *forbidden* to submit himself to death . . . My friends and dear ones, heed my words for they are pleasant, and may your eyes be enlightened. The complete Torah as we have it is accessible to all of Israel, for what one is commanded there to 'arise and do' one *must* do, and what is commanded there not to do one must beware of doing. But our sages have said that a sin for the sake of Heaven is greater than a *mitsvah* that is not for the sake of Heaven, as Jael wife of Heber the Kenite proved. This could not be expounded in the Torah, because it is governed by the circumstances of time and place and by the soul's desire to do the will of God, blessed be He . . . So it came about for our Father Abraham, who knew with certainty that he was committing sin in offering himself to death, and the punishment for sin is Hell. In spite of this, to sanctify His Great Name, he offered his life in this world and in the next, and committed a sin for the sake of Heaven. Now since this was a sin which did not accord with the Torah, it could not be reported in the Torah explicitly. For sin is for the sake of Heaven only when it is committed in pursuit of the inner truth in the service of God, blessed be He. This cannot be understood or likened to another sin. It applies only to the esoteric truth, concealed in the innermost chamber of the heart.[16]

The classic example of preference for God's will over the way of halakhah is the delaying of the time of prayer, which was practised in many hasidic circles. This, incidentally, is a practice that the Rabbi of Dynow fervently opposes, arguing that it is like eating *matsah* after Passover or sitting in a *sukah* after Tabernacles,[17] as in the well-

[14] *Agra dekhalah* on 'Re'eh', 96*a*; on 'Shofetim', 90*b*.
[15] Ber. Rabah, ch. 38 and Pes. 118*a*.
[16] *Agra dekhalah*, on 'Noaḥ', 71*b*–*c*.
[17] *Sur mera*, comments 36 and 100, pp. 9*b* and 27*a*.

known formulation of the idea by R. Hayyim of Volozhin.[18] It is true that there were some eminent rabbinic authorities who managed, by way of *pilpul*, to justify this practice,[19] but there is no doubt that the hasidim did not require such *post facto* halakhic excuses to adopt it. As the Rabbi of Izbica writes: 'In every generation the man who is the zaddik of the generation perceives the will of God, blessed be He . . . and the Holy Jew (of Przysucha) in his generation perceived the will of God blessed be He, in delaying the time of prayer, relying on the verse,[20] 'Ye shall not do so unto the Lord your God'—'so' implying a lifeless permanence. Seeing the will of God in this, he delayed his prayer . . . although this could change in accordance with changing circumstances.[21] In other words, this practice also depends upon time and place, and, as he declares elsewhere,[22] renewal must take place day after day, but in time daily renewal becomes a fixed routine that must itself be changed . . . (for more on the Rabbi of Izbica and his book see below).

In the same vein, R. Asher of Karlin states explicitly: 'The requisite, heartfelt divine service is governed by the circumstances of place and time. And although the time of prayer is fixed in the dicta of our sages and is communicated to all, yet there is a time that is within time, communicated to the heart.'[23]

It is related that, when R. Leibele Eger (disciple of the Rabbi of Izbica; d. 1888) was about to visit his father and grandfather, the mitnaggedim R. Solomon and R. Akiva Eger, he asked his hasidic *rebbe*, Menahem Mendel of Kotsk, how he would explain to them the halakhic basis for delaying the time of prayer.[24] Significantly, he sought no such halakhic explanation for himself. When it was pointed out to him once that the sun had already set and the stars were out, and what was to become of prayer, he replied: 'I do not pray to the sun, nor to the moon nor to the stars.' This approach

[18] See R. Hayyim of Volozhim, *Nefesh haḥayim* (Vilna, 1824), ch. 4 of the section between gate 3 and gate 4. The book was first published in Vilna–Grodno in 1824, and the Rabbi of Dynow wrote the comment referred to above (n. 17) at about the same time. That similar ideas should occur to individuals who are very remote from, or even opposed to, one another, and where mutual influences can be ruled out, is hardly surprising, as I pointed out elsewhere with regard, for example, to R. Hayyim of Volozhin and the Besht, and in contrast to the far-reaching claims made by Y. Liebes (see Y. Mondshine, 'On "R. Nahman of Bratzlav's *Hatikun Hakelali* and his Attitude towards Sabbateanism"' (Heb.), *Zion*, 47 (1982), 220–1 and n. 81).

[19] Some of these justifications were collected by A. Wertheim in his *Halakhot vahalikhot baḥasidut* (Jerusalem, 1960), 88–93. See also I. Alfasi, 'Ha*Shulḥan arukh* bikhal ḥasidim', *Mahanayim*, 97 (1965), 53–8. There are numerous others, and I shall mention only a few. For the Przysucha (Pshiskha), school see Y. K. K. Rokotz, *Tiferet hayehudi* (Piotrkow, 1912), 37–8, ss. 80–1; for Habad see Y. Mondshine, *Migdal oz* (Kfar Habad, 1980), 340–78 (where R. Shneur Zalman of Lyady is quoted as saying that the greatest zaddikim do not delay, lesser zaddikim delay, and ordinary people must not delay the time of prayer); see also R. Yeḥezkel Faigin, 'Reply' (Heb.), *Hatamim*, 8 (Warsaw, 1937), 69–70.

[20] Deut. 12: 4.

[21] Mordecai Joseph Leiner of Izbica, *Mei hashilo'aḥ* (2 vols., Vienna, 1860; Lublin, 1922), ii. 29*a*. Notably, some decades later, in 1906, the *admor* R. Abraham Mordecai of Gur instructed his followers to stop delaying the time of prayer. Cf. *Tiferet hayehudi*, 39, s. 82, where 'the zaddikim of the generation' are said to have restored prayer and other *mitsvot* to their proper time. The author links this with the Rabbi of Kotsk's statement that there is a certain path which only the select few can follow, but if the majority of people should walk it, the path would become obstructed and they would have to return to the old road, praying and observing all other *mitsvot* in their proper time.

[22] *Mei hashilo'aḥ*, i. 35*a*; cf. 24*b*–*c*.

[23] See his 'Order of the Day' (*seder hayom*) in *Beit Aharon* (Brody, 1875), 10.

[24] See the sources cited in *Lahavot kodesh*, 151.

stems from a change in the perception of the function of prayer which took place in hasidism and has been discussed extensively in the scholarly literature. By way of illustration (and in a negative mode) I shall merely quote the following remark of R. Judah Leib of Gur ('the *Sefat Emet*'): 'Our sages said that the prayer of the individual is not "heard" (answered) unless it is recited together with the entire congregation. This is surprising, since the best worshippers often pray in solitude! The hasidic answer to this is that our prayer is not being offered in order that we should be "heard" (answered).'[25]

Turning from prayer to Torah study: although the halakhah states that he who is able to study Torah without working for his livelihood is obliged to do so,[26] hasidism prefers to submit such questions to the test of the heart and recognition of God's will. Consequently the issue became the subject of internal controversy. The Rabbi of Zhidachov and the Rabbi of Dynow were divided on this point, the latter belittling the importance of work for one's livelihood but admitting that sometimes one can be misled into neglect of business by the evil inclination to pride.[27] Similarly, it was the opinion of the Rabbi of Izbica that sometimes such conduct could emanate from the *kelipah* of idleness, although ostensibly it was from faith and trust in God.[28]

R. Asher of Karlin, too, wrote to one of his followers who wanted to dedicate himself to his studies rather than work, telling him that to work for his livelihood, and so to be in a position to give charity and support to others, was better for him than weeks and years of studying Torah.[29]

Here too, understanding the will of God overrides adherence to the strict rule of halakhah, and even, to some extent, the hasidic censure of concern for one's livelihoood, which distracts the individual from his study and prayer.[30] On the other hand we may note that according to the *siddur* of R. Shneur Zalman of Lyady (and it is possible that the idea derives from the teaching of R. Jeḥiel Michel of Zloczow), there are individuals so deranged by the grief of exile and poverty that they are incapable of praying at all, 'and this is better for them than if they were praying in a state of total

[25] His letter, published in R. Judah Leib of Gur, *Otsar mikhtavim uma'amarim* (Jerusalem, 1986), 74. There is a remarkable similarity between what is considered to be the innovative and uniquely hasidic conception of prayer (see e.g. Rivka Schatz-Uffenheimer, *Haḥasidut kemistikah* (Jerusalem, 1968), ch. 6) and the following statement by none other than the Gaon of Vilna (Elijah b. Solomon Zalman, *Shenot Eliyahu* (Lemberg, 1799), 'Mishnayot-berakhot', ch. 5, mishnah 1): 'Prayer should not be intended to gratify the personal needs of the individual; rather one should pray that the whole of Israel should attain to a state of perfect harmony, restoring to perfect harmony the "Congregation of Israel" (*keneset yisrael*) in the realm above'. According to the Gaon, only the prayer 'O my God! guard [my tongue etc.]' (*Elohai netsor*) at the end of the Eighteen Benedictions refers to the personal needs of the individual. Cf. R. Hayyim of Volozhin, *Nefesh haḥayim*, gate 2, chs. 11–15, and above, n. 17.

[26] See R. Shneur Zalman of Lyady, *Hilkhot talmud torah* (Shklov, 1794), ch. 3; cf. id., *Torah or* [Kopys, 1836; Zhitomir, 1862] (Brooklyn, NY, 1984), 98*c*, on the person who is able to study Torah but does not.

[27] R. Zevi Elimelekh's commentary on *Sur mera*, comments 30 and 55–6, pp. 7*b* and 15*a–b*, and cf. the main text by R. Zevi Hirsch of Zhidachov.

[28] See *Mei hashilo'aḥ*, ii. 36*b*.

[29] See *Beit Aharon*, 294, where it is evident that he forced many of his followers to adopt this attitude.

[30] This is a common theme throughout the literature. See e.g. R. Dov Ber Shneuri of Lubavitch (the Mitteler Rebbe), *Derekh ḥayim* [Kopys, 1819], (Brooklyn, NY, 1955), introd., and cf. the commentary on this by R. Dov Ber's disciple, R. Hillel of Parichi, in R. Dov Ber Shneuri of Lubavitch, *Likutei be'urim* (Warsaw, 1868), the last section of the book.

self-abnegation . . . for this [their grief and pain] is the main intention.'[31] In other words, even distraction from prayer has a positive value in the process of weighing up all the factors and circumstances which govern the decision on how to act.

The same applies to charity: the sages decreed that a man should not give to charity more than a fifth of his wealth,[32] and yet R. Shneur Zalman of Lyady allows, even recommends, the dissipation of all one's worldly possessions to charity, and this essentially for reasons of hasidic piety rather than halakhah.[33] Similarly, the Rabbi of Lyady argues that in our time we are obliged to ransom captives even when the captors demand more than the captives are worth (although the Mishnah specifically forbids this,[34] and there are those who see this principle as an example of hasidic piety overriding halakhah.[35]

We have dealt with the three central issues of study, prayer,[36] and charity, but the same rule applies to everything pertaining to Torah: hasidism will always examine deeds in the light of the will of God and the instinctive inclination of the individual,

[31] R. Shneur Zalman of Lyady, *Seder tefilot mikol hashanah* (Zhitomir, 1863), 157 (the end of the section 'Kavanat hamikveh'). Hielman in *Beit rabbi*, i. 3*a*, notes that 'What is said in the *Siddur* at the end of "Kavanat hamikveh" is a tradition which he received from . . . R. Jeḥiel Michel [of Zloczow]', and he seems to be referring to our passage. See also R. Shneur Zalman of Lyady, *Torah or*, on 'Noaḥ', 8*c*, the discussion on the verse (S. of S. 8: 7) 'Many waters cannot quench love.' The same idea is stated in similar terms by a number of other hasidic leaders, in response to complaints by their followers to the effect that preoccupation with material hardship was preventing them from study and prayer. R. Israel of Ruzhin, for example, replied: 'How do you know that the Holy One, blessed be He, desires your study and prayer? He may prefer your broken heart' (J. L. Levin, *Ḥasidim mesaperim* (3 vols.; Jerusalem, 1979), i. 40). Similarly, R. Levi Isaac of Berdichev is reported as saying: 'Perhaps the Holy One, blessed be He, does not require either your prayer or your study? Perhaps He desires your material concerns and endeavours?' (*Ḥasidim mesaperim*, i. 43).

[32] Ket. 67*b*.

[33] See *Likutei amarim*: *Tanya* [Slavuta, 1796; Vilna, 1900], bilingual edn, trans. N. Nindel, N. Mangel, Z. Pesner, and J. Schochet (London, 1973), 'Igeret hakodesh', ch. 10; 'Igeret hateshuvah', ch. 3. The Baal Shem Tov is also said to have set aside for charity more than a fifth of his income, justifying this by the claim that to give to charity is his pleasure, and no limit is set on the amount which one may spend on pleasures. R. Mendel of Vizhnitz, on the other hand, said that he would rather transgress the command of the sages and lose his share in the World to Come than deny charity to the poor and secure his share in Gan Eden (Levin, *Ḥasidim mesaperim*, i. 128).

[34] Gitin, 4: 6.

[35] See the letter of J. A. Kamelhar in *Yagdil torah*, no. 63 (New York, Kislev–Tevet 5745 [1985–6]), where he argues that R. Shneur Zalman of Lyady considered the mishnaic rule incompatible with hasidic piety, but while at the time of the Mishnah it was reasonable not to pay an exorbitant ransom on the grounds of 'restoring the world to good order' (*tikun ha'olam*), at the present time it is precisely for the sake of 'restoring the world to good order' that one should take pity on the children of Israel and stretch one's resources beyond the limit of capacity as set by the Mishnah.

[36] The insistence on preserving the essential quality of prayer—service of God which comes from the heart—gave rise to a number of extraneous practices which were not altogether straightforward from the halakhic point of view. These included the setting of regular periods of study (and even eating) before prayer, in order to improve the quality of prayer. The Habad prayer book *Sidur torah or* (numerous editions were published between Vilna, 1887 and Brooklyn, NY, 1987) contains the approbation (originally printed in 'Sidur hayashan' [Shneur Zalman of Lyady's *Sedur tefilot mikol hashanah*, Kopys, 1822 edn.]) of R. Judah Leib, brother of R. Shneur Zalman of Lyady, in which he quoted his brother 'who had heard from etc.' (which may be a reference to the Besht) that he used to mock the grammarians of recent generations who pronounced grammatically those words of the daily service which were not usually pronounced according to the rules of grammar, 'thereby obscuring the essential feature of prayer which is that it should be "with intention"'. Indeed, meticulous care with the pronunciation of words in prayer has always been a characteristic of mitnaggedic piety.

both of which change according to the circumstances of time and place. This is the fluidity to which I refer in the title of the present chapter.

In this context it is important to mention the book *Mei hashilo'aḥ* by R. Mordecai Joseph of Izbica (pupil of Rabbi Simḥah Bunem of Przysucha; d. 1853–4).[37] The principal motif in his book is the notion expressed by a particular reading of Ps. 119: 126, which is taken to mean: 'It is time to work for the Lord by making void the Law.' This is the response to the individual's insight into the true will of God[38] whereby many sins related in the Bible were in fact pure acts which were carried out at the wrong time—errors of timing rather than sins as such. All the admonitions in the Torah against making molten gods, graven images, idols of silver and of gold—all these are interpreted by the Rabbi of Izbica as warnings against adherence to rigid rules and ancestral traditions.[39] Thus he explains the verse (Lev. 19: 31) 'Regard not them that have familiar spirits' (*ha'ovot*) as meaning 'Regard not the fathers' (*ha'avot*).[40] Indeed, many hasidic leaders had made a point, as if on principle, of departing from the customs of their forebears.

Nevertheless, the Rabbi of Izbica repeatedly warns against ingenious reinterpretation of the plain sense of the Torah even when the intention is good.[41] He states that even when offering oneself as a sacrifice for the sake of the sanctification of God's name, one should examine one's motives closely and be sure that one's deeds and heart are truly directed towards Heaven.[42] He often preaches that it is necessary to enter into doubts and not to flee from them, while at other times he warns that one should not put oneself in a place of danger.[43]

The same sentiment is expressed in a discourse by R. Shneur Zalman of Lyady, who warns that this type of divine service is fraught with danger and requires caution and great circumspection, since not all circumstances are equal and not every mind is capable of withstanding such trials. The worshipper is like a man walking a tightrope across a chasm, with 'do not be wicked' on the one side and 'do not be foolish' on the other.[44] And we are well aware that the admonition 'do not be foolish' does not occur in the legal code of the *Shulḥan arukh*.

[37] The teaching of the Rabbi of Izbica has been the subject of a number of scholarly studies: J. G. Weiss, 'Torat hadeterminism hadati le R. Mordekhai Yosef Leiner meIzbica', in *Sefer yovel le Yitsḥak Ber* (Jerusalem, 1961), 447–53; id., 'A Late Jewish Utopia of Religious Freedom', in id., *Studies in Eastern European Jewish Mysticism* (Oxford, 1985), 209–48; Rivka Schatz-Uffenheimer, 'Autonomiah shel haru'aḥ vetorat mosheh', *Molad*, 21: 183–4 (1963), 554–61; M. Faierstein, *All Is in the Hands of Heaven: The Teachings of Rabbi Mordecai Joseph of Izbica* (New York, 1989); id., 'Personal Redemption in Hasidism', in the present volume. All these leave considerable scope for further research into the original and remarkable teachings of the Rabbi of Izbica.

[38] See *Mei hashilo'aḥ*, i. 52*a–b*, 30*d*.

[39] See ibid. i. 30*d*, 38*a–b*, 48*a*, 57*c*; ii. 20*c–d*, 27*a*, and in numerous additional passages.

[40] Ibid. 16*d*.

[41] Ibid. i. 39*b–c*; ii. 30*d*, and cf. ibid. ii. 30*a–b*, where Joshua's innocence is seen as preferable to the 'sin for the sake of Heaven' committed by the spies.

[42] Ibid. ii. 21*a*.

[43] Ibid. i. 15*c–d*, 46*a–b*, 62*b*; ii. 16*c*.

[44] See *Ma'amrei Admor haZaken*: *Inyanim* (Brooklyn, NY, 1983), 394–401. This may be the origin of the saying, ascribed to R. Shneur Zalman of Lyady, that 'to be a fool is prohibited from the Torah'. In the name of R. Naphtali of Ropczyce (Ropshits) and others it was said that one should always be *gut*, *frum*, and *klug* (good, pious, and clever) at the same time, since the person who is good but neither pious nor clever is

In the pamphlet *Igeret viku'aḥ vehashalom*, attributed to one of the early followers of the Habad school,[45] it is explained that the mitnaggedim may be regarded as 'righteous men' who do not deviate from the straight line of the law, whereas the hasidim may be regarded as 'penitents', seekers after the Lord who are capable of deviating from the letter of the law for His name's sake, like that laundryman in the Gemara who took his own life for the love of God and was accepted into the life of the World Hereafter.[46] Such is the case with other acts which run contrary to the halakhah but are occasioned by the love of God.

Similarly, the Rabbi of Izbica suggests that the House of Ephraim and the House of Judah were hostile towards one another because they represented the conflict between the devotees of halakhah on the one hand, and those who know the law well but look to the will of God and seek the *inner* truth on the other hand. They serve the Lord in a particular way, not simply because this is how it has always been done before but since it is their wish to know what is the will of God at *this* very moment, and perhaps what was right for yesterday is not right for today, and perhaps today is the 'time to work for the Lord by making void the Law', which is not the way of halakhah.[47]

It is obvious that divine service which is performed in such a flexible and fluid manner can both raise and lower the spiritual level of the hasid, and may even lead to a collapse: ' "In" today and "out" tomorrow'—in the words of that Habad hasid quoted above.[48] A lucid formulation of this idea is to be found in the teaching of R. Leibele Eger, who derives it from the statement in the Mishnah that 'all that engage in the rite of the (Red) Heifer from the beginning until the end, render garments unclean'—although the Heifer herself purifies![49] As he explains it: all those who engage in the purification of their souls and desire to draw near to holiness 'from the beginning until

an adulterer, the one who is pious but neither good nor clever is a fool, and the one who is clever but neither pious nor good is a heretic. Many popular hasidic sayings condemn the *frumer*. The most pertinent is R. Menahem Mendel of Kotsk's definition of the *frumer* as one who makes the essential trivial and the trivial essential (*Si'aḥ sarfei kodesh*, i. 75). J. G. Weiss ('Reshit tsemiḥatah shel haderekh haḥasidit'), *Zion*, 16 (1951), 89–90) and A. Rubinstein (*Hebrew Encyclopaedia*, xx (1971), s.v. 'Rabi Israel ben Eliezer Ba'al Shem', 590; id., 'Al rabo shel haBesht ve'al haketavim shemehem lamad haBesht', *Tarbiz*, 48 (1978–9), 153 n. 23) speculated on the precise meaning of 'the wisdom of the Besht' (*ḥokhmat haBesht*), an expression which occurs in a certain passage in *Shivḥei haBesht*. It seems to me that it refers simply to divine service which is executed sensibly, as explained above.

45 About him see J. Mondshine, *Migdal oz*, 347.

46 Ket. 103*b*.

47 See *Mei hashilo'aḥ*, i. 14*d*–15*a*, and 28*d*, where the tribe of Judah is characterized as lacking a fixed mode of conduct and wavering between righteousness and penitence. Cf. ibid. 29*c*, where the same tribe is described as superior to all the others, and this is offered as the reason why the messiah will emerge from within its ranks. See also ibid. 42*b*–*c*, where the verse in Eccles. 12: 12 'be admonished: of making many books there is no end' is taken to mean that good conduct cannot be expounded in books, and one must understand the will of God, and direct oneself towards it, according to the variable conditions of time and circumstance.

48 See above p. 303. In the same vein, the Rabbi of Dynow is reported as saying (Levin, *Ḥasidim mesaperim*, i. 21) that only a mountain—an inanimate mass of soil—can be permanently elevated without ever coming down. By contrast, a good horseman must know how to fall off his horse. And R. Zevi Hirsch of Zhidachov (*Beit Yisrael*, 37*a*) said that only the Holy One, blessed be He, can remain permanently in the state of holiness, but man who is flesh and blood must fall from time to time, 'sometimes walking forward, sometimea backward, depending on the time and circumstances'.

49 *Parah*, 4: 4.

the end' render themselves unclean—since throughout their lives they are subjected to various distractions and temptations by all kinds of worldly delights. But 'she herself purifies'—by means of these very distractions and temptations one overcomes all the forces which are contrary to holiness and attaches oneself to the true joys and delights of Torah and *mitsvot*. For the essence of purification and holiness which make a man worthy of receiving Torah is to be subjected to all kinds of distractions which seek to separate him from holiness. By his struggle to subdue them, his holiness is consolidated. Only at the end of this process does it become clear that all his defilements and 'descents' from the state of holiness were for the purpose of ascending[50] (and to complete the depiction of the hasid by the same follower of the Habad school who was quoted above—'"In"' today and "out" tomorrow, but in the end he pushes his way "in"').

Such ordeals are the lot of the conscientious hasid who has no book of rules to guide him. This notion, too, is lucidly expounded in the teaching of the Rabbi of Dynow when he refers to King David's appeal to God: 'Preserve my soul for I am a hasid,'[51] meaning that being a 'hasid' renders him needful of greater protection. This suggests that the ordinary person, when confronted by the evil inclination inciting him to sin and telling him that he would thereby be fulfilling a commandment, can ask his rabbi or consult the holy texts to discover whether this act does indeed fall within the 613 commandments and their ramifications. But if the one tempted is a hasid, this advice will not avail him, because the evil inclination will say to him: 'To be sure this "commandment" is not expounded in any book, but you are a hasid and you practise the kind of piety which takes precedence over the letter of the law. You must perform this "commandment" even though it is not written in the Torah or the words of our sages.'[52]

The conscientious hasid cannot resolve his doubts even by choosing to follow the example of his hasidic master; it is precisely in the sense of 'Do not imitate your leaders' that R. Elimelekh of Lyzhansk had interpreted the verse (Lev. 19: 4) 'Turn ye not unto idols',[53] and the Rabbi of Dynow is unequivocal in his condemnation of those who imitate the actions of the zaddikim, whether in eating to excess or in abstinence and fasting.[54] Yet there are some hasidic teachings which insist that there are occasions when it is desirable to model oneself on one's teacher.[55] The greatest of all hasidic authorities, the Baal Shem Tov himself, had instructed all his followers to 'raise' their 'straying' or evil thoughts and attributes, yet subsequent leaders of hasidism, who regarded themselves as his faithful disciples, were wont to say that *according to the way of the Baal*

[50] R. Judah Leib Eger, *Torat emet* (Lublin, 1890), on 'Ḥukat', 170–1.

[51] Ps. 86: 2.

[52] *Agra dekhalah*, on 'Korah', 56*a*–*b*. The text is introduced as: 'that which I have heard by way of *derush* (a homiletic insight) . . . Nevertheless, the enlightened reader would realize that this sort of temptation by the evil inclination is not uncommon.'

[53] Elimelekh of Lyzhansk, *No'am Elimelekh* [Lemberg, 1788], on 'Kedoshim', 330, on 'Emor', 347; *Or Elimelekh*, ed. A. E. M. Pakscher (Jerusalem, 1984), 150. R. Elimelekh's comment is quoted also by the Rabbi of Zhidachov in his *Sur mera*, 26*a*.

[54] *Agra dekhalah*, on 'Ekev', 92*a*–*b*.

[55] See S. Z. Breitstein, *Siḥot ḥayim* (Piotrkow, 1914), 54, in the names of R. Hayyim Meir of Mogielnica and R. Eliezer of Kozienice. See also Y. Meir, *Gedolim tsadikim* (Kalusz, 1932), at the end, where it is stated in the name of R. Meir of Peremyshlany that one may imitate the zaddikim, but only when their actions are 'bitter', not when they are 'sweet'. Cf. N. N. Donner, *Sha'arei ha'emunah* (Warsaw, 1901), 47, where the author points to the absurdities which may be committed out of mindless adherence to the principle of imitating the zaddikim.

Shem Tov, Heaven forbid that everyone should act thus![56] This is the extent to which the hasid lacks any guidance if he wants to walk with confidence in a sure path.

R. Naphtali of Ropczyce, who fulminated against many of the hasidic irregularities in halakhic practice,[57] was himself no less 'subtle' or ingenious in his pursuit of the *inner* truth of God's will (*arum beyirah*), as a brief statement of his will illustrate clearly: one of his young followers received from him instructions for the order of his day, a precise and detailed order of worship, and when the hasid turned to go, the Rabbi recalled him and said: 'But sometimes you must do the *exact* opposite.'

And the Rabbi of Przysucha, as was his wont, summarized the entire issue in the briefest of forms: 'There are no rules in divine service, and even this rule is not a rule.'[58]

I hope that I have succeeded in demonstrating the instability, indeed the fluidity, of categories in hasidism, which by its very nature resists the imposition of constant and firm definitions. My argument runs contrary to such scholarly attempts as have been made in recent times to mould hasidism into rigid patterns: the authenticity of diverse traditions is measured by criteria derived from artificial models, and if the traditions do not fit neatly into one or another of these patterns they are rejected, or else presented as a new current of hasidic thought distinguished by a structure of its own.[59]

[56] R. Shneur Zalman of Lyady (*Tanya*, ch. 28) believed that the 'raising' of 'straying' thoughts was intended only for the zaddikim, and R. Meshullam Phoebus Heller of Zbarazh held the same view (*Yosher divrei emet* (Munkacz, 1905), i, ch. 16, 16*a*, and ii, ch. 3, 24*a*). R. Ze'ev Wolf of Zhitomir was similarly inclined to the opinion that ordinary people neither do nor should attempt to 'raise' their thoughts (see *Or hame'ir* [Korets, 1798] (Warsaw, 1883), on 'Vayeshev', 39; on 'Shir hashirim', 31, 41; on 'Tazri'a' 44; on 'Ruth', 34; on 'Masei', 83; on 'Devarim', 6, and elsewhere). In Bratslav hasidism, R. Nahman advances the view that the zaddik 'raises' such thoughts (*Likutei moharan* [2 vols.; Ostrog, 1808; Mogilev, 1811] (1 vol.; Jerusalem, 1969), part 1, *torah* 96) while advising everyone else to ignore them during prayer (*Siḥot haran* [in *Shivḥei haRan*], s. 72), and R. Nathan Sternhartz states that the majority of people should ignore their 'straying' thoughts, but the great zaddikim must 'grasp' and 'raise' them (*Likutei halakhot* [8 vols.; Zolkiew (Zholkva), 1846; Lemberg, 1861] (Jerusalem, 1970), *Yoreh de'ah*, 'Hilkhot shilu'aḥ haken', 4: 2). The Rabbi of Dynow never tires of warning that 'raising' thoughts is the exclusive domain of the zaddikim (see his commentary on *Sur mera*, no. 1 following comment 86, and comment 147; *Agra dekhalah*, on 'Ki tetse', 104*a*; on 'Kedoshim', 40*d*; on 'Re'eh', 96*c*–97*a*; *Agra defirka* [Lemberg, 1868] (Munkacz, 1942), no. 140, 17*c*–*d*; *Derekh pikudeikha* (Jerusalem, n.d.), 25, 159, 173–4. However, in a number of instances he discusses the 'raising' of straying thoughts without specifying the type of person who should engage in this task (see *Agra dekhalah*, on 'Shemini', 34*a*; on 'Metsora', 37*a*–*b*; on 'Re'eh', 97*c*–*d*; on 'Shofetim', 102*a*–*b*; *Likutei Mahartsa* (Jerusalem, 1972), no. 188, 37; *Benei yisakhar*, on 'Tishrei', no. 12, 35*c*–*d*. A clear statement in favour of 'raising' thoughts, as well as an explanation of the technique of 'raising' can be found in the works of R. Zevi Hirsch of Zhidachov (see *Peri kodesh hilulim* (Lemberg, 1865), 11*a*–*c*, and *Beit Yisrael*, 41*a*–*b*). R. Isaac of Komarno followed the same line (see *Shulḥan hatahor* (Tel Aviv, 1963) 76–8, 126, and the references in the *Hebrew Encyclopaedia*, vii. 799).

[57] See the chapter dedicated to him in J. A. Kamelhar, *Dor de'ah* (Bilgoraj, 1933), 236 ff., where he is said, however, to have requested that no merit should be ascribed to him on his tombstone other than that he was 'subtle in God-fearing' (*arum beyirah*) as defined below, in the main text. As regards the statement quoted there in his name, see a variant tradition in the appendix below.

[58] Levin, *Ḥasidim mesaperim*, iii. 28 (drawn from Rokotz, *Tiferet hayehudi*, 93, 42).

[59] Examples of this abound. See Schatz-Uffenheimer, *Haḥasidut kemistikah*, 88, where the failure to distinguish between, on the one hand, prayer for the satisfaction of a particular personal need and, on the other hand, the concern for one's personal needs at the time of prayer results in the notion of a clash between the Mezhirech and the Korets 'schools' (ibid. 95, 139 ff.); id., 'Antispiritualizm baḥasidut', *Molad*, 20: 171–2 (1962), where, through selective quotation (e.g. disregard for the issue of 'sifting out the sparks' (*berur hanitsotsot*) in R. Shneur Zalman of Lyady's *Tanya* (cf. *Tanya*, ch. 37 with 'Antispiritualizm', 520), an issue whose presence in the book does not accord with the main thesis of the article), or

Not all the differences of opinion between one zaddik and another stem necessarily from coherent differences in overall orientation, just as not all the many discrepancies that may be found within the body of teachings associated with each of these zaddikim stem necessarily from poor presentation and lack of coherence. Rather, it is the nature of fluid things that they cannot be fixed permanently and exist in rigid form; today they are thus and tomorrow otherwise; one individual may be instructed to act in a certain fashion, his fellow in another.[60]

This applies to the vast literature which comprises the teaching of R. Shneur Zalman of Lyady. His grandson (and intimate disciple) R. Menahem Mendel of Lubavitch (the Tsemaḥ Tsedek), unequalled as an elucidator of his grandfather's methods, writes with regard to a certain discourse of R. Shneur Zalman's that it is based on the teachings of one kabbalistic school, whereas another discourse is based on the teachings of another.[61] This is true particularly of the discourses which deal with divine service. The grandson explains that a certain statement of his grandfather was 'an ad hoc instruction. Since I remember well to whom it was addressed, I know that it was intended to dissuade that person from overreaching his own grasp and from excessive ecstasy in prayer.'[62]

through distortive quotation (e.g. the insertion of the phrase 'during divine service!' ('Antispiritualizm', 523) where the text clearly states '*not* during divine service' (*Tanya*, ch. 27), the author defines the structure of hasidic thought and then proceeds to exclude the *Tanya* from it as an 'anti-hasidic document' ('Antispiritualizm', 516). The same applies to J. G. Weiss's suspicion ('The Kavvanoth of Prayer in Early Hasidism', in id., *Eastern European Jewish Mysticism*, 108–9 and n. 45, 121–2), that a certain parable, ascribed to the Besht by one of the Maggid of Mezhirech's most eminent disciples, could not have been told by the Besht since it is incompatible with what Weiss defines as the authentic teaching of the Besht on the subject. The notion that what is authentic or inauthentic in any body of hasidic teachings, what is said in earnest or is merely offered as lip-service, apologetics, or in the heat of a polemic, can be identified by means of 'the intuition which one acquires through reading the sources' (Schatz-Uffenheimer, 'Antispiritualizm', 513) is untenable, since the intuition of the scholar cannot always be trusted (for examples of its failure see Schatz-Uffenheimer, *Haḥasidut kemistikah*, 65 n. 36, where the spiritual ostentation associated with the desire to lay *tefilin* during the afternoon service was not recognized as underlying the hasidic text under discussion; or 167, where the admonition of R. Joseph Caro's 'Maggid' (in Caro's *Maggid meisharim* [Lublin, 1645] (Jerusalem, 1960), 6) was mistaken for an admonition by the Maggid of Mezhirech to his disciple R. Jeḥiel Michel of Zloczow).

[60] For an example of this see below, the discussion around n. 62. Much of the entry on hasidic thought in the *Hebrew Encyclopaedia* has resulted from the deployment of the scholarly method discussed above (n. 59) which discerns imaginary 'internal contradictions' in hasidic texts. This is the method which has led also to the theory of the 'two-faces'—the esoteric and the exoteric—of the Habad teaching, a theory which arises from fundamental misunderstandings and confusions (such as the failure to distinguish between 'straying thoughts' (*maḥashavot zarot*) and sinful thought (*maḥshevet averah*) (ibid. 812), from the disregard for texts which are incompatible with the thrust of the scholarly argument (such as the issue of 'raising the sparks' in ch. 37 of *Tanya*, and cf. I. Tishby and J. Dan, 'Torat haḥasidut vesifrutah', *Hebrew Encyclopaedia*, xvii (1965), 790), or from the distortion of texts for the sake of the argument (as in the interpolation of the phrase 'a perfect zaddik' (*tsadik gamur*) in a passage which deals with 'straying thoughts' in order to create an internal contradiction in the doctrine of R. Shneur Zalman of Lyady. See Tishby and Dan, 'Ḥasidut', 793).

[61] See his observations regarding the various kabbalistic conceptions of the *sefirot* in his *Or hatorah: Ma'amrei Razal ve'inyanim* (Brooklyn, NY, 1983), 258 ff., 285 ff.; id., *Be'urei haZohar* (2 vols.; Brooklyn, NY, 1978), ii. 963–4.

[62] *Or hatorah; Bereshit–Devarim*, on 'Genesis' (Brooklyn, NY, 1970), 1207, and cf. 2027. For the question whether or not R. Shneur Zalman's ad hoc instruction was addressed to R. Aaron Halevi of Starosielce see Hielman, *Beit rabbi*, 134.

As for 'sin for the sake of Heaven', which certain scholars have 'uncovered' in the writings of Moses Hayyim Luzzatto and in hasidism alike, detecting in both a whiff of the 'Sabbatean heresy',[63] one cannot rely on their judgement as to who was a Sabbatean and what could be construed as heresy, especially considering that the pronouncements of R. Jacob Emden on this subject were never widely accepted, and most of the books in which he found Sabbatean heresy were not proscribed from the community of Israel. Or we may take the example of the hasidic *rebbe*s of Munkacz and Satmar who in the last generation denounced many eminent and worthy individuals as heretics, but for all their protestations failed to impair the respectability of their colleagues of Belz and of Gur who were the main targets for their attacks.

Sometimes it seems that, in the opinion of some scholars, the followers of hasidism spent most of their time studying Sabbateanism, and the remainder of their time they devoted to obscuring and camouflaging this pursuit. Yet the Rabbi of Dynow in his teachings, which were published and became popular books, did not hesitate to deal openly with 'sin for the sake of Heaven',[64] a concept which, like the notions that 'It is time to work for the Lord by making void the Law'[65] and 'In all your ways know Him—even in an act of sin',[66] is based on classical rabbinic tradition.

The fundamental difference between the hasidic 'sin for the sake of Heaven' which is an act of piety and 'sin for the sake of Heaven' which is an impious act is as follows: the hasidic 'sin' is committed out of complete surrender to the will of God and His commandments, and therefore it is expressed in the exaltation of form over matter, spirit over flesh, with unstinting prayer, charity that exceeds the requirements of the halakhah, and other such extravagances in which the soul delights while the body suffers. As for the Sabbateans (extremists) and their hangers-on, although they exalt the spirit with their lips and have been labelled spiritualists, their sins are acts of lust, which the body craves but which are distasteful to the refined soul.

Professor Tishby and Professor Schatz have both commended the courage of the hasidim who did not follow their method to its logical conclusion, and did not breach altogether the wall of the halakhah and its prohibitions.[67] But it is clearly evident that the wall of halakhah was never breached, not because of 'the historic responsibility towards the People of Israel and its halakhic tradition', in the words of Professor Schatz, but rather because hasidism aspires to fulfil nothing other than the will of God, and the will of God consists in nothing other than that His Law and His commandments should be observed. Thus the Rabbi of Dynow writes:

A sin for the sake of Heaven is greater than a *mitsvah* that is not for the sake of Heaven. This could not be expounded in the Torah because it is governed by the circumstances of time and

[63] See Tishby and Dan, 'Ḥasidut', 783, 798; I. Tishby, *Netivei emunah uminut* (Ramat Gan, 1964), 182–5.

[64] 'A sin [committed] for the sake of Heaven (*averah lishmah*) is as great as [or: greater than] a *mitsvah* which is [performed] for ulterior motives (*shelo lishmah*)' (Hor. 10*b*; Naz. 23*b*). This concept, which is always positive, must be distinguished from the utterly negative concept of 'a *mitsvah* which is arrived at through sin' (*mitsvah haba'ah ba'averah*) (Ber. 47*a*, and elsewhere). The two concepts are often confused with one another, not least through the misleadingly titled essay by the late G. Scholem ('Mitsvah haba'ah ba'averah', *Keneset*, 2 (1937), 347–92; pub. in Eng. as 'Redemption through Sin', in id,. *The Messianic Idea in Judaism* (New York, 1971), 78–141).

[65] Ps. 119: 126, and cf. Ber. Mishnah 9: 5.

[66] Prov. 3: 6, and cf. Ber. 63*a*.

[67] Tishby and Dan, 'Ḥasidut', 806; Schatz-Uffenheimer, *Haḥasidut kemistikah*, 154.

place and the soul's desire to do the will of God, blessed be He. It is on account of this love of God, blessed be He, that the soul will consent even to descend into Hell and endure everlasting shame, if only His great name be sanctified thereby. And we have heard that the lovers of God, blessed be He, in our own generation, said: even if we knew for certain that the reward for keeping commandments were Hell, and the reward of sin were Paradise, in spite of this, we would prefer to keep the commandments of the Creator, blessed be He.[68]

APPENDIX

The concept of 'sin for the sake of Heaven', and the facility for departing from the strict rule of halakhah in order to comply with the divine will which is not fixed but must be sought out in every changing circumstance of time and place, occur in other sources as well. I have assembled and reproduced them here—without much elaboration—in order to put in perspective the statements of R. Zevi Elimelekh of Dynow on this score.

1. *Tsava'at haRibash* [n.p. (Ostrog?), 1793; Zolkiew, 1795], ed. J. I. Schochet (Brooklyn NY, 1975), s. 46. 15–16: '"It is time to work for thee, Lord: for they have made void [understood as: by making void] thy law" (Ps. 119: 126). [This means] that there are times when the fulfilment of a *mitsvah* entails a small element of transgression and one should pay no heed to the evil inclination in its endeavours to stop one from fulfilling that *mitsvah*; rather one should say to the evil inclination: Surely, it is not my intention to provoke the Lord in fulfilling this *mitsvah*, etc., for if I knew that the Creator did not wish me to do so, I would not have fulfilled it, since all I want is to please the Creator, blessed be He, by means of this *mitsvah* etc. But in all events, one should discern for oneself whether to fulfil this *mitsvah* or not.'

2. Ibid. s. 65. 20: 'One should carry out one's [pious] deeds in secret, so that people may not realize that one is engaged in acts of piety. However, if one has not reached a high level [of piety] one should carry out such deeds in public, for if one were to follow the ways of the world in public while striving to be pious in private only, one might be seduced by the ways of the world and end up acting impiously out of the desire to act piously.'

3. In the name of hasidic leader R. Israel of Ruzhin (1796–1850), the story is told of a certain young man who was living at his father-in-law's house in a mitnaggedic town. He had promised his father-in-law on a handshake (which has the validity of an oath) that he would not travel to visit the Maggid of Mezhirech but his desire to go could not be restrained; he broke his promise and travelled to Mezhirech on more than one occasion. His father-in-law consulted the town's rabbi and was told that according to the halakhah his daughter must be divorced from her husband. Once the couple were divorced, the young man was thrown out of his father-in-law's house and remained penniless. He lived in the *beit midrash* until he fell ill and died. The Rebbe of Ruzhin concluded the story with the following insight: 'When the messiah comes, this young

[68] *Agra dekhalah*, on 'Noaḥ', 71*b*–*c*.

man will take his case to a court of law presided over by the messiah himself. He will summon his father-in-law and charge him with having caused his death but the father-in-law will defend himself on the grounds that he had simply followed the ruling of the town's rabbi. The town's rabbi will be summoned next and he will point to the halakhic basis for his ruling. The messiah will then wish to know why the young man had broken his promise to his father-in-law, and the young man will plead: I was very eager to visit the Rebbe! The messiah will pronounce as follows. To the father-in-law he will say: You followed the ruling of the town's rabbi and you have acted justly. To the rabbi he will say: You ruled according to the halakhah and you have acted justly. But I—the messiah will say—I have come to those who have acted unjustly!' (R. Solomon Tellingator, *Tiferet Yisrael* (Jerusalem, 1945), 35–8.) The same story occurs, with some variations, in R. Yoshe Shoḥet of Brisk, *Kitvei R. Yoshe Shoḥet* (Jerusalem, 1981), 59–60, where the messiah's answer is a play on the Yiddish word *umgerekht* meaning both 'unjust' and 'unexpected', that is to say, the messiah will come unexpectedly, to an unsuspecting, unjust world!

4. The hasidic leader R. Abraham of Slonim (1804–84) in his book *Yesod ha'avodah* (Jerusalem, 1989), 120, elaborates on the talmudic statement that 'a transgression committed for the sake of Heaven is greater than a *mitsvah* carried out for some other sake' (Hor., 10*b*). He makes the following, rather surprising, comment: 'You should know that a transgression for the sake of Heaven may be preferable even to a *mitsvah* for the sake of Heaven, as, for example, when the transgression enhances the greater dignity and sanctity of the name of the Lord, blessed be He'. In support of this he adduces the talmudic dictum: 'It is better for one letter of the alphabet to be obliterated from the Torah if the name of Heaven is [thereby] sanctified in public' (Yeb., 79*a*).

5. The hasidic leader R. Zaddok Hacohen of Lublin (1823–1900), a disciple of R. Mordecai Joseph Leiner of Izbica (discussed above, p. 310), makes the original statement that an individual who has committed a transgression for the sake of Heaven must atone for his transgression even though by means of it he has performed an extremely important *mitsvah* (see *Tsidkat hatsadik* (Lublin, 1902; 1913), 39, s. 128). In another of his books (*Peri tsadik* (Lublin, 1934), on 'Vayelekh', 187) he writes that when the individual is unable to 'fall', he is not able to 'ascend' either. It is precisely his 'descent' or 'fall' that intensifies his devotional work and invests him with greater spiritual force, and this is how the verse 'For a just man falleth seven times, and rises up again' (Prov. 24: 16) is to be understood: the falls enable him to stand up and rise (cf. above, pp. 311–12).

6. In one of his teachings R. Shneur Zalman of Lyady differentiates the divine service of the hasidim from that of the mitnaggedim, depicting the latter as static and frozen. He weaves this observation into a comment on the verses: 'Let thy *Thummim* and thy *Urim* be with thy holy one [in the original Hebrew—thy *ḥasid*] . . . smite through the loins of them that rise against him' (Deut. 33: 8–11). '"Thy *Thummim*" [the term *Thummim* deriving from a stem meaning 'perfection', 'wholeness']—these are the ones who serve the Lord perfectly and wholeheartedly . . . even though there is no fire in their hearts; 'thy *Urim*' [the term *Urim* deriving from a stem meaning 'fire']—these are the ones who are kindled with the fire of ecstasy—all this belongs to "thy hasid" . . . But "loins"—these are the upper part of the body . . . which does not move at all but

stays always in the same position . . . these are the ones who observe all the *mitsvot* in a manner "taught by the precept of men" [*mitsvat anashim melumadah*] (Isa. 29: 13), and they stay always in the same position because their hearts are devoid of inner intention and do not know how to serve the Lord in truth. They imagine that they are true but in fact they hate truth. These people are called "them that rise against him"—they rise against those who are true [in their divine service], the *Thummim* and the *Urim*' (*Ma'amrei Admor haZaken:—Ethalekh Liozno* (Brooklyn, NY, 1957), 55).

7. This elasticity of categories, and the rejection of all rigid definitions of divine service, find concrete expression in R. Isaac Bendery's account of his father-in-law, the hasidic leader R. Joseph of Radziwillow (1820–75, a great-grandson of R. Jeḥiel Michel of Zloczow who was a disciple of the Besht, and himself a follower of R. Israel of Ruzhin). According to R. Isaac, R. Joseph of Radziwillow once told him that in his youth he used to set a fixed time for each of his activities, hour by hour, day by day—a fixed time for preparation for prayer, for prayer, for study, and so on. Once he had set a time for any particular activity, nothing would move him to change it. One sabbath, during the reading of the Pentateuchal portion of 'Bo', on hearing the verse 'and we know not with what we must serve the Lord, until we come thither' [(Exod. 10: 26), understood here as meaning that it is impossible to know in advance what manner of service the Lord may require of us], he understood that he had been wrong to set his schedule in advance, and that he should rather consider afresh and decide how to act at every moment of each day. From that time on he refrained from setting his daily schedule in advance. Some years later, however, when his son-in-law R. Isaac was visiting Radziwillow again, R. Joseph declared that whenever he knew in advance that on a particular day, at a particular time, he was going to recite Zohar, and when that time arrived he was indeed reciting Zohar as anticipated, the session would be particularly productive. R. Isaac, who wondered how his father-in-law could possibly know in advance that he was going to be reciting Zohar on a particular day, reminded him of his earlier decision to follow the verse 'and we know not' etc. by refraining from planning his actions in advance. R. Joseph replied with a story. The disciples of R. Naphtali of Ropczyce once asked their master to set them a regular daily schedule of divine service. He answered as follows: Abraham the Patriarch was so distinguished in serving the Lord with the attribute of *ḥesed* that the evil inclination was forced to resort to the same attribute in opposing him. Isaac the Patriarch distinguished himself by serving the Lord with another attribute, *gevurah*, in opposition to which the evil inclination had had no previous experience. Jacob the Patriarch in his turn adopted yet another attribute, and so did all the zaddikim who have lived since then—each would open up a new righteous path, unfamiliar to the evil inclination. But now the evil inclination has come to know all the paths, and one may no longer stick to the same path but rather one should seek a new path each day. This is why I am unable to set you a regular schedule of divine service, for the days are not all the same, and while you should act in one way today, you should act in another way tomorrow (cf. the tradition reported in his name above, around n. 57). With this R. Joseph concluded his story and assured his son-in-law that he need not query his departure from an earlier mode of operation, and that, since the time when he had decided to refrain from planning his actions in advance, he had undergone

several other changes, sometimes acting this way, sometimes another. (See *Kovets siftei tsadikim*, 3 (Jan.—Shevat 1991), 21–3.)

8. *Yad avi shalom* (Warsaw, 1882) is an unusual work. The author, R. Meir Zevi of Zamosc (b. 1823 or 1833), was a ritual slaughterer in his town and a follower first of R. Menahem Mendel of Kotsk and later of R. Menahem Mendel of Lubavitch (the Tsemaḥ Tsedek). The book is distinguished not as a display of scholarship or any other intellectual quality but rather as a reflection of the author's 'ordinary hasid' mentality. He is engaged in constant conflict both with himself and with his environment, in the endeavour to serve the Lord in an authentically hasidic way. The inner struggles of the ordinary follower of hasidism are not often recorded in the literature of the movement, and this is what makes R. Meir's book so unusual.

On page 74 he explains the reason why the hasid must take great care to ensure that he does not 'fall'. Like R. Zevi Elimelekh of Dynow (cf. above, p. 312), he derives this idea from the verse 'Preserve my soul for I am a hasid' (Ps. 86: 2). He argues that such caution is necessary since, for the hasid, not all occasions are the same: sometimes he prays in ecstasy and contemplation, at other times he simply recites his prayers as fast as possible; sometimes he throws himself deep into his studies, at other times he studies little, as circumstances require; sometimes he sleeps till noon, at other times he stays up all night; sometimes he refrains from eating, at other times he indulges in food; sometimes he mixes with society, at other times he withdraws from it completely; and sometimes he contravenes the rule of halakhah as, for example, when he fails to observe the prescribed times of prayer,

> but he does this genuinely for the sake of uniting the Holy one, blessed be He, with his Presence, as is required at that time and circumstance . . . and in this departure from the rule of halakhah he must take great care (or, echoing the verse in Ps. 86—he must take care to 'preserve' his soul) lest he should be transgressing for his own sake, to gain honour or pleasure, for if, Heaven forbid, he was to direct his action to his own advantage, he might fall, Heaven forbid, into a deep pit never to rise from it again. This is so because he conducts himself in a disorderly fashion, unlike the mitnagged who follows the order of each day precisely . . . Therefore, all those who follow the hasidic way must take great care to 'preserve' themselves; they must penetrate the surface of things and weigh them up in their own minds, making sure that they are acting not in their own interest but only to please Him, blessed be He.

9. For hasidic departures from the strict rule of halakhah see Kamelhar, *Dor de'ah*, the chapter dedicated to R. Simḥah Bunem of Przysucha, where the author condemns the 'hasidic digressions' from the rule of halakhah in no uncertain terms. However, his condemnations were omitted from subsequent editions of the work, largely as a result of the remarks by R. Meir Jeḥiel Halevi of Ostrowiec, to the effect that Przysucha hasidism had long abandoned the practice of 'digression' and was now toeing the line advocated by R. Isaac Meir of Gur (author of *Ḥidushei haRim*), urging a return to the full rigour of the *Shulḥan arukh*. See on this Y. Mondshine, *Hatsofeh ledoro* (Jerusalem, 1987), 243–4. Similarly, R. Naphtali Zevi Berlin ('HaNatsiv') of Volozhin published a letter in the newspaper *Kol maḥazikei ḥadas* (Cracow, 15 Jan. 1884) in which he outlined what he considered to be the way in which adherence to religion may be strengthened. In it he said:

One should make a point of following precisely the opinion of our sages, namely the Talmud and the *Shulḥan arukh*, rather than digressing from it on the instruction of some eminent and saintly individual who imagines that his is the more appropriate route to divine service. Many of the God-fearers, upholders of religion of our time, follow their own path to the love of God, even where it does not accord with the Talmud and the *Shulḥan arukh*. They rely in this on the statement of the sages [San., 106*b*]: 'The All Merciful seeks out the heart' (*raḥmana liba ba'ei*) but it leads them to numerous transgressions, sins which are all 'for the sake of Heaven', to enable them to attain to the love of God of which they speak so much.

This passage is accompanied by an editorial comment which reads as follows:

The eminent author must forgive us for suggesting that the old spirit of mitnaggedic opposition to hasidism is speaking from his throat. Many people have been misled into thinking that the hasidim transgress the rules and regulations of the *Shulḥan arukh*, Heaven forbid. But those days [in which this used to occur] are long forgotten. The enlightened must realize that in truth, the hasidim are scrupulous in their observance of the halakhah. It is abundantly evident that those who have been inspired by the belief in the zaddikim and who have followed the teachings of hasidism are reinforcing religion, and they go out of their way to marry off their daughters to rabbinic scholars, in complete disregard for the spirit of the time.

(R. Israel Meir Hakohen, the Hafets Hayyim, uses a similar argument in support of the hasidim of his time: 'Even if they do commit some errors, essentially they uphold the Lord's Law wholeheartdly, and they raise their children to be God-fearers and marry off their daughters to those who keep the Law and observe the *mitsvot*; what else could one wish for' (R. Arieh Leib Cohen, *Derakhav, nimukav vesiḥotav shel haḤafets Ḥayim* (Warsaw, 1937), 18).

NINETEEN

R. Naphtali Zevi of Ropczyce ('the Ropshitser') as a Hasidic Leader

YOSEPH SALMON

WHAT we know of the life of R. Naphtali Zevi Horowitz of Ropczyce is drawn mainly from collections of hasidic hagiography published many years after his death. These are: *Devarim arevim* (Munkacz, 1903–4); *Eser tsaḥtsaḥot* (Piotrkow, 1910); and *Ohel Naftali* (Lemberg, 1910). The hagiographical literature of hasidism—a large body of oral traditions committed to writing long after the events they describe—is highly problematic and its validity as historical source material has been frequently questioned, not least in connection with the figure of Israel Baal Shem Tov (the Besht), the founder of hasidism. Reports of his activities were circulating by word of mouth for several decades but they were not printed until 1814, some fifty-five years after his demise.[1] No methodology for the exploitation of such source material has yet been proposed, and an examination, for example, of G. Scholem's classic biographical study of the Besht[2] reveals that he utilized almost every possible exegetical instrument to extract historical information from *Shivḥei haBesht.* Although in the case of R. Naphtali of Ropczyce a much longer period had elapsed before his 'life' was committed to writing, we are fortunate in having at our disposal a number of contemporary or near-contemporary sources, including his own correspondence with his circle of associates (*Imrei shefer* (Lemberg, 1874)). Furthermore, it is possible to cross-check the information contained in the hagiographical collection *Ohel Naftali* against other hagiographical works written in R. Naphtali's own times. D. Ehrman, who first gathered all this material between 1881 and 1903, presents a wide range of traditions and notes all his sources. Additional information is contained in the responsa volume entitled *Derekh yivḥar* (Munkacz, 1893) by Hayyim Bezalel Panet, where the redactor, Dov Friedman, also supplies his sources.

In general, my approach in utilizing these traditions has been to distinguish between didactic material, which offers virtually no insight into the historical reality of R. Naphtali, and such concrete historical details as do occasionally occur in the tales,

The research on which the present paper is based was facilitated by a grant from the Memorial Council for Jewish Culture.

[1] Dov Ber b. Shmuel of Limits (Luniets), *Shivḥei haBesht* [Kopys, 1814], pub. in Eng. as *In Praise of the Baal Shem Tov*, trans. D. Ben-Amos and J. R. Mintz (Bloomington, Ind., 1970).

[2] G. Scholem, 'Demuto hahistorit shel R. Israel Baal Shem Tov', *Molad*, 18: 144–5 (1960), repr. with some revisions in id., *Devarim bego* (Tel Aviv, 1975), 287–324.

furnishing the background against which the plots are developed. The historical details are usually incidental to the tales, and this, on the whole, lends them greater credibility, particularly as in many cases they can be verified by comparison with parallel sources. This is especially true of references to disagreements between R. Naphtali Zevi, his teachers, and his disciples. It goes without saying that any composite historical image which emerges from all the available sources is bound to reflect nothing more than the way in which R. Naphtali was perceived either by his contemporaries or by later generations. The historian's task is to distinguish between the different layers of this hagiographical tradition, a tradition which is, after all, a unique repository of information about the social history of hasidism.

It is worth remembering that R. Naphtali's homiletic writings were published long before any of the hagiographical works about him. His two homiletic works, *Ayalah sheluḥah* (Lemberg, 1862) and *Zera kodesh* (Lemberg, 1868), appeared many years after his death (in 1827) since he did not allow them to be published. They were printed on the authority of R. Hayyim Halberstam of Zanz who justified his action by the precedent of the posthumous publication of the Ari's teachings against his own instructions. It seems that R. Hayyim Halberstam was related to R. Naphtali Zevi—one of his descendants refers to R. Naphtali Zevi as 'my distinguished forebear (*adoni avi zekeni*)'.[3]

1. A BIOGRAPHICAL SKETCH

R. Naphtali Zevi was born on the festival of Shavuot 1760, the day on which Israel Baal Shem Tov died; and hasidic tradition has ascribed great symbolic significance to this fact.[4] The Horowitz family was a distinguished one: Naphtali Zevi's father, R. Menahem Mendel, had served in the rabbinate of Lesko in central Galicia (in hasidic tradition he became known as 'R. Menahem Mendel, *av beit din* (president of the rabbinical court) of Linsk' (as Lesko was known in Yiddish), and his grandfather, R. Isaac Halevi b. Jacob Jokel Horowitz, or Itsikel Hamburger, as he was often called, was the rabbi of the amalgamated communities of Altona, Hamburg, and Wandsbeck known by their Hebrew acronym as 'Ahu'.[5] As a boy, R. Naphtali Zevi studied under both his grandfather and his uncle, R. Meshullam Igra of Tysmenitsa, who was president of the rabbinical court of Presburg. Some of his fellow students were to become leading rabbis, including Jacob of Lysa (the author of *Ḥavat da'at*) and Mordecai Banet (head of the rabbinical academy of Nikolsburg and chief rabbi of Moravia).

It seems that R. Naphtali Zevi became interested in hasidism under the influence of his father, who presented him to R. Elimelekh of Lyzhansk and, perhaps even earlier, to R. Jeḥiel Michel of Zloczow, who was a disciple of the Besht himself. R. Naphtali Zevi was in contact with those leaders of hasidism who had been disciples of the Maggid of Mezhirech—R. Mordecai of Neskhiz, R. Meshullam Phoebus of Zbarazh, R. Elimelekh of Lyzhansk, and R. Levi Isaac of Berdichev. His principal mentors were R. Jeḥiel Michel of Zloczow and R. Elimelekh of Lyzhansk, the latter having consoli-

[3] See R. Hayyim Halberstam's approbation in Naphtali Zevi Horowitz of Ropczyce, *Zera kodesh* (Lemberg, 1868). It was he who gave the book its title.

[4] *Eser tsaḥtsaḥot*, collected and edited by Israel Berger (Piotrkow, 1910), 83.

[5] Ibid. 83–4.

dated the hasidic movement in Poland after the death of the Maggid of Mezhirech and the departure of R. Samuel Shmelke Horowitz from the rabbinate of Sieniawa to become rabbi of Nikolsburg in 1773. R. Naphtali Zevi was also associated with three leading figures in Polish hasidism—R. Jacob Isaac, the Seer of Lublin, R. Israel of Kozienice, and R. Menahem Mendel of Rymanow—all disciples of R. Elimelekh of Lyzhansk. When all three died within the space of one year (1814–15), R. Naphtali Zevi assumed the leadership of the movement in Galicia, principally in western and central Galicia; but he never became supreme leader of Polish hasidism as a whole (see below).

R. Naphtali Zevi was famous for his sharp intellect. His works feature kabbalistic, hasidic, and ethical themes and contain novel homiletic insights. More than one hundred of his descendants became hasidic leaders (*admorim*) in communities as far apart as Romania, Bukovina, America, and the Land of Israel.

R. Naphtali Zevi was rabbi of Ropczyce, Lesko, and the whole of the Sanok province simultaneously, notwithstanding the wide dispersal of the Jewish villages and townships of this area. He also headed the Galician and Hungarian branch of the 'Rabbi Meir Ba'al Hanes Charity Fund' for the needy of the Land of Israel. He was very active in communal affairs and played an important part in the selection of rabbis for the Jewish communities in his area, often securing rabbinical appointments for members of his own family.

R. Naphtali Zevi's first wife came from a wealthy family in Brody; his second wife was the daughter of R. Zevi Goldhammer of Dukla. His divorce from his first wife is treated quite extensively in hasidic folklore since it was authorized by his teacher, R. Jeḥiel Michel of Zloczow, and, according to another tradition, by the Seer of Lublin himself.[6] Among R. Naphtali Zevi's closest friends were R. Zevi Hirsch of Zhidachov and R. Israel of Ruzhin. His main disciples were R. Hayyim Halberstam of Zanz, Sar Shalom of Belz, R. Shalom Rosenfeld of Kaminka and R. Zevi Elimelekh of Dynow. R. Naphtali Zevi was involved in many disputes, among others with the 'Holy Jew' of Przysucha and R. Solomon Leib of Leczna (Lenchna), as well as with his own disciple, R. Zevi Elimelekh of Dynow.[7]

The immediate heir to what became the Ropczyce dynasty was R. Naphtali Zevi's son-in-law R. Asher Isaiah Rubin. His son, R. Eliezer, who founded the Dzieckowitz (Dzikow) dynasty, was also a famous hasidic leader; he began his activities as an *admor* only after R. Asher Isaiah Rubin's death.[8]

2. R. NAPHTALI ZEVI'S CONVERSION TO HASIDISM

Hasidic tradition gives extensive coverage to R. Naphtali Zevi's conversion to hasidism. Since he was related to two of the most eminent scholars of the time, who actively

[6] *Ohel Naftali*, collected and ed. Abraham Hayyim Simḥah Bunem Michelsohn (Lemberg, 1911), s. 8, 5; *Eser tsaḥtsaḥot*, s. 23, 88.

[7] Jekutiel Aryeh Kamelhar, *Dor de'ah* [Bilgoraj, 1933] (Jerusalem, 1970), 240–1. See also *Eser tsaḥtsaḥot*, s. 29, 89–90.

[8] M. Wunder, *Entsiklopediah leḥakhmei Galitsiah* (Jerusalem, 1984), s.v. 'R. Naftali Zevi', 300–6, and 'Eliezer ben Rabbi Naftali Zevi', 163–4.

opposed the movement, R. Itsikel Hamburger and R. Meshullam Igra, and since moreover his lineage could be traced to the famous R. Isaiah Horowitz, author of *Shenei luḥot haberit*,[9] R. Naphtali Zevi was clearly regarded as an important 'catch' for hasidism.

According to one account of his conversion, R. Naphtali Zevi's father had taken him to receive a blessing for his barmitzvah from R. Elimelekh of Lyzhansk.[10] Another version claims that he came to R. Elimelekh as an adult in order to join his circle of disciples but was denied admission because of his distinguished family background, which was considered undesirable in the new movement. This version is extremely strange since R. Elimelekh himself was the scion of an eminent rabbinical family, as were many of the second- and third-generation leaders of hasidism.[11] Yet another version has it that R. Elimelekh rejected R. Naphtali Zevi as an act of vengeance against R. Naphtali Zevi's father, who had poked fun at R. Elimelekh and his brother R. Zusya during their early itinerant years.[12] Can one conclude from all these diverse traditions that R. Naphtali Zevi had to struggle to be admitted into the hasidic movement? Apparently his father, R. Menahem Mendel, had himself converted to hasidism at an earlier stage, and it may well be that he was the one who took R. Naphtali Zevi to R. Jeḥiel Michel of Zloczow when he became *bar mitsvah*.[13]

Another account corroborates the evidence that R. Menahem Mendel of Lesko's home was a meeting place for eminent hasidic masters. These included R. Aryeh Leib 'the Zeide' (Grandfather) of Shpola, R. Mordecai of Neskhiz and, as we have seen, R. Elimelekh of Lyzhansk and his brother R. Zusya during their early itinerant days, as well as, later on, R. Simḥah Bunem of Przysucha.[14] In fact, R. Menahem Mendel's house in Lesko seems to have functioned as a *kloiz*, not unlike the famous *kloiz* in Brody, and it may well be that a circle of pietists had formed there, of the type that immediately preceded and was contemporaneous with the rise of the hasidic movement.[15] If these traditions are trustworthy then it can be assumed that R. Menahem Mendel's *kloiz* existed already in the 1760s, and that it followed him to Lesko when he was appointed rabbi there in 1782. However, it is worth noting that R. Menahem Mendel's extant writings, the earliest of which date from 1799, show no trace of hasidic

[9] For the genealogy, see *Ohel Naftali*, s. 393, 139–48, repr. in *Hitorerut hatefilah* (New York, 1982); Jacob Shwerdsharf, *Geza, tarshishim* (Lemberg, 1905), repr. in *Naḥalat Tsevi: Bamah lemishnat haḥasidut vetoledoteihah*, i (Bnei Brak, 1989), 107–24. See also *Ohel Naftali*, s. 1, 5.

[10] This version contradicts another which claims that at this age he was presented to R. Jeḥiel Michel of Zloczow. See *Ohel Naftali*, s. 1, 5.

[11] R. Jeḥiel Michel of Zloczow was a grandson of R. Isaac Hayot, the head of the rabbinical court in Prague; see *Dor de'ah*, 1, 83.

[12] *Ohel Naftali*, s. 13, 8. This version also appears in Abraham Hayyim Simḥah Bunem Michelsohn, *Ohel Elimelekh* (Jerusalem, 1948), s. 38, 10, in the name of Abraham Segal of Ittingen, head of the yeshivah in Dukla. The visit is mentioned again in *Ohel Naftali*, s. 14, 8. *Eser tsaḥtsaḥot*, s. 16, 86–7 has a slightly different version.

[13] For R. Menahem Mendel being a disciple of R. Jeḥiel Michel of Zloczow, see the testimony of R. Simḥah Bunem of Przysucha in *Ohel Naftali*, s. 14, 8. It is clear that the third- and fourth-generation hasidic leaders who used to attend his court included R. Simḥah Bunem himself. Cf. *Ohel Elimelekh*, s. 39, 10–11; *Ohel Naftali*, s. 4, 5.

[14] *Ohel Naftali*, s. 9, 6, 7; s. 13, 8; *Ohel Elimelekh*, 10, 11.

[15] *Ohel Naftali*, s. 19, 12–13. Regarding the circles of pietists, see J. G. Weiss, 'A Circle of Pneumatics in Pre-Hasidism', *Journal of Jewish Studies*, 8 (1957), 199–213, repr. in id., *Studies in Eastern European Jewish Mysticism* (Oxford, 1985), 27–42.

influence.[16] One of his disciples, R. Ezekiel Panet, who later became rabbi of Alba-Iulia in Transylvania, had turned to hasidism under his influence and was introduced by him to R. Menahem Mendel of Rymanow. In his biography of R. Ezekiel Panet, based on family traditions and published in Hayyim Bezalel Panet's *Derekh yivḥar* (Munkacz, 1893), R. Issachar Ber Friedman reports that R. Menahem Mendel of Lesko headed a *kloiz* in which the kabbalistic system of Moses Cordovero and the writings of Moses Zacuto on the Zohar were studied, as well as the *Zohar ḥadash* and Lurianic kabbalah: 'He [R. Menahem Mendel of Lesko] studied with him [R. Ezekiel Panet] both revealed and esoteric wisdom. He revealed to him the secrets of Torah and the spirit of God rested on him. The Gates of Understanding (*sha'arei binah*) were opened before him and he was able to stroll through the "Orchard of Pomegranates" (*pardes rimonim*) by which the secrets of Torah may be understood.'[17]

According to hasidic tradition, some of the greatest Torah scholars of the time had been trained at this *kloiz*. Candidates for admission were examined in order to ascertain that they possessed sufficient 'acuteness of intellect and wide erudition in matters of holiness', that is, in kabbalah. A successful candidate would become 'a colleague to those who fear God and can manipulate His Name'.[18] The group was also distinguished by adopting the 'Sefardi'-kabbalistic rather than the indigenous Ashkenazi prayer rite.[19]

There is, however, another tradition concerning R. Menahem Mendel's connection with the hasidic movement which contradicts all the accounts above. According to this tradition, R. Menahem Mendel, like his father-in-law R. Itsikel Hamburger and his brother-in-law R. Meshullam Igra, was a staunch opponent of Beshtian hasidism. He first came in contact with the movement when one of his sons, who lived in Berdichev, became involved in the Haskalah movement which emanated from Berlin. R. Naphtali Zevi—by that time a frequent visitor to the court of R. Elimelekh of Lyzhansk—advised his father to consult R. Jeḥiel Michel of Zloczow, since he, by virtue of his great piety and holiness, would be able to overcome the powers of evil which had led his own brother astray. R. Menahem Mendel took his son's advice and consequently became an enthusiastic follower of R. Jeḥiel Michel, notwithstanding the objections of both his father-in-law and his brother-in-law.[20] This tale, which echoes the early nineteenth-century conflict between hasidim and maskilim in Galicia, appears to be of relatively late provenance and is, perhaps, less reliable than the rest.

Another source suggests a connection between R. Menahem Mendel of Lesko and R. Menahem Mendel of Rymanow. Despite his seniority and status, R. Menahem Mendel of Lesko accepted the authority of R. Menahem Mendel of Rymanow, recognizing his superior kabbalistic knowledge.[21] In any event, from his approbation (*haskamah*) of Zechariah Mendel of Jaroslaw's *Darkhei tsedek* (1796), it is clear that by

[16] See appendix to R. Naphtali Zevi, *Ayalah sheluḥah* (Podgorze, 1903), and the appendix to the earlier *Zera kodesh*.

[17] *Ohel Naftali*, s. 19, 12. The reference is clearly to Moses Cordovero's *Pardes rimonim* and to Moses Zacuto's *Sha'arei binah*. The story first appears in Hayyim Bezalel Panet's *Derekh yivḥar* (Munkacz, 1893), in the introd., the section on 'The Biography of R. Ezekiel Panet'.

[18] *Ohel Naftali*, s. 19, 12. See also Ezekiel Panet's 'Responsum mareh Yeḥezkel', in *Ayalah sheluḥah* (Budapest, 1943), 88–96.

[19] *Ohel Naftali*, s. 227, 72.

[20] Ibid.

[21] Ibid., s. 26, 18. See also Jekutiel Aryeh Kamelhar, *Em lebinah* (Warsaw, 1904), 30.

the turn of the eighteenth century R. Menahem Mendel of Lesko was already well known as an adherent of hasidism.[22]

From all these sources it emerges clearly that R. Naphtali Zevi's father was a follower of hasidism and may have acted as an intermediary between the older form of mystical, pietistic hasidism and the new movement.[23] However, there is evidence that not all of R. Menahem Mendel's sons became followers of hasidism, and at least one of them, R. Jacob Yukel, the head of the rabbinical court of Bolechow, was an opponent of the movement.[24]

R. Naphtali Zevi's lineage is treated somewhat ambivalently in the hagiographic literature of hasidism. Some sources have it that he used to boast of his ancestry while according to others he saw his distinguished pedigree as an impediment.[25] We shall return to this point below.

In hasidic sources, R. Naphtali Zevi's relationship with the opponents of hasidism (mitnaggedim) is dealt with at length. From various sources it appears that he was in contact with a number of the leading rabbis of his time, some of whom, as we have seen, were relatives, while others had been his teachers. He certainly did not reject the value of erudition in the 'revealed', normative aspects of Torah. He refused, for example, to come out against R. Zevi Hirsch Heller, the head of the rabbinical court of Brugl (Brzesko) and Otuda (Old Buda), who was harassing the hasidim of his region; R. Naphtali Zevi argued that 'the Torah stands by him like a pillar of íron and will not allow any harm to come to him!'[26] Nor did he distance himself from his brother R. Jacob Yukel, who remained antagonistic to hasidism all his life; he even travelled in his company to visit R. Zevi Hirsch of Zhidachov.[27] All this does not mean that R. Naphtali Zevi was passive in his attitude to anti-hasidic circles. In a letter to R. Jacob Orenstein (the author of *Yeshu'ot Ya'akov*) he insisted that 'the zaddikim are the true leaders of the generation and it is on their account that the world exists'.[28] He is also reported to have said: 'Young men! Ḍo you know that people say that the mitnaggedim will return to this world [by way of the transmigration of souls] in the shape of dogs? It is true!'[29] From these statements it is clear that his attitude to the mitnaggedim was ambivalent.

3. HIS MENTORS IN HASIDISM

The precise nature of the teacher–disciple relationship in hasidism is still far from clear. It was always complex, since it existed outside a formal yeshivah framework. The situation is further complicated by the fact that hasidic leaders were in the habit of claiming many of their predecessors and colleagues as personal teachers. Such claims were rarely made during the actual period of alleged discipleship, and they tend to reflect personality developments in later life. The hagiographical sources usually rely

[22] Zechariah Mendel of Jaroslaw, *Darkhei tsedek* (Lemberg, 1796), 'Approbations' section. Cf. Moses Hayyim Ephraim of Sudylkow, *Degel maḥaneh Efrayim* [n.p., 1808], 'Approbations' section.

[23] For ideological parallels between hasidism and other groups in the early days of the movement, see M. Piekarz, *Biyemei tsemiḥat haḥasidut: Megamot ra'ayoniyot besifrei derush umusar* (Jerusalem, 1978).

[24] *Ohel Naftali*, s. 335, 121.

[25] *Eser tsaḥtsaḥot*, s. 31, 90.

[26] *Ohel Naftali*, s. 299, 111.

[27] Ibid., s. 335, 121.

[28] Ibid., s. 279, 100.

[29] *Eser tsaḥtsaḥot*, s. 35, 91.

on subjective statements made by each 'disciple' at that stage of his life at which he had attained independent status as a leader in his own right: it was from the perspective of hindsight that he would identify his hasidic teachers.

R. Naphtali Zevi serves as an excellent example of this. He saw himself as a disciple of R. Elimelekh of Lyzhansk as well as of R. Elimelekh's disciples: R. Menahem Mendel of Rymanow, R. Israel of Kozienice, and R. Jacob Isaac the Seer of Lublin. In some respects he also considered himself a disciple of R. Jeḥiel Michel of Zloczow and R. Meshullam Phoebus of Zbarazh. He refers to R. Elimelekh and R. Menahem Mendel of Rymanow in equally respectful terms, frequently acknowledging their influence by such formulas as: 'as I heard from my master and teacher R. Elimelekh, of blessed memory',[30] or, with a higher honorific, 'as the holy rabbi, my master and teacher, R. Elimelekh, of blessed memory, had explained'.[31] The same formula is used in reference to R. Menahem Mendel of Rymanow[32] and R. Jeḥiel Michel of Zloczow.[33] R. Israel, the Maggid of Kozienice, testifies that R. Naphtali Zevi was R. Elimelekh's outstanding disciple and that 'the Gaon, R. Elimelekh studied his whole book with him [R. Naphtali Zevi] after he [R. Elimelekh] died'.[34] The hagiographical works on R. Elimelekh and R. Naphtali Zevi, *Ohel Elimelekh* and *Ohel Naftali* respectively, share many motifs in common, a fact which seems to strengthen the claim that the two were intimate friends, at least in the eyes of their disciples.

R. Naphtali Zevi insisted that only three men deserved the title of 'father of Polish hasidism': the Seer of Lublin, R. Israel of Kozienice, and R. Menahem Mendel of Rymanow.[35] In making this assertion he classified himself as belonging to the second generation of R. Elimelekh of Lyzhansk's disciples and, indeed, this is compatible with his view of himself as a disciple of R. Elimelekh's three other disciples.[36] However, he clearly did not consider them to be his exclusive mentors; his self-proclaimed association with R. Jeḥiel Michel of Zloczow and R. Levi Isaac of Berdichev reveals his need to be associated more directly with those who were closer to the Besht and the Maggid of Mezhirech.[37] In any event, hasidic tradition strongly indicates that R. Naphtali Zevi made a distinction between the authority which he received from the earlier masters and that which he received from the three Polish 'founders'; his relationship with the latter was complex and ambivalent.

If we try to gauge R. Naphtali Zevi's evaluation of the three 'founders' from the honorific titles by which he refers to them, then the one he admired most was R. Menahem Mendel of Rymanow. R. Naphtali Zevi calls him 'my master, the holy rabbi, our master and teacher'.[38] In one instance he claims that R. Menahem Mendel's statements 'are the words of the living God'.[39] Did his admiration stem from his acknowledgement of

[30] *Zera kodesh*, on 'Noaḥ', 5*b*; *Ayalah sheluḥah* (Lemberg, 1862), 11*b*, 16*a*.

[31] *Zera kodesh*, on 'Ki tetse', 138*a*; on 'Koraḥ', 120*a*.

[32] *Ayalah sheluḥah* (Lemberg, 1862), 10. *Zera kodesh*, on 'Pinhas', 125*b*.

[33] *Zera kodesh*, 33*b*.

[34] *Ohel Naftali*, s. 278, 100.

[35] Ibid., s. 138, 48.

[36] For his claim that he was ordained as an *admor* by the Seer of Lublin, see *Ohel Naftali*, s. 331, 119.

[37] Ibid., s. 61, 27. For his visits to R. Jeḥiel Michel of Zloczow, see also D. Ehrman, *Devarim arevim*, (Munkacz, 1803–4), 37*b*, and the passages quoted in his name in *Zera kodesh*, on 'Ki tisa', 70*b*.

[38] *Ayalah sheluḥah* (Lemberg, 1862), 10; *Zera kodesh*, on 'Pinhas', 125*b*. This is corroborated by *Derekh yivḥar*, s. 2.

[39] *Zera kodesh*, 60*a*.

the hasidic tradition whereby R. Menahem Mendel received the soul of R. Elimelekh of Lyzhansk when the latter died? This was a spiritual attribute of which R. Naphtali Zevi himself boasted, and it may be alluded to in his epitaph: 'unique in his generation in divine wisdom'. All the other founders of Polish hasidism are credited with lesser qualities: the Seer of Lublin with 'clear sight'; R. Israel of Kozienice with 'the power of the heart'; and R. Abraham Joshua Heschel of Apta with 'the power of the mouth'.[40] The hasidic sources frequently tell of consultations between R. Menahem Mendel of Rymanow and R. Naphtali Zevi when they discussed matters which others could not understand.[41] R. Ezekiel Panet gives explicit testimony on the relationship between the two in a letter to his father written in 1765: 'At R. Menahem Mendel's home, the zaddik, the rabbi of Ropczyce [i.e. R. Naphtali Zevi] stands beside him and attends him as one of the pupils.'[42]

However, the relationship between R. Menahem Mendel and R. Naphtali Zevi was complex and strained. Hasidic tradition relates that when sickness broke out in a certain town and the townsfolk appealed to R. Menahem Mendel of Rymanow for help, he advised them to complain to R. Naphtali Zevi who had brought it on by exorcizing spirits during prayer.[43] A more serious dispute between the two centred on what was primarily a political issue, but its implications concerned their conflicting views of messianic redemption. R. Menahem Mendel believed that the Napoleonic wars were the final struggle of Gog and Magog which was to precede the advent of the messiah. He disagreed on this with his colleagues R. Israel of Kozienice and the Seer of Lublin. The Seer was determined to force the messiah to come but insisted that this should be done without Napoleon's help,[44] and R. Naphtali Zevi sided with him against R. Menahem Mendel. The latter bore a grudge and was only pacified by the intervention of R. Israel of Kozienice.[45] Another story tells that R. Menahem Mendel once ordered R. Naphtali Zevi to study a passage of Mishnah with a group of hasidim. His exposition of the passage was so outstanding that on hearing it the hasidim recited the benediction over the Torah. On another occasion, hearing R. Naphtali Zevi make an insightful remark, R. Menahem Mendel pronounced him a sage. To this R. Naphtali Zevi retorted that since R. Menahem Mendel himself was a holy man and not a sage, he could have no understanding of such matters, 'and how could he judge me?' Understandably, R. Menahem Mendel was furious and R. Naphtali Zevi had to beg for forgiveness.[46] Another tradition points to the difference between R. Menahem Mendel's understanding of the nature of piety and that of R. Naphtali Zevi. This centred on the question of whether prayer should be offered in a state of abjection or from joy. R. Naphtali Zevi held the latter view. According to another report, R.

[40] *Em lebinah*, 28.

[41] Ibid. 40–1.

[42] Ezekiel Panet, *Mareh Yeḥezkel* (Siget, 1875), s. 104.

[43] *Ohel Naftali*, s. 29, 19.

[44] When the Seer failed to bring the messiah on Passover 1813, he blamed his failure on his colleagues but not on R. Naphtali Zevi.

[45] See *Ohel Naftali*, s. 52, 25–6. For another version see ibid., s. 73, 30, where R. Naphtali Zevi's position on this matter is given greater emphasis than that of his teachers, R. Israel of Kozienice and the Seer; cf. *Eser tsaḥtsaḥot*, s. 17, 87. For other sources, see I. Alfasi, *Haḥozeh miLublin* (Jerusalem, 1969), 97–104 nn. 5, 12. For a detailed and different account, see Abraham Hayyim Simḥah Bunem Michelsohn, *Ateret Menaḥem* (Bilgoraj, 1910), 38–9.

[46] *Ohel Naftali*, s. 70, 29.

Naphtali Zevi accepted R. Menahem Mendel's authority in all matters concerning the inner meaning of Torah and its secrets.[47] It also appears that before R. Naphtali Zevi was appointed to the rabbinate, R. Menahem Mendel supported him financially.[48]

R. Naphtali Zevi's relationship with R. Jacob Isaac of Lancut, the Seer of Lublin, was no less ambivalent. He consistently refers to him by lesser titles than he affords either R. Elimelekh or R. Menahem Mendel of Rymanow, merely saying: 'I have heard from the *admor* of Lublin',[49] or 'When the rabbi, our master and teacher R. Jacob Isaac of Lancut was reciting the Amidah prayer during the afternoon service'.[50] On the other hand, the Seer accused R. Naphtali Zevi of frivolity, and pleaded with him to mend his ways without success.[51] Anecdotes about clashes between the two are scattered throughout the hagiographic literature. The Seer opposed the match that R. Naphtali Zevi had made for his daughter with R. Asher Isaiah Rubin, but he later relented and remarked that a sage (R. Naphtali Zevi) was greater than a prophet (himself).[52] On another occasion the Seer announced that the prophet Elijah had visited R. Naphtali Zevi—an announcement much to the irritation of the latter, who resented his affairs being made public.[53] Nevertheless, the Seer's relationship to R. Naphtali Zevi was that of a teacher-colleague. Of all the Seer's disciples it was R. Naphtali Zevi who, according to hasidic tradition, knew in advance the day of the Seer's death, and it was he who arranged for his burial and overcame all the difficulties involved.[54] Above all, R. Naphtali Zevi claimed that it was the Seer who ordained him as *admor* in his youth, when they met on a visit to R. Jeḥiel Michel of Zloczow.[55]

Unfortunately, the sources do not reveal much about the relationship between R. Naphtali Zevi and R. Israel of Kozienice. R. Israel is said to have stated that R. Naphtali Zevi was the most faithful explicator of the book *No'am Elimelekh*, in which he had been instructed by the author, R. Elimelekh of Lyzhansk.[56] Elsewhere we read that R. Naphtali Zevi asked R. Israel to protect him from R. Menahem Mendel of Rymanow's anger during their dispute over the messianic significance of the Napoleonic wars.[57]

R. Naphtali Zevi spent an entire year in the home of R. Mordecai of Neskhiz, but the sources do not elaborate on the relationship between them. There is also mention of a visit by R. Naphtali Zevi, together with R. Abraham Joshua Heschel of Apta, to the court of R. Israel of Ruzhin. Apparently, R. Abraham Joshua admired R. Naphtali Zevi as 'a sage',[58] and taught him esoteric hasidic theories. This would suggest that R. Naphtali Zevi was a close disciple also of R. Abraham Joshua Heschel.[59] It is doubtful

[47] Ibid., s. 52. 25–6.

[48] Ibid., s. 345, 128. See also *Derekh yivḥar*, 6–7, for a letter from Ezekiel Panet to Menahem Mendel of Rymanow.

[49] *Zera kodesh*, on 'Vayishlaḥ', 27*b*.

[50] Ibid., on 'Tetse', 139*b*. Tal points out that R. Naphtali Zevi's relationship with the Seer was that of disciple/colleague; see S. Tal, *Rabbi Naftali meRopshits* (Jerusalem, 1983), 15.

[51] *Ohel Naftali*, s. 349, 124.

[52] Ibid., s. 341, 122; see also s. 361, 129.

[53] Ibid., s. 97, 36.

[54] Nathan Ortner, *Rabbi Tsevi Elimelekh MiDinov* (Bnei Brak, 1972), i. 53 n. 24. See also *Ohel Naftali*, s. 72, 30–1, and cf. *Devarim arevim*, 37*b*.

[55] Ibid. 37, 38.

[56] *Ohel Naftali*, s. 278, 100.

[57] Ibid., s. 52, 25–6.

[58] *Eser tsaḥtsaḥot*, s. 57, 95.

[59] For R. Naphtali Zevi's visit to R. Abraham Joshua Heschel of Apta when he was in Medzibezh, see *Imrei shefer* (Lemberg, 1884), 8*a*.

whether there is anyone else in the history of hasidism who received direct instruction from as many teachers and mentors as did R. Naphtali Zevi.

R. Naphtali Zevi's relations with peers and disciples were also complex. His two closest colleagues were R. Zevi Hirsch of Zhidachov and the younger R. Zevi Elimelekh of Dynow. A certain amount of tension developed between them following the death of 'the three shepherds', the Seer, R. Menahem Mendel, and R. Israel of Kozienice, when the question of succession arose. Although R. Naphtali Zevi was the senior disciple, R. Zevi Hirsch of Zhidachov claimed the title of heir. This offended R. Abraham Joshua Heschel, the oldest Polish *admor* who, as a resident of Medzhibezh in Podolia, was unable to assume the leadership in Poland. Hasidic tradition has it that R. Naphtali Zevi defended R. Zevi Hirsch of Zhidachov because he believed his prayers to be as efficacious as those of R. Elimelekh of Lyzhansk.[60] On the other hand, a letter written by R. Zevi Hirsch during an illness to R. Naphtali Zevi to ask him to pray on his behalf reveals the deep respect he felt towards him; he attributed his recovery to R. Naphtali Zevi's prayers.[61] From the terms of address in the letter it is clear that R. Zevi Hirsch regarded R. Naphtali Zevi as his friend and colleague rather than teacher or mentor, although he describes him as capable of operating in the upper worlds at the highest level: 'the most illustrious zaddik at the feet of the [divine] chariot, a zaddik who is the foundation of the world, who encompasses, and combines with, the special alabaster of the Only One, to incline divine mercy towards the unique nation on earth'.[62] Nevertheless, there is evidence of some rivalry between the two, and it seems that R. Naphtali Zevi was the more successful in attracting followers.[63]

By contrast, R. Naphtali Zevi's relationship with R. Zevi Elimelekh of Dynow was complex and acrimonious. The latter had set himself up as an *admor* and attracted followers in his own right.[64] Both he and R. Naphtali Zevi had been outstanding disciples of R. Menahem Mendel of Rymanow, but Zevi Elimelekh was the younger of the two.[65] Hasidic legend claims that R. Naphtali Zevi's objection to the leadership of R. Zevi Elimelekh was prompted simply by the desire to prolong his friend's life, since he knew the preordained length of R. Zevi Elimelekh's career as an *admor*, and hoped to postpone his death by delaying the start of his term of office.[66] Be that as it may, the antagonism between the two was given extreme expression in the belief held by Dynow hasidism that R. Naphtali Zevi had doubted the ability of their dynasty to sustain itself because R. Zevi Elimelekh's lineage was not sufficiently distinguished. These reservations about R. Zevi Elimelekh's qualifications for leadership are said to have provoked the Seer's anger.[67]

60 Ortner, *R. Tsevi Elimelekh*, 162. See also Israel Berger, *Eser kedushot* [Warsaw, 1902; Piotrkow, 1906] (Tel Aviv, 1973), s. 33, 19.

61 *Ohel Naftali*, s. 200, 62; s. 201, 63. See also *Imrei shefer*, 13–14.

62 *Imrei shefer*, 13.

63 *Ohel Naftali*, s. 371, 131. For the rivalry over the hasidim of R. Isaac Taub of Kalow who died in 1821, see also *Dor de'ah*, ii. 119 and n. ad loc.

64 Ortner, *R. Tsevi Elimelekh*, 162–3. For R. Naphtali Zevi's irritation with R. Zevi Elimelekh at an earlier period, see ibid. 41. R. Naphtali Zevi was angry with R. Zevi Elimelekh's pretentious behaviour while at the court of the Seer, in the presence of the senior disciples. It is possible that the dispute led R. Zevi Elimelekh to accept the post of rabbi in Munkacz in 1825. After R. Naphtali Zevi's death he returned to Galicia in 1829.

65 See *Derekh yivḥar*, introd., s.2.

66 *Ohel Naftali*, s. 46, 24.

67 Ortner, *R. Tsevi Elimelekh*, 164.

R. Zevi Elimelekh's rejection of R. Naphtali Zevi's authority is clearly evident in the affair of R. Solomon Leib of Leczna (Lenchna), who was excommunicated by R. Naphtali Zevi for reasons which are not altogether clear.[68] Some sources connect the affair with the Seer's struggle against the 'Holy Jew' of Przysucha, in which R. Naphtali Zevi sided with the Seer,[69] while others claim that the antagonism towards R. Solomon Leib began when he presumed to act as an *admor* in the town of Bukowsko, in the Galician district of Sanok which was part of R. Naphtali Zevi's territory. Indeed, it was as a result of this contoversy that R. Solomon Leib eventually moved to Leczna, in the Lublin province of Poland. Hasidic folklore glosses over the whole affair with the explanation that R. Naphtali Zevi's apparent antagonism was only to cover up his real affection for R. Solomon Leib.[70] In any event, it is reasonable to assume that, in refusing to side with R. Naphtali Zevi on the question of R. Solomon Leib, R. Zevi Elimelekh was following the advice of R. Menahem Mendel of Rymanow, or, more likely, of R. Abraham Joshua Heschel of Apta, who had been his teacher and predecessor in the rabbinate of Dynow.[71] R. Naphtali Zevi's stand in the controversy with R. Solomon Leib was unacceptable even to his closest associates, including his son, R. Eliezer of Dzieckowitz (Dzykow) and his disciple, Sar Shalom of Belz.[72] But in spite of the antagonism between R. Zevi Elimelekh and R. Naphtali Zevi, hasidic tradition depicts R. Zevi Elimelekh as the one who sat by R. Naphtali Zevi's deathbed.[73]

R. Naphtali Zevi's relationship with R. Jacob Isaac 'the Holy Jew' of Przysucha was also problematic. The 'Holy Jew' had already attracted the antagonism of the Seer of Lublin, for reasons which are not entirely clear. Was it simply because he had set himself up as an *admor* in the Seer's lifetime, or was there also an ideological disagreement between them? In any event, against R. Menahem Mendel of Rymanow's wishes,[74] R. Naphtali Zevi sided with the Seer of Lublin. Notably, R. Naphtali Zevi's mother disapproved of her son's attitude and attempted to modify it.[75]

The most important of R. Naphtali Zevi's disciples were R. Hayyim Halberstam of Zanz, R. Shalom Rosenfeld, the rabbi of Kaminka, and, to a lesser degree, R. Ezekiel Panet, the rabbi of Transylvania.[76] R. Hayyim spent many years with R. Naphtali Zevi, but he does not refer to him as 'my master and teacher', preferring the rather impersonal formula, 'I heard from the Ropshitser Rebbe'. By contrast, when he mentions R. Zevi Hirsch of Zhidachov he never fails to accord him the honorific title 'my master

[68] *Ohel Naftali*, s. 114, 40. On the reasons for the ban and for the connection with R. Naphtali Zevi's relationship with R. Solomon and R. Zevi Elimelekh, see Ortner, *R. Tsevi Elimelekh*, 262–7, and n. 6 ad loc.

[69] Ortner, *R. Tsevi Elimelekh*, 265–8, 271–2. See also Tal, *R. Naftali*, 25.

[70] Ortner, *R. Tsevi Elimelekh*, 267–8. Hasidic legend has it that R. Naphtali Zevi changed his mind before he died (ibid. 274–5); see *Ohel Naftali*, ss. 111, 180.

[71] *Ohel Naftali*, s. 131, 46. R. Zevi Elimelekh explained his support for R. Solomon Leib by reference to the occasion when, in his presence, R. Solomon Leib entered R. Joshua of Dynow's room. R Joshua stood up to greet R. Solomon Leib, observing that the prophet Elijah had come in with him; ibid. ss. 111–12, 40. See also Israel Berger, *Eser atarot* (Piotrkow, 1910), 25, s. 20; Ortner, *R. Tsevi Elimelekh*, 267–9.

[72] *Ohel Naftali*, s. 327, 117; Ortner, *R. Tsevi Elimelekh*, 269–70 n. 14.

[73] M. S. Geshuri, 'Lancut ir hilulah', in *Sefer Lancut* (Tel Aviv, 1963), 50.

[74] For R. Naphtali Zevi's warning to the 'Holy Jew', see *Ohel Naftali*, s. 137, 48.

[75] Ibid., s. 134, 47.

[76] *Dor de'ah*, iv. See also *Derekh yivḥar*, 6 (my own pagination. Y. S.); I. J. Cohen, 'Teshuvot *Mar'eh Yeḥezkel* me'et R. Yeḥezkel Panet', in *Mekorot vekorot* (Jerusalem, 1982), 295–307.

and teacher'. Another tradition points to a certain amount of tension between R. Hayyim of Zanz and R. Eliezer of Dzieckowitz, R. Naphtali Zevi's son: R. Eliezer's sons are said to have been critical of their father for not going to Zanz for Rosh Hashanah as he had formerly gone to Lublin. He answered them: 'R. Hayyim's service of God may be superior to the Lublin service, but as far as [spiritual] (*hasagot*) grasp is concerned, he does not reach the soles of the feet of the Rebbe of Lublin.'[77] As for R. Shalom Rosenfeld, in a letter to him written in 1822 R. Naphtali Zevi implies that he had encouraged R. Shalom to accept the rabbinate of Jaraczew, and he directs his disciple to conduct his life in joy, inviting him to Ropczyce for the coming festival and assuring him that he has prayed for his and his family's welfare.[78]

R. Naphtali Zevi willed his court in Ropczyce to his son-in-law R. Asher Isaiah Rubin, but R. Asher never achieved the influence throughout Galicia that his father-in-law had enjoyed. R. Naphtali Zevi exerted his influence to obtain rabbinic appointments in a number of communities for his sons; the most successful was R. Eliezer, who established a new hasidic dynasty in Dzieckowitz. However, like the hasidic courts of Lesko, Rymanow, and Lublin, the court at Ropczyce was unable to secure its own future by means of direct hereditary succession.

4. THE SOURCE OF HIS AUTHORITY

On the authority that R. Naphtali Zevi claimed as the source of his leadership we have both his own statements and remarks attributed to him by his disciples. Most notably, his image of himself and that created by others were very different.

As noted above, R. Naphtali Zevi was proud of his rabbinical lineage—an asset to anyone in a society that puts a high value on normative Torah study. His line of descent included his grandfather, R. Itsikel Hamburger, and R. Meir of Tiktin (Tykocin), and it could be traced back to the famous R. Isaiah Horowitz, who lent it an additional kabbalistic dimension. Did R. Naphtali Zevi's pride in this line of descent imply that he believed himself an heir to the power of prophecy, at least at the level of 'revelations by the Shelah' (as R. Isaiah Horowitz was known, from the acronym of the title of his famous work)? It is of interest that the Seer of Lublin in fact attributed such powers to R. Naphtali Zevi,[79] although, according to one hasidic tale, R. Naphtali Zevi himself made light of the matter and was even angry that the Seer had mentioned it in public.[80] R. Zevi Hirsch of Zhidachov, on the other hand, denied that the capacity for receiving such revelations was hereditary and claimed that he himself had enjoyed 'a revelation of the Shelah', a claim on which he grounded his own aspirations to become the supreme leader of Galician hasidism after the death of the 'three shepherds'.[81] The motif of denigration of lineage runs through the whole of hasidic tradition. Indeed, R.

[77] *Ohel Naftali*, s. 84, 32.

[78] R. Naphtali Zevi to R. Shalom Halevi of Kaminka, *Imrei shefer*, 13–14.

[79] *Ohel Naftali*, s. 41, 23, and s. 97; *Eser tsaḥtsaḥot*, s. 58, 95.

[80] The story has it that the Seer once said to R. Naphtali Zevi, 'On Shemini Atseret last, the Shelah visited you.' R. Naphtali Zevi agreed, but said that the Shelah had been angry with him and had not talked to him. 'Is that possible?' asked the Seer. 'Yes', answered R. Naphtali Zevi, 'he stood at the bookcase with his back to me.' Tal, *R. Naftali*, 106.

[81] *Ohel Naftali*, s. 94.

Naphtali Zevi's teacher, R. Meshullam Phoebus of Zbarazh, complained on one occasion that his disciple was utilizing his distinguished ancestry in his divine service; R. Meshullam's own view was that this merit could carry no weight in the divine sphere. Hasidic tradition defuses the tense issue of R. Naphtali Zevi's lineage by reversing its thrust, claiming that it had led him to greater humility and severe self-examination against the standards which had been set by his illustrious forebears. As R. Naphtali Zevi himself said: 'I see how lowly I am and recognize my worthlessness. That is what lineage does.'[82]

Since R. Naphtali Zevi's prestigious lineage was on the maternal side, he adopted his mother's maiden name, Horowitz. Hasidic tradition relates that his paternal grandfather had been uncertain about the desirability of his son's marriage to the eminent R. Itsikel Hamburger's daughter because of the disparity of their lineages. Even after he overcame his hesitation on this score, he still wanted to withdraw from the match on hearing that the bride-to-be was ugly. But the groom, R. Menahem Mendel—R. Naphtali Zevi's father—insisted on going ahead because of the bride's fine character. It was for this reason that he was blessed with such a pious son.[83] R. Naphtali Zevi's mother Beyleh was to play an important part in all her son's public activities by virtue of her great wisdom; a closer study of her role may well change our evaluation of women's position in hasidic society.

R. Naphtali Zevi was clearly ambivalent about his lineage. He certainly exploited it occasionally, claiming, for example, that 'there is no other man in the whole world with a lineage such as mine, on both the maternal and the paternal sides', He is even said to have claimed that 'forty of his ancestors were as good as the Besht', thus raising his own status above that of the direct descendants of the founder of hasidism. Did he mean to rebut the claims of others who could trace their lineage back to the Besht or the Maggid of Mezhirech, such as Moses Hayyim Ephraim of Sudylkow, R. Nahman of Bratslav, or perhaps R. Israel of Ruzhin? The fact that R. Naphtali Zevi always concluded discussions of lineage with a joke or a witticism strengthens the suggestion that he was, in fact, disparaging those leaders of hasidism who claimed a distinguished hasidic lineage.[84] What is clear is that as far as R. Naphtali Zevi was concerned, illustrious lineage or possession of a 'holy soul' were not the prerogative of the hasidim. This explains his quote from R. Elimelekh of Lyzhansk, who said that a soul as holy as that of R. Nathan Adler—the controversial Frankfurt rabbi and kabbalist—has not come down to earth for many years, except for R. Israel Baal Shem Tov, of blessed memory'.[85] From this it follows that a 'holy soul' need not be the soul of a hasidic zaddik, and that eminent Torah scholars were highly esteemed by the founders of hasidism. The whole question of the relationship between the leaders of hasidism and traditional rabbinical scholars requires re-evaluation, particularly as far as Poland and Galicia are concerned.

Apart from his lineage, R. Naphtali Zevi derived his authority from the merit of his teachers and mentors. For example, he claimed that when he reached the age of 13 his father took him to R. Jeḥiel Michel of Zloczow, and 'R. Michel put the *tefilin* on his head. The rabbi of Ropczyce said that he thereby tied him to an upper world from

[82] Ibid., s. 362, 128. [83] Ibid. 11; s. 227, 105–6. [84] See ibid., ss. 361, 362, 385.
[85] Ibid., s. 127, 45–6. See also I. J. Cohen, 'HaḤatam Sofer vehaḥasidut', *Sinai*, 69 (1971), 164–5.

which he could never be detached.'[86] This attempt to anchor his authority in a hasidic master who was senior even to R. Elimelekh of Lyzhansk—the founding father of Polish hasidism—and who was a disciple of the Besht himself was clearly intended to establish R. Naphtali Zevi in the highest echelons of the hasidic hierarchy. Elsewhere R. Naphtali Zevi claims that R. Levi Isaac of Berdichev had assured him that he would become an *admor* and wished to bless him, but that he had refused to accept the blessing and later regretted his refusal.[87] The same search for legitimacy finds further expression in the statement attributed to R. Hayyim Halberstam of Zanz: 'The holy rabbi of Ropczyce was born on the same day on which the holy Besht died, and in him was realized the verse, "The sun rises and the sun sets"' (Eccles. 1: 5).[88]

R. Naphtali Zevi claimed that his authority was bestowed on him by R. Isaac Jacob, the Seer of Lublin, before the latter had himself become famous as a zaddik.[89] But he still considered R. Elimelekh of Lyzhansk and R. Menahem Mendel of Rymanow as his main teachers in hasidism. Hasidic tradition inflates the importance of his relationship with R. Elimelekh by claiming that R. Naphtali Zevi's ability to perform miracles equalled that of R. Elimelekh, that he acquired his powers and skills directly from R. Elimelekh, and that he was R. Elimelekh's most faithful explicator.[90] The same tradition attributes to R. Elimelekh the statement that R. Naphtali Zevi achieved the power of prophecy at the level of 'revelation of Elijah'.[91]

The same magical and parapsychological activities which had characterized the career of the Besht and were evident in the lives of R. Elimelekh and the Seer of Lublin were also attributed to R. Naphtali Zevi. These included the power to abrogate evil decrees, to destroy the enemies of the Jews, and to exorcize evil spirits; the ability to see from afar and to gain access to secret knowledge.[92] Apparently, R. Menahem Mendel of Rymanow, who had taught R. Naphtali Zevi the spiritual, inner meaning of Torah, was critical of him for practising his supernatural skills.[93]

Another source from which R. Naphtali Zevi drew his authority was his 'wisdom'. The precise nature of this is never clearly defined but it is evident that neither of his teachers, R. Menahem Mendel of Rymanow and the Seer, possessed this quality, since R. Naphtali Zevi described both as *zaddikim* ('righteous') rather than *ḥakhamim* ('wise').[94] According to one source, the Seer himself differentiated the quality of prophecy which people attributed to him from the quality of wisdom with which R. Naphtali Zevi was endowed, and he stated that, according to tradition, the 'wise man' is superior to the 'prophet'.[95] Was the Seer referring to wisdom in worldly affairs, as is suggested by the sharpness of R. Naphtali Zevi's response, or did he have in mind the

[86] *Ohel Naftali*, 5. [87] Ibid., s. 61, 27. [88] Ibid. 5. [89] Ibid., s. 331, 119.

[90] *Ohel Elimelekh*, s. 40, 11. See also *Sipurei nifla'ot* (Tel Aviv, 1969), 257. For the story as related by R. Israel of Kozienice, see *Ohel Naftali*, s. 278, 108. [91] Ibid., s. 106, 40.

[92] For his ability to foretell the sex of an unborn child, see ibid., s. 34, 20; for exorcisms, see ibid. 19; for seeing from after, ibid. 20, s. 50, 24–5; for cursing Israel's enemies, ibid., s. 31, 20; for healing the sick, ibid., s. 40, 23; s. 90, 34; s. 158, 53; for foretelling the future, ibid., s. 53, 26; for exposing secret deeds, ibid., s. 92, 34–5; s. 50, 24–5.

[93] *Ohel Naftali*, s. 36, 21. For R. Menahem Mendel's rebuke, see ibid., s. 29, 19.

[94] Ibid, s. 70, 29. With relation to the Seer, cf. ibid., s. 118, 42–3. Similarly ibid., s. 365, 129. For all these as related by R. Abraham Joshua Heschel of Apta, see *Eser tsaḥtsaḥot*, s. 57, 95.

[95] *Ohel Naftali*, s. 365, 129.

ability to penetrate the hidden meaning of the Torah, as is suggested further on in the discussion? The second possibility is problematic, since the source makes no mention of R. Menahem Mendel of Rymanow, who was, after all, R. Naphtali Zevi's chief instructor in the hidden meaning of Torah.

Characteristically of early hasidism, R. Naphtali Zevi did not produce any halakhic works, notwithstanding his well-attested training in this field, and despite the fact that both his teachers and his colleagues were outstanding Torah scholars. This is highlighted in a tradition according to which R. Naphtali Zevi's mother reproached R. Ezekiel Panet for failing to commit her son's teachings to writing as he had done for R. Menahem Mendel of Rymanow. R. Ezekiel replied that 'her son's teachings were Torah without clothing'.[96] This suggests that R. Naphtali Zevi did not concern himself with the external 'clothing' of Torah—halakhah and normative explanations, as the term is usually defined in hasidic literature—but rather with the inner, naked spiritual core of Torah. This is reiterated in the following comparison between the Seer and R. Naphtali Zevi: 'He [the Seer] was brought into this world in order to effect *tikun* on the revealed aspects [of Torah] because he had already effected *tikun* on the esoteric aspects in a previous existence, whereas the holy rabbi of Ropczyce had come into the world in order to effect *tikun* on the esoteric aspects because he had already effected *tikun* on the revealed aspects in a previous incarnation.[97] From this it follows that R. Naphtali Zevi's main task in his present incarnation was to further the understanding of the inner meaning of Torah.

All this may provide the context in which to place the following tradition concerning R. Hayyim of Zanz. He was asked by his disciples why, whenever he cited R. Naphtali Zevi who was his foremost teacher, he referred to him by the formula 'I heard from the Rabbi of Ropczyce', whereas whenever he cited R. Zevi Hirsch of Zhidachov, with whom his relationship was less intimate, he used the more personal formula, 'I have heard from my master and teacher'. R. Hayyim answered that he understood 'a little' of what he had heard from R. Zevi Hirsch, but with regard to R. Naphtali Zevi, 'I did not even begin to understand him.'[98] On another occasion, R. Hayyim is reported as saying, 'The sages say, even if you learn as little as one letter from another person [you are required to address him as "My master and teacher"]. The Ropczicer taught me the fear of Heaven, but I do not possess [as little as] one letter of it nor even the stroke at the end of the [smallest] letter *yod*.'[99] This may point to the nature of R. Naphtali Zevi's unique 'wisdom'—'to be cunning in the fear of Heaven'. Since he did not teach R. Hayyim even 'one letter' of normative Torah, it would seem that R. Naphtali Zevi was known for his expertise in the esoteric inner meaning of Torah, a fact which emerges from numerous other sources. Indeed, R. Menahem Mendel of Rymanow is said to have congratulated him on his achievement in this sphere: 'Happy are you and happy is your lot, for you have reached such a high level of insight into the divine realm that you are able to reveal the secrets of Torah.[100]

[96] Ibid., s. 25, 18. The source is *Derekh yivḥar*, 6–7 in the note, citing R. Moshe Panet of Desh, Ezekiel Panet's grandson.
[97] *Ohel Naftali*, s. 140, 48.
[98] Ibid., s. 368, 130.
[99] Ibid., s. 389, 138–9.
[100] Ibid., s. 36, 21.

Hasidic tradition stresses this aspect of R. Naphtali Zevi's reputation in connection with his appointment to the rabbinate of Ropczyce. In order to obtain the appointment he required the assistance of R. Menahem Mendel of Rymanow who enlisted a 'proclamation from heaven'.[101]

Although R. Naphtali Zevi was 'ordained' by the Seer of Lublin, the Seer does not appear to have initiated him into the speculative teachings of hasidism. R. Naphtali Zevi's own statements imply that his teacher in the 'inner meaning of Torah' (i.e. kabbalah) was R. Menahem Mendel of Rymanow, while his main teacher in hasidic doctrine was R. Abraham Joshua of Apta.

Ordination in this context could take one of several forms. A disciple could be ordained by way of a blessing such as R. Naphtali Zevi received from the Seer of Lublin; another way was for the teacher to 'bind' him to the upper worlds, as did R. Jeḥiel Michel of Zloczow; still another was to transmit a certain body of knowledge to the disciple, as did R. Elimelekh of Lyzhansk and R. Menahem Mendel of Rymanow; yet another was to initiate him into the secret doctrines of hasidism, as in the case of R. Abraham Joshua of Apta.

R. Naphtali Zevi's two main disciples, Sar Shalom of Belz and R. Hayyim of Zanz, both claimed that he had given them his blessing and had also transmitted to them the esoteric doctrines of hasidism.[102] We are also told that R. Naphtali Zevi had ordained as *admorim* both R. Zevi Hirsch of Rymanow and R. Yitzhak Isaac of Zhidachov. The latter attributed his ordination by R. Naphtali Zevi to his having emulated him in every detail: 'My hand never left his and I followed his every move.' R. Naphtali Zevi also revealed to him the secret of *shirayim* (the leftover food) of the zaddikim.[103] From all these testimonies it appears that after the death of the 'Holy Jew' of Przysucha in 1813 and the 'three shepherds' in 1814–15, R. Naphtali Zevi became the central authority for Galician hasidism, although he was never formally appointed to any such post.[104] It is also evident that, although he began to attract followers during the lifetime of his teachers, this did not generate any tension among them, a fact which may indicate that he did not challenge their authority but managed to maintain the balance of hierarchical obligations which developed between him and them.

5. THE HASIDIC LEADER AND HIS COMMUNITY

Following the death of the three acknowledged leaders of Polish hasidism,[105] the opportunity arose to create a single, united centre of authority for the hasidic movement of the entire region. However, a meeting of regional leaders was unable to reach any agreement. It seems that R. Naphtali Zevi—the most senior figure among them—was prepared to take on the position of supreme leader but his eccentric personality was held against him, particularly in the light of his numerous and acrimonious disputes

[101] *Ohel Naftali*, s. 36.

[102] Ibid., s. 38, 22; s. 42, 23; see also Tal, *R. Naftali*, 38.

[103] *Ohel Naftali*, s. 100, 36–7.

[104] According to a tradition reported by Kamelhar, R. Naphtali Zevi requested that R. Menahem Mendel of Rymanow should bless him, but the latter emphasized that his principal heir was to be R. Zevi Hirsch of Rymanow; see Gershon Kamelhar, *Mevaser tov* (Podgorze, 1900), 8 n. 8.

[105] These were the only three whom R. Naphtali Zevi recognized as the leaders of Polish hasidism.

with so many of his colleagues.[106] R. Zevi Hirsch of Zhidachov made an explicit bid for the leadership and even appealed to R. Naphtali Zevi for support on the grounds that the Shelah, one of R. Naphtali Zevi's own distinguished ancestors, was 'visiting' him regularly. Apparently R. Abraham Joshua of Apta took umbrage at R. Zevi Hirsch's presumption; he himself would have been considered the natural candidate had he not moved to distant Podolia. Of all the *admorim* present, it was R. Naphtali Zevi who took up R. Zevi Hirsch's defence and stressed his special qualities—humility, and the ability to pray as effectively as R. Elimelekh of Lyzhansk.[107] However, it seems that R. Naphtali Zevi was attempting to unify the hasidic movement of western Galicia around himself, despite the fact that Polish hasidism had been divided since R. Elimelekh's time. The main obstacle to the realization of R. Naphtali Zevi's aspirations was his disciple R. Zevi Elimelekh of Dynow, who refused to accept his authority and set about establishing a dynasty of his own.[108] This failure, however, did not prevent R. Naphtali Zevi from placing his descendants and disciples in positions of leadership throughout western Galicia and thus establishing, to some degree at least, the hegemony of the Ropczyce line, albeit without containing it within the framework of a single dynastic line of succession.

There are contradictory testimonies concerning R. Naphtali Zevi's own understanding of the responsibilities of the leader towards his community. This may indicate that his approach was pragmatic, altering in response to specific conditions and changing circumstances. On the one hand, we are told that 'the Rabbi of Ropczyce wakes up early in the morning and prays that all who need salvation should find it wherever they are rather than travel to Ropczyce and so come to believe that they have been saved by the Rabbi of Ropcyzce'.[109] However, 'anyone who stays at home and does not travel to the zaddikim does not know the way of God'.[110] Perhaps he distinguished between salvation in material affairs and spiritual salvation.

R. Naphtali Zevi fulfilled the functions of the zaddik as they had been formulated by his teacher, R. Elimelekh of Lyzhansk. He performed miracles and abrogated evil decrees which threatened to harm the Jews; like the Seer of Lublin, he practised 'seeing from afar' and admonished the hasidim for their secret transgressions which he, as a zaddik, could see clearly; he was endowed with divine inspiration, could see into the future, and heal the sick. He was also able to activate the flow of divine grace to counter the forces of evil by stimulating the upper worlds from below.[111] Hasidic tradition relates that R. Naphtali Zevi deliberately interrupted R. Elimelekh's meditation of the upper worlds so that he should be free to take an interest in events on earth.[112] This is the thrust of his statement to R. Jacob Orenstein, the non-hasidic rabbi of Lemberg and author of *Yeshu'ot Ya'akov*: 'The zaddikim are the eminent men of the generation and the world exists by their merit.'[113] According to R. Eliezer of

[106] *Ohel Naftali*, s. 94; cf. *Eser kedushot*, s. 33, 10.

[107] *Ohel Naftali*, s. 94; cf. *Eser kedushot*, s. 33, 10.

[108] For this affair, see above, s. 4.

[109] *Ohel Naftali*, s. 40, 23.

[110] Ibid., s. 64, 28.

[111] *Ayalah sheluḥah* (Bnei Brak, 1972), on 'Mikets', 19.

[112] See *Devarim arevim*, s. 39, 21. The story can be interpreted otherwise: R. Naphtali Zevi may have feared that if R. Elimelekh continued his prolonged meditation on the upper worlds he would die, and he wanted to save him.

[113] *Ohel Naftali*, s. 279, 100.

Zhidachov, he once said that even if a person is not pious but cleaves to a zaddik, his actions become holy; but if he does not cleave to a zaddik, however pious and God-fearing he may be, his actions are profane.[114] Notwithstanding this severe indictment of the non-hasid, R. Naphtali Zevi maintained contact with important rabbis who did not accept hasidism and even with those who were antagonistic to it. This is true not only with regard to his uncle R. Meshullam Igra but also with regard to other Galician rabbis such as Jacob Orenstein. Certain of his utterances give the impression that R. Naphtali Zevi saw himself as the zaddik of the generation, capable of 'drawing all the [divine] sparks out of the inanimate, the vegetative, the animate, and the human worlds—out of every material object'. Addressing himself to R. Zevi Elimelekh of Dynow, he went on to say that 'the zaddik of the generation is capable of drawing out of every individual his own particular attributes and virtues'.[115] Consequently, the zaddik not only elevates his follower's actions, purifiying and elevating the holy sparks around him, but he also atones for his sins: 'The zaddik believes that he has sinned and repents; by doing so he atones for the sins of the people.'[116] Elsewhere the zaddik is described as the one who fights God's battle against wickedness and heresy:

The term *metsora* (leper) is made up of the words *motsi ra* [literally, 'brings out evil', interpreted in the classical rabbinic sources as 'talks slander'], as it is written in the books. We apply it to the person who suffers because the Divine Presence is in exile. He wishes to defeat the wicked and the heretics and to remove the thorns from the vineyard of God, the Lord of Hosts of Israel, because the task of the zaddik is to abrogate judgements and harsh decrees so that they should not affect the Jews.[117]

Some believe that this statement was directed against the maskilim.[118] In any event, there is evidence that R. Naphtali Zevi wanted to restore hasidism to its pristine state of purity at the time of the Besht, when the movement was confined to the ranks of the spiritual élite. The divisions within the leadership and his own failure to impose his authority even on his own disciples may have prompted R. Naphtali Zevi to advocate a return to pre-Beshtian, non-hasidic, rabbinic Judaism, devoted exclusively to the outer 'wrappings' of Torah as presented by the *Shulḥan arukh*. This change of direction appears to have encountered some resistance among his disciples, and at least one, R. Meir of Apta, author of *Or lashamayim*, is said to have prevailed upon him to desist from this line of advocacy.[119]

The hasidic leaders in Galicia often fulfilled the functions of both *admor* and rabbi, particularly in the smaller communities, and in this R. Naphtali Zevi was no exception. The *admorim* strove to control the rabbinate either by serving as rabbis themselves or by ensuring that the rabbinical posts within the orbit of their influence should be occupied by their own protégés. Apparently R. Naphtali Zevi was particularly aggressive in this respect. He himself was the rabbi of Ropczyce, a position he obtained with the help of R. Menahem Mendel of Rymanow;[120] he inherited the rabbinate of Linsk (Lesko) and the province of Sanok from his father, in turn passing it on to his son, who later

114 *Eser tsaḥtsaḥot*, s. 48, 93; cf. *Ohel Naftali*, s. 67, 28–9.
115 *Ohel Naftali*, s. 273, 98.
116 Ibid., s. 59, 27.
117 *Zera kodesh*, on 'Metsora', 8*b*.
118 Tal, *R. Naphtali*, 29.
119 *Dor de'ah*, ii. 237, 241.
120 *Ohel Naftali*, 6.

passed it on to his grandson.[121] In Debice (Dembits) R. Naphtali Zevi made the householders undertake on oath to appoint one of his progeny to the rabbinate after his death.[122]

Similarly, R. Naphtali Zevi's son, R. Eliezer, who was appointed rabbi of Dzykow thanks to his father's intervention, succeeded in placing his many sons in rabbinical posts throughout the region. All this, however, led to the fragmentation of the Ropczyce dynasty and blurred the hierarchical distinctions within its structure. Every one of these rabbis directed a hasidic 'court' of his own, while at the same time often enjoying the patronage of a senior hasidic authority. Thus we read that R. Reuben, the rabbi of Debice, and R. Moysheleh, the rabbi of Rozwadow, deferred to R. Meir of Dzykow, R. Naphtali Zevi's grandson.[123]

R. Naphtali Zevi was equally concerned to place his disciples in positions of authority. This is evident from a letter he sent to his pupil R. Shalom Halevi of Kaminka, encouraging him to accept a rabbinical post: 'You would do well to take on the burden of the rabbinate of Jaryerzow, for at present it is a great *mitsvah* to supervise and guide the public and to make peace between neighbours and spouses, and in this way to serve God.' He offered his patronage to R. Shalom and promised to pray for his welfare, while at the same time reprimanding him for sinking into melancholy.[124] R. Naphtali Zevi had himself received a similar letter of encouragement from R. Moses Hayyim Ephraim of Sudylkow, the author of *Degel maḥaneh Efrayim*, on the occasion of his own accession to the rabbinate. Interestingly enough, the Ropczyce tradition of placing both sons and disciples in rabbinical positions finds expression also in a letter by R. Hayyim of Zanz, addressed to the same R. Shalom Halevi, in which he asks him to find a rabbinical appointment for another of the Ropczyce clan 'because of your great love for the house of our holy master and teacher, the rabbi of Ropczyce'.[125] There are other sources which testify to R. Naphtali Zevi's concern to establish his authority over the rabbis and other communal functionaries such as ritual slaughterers, throughout the region.[126]

6. PUBLIC ACTIVITIES

R. Naphtali Zevi attempted to influence Jewish public opinion in Galicia against Napoleon while at the same time waging war on the Haskalah movement. Was there a connection between these two campaigns? In Russia, R. Shneur Zalman of Lyady had clearly combined them in his opposition to Napoleon, but there is no evidence that the hasidic leaders of Galicia associated Napoleon with the threat of Jewish Enlightenment. It seems that the differences of opinion regarding Napoleon between, on the one hand, R. Menahem Mendel of Rymanow and, on the other, the Seer of Lublin, R. Israel of Kozienice, and R. Naphtali Zevi, reflected their respective stances on the messianic issue. R. Menahem Mendel believed that all efforts should be made to hasten the

[121] Ibid. 18. He was helped in his attempt to become rabbi of Lesko by R. Ezekiel Panet; see *Dor de'ah*, iv. 219.

[122] *Ohel Naftali*, s. 75, 31; *Eser tsaḥtsaḥot*, 84.

[123] H. Harshoshanim *et al.* (eds.), *Radomshil rabati* (Tel Aviv, 1971), 20.

[124] *Imrei shefer*, 13*b*.

[125] Ibid. 16*a*–*b*.

[126] *Ohel Naftali*, s. 196, 61.

messianic advent by means of Napoleon. The Seer, on the other hand, tried—albeit unsuccessfully—to 'bring the messiah' in 1813, but without the help of Napoleon.

R. Naphtali Zevi was also active in the struggle against government legislation which had a detrimental effect on the Jewish community. This included the institution of special taxes on meat, candles and marriages, as well as the legislation designed to Germanicize the Jews, particularly after the Congress of Vienna in 1815.

Ways could be found round this new legislation: led by their rabbis, the Jews avoided civil registration of marriages; they kept secret the existence of small prayer-houses; they took their disputes to arbitration in the Jewish courts rather than resorting to civil litigation; secret Hebrew printing shops operated clandestinely; money was still collected and sent to the Holy Land in defiance of government prohibition; birth records were tampered with in order to avoid military duty; Jewish tax farmers were excommunicated; and the rabbis forbade the consumption of meat, in order both to evade the new tax and to exert pressure on the tax farmers and the government. Since the maskilim were collaborating with the government in the implementation of the 'decrees' and often informed the authorities of these clandestine activities, they were bitterly hated and feared. The Haskalah movement was regarded as a threat to religious tradition, not only in terms of halakhic observance but also with regard to the status of kabbalah of which the maskilim were particularly critical.

In his *Hasidism and the Jewish Enlightenment*, Raphael Mahler quotes an 1824 report of the investigation into the activities of R. Zevi Hirsch of Zhidachov which was occasioned by the seizure of one of his letters to R. Naphtali Zevi. The letter was passed on to the maskil Joseph Perl for examination, and he ruled that it expressed 'evil intentions'. The hasidim suggested that the letter should be subjected to rabbinical scrutiny, and this resulted in the verdict that the only difference between the hasidim and their mitnaggedic opponents was their prayer rite. According to a report by the commissar of the Brody province in 1827, R. Naphtali Zevi was summoned officially to defend himself against the accusations of the maskilim.[127] The ruling on this occasion was that the Toleranz Patent of 1788, reaffirmed in 1814, applied to the Jewish religion as a whole, including hasidism; hasidism was to be tolerated, therefore, so long as it kept in line with 'political regulations'. It is noteworthy that R. Naphtali Zevi was assisted in his appeal to the authorities against the slanders of the maskilim by the non-hasidic R. Jacob Orenstein.

R. Naphtali Zevi's attitude to the government informers among the maskilim is abundantly clear from his own writings:

> As we can see, even in our own times the heretics, may their name be blotted out, wish to prevent us from following the customs of the zaddikim and the hasidim by forbidding us to pray or meet together and by other decrees aimed at preventing us from serving God. However, all their efforts cannot undermine the fundamental principles of faith and religion, since God requires of us that we serve him with our hearts, and He combines our good intentions with our deeds. For all our good deeds, and all the restrictions which we impose upon ourselves [in order to avoid sin] are the products simply of our limited intelligence. They appear to us to be the most important [aspect of divine service] and we therefore believe them to be

[127] R. Mahler, *Hasidism and the Jewish Enlightenment* (Philadelphia, 1985), 83.

the only appropriate way in which to serve God. Therefore, if anyone comes and tries to stop us, God becomes angry and wreaks vengeance on him, saying, 'How dare you stand against Me to take away from My beloved children the good and upright laws and customs which I have given them for their benefit and pleasure? I consider this an abrogation of the Torah and the commandments themselves.' This is the meaning of the biblical verse [Ps. 99: 8] 'And he takes vengeance on their deeds (*alilotam*)', that is, He takes vengeance over those things which His children and infants [a play on the word *alilotam*] do in order to afflict themselves and thus to fulfil their desire for the One they love.[128]

7. CONCLUSION

Students of hasidism often divide the hasidic movement into distinct and even contrasting strands: popular as opposed to élitist, intellectual hasidism; hasidism based on faith as opposed to mystical hasidism; practical as opposed to spiritual zaddikism. None of these categories, however, is helpful in understanding the personality and teachings of R. Naphtali Zevi. His own statements as they have come down to us do not fall into any of these broad categories, and they appear to defy any clear-cut characterization. Alongside his emphatically stated view that the zaddik is responsible for both the spiritual and the material welfare of his flock, we find his disapproval of those hasidim who turn to their zaddik for advice on temporal matters. He appears to view the community as wholly dependent on the zaddik, and yet some of his remarks suggest that he may have qualified or even abandoned that view. He often stressed his own special spiritual powers, and yet was unhappy to learn that they were being discussed publicly.

He believed that hasidism was the highest form of Judaism, and yet he called for a return to normative Judaism. One can only conclude that R. Naphtali Zevi was uncertain that hasidism was indeed the only authentic expression of Judaism. He was proud of his non-hasidic forebears and claimed that they were no less virtuous than the Besht himself. Although he endeavoured to maintain his position of power and influence, he was able to resign himself to losing both; he was prepared to submit to the authority of R. Zevi Hirsch of Zhidachov and did not appoint a successor to his 'seat' at Ropczyce, nor did he ensure that his 'court' would occupy a central position in Galician hasidism. Few indeed are the hasidic leaders to whom were attributed spiritual powers such as were attributed to R. Naphtali Zevi, and yet his powers had little tangible or long-lasting effect. Can these apparent contradictions be explained by the complexity of his personality, so irresolute as to be incapable of effective leadership? Or was his failure to leave a more permanent mark an outcome of the leadership crisis of Polish hasidism in general? It is not impossible that the regional structure which developed in Polish hasidism, with the various courts becoming attached to local rabbinates, made it impossible for the Ropczyce line to emerge as the central authority throughout the region.

R. Naphtali Zevi's speculative teachings show no evidence of radical tendencies in any direction. In a letter to his cousin containing his spiritual will, he wrote: 'Our only light is this Torah [and our only task is] to study it diligently and to constantly review

[128] *Imrei shefer*, 6*b*.

what we learn. This applies even to the ethical books which are pleasant to read and which you should memorize well. You should study *Tana devei Eliyahu* constantly and not immerse yourself in the *mikveh* too frequently, particularly not during the winter. Do not scatter [your money] too much and do not miss the prescribed times for the recitation of the Shema and the prayer services. From time to time you should visit the scholars and be happy at all times.'[129]

[129] *Dor de'ah*, 240; *Ohel Naftali*, s. 337.

PART V

THE HASIDIC TALE

TWENTY

New Light on the Hasidic Tale and its Sources

GEDALIAH NIGAL

HASIDIC literature can be classified in two main categories, homiletic-speculative, usually originating in the sermons delivered by the hasidic teachers to the gatherings of the hasidim at the courts and containing ethical, kabbalistic, and hasidic teachings, and narrative, comprising numerous collections of tales. Although research has addressed itself to both categories, it seems to me that the tales, the more popular of the two genres, have not been given the scholarly attention they deserve. A number of important studies have appeared in recent years,[1] but many questions remain unanswered. This chapter is an attempt to address three cardinal questions:

1. What constitutes the literary form to which we refer as a hasidic tale?
2. When did 'the tale' first emerge in hasidism?
3. On which literary sources did the authors of the tales draw, and how did these sources contribute to the development of the genre?

These questions are, of course, interconnected, and the answer to any one of them will constitute a partial answer to the others.

The figure of the Baal Shem Tov ('the Besht', as he is known in Hebrew), the founder of hasidism, is crucial to the discussion throughout. His personality is inseparably connected with the emergence of the hasidic tale and its subsequent development.

One important fact that must be borne in mind is that the *printed* hasidic tale was preceded by an earlier stage of oral dissemination. This is attested to by allusions to and even the appearance of complete tales in other genres long before the emergence of the narrative literature of hasidism in print. For example, Ephraim of Sudylkow, a grandson of the Besht and the author of *Degel maḥaneh Efrayim*,[2] refers to tales that his grandfather used to tell. Aaron Samuel Hakohen in his *Kore merosh* supplies the nucleus of a biographical tale about the Besht in his references to the Besht's visit to his father-in-law and to his ability to understand the song of birds.[3] From other reports in

[1] See J. Dan, *Hasipur haḥasidi* (Jerusalem, 1975); id., *Hanovelah haḥasidit* (Jerusalem, 1966); M. Piekarz, *Ḥasidut Braslav* (Jerusalem, 1972); G. Nigal, *Hasiporet haḥasidit: Toledoteihah venose'eihah* (Jerusalem, 1981); Y. Mondshine, *Shivḥei haBesht: Ketav yad* (Jerusalem, 1982), introd. 65–8.

[2] See Moses Hayyim Ephraim of Sudylkow, *Degel maḥaneh Efrayim* (Korets, 1810), on 'Vayeshev', 22*c*; G. Scholem, 'Demuto hahistorit shel R. Yisrael Baal Shem Tov', *Molad*, 18: 144–5 (1960), 343, repr. in id., *Devarim be go* (Tel Aviv, 1975), 311.

[3] See *Kore merosh* (Berdichev, 1811), 60*c*–60*d*; G. Nigal, 'Al R. Aharon Shemuel Hakohen: mitalmidei haMagid miMezhirech', *Sinai*, 78 (1976), 257. See also Scholem, 'Demuto', 340 and 341 n. 10, who mistakenly attributed *Kore merosh* to Joel Heilprin, Aaron Samuel's father-in-law.

various anthologies of speculative hasidic teaching it becomes clear that the Besht was indeed in the habit of telling stories, many of them about himself.[4]

The writings of Jacob Joseph of Polonnoye,[5] a friend and disciple of the Besht, were the first hasidic books to appear in print (1780–2) and they provide important evidence on the nature of the oral transmission of tales in hasidism. While the importance of R. Jacob Joseph's books for understanding the socio-religious doctrines of hasidism has long been established, their importance for reconstructing the development of the hasidic tale has been overlooked. Some scholars argue that the year 1814, when *Shivḥei haBesht* (In Praise of the Baal Shem Tov) first appeared in print, marks the beginning of the printing history of the hasidic tale,[6] but they do not take account of the six well-developed and important tales in Aaron of Opatow's *Keter shem tov*,[7] which was published some twenty years earlier. Moreover, it is now becoming clear that the allusions to tales in the works of R. Jacob Joseph of Polonnoye not only indicate that the oral transmission of tales was widespread already during the lifetime of the Besht, but they also constitute the earliest publication of tales in hasidism.

These allusions are not immediately recognizable as references to tales, and I myself have overlooked them in the past. In my book *Manhig ve'edah* (The Leader and the Community),[8] I collected all the parables which are scattered throughout R. Jacob Joseph's works, but did not realize the significance of the tale-fragments concealed in his long homilies.

R. Jacob Joseph's allusions to the tales associated with the Besht may be characterized by three key features. All are brief, consisting of mere allusions to stories. All refer to past events, usually episodes in the life of the Besht. Finally, all are used as examples or illustrations of doctrinal points, either mystical or magical, which are being integrated into mainstream hasidic thought.

The following are examples of such allusions:

1. In his *Tsafenat pa'neaḥ*,[9] R. Jacob Joseph argues that our world is full of *kelipot* ('shells' or 'husks', that is, forces of evil); were it not for the *kelipot* one would be able to see from one end of the world to the other and also hear heavenly voices. In support of this claim, Jacob Joseph writes as follows: 'My master [the Besht] is the proof; he could see afar and hear heavenly voices as has been truly proven.'

2. In his *Ben porat Yosef*,[10] R. Jacob Joseph discusses the ability of his teacher to forecast future events and adds: 'I have heard something similar from my teacher, of blessed memory. If he saw a person studying some passage from the Mishnah, he

[4] See e.g. Aaron of Opatow, *Keter shem tov* (2 vols.; Zolkva (Zolkiew), 1794–5), ii. 30; *Sefer Ba'al Shem Tov*, ed. Simon Menahem Mendel of Govartchov (Gowarczwow) (2 vols.; Lodz, 1938), i, introd.; s. 'Me'irat einayim', para. 8

[5] On his works see G. Nigal, *Manhig ve'edah* (Jerusalem, 1962); Jacob Joseph of Polonnoye, *Ketonet pasim*, ed. G. Nigal (Jerusalem, 1985), 1–50; Jacob Joseph of Polonnoye, *Tsafenat pa'neaḥ*, ed. G. Nigal (Jerusalem, 1989), 1–50.

[6] See Dan, *Hasipur haḥasidi*, 34 *et passim*.

[7] See G. Nigal, 'Makor rishoni lesifrut hasipurim haḥasidit: Al sefer *Keter shem tov* umekorotav', *Sinai*, 79 (1976), 132–46.

[8] Nigal, *Manhig ve'edah*, 113–36.

[9] Jacob Joseph of Polonnoye, *Tsafenat pa'neaḥ* (Korets, 1782), 18*d*.

[10] Id., *Ben porat Yosef* (Korets, 1781), on Shabbat Teshuvah of the year 1767, 96*a*.

would tell him what was to happen in the future, in the actual physical sense, as indeed happened on one occasion.'

3. Another homily in *Tsafenat pa'neaḥ* considers a philosophical problem: does the zaddik's ability to temper God's judgement by abrogating His decrees mean that the divine will is susceptible of change? An answer is offered in the name of Ahijah the Shilonite, the Besht's heavenly mentor,[11] and R. Jacob Joseph concludes the section with a reference to a tale connected with the Besht: 'Similarly, I have heard of an incident which was reported in his name and cited as evidence in this connection.'[12]

All the passages quoted above contain allusions, albeit brief ones, to specific events. R. Jacob Joseph, who was not given to the art of narrative writing, had little interest in recording the incidents in full, but there can be no doubt that he alluded to events of which full narrative accounts were circulating orally among the disciples and associates of the Besht. The characteristic features of an allusion as presented above are clearly evident in all three instances, demonstrating that, right from the start, a strong connection existed between the tales and the speculative teachings of hasidism.

This connection, which has been questioned by some scholars, precludes the possibility that the hasidic tale was a mere by-product of later theories concerning the role of the zaddik in hasidism.[13] The overwhelming majority of the motifs and subject-matters that feature in the later hasidic tale are present already at this early phase, as is the positive approach to the tale which is articulated in the notion of its 'sanctification'.[14] The difference between the early allusions to narrative material and the later, fully developed tales is quantitative, not qualitative.

Two well-known parables of the Besht[15] have attracted the attention of scholars in the past.[16] What has escaped their attention, however, is that, unlike other homilists who used parables for didactic purposes, the Besht used to relate them to events in his own life. Furthermore, he was unique among contemporary homilists in introducing into his teachings not only parables but also autobiographical tales, which were later retold by his followers. In this respect he shows greater affinity with fellow *ba'alei shem* ('masters of the divine name') than with contemporary preachers and homilists.[17]

The third passage from R. Jacob Joseph's works quoted above cited the opinion of Ahijah the Shilonite. This is not the only appearance in this literature of the heavenly mentor in his capacity of the Besht's instructor in doctrinal matters.[18] Scholars have been particularly drawn to two short but important passages at the end of *Toledot Ya'akov Yosef*,[19] which refer to Ahijah the Shilonite's role in the Besht's attempted

[11] On Ahijah the Shilonite as the Besht's mentor, see G. Nigal, 'Moro verabo shel R. Yisrael Ba'al Shem Tov', *Sinai*, 76 (1976), 150–9.

[12] *Tsafenat pa'neaḥ*, on 'Mishpatim', 62*d*.

[13] See Dan, *Hasipur haḥasidi*, 53.

[14] For the theory of the 'sanctification of the tale', see ibid. 40 ff.; Piekarz, *Ḥasidut Braslav*, 85–101.

[15] See Jacob Joseph of Polonnoye, *Toledot Ya'akov Yosef* [Korets, 1780] (Jerusalem, 1966), 96*b*; *Tsafenat pa'neaḥ*, 20*b*.

[16] See Scholem, 'Demuto', 348, 350.

[17] See *Encyclopedia Hebraica*, ix. 263–4, s.v. 'ba'al shem'; *Encyclopedia Judaica*, iv. 5–7. See also J. Guenzig, *Die 'Wundermänner' im jüdischen Volke* (Antwerp, 1921), and G. Nigal, *Magic, Mysticism and Hasidism* (Northvale and London, 1994), ch. 1.

[18] See *Toledot*, on 'Noaḥ', 13*b*; on 'Devarim', 161*a*; *Tsafenat pa'neaḥ*, 16*c*, 62*c*, 83*b*; *Ketonet pasim*, 47*a et passim*.

[19] See *Toledot*, 201*a*.

emigration to Erets Yisrael. These passages, too, must be considered as allusions that unite a concrete event with a point of doctrine. Furthermore, in a letter to his brother-in-law, Gershon of Kutow, which appears at the end of *Ben porat Yosef*,[20] the Besht alludes to Ahijah the Shilonite, presuming the identity of his heavenly mentor to be known to R. Gershon, to R. Jacob Joseph who was to deliver the letter, and presumably to all his other associates. If we add this to the evidence cited above, it would seem probable that a full narrative account—in effect, a tale—about the relationship between the Besht and Ahijah the Shilonite was current in the Besht's circle even during his lifetime, and that he himself was its first narrator.

As a rule, the late appearance of a hasidic tale in print need not preclude the possibility that it is of ancient provenance. It is reasonable to assume, for example, that many of the tales which were first published in *Shivḥei haBesht* had originated during the lifetime of the Besht and were told many times before they finally reached the anthologist, R. Dov Ber of Linits. An example of this is a tale reported in the name of Jacob Joseph of Polonnoye in *Shivḥei haBesht*,[21] that describes R. Alexander, the Besht's scribe and the father-in-law of Dov Ber of Linits, lagging behind the Besht and his party in Paradise. Notably, the same tale appears also in the homilies of Jacob Joseph of Polonnoye[22] which were published some thirty-five years prior to the publication of *Shivḥei haBesht*. This is an example of a tale which is first recorded by the original narrator, only later to be reproduced in his name by the 'professional' anthologist.

Another example provides a further illustration of this point. Some scholars have argued that the tales concerning the Besht's abortive attempt to emigrate to Erets Yisrael are of late provenance and were fabricated by Michael Levi Rodkinson, Isaac Jeḥiel Safrin of Komarno, and others.[23] However, in addition to the early allusions to this event which were mentioned above, further narrative evidence may be cited to confirm its historicity. I am referring to a passage in R. Jacob Joseph's *Ketonet pasim*, a book which, though clearly written before 1782, was never published in the lifetime of the author but appeared in print in Lemberg as late as 1866. The passage is remarkably consistent with the accounts of the event in the tales which are alleged to be of late nineteenth-century provenance.

If a person realizes that he is in the throes of 'smallness' and cannot concentrate his thoughts [in prayer] because strange thoughts overcome him, then he should pray like a young child, out of the printed text, as my teacher [the Besht] testified concerning himself, that when he

[20] See *Ben porat Yosef*, 100*a*; Abraham Rubinstein, 'Igeret haBesht leR. Gershon miKutov', *Sinai*, 67 (1970), 120–39; Y. Mondshine, 'Nusaḥ kadum shel igeret aliyat haneshamah lehaBesht', *Migdal oz* (Kfar Habad, 1980), 119–26.

[21] Dov Ber b. Shmuel, *Shivḥei haBesht*, ed. S. A. Horodecky (Tel Aviv, 1947), 52.

[22] *Ben porat Yosef*, 13*a*.

[23] See Nigal, *Hasiporet haḥasidit*, 280–92; M. L. Rodkinson, *Adat tsadikim* [Lemberg, 1864], repr. in G. Nigal (ed.), *Sipurei Michael Levi Rodkinson* (Jerusalem, 1988), 15–97; Isaac Judah Jeḥiel Safrin of Komarno, *Netiv mitsvoteikha* [Lemberg, 1858] (Jerusalem, 1983), 'Shevil ha'emunah', 4*a*; Abraham Isaac Sperling, *Ta'amei haminhagim umekorei hadinim* (Jerusalem, 1957), 292; Nathan Neta Donner, *Derekh ha'emunah uma'aseh rav* (Warsaw, 1899), 35; Isaac Dov Ber b. Zevi Hirsch, *Emunat tsadikim* [Warsaw 1900] pub. as *Kehal ḥasidim heḥadash* [Lemberg, 1902], s. 23. See also Scholem's remarks regarding the Zaddik of Komarno in his 'The Neutralization of the Messianic Element in Early Hasidism', *Journal of Jewish Studies*, 20 (1969), 35, repr. in id., *The Messianic Idea in Judaism* (London, 1971); see 185.

was in such a state while in another country . . . he adhered to the letters . . . And he ruled that every individual should do the same until he can return to a higher state . . . Similarly, I have heard from my master concerning himself that after the above-mentioned descent, he enjoyed a double ascent, even with regard to temporal matters.[24]

This passage, too, contains allusions to a tale that relates to matters of doctrine. Unless my reading is mistaken, it refers to the spiritual crisis which the Besht experienced following the failure of his plan to emigrate to the Holy Land. I believe that the allegedly late and historically 'unfounded' account of his request on this occasion that his scribe should recite the alphabet with him, as well as the reference to his subsequent spiritual ascent, are, in fact, alluded to in this passage from *Ketonet pasim*.

To complete the picture, we must now turn to the question of the sources of the hasidic tale. As suggested above, the origins of the tale in hasidism are connected with the personality of the Besht. In a unique fashion, the Besht combined the characteristic features of several types of religious leader: He was a 'master of the divine name', a preacher, and a charismatic teacher. The telling of autobiographical tales, particularly reports of miracle-working, is a tradition associated specifically with the 'masters of the divine name' Long before the time of Israel Ba'al Shem Tov, there were other 'masters' whose reputation as miracle-workers owed much to their own endeavours to publicize their feats by means of telling autobiographical tales to their associates.

The most prominent feature of the hasidic tale, both early and late, is almost invariably the miraculous feat performed by a mystical or magical figure endowed with superhuman powers. Although the miracle may benefit no one other than the miracle-worker himself, by and large the beneficiaries are others in need of help—seeking offspring, good health, an assured livelihood, and the like.[25] At first glance, the literary model for this type of tale would appear to be the Bible, where the prophets are often portrayed as miracle-workers. However, since the gaonic period, and perhaps even earlier, miracle-workers of this type have been known as *ba'alei shem*, 'masters of the divine name', a title which, in the eighteenth century, was conferred upon the founder of hasidism. The systematic examination of thousands of hasidic tales reveals that they contain most of the motifs and subject-matters which have featured in the tales of the *ba'alei shem* throughout the ages.[26] This must be the outcome of the process whereby, after the time of the Besht, hasidic zaddikim simply displaced *ba'alei shem* in the public consciousness. They, too, used divine names to bring salvation both to individuals and to the community;[27] the only difference between the types was nomenclature—the hasidic zaddikim were simply no longer referred to as *ba'alei shem*.[28] In the course of

[24] *Ketonet pasim*, 298.

[25] In hasidic thought, the zaddik is concerned with children, life (i.e. health) and food (i.e. livelihood). See Elimelekh of Lyzhansk, *No'am Elimelekh* [Lemberg, 1788], ed. G. Nigal (2 vols.; Jerusalem, 1978), i, introd. 24–56.

[26] For a detailed discussion of many of these motifs and subject-matters see Nigal, *Hasiporet haḥasidit*, part ii, chs. 1–16.

[27] For the use of the divine name see E. E. Urbach, *The Sages: Their Concepts and Beliefs* (Jerusalem, 1979), 124–34.

[28] After the Besht's time, nothing more is heard of *ba'alei shem* in eastern Europe, even though they do survive in other regions. Seckel Wormser, for example, the *ba'al shem* of Michelstadt, was still active in Germany at the beginning of the 19th cent.

time, incantations of divine names became less popular and were eventually replaced by the blessings and prayers of the zaddik,[29] while certain other characteristics of the historical *ba'alei shem* never entirely disappeared from zaddikism.

In most *ba'alei shem* stories, the heroes are portrayed as possessing superhuman powers such as the ability to transport themselves over great distances,[30] to inflict injury on their enemies, or even to cause their premature death;[31] they can revive the dead,[32] exorcize demons,[33] heal the sick,[34] inflict paralysis,[35] and much more. Some of these powers are mentioned in a responsum which R. Hai Gaon sent to Kairouan in reply to an enquiry about *ba'alei shem*;[36] others are described in the *Aḥima'ats Scroll* of Ahima'ats ben Paltiel, which records the author's family history in southern Italy in the tenth and eleventh centuries.[37] Apparently, interest in *ba'alei shem* was exported from Italy to Germany with the northward migration of a number of prominent Italian Jewish families in the tenth century,[38] and it is not surprising, therefore, that we find miracle-tales involving *ba'alei shem* in the narrative texts of the medieval German pietists—the Ashkenazi hasidim.[39]

To the characteristic motifs and subject-matters which were integrated into the hasidic tale from the medieval *ba'alei shem* stories must be added those which it absorbed from the magical tales of the sixteenth-century circle of Safed kab-

[29] Menahem Nahum of Chernobyl (*Me'or einayim* [Polonnoye, 1810], on 'Naso', 40*d*) writes: 'The Besht, may his soul rest in paradise, cured [the sick] only by his special meditations [on the divine name].' Moses Hayyim Ephraim of Sudylkow (*Degel maḥaneh Efrayim*, on 'Vayishlaḥ' 19*c*) reports in the name of his grandfather, the Besht, that 'on one occasion he passed through the river Dniester without using any divine name. He just placed his belt [on the water] and the waters parted so that he could pass. He said that it was [his] great faith that had enabled him to pass.' Similarly, Isaac Judah Jeḥiel Safrin of Komarno (*Notser ḥesed* [Lemberg, 1855], 43*b*) emphasizes that 'he [i.e. the Besht] never used any divine name'.

[30] For the ability to cover great distances magically, see Sanh. 95*a*; Ḥul. 91*b*; *Halakhot gedolot*, ed. Azriel Hildesheimer (Berlin, 1850–2), 337–8; *Maise bukh* [Basle, 1602] (Nuremberg, 1863), 50*a*; G. Scholem, 'Ma'amar al ha'atsilut hasemalit leR. Yitzḥak Hakohen b. R. Ya'akov z.l.: Mofet hador', *Mada'ei hayahadut*, 2 (Jerusalem, 1927), 254; A. Marmorstein, 'Beiträge zur Religionsgeschichte und Volkskunde', in *Jahrbuch für jüdische Volkskunde* (Berlin, 1923), 316. See also Nigal, *Hasiporet haḥasidit*, 88–90.

[31] For inflicting injury on enemies, see e.g. Ahimaaz b. Paltiel, *Megilat Aḥima'ats*, ed. B. Klar (Jerusalem, 1974), 22; Jephthah Joseph Yozpa Shamash, *Ma'aseh nisim* (Amsterdam, 1696), s. 7, 13*a*. On causing premature death, see the responsum of Rav Ḥai Gaon in Benjamin Menasseh Lewin, *Otsar hage'onim* (13 vols.; Haifa, Jerusalem, 1928–62), iv (on Ḥag.), 16 ff.

[32] See *Megilat Aḥima'ats*, 15, 22; *Ma'aseh nisim*, 27*b*–29*b*; *Maise bukh*, 50*b*.

[33] For the exorcism of spirits, see *Megilat Aḥima'ats*, 18, 47, and cf. Me'ilah, 17*b*.

[34] For curing the sick, see Jacob Emden, 'Igeret Purim', Bodleian Library, Oxford MS 2190, 7; G. Nigal, *Sipurei dibuk besifrut Yisrael* (Jerusalem, 1983), 108.

[35] See responsum of Rav Hai Gaon, in *Otsar hage'onim* on Ḥag., 16 ff.

[36] See Eliezer Ashkenazi (ed.), *Ta'am zekenim* (Frankfurt on Main, 1854), 54–8; *Otsar hage'onim*, on Ḥag., 16 ff. (responsum of Rav Hai Gaon); cf. A Neubauer, *Seder haḥakhamim vekorot ha'itim* [2 vols.; Oxford 1877–95] (2 vols. in 1; Jerusalem, 1967), ii. 78, regarding the Babylonian sage, a contemporary of Rav Hai Gaon, 'who used to open locks by use of the divine name'.

[37] See *Megilat Aḥima'ats*, e.g. 12, 13, 15, 18, 22, 23. In Abraham b. Azriel, *Sefer arugat habosem*, ed. E. E. Urbach (Jerusalem, 1947), 18, both Shefatyah and his son Amitai are called *ba'alei shem*.

[38] See A. Grossman, 'Hagiratah shel mishpaḥat Kalonymos me'Italiah leGermaniyah', *Zion*, 40 (1975), 154–85.

[39] See e.g. N. Bruell, 'Beiträge zur jüdischen Sagen- und Sprachkunde in Mittelalter', *Jahrbücher für Jüdische Geschichte und Literatur*, 9 (1889), 32–3.

balists.[40] These include the exorcism of dybbuks, the ability to identify transmigrated souls, and the ability to read specific sins on the physiognomy of sinners. The Safed tale itself had assimilated many elements of the earlier *ba'alei shem* stories and, by infusing them with original material, created a new narrative genre which became known as a *shevaḥ* ('praise'), comparable to the non-Jewish hagiography. Although throughout this literature neither Isaac Luria nor Hayyim Vital is ever referred to as a *ba'al shem*, in terms of subject-matter the Safed tales nevertheless constitute a subcategory of the *ba'alei shem* stories. The indebtedness of the hasidic tale, particularly of *Shivḥei haBesht*, to the Safed 'praises' has been demonstrated and is discussed at length elsewhere.[41]

From the sixteenth century on, the narrative literature concerned with exorcising dybbuks begins to proliferate.[42] This body of literature, too, must be seen as a subcategory of the *ba'alei shem* stories. Its influence on the hasidic tale is evident in that the exorcists featured in the hasidic tales are usually[43] described as *ba'alei shem*.[43] In *Shivḥei haBesht*, for example,[44] one of the Besht's first public acts, if not his very first, is to exorcize a dybbuk from a demented woman. The dybbuk is said to have told the Besht that he was not afraid of him since it had been decreed in Heaven that the Besht would not be permitted to use divine names before reaching the age of 36. Realizing that he was 36, and that the time had come for him to step into the public arena, the Besht employed a scribe to write magical amulets which he gave to the sick who now began to flock to him in search of cures.[45]

Of particular interest are the special talents and attitudes to stories ascribed to the few *ba'alei shem* who are known to have operated at or near the time of the Besht.[46] There were at least two who shared many characteristics with the Besht: Samuel Essingen,[47] a famous early eighteenth-century *ba'al shem* who lived in Lippe (Westphalia) in Germany, and Jonathan Eybeschuetz,[48] a well-known rabbi and halakhic authority in Metz and Altona during the same period. Like the Besht, they combined the qualities of spiritual leader, teacher, and *ba'al shem*. There is ample evidence to suggest that both used to tell autobiographical stories, and that they saw to it that their tales, especially those concerned with miracle-working, should be disseminated either by way of letters or through the publication of chap-books. Samuel Essingen instigated the publication and distribution of a chap-book entitled *Ma'aseh nora zakah berurah* (A

[40] See *Shivḥei ha'Ari* (Ostrog (Ostraha), 1794). For Shlomel of Dreznitz and his letters, see Meir Benayahu, *Sefer toledot ha'Ari* (Jerusalem, 1967), 41–60.

[41] See Nigal, *Hasiporet haḥasidit*, 26–7.

[42] See Nigal, *Sipurei dibuk besifrut Yisrael*.

[43] See id., 'Sipurei dibuk basipur haḥasidi', *Sefer Bar-Ilan*, 24–5 (1989), 51–60.

[44] *Shivḥei haBesht*, 52–3.

[45] Ibid. 53.

[46] For Naphtali Katz, a rabbi, kabbalist, and *ba'al shem* who lived a little before the Besht, see G. Nigal, 'Al R. Naftali Kats miPosen', *Sinai*, 92 (1983), 91–4.

[47] Samuel Essingen served as rabbi of Warendorf and the county of Lippe (Westphalia) from 1742 until *c.*1753. He was a kabbalist and *ba'al shem*.

[48] Jonathan Eybeschuetz served as rabbi in Altona and Metz and was recognized as a halakhic authority. In a chap-book describing the exorcism of a dybbuk in Detmold (*Ma'aseh nora zakah berurah* (n.p., n.d.), repr. in G. Nigal, *Sipurei dibuk besifrut Yisrael*, 107–14), the dybbuk lists Eybeschuetz as one of three famous *ba'alei shem*. Jacob Emden, Eybeschuetz's bitter opponent, remarks about him that 'people held him to be a *ba'al shem* and one who worked with amulets' (*Sefer hitabekut* [Lvov, 1877], 36).

Terrible Story . . .)[49] which described his experiences with a dybbuk, and Jonathan Eybeschuetz actively publicized his own miraculous feats by means of letters which his pupils sent abroad,[50] as well as through an anonymous chap-book in German which related the miracles he had worked while serving as a rabbi in Metz.[51]

It is not unreasonable to assume that the Besht was well acquainted with the narrative literature of earlier generations, through either reading or hearing such tales. Whether consciously or not, he clearly drew heavily on this earlier literature in his own parables and stories. A good example of this is his well-known parable of the four ministers appointed to guard the Royal treasury.[52] This was drawn either from *Olelot Efrayim* by Ephraim of Luntshits,[53] which enjoyed great popularity at the time and was quoted frequently by Jacob Joseph of Polonnoye,[54] or directly from the medieval ethical treatise in which it first occurred, *Ḥovot halevavot*.[55] Moreover, whether directly or not, the Besht was also acquainted with non-Jewish literary motifs of which he clearly made use in his own tales and parables. An example of this is the parable of the humble merchant's wife,[56] which, in my opinion, was drawn from the *Maise bukh* or similar works.[57] Admittedly, alongside this early material, *Shivḥei haBesht*, and the hasidic tales in general, contain motifs, subject-matters, and even fully developed stories which are attributed to the Besht at a later date even though they could not have been told in his own lifetime. The example of the cycle of *Adam ba'al shem* tales[58] which found their way into *Shivḥei haBesht* is by no means unique. I have identified a tale in *Shivḥei haBesht*,[59] which, according to R. Jacob Emden, had been told several decades earlier about R. Jonathan Eybeschuetz.[60] The story about Eybeschuetz, who was also known as a *ba'al shem*,[61] was apparently circulating in his pupils' letters, which eventually reached eastern Europe, where the Besht was famous. Those who heard the story there automatically assumed that the *ba'al shem* referred to must have been the Besht.

Fuller documentation of this process may well emerge once the abundant narrative material preceding hasidism is examined and compared with the corpus of hasidic tales. For the time being, it is possible to demonstrate that the hasidic tale had assimilated all the narrative materials that were accessible to it, particularly the tales about the miraculous feats of *ba'alei shem* of past centuries. It was the positive, even enthusiastic recep-

[49] Samuel Essingen's chap-book (*Ma'aseh nora zakah berurah*) arrived at the National and University Library in Jerusalem from the library of the Ets Hayyim Synagogue in Amsterdam. I reprinted it in my *Sipurei dibuk besifrut Yisrael* (Jerusalem, 1983), 10–14

[50] See Jacob Emden, *Beit Yehonatan hasofer* (Altona, 1763?), 9; *Sefat emet uleshon zehorit* (n.p., 1772), 28*a* (my pagination; the book has none).

[51] *Sefat emet uleshon zehorit*, 18*a*. See also Yekutiel Judah Greenwald, *Harav R. Yehonatan Eybeschuetz* (New York, 1954), 38.

[52] *Toledot*, on 'Tsav', 96*b*.

[53] See Ephraim Solomon b. Aaron of Leczyca (Luntshits), *Olelot Efrayim* [Lublin, 1590] (Prague, 1619), s. 236, 59*c–d*.

[54] See Nigal, *Manhig ve'edah*, index of books and authors, 156.

[55] See Baḥya ibn Pakuda, *Ḥovot halevavot* [Jerusalem, 1928], trans. as *The Book of Direction to the Duties of the Heart*, ed. and trans. M. Mansoor (London, 1973), 'Sha'ar hateshuvah', ch. 6.

[56] On this story, see Dan, *Hasipur haḥasidi*, 40–6; Piekarz, *Ḥasidut Braslav*, 104.

[57] See *Maise bukh*, 70*b*–71*b*. Piekarz (*Ḥasidut Braslav*, 104) has already made this point.

[58] For a detailed discussion of this see C. Shmeruk, 'Hasipurim al R. Adam Baal Shem vegilguleihem benusḥe'ot sefer *Shivḥei haBesht*', *Zion*, 28 (1963), repr. in id., *Sifrut yidish bePolin* (Jerusalem, 1981), 119–46.

[59] See *Shivḥei haBesht*, 127–8.

[60] See *Beit Yehonatan hasofer*, 9*b*.

[61] See above, n. 48.

tion by the Besht and his colleagues of these early literary models, and their method of incorporating the tales in the broader ideological framework of hasidic doctrine, that made possible not only the integration of earlier narrative materials into hasidism, but also the creative development of the tale genre for a period of approximately two centuries.

In conclusion, the main arguments presented here are as follows. The hasidic tale was disseminated orally long before it appeared in print. The process of oral dissemination began in the lifetime of the Besht, who was much given to telling stories about himself. The tradition of telling autobiographical tales was inherited from *ba'alei shem* of earlier times, some of whom are known not only to have told miracle-stories about themselves but also to have publicized them, either by word of mouth or in print. Most of the motifs and subject-matters characteristic of these *ba'alei shem* stories were assimilated by the hasidic tale, which must be seen as the direct continuation of an earlier narrative tradition, albeit in a novel, expanded mode: integration of the tale into the ideological framework of hasidism, with the connection between tale and doctrine being forged as early as the very beginning of the movement. This connection was articulated in the notion of the 'sanctification of the tale', and it is evident in the numerous allusions to such tales which occur in R. Jacob Joseph's works, where they are used to illustrate various points of doctrine. It thus follows that the hasidic tale was not a by-product of later developments in the doctrine of the zaddik but rather resulted from the evolution of *ba'alei shem* stories into stories by and about the zaddikim, with the hasidic zaddik himself representing a new stage in the development of the ancient *ba'alei shem* tradition. All these factors, together with the very growth of hasidism and the concomitant proliferation of its zaddikim in the course of time, generated intense literary creativity and culminated in the production of thousands of tales, anthologized in several hundred volumes.

TWENTY-ONE

The Source Value of the Basic Recensions of *Shivḥei haBesht*

KARL ERICH GRÖZINGER

IN spite of its admittedly legendary character, *Shivḥei haBesht* has served the scholars of early hasidism as an important, if not the main, basis for their reconstructions of the beginnings of the movement in the eighteenth century. Modern hasidic scholarship should therefore address itself to the question of the source value of the text of this important and early collection of narrative hasidic lore.

The text is available in two versions, the Hebrew version published in Kopys in 1814, our understanding of which has been much enhanced by the publication of the important Mondshine edition,[1] and the Yiddish version published in Korets in 1815.[2] This has given rise to a number of questions:

1. Is the Yiddish Korets edition a paraphrastic translation of the Hebrew Kopys edition,[3] or does it represent an earlier, independent tradition?[4]
2. Did the editor of the Hebrew edition deliberately understate the notion of the founder of hasidism as a *ba'al shem* engaged in magical practices?[5]
3. Is it possible to discern in the book an early stratum of 'authentic' tales in which the subtle supernatural element is totally dependent on the subjective perception of spectators and narrators, since nothing extraordinary takes place on the plane of external reality?[6] If this is so, then the more extravagantly fantastical tales could be distinguished from the 'authentic' core as belonging to the universal genre of hagiography.

[1] Y. Mondshine, *Shivḥei haBesht: Ketav yad* (Jerusalem, 1982).

[2] The Hebrew date given in the Korets edition is 5576, and according to the title-page this is a reprint of an edn. published in Ostrog earlier in 1815, corresponding to 5575 in the Jewish calender. The considerable differences between this Yid. version and the Kopys Heb. edn are described in A. Ya'ari, 'Shetei mahadurot yesod shel *Shivḥei haBesht*', *Kiryat sefer*, 39 (1964), 249–72, 394–407, 552–62. Ya'ari concludes that the Yid. version is independent of the Heb. Kopys, 1814 edn.

[3] Mondshine, *Shivḥei haBesht*, 41.

[4] Ya'ari, 'Shetei mahadurot yesod'.

[5] Cf. C. Shmeruk, 'Hasipurim al R. Adam Baal Shem vegilguleihem benuṣhe'ot sefer *Shivḥei haBesht*', *Zion*, 28 (1963), 98, repr. in id., *Sifrut yidish bePolin* (Jerusalem, 1981), 119–46; G. Scholem, 'Demuto hahistorit shel R. Yisrael Baal Shem Tov', *Molad*, 18: 144–5 (1960), 340, repr. in id., *Devarim bego* (Tel Aviv, 1975), ii. 296 f.; K. E. Grözinger, 'Baal Shem oder Ba'al Hazon, Wunderdoktor oder Charismatiker: Zur frühen Legendenbildung um den Stifter des Hasidismus', *Frankfurter judaistische Beiträge*, 6 (1978), 71–90.

[6] See J. Dan, *Hasipur haḥasidi* (Jerusalem, 1975), 88 f.

All these questions would have a bearing on any attempt to gauge the source value of the tales as they have come down to us.

Numerous scholars, such as B. Dinur,[7] I. Halpern,[8] A. Ya'ari,[9] A. J. Heschel,[10] J. G. Weiss,[11] I. Bartal,[12] and J. Barnai,[13] have all pointed to historical connections between the tales and extraneously verifiable facts and I do not wish to question the value of their work. However, Bartal has remarked that the problem of the reliability of such historical facts as are contained in the hasidic tales is a complex one:

It is connected . . . with the difficulty of distinguishing between, on the one hand, the literary elements of structure and theme and, on the other hand, historical material which is unique or bound to a specific and well defined period. The hasidic tale uses historical material ahistorically; it is liable to combine separate elements, to antedate events and to mingle the natural with the supranatural, the earthly with the celestial.[14]

In what follows I shall focus not on the few points of contact between the tales and external events but rather on the mass of narrative material that has defied critical analysis by modern historians and that cannot be evaluated by rationalistic criteria. For it is precisely this 'literary' material, often irrational, that was most important to the hasidic narrators and their audiences.

For the purpose of the present discussion, the two versions—the Yiddish and the Hebrew—must not be regarded as coherent bodies of text, each displaying its own consistent overall tendency. Rather, I would like to suggest that each version in itself represents two or more totally different strands of thought. *Shivḥei haBesht* is a collection of individual tales, told by a considerable number of distinct individuals. We should therefore consider each tale on its own, and be prepared to encounter contradictions between them even within each of the two basic recensions of the text. Similarly, we must be alert to the possibility that points of convergence as well as of difference may be located across the lines that demarcate the two basic divisions of textual tradition.

I propose to look for criteria of differentiation within the corpus of the tales itself. Such criteria would permit qualitative differentiation of the tales while at the same time enabling us to evaluate each tale and locate it within the spiritual and social framework of the narrator, beyond or in addition to its narrative substance. In other words, we should not only listen to the words of the narrator but also note the form he gives to his tales. Awareness of the form would enable us to gauge the level of transmission and fully grasp the message being transmitted. For the transmission of the tales is comparable to

7 *Bemifneh hadorot* (Jerusalem, 1955), 188–92.

8 'Gezerot Woszczylo', *Zion*, 22 (1957), 56–67, repr. in id., *Yehudim veyahadut bemizraḥ Eiropah* (Jerusalem, 1969), 277–88; id., *Ha'aliyot harishonot shel haḥasidim le'Erets Yisrael* (Tel Aviv, 1947).

9 'Shetei mahadurot yesod', 259, 402, 560; cf. id., 'Serefat haTalmud beKamenets Podolsk', *Sinai*, 42 (1957–8), 294–306.

10 *The Circle of the Baal Shem Tov: Studies in Hasidism*, ed. S. H. Dresner (Chicago, 1985), on R. Gershon Kutover, 44–112, and on Nahman Kosover, 113–51.

11 *Studies in Eastern European Jewish Mysticism* (Oxford, 1985), 27–42.

12 'Aliyat R. Eleazar me'Amsterdam le'Erets Yisrael bishnat 1740', in *Meḥkarim al toledot yahadut Holland*, 4 (1984), 7–25.

13 'Al aliyato shel R. Avraham Gershon miKutov le'Erets Yisrael', *Zion*, 42 (1976–7), 110–19; id., 'Some Clarifications on the Land of Israel's Stories of "In Praise of the Baal Shem Tov" ', *Revue des études juives*, 146 (1987), 367–80.

14 Bartal, 'Aliyat R. Eleazar', 7 ff.; cf. Barnai, 'Some Clarifications', 379.

normal speech: a message may be put in the form of a question or a statement, a joke or a riddle. The story is the same, but the form conveys additional information that may be more important than the message itself. Only by discerning the form can the meaning be precisely understood. Let me exemplify this point.

The Kehot Publication Society in Brooklyn published in 1967 a small booklet by Zalman Aryeh Hilsenrad entitled *The Baal Shem Tov: His Birth and Early Manhood*, a book which could be taken as a modern American Lubavitch version of *Shivḥei haBesht*. On page 43 we find the following heading: 'The Besht's Mission is Revealed to Him'. The author reports this revelation as follows:

> On his thirty-sixth birthday, it was revealed to the Baal Shem Tov from on High that he had a unique mission in this existence . . . to bring a new light and instill a new spirit in our people through a somewhat different approach to our faith . . . a way of life which we call now Chasidus . . . Many young and older men, learned and unlearned, streamed to Mezshbozsh to learn this new way . . . numbered among his thousands of disciples were the most highly esteemed Rabbis and Talmudic scholars. The greatest of them, Rabbi Ber of Mezritzch, later became the Besht's successor and the teacher of the celebrated Rabbi Schneur Zalman of Liady, the founder of Chabad-Lubavitch Chasidus . . .[15]

Every reader of *Shivḥei haBesht* would recognize the tale on which the author based his account. This is the tale which reports that, after having been told during the night (presumably in a vision) 'that he was already 36 years old', the Besht calculated his age and discovered that this was indeed the case,[16] and he then proceeded to cure a madman (or woman). At this point he put behind him his humble employment as a *melamed* and appointed R. Alexander Shoḥet to be his scribe, since he was now permitted 'to practise with holy names'.[17]

There is no doubt that the author of the American version was well aware that the original version was a revelation-tale, aimed at highlighting the complete change in the life of the Besht when he emerged from anonymous seclusion and embarked on a career in public life. In other words, both authors, the American and the eastern European, point to the significance of this turning-point in the life of the Besht by selecting the narrative form of the revelation-tale. Nevertheless, the two versions differ considerably in content, especially in regard to the social function of the Besht. According to the original version he revealed himself as a *ba'al shem* who cured the sick and the mad, while in the New York version the Besht appears as an initiator of a new approach to the Jewish faith who establishes a new 'way of life'. This is a modern notion, and indeed a distinctly American one.

The use of the same literary form, that of the revelation-tale, would seem to indicate that both authors have a common aim: to define by implication the broadest outlines of the role and personality of their hero. Now a religious hero can only be 'revealed' once. On the occasion of his revelation at the start of his career, he must emerge fully and

[15] Zalman Aryeh Hilsenrad, *The Baal Shem Tov: His Birth and Early Manhood* (based upon Chasidic lore compiled and translated) (New York, NY, 1971), 44.

[16] Dov Ber b. Shmuel of Linits (Luniets), *Shivḥei haBesht* (Kopys, 1814), 5*a*; pub. in Eng. as *In Praise of the Baal Shem Tov*, trans. and ed. D. Ben-Amos and J. R. Mintz (Bloomington, Ind., 1970), 36.

[17] *In Praise*, 34; *Shivḥei haBesht* (Kopys), 4*d*.

precisely in the particular role that his final mission eventually assumes. In our case, while the original *Shivḥei haBesht* version launches the founder of hasidism as a *ba'al shem*, the American Lubavitch version turns him into the charismatic teacher of a new approach to Jewish faith.

Only one revelation, reported in one revelation-tale, may be allocated to each particular type of religious hero. A new revelation-tale would be required only when a new type of hero, with a new role, has entered the arena. This is precisely why Zalman Hilsenrad was compelled to compose a new revelation-tale rather than simply translate the Hebrew or Yiddish versions into English; he had to rewrite the story in order to accommodate the new type of religious hero that has emerged in Habad-Lubavitch. However, he retained the form of the revelation-tale because this particular form best expressed what he considered to be the Besht's ultimate mission. By using this form, the narrator is transmitting an additional message to his audience that facilitates the proper evaluation of the narrative substance of the tale.

Since we can expect only one revelation-tale, promoting a particular religious type, to be associated with any one religious hero, where there are more such tales we have grounds to suspect that a new religious type is being promoted, and that the role of the hero is being defined in a new and different way.

In contrast to the revelation-tale, there are other tale types that require continuous reiteration. These depict repeated demonstrations of skills that are associated with the mission of the hero. For example, a *ba'al shem* might be expected to perform numerous exorcisms or healings. The tales reporting these would assume their own characteristic narrative form. The same is true for performance-tales associated with other religious types, such as the person who can prescribe a *tikun*, or the prophet uncovering the sins of his fellow-men, or the advocate pleading before the heavenly court.[18]

In what way is this differentiation of narrative forms useful for assessing the source value of *Shivḥei haBesht*? If we agree, for example, that a revelation-tale should occur only once in any biography of the religious hero, then the very presence of a second revelation-tale in *Shivḥei haBesht* should raise our suspicions and point to the possibility that there may have been differences of opinion regarding the nature of the Besht's mission, and that these are reflected in the work. I am referring to the story of a pupil of R. Gershon of Kutow who was compelled by a series of accidents and mishaps to spend the sabbath with the Besht in his village.[19] Here the Besht emerges from obscurity not as a *ba'al shem* but rather as a charismatic teacher of the mysteries of Torah. Consequently, he does not embark on the career of a healer, as he does in the earlier

[18] Cf. my articles, 'Ba'al Shem oder Ba'al Hazon'; 'Die hasidischen Erzählungen: Ihre Formen und Traditionen', *Frankfurter judaistische Beiträge*, 9 (1981), 91–114; 'Sündenpropheten: Halachaprophetie im Judentum Osteuropas', *Frankfurter judaistische Beiträge*, 15 (1987), 17–46; 'Himmlische Gerichte, Wiedergänger und Zwischenweltliche in der ostjüdischen Erzählung', in K. E. Grözinger, S. Moses, and H. D. Zimmermann (eds.), *Franz Kafka und das Judentum* (Frankfurt on Main, 1987), 93–112; for the form-critical method see also my 'Die Gegenwart des Sinai: Erzählungen und kabbalistische Traktate zur Vergegenwärtigung des Sinai', *Frankfurter judaistische Beiträge*, 16 (1988), 143–83; Esther Alexander-Ihme, '"Warum wird eine Geschichte erzählt?" Überlegungen zur Bedürfnisstruktur der Erzählungen von der "Rache der Leiche" und "Rache des Toten"', *Frankfurter judaistische Beiträge*, 16 (1988), 185–99; id., '"A Yid shmadt sikh nit": Apostasie, Judenmissionsnot und Taufe in jüdischen Volkserzählungen', *Frankfurter judaistische Beiträge*, 15 (1987), 47–89.

[19] *In Praise*, 28; *Shivḥei haBesht* [Kopys], 4*a*.

revelation-tale, but is appointed to be rabbi and teacher of the community of the 'great hasidim' of Kutow.

If we accept the premiss of one revelation-tale per hero, then we have to conclude that the narrator of this second revelation-tale in *Shivḥei haBesht* must have wished to define the Besht's mission quite differently from the first narrator. This suggests the presence of at least two conflicting views of the Besht's mission within the *Shivḥei haBesht* itself, one defining him as a *ba'al shem* and the other as a charismatic teacher of Torah. The first narrator sees the Besht as something like a latter-day physician, while the second regards him as the founder of a new religious community. My belief is that such a conflict of opinions did take place in reality.[20] There were those in the first, second, and third generations of hasidism, and even among the companions of the Besht himself, who preferred to see him primarily as a *ba'al shem*, while others regarded him as a charismatic teacher.

Moreover, the original manuscript of *Shivḥei haBesht* by Dov Ber of Linits, which begins with the words 'I heard about the beginnings from my father-in-law . . . Alexander Shoḥet' constitutes the second opening of the book.[21] It follows on from a cluster of parallel traditions, marked by the influence of '*admor*', which now form the first opening of *Shivḥei haBesht*.[22] At the start of Dov Ber's manuscript, therefore, we find an account of the beginnings of the Besht's career that emanates from Alexander Shoḥet, his first scribe. It is in this section of the book that the *ba'al shem*-type revelation-tale appears, as was discussed above. The remaining Alexander Shoḥet traditions are similarly preserved in tales that promote the *ba'al shem* aspect of the Besht, depicting him as exorcizing spirits, struggling with demons, and curing the sick.[23] The

[20] This appears to clash with the common and more harmonistic viewpoint whereby the Besht began his career as a *ba'al shem* and developed later into a charismatic teacher (Dubnow), or the view whereby he was, throughout his career, both a *ba'al shem* and a charismatic (Scholem, 'Demuto', 292 ff., 338 ff.). But this is not the point I wish to stress here. Rather, there were different opinions among the early followers regarding the quality of the Besht. It is precisely these conflicting opinions that may serve the historian for his own reconstruction of the 'historical' Besht.

[21] *In Praise*, 32; *Shivḥei haBesht* [Kopys], 4*c*.

[22] The end of the '*admor*' traditions is marked by the words: 'Up to this point I heard the unfolding of these events in the name of *admor* . . . The other events and miracles that occurred I shall print according to the manuscripts that I obtained.' *In Praise*, 31; *Shivḥei haBesht* [Kopys], 4*b* (end of page).

[23] The *ba'al shem* traditions are reflected in those tales in which the miracle-worker offers help to those suffering worldly distress. These are distinct from the tales that depict the hero as offering spiritual assistance by way of *tikun*, ethical instruction, and teaching as well as by representing both individuals and communities in the heavenly court. The Alexander traditions about the Besht include the following tales: *In Praise*, 32; *Shivḥei haBesht* [Kopys], 4*c* (Alexander and Zevi, the Besht's scribes); *In Praise*, 33; *Shivḥei haBesht* [Kopys], 4*c* (Alexander's fingernails); *In Praise*, 34; *Shivḥei haBesht* [Kopys], 4*d* (the Besht exorcises a madwoman); *In Praise*, 35; *Shivḥei haBesht* [Kopys], 4*d* (the Besht banishes demons to the attic); *In Praise*, 35; *Shivḥei haBesht* [Kopys], 5*a* (the Besht brings rain) (cf. *In Praise*, 123; *Shivḥei haBesht* [Kopys], 15*a*); *In Praise*, 36; *Shivḥei haBesht* [Kopys], 5*a* (curing a madwoman, revelation, and the beginning of the Baal Shem's career); possibly also *In Praise*, 37; *Shivḥei haBesht* [Kopys], 5*a* (exorcising demons from a house), and *In Praise*, 37; *Shivḥei haBesht* [Kopys], 5*b* (a cure refused), which seems to represent the end of the 'Beginnings told by Alexander'; *In Praise*, 40; *Shivḥei haBesht* [Kopys], 5*c* (conflict with a physician); *In Praise*, 44; *Shivḥei haBesht* [Kopys], 6*a* (the stolen horse); *In Praise*, 123; *Shivḥei haBesht* [Kopys], 15*a* (the Besht's encounter with a witch); *In Praise*, 200; *Shivḥei haBesht* [Kopys], 26*a* (competing for an *arenda*); *In Praise*, 210; *Shivḥei haBesht* [Kopys], 27*b* (call to flight because of bandits). The single exception is the story of the Besht's incomplete revelation (to which I refer as the first 'epiphany') to R. David of Kolomyya, *In Praise*, 45; *Shivḥei haBesht* [Kopys], 6*b*. But here the informant is R. Gedaliah.

same is true of the tale recorded in the name of the Besht's second scribe, Zevi Hirsch.[24]

It would appear, therefore, that the two scribes were unable or unwilling to see the Besht as anything other than a *ba'al shem*. In other words, they reported only those activities of the Besht that they personally found worthy of note because they fitted into their own *Weltanschauung*. This is confirmed by a well-known statement in the Yiddish version of the book that there were people who were not able to see in the Besht anything more than a mere *ba'al shem*. The passage reads as follows: 'The Rav Besht . . . revealed to his most eminent men the secret of which they were not to give away anything during his lifetime, namely, what his life was really like, so that this should remain totally concealed from people, in order that the whole world should regard him as a mere *ba'al shem* and nothing more.'[25]

Another expression of the *ba'al shem* view of the Besht is to be found in the *Adam ba'al shem* traditions. These traditions are hardly compatible with the opening *admor* tales, not only in the Yiddish but even in the Hebrew version which lacks the overall magical flavour of the Yiddish text. The aim of these Adam traditions is to integrate the Besht into a historical chain of *ba'alei shem* who were all in possession of magical writings by which they could accomplish miraculous feats, as is explicitly stated in the Yiddish text: 'All the miraculous deeds and wonders accomplished by the Besht were derived entirely from these writings which had come to him from the *ba'al shem tov* R. Adam.'[26] It is essential to realize that these Adam traditions do not belong with the rest of the *admor* prologue which aims at presenting the Besht in a totally different light. By contrast with the rest of the introductory tales, the Adam traditions are reported in the name of R. Shimshon, the son of R. Jacob Joseph of Polonnoye. R. Shimshon may well have heard them from R. Alexander Shoḥet, of whom it is reported in *Shivḥei haBesht* that he was a regular guest at the house of Jacob Joseph, R. Shimshon's father.[27]

In contrast to R. Shimshon, R. Jacob Joseph was reluctant to draw attention to the *ba'al shem* qualities of the Besht, for only one of the fourteen tales reported in his name may be classified as depicting the *ba'al shem* functions of his master.[28] R. Jacob Joseph was more interested in the prayer, teachings, and remarkable visionary powers of the

24 *In Praise*, 144; *Shivḥei haBesht* [Kopys], 18*a* (the Besht procures a dowry).

25 *Shivḥei haBesht* [Korets], 23*a*.

26 Ibid. 10*a*.

27 Ibid.

28 *In Praise*, 107; *Shivḥei haBesht* [Kopys], 12*d* (the Besht banishes demons from a synagogue). It should be noted, however, that, once again, the first narrator named is R. Gedaliah, the 'rabbi of the community'. The other tales are: *In Praise*, 50; *Shivḥei haBesht* [Kopys], 7*a* (the Besht's trembling in prayer); *In Praise*, 61; *Shivḥei haBesht* [Kopys], 8*b*, end (R. Jacob Joseph recognizes the greatness of the Besht); *In Praise*, 129; *Shivḥei haBesht* [Kopys], 15*d* (the Besht's *devekut*); *In Praise*, 133; *Shivḥei haBesht* [Kopys], 16*c* (*tikun* for a fish and a dog); *In Praise*, 186; *Shivḥei haBesht* [Kopys], 24*a* (the Besht comes to R. Zevi in a dream); *In Praise*, 190; *Shivḥei haBesht* [Kopys], 24*c* (the Besht's dictum about his intervention in the war of the Greeks and the Israelites); *In Praise*, 196; *Shivḥei haBesht* [Kopys], 25*c* (the Besht's prophetic evaluation of an amulet and his dictum about his own qualities); *In Praise*, 197; *Shivḥei haBesht* [Kopys], 25*c* (the Besht's evaluation of a *tsitsit*); *In Praise*, 199; *Shivḥei haBesht* [Kopys], 26*a* (the Besht pronouncing story-telling to be equal to the study of *ma'aseh merkavah*); *In Praise*, 206; *Shivḥei haBesht* [Kopys], 26*d* (the Besht's dictum about the celestial garments); *In Praise*, 206; *Shivḥei haBesht* [Kopys], 26*d* (the Besht's dictum about his *mikveh* visions).

Besht. All these clearly accorded with his own conception of the mystical–social function of the hasidic leader.[29]

A possible reflection of these conflicting perceptions of the Besht may be seen in R. Jacob Joseph of Polonnoye's criticism of Alexander Shoḥet. I refer to his tale of the Besht's dream that he walked to the Tree of Life in the company of his followers. Alexander Shoḥet lagged behind and did not succeed in following the Besht to the end of the journey.[30] Could this rebuke suggest that Alexander Shoḥet was being faulted for viewing the Besht as a mere *ba'al shem*?

Notwithstanding Dov Ber of Linits's loyalty to his father-in-law Alexander Shoḥet, there is no doubt that he was subject to Jacob Joseph's influence when he reported his reservations with regard to R. Alexander. We shall soon note yet another example of the influence of R. Jacob Joseph on the author of *Shivḥei haBesht*.

In opposition to R. Alexander's view, another definition of the Besht's mission can be traced to the cluster of *admor* traditions at the beginning of the Hebrew version of *Shivḥei haBesht*, traditions which are clearly independent of the cycle of Adam tales. The *admor* traditions section begins with a typical announcement-tale concerning the messianic child who has been born to saintly old parents. The announcement by the heavenly messenger Elijah defines the mission of the child as 'to bring light to Israel', in fulfilment of the prophecy of 'Israel in whom I will be glorified' (Isa. 49: 3).[31] The beginning of the Besht's public mission is described at the very end of the *admor* traditions section, in the account of the luminous revelation of the Besht and his enthronement as a charismatic teacher of Torah.[32]

There can be no doubt that this is a carefully crafted composition, beginning with the announcement-tale ending with the account of revelation, and with intermediate infancy-tales infusing the entire *admor*-text with messianic significance.

Other tales in *Shivḥei haBesht* demonstrate this to have been the clear-cut intention of the editor. One of these is the account of David Furkes's prayer on the Day of Atonement after he had been put to shame by the Besht in front of the entire community.[33] In the Yiddish version this takes the form of a duel narrative, a verbal contest between the two protagonists, one aiming to bring about the coming of the messiah, the other opposing this plan.[34] In the Yiddish version, not only does the Besht curtail R. David Furkes's messianic endeavours by disrupting his meditations but he also declares explicitly that the time is not ripe for the advent of the messiah; rather, it is time for greater fraternization among Israel. Thus, the Yiddish version appears to promote the notion that the present time is devoid of any messianic quality. The Hebrew

[29] A similar position is taken by Immanuel Etkes when he states: 'It seems that different aspects of the Besht's personality attracted different people. Rabbi Nachman of Horodenko became a disciple of the Besht after he learned from him how to overcome "*machshavot zarot*". Previously, Rabbi Nachman had failed in his efforts to cope with this obstacle by asceticism, the method which was common in pre-Beshtian hasidism. The Maggid was attracted to the Besht after he saw how the Besht had turned the study of kabbalah into a mystical experience . . . HaMochiach of Polna claimed that he possessed some unique spiritual powers, but acknowledged the superiority of the Besht in this matter and tried to learn from him.' I. Etkes, 'Hasidism as a Movement: The First Stage', in B. Safran (ed.), *Hasidism: Continuity or Innovation?* (Cambridge, Mass. 1988), 12 f.

[30] *In Praise*, 33; *Shivḥei haBesht* [Kopys], 4*c*.

[31] *In Praise*, 11; *Shivḥei haBesht* [Kopys], 1*c*.

[32] *In Praise*, 28–31; *Shivḥei haBesht* [Kopys], 4*a*–*b*.

[33] *In Praise*, 52; *Shivḥei haBesht* [Kopys], 7*b*.

[34] *Shivḥei haBesht* [Korets], 8*a*.

version, on the other hand, contains neither the duel narrative nor any reference to the messiah's coming. The author of this version clearly did not wish to depict the Besht as opposing the view that the advent of the messiah was imminent.

The same divergence of views seems to be reflected in the two parallel versions of the infancy-tale that features the Besht's encounter with a werewolf (*volkelak*).[35] The Hebrew version states that 'Satan understood what must come to pass, he was afraid that the time was approaching when he would disappear from the earth'.[36] This messianic nuance is absent from the Yiddish version, but it fits well with the underlying tendency of the *admor* traditions. Yet another testimony, reported in the name of Menahem Nahum of Chernobyl in the Hebrew version but altogether absent from the Yiddish version, echoes the view that the Besht's mission was messianic. In the tale concerning the burning of the Talmud as a result of the Sabbatean/Frankist accusations, the messiah himself addresses the Besht as follows: 'I do not know whether you will open this [heavenly] gate, but if you do, redemption will certainly come to Israel.' R. Menahem Nahum remarks that 'this was the gate of the palace of the Bird's Nest through which no one has ever passed, save the Messiah'.[37] Once again, the difference between the two versions testifies to the presence of dissenting views among the early narrators regarding the messianic nature of the Besht's mission.

Finally, I should like to suggest that further discrepancies between the two versions may derive from controversy concerning the true succession to the Besht. Here again, it seems that R. Jacob Joseph of Polonnoye's influence on the Hebrew version is readily apparent. For example, there are considerable differences between the Hebrew and Yiddish accounts of the initiation of Dov Ber, the Great Maggid of Mezhirech, by the Besht.[38] If we bear it in mind that the central part and climax of this tale is the nomination of a successor to the master, the significance of the differences between the two versions is clear.

The Besht's initiation of the Maggid in the secret lore is accorded much greater significance in the Yiddish text than in the Hebrew. The Yiddish version twice stresses the unique position of the Maggid relative to his peers. The Besht says of the Maggid: 'He is a great and receptive man. Out of him I shall be able to make more than out of all my other followers!'[39] And again: 'I have never seen a vessel as receptive as this one. I wish I could learn with all of you as I did with him, but I know that no one is as receptive as him!'[40]

In addition, the Yiddish text refers to the event as the 'true transmission of Torah' from the Besht to the Maggid.[41] It compares the revelation of Torah at Sinai to the transmission of Torah to the Besht, and thus in turn to the Besht's transmission of

[35] *In Praise*, 11–13; *Shivḥei haBesht* [Kopys], 1*d*; *Shivḥei haBesht* [Korets], 2*c*.

[36] *In Praise*, 12; *Shivḥei haBesht* [Kopys], 1*d*.

[37] *In Praise*, 58; *Shivḥei haBesht* [Kopys], 8*a*, 8*d*–9*a*. One should mention here the Besht's famous letter to R. Gershon of Kutow, published by R. Jacob Joseph as an appendix to his *Ben porat Yosef* [Korets, 1781], in which the Besht reports that the messiah himself told him that his coming would depend on the dissemination of the Besht's teaching throughout the world. Cf. Dinur, *Bemifneh hadorot*, 181–8, where all the evidence is presented in support of the view that according to early hasidic literature the Besht's mission was messianic.

[38] *In Praise*, 81–4; *Shivḥei haBesht* [Kopys], 9*a*–*c*; *Shivḥei haBesht* [Korets], 11*a*–12*a*.

[39] *Shivḥei haBesht* [Korets], 11*b*, end.

[40] Ibid. 11*d*.

[41] Ibid., end.

Torah to the Maggid. Finally, the Maggid confesses proudly: 'All this I have received from the Besht.[42]

The Hebrew version does not acknowledge the unique qualities of the Maggid. On the contrary, a certain remark in the name of R. Jacob Joseph of Polonnoye presents the event from a different perspective. The Besht is said to have taught Torah to R. Jacob Joseph in much the same way as to the Maggid or even more wondrously in that at R. Jacob Joseph's inauguration the sound of musical instruments could be heard.[43] In the light of this remark, the initiation of the Maggid in his account of the event appears less as the inauguration of the Besht's future successor and more as the initiation into the group of one disciple among others.[44] Thus the Hebrew text diminishes the role of the Maggid and enhances that of R. Jacob Joseph. Similar promotion of R. Jacob Joseph's importance can be detected in the Hebrew version of the tales concerning his primary vocation as a rabbi.[45]

We may conclude that the divergent evaluations of the early heroes of hasidism in the first eastern European accounts of the beginnings of the movement are no different in scope or intent from the modern Brooklyn re-evaluation. Each version provides an individual evaluation of the early protagonists and their relationship to one another. Consequently, the tales constitute a testimony of each narrator's personal views rather than a historical account of the events that he purports to retell. This becomes especially evident when we bear in mind that much of this material is presented in the mould of schematic tale-type rather than as a historical record of unique events.

However, since the eastern European accounts are closer to the events than the American version in both time and circumstance, they can shed more light on the question of the immediate success of hasidism. For the success of a popular movement depends less on the historical personalities of its founding fathers and more on the impressions of these leaders that are implanted in the consciousnesses of their disciples and followers. These impressions are coloured by the personal ambitions and rivalries of the disciples, and by the sense of the social and spiritual needs of the wider community, such as the need for help and guidance in worldly affairs, or for technical expertise concerning the transmigration of souls or in uncovering the spiritual dimension of Torah. These are precisely the needs that the tales of *Shivḥei haBesht* address.[46]

[42] *Shivḥei haBesht* [Korets], 12*a*.

[43] *In Praise*, 83 f. *Shivḥei haBesht* [Kopys], 9*c* top.

[44] In spite of this fact, both the Heb. and the Yid. versions report the statement of R. Jeḥiel Michel of Zloczow whereby after the death of the Besht, 'the same streams of wisdom that formerly ran to the Besht now led to the rabbi, the Maggid'; *In Praise*, 185; *Shivḥei haBesht* [Kopys], 24*a*; *Shivḥei haBesht* [Korets], 21*c*.

[45] In the Heb. version, the tales about R. Jacob Joseph's vocation are combined into one cycle of thirteen units, while the Yiddish version offers only nine tales which are split up into two single tales and a smaller cycle of seven tales. Only the Heb. version contains the Besht's letter to R. Jacob Joseph, which is very flattering to the latter (*In Praise*, 66; *Shivḥei haBesht* [Kopys], 7*a*—the second p. 7 of erroneous pagination). Finally, only the Heb. version contains the 'praise' of R. Jacob Joseph's saintly way of life (*In Praise*, 69; *Shivḥei haBesht* [Kopys], 7*c*, [second 7]).

[46] I therefore fully agree with Joseph Dan when he states: 'What happened in reality when the Besht was visiting a particular place and performing a particular act—it seems that we shall never know, and from the literary point of view, this makes no difference whatsoever.' See *Hasipur haḥasidi*, 89. The question is less one of 'historical' material versus 'unhistorical' material but of authenticity versus inauthenticity in respect of the narrators' cultural and temporal milieu. As these hagiographic tales were shaped in a cultural atmosphere close to the events that they purport to depict, they reflect the social and spiritual

Greater understanding of the rapid growth of the hasidic movement may derive from discerning within the tales the factors that stimulated the emergence of divergent impressions and views of the early history of the movement. This may prove to be more productive than the search for external corroboration for the tales. It is here, it seems to me, that we may locate the greatest value of *Shivḥei haBesht* as a source material.

needs of the society in which hasidism grew; the American version likewise reflects the perceived needs of its own time. In other words, *Shivḥei haBesht* depicts more exactly what the narrators of the first generations of hasidim expected of their leaders than what those leaders achieved in reality. To quote, once again, the historian Jacob Barnai: 'In the stories . . . different and even contradicting trends [can be identified], trends which are derived from the nature of the narrators rather than from the factual events' ('Some Clarifications', 379).

PART VI

THE HISTORY OF HASIDIC HISTORIOGRAPHY

TWENTY-TWO

The Imprint of Haskalah Literature on the Historiography of Hasidism

ISRAEL BARTAL

HASKALAH literature and the historiography of hasidism have always been interrelated. The maskilim and their writings had an enormous effect on the evolution of modern hasidic scholarship, while the depiction of hasidism in Haskalah literature bears the imprint of certain modern historiographical sensibilities and conventions.

The early historians of hasidism clearly drew most if not all of their information about the movement from maskilic texts. I. M. Jost, the author of the first history—a work conceived in the spirit of *Wissenschaft des Judentums*—culled much of his material from the writings of the maskilim Joseph Perl and Judah Leib Miesis.[1] His other sources, Peter Beer and Henri Grégoire, had relied almost exclusively on Perl and on Israel Loebel.[2] Beer himself, and Heinrich Graetz, had drawn extensively on the autobiography of the maskil Solomon Maimon.[3] Thus, practically all the early attempts to

[1] On Jost and the hasidic movement see R. Michael, *I. M. Jost: Avi hahistoriografiah hayehudit hamodernit* (Jerusalem, 1983), 67–8. Jost's main source was Joseph Perl's anti-hasidic German treatise, *Über das Wesen der Secte Chassidim*, written in 1816. The unpublished manuscript of this was sent to Jost in 1828 (see S. Dubnow, *Toledot haḥasidut* [Tel Aviv, 1930–1] (Tel Aviv, 1960), ii. 379–80). Perl's work was published only in 1977 as J. Perl, *Über das Wesen der Sekte Chassidim* [*sic*], ed. A. Rubinstein (Jerusalem, 1977). Jost's other Haskalah source was Judah Leib Miesis's *Kinat ha'emet* (Vienna, 1828).

[2] Peter Beer, *Geschichte, Lehren und Meinungen aller bestandenen und noch bestehenden religiösen Sekten der Juden* (2 vols.; Brünn, 1823), ii. 197–259; H. Grégoire, *Histoire des sectes religieuses* (2 vols.; Paris, 1810). Even though Israel Loebel was a mitnagged rather than a maskil, his anti-hasidic propaganda reached the maskilim in a version adapted to suit their own purposes and translated into German, through the intermediacy of a number of Haskalah activists. On the maskilic version of Loebel's polemical writings, published in Frankfurt on Oder in 1799, see Dubnow, *Toledot haḥasidut*, 289–90; M. Wilensky, *Hasidim umitnaggedim* (2 vols.; Jerusalem, 1970), 258–61. This German adaptation of Loebel's work was republished by the maskilim in the periodical *Shulamith* in 1807. See on this R. Michael, 'Terumat ketav ha'et *Shulamit* lahistoriografiah hayehudit haḥadashah', *Zion*, 39 (1974), 93–5. According to Michael, it is unlikely that Loebel would have collaborated with radical maskilim, since he opposed their views violently and wrote explicitly against them. On Perl's attempt to publish a second edition of Loebel's *Sefer vikuaḥ* [Warsaw, 1798], repr. in Wilensky, *Hasidim umitnaggedim*, ii. 266–325, see R. Mahler, *Hasidism and the Jewish Enlightenment* (Philadelphia, 1985), 127.

[3] Graetz mentions the work of the Warsaw maskil Jacob (Jacques) Calmanson, *Essai sur l'état actuel des Juifs de Pologne et leur perfectibilité* (Warsaw, 1796), as well as Grégoire's *Sectes religieuses*; see H. Graetz, *Geschichte des Juden* (11 vols.; Leipzig, 1853–70), xi. 592–608, pub. in Eng. as *History of the Jews* (5 vols, London, 1901), v. 396–418. Solomon Maimon was not a member of any Haskalah group, yet his autobiography is permeated with Haskalah views. See Solomon Maimon, *Salomon Maimons Lebensgeschichte* [Berlin, 1793] pub. in Eng. as *The Autobiography of Solomon Maimon*, trans. J. Clark Murray (London, 1954). App. 2 of this edn. (166–79), which deals with the author's early encounter with hasidism, was reprinted in G. D. Hundert (ed.), *Essential Papers on Hasidism* (New York, 1991), 11–24.

explain hasidism historically had gestated in the minds of scholars who were strongly imbued with Haskalah ideas and who wrote under its direct impact. Even some of Simon Dubnow's observations and insights undoubtedly originated in the tradition of maskilic discourse about hasidism.

Alongside this ideological impact, both direct and indirect, of the maskilim and their writings on the early historians of hasidism, the decline of the Haskalah as a viable intellectual and social movement signalled the beginning of another relationship between modern hasidic historiography and the literary legacy of the maskilim: hasidic historians began to utilize Haskalah literature as historical source material. Haskalah literature is virtually the only or at any rate the richest source of information we possess about the social, political and economic orientation of hasidism. The studies of Raphael Mahler, Chone Shmeruk, and Mordechai Levin are but a few examples of this intensive, and highly effective, utilization of Haskalah sources, both Hebrew and Yiddish, by the modern historians of hasidism.[4]

Admittedly, Haskalah literature was extremely hostile to the hasidic movement; but this should not obscure the fact that it was at the same time the first systematic expression of a modern European critical interest in the new phenomenon of hasidism. This interest was prompted primarily by the desire to collect the evidence against a movement which was perceived to be an ideological rival. It was thus focused on areas of concern which were central to Haskalah ideology but alien or marginal to hasidism. The maskilim raised the questions, for example, of the socio-economic implications of the hasidic movement; of its origins in earlier periods of Jewish history; and they strove to account for its apparently inexplicable, from their point of view, success and rapid expansion throughout eastern Europe. Some of the answers they formulated, and many of their other observations and views, may seem to us simplistic or shallow, yet they were the answers and observations of modern European witnesses, and as such they are historically significant.

Many of the maskilim had been affiliated with hasidism in their youth but had 'liberated' themselves from it in later life. Their mature understanding of the movement was conditioned, therefore, by the experience of having metamorphosed from being naïve traditional believers to modern, critical students of Judaism.[5] However, since the Haskalah movement of their time was associated with an early stage of Jewish modernization, they were not as yet committed to any of the anachronistic 'hidden agendas' of later historiography—neither the nationalistic variety, striving to integrate the hasidic phenomenon into a broader conception of national history,[6] nor the Ortho-

[4] Mahler, *Hasidism and the Jewish Enlightenment*; id., *Divrei yemei Yisrael: Dorot aḥaronim* (6 vols.; Tel Aviv, 1976), vi. 11–85; C. Shmeruk, 'Mashma'utah haḥevratit shel hasheḥitah haḥasidit', *Zion*, 20 (1955), 47–74; id., 'Haḥasidut ve'iskei haḥakhirut', *Zion*, 35 (1970), 182–92; M. Levin, *Erkhei ḥevrah vekalkalah ba'ideologiah shel tenu'at haHaskalah* (Jerusalem, 1975).

[5] The maskilim whose writings had the most enduring impact on modern hasidic historiography are Joseph Perl and Abraham Dov Ber Gottlober.

[6] The most important scholarly attempt to integrate the hasidic movement into a Zionist interpretation of Jewish history was Benzion Dinur's. See his Hebrew collection of essays *Bemifneh hadorot* (Jerusalem, 1955), where the theme is prominent throughout (an English version of one relevant section of this book appeared in Hundert (ed.), *Essential Papers*, 86–208). In the conclusion to his seminal study of the origins of hasidism and its social and messianic foundations, Dinur argued, for example, that 'the immigration [of the hasidim to Erets Yisrael] was an organic part of the course of redemption on which the [hasidic] movement endeavoured to lead the people, diverting the messianic energy to new channels' (*Bemifneh hadorot*, 227).

dox variety, reducing the struggle between hasidism and mitnaggedism to 'a struggle for the sake of Heaven' in which everyone within the traditionalist camp was right.[7] Most of the maskilim adopted an 'open agenda' that displayed their strong and unabashed anti-hasidic bias, which undoubtedly distorted their image of hasidism, but their accounts of the movement were free from the apologetics which mark so much of the work of their successors.

In order to appreciate the scope and nature of the maskilic distortion of hasidism, it would be useful to identify the main characteristics of the accounts of the movement by Haskalah authors. First, the presentation is selective: some features are highlighted repeatedly while others, well attested in a variety of other sources, are altogether absent. This is evident, for example, in the one-dimensional, trivial stereotyping of the leaders of hasidism. They are invariably characterized by the same fixed set of well-known traits, to the virtual exclusion of individual orientation or the variety of views, styles and practices within the hasidic leadership. Similarly, the spiritual dimension of the movement is often satirized or parodied; quasi-hasidic lore and aphorisms are fabricated in order to mock their alleged creators and their inner world. Penetrating the reality of hasidic spirituality on the basis of this image is comparable to attempting to paint a portrait from a rough pencil sketch: some lines are clear, some are exaggerated, and some are not in the picture at all.

Secondly, Haskalah literature presents a picture that is at once both particular-regional and universal. It presents the reader with what appears to be an authentic depiction of a specific hasidic milieu, enhanced by allusions to local events, persons, and names, while attributing to this milieu traits which are presumed to be universal within hasidism. Sometimes, as in the case of *Megaleh temirin* by Joseph Perl, the maskilic author applies what is in reality a highly specific, local set of characteristics to a vast region of hasidism. This is how the historian Jost 'knew' that the teachings of R. Nahman of Bratslav typified the hasidic movement as a whole: texts sent to him by Perl had told him so.[8]

Thirdly, Haskalah literature is in some respects a response—both explicit and implicit—to the hasidic movement. The response is at least in part polemical since, with several important exceptions, Haskalah usually construes hasidism as its own antithesis. This juxtaposition of the two movements inevitably highlights the sharp contrasts between them and obscures all else; the subtlety of intermediate states—'neutral' issues which are of no direct relevance to the polemic between rival ideologies—disappears from view altogether. If hasidism is perceived as an antithesis then it functions as the 'negative' of a 'positive' self-image of Haskalah. The resulting distortion of hasidism—the crude lines of caricature, the blurred distinction between the specific and the universal, as well as the total exclusion from view of all points of contact or affinity rather than contrast between the two 'rivals'—is thus determined almost exclusively by the Haskalah's own perceptions and ideals.

[7] See e.g. the idyllic description of hasidic–mitnaggedic encounters by the ultra-Orthodox writer R. Jacob Lipschitz in his *Zikhron Ya'akov* (3 vols.; Kovno, Slobodka, 1924–30), i. 16. On Orthodox historiography in this connection see I. Bartal, 'Zikhron Ya'akov leRabi Ya'akov Lipschitz: Historiografiah ortodoxit?', *Milet: Meḥkerei haUniversitah haPetuḥah betoledot Yisrael vetarbuto*, 2 (Tel Aviv, 1984), 409–14.

[8] See Dubnow, *Toledot haḥasidut*, 399, and cf. Michael, *Jost*, 67–8, who argues that Jost was not influenced by Perl's anti-hasidic stance.

Since *Wissenschaft des Judentums* and modern Jewish historiography have always been associated with Haskalah thinking, they have adopted much of the maskilic posture towards hasidism. Certain observations, ideological constructs, focal points of interest, and data on the socio-economic aspects of the hasidic movement that originated in the writings of the early maskilim have found their way to modern scholarship on hasidism. Some of these were taken over uncritically, some were adapted to conform with alternative ideological stances, while others have been transmitted dialectically, generating counter-Haskalah claims about the nature of hasidism. This continuity of Haskalah preoccupations and motifs can be amply demonstrated in the historical writings of Jewish radicals, who made extensive use of the Haskalah's critique of Jewish autonomy and adopted its views of society, the economy, culture, and politics; at the same time, it is evident also in the work of those historians who utterly rejected the radicals' interpretation of hasidism. There is no doubt that, as the first modern Jewish school of thought to confront hasidism and to address it, the Haskalah has left its mark on every subsequent interpretation of hasidic history. Moreover, the close relationship between Haskalah literature and modern historiography on hasidism is manifest even in the fictional depiction of hasidism in modern Hebrew and Yiddish literature. Indeed, it is legitimate to ask which came first: the fictional image or the historical interpretation of hasidism within the literary tradition of the Haskalah.

In what follows I can give no more than a few examples to illustrate the profound influence of Haskalah literature on modern historiography on hasidism. I deal first with some interpretative models that were formulated by the maskilim and have endured in subsequent histories of hasidism, and then evaluate a number of 'facts' which originated in maskilic accounts and have entrenched themselves in modern hasidic historiography. I conclude with a brief overview of works that display the full range of affinities between Haskalah literature and modern historiography.

Simon Dubnow acknowledges Graetz as 'the first historian to shift the study of Hasidism from the domain of beliefs and opinions to that of historical development'. However, this tribute is immediately followed by reservations which qualify Dubnow's appreciation of Graetz's scholarly achievement: 'But he adopted toward the subject of his enquiry the attitude of prosecutor rather than impartial historian. His hatred of the kabbalah and of mysticism in general enabled Graetz to grasp only the negative side of Hasidism.'[9] Dubnow goes on to criticize Graetz for the paucity of historical documentation of which he made use. This, he argued, prevented Graetz from generating any theoretical framework for the study of hasidism. He himself has been praised by a contemporary scholar in terms which were as qualified as those which he had applied to Graetz.[10] Modern scholars, however, concur in the opinion that Dubnow, the 'father of the history of Hasidism', was in fact much less hostile to his subject-matter than Graetz and more critical of the anti-hasidic sources available. Nevertheless, and however refined his methodology, Dubnow belonged to the same historiographical tradition. He shared many of the presuppositions of the maskilim, as well as their subjective percep-

[9] Dubnow, *Toledot haḥasidut*, 401.

[10] Z. Gries, 'Hasidism: The Present State of Research and Some Desirable Priorities', *Numen*, 34: 1 (1987), 192.

tion and selective vision. Admittedly, he endeavoured to dispel the popular Haskalah notion of the link between the Sabbatean heresy and hasidism (a link often emphasized by later historians, citing the evidence of Perl's maskilic circle). Time and again he stressed the need for caution in the utilization of anti-hasidic source material, whether mitnaggedic or maskilic. He felt that his methodology enabled him to distinguish between reliable and unreliable strands of evidence in this type of polemical material. For example, he introduced his analysis of a mitnaggedic report on the hasidic court of R. Hayyim Haikel of Amdur with the following methodological remarks:

> In contemporary mitnaggedic writings we find a description of the household of a certain hasidic leader which might be taken as typical of the majority of the hasidic courts at that time if not for the anti-hasidic bias of the author. However, so long as we are fully aware of this problematic factor, we are entitled to utilize this contemporary account by an individual who recorded everything he saw and heard but embellished the authentic evidence with his own interpretations. Let us consume the factual core while discarding the interpretative outer shell.[11]

In spite of this, much of Dubnow's interpretation of the socio-economic context of hasidism and his overtly dismissive attitude to its spiritual world originate in his maskilic sources. The same can be said of most of his successors, right down to the present generation of historians of hasidism. I should like to demonstrate this by examining a number of scholarly claims and characterizations of hasidism, tracing them back to their Haskalah antecedents.

1. *Hasidism was a 'mass' or 'popular' movement.*[12] This seems to me to be an inversion of the negative maskilic image of hasidism, and it clearly derives from virtually the same body of evidence and speculation. While the maskilim had disparaged the hasidic phenomenon by associating it with the lowest strata of Jewish society, later nationalist and populist historiography celebrated it as signalling by this very trait the rejuvenation of a decaying people that constituted the basis for the emergence of a new society in a reformed world.

2. *The non-productive character of hasidic society has its roots in specifically hasidic theological factors.*[13] This major Haskalah claim has found its way into the sociological literature on traditional eastern European Jewish society. Its validity is questionable, to say the least, in view of the extensive involvement of the hasidim in the full range of Jewish economic enterprises in eastern Europe.[14] It originates in an old, widely entertained European notion of the correlation between modern ideas and the modern econ-

[11] Dubnow, *Toledot haḥasidut*, 367.

[12] For two representative Haskalah characterizations of the hasidic community as comprising the poor and uneducated sections of Jewish society see I. B. Levinsohn (Ribal), 'Emek refa'im', in id., *Yalkut Ribal* (Warsaw, 1878), 121 (set in early 19th-cent. Volhynia), and Y. L. Gordon, 'Aḥarit simḥah tugah' (Happiness Ends in Sadness), in id., *Kol kitvei Y. L. Gordon* (2 vols.; Tel Aviv, 1953–60), ii. 16–17. On the historical setting of Gordon's short story (Pinsk and Karlin–Stolin, Belorussia, mid-19th cent.) see I. Bartal, 'Halo-Yehudim veḥevratam besifrut ivrit veyidish bemizraḥ Eiropah bein hashanim 1856–1914' (Ph.D. thesis, Hebrew University of Jerusalem, 1980), 18–25; M. Stanislawski, *For Whom Do I Toil? Judah Leib Gordon and the Crisis of Russian Jewry* (New York, 1988), 84–5.

[13] See Dubnow, *Toledot haḥasidut*, 354–67. Most of his sources for this are the writings of the mitnaggedim, but he cites only Perl's German anti-hasidic tract.

[14] This was shown by Shmeruk in the studies cited in n. 3 above. It should be pointed out that Dubnow recognized the economic impact of the hasidic courts on a number of towns and townlets in eastern

omy. The fact that some religious, mystically oriented Jewish élites, including the hasidic leadership, were fully engaged in devotional rather than productive economic activities did not preclude the bulk of their hasidic following from pursuing material prosperity by mundane action. Many historians have resorted to the image of the 'merry paupers' in characterizing the socio-economic orientation of the hasidic movement as a whole. This image, however, represents only a small element of the large and socially heterogeneous hasidic community in eastern Europe.

3. *Hasidism weakened the traditional framework of Jewish self-government in eastern Europe*. This is another Haskalah claim which survived well into the recent historiography of hasidism. Jacob Katz, for example, has argued that 'the community of hasidism grew, if not on the ruins of the traditional institutions of society, at least at their expense'.[15] Perl, Isaac Erter, and all their maskilic followers would have endorsed this statement fully. But at the same time Haskalah authors also argued that hasidism revitalized traditional society and helped preserve its cohesion at a time of political instability and social transformation.[16] This ambivalence on the part of the maskilim is not surprising given the Haskalah's own ambivalence towards the traditional framework of Jewish corporate life within the nascent modern European state. In reality, the effect of hasidism on traditional Jewish society and its institutions was neither to undermine nor to bolster them, and this, surprisingly enough, can be argued from the selfsame body of Haskalah writings. The maskilim fully grasped the implications of political change; they recognized the potential for opposition to the new reforms in the informal voluntary organization of hasidism. Their clash with hasidism was a clash between rival élites, each striving to capture the leadership and institutions of the old corporate order. Thus the notion of hasidic agitation undermining the traditional order of society which is common in the polemical literature of the Haskalah represents above all a mirror image of the central maskilic enterprise itself.

4. *The unbridgeable gap between the hasidic world-view and the intentions and policies of the state*. The historians of hasidism have tended to rely uncritically on Haskalah claims to this effect. Often their own ideological leanings have helped to reinforce this view, and they attributed to the hasidim the political edge of social activism or even radical-

Europe (see *Toledot haḥasidut*, 361–2), but he regarded this as a negative factor. See on this I. Bartal, 'Le'an halakh tseror hakesef? Habikoret hamaskilit al hebeteihah hakalkaliyim shel haḥasidut', in M. Ben-Sasson (ed.), *Dat vekalkalah: yaḥasei gomelin* (Jerusalem, 1995).

15 J. Katz, *Masoret umashber* (Jerusalem, 1958), pub. in Eng. as *Tradition and Crisis*, trans. B. D. Cooperman (New York, 1993), 212.

16 See e.g. Gottlober's description of a united hasidic, mitnaggedic, and maskilic front responding to the Jewish reform projects of the Russian government, in A. B. Gottlober, *Zikhronot umasa'ot*, ed. R. Goldberg (2 vols.; Jerusalem, 1976), i. 173–8. Gottlober's account corroborates Ettinger's claim to the effect that hasidism strengthened traditional society: 'Gradually it became clear that the Hasidic leadership was capable of contributing to the strengthening of the unity of Jewish society as a whole' (S. Ettinger, 'The Hasidic Movement: 'Reality and Ideals', in H. H. Ben-Sasson and S. E. Hinger (eds.), *Jewish Society through the Ages* (New York, 1971), orig. pub. in *Cahiers d'histoire mondiale: Journal of World History*, 11: 1–2 (1968), 251–66; repr: in Hundert (ed.), *Essential Papers*, 227. Cf. I. Halpern, 'R. Levi Yitsḥak miBerdichev ugezerot hamalkhut beyamav', in id., *Yehudim veyahadut bemizraḥ Eiropah* (Jerusalem, 1969), 343–7; A. Rapoport-Albert, 'Hatenu'ah haḥasidit aḥarei shenat 1772: Retsef mivni utemurah', *Zion*, 55 (1990), 226–8; E. Lederhendler, *The Road to Modern Jewish Politics* (New York, 1989), 70.

ism. However, it has long been known that the maskilic analysis of political loyalties and alignments was based to a considerable extent on little more than wishful thinking; in fact, the absolutist state and the hasidic community managed to reach, and to maintain, a *modus vivendi* that is well documented in a number of state archives.[17]

5. *The juxtaposition of hasidism and the Haskalah.* Many historical studies have set hasidism in the wider context of early modern Jewish history. Consequently, the rise of hasidism is usually, and rightly, juxtaposed with the emergence of the Haskalah. This, however, has meant that historians have found it virtually impossible to move away from the dichotomy between the two movements that was first posited by Haskalah authors and to deal with hasidism in its own terms. Even Orthodox historiography has produced its own version of this dichotomy in presenting the relationship between the Haskalah and hasidism as a personal clash between Moses Mendelssohn and the Baal Shem Tov.[18]

Haskalah literature has similarly given rise to a variety of other claims and notions that are still commonly encountered in the historiography of hasidism, even though they cannot be substantiated and are sometimes directly countered by the evidence of hasidic and other contemporary sources. These include, for example, the supposition that *Shivḥei haBesht* was a major instrument for the dissemination of hasidism,[19] that hasidic leadership has continued since the time of the Baal Shem Tov in a single dynastic line of succession;[20] that early hasidism assigned a special role to women; and that its ethical teaching had an impact on Jewish family life.[21] Many of these doubtful claims have their origins in the invaluable but rather subjective accounts of hasidism supplied by a long line of Haskalah-inspired authors from Perl on.

Finally, I should like to draw attention to the affinities between hasidic historiography and the legacy of the Haskalah that emerge clearly from the comparative study—here outlined in brief—of two major Haskalah depictions of hasidism. One is *Emek refa'im*, a satire by Isaac Ber Levinsohn ('Ribal') written in the second decade of the nineteenth century, and the other is Judah Leib Gordon's short story entitled 'Aḥarit simḥah tugah' written in the second half of the same century. The probable setting of the former is Volhynia while the latter depicts Belorussian hasidism. Both works interpret various aspects of hasidism and the Haskalah in terms that have become well

[17] See the memoranda of Joseph Perl from the Austrian archives in R. Mahler, *Haḥasidut vehaHaskalah* (Merhavya, 1961), 397–471. That in many cases the authorities were much more favourable to the hasidim is evidenced by archival material from Galicia (ibid. 87–131, 155–86) and from Russia (see Abraham Mapu, *Mikhtevei Avraham Mapu*, ed. B. Dinur (Jerusalem, 1970), 288). A typical maskilic depiction of the collaboration between the authorities and the maskilim in the campaign against hasidism in Belorussia is to be found in Gordon, 'Aḥarit simḥah', 52–60, 65–8, 76–7.

[18] See I. Bartal, 'Shimon hakofer: Perek behistoriografiah ortodoksit', in I. Bartal, E. Mendelsohn, and C. Turniansky (eds.), *Keminhag Ashkenaz uPolin: Sefer yovel leChone Shmeruk* (Jerusalem, 1994), 241–66.

[19] See Y. Mondshine, *Shivḥei haBesht: Ketav yad* (Jerusalem, 1982), 54–7; cf. Dubnow, *Toledot haḥasidut*, 42, where the book is described as one of the 'holy scriptures' of the hasidim.

[20] See Rapoport-Albert, 'Hatenu'ah haḥasidit'.

[21] See id., 'On Women in Hasidism: S. A. Horodecky and the Maid of Ludmir Tradition', in A. Rapoport-Albert and S. J. Zipperstein (eds.), *Jewish History: Essays in Honor of Chimen Abramsky* (London, 1988), 495–525.

established in modern historiography. Ribal's satire constructs a model of the hasidic court that accounts for the emergence of the institution of the zaddik and offers several mundane explanations of the spread of hasidism. It deals at length with hasidic penetration into traditional communal institutions, portraying it as a technique which enabled the movement to establish its power bases within the existing structures of local societies and associations. Thus *Emek refa'im* presents a historical explanation of the spread of hasidism which is not so different in essence from the explanations put forward by Joseph Weiss, Israel Halpern, Chone Shmeruk, and others. He maps out the course of the hasidic takeover of one communal office after another until all the basic functions of the *kahal* were effectively controlled; he singles out the role played by Jewish leaseholders in the early stages of hasidism; he dwells on the impact of hasidism on women and on the young; he identifies the relationship between the hasidic leadership and the feudal system, placing it within the context of traditional corporate affiliations. Ribal's analysis abounds in concrete historical examples and allusions to authentic hasidic figures. It offers a schematic periodization of hasidic history and displays, despite its polemical tone, a rational historical approach that is clearly focused on major issues in the sociology of east European Jewry.

Gordon's short story, based on a concrete historical event—the expulsion of the Karliner Rebbe from Pinsk to Stolin in 1864—paints a detailed picture of a Lithuanian hasidic court. It contains numerous observations on socio-economic affairs, most of which have made their way into current histories of hasidism. These include, for example, the remark that hasidism appealed primarily to the young; the discussion of territorial and financial rivalries between the various hasidic courts; the identification of the social origins of the movement in the lower strata of Jewish society; the evaluation of the impact of hasidism on Jewish family life as negative and destructive; the characterization of hasidism as an intercommunal informal organization, and so on.[22]

I selected these particular maskilic texts in order to demonstrate that Haskalah literature and modern hasidic historiography share not only a certain body of historical data but also their basic interpretative schemes and insights. Furthermore, both Ribal and Gordon serve to justify my opening claim that the maskilic authors' preoccupation with the socio-economic aspects of hasidism was the product of their essentially modern, western European outlook and formed an integral part of it. Both Ribal and Gordon produced a grossly distorted picture of the inner world of hasidism, although they fully understood the influence of religious belief on society and social behaviour.

The time is ripe for a reappraisal of Haskalah literature as a rational mode of contention with a rival ideology. To my mind, in their endeavour to decipher its codes, the maskilim had made an invaluable contribution to the study of hasidism. They concerned themselves with precisely the same issues that were later to concern the modern historians of hasidism. Their writings must now be reread and rehabilitated, not only as repositories of precious historical information but also as analytical discourses, full of historical insights and shrewd observations about the nature and development of hasidism. All these have been devalued by the shift away from the Haskalah's fierce

[22] Gordon, 'Aḥarit simḥah', 18.

rationalistic critique of hasidism and the enthusiastic endorsement of the movement by neo-Romantic or nationalistic historiography which saw it as a vital manifestation of 'authentic' Judaism. Let us not forget that not only the historians' fallacies owe their origins to the literature of the Haskalah, but also their soundest and most penetrating insights into hasidic life and lore.

TWENTY-THREE

The Historiography of the Hasidic Immigration to Erets Yisrael

JACOB BARNAI

THE first waves of hasidic immigration to Erets Yisrael have attracted the attention both of scholars of hasidism and of historians of the Jewish *yishuv* in Erets Yisrael. Hasidic scholarship has viewed the subject as an interesting and somewhat obscure chapter in the history of hasidism, while the historians of the *yishuv*, most of whom were associated with either the Zionist or the Orthodox currents in Jewish historiography, have perceived the hasidic immigration as an important element of the 'proto-Zionist' trend which proved the centrality of Erets Yisrael to Diaspora Jews even before Zionism. While the scholars of hasidism have set the issue in the context of the overall history of the hasidic movement, historians of the *yishuv*, under the impact of various trends within the Zionist movement and orthodox Jewry, have treated it primarily as an ideological issue.[1]

The present chapter is an attempt to survey and evaluate these two distinct traditions in the historiography of the subject.

At the beginning of the seventeenth century, after a long period of prosperity during the sixteenth century, the Galilean towns, especially Safed and Tiberias, were depleted of their Jewish populations. The Jews of these towns (mostly Sefardim, with some Mustarabians—Jews native to the Land of Israel who had adopted the language and lifestyle of their Arab neighbours—and Ashkenazim) dispersed throughout the Ottoman Empire, and some of them settled in Jerusalem. Among the new settlers were a few Ashkenazim from Safed whose move to Jerusalem was carefully recorded in a minute-book (*pinkas*), still unpublished, which listed their names and communal institutions.[2]

By the beginning of the eighteenth century the tide had changed. Economic hardship and pressure from the authorities led to a mass exodus of Jews from

[1] See Jacob Barnai, 'Trends in the Historiography of the Medieval and Early Modern Period of the Jewish Community in Erets-Israel' (Heb.), *Cathedra*, 42 (1987), 87–120; Jacob Katz, *Le'umiyut yehudit* (Jerusalem, 1979), 230–8. The main sources of information on the hasidic immigrations to Erets Yisrael are as follows: (a) the letters of the hasidim from and to Erets Yisrael; (b) hasidic tales; (c) more generally, both hasidic and rabbinic works written and published in eastern Europe during this period; (d) various non-hasidic sources, such as the Ottoman documents and the *pinkas* (minute-book) of the officials from Erets Yisrael in Istanbul. See Jacob Barnai, 'Some Clarifications on the Land of Israel's Stories of "In Praise of the Baal Shem Tov"' *Revue des études juives*, 146 (1987), 367–80.

[2] MS Jewish Theological Seminary, New York, Adler collection 74.

Jerusalem.[3] The Ashkenazi community collapsed and its membership dispersed. A few returned to the Galilee, which at this time was being redeveloped by Sheikh Dahir Al Umar.[4]

During the eighteenth century there was a continuous influx of eastern European immigrants to Erets Yisrael, and most of them settled in the Galilee. Many had come from Brody and its vicinity, where the Besht and his followers were active and where the hasidic movement began. Indeed, some of the immigrants belonged to the Besht's immediate circle of associates. They came during the period when hasidism was only just beginning and long before it became a mass movement.

In 1747 the brother-in-law of the Besht, R. Gershon of Kutow, immigrated to Erets Yisrael, settling first in Hebron and later in Jerusalem. In 1765 some of the Besht's close associates travelled together with a larger group of immigrants from eastern Europe, and they settled in Tiberias and Safed.

The largest group of hasidic immigrants, together with many non-hasidic Jews, came in 1777 (after the death of both the Besht in 1760 and R. Dov Ber of Mezhirech in 1772). This group, too, settled in the towns of the Galilee. The hasidic immigration to Erets Yisrael continued to the end of the eighteenth and during the whole of the nineteenth centuries. Among the immigrants were a number of prominent figures in the hasidic movement.

Three main tasks confront scholars who are concerned to explain this phenomenon and to assess its historical significance:

1. to identify the background and causes of the hasidic immigration;
2. to describe the immigration and settlement of the hasidim;
3. to consider the impact of the immigration both on the Jewish *yishuv* in Erets Yisrael and on the hasidic movement in eastern Europe.

The second of these tasks is now more or less accomplished. We can reconstruct the events in detail from ample historical documentation: the journey of the hasidim to Erets Yisrael has been mapped out; their initial settlement, the patterns of communal organization which they created, and full details of the funds which were raised in eastern Europe for their maintenance in the Holy Land are all known. But as far as the other two tasks are concerned, the historical sources are more equivocal. At best they leave much scope for divergent interpretation, at worst they attract blatant ideological bias.

The first historian to pay special attention to the hasidic immigrations to Erets Yisrael was Simon Dubnow, who dedicated one of his earliest articles to this subject.[5] Dubnow, then, clearly ascribed some importance to the phenomenon of the hasidic immigration to the Holy Land. This may reflect not only his interest in the hasidic movement as a historical phenomenon but also the shift in his ideological orientation

[3] Meir Benayahu, 'The Ashkenazi Community of Jerusalem, 1647–1747' (Heb.), *Sefunot*, 2 (1958), 128–89; Minna Rozen, 'The Nakib al Ashraf Mutiny in Jerusalem (1702–1706)' (Heb.), *Cathedra*, 11 (1982), 75–90; Jacob Barnai, *The Jews in Erets-Israel in the 18th Century* (Heb.) (Jerusalem 1982), 164–9; Adel Manna, 'The Rebellion of Nakib Al-Ashraf in Jerusalem' (Heb.), *Cathedra*, 53 (1989), 49–74.

[4] Amnon Cohen, *Palestine in the Eighteenth Century* (Jerusalem, 1973), 7–18, 30–52.

[5] Simon Dubnow, 'Haḥasidim harishonim be'Erets Yisrael', *Pardes*, 2 (1894), 201–4.

that had occurred a few years prior to the publication of the article. In the early 1880s, at the start of his career as a historian, Dubnow still believed in universalism rather than Jewish nationalism and particularism; only in the second half of the decade did he adopt a Jewish nationalist outlook.[6] It should be noted that, when Dubnow published his article in 1894, little historical documentation was available to him. Only a few of the hasidic letters concerned with the immigration to Erets Yisrael were known at that time, and there was no information whatsoever about the Jews of Palestine during this period. Nevertheless, Dubnow managed to reconstruct from this inadequate source material an interesting sequence of events that he attempted to interpret. Virtually all his conclusions, whether or not they were based on the documents before him, were taken up by subsequent historians. Only in recent times have scholars begun to re-examine Dubnow's ideas, rereading his sources and making use of a growing body of fresh evidence.

Dubnow reveals his critical attitude to the hasidic movement in general, and to the hasidic immigration to the Holy Land in particular, at the very beginning of his article. He asks rhetorically: 'Who led this pillar of cloud [the hasidim] to the pillar of fire [Erets Yisrael], the fire of religion that had illuminated the whole world thousands of years ago? Who introduced the darkness of belief [hasidism] to the land where the light of Torah had shone on Israel and on all the nations?'[7] Dubnow sets the hasidic immigration to Erets Yisrael in the context of the Jewish mystical tradition, presenting the immigration of the hasidim as a direct sequel to the sixteenth-century immigration of the mystics to Safed, and assuming the traditional mystical motivation to have been the main reason for the hasidic immigration to Erets Yisrael too. He writes emotively:

> This meeting [of the pillars of cloud and fire] in the Land of Israel was not the first one. The founders of practical kabbalah had all walked in the ruins of Safed, Hebron, and Jerusalem: R. Joseph Caro, the Ari [R. Isaac Luria], R. Moses Cordovero, R. Hayyim Vital, and their followers. In the village of Ein Zeitim and in the *ḥiklei tapuḥim* [a kabbalistic term, literally 'apple orchards'] around the city of Safed a powerful voice was often heard in the silence of the night; frightful spectacles were witnessed, and wondrous secrets were revealed. In the ruins of Mount Zion, in the desolation of Judea and the Galilee, troops of spirits and transmigrated souls (*gilgulim*) had found their resting place. The enlightening atmosphere of Erets Yisrael was filled with both holy and impure souls. From this wonderland a great movement arose and shook the Jewish world in the seventeenth century: the belief in Shabbetai Zevi . . . As this movement died out, another was emerging in Poland—hasidism—which resembled it in essence but not in style. Finally, at the end of the eighteenth century, the hasidic movement reached Erets Yisrael to prostrate itself at the tomb of its ancient mother—practical kabbalah.[8]

Dubnow clearly sees the immigration of the mystics in the sixteenth century, the Sabbatean movement in the seventeenth century, and the hasidic immigrations in the eighteenth century as three links in the chain of Jewish mystical tradition that is firmly connected to the Holy Land. He explains the connection between Sabbateanism and the hasidic immigrants by the observation that R. Gershon of Kutow, who came to

[6] Reuven Michael, 'Jost, Graetz, and Dubnow on the Singularity of Jewish History' (Heb.), in S. Almog *et al.* (eds.), *Transition and Change in Modern Jewish History: Essays Presented in Honor of Shmuel Ettinger* (Jerusalem, 1987), 521.

[7] Dubnow, 'Haḥasidim harishonim be'Erets Yisrael', 201.

[8] Ibid. 201–2.

Jerusalem in 1754, was appointed head of its small Ashkenazi congregation. This congregation included immigrants from R. Judah Hasid's group who had come to Jerusalem at the turn of the century, and who were known to be Sabbateans.

This connection leads Dubnow to his second motivation for the hasidic immigrations to Erets Yisrael: the messianic factor. This, of course, is one of the most problematic and controversial issues in the historiography of hasidism.[9] In his comprehensive history of the hasidic movement, Dubnow suggested that in hasidism the idea of 'personal redemption' had replaced the notion of 'national redemption'.[10] This general thesis finds its expression also in the article dedicated to the hasidic immigrations to Erets Yisrael. Dubnow points out that the immigrants were motivated by the desire to hasten the process of redemption,[11] a desire which was alien to the essential teaching of hasidism and much closer to the tradition of 'practical kabbalah'. He thus presents the hasidic immigrants as outsiders in relation to their own camp:

> It is quite possible that among the many hasidim of the circles of the Besht and the Maggid of Mezhirech there were some who were more attracted by the kabbalah of the Ari and who were engaged in speculation as to the date of redemption. These individuals travelled to Erets Yisrael, and their colleagues and allies were to follow them.[12]

Dubnow, then, sees the immigrants as an élite group within hasidism, a view which has been expressed in modern scholarship as well, especially by Israel Bartal.[13] It is doubtful whether the hasidic immigrants were more attracted to Lurianic kabbalah than their colleagues who remained in eastern Europe, but the main question is whether or not there is any basis for Dubnow's assumption that the first hasidic immigrants had gone to Erets Yisrael out of purely messianic motives. He offers only one piece of evidence to substantiate this claim: a letter written by R. Meshullam Phoebus Heller of Zbarazh.[14]

R. Meshullam was a disciple of the Maggid of Mezhirech, of R. Menahem Mendel of Peremyshlany, and of R. Jeḥiel Michel of Zloczow.[15] He was among the authors and publishers of *Likutim yekarim*,[16] one of the first hasidic books to present the ideas of the earliest hasidic leaders to a wider public. In his search for the messianic motives of the hasidic immigrants to Erets Yisrael, Dubnow relied heavily on a single passage in a long pastoral letter written by R. Meshullam to one of his friends and published in *Likutim yekarim*. The letter is assumed to have been written in 1777, the year of the largest hasidic immigration to Erets Yisrael.[17] Since it is crucial to the understanding of

[9] B. Dinur, *Bemifneh hadorot* (Jerusalem, 1955), 81–227; G. Scholem, *Major Trends in Jewish Mysticism* (New York, 1954), 325–50; id., 'The Neutralization of the Messianic Element in Early Hasidism', *Journal of Jewish Studies*, 20 (1969), 25–55, repr. in id., *The Messianic Idea in Judaism* (London 1971), 176–202; Tishby, 'Hara'ayon hameshiḥi vehamegamot hameshiḥiyot bitsemiḥat haḥasidut', *Zion*, 32 (1967), 1–45.

[10] Simon Dubnow, *Toledot haḥasidut* (Tel Aviv, 1930–1), 7, 60–2.

[11] Dubnow 'Haḥasidim harishonim be'Erets Yisrael', 205.

[12] Ibid.

[13] I. Bartal, 'Tsemiḥato shel hayishuv hayashan vehatifroset hayishuvit shelo', *Hahistoriah shel Erets Yisrael*, 8 (1983) 197–217.

[14] Dubnow, 'Haḥasidim harishonim be'Erets-Yisrael', 203.

[15] See Dubnow, *Toledot haḥasidut*, 323–4; Dov Ber b. Shmuel of Linits (Luniets), *Shivḥei haBesht*, ed. S. A. Horodecky (Tel Aviv, 1947), 101.

[16] *Likutim yekarim* (Lemberg, 1792).

[17] Haya Stiman-Katz, *Reshitan shel aliyot ḥasidim* (Jerusalem, 1987), 8.

Dubnow's messianic explanation of the hasidic immigration, I translate the relevant passage from the original Hebrew in full.

I would like to urge you and those around you who pay heed to what I say to strive hard in the service of God, each according to his ability, as each person must always seek eagerly for new methods of stirring his heart afresh, and each must strive to serve the Lord at all times. *But now we have seen and heard that many people, some of whom are perfect in their deeds, are travelling to the Holy Land* [my emphasis—J.B.], and some have already gone, and the perfect ones who have gone are well known to have been imbued with the Holy Spirit and with much learning, both in the revealed and in the hidden aspects of Torah. With them are many of the poor flock of the Diaspora. Surely, this means that there is now a great seeking of Zion, the like of which has not been felt before. And this great awakening must have come from God, and it surely means that [Redemption] is coming soon, may God bring it speedily in our own time, Amen. Therefore, no one knows what the next day may bring, and so why should you be troubled by future misfortune, especially the misfortune of this world; why should you concern yourself with the question of how to live out your allotted seventy years in wealth, and how to marry off your daughters, as most people do. It would be better for you to spend as little time as possible on business affairs, and to occupy yourself with Torah and divine service, of which the essence is prayer. I do not need to remind you of this, since you already know it from the writings of the Ari on the subject of the task of sorting out holiness from impurity, a task which is carried out every single day, to be accomplished with the coming of the messiah, may he come speedily in our own time.[18]

Dubnow deduced from this fragment that 'another important reason for the hasidic immigrations to the Holy Land was the hope of advancing Redemption' and 'bringing the messiah by implanting the ideas of the Besht in the soil of the Land of Israel'.[19] Although R. Meshullam was not an immigrant himself, his letter appears to offer an important insight into the background of the hasidic immigration to Erets Yisrael. Nevertheless, while the letter should certainly be taken into consideration, its apparent messianic fervour must be treated with caution, since such statements of messianic hope as it contains often turn out to be little more than messianic rhetoric.

Haya Stiman-Katz has recently brought to light several additional sources of this nature which seem to point to the messianic motivation of the hasidic immigrants.[20] However, as she herself observes, these are virtually indistinguishable from traditional kabbalistic formulations of messianic hope which address the issue in terms of *tikun* (restoring the world to a state of harmony), the raising up of Shekhinah and the role of the zaddik in hastening redemption.

Moreover, it is difficult to find in R. Meshullam's letter any evidence for the messianic background of the rise of hasidism. Rather, it seems to furnish support for the Dubnow–Scholem thesis whereby hasidism represented an attempt to diffuse messianic tensions and to redirect them to personal devotional channels such as prayer.[21]

[18] *Likutim yekarim*, 26.

[19] Dubnow, 'Haḥasidim harishonim be'Erets Yisrael', 205.

[20] Stiman-Katz, *Reshitan shel aliyot ḥasidim*, 5, 8; Dinur, *Bemifneh hadorot*, 227.

[21] S. Dubnow, *Toledot haḥasidut* (Tel Aviv, 1960), 62–3; G. Scholem, 'The Neutralization of the Messianic Element in Early Hasidism', *Journal of Jewish Studies*, 20 (1969), 25–55, repr. in id., *The Messianic Idea in Judaism* (New York, 1971), 176–202.

In his study of the messianic idea in early hasidism, Isaiah Tishby argued that the messianic factor was clearly in evidence,[22] and he tried to demonstrate this on the basis of two works by R. Simḥah of Zalozhtsy and R. Perets b. Moshe respectively. One important fact to which Tishby did not draw attention is that both authors were among the hasidic immigrants to Erets Yisrael. Surely, the connection between the active messianic agitation, which he found in both their works, and the immigration of the authors to Erets Yisrael should be highlighted. This must be seen in the context of other works which, as I have demonstrated elsewhere, link the hasidic immigrations to Erets Yisrael in the middle of the eighteenth century with the Sabbatean crisis and the messianic expectations associated with the year 5500 (1740).[23]

Israel Bartal, too, is of the opinion that 'the first immigrations of the hasidim, which took place during the Besht's lifetime and close to his death, were connected to messianic tension. However, this tension does not manifest itself in any distinctively hasidic messianic ideology, but rather in the overall impact of the Sabbatean upheaval and the hasidic methods of dealing with it.'[24] Bartal is not specific about the messianic background of the hasidic immigrants of 1777. He emphasizes the élitism and sense of mission towards the People of Israel that characterize this group.[25] In general, I agree with his assertion that the first hasidic immigrants were inspired by ideas which were widespread in eastern Europe during the post-Sabbatean period.

Israel Halpern in his study of the hasidic immigrations to Erets Yisrael completely ignored the messianic factor, and concentrated on more pragmatic considerations which will be discussed below.[26] But his appendices suggest that he accepted both Dubnow's and Scholem's views concerning the 'neutralization' of the collective messianic tension in early hasidism as reflected in the writings of R. Menahem Mendel of Vitebsk.[27] Halpern pointed out that the idea of personal redemption took precedence over the collective redemption of Israel. We can thus discern a certain difference between his view and Dubnow's regarding the significance of messianic ideas as a motivating factor in the hasidic immigration to Erets Yisrael.

Mordechai Eliav, on the other hand, emphasized the importance of the messianic factor in hasidism, a movement that he viewed as wholly connected to Erets Yisrael.[28] While listing other factors mentioned by Dubnow and others as possible reasons for the hasidic immigrations, Eliav stressed the overall centrality of Erets Yisrael in hasidic thought and practice, thereby placing himself within the tradition of Zionist historiography, especially its national–religious strand.[29]

The mystical kabbalistic factor which Dubnow explained historically has been re-examined by Moshe Idel. Idel believes that a careful reading of R. Menahem Mendel of Vitebsk's writings would show clearly his powerful mystical orientation. He

22 Tishby, 'Hara'ayon hameshiḥi', 1–45.

23 Barnai, *The Jews*, 32 ff.

24 Bartal, 'Tsemiḥato shel hayishuv', 198.

25 I. Bartal, 'The Old Yishuv in Erets-Israel' (Heb.), *Sekirah ḥodshit*, 3–4 (1981), 24–33.

26 I. Halpern, *Ha'aliyot harishonot shel haḥasidim le'Erets Yisrael* (Tel Aviv, 1947), 1–20.

27 Ibid. 38.

28 Mordechai Eliav, *Erets-Israel and its Yishuv in the Nineteenth Century, 1777–1917* (Heb.) (Jerusalem, 1978), 75–8.

29 See Barnai, 'Trends', 95–6, 114–19.

raises the possibility that radical mystics in the hasidic camp preferred to settle in Erets Yisrael, perhaps in order to escape censure from their more conservative colleagues in the Diaspora.[30]

Reviewing all these opinions, and the sources cited in their support, one must acknowledge that there exists a certain amount of concrete evidence to suggest that both the mystical and the messianic factors first identified by Dubnow were important motivations for the hasidic immigrations to the Holy Land, although it is the mystical rather than the messianic orientation of the immigrants that is more amply and unequivocally attested.

The third factor identified by Dubnow, and the most important one in his view, was the desire to create a *centre for hasidism* in Erets Yisrael.[31] Dubnow did not adduce any evidence in support of this thesis, although it is, of course, connected with his overall theory of the plurality of autonomous 'centres of Judaism', a theory which informs his historiographical work in general and by which he explained the entire course of Jewish history in terms of the rise and fall of discrete centres of Jewish life. He saw the attempt to establish a hasidic centre in Erets Yisrael as unsuccessful:

> But if we ask the question: Did the leaders of this settlement in Erets Yisrael and their supporters abroad achieve their main goal of the establishment in Erets Yisrael of a spiritual centre from which the streams of hasidism would flow outwards, we must answer: No. [32]

The view whereby the early hasidim had tried to establish in Erets Yisrael a 'centre' from which to inspire a new movement in Judaism was put in sharper focus and elaborated on by Horodecky.[33] While Dubnow saw the immigrants as a minority group, Horodecky claimed that they represented the ideology of the hasidic movement as a whole, a movement whose spiritual centre was located in Erets Yisrael. He saw R. Gershon of Kutow's immigration (1747) as a mission to spread the ideas of the Besht in the Holy Land. Relying on certain passages in the correspondence between R. Gershon and the Besht, he argued that Erets Yisrael was conceived by both as the spiritual centre of hasidism; from there its light would spread out to the whole Diaspora.[34] It was in this context that he placed also all the hasidic tales concerning the Besht's own abortive attempt to immigrate to Erets Yisrael.

At first glance these tales seem to belong to a contemporary typology of famous and saintly men, such as the Vilna Gaon and the Ḥida (R. Hayyim Joseph David Azulai), all of whom were said to have tried to immigrate to Erets Yisrael. However, a careful reading of the hasidic sources, especially of *Shivḥei haBesht*, suggests that all the references to the Besht's attempt to reach the Holy Land are very likely to be based on fact. Gedaliah Nigal, who has recently examined these hasidic tales in detail, considers that 'there is no reason to doubt the historical fact of the Besht's attempt to immigrate to

[30] Lecture delivered at Harvard University in Oct. 1985.

[31] Dubnow, 'Haḥasidim harishonim be'Erets Yisrael', 206.

[32] Ibid. 214.

[33] S. A. Horodecky, *Haḥasidut vehaḥasidim* [4 vols.; Tel Aviv, 1928–43] (Tel Aviv, 1951), i. 53–6; id., *Olei Tsion* (Jerusalem, 1947), 133–92; id., 'Haḥasidim be'Erets Yisrael', *Hashiloaḥ*, 8 (1901–2), 486–97.

[34] Horodecky, *Olei Tsion*, 136–41.

Erets Yisrael; not only did he yearn to immigrate, but he actually started out'.[35] Nevertheless, the evidence for this is inconclusive.

In his *History of Hasidism* Dubnow added a fourth motive to the list of factors underlying the hasidic immigrations. This was the persecution of the hasidim by the mitnaggedim.[36] In Dubnow's view, it was this persecution that prompted R. Menahem Mendel of Vitebsk to establish a hasidic centre in Erets Yisrael. Horodecky concurs: 'Persecution in Vilna aroused a desire in R. Menahem Mendel and his three friends to travel to Erets Yisrael—the land which had given birth to Sefardi kabbalah and where the Besht had also wished to end his days.'[37]

Halpern, who did not refer to any ideological motives (whether mystical or messianic), agreed, albeit cautiously, with his predecessors as to the practical motivation of the immigrants: the wish to escape persecution by the mitnaggedim and to establish a centre for the hasidic movement in a more auspicious environment. He considered this to be an additional factor to the traditional Jewish ideal of pilgrimage or immigration to the Holy Land:

> What moved R. Menahem Mendel and his companions to immigrate to Erets Yisrael? . . . The answer is simple: the desire to 'awaken the mercy of God, to pray for all of Israel'. It is not impossible that persecution by the mitnaggedim had played an important part, and the immigrants may have been inspired by the desire to create a centre for hasidism, to invest the new ideology with the sanctity of the Holy Land.[38]

Halpern suggested yet another motivation for the immigration: 'The Polish state . . . had suffered devastating blows which impoverished and weakened the Jewish community.'[39] The Jewish masses were ready to emigrate wherever the wind would carry them, but neither the Prussian nor the Austrian authorities would accept any Jewish immigrants. The Holy Land was an alternative destination.

Dinur discusses the hasidic immigrations to Erets Yisrael at great length. In keeping with his overall historiographical concerns, he places the immigrations in two contexts:

1. the centrality of Erets Yisrael to Jewish history in general;
2. hasidism as a messianic movement.

He argues that, at the outset, the Besht and his associates promoted the ideal of immigration to the Holy Land as a catalyst for redemption. However, once his own attempt to reach Erets Yisrael had failed, the Besht revised his view; the decision of his close associate, R. Jacob Joseph of Polonnoye, against immigration reflected this revised position.[40]

35 G. Nigal, *Hasiporet haḥasidit: Toledoteihah venos'eihah* (Jerusalem, 1981), 280–92; Dinur, *Bemifneh hadorot,* 192 ff.; I. Bartal, 'Aliyat R. Eleazar me'Amsterdam le'Erets Yisrael bishnat 1740', *Meḥkarim al toledot yahadut Holland*, 4 (1984), 7–25; Barnai, 'Some Clarifications', 367–80; Mark Verman, 'Aliyah and Yeridah: Journeys of the Besht and R. Nachman to Israel', in D. Blumenthal (ed.), *Approaches to Judaism in Medieval Times* (Atlanta, 1988), iii. 159–71.

36 Dubnow, *Toledot haḥasidut.*

37 Horodecky, 'Haḥasidim', 488.

38 Halpern, *Ha'aliyot harishonot*, 20–1.

39 Ibid. 22; Shmuel A. Cygielman. 'The Proposals of M. Butrymowicz for the Correction of the Jews of Poland and Lithuania in the Late 18th Century' (Heb.), in *Israel and the Nations: Essays Presented in Honor of Shmuel Ettinger* (Jerusalem, 1988), 91–3.

40 Dinur, *Bemifneh hadorot*, 192–227.

The Besht now advocated a new path to salvation as an alternative to going to the Holy Land: the merit of the entire generation. However, this was only a temporary stage in the development of the messianic teaching of hasidism. The next generation witnessed the successful immigration of hasidic leaders and their followers to Erets Yisrael, a move which was conceived as a means of hastening the redemption. Dinur's explanation of this return to the original teaching was that the generation after the Besht was frustrated by the failure of redemption to materialize through his own endeavours.[41]

Eliav has synthesized all the arguments surveyed above. Although he found some messianic elements in hasidism, he followed Dubnow and Scholem in classifying them as neutralized. He concluded: 'At any rate, hasidism viewed the emigration from the lands of the Diaspora, the inherent sanctity of the Land [of Israel] and its resettlement as factors which would speed up the advent of redemption.'[42] In addition, Eliav saw the hasidic settlement in the Holy Land as a wholly new phenomenon. He accepted Dubnow's view of it as a hasidic 'centre', but did not go as far as Horodecky; he rejected, for example, Horodecky's suggestion that R. Gershon of Kutow's immigration was prompted by the desire to establish such a centre there, and instead placed R. Gershon's immigration in the context of 'the immigrations of earlier kabbalists and pietists'[43] (although this was not quite compatible with his view of the hasidic immigration as a novel phenomenon).

This raises the questions of the extent and ideology of Jewish immigration from Europe to the Land of Israel before the beginning of the hasidic movement and particularly after Shabbetai Zevi. It seems to me that Eliav's evaluation of the hasidic immigrations as a novel phenomenon is a product of the national–religious elements in Jewish historiography. Religious Zionism seeks its roots in the immigration to the Holy Land of both the hasidim and the mitnaggedic followers of the Vilna Gaon (the *perushim*), adopting both groups as its direct spiritual ancestors.[44] It cannot trace its ancestry to the heresy of Sabbateanism and does not, therefore, accept Dinur's view whereby the immigration of the Sabbatean Judah the Pious and his followers (1700) was the turning point of modern Jewish history and a precursor of modern Zionism.[45] In fact, neither the immigration of the hasidim nor that of the *perushim* was the natural precursor of the ideology of religious Zionism. With regard to hasidism this can be exemplified by the following admission by Yitsḥak Werfel: 'It was especially necessary to emphasize the hasidic factor in Zionism . . . There were very few who saw the roots of Zionism in hasidism. This view seems to me highly probable. I have tried to base my book on it.'[46]

As for the immigration of the *perushim*, it, too, has been the subject of controversial interpretation by Orthodox Zionists,[47] while non-Zionist Orthodox historiography has similarly claimed it for its own ancestry. The Orthodox Zionists argue that both the hasidim and the *perushim* who came to Erets Yisrael from eastern Europe at the end of

41 Dinur, *Bemifneh hadorot*, 199–225.
42 Eliav, *Erets-Israel*, 75.
43 Ibid.
44 See Barnai, 'Trends', 94–5, 114–19.
45 Dinur, *Bemifneh hadorot*, 26–9.
46 Yitsḥak Werfel (Raphael), *Haḥasidut ve'Erets Yisrael* (Jerusalem, 1940), foreword, 149–50.
47 Yosef Yoel Rivlin, 'HaGra vetalmidav beErets Yisrael', in J. L. Maimon (ed.), *Sefer HaGra* (2 vols.; Jerusalem, 1964), 111–62; Aryeh Morgenstern, *Messianism and the Settlement of Erets-Israel* (Heb.) (Jerusalem, 1985); id., *Redemption in a Natural Way* (Heb.) (Elkana, 1989); I. Bartal, 'Note' (Heb.), *Cathedra*, 31 (1984), 159–71; id., 'Messianism and Historiography', *Zion*, 52 (1987), 117–30.

the eighteenth century and in the course of the nineteenth were the true pioneers of Zionism, thereby denying this title to the secular immigrants who began to arrive only at the end of the nineteenth century. Altogether, the Orthodox historiographical discourse about hasidism is clearly focused on Erets Yisrael.[48]

On the other hand, some scholars have stressed the negative attitude of the hasidic movement toward political Zionism in the late nineteenth and early twentieth centuries, presenting it as a break from the earlier hasidic ideal of settlement in the Holy Land for religious reasons. Horodecky, for example, remarked: 'It is interesting to note the dramatic difference between the attitude of the eighteenth century hasidim and that of contemporary hasidism.'[49]

In my opinion, this does not constitute any break or inconsistency in the hasidic orientation towards Erets Yisrael, since there is no connection between the traditional medieval ideal of immigration to the Holy Land and the ideals of modern Jewish nationalism; on the other hand, the hasidic opposition to Zionism can hardly be construed as an objection to the traditional religious ideal of settlement in Erets Yisrael.

I would like to suggest that, in contrast to all these ideologically charged views and debates, a dispassionate analysis of the political situation in the Ottoman Empire and in Palestine during this period can shed new light on the background of the hasidic immigrations. The following observations can serve as examples:

1. The Russo-Turkish war of 1768, which ended with the signing of the Kügik–Kayanarci treaty, enabled immigrants to reach Palestine more easily by way of Turkey.
2. The end of the war in Palestine between Dahir Al Umar and Ali Bey in 1775, and the rise to power of Ahmed Jazar Pasha, stabilized the region and thereby facilitated hasidic immigration and settlement.

Both factors may well account for the timing of the great hasidic immigration of 1777.

As for the historical significance of the hasidic immigrations and their impact on the hasidic movement as well as on the Jewish *yishuv* in Erets Yisrael, scholars are divided in their evaluation. Dubnow believed that the hasidim had failed totally in their attempt to establish a hasidic centre in Erets Yisrael.[50] Horodecky reached a different conclusion. In his view, the arrival of the hasidic immigrants had a great impact on the *yishuv*:

> In Erets Yisrael, R. Menahem Mendel and his followers were received with great respect. Not only did the Jews of Jerusalem and Tiberias invite them to leave Safed and to settle in their midst, but in addition the sultan bestowed power and freedom on the entire community.[51]

Halpern maintained that the continued involvement of the hasidic leaders from Erets Yisrael in the affairs of their followers in eastern Europe by means of correspondence did turn the Holy Land into a veritable centre of hasidism,[52] but he noted the diffi-

[48] See e.g. Yeḥiel Gertenstein, *The Besht's Pupils in Erets-Israel* (Heb.) (Tel Aviv, 1982); David Assaf, 'MiVolin liTsfat: Deyokano shel R. Avraham Dov me'Ovruch kemanhig ḥasidi bamaḥatsit harishonah shel hame'ah hatesha'esreh', *Shalem*, 6 (1992), 223–79.

[49] Horodecky, 'Haḥasidim', 497; Isaac Alfasi, *Haḥasidut Veshivat Tsiyon* (Tel Aviv, 1986).

[50] Dubnow, 'Haḥasidim harishonim be'Erets Yisrael'.

[51] Horodecky, 'Haḥasidim', 497.

[52] Halpern, *Ha'aliyot harishonot*, 21, 37.

culties experienced by the settlers in acclimatizing to local conditions, difficulties which were evidenced in their move from Safed to Tiberias and in their quarrels with the local communities, both Sefardi and Ashkenazi. Eliav, on the other hand, believed that, while the hasidim did not succeed in creating a 'centre' for their movement in Erets Yisrael, their settlement in the Galilee did provide a strong base for the integration of future immigrants and facilitated the continued Jewish settlement of the Holy Land. In contrast with Dinur, who viewed the Sabbatean R. Judah the Pious and his associates who immigrated to Erets Ysrael in 1700 as the precursors of modern Zionism, Eliav regarded the immigration of this Sabbatean group as an isolated episode,[53] and presented the hasidic immigrants as the true forerunners of Zionism. However, Eliav's argument is focused on what he terms 'the continuity of Jewish immigration after 1777', a factor which he adopts as his chief criterion in assessing the long-term effect of the phenomenon. This is problematic since the immigration to Erets Yisrael of various groups and individuals from all over the Jewish Diaspora was continuous throughout the eighteenth century. The hasidic immigrants constituted no more than a link in this long chain of immigration. Eliav's problematic thesis is clearly informed by his Orthdox Zionist ideology.

More recently, Bartal has suggested that the most distinctive contribution of the hasidic immigration to *yishuv* life was the establishment of the systems of *ḥalukah* (distribution of funds raised by Diaspora Jewry in support of the Jewish inhabitants of the Holy Land) and *kolelim* (groups of Ashkenazi Jews residing in the Holy Land, organized by common European countries or districts of origin) in the nineteenth century.[54] According to Bartal, the hasidim and later on the *perushim*, can thus be regarded as the founders of the old *yishuv*. Like Eliav, he recognizes the importance of the hasidic immigrations to the history of the *yishuv*. However, Bartal's interpretation of the facts is quite different from Eliav's. Eliav saw the hasidim as the founders of the new *yishuv* and the modern Jewish settlement in Erets Yisrael, while Bartal sees them as the founders of the old *yishuv*, whose historical and ideological origins are totally different.

The historiography of the immigration of both the hasidim and the *perushim* has become a popular subject of debate in recent years. Much effort has been invested in the presentation of immigration to Erets Yisrael as the primary goal of both movements. Nevertheless, modern hasidic scholarship has made it patently clear that the main goal of the hasidim was to generate a new approach to divine service rather than to promote any novel *quasi*-Zionist orientation towards the Holy Land.

Recent research has highlighted the full complexity of the issue. Immanuel Etkes,[55] for example, connects the hasidic settlement in Erets Yisrael with the change in the balance of power and ideology within the hasidic leadership of eastern Europe. He points out that the leaders of the hasidic immigrants, despite the fact that their residence in the Holy Land had invested them with new authority, failed in their attempt to continue to function as leaders to their followers abroad. The hasidic immigration thus stimulated, however unintentionally, the emergence of a new local leadership in eastern Europe. This is evidenced, for example, by the rise to leadership of R. Shneur Zalman of

[53] Eliav, *Erets-Israel*, 84.

[54] Bartal, 'Tsemiḥato shel hayishuv', 198.

[55] I. Etkes, 'Darko shel R. Shne'ur Zalman miLiadi kemanhig shel ḥasidim', *Zion*, 50 (1986), 321–54; id., 'Aliyato shel R. Shne'ur Zalman miLiadi le'emdat manhigut', *Tarbiz*, 54 (1985), 429–39.

Lyady. Etkes attributes the failure of the immigrant leaders to maintain their authority over the hasidim in eastern Europe to the lack of personal contact which is a vital feature of the relationship between the hasidic leader and his followers.

Mordecai Wilensky has recently discovered a large collection of documents relating to the hasidic settlement in Erets Yisrael and has published some of them.[56] This new material has greatly enriched our knowledge and understanding of the subject. In his introduction Wilensky deals with some of the historiographic questions relating to the hasidic immigration. On the basis of new documents, he argues against the view that the immigration of the hasidim contained a messianic element. His research contributes also to the understanding of the relations between the hasidic leaders who emigrated to Erets Yisrael and those who remained in eastern Europe, especially R. Shneur Zalman of Lyady.

Wilensky puts in sharper focus some of the points concerning the dispute between the hasidim and the mitnaggedim as well as between the hasidim and the Sefardim in Tiberias. He also succeeds in extracting from the documents important information on the economic situation in Palestine at the end of the eighteenth century.[57]

Yaakov Hisdai has placed the hasidic immigration in the context of all the Jewish immigrations from eastern Europe in the eighteenth century.[58] He puts forward the following arguments.

1. The eighteenth-century hasidic immigration was paralleled by a mitnaggedic immigration.
2. The two groups were motivated by different sets of considerations: the hasidic immigrants perceived themselves as an élite within the movement while the mitnaggedim were inspired by powerful messianic longings.
3. Some of the Ashkenazi immigrants in the mid-eighteenth century can be classified as mitnaggedim even though the birth of Lithuanian mitnaggedism is usually associated with the outbreak of the first wave of denunciations and excommunications of all the followers of hasidism in 1772; the opposition to hasidism had begun before that date.

Hisdai attempts to map out the places of origin of all the immigrants (Brody, Vilna, and environs) and to identify their ideological stance (anti-Sabbatean), their primary destination (Safed), and their common notions of Erets Yisrael. He defines the characteristics of the mitnagged in Erets Yisrael, distinguishing him from his eastern European counterpart, and he raises a number of important questions such as when did the immigration of the hasidim and the mitnaggedim respectively begin? What and how varied was the attitude of the immigrants toward Sabbateanism?[59] These questions cannot be answered fully at the present time; rather, they serve to highlight the need for further research.

Finally, two students at the Hebrew University of Jerusalem have recently examined

[56] Mordecai Wilensky, *Hayishuv haḥasidi biTeveriah* (Jerusalem, 1988). [57] Ibid. 11–32.

[58] Yaakov Hisdai, 'Early Settlement of "Hasidim" and of "Mitnaggedim" in Palestine' (Heb.), *Shalem*, 4 (1984), 231–70.

[59] I hope to deal with these questions elsewhere.

the hasidic letters from Erets Yisrael as historical source material.[60] Their preliminary conclusions raise serious doubts with regard to the very credibility of the letters.

It seems to me that, in addition to these serious bibliographical considerations, future historical research in this field should be concentrated on the following issues:

1. the precise background of the hasidic immigration and the full range of factors—political, economic, sociological, and ideological—which led to it;
2. a sociological analysis of the immigrant community in Erets Yisrael;
3. a clearer differentiation of the distinct waves of hasidic immigration in the course of the nineteenth century, in the context of the history of the *yishuv* during this period.

[60] Raya Haran, 'The Authenticity of Letters Written by Hasidim in Erets Yisrael' (Heb.), *Cathedra*, 55 (1990), 22–58; id., 'On the Copying and Transmission of Hasidic Letters' (Heb.), *Zion*, 56 (1991), 299–320; id., 'What Motivated Hasidic Jews to Emigrate to Erets Israel?' (Heb.), *Cathedra*, 76 (1995), 77–95; Nahum Karlinsky, 'The Hasidic Epistles from Erets-Israel; The Text and Context: A Reconsideration' (Heb.) (M.A. thesis, Hebrew University of Jerusalem, 1989). See also Z. Gries, 'Hasidism: The Present State of Research and Some Desirable Priorities', *Numen*, 34: 1 (1987), 101–3; A. Rapoport-Albert, 'Hatenu'ah haḥasidit aḥarei shenat 1772: Retsef mivni utemurah', *Zion*, 55 (1990), 226; I. Alfasi, *Haḥasidut veshivot Tsiyon* (Tel Aviv, 1986); Y. Mondshine, 'Igrot Erets Yisrael', in id. (ed.), *Kerem Habad*, 4/2 (1992), 269–315; id., 'The Authenticity of Hasidic Letters' (Heb.), *Cathedra*, 63 (1992), 65–97; 64 (1992), 79–97; D. Assaf, '*Yesod Ha-Ma'ala*: A New Chapter in the Historiography of Hasidism in Erets-Israel' (Heb.), *Cathedra*, 68 (1993), 57–66; A. Surasky, *Yesod hama'alah* (2 vols.; Bnei Brak, 1991); I. Bartal, *Galut ba'arets* (Jerusalem, 1994); J. Barnai, *Historiografiah ule'umiyut* (Jerusalem, 1995); M. Yizra'eli, *Haḥasidim harishonim beyishuv Erets Yisrael* (Jerusalem, 1995).

TWENTY-FOUR

Martin Buber and Gershom Scholem on Hasidism: A Critical Appraisal

MOSHE IDEL

I

THE divergences between Buber and Scholem on the nature of kabbalah and hasidism and the appropriate methods for exploring their literatures are well known, since both parties were concerned to state them in print.[1] It should be sufficient, therefore, to review their divergent positions as briefly as possible.

1. As his *Ecstatic Confessions* would testify, Buber was concerned from the very beginning with the phenomenon of mysticism in general. His enterprise in the field of hasidism was an integral part of a philosophical-experiential orientation which gravi-

Thanks are due to Ada Rapoport-Albert for refining the English of this chapter as well as for her helpful suggestions concerning its content.

[1] M. Buber, 'Interpreting Hasidism', *Commentary*, 36: 3 (Sept. 1963), 218–25; G. Scholem, 'Martin Buber's Interpretation of Hasidism', in id., *The Messianic Idea in Judaism* (New York, 1971), 228–50. This is an expanded version of the article originally published in *Commentary*, 32 (1961), 305–16.

On the controversy see R. Schatz-Uffenheimer, 'Man's Relationship to God and World in Buber's Rendering of Hasidic Teachings', in Paul Schilpp and Maurice Friedman (eds.), *The Philosophy of Martin Buber* (La Salle, Ill., 1967), 403–35, and her introd. to *Haḥasidut kemistikah* (Jerusalem, 1968), 10–18; see also Michael Oppenheim, 'The Meaning of Hasidut: Martin Buber and Gershom Scholem', *Journal of the American Academy of Religion*, 49: 3 (1981), 409–21; Steven D. Kepnes, 'A Hermeneutic Approach to the Buber–Scholem Controversy', *Journal of Jewish Studies*, 38 (1987), 81–98; Samuel H. Dresner's introd. to Abraham Joshua Heschel, *The Circle of the Ba'al Shem Tov: Studies in Hasidism* (Chicago, 1985), pp. xvi–xix, and D. Biale, *Gershom Scholem, Kabbalah and Counter-History* (Cambridge, Mass., 1982). Buber's view of hasidism, and Scholem's critique of this view, are discussed in Grete Schaeder, *The Hebrew Humanism of Martin Buber*, trans. N. J. Jacobs (Detroit, 1973), 287–338; Rahel Shihor, 'Buber's Method in his Research of Hasidism' (Heb.), *Da'at*, 2–3 (1978–9), 241–6. In Maurice Friedman's 'Interpreting Hasidim: The Buber–Scholem Controversy', *Leo Baeck Institute Year Book*, 33 (1988), 449–67 the evolution of Scholem's attitude to Buber's presentation of hasidism is surveyed stage by stage.

On Scholem and hasidism see Louis Jacobs, 'Aspects of Scholem's Study of Hasidism', in Harold Bloom (ed.), *Gershom Scholem* (New York, 1987), 179–88, and Rivka Schatz-Uffenheimer, 'Perush haḥasidut kevitui lahashkafah ha'idealistit shel Gershom Scholem', in *Gershom Scholem: Al ha'ish ufo'olo* (Jerusalem, 1983) (trans as 'Gershom Scholem's Interpretation of Hasidism as an Expression of his Idealism', in Paul Mendes-Flohr (ed.), *Gershom Scholem: The Man and his Work* (New York, 1994), 48–62.

See also Isaiah Tishby's stand on both Buber's and Scholem's views of the neutralization of messianism in hasidism, in 'Hara'ayon hameshiḥi vehamegamot hameshiḥiyot bitsemiḥat haḥasidut', *Zion*, 32 (1967), 1–45.

tated towards the orient, following the *fin de siècle* fashion of his time.[2] Scholem's frame of mind was quite different, since the starting point of his considerations was the continuum of Jewish mysticism and its particular dynamics as a specific type of mysticism, and the historical and philological questions that derived from this.[3]

2. Buber's approach is phenomenological; he is interested primarily in the religious characteristics of a certain type of mysticism, and only secondarily in its historical genesis.[4] His discussions centre on the spiritual parameters of hasidic mysticism and touch on historical points only tangentially.[5] By contrast, Scholem's interest in hasidism is primarily historical, since he regards it as the last phase of a long Jewish mystical tradition whose complete history he strove to map out. Thus, the relationship between hasidic ideas and earlier mystical thought—in his view almost exclusively the Lurianic and Sabbatean schools—is crucial to Scholem's understanding of hasidism.[6]

3. Scholem's approach differed from Buber's even in regard to the phenomenological understanding of hasidism. Scholem was more concerned with theological issues, such as the importance of the ideal of *devekut* and the place of pantheism,[7] while Buber was concerned with experiental issues in his early mystical phase,[8] turning later to the dialogical approach.[9]

4. These divergent approaches directed the two scholars to two different types of hasidic sources: for Scholem, focusing on hasidic theology, the pertinent body of texts was the speculative, homiletic writings of the masters of hasidism.[10] Buber, on the other hand, who was interested in the living expressions of hasidic phenomena, in the realization of the hasidic experience in daily life and popular literature, focused on the legends surrounding the lives of the hasidic masters, and it was this type of literature that became the basis for his interpretation of hasidism.[11]

5. Guided by his phenomenological approach, Buber ultimately reached the view that hasidism expressed the quintessence of Judaism. Other types of Jewish spirituality, such as kabbalah and apocalypticism, were for him not essential components of the

[2] See P. Mendes-Flohr, 'Fin-de-Siècle Orientalism, the Ostjuden and the Aesthetics of Jewish Affirmation', in *Studies in Contemporary Jewry* (Bloomington, Ind., 1984), 96–139.

[3] See Scholem, *Major Trends*, 327–31.

[4] Buber, 'Interpreting', 218, 221. In his *Hasidism* (New York, 1948), 6–7, 13–17, and elsewhere throughout the book, Buber explicitly relates hasidism to Sabbateanism; but even when he points to the historical relationship between the two movements he does not suggest that there were Sabbateans among the founding fathers of hasidism. This claim is implicit in some of Scholem's discussions of the same topic and more explicit in Isaiah Tishby, 'Between Sabbateanism and Hasidism: The Sabbateanism of the Kabbalist R. Jacob Koppel Lifshitz of Mezhirech' (Heb.), in his collection of essays, *Netivei emunah uminut* (Ramat Gan, 1964), 204–26, esp. 225–6.

[5] This seems to be the general character of Buber's *Hasidism*.

[6] See his *Major Trends in Jewish Mysticism* (New York, 1954), 327–31. See also J. Dan, 'The Historical Perceptions of the Late Professor Gershom Scholem' (Heb.), *Zion*, 47 (1982), 170–1. Cf., however, Scholem's remark on Cordovero's theosophy (see p. 402 below).

[7] See 'Devekut, or Communion with God', *Review of Religion*, 14 (1949–50), 115–39, repr. in id., *The Messianic Idea*, 223–7.

[8] The experiential *Erlebnis* phase is well represented by his *Ecstatic Confessions* [1909], ed. P. Mendes-Flohr (San Francisco, 1985).

[9] Buber, 'Interpreting', 218.

[10] Scholem, 'Martin Buber's Interpretation', 233–4.

[11] Buber, 'Interpreting', 219–20.

Jewish religion.[12] In principle, Buber was looking for the perennial element in hasidism that could nourish his own religiosity. Scholem's historical and critical considerations, on the other hand, led him to a theological stance that defined most expressions of Jewish mysticism as authentic Jewish phenomena, in line with his pluralistic vision of Judaism. Buber's romantic posture is conspicuously different from Scholem's critical approach; indeed, Scholem himself pointed out that Buber had ignored some of the more distasteful aspects of hasidism, most strikingly its magical components.[13]

Notwithstanding the crucial differences discussed above, these two great scholars did share certain important common ground. Both aspired to understand the essence of hasidism not only as scholars but as public figures; they considered Jewish mysticism a possible bridge between tradition and the Jewry of the present. Their exposition of the writings of the past was a crucial aspect of their vision of national revival; it was a creative cultural act, intended to generate a new relationship to the Jewish tradition, to coexist with if not to replace the traditional relationship of Orthodoxy.[14] I would like to examine in detail the main points of agreement between them.[15]

The three main features which are common to Buber's and Scholem's expositions of hasidism are: (*a*) an approach which I propose to call proximism, (*b*) the assumption that kabbalah is a gnostic type of mystical lore, and (*c*) reductionism. Let me start with proximism, which seems to be the most important.

(a) Both Buber and Scholem were in agreement that hasidism had to be understood as part of a longer historical process whose crucial turning point was the diffusion of Lurianism and its messianic explosion in Sabbateanism and Frankism. In their understanding, the emergence of hasidism was historically related to the spiritual situation of the Jews in Poland after the decline of these movements. In other words, they saw hasidism as a response to a great spiritual crisis. In principle, the nexus between messianic Lurianism in its heretical forms and hasidism is essential to the historical explanations advanced by both scholars.[16] Proximism may take two different forms. One is reactive, assuming that a later phenomenon is a reaction to the challenges posed by an earlier one. On the other hand, proximism may point to a relation of some continuity between two consecutive phenomena; thus hasidism can be seen not only as a reaction to certain elements of heretical Sabbateanism, but also as its continuation as far as other elements are concerned. Scholem espoused the two forms of proximism,[17] whereas Buber was more inclined to the reactive variety.[18]

[12] Buber defined hasidism as the place where the 'primal Jewish reality', embodying the 'inner truth' of Judaism, may be found. See Martin Buber, *Hasidism and Modern Man* (New York, 1966), 59; Mendes-Flohr, 'Fin-de-Siècle', 115–16. On the nature of gnosticism and apocalypticism see Buber, *Hasidism and Modern Man*, 27.

[13] Scholem, 'Martin Buber's Interpretation', 231; Buber, *Hasidism*, 79–81, 142–4; id., 'Interpreting', 225.

[14] See Buber, 'Interpreting', 218; Oppenheim, 'Meaning of Hasidut', 409.

[15] I shall not deal with those points of agreement which were discussed by Scholem himself; see his 'Martin Buber's Interpretation', 236–7. See also Buber, 'Interpreting', 221–2.

[16] See e.g. Buber, *Hasidism*, 6–7.

[17] See Scholem, *Major Trends*, 327–31; Dan, 'Historical Perceptions', 170–1; Scholem, 'Devekut', 223–5. See also n. 29 below.

[18] See e.g. Buber, *Hasidism*, 6–7, where hasidism is described as a 'counter-movement'.

(b) Scholem, and under his influence also Buber,[19] considered kabbalah a gnostic phenomenon.[20] For Buber, particularly in his later years, the characterization of the whole of the kabbalistic tradition as gnostic was not devoid of certain negative connotations, since, according to him, it was precisely this feature of kabbalah that estranged the mystics from the real world, where he located the arena for the most authentic encounter between God and man.[21] Scholem also had certain reservations with regard to the emanative structure in kabbalah, though these comprise only a marginal element of his vast scholarly enterprise. According to Scholem, the emanative system of theosophical kabbalah was detrimental to the viability of this type of mysticism.[22] Although the respective religious concerns of Scholem and Buber were quite different, in evaluating the great gulf separating man from God, it seems that both agreed as to the novelty in Judaism of the median structure of emanation, and this accounted for their common perception of kabbalah as gnostic. Scholem had stamped kabbalah with the mark of gnosticism at the very beginning of his scholarly career, drawing on what was then the modern vocabulary of the academic study of religion; Buber, who was critical of kabbalah for its schematization of the divine mystery, himself schematized the discipline by describing it as a singular, anti-dualistic form of gnosticism.

The assumption shared by both Buber and Scholem as regards the gnostic structure of kabbalistic thought is one of the most important hypotheses about the nature of Jewish mysticism which has ever been formulated by a Jewish scholar, and in my opinion the most problematic one. If it can be proved erroneous—and for the time being I see no historical or philological reason for accepting it—then the entire issue of the relationship between kabbalah and hasidism would need to be examined afresh, with a new set of concepts and criteria.

(c) Buber's characterization of the whole of kabbalah as gnostic, and his frequent references to this feature when comparing hasidism and kabbalah, render his approach monolithic, and subsequently reductionist; this can be illustrated by his presentation of hasidism as a single, unified phenomenon.[23] Buber's comparison between the huge literary corpuses of hasidism and kabbalah is a daring spiritual enterprise, which, curiously enough, Scholem never challenged. Buber contrasted hasidism with its kabbalistic-gnostic 'core', which he implicitly identified with Lurianism,[24] entirely overlooking the

[19] See Buber, *Hasidism*, 138–42; Scholem, 'Martin Buber's Interpretation', 232.

[20] David Biale notes the importance of gnosticism to Scholem's exposition of the nature of kabbalah, in *Gershom Scholem*, 51–64, 65–7, 71–2, and esp. 89–91, where he deals with the controversy between Scholem and Buber on the place of gnosticism in hasidic thought. On Scholem and gnosticism see Bloom, in *Gershom Scholem*, 207–20. For my critical evaluation so far of Scholem's emphasis on the role of gnosticism in the constitution of kabbalah see M. Idel, *Kabbalah: New Perspectives* (New Haven, 1988), 30–2; id., 'The Problem of the Sources of the *Bahir*' (Heb.), in J. Dan (ed.), *The Beginnings of Jewish Mysticism in Medieval Europe, Meḥkerei Yerushalayim bemaḥshevet Yisrael*, 6 (Jerusalem, 1987), 55–72.

[21] M. Buber, *Der Jude und sein Judentum* (Cologne, 1963), 194–7.

[22] See the very beginning of Scholem's seventh unhistorical statement: 'The doctrine of emanation is to be considered as the special misfortune of Kabbalah.' 'Zehn unhistorische Sätze über Kabbala', in *Geist und Werk: Zum 75. Geburtstag von Dr. Daniel Brody* (Zurich, 1958), 211.

[23] Buber was well aware of the diversity of hasidic thought and legend, as is evidenced by his anthologies of hasidic tales and by his introductions to these volumes. When discussing the movement as a religious phenomenon, however, he ignores the implications of this diversity and presents the religious core of hasidism as a unified doctrine.

[24] Buber, *Hasidism*, 140–1; id., 'Interpreting', 219.

diversity of each of these kabbalistic schools of thought. Scholem, who was acquainted with the diversity of kabbalistic thought, was uncritical of this because he himself was convinced that the only kabbalistic school to be taken into serious consideration when attempting to explain the emergence of hasidism was the Lurianic one.[25] Although he was well aware that the kabbalistic tradition could not be reduced to mere Lurianism, it was Lurianism alone that featured in his own analysis of hasidism.

Last but not least, Buber and Scholem were in disagreement over the type of hasidic literature which was most likely to reveal the true nature of hasidism. Buber considered the corpus of legend more representative of what he considered to be essential hasidism,[26] whereas Scholem gave preference to the movement's speculative literature.[27] Moreover, neither acknowledged the other's preferred literary corpus as in any way capable of yielding an authentic characterization of hasidism. Each argued that his sources alone captured the true nature of hasidism. Thus, the implicit assumption of both was that hasidism must be seen as a unilateral type of mysticism—legendary and dialogical according to Buber, pantheistic and speculative according to Scholem.

As far as I am aware, neither Buber nor Scholem was ready to offer an interpretation that could accommodate the different aspects of this richly variegated religious phenomenon. The assumption that the truth was located in but one of the two available sets of sources seems problematic and naïve, but it was clearly shared by the two modern giants of mystical scholarship. Rather than advocating dogmatically the importance of one type of literature to the exclusion of another, a more fruitful approach might have been to uncover, without entering into a harmonistic frame of mind, what was common to both these types of literature.

I would like to propose, and I cannot elaborate on this proposal within the confines of the present discussion, that the speculative literature of hasidism reflects mainly the mystical relationship between the zaddik and the Divine, whereas the narrative writings reflect the social dimension of hasidism, namely the relationship of the mystic who returns from his mystical experience to the social sphere in order to contribute to the improvement and welfare of his community. Thus, the question of which particular type of hasidic literature is more representative of its essence may be solved by the proposition that different topics are dealt with in different types of literature.[28] Buber, who described hasidism as capable of living with paradoxes without needing to resolve them, could not imagine that hasidism might have been transmitting its messages on more than one wavelength.

II

In lieu of, or to a certain extent in addition to, Scholem's and Buber's essentially historical explanations, I should like to propose a less historical explanation of the rise of the

[25] Scholem rejected Buber's claim that hasidism had neutralized the gnostic elements of kabbalah and argued that only the messianic elements had been neutralized; see his 'Martin Buber's Interpretation', 241.

[26] Buber, 'Interpreting', 219–20.

[27] Scholem, 'Martin Buber's Interpretation', 233–4.

[28] This issue cannot be elaborated on here; it deserves a separate discussion.

hasidic movement. My basic assumption is that notwithstanding the fact that Lurianism, Sabbateanism, and kabbalistic *musar* literature (ethical and moralistic writings) all displayed a certain affinity of religious atmosphere and genre with hasidism and were closest to it in both time and space, the alternative sources which were available to the hasidic masters in the construction of their own spiritual configurations were both more numerous and more diverse. In print, more kabbalistic works were available to them than Sabbatean ones, more pre-Lurianic writings than Lurianic ones; and as for the kabbalistic *musar* literature, its popularity and admittedly immense influence must be placed in a larger context so as to permit a fuller acknowledgement of the parallel influence of purely theological works. These works, available in print, were instrumental in opening up kabbalistic doctrines to a wider public no less than the popular *musar* works.[29]

Let me state at the outset that I do not envisage the emergence of hasidism as a battle of books, ancient versus modern, in the mould of the eighteenth-century literary debates in England. The wide dissemination of a certain book or group of books was not in itself sufficient to account for a major spiritual phenomenon. Such an explanation of the rise of hasidism would be simplistic and no less blinkered than the explanations that I am trying here to counter. The quantitative criterion is meaningful only if it is corroborated by a qualitative one. In other words, I would consider the impact of one set of works as decisive in comparison with that of another, only if, in addition to its wider dissemination, it could be shown to be advocating a new type of ideology or theology. Consequently, the difference between presentation of a certain mystical paradigm in a popular ethical treatise and its presentation in an abstruse theological work seems to me to be only secondary.

The real issue, which goes beyond my emphasis on the sheer variety of available sources, is that the founders of the hasidic movement had access to a long series of written mystical materials which preceded the emergence of the Lurianic school and must be recognized as equally decisive in the formation of hasidism, notwithstanding the long time that had elapsed since their composition. Theoretically, the whole range of Jewish cultural traditions was available to the early hasidic masters, from the Bible to the most recent Sabbatean and Frankist innovations. Since I do not see why anyone should have preferred the more recent 'heretical' series of texts and concepts to the earlier and more authoritative materials, the emphasis placed by both Buber and Scholem on the crucial relevance of the 'modern' Sabbateans as against the 'ancient' authorities must be seen to have derived, at least to a certain degree, from a preconceived historiosophical model, though neither of them ever set it out in a systematic way. In order to be free of any such historiosophical constraints when attempting to pinpoint the most important factors that contributed to the formation of hasidism, we should allow for the widest range of possible factors before selecting any one as the most influential.

This amounts to a broader view of the relevance of the history of Jewish mysticism

[29] Among the kabbalistic works available in print were Cordovero's *Pardes rimonim* and Abraham Azulai's *Ḥesed le'Avraham*. For the influence of these works on hasidism see M. Idel, 'Die Rezeption der Kabbala in der zweiten Hälfte des 18. Jahrhunderts', *Hebräische Beiträge zur Wissenschaft des Judentums*, 1–2 (1986), 147, 152–7, trans. as 'Perceptions of the Kabbalah in the Second half of the Eighteenth Century', *Journal of Jewish Thought and Philosophy*, 1 (1991), 56–114; see 77–9, 89–103. Scholem, 'Martin Buber's Interpretation', 241. Cf. Scholem, 'Devekut', 223–5.

to the understanding of hasidic mystical thought. It seems to me that the central question in the development of Jewish mysticism is not the links between the various schools within a historical continuum in which the Zohar necessarily precedes the expulsion from Spain, the expulsion precedes (and thus explains) Lurianism, and Lurianic kabbalah precedes Sabbateanism which in turn is 'necessarily' followed by hasidism. In lieu of this developmental model I propose to discern in each manifestation of the Jewish mystical tradition, including hasidism, a series of choices made out of a variety of available alternatives. Divergent mystical paradigms had been available since the earliest literary expression of Jewish esotericism in talmudic times, and these were enriched by the medieval Jewish mystics.[30] By the thirteenth century, a variety of mystical paradigms had crystallized into several articulated mystical schools that can be defined phenomenologically, historically and geographically.

Kabbalah, for example, appeared at the end of the twelfth century in several distinct literary formulations, all of which are extant today. None of the variegated developments in the kabbalah of the thirteenth century had disappeared completely, in that they survived at least as literary documents that could surface and fructify the spiritual lives of later kabbalists. The assumption that Lurianism alone, or any other particular type of kabbalistic thought, was the single major drive behind all subsequent developments in Jewish mysticism, including Sabbateanism, is an oversimplification that has become all too prevalent in the literature of modern scholarship.[31]

Only the coexistence in Jewish mysticism of a variety of mystical paradigms can explain how hasidism was able to put back into circulation a whole range of mystical concepts which were either marginal to or altogether absent from Lurianism and Sabbateanism. How can anyone explain the centrality in hasidism of the concepts of *hitbodedut, hishtavut, hitpashetut hagashmiyut, bitul hayesh*, and *hitkalelut*, or extreme formulations of *unio mystica*, merely as a continuation of or a reaction to Lurianism and Sabbateanism, where all these mystical concepts were of little or no importance at all? In addition to Lurianism and Sabbateanism, the major speculative paradigms which were available to the hasidic masters before the middle of the eighteenth century were as follows:

1. The *heikhalot* literature.

2. Early kabbalah, which consisted mostly of Castilian treatises written in the thirteenth century, in the generation of the Zohar, and the Zohar itself. Let me quote in this connection only one pertinent passage from R. Meshullam Phoebus of Zbarazh's *Yosher divrei emet*, where we read: 'On the issue of the study of the writings of Luria, Blessed

[30] The suggestion that several mystical paradigms had been available in a variety of Jewish sources since the tannaic period cannot be elaborated on here. It is sufficient to point to talmudic literature which contains what Kadushin has termed 'normal mysticism', to the *heikhalot* literature, to the substantially different theories of *Sefer yetsirah*, and to the esoteric trends which generated medieval kabbalah. Moreover, the *heikhalot* literature itself represents a number of distinct strands of thought, as has emerged from studies by Joseph Dan, e.g. 'Anafiel, Metatron and the Creator' (Heb.), *Tarbiz*, 52 (1983), 456–8. See also Idel, *Kabbalah*, 74–111, and it is quite evident that the views expressed in the book *Sefer habahir*, ed. R. Margaliot (Jerusalem, 1978), differ substantially from those of the Provençal kabbalists. These issues will be discussed in greater detail in a forthcoming study of the emergence of kabbalah in Europe.

[31] This requires detailed discussion which cannot be undertaken here; see n. 55 below.

be his memory, I know that you will not undertake it alone, without a [master who is] greater than you, but you cannot find anyone. However, you should study *Sefer sha'arei orah* and *Ginat egoz* and, most of all, the Book of the Zohar and the *Tikunim*.'[32]

3. Besides Lurianic kabbalah, whose importance to hasidic masters is fully recognized by modern scholars, Cordoverian kabbalah was also highly influential. In print, it was no less available than the Lurianic corpus, and it circulated more widely than did the doctrines of Luria. It penetrated eastern Europe through two channels: through Cordovero's own speculative works, and through the popular expositions of his views that appeared in the *musar* literature.[33]

4. The mystical theories of the Maharal of Prague, which had been available in print for several decades, drawing on the authority of that highly respectable author and offering a less technical and more accessible world-view than that of all the kabbalistic treatises. Byron Sherwin and Bezalel Safran have pointed to the deep affinity between some of the Maharal's concepts and certain hasidic doctrines, and there is no doubt that this is a fertile field for future research on the emergence of hasidic mysticism.[34]

5. Renaissance kabbalah. This is a combination of Spanish kabbalah and various philosophies, from medieval Aristotelianism and Neoplatonism to Hermeticism and Renaissance Neoplatonism.[35] Although the impact of this type of kabbalah on further developments in Jewish mysticism has not been investigated closely, I venture to suggest that its influence was considerable. This was mostly an indirect influence, through the integration of some ideas of Renaissance kabbalah by Cordovero,[36] but there was possibly also a direct influence on eighteenth-century kabbalistic authors through the intermediacy of kabbalists such as Solomon Delacrut who had studied in Italy during the sixteenth century and whose works had been in print for a very long time. This, too, must be pursued in future studies of the emergence of hasidism. For the time being it seems obvious that the amalgam of kabbalah, philosophy and magic characteristic of some Renaissance figures can be detected also during the period of the crystallization of hasidism in the manuscript writings of Solomon Maimon, who came from the same area in which hasidism flourished.[37]

6. The Polish kabbalah of the first half of the seventeenth century, written by

[32] Meshullam Phoebus Heller of Zbarazh, *Yosher divrei emet* [Munkacz, 1905], para. 39; printed together with *Likutim yekarim* [Lemberg, 1792], ed. Abrahem Isaac Kahan (Jerusalem, 1974), 132*b*.

[33] See Idel, 'Die Rezeption', 147, 152–7, and cf. n. 42 below.

[34] See Byron Sherwin, *Mystical Theology and Social Dissent: The Life and Works of Judah Loewe of Prague* (London, 1982), 130–3, 138–40; Bezalel Safran, 'Maharal and Early Hasidism', in id. (ed.), *Hasidism: Continuity or Innovation?* (Cambridge, Mass., 1988), 47–144.

[35] See M. Idel, 'The Magical and Neoplatonic Interpretations of the Kabbalah in the Renaissance', in B. D. Cooperman (ed.), *Jewish Thought in the Sixteenth Century* (Cambridge, Mass., 1983), 186–242; id., 'The Magical and Theurgical Interpretation of Music in Jewish Sources from the Renaissance to Hasidism' (Heb.), *Yuval*, 4 (1982), 33–62.

[36] See M. Idel, 'Jewish Magic from the Renaissance Period to Early Hasidism', in J. Neusner, E. S. Frerichs, and P. V. McCracken Flesher (eds.), *Religion, Science, and Magic* (New York, 1989), 82–117.

[37] For my analysis so far see Idel, 'The Magical and Theurgical Interpretation', 57–60, and id., 'Jewish Magic', 100–6.

kabbalists such as R. Samson Ostropoler, R. Nathan Neta of Cracow and R. Aryeh Leib Pryluk.[38]

7. The ecstatic kabbalah which developed in Italy and in the east during the thirteenth and fourteenth centuries. This was still available in manuscripts which circulated in eighteenth-century Poland and could have influenced hasidism directly as well as indirectly, through the earlier influence of this school on the kabbalah of Safed.[39] Some of the concepts associated with the mystical path of hasidism derive ultimately from the interest of ecstatic kabbalah in methods by which to attain the mystical experience. It is also possible to detect some structural affinities between hasidic hermeneutics and the hermeneutics characteristic of ecstatic kabbalah, all of which have been ignored by modern scholarship.[40]

8. Medieval philosophy as formulated mostly by Maimonides, but also the more Neoplatonically inclined variety, such as could be found in the works of R. Abraham Ibn Ezra, R. Judah Halevi, or R. Isaac Abravanel.

I have enumerated only the most important bodies of medieval and post-medieval speculative literature that were available in more than one way to the early Polish hasidim. There is no doubt that they were also acquainted with at least some of the twelfth- and thirteenth-century pietistic theology formulated in the Rhinelands.[41] It is only if we take into account the entire range of paradigms—what I would like to call the mystical panorama—and the possible interplay of all its elements with one another, that we shall arrive at sounder and more responsible answers to the question of the emergence of the complex phenomenon of hasidic mysticism.

III

Against Buber's and Scholem's proximist explanations as discussed above, I should now like to propose a panoramic approach. Its thrust is that hasidism cannot be understood as a reaction to any physical or spiritual crisis but rather as the result primarily of the interaction between a long series of paradigmatic spiritual concepts and a variety of social factors. This presupposes the existence of an established educational pattern which introduced the student first to the study of the Bible and its commentators, then

[38] These works were printed long before the emergence of hasidism and were quoted by the early hasidic masters. On their kabbalah see Gershom Scholem, *Sabbatai Sevi: The Mystical Messiah*, trans. R. J. Z. Werblowsky (Princeton, 1973), 79–86; Yehuda Liebes, 'Mysticism and Reality: Towards a Portrait of the Martyr and Kabbalist, R. Samson Ostropoler', in I. Twersky and B. Septimus (eds.), *Jewish Thought in the Seventeenth Century* (Cambridge, Mass, 1987), 221–55; id., 'Jonah as the Messiah ben Joseph' (Heb.), in J. Dan and J. Hacker, (eds.), *Studies in Jewish Mysticism, Philosophy and Ethical Literature Presented to Isaiah Tishby* (Jerusalem, 1986), 269–311.

[39] See M. Idel, *Studies in Ecstatic Kabbalah* (Albany, NY, 1988), 126–34.

[40] This thesis will be the subject of a future study. For the time being, see M. Idel, 'Universalization and Integration: Two Conceptions of Mystical Union in Jewish Mysticism', in M. Idel and B. McGinn, (eds.), *Mystical Union and the Monotheistic Faith: An Ecumenical Dialogue* (New York, 1989), 32–3, 37, and Amos Goldreich's important observation in his edition of R. Isaac of Acre's *Sefer meirat einayim leRabi Yitsḥak demin Ako* (Jerusalem, 1984), 399–400.

[41] Idel, *Kabbalah*, 88–96.

to the basic halakhic texts, and only rarely, at the summit of the ideal curriculum, to a variety of mystical sources. Access to the mystical teachings was not always achieved directly, through the major *chefs d'œuvre* of kabbalah, but also through the more popular presentations of kabbalistic ideas in the ethical and moralistic literature, saturated as it was by Cordoverian kabbalistic concepts.[42] In principle, the study of complex kabbalistic texts, whether in print or in manuscript, was the prerogative of a small élite group. I can only assume that access to heretical kabbalah—Sabbatean or Frankist—was extremely limited, not only on the grounds of theological inhibition but also because of the limited diffusion of heretical texts.

In what follows I shall present my arguments in favour of the panoramic approach to the sources that moulded hasidic mysticism. The proximist approach, whether it advocated a relationship of reaction or continuation between hasidism and its immediate kabbalistic predecessors, was based on the assumption that the mystical works that exerted a decisive influence on the hasidic masters were all Lurianic, or perhaps to some extent Sabbatean versions of Lurianism. The scholars who advocated this approach implicitly excluded the possibility of interplay between different strands of kabbalistic literature, the only notable exception being Mendel Piekarz, who has stressed the importance of kabbalistic *musar* works. However, even he did not notice that some of the important 'hasidic' ideas which he traced back to these *musar* works originated in Cordoverian rather than Lurianic kabbalah.[43] Piekarz has made a significant contribution to our understanding of hasidism by demonstrating the importance of types of books other than the purely kabbalistic as possible sources for hasidic mystical concepts. However, he did not realize that the mystical paradigms which underlay the *musar* works he was consulting were not necessarily or even predominantly of Lurianic or Sabbatean origin. Although Piekarz's important work has undermined Scholem's Sabbatean thesis by pointing to a more variegated literature as the likely source of many hasidic concepts, his findings do not preclude the proximist explanation of the rise of hasidism, in that they point to a link of direct continuity between kabbalistic *musar* literature and hasidism.

While hasidism clearly drew on Lurianic kabbalah and on the ethical and moralistic *musar* writings—bodies of literature which were based overtly on Zoharic ideas and were sometimes even considered to be nothing more than profound interpretations of the Zohar—no serious scholar acquainted with hasidic texts would argue that hasidism ignored the Zohar itself. Although they were aware of the indispensability of Luria for the 'correct' understanding of the Zohar, hasidic masters nevertheless continued to compose their own original commentaries on this work. Beginning with the disciples of the great Maggid of Mezhirech, the literary genre of Zohar commentary flourished and infiltrated a large number of hasidic writings, almost all of which have been ignored by

[42] This point, which emerges clearly from any inspection of the sources, has not been appreciated fully by modern scholars who have attempted to account for the emergence of hasidic mystical thought. See e.g. the important study by Mendel Piekarz, *Biyemei tsemiḥat haḥasidut: Megamot ra'ayoniyot besifrei derush umusar* (Jerusalem, 1978), who seems to overlook this cardinal point, failing altogether to distinguish between the *musar* works which were profoundly influenced by Cordovero's kabbalah and those which drew on the Lurianic literature.

[43] See Idel, 'Die Rezeption'; B. Sack, 'An Inquiry into the Influence of R. Moses Cordovero on Hasidism' (Heb.), *Eshel Be'er Sheva*, 3 (1986), 229–46.

modern scholars of hasidism. This genre constitutes only one obvious demonstration of the coexistence within hasidism of different strata of kabbalistic literature, despite the fact that the hasidic masters themselves considered the latest developments in matters of kabbalah as the most profound and authoritative.

The question may be asked, is it possible to reconstruct the mystical panoramas that lay before the individual hasidic masters? I should like to stress that I do not believe the mystical panorama of the Baal Shem Tov to have been identical, or even similar, to that of the great Maggid. We must assume the existence of a whole range of panoramic views, each the product of the educational background and spiritual idiosyncrasies of the individual. No single presentation of such factors can be presumed to have functioned as the basic, universal panoramic view. However, in order to refrain from the excessive atomization of the academic discourse on the sources of hasidism, I shall outline the model of a broader landscape whose crucial features were shared, wholly or partially, by some or all of the hasidic masters.

As in viewing a physical landscape, the process of observing this spiritual landscape entails not only comprehensive or holistic perceptions but also linear connections between one point and another, the peculiar shift from one to the other determining also the unique quality of each spectator's vision. So, for example, if a person became acquainted first with Cordoverian kabbalah and only then with the Lurianic teaching, this could well affect his understanding of the very nature of Lurianism;[44] and the reverse would also be true. At times, the fascination with, or even fixation on, one attractive idea or cluster of ideas found in a particular kabbalistic source could well nourish a hasidic master for years, while all other points on the landscape would linger in view without affecting his perception substantially, however important or eye-catching they might be in themselves. Surely, the eighteenth-century masters of hasidism were not able to take in each and every detail of this vast landscape; no doubt, there were numerous blind spots which escaped their attention altogether. Moreover, an idiosyncratic perspective would yield an idiosyncratic view, and some of the masters had clearly misunderstood or distorted the 'real' spiritual concerns of the original sources. However, despite these limitations, there is no reason why we should exclude from their field of vision all but those developments of Jewish mysticism which were nearest to their own time.

A panorama exists objectively in the external reality of the spectator, but his perception depends on the peculiarities of his subjective stance. He recreates the landscape in his own consciousness, and thus it becomes not merely an internal reproduction of external sites but a synthesis of personal perceptions. In other words, the hasidic masters did more than merely select what they liked from among the discrete materials and paradigms which were available to them; they also synthesized them afresh. Thus, they built a series of distinct structures, based on a variety of syntheses of what was essentially the same range of older paradigms. Most of the materials out of which the new

[44] For the resolution, included in the anti-hasidic ban of Brody, that limited the study of Lurianic kabbalah to men over 40, and of Cordoverian kabbalah to men over 30, see Tishby, 'Hara'ayon hameshiḥi', 4–5; M. Idel, 'On the History of the Interdiction to Study Kabbalah before the Age of Forty', *AJS Review*, 5 (1980), 14–15, and cf. Solomon of Lutsk, introd. to Dov Ber of Mezhirech, *Maggid devarav leYa'akov*, ed. R. Schatz-Uffenheimer (Jerusalem, 1976), 1–2.

structures were built were accessible to all the early masters of hasidism, but the location of each component and the precise weight which was laid upon it may have differed substantially in each case. It is only when we acknowledge the full range of paradigms available to all the hasidic masters that we can begin to explain the presence in hasidism of concepts alien to both Lurianism and Sabbateanism as something new rather than as a mere reaction to earlier concepts or an attempt to neutralize them.

By way of illustration, let me compare the different solutions that the panoramic and the proximist approaches can supply to three central and highly controversial questions.

According to both Buber and Scholem, hasidism neutralized the messianic elements inherent in Lurianic kabbalah as a reaction against the fateful collapse of Sabbateanism. Lurianism had to be stripped of its putative messianic nature in order to function effectively in the new 'critical' conditions of mid-eighteenth-century Poland.[45] Scholem suggested, therefore, that the value of *devekut*, essentially confined to the inner process of individual redemption, had come to replace the collective messianism of the Lurianic school.[46] In principle, I accept Scholem's phenomenological diagnosis of what was most highly valued in hasidism,[47] although I deeply disagree with his historical explanation of this. Moreover, I question Scholem's very characterization of the Lurianic school as acutely messianic. As far as I am aware, neither he nor Buber has ever furnished any evidence in support of the claims that the hasidic masters were reacting against the allegedly acute messianism of their Lurianic and Sabbatean predecessors; nor am I aware of a single messianic passage stemming from Lurianic circles which was interpreted in hasidism in such a way as to smooth its 'acute' messianic edge. On the other hand, it can easily be demonstrated that it was not only the notion of collective messianism that was put aside, neglected or reinterpreted by the leading masters of early hasidism. This was true also of the messianically charged concepts of Erets Yisrael and the Temple, which were understood in hasidism as referring to personal perfection. Even the sacrosanct ten *sefirot* of theosophical kabbalah became, for most of the early hasidic masters, allegories of inner psychological states.[48] Thus it seems to me

[45] See Buber, *Hasidism*, 112–16; G. Scholem, 'The Neutralization of the Messianic Element in Early Hasidism', *Journal of Jewish Studies*, 70 (1969), repr. in id., *The Messianic Idea*, 178–202. Scholem's paper is a response to Tishby, 'Hara'ayon hameshiḥi', and cf. the more extreme formulation of Scholem's stance in R Schatz-Uffenheimer, 'Self-Redemption in Hasidic Thought', in R. J. Z. Werblowsky and C. J. Bleeker (eds.), *Types of Redemption* (Leiden, 1970), 207–12.

[46] Scholem, 'Neutralization of the Messianic Element', 180–202.

[47] I am inclined to accept Scholem's stand on this point, since the material adduced by Tishby in 'Hara'ayon hameshiḥi' is scanty and hardly representative. Although Tishby's evidence is convincing as regards the propensity to Lurianic eschatology of many non-hasidic kabbalists who were contemporary with the early phases of hasidism—a propensity much greater than Scholem would admit, the relative paucity of comparable hasidic material is surprising. See also R. J. Z. Werblowsky's 'Mysticism and Messianism: The Case of Hasidism', in *Man and his Salvation: Essays in Memory of S. G. F. Brandon* (Manchester, 1973), 305–13.

[48] This point was recognized by Scholem in 'Neutralization of the Messianic Element', 200, where he attributed the tendency to kabbalistic preachers, apparently active in the 16th–17th cents. However, Scholem did not show precisely what was novel in the hasidic spiritualization of these concepts, nor did he explain why messianism should have been spiritualized in hasidic circles as a fresh reaction to the heretical messianic doctrine if the tendency to spiritualize messianism had been present long before. See Idel, *Studies in Ecstatic Kabbalah*, 100–1; id., 'The Land of Israel in Medieval Kabbalah', in Lawrence A. Hoffman (ed.), *The Land of Israel: Jewish Perspectives* (Notre Dame, Ind., 1986), 178–80. On the spiritualization of the sefirotic ontology of theosophical kabbalah, which was already evident in 13th-cent. ecstatic kabbalah, and its early hasidic manifestations see Idel, *Kabbalah*, 146–53.

that what hasidism neutralized was the messianic idea *in general*, not only its Lurianic formulation. Hasidism did not engage in a battle specifically against Sabbateanism. Rather, its messianic posture was part and parcel of a larger scheme or religious paradigm which can be characterized as devotional, a historical mysticism, free from any concrete geographical ties.[49] While some aspects of this scheme had also served for polemical purposes, as did the attempt to counteract the heretical messianism of the Sabbateans and Frankists, it would nevertheless be false to reduce the entire scheme to a resolution of these quandaries alone. Since concepts such as *sefirot*, Erets Yisrael or the Temple did not originate in Sabbateanism and were free from any particular Sabbatean connotations, it would seem more reasonable to explain the spiritualization of these concepts in hasidism as originating in an earlier kabbalistic paradigm, where they had long been interpreted spiritually.

According to Scholem, *devekut*—a mystical value which represents the way to personal redemption—had come to replace the messianically charged Lurianic ideal of *tikun*. However, the mystical ideal of *devekut* did not originate in hasidism; it had existed in schools of Jewish philosophy as early as the thirteenth century,[50] and in the contemporaneous ecstatic kabbalah of Abraham Abulafia.[51] It would be very difficult indeed to ascribe to thirteenth-century sources the tendency to neutralize an ideal of active messianism; it is highly improbable in the case of the philosophers and verging on the absurd in the case of Abulafia, who had conceived of himself as a messiah and did not refrain from acting in this capacity in the public arena.[52] His own 'acute' messianism was not incompatible with the presentation of the personal union with God, or with the agent intellect, as a redemptive act, quite independently of the collective experience of the messianic advent.[53] We may infer from this example that the spiritual interpretation of messianism, or the 'neutralization' of the messianic idea in Jewish mysticism, was not new, at least not on the phenomenological level. Thus, we may assume that, at least in principle, the spiritual panorama which stretched before the masters of hasidism could include an area where *devekut*, but not *tikun*, was considered an eschatological endeavour. To assume this, it is not strictly necessary to prove that the entire paradigm of ecstatic kabbalah was known to the hasidim and used as an alternative to 'messianic' Lurianism. It would be sufficient to show that the importance of *devekut* as the paramount mystical value was accepted by them, even without any 'reactive' connection to Lurianic or Sabbatean kabbalah. This might have shaped their consciousness by way of an inner and organic development while external factors—historical, geographical, or theosophical—became marginal by comparison with their spiritual attainment at the moment of mystical experience. Thus, it is possible to

[49] See M. Idel, 'Some Conceptions of the Land of Israel in Medieval Jewish Thought', in Ruth Link-Salinger (ed.), *A Straight Path: Studies in Medieval Philosophy and Culture: Essays in Honor of Arthur Hyman* (Washington, 1968), 137–41.

[50] M. Idel, 'Types of Redemptive Activity in the Middle Ages' (Heb.), in Zvi Baras (ed.), *Messianism and Eschatology* (Jerusalem, 1983), 254–8; Werblowsky, 'Mysticism and Messianism', 308.

[51] Scholem, *Major Trends*, 140–1; Idel, 'Types of Redemptive Activity', 259–63.

[52] Scholem, *Major Trends*, 127–8; Idel, *Studies in Ecstatic Kabbalah*, 45–61. Cf. also Werblowsky's view that concepts related to historical and collective messianism coexisted in hasidic writings with the spiritual interpretation of messianism (Werblowsky, 'Mysticism and Messianism', 311–13).

[53] See Idel, *Studies in Ecstatic Kabbalah*, 6–18.

envisage a situation in which *devekut* moves to the centre of the mystical arena; this results in a complete restructuring of mystical thought along the lines of ecstatic kabbalah, despite the fact that the details of this type of mysticism may not be entirely known. The shift of focus to the spiritual value of *devekut* could automatically reduce the importance of the external factors in religion, including the dimension of historical time in connection with the eschaton.

A similar exercise can also be carried out in connection with the ideal of pantheism or, according to some scholars, immanentism—another important and controversial issue in hasidic theology. According to Scholem, pantheism is characteristic of hasidic thought,[54] and more recently Rachel Elior has proposed considering immanentism as a singular feature of hasidism.[55] However, this concept was not an innovation of the hasidic masters, but had been formulated long before them in older strands of kabbalah. As the hasidim themselves have acknowledged,[56] and as Scholem has rightly pointed out,[57] the direct source from which pantheistic and panentheistic formulations in hasidism were drawn was the views of R. Moses Cordovero. Thus, hasidism does not constitute a dramatic departure from any universally accepted view of God's transcendence; the hasidic masters simply preferred one available theological paradigm to another, in this case the more theistic Lurianic one. Moreover, one of the important illustrations of the immanentist perception in hasidic literature—the experience of contemplating God when observing a woman—was clearly extracted from the work of R. Elijah de Vidas, a disciple of Cordovero, who had quoted it from a lost treatise by R. Isaac of Acre, a kabbalist profoundly influenced by ecstatic kabbalah.[58] Although there is scope for further discussion of the peculiarities of hasidic pantheism or immanentism, the literary sources from which it was drawn are in full view.

That hasidic mysticism revolved round *devekut*, which was understood, at least in some cases, as *unio mystica*, while at the same time opting for a pantheistic theology is no mere accident. *Unio mystica* and pantheism were integrated already in the mystical paradigm of ecstatic kabbalah as two correlative concepts: it was possible to unite with God precisely because He permeated the whole of reality, and the continuous diffusion of the Divine facilitated the mystical encounter.[59]

The poverty of the proximist approach may be illustrated further by a more specific example. In attempting to identify R. Adam Ba'al Shem who, according to *Shivḥei haBesht*, had passed on his esoteric writings to the founder of hasidism, Scholem proposed that this legendary figure was one and the same as a certain Sabbatean author.[60] Nothing in the legends connected to this figure had suggested this identification; Scholem's resort to such a far-fetched explanation was undoubtedly based on his preconception of the importance of Sabbatean figures for the genesis of hasidism. As Chone Shmeruk has convincingly shown, the prehistory of the R. Adam legends can be

54 See Scholem, 'Devekut', 223–5.

55 R. Elior, 'Hazikah shebein kabalah laḥasidut: Retsifut utemurah', *The Proceedings of the Ninth World Congress of Jewish Studies* (Jerusalem, 1986), 107–14. Elior, apparently following Scholem, implicitly assumes that the only type of kabbalah to be taken into account as a point of reference for hasidic thought is the Lurianic one; see 108–9.

56 See Idel, 'Die Rezeption'.

57 Scholem, 'Devekut', 223.

58 See Idel, *Studies in Ecstatic Kabbalah*, 115–19.

59 Idel, *Kabbalah*, 154. See Scholem, 'Devekut', 223–4.

60 Scholem, *Major Trends*, 332–4.

traced to long before the emergence of either hasidism or Sabbateanism, in the early seventeenth century.[61] This once again highlights the need to allow for the possibility of richer sources of influence on early hasidism than either Scholem or Buber was willing to entertain.

The present chapter calls for the greater integration of the study of hasidic mysticism into the broader framework of Jewish mysticism in general. This could be achieved by the examination of all the mystical possibilities of the past that were open to the early founders of hasidism. Although the merit of such an approach has been acknowledged in principle here and there, in practice modern scholarship has hardly resorted to it at all.[62] In addition, phenomenological and comparative approaches should be adopted in order to interpret hasidism as a mystical paradigm in itself, alongside all other mystical paradigms, both Jewish and non-Jewish. This should take precedence over Scholem's historical approach, which reduced hasidic mysticism to a mere solution to a crisis and presented it as a potential source for the revitalization of Judaism today.[63] Important as both these concerns may be, they detract from the independent value and full stature of hasidism. Hasidism is to be understood not so much as a reaction or a solution to immediate crises, but rather as a synthesis of diverse mystical paradigms that were available in most of the preceding strands of Jewish mysticism.[64] Its vitality derives not so much from the fact that it provided an effective answer to a particular historical situation but from the ability to exploit the achievements of previous generations of Jewish mystics who had supplied the materials out of which a new mystical edifice could be built.[65] The precise nature of this edifice still awaits a more nuanced phenomenological description, which should identify those of its features which were most relevant to the spiritual demands of eastern European Jews and their descendants.

[61] C. Shmeruk, *Sifrut yidish bePolin* (Jerusalem, 1981), 119–39.

[62] Martin Buber, Joseph Weiss, Rivka Schatz-Uffenheimer, and other scholars writing on early hasidism all considered the question of the kabbalistic sources of hasidism a minor issue, in line with their common preconception that hasidism was simply a continuation or interpretation of, or in some ways a reaction to, Sabbatean Lurianism. Although Schatz-Uffenheimer did acknowledge the need to examine also the relevance of other kabbalistic sources, she did not do so (see her *Haḥasidut kemistikah*, 11). Only more recently, in studies by Tishby, Pechter, Sack, and Nigal, have the kabbalistic sources of hasidism been discussed in greater detail (e.g. Sack, 'An Inquiry'). However, rather than attempting to reconstruct the hasidic panorama of earlier kabbalistic materials, these studies focus on sporadic relations between the two bodies of literature.

[63] See Immanuel Etkes's critique of this view of hasidism as a popular response to a situation of crisis in 'Hasidism as a Movement: The First Stage', in Safran (ed.), *Hasidism: Continuity or Innovation?*, 1–26, esp. 23.

[64] The view that Jewish mysticism is capable of generating spiritual resolutions of historical crises is characteristic of Scholem and his students. See e.g. Dan, 'Historical Perceptions', 170–1, which stresses the importance of the historical crisis of the expulsion from Spain to the emergence of Lurianic kabbalah. I disagree also with Scholem's explanation of this; see my 'Universalism and Particularism in Kabbalah: 1480–1650', in D. B. Ruderman, *Essential Papers on Jewish Culture in Renaissance and Baroque Italy* (New York, 1992), 324–44 and *Kabbalah*, 264–6. See also Ivan Marcus, 'Beyond the Sefardic Mystique', *Orim*, 1 (1985), 40–7.

[65] Werblowsky, 'Mysticism and Messianism', 307.

TWENTY-FIVE

Yitzhak Schiper's Study of Hasidism in Poland

CHONE SHMERUK

By the beginning of the Second World War, Yitzhak (Ignacy) Schiper was a recognized authority on Polish Jewish history. We know now that in the very midst of the war, while incarcerated in the Warsaw ghetto, Schiper kept up his research and continued to write, persisting up to the very end.

A description of Schiper at that time appears among Emanuel Ringelblum's notes from the Warsaw ghetto, and brief and imprecise remarks about Schiper's wartime writings are also to be found in two memorial volumes, one in Hebrew and one in English, which were published in Schiper's honour. Ringelblum, who knew Schiper quite well, mentioned that Schiper had been working on several studies. One was a comprehensive work on the Khazars and their role in the earliest phase of Jewish settlement in eastern Europe—a topic which had occupied him in the years before the war. 'His other work written during the present war,' Ringelblum wrote, 'was a history of hasidism in the nineteenth century. This work was based on records of the Jewish community of Warsaw and on Polish archival material. These two works, together with a manuscript on Jewish autonomy and a number of other very valuable items, have been lost.'

It now appears that most of Schiper's manuscript on hasidism did in fact survive. Two of the original three bulky notebooks into which Schiper had copied his completed work were discovered several years ago by a young student of Hebrew at Warsaw University, Zbigniew Targielski. The two notebooks contain a total of 330 pages of Polish text, which Targielski has now published with his own introduction.[1] I should like to take this opportunity to express heartfelt thanks to Mr Targielski for identifying and rescuing the manuscript, as well as for permitting me to use material from what was, at the time of writing, his as yet unpublished introduction. Schiper's monograph is a brand plucked from the fire, a remnant of the fine historiographical literature produced by Polish Jewry, and testimony to the author's refusal to abandon the historian's mission even in the face of disaster and destruction.

The cover page of the first notebook is missing, but the front page of the second bears Schiper's own name and leaves no doubt that this is indeed Schiper's own

In this chapter Polish forms of place names are used.

[1] Ignacy Schiper, *Przyczynki do dziejów Chasydyzmu w Polsce*, introd. and notes by Zbigniew Targielski (Warsaw, 1992).

manuscript. The study is entitled *Przyczynki do dziejów Chasydyzmu w centralnej Polsce* ('Toward a history of hasidism in central Poland'). Schiper, in his own introduction to the work, defines 'central Poland' as 'the territory of the former Polish Kingdom': 'obszar byłego Królestwa Polskiego.'

There is no doubt that this is the work to which Ringelblum referred, not entirely accurately, in the passage I quoted earlier. Schiper himself, in introducing his study, notes that it was written in the Warsaw ghetto. Its recorded date of completion, which we read today with a shudder, was 'October of the terrible year 1942'. Schiper's words are sobering:

> We have written this study during stormy days, in the midst of the disaster facing Polish Jewry. As of now we cannot tell how it will end. The freshly inflicted wounds burning within us make it difficult to view our chosen subject with the necessary perspective. We may well ask, in fact, whether this subject still holds any importance in light of the tragedy that has befallen us and is occurring before our very eyes.

In early July 1943, less than a year after completing his book, Yitzhak Schiper met his death in the camp at Majdanek, outside Lublin.

The two surviving notebooks contain six chapters. The last one, the sixth, lacks a conclusion, but a reading of the chapter suggests that only a few pages are missing. We have no way of knowing how many further chapters were contained in the third notebook, or what topics they may have covered.

From the title of the work it is clear that Schiper aimed at presenting a history of the hasidic movement specifically in central Poland, in contrast with Simon Dubnow's well-known book which covered all of pre-partition Poland. And whereas Dubnow dealt with the period ending in 1815, Schiper extended his own study beyond that date.

The first chapter is a description of the earliest eighteenth-century 'focal points' (*ogniska*) of hasidism within the bounds of what Schiper calls central Poland. Such 'focal points' existed in the 1760s in several towns near Lublin: Ryczywół, Lubartów and, somewhat later, Sieniawa. In the 1770s hasidic activity spread to Opatów, known in Yiddish as Apt; to Żelechów; and to Nowy Dwór. During that decade we also detect the first signs of the movement's penetration into Praga, across the Vistula from Warsaw. The last twenty years of the century saw the rise of six new centres: Lelów, Przysucha, Kozienice, Czechów, and Lublin. Nevertheless, Schiper is of the opinion that, until the end of the eighteenth century, 'the Hasidic movement in Poland could not boast any significant successes'. The majority of the Jewish population, he asserts, were still anti-hasidic.

It should be pointed out that the locations mentioned are considered centres of hasidic activity solely because the rabbis officiating there were identified with the movement. Among them were R. Shmuel (Shmelke) Horowitz, who served as rabbi in Ryczywół from 1754 to 1766, and in Sieniawa from 1766 to 1773; R. Levi Isaac of Berdichev, who served first in Lubartów and later in Żelechów; R. Abraham Joshua Heschel, whose residence in Apt dated from before 1786; 'the Jew' of Przysucha; R. Israel of Kozienice; and the Seer of Lublin, who had lived in Czechów before moving to Lublin. These were some of the most distinguished figures in the history of hasidism, though not all of them remained in central Poland.

In his second chapter, which discusses the nature of hasidism in Poland during the second half of the eighteenth century, Schiper contends that the main proponents and leaders of the movement had come originally from Galicia, or else were heavily influenced by the Galician movement, particularly by R. Elimelekh of Leżąsk. This led them to adopt the idea of the zaddik as set forth in R. Elimelekh's book *No'am Elimelekh*, which was widely read in Poland. Schiper argues that it was not so much the philosophical as the more 'practical' aspects of hasidism that determined the specific course of its development in Poland. By the 'practical' aspects he means such elements as healing, atonement for sins, ecstatic prayer, joy in worship, and a negative attitude to scholasticism. Even more important, he writes, was the influence of the hasidic masters themselves, who were charismatic and dynamic figures. They and their entourage of disciples—the hasidic 'courts'—were magnets that attracted growing numbers of adherents, while setting a pattern of inner cohesion that was characteristic of Polish hasidism.

The third chapter deals with the historical and social background underlying the emergence of hasidism as a mass movement. The discussion here revolves around the activities of Judah the Pious of Siedlce, of Hayyim Malakh and of Gedaliah of Siemiatycze. Schiper also discusses the Polish ramifications of the notorious controversy between R. Jonathan Eybeschuetz and R. Jacob Emden, as well as the history of the Frankist sect. It is Schiper's view that these men and the groups around them were largely responsible for popularizing kabbalistic study in the years before the rise of hasidism. But the esteem in which kabbalah came to be held was counterbalanced by what Schiper chooses to call 'talmudism', a reference to classical rabbinic scholasticism.

The events surrounding the conversion of Jacob Frank and his sect to Catholicism served to heighten Jewish suspicion of any sort of religious deviation. This absolute vigilance against heresy was an important factor in hasidism, too, despite the movement's roots in earlier, less successful mystical trends. Schiper credits these previous trends with having introduced a number of important motifs which were later incorporated in hasidism: a love for and pilgrimages to the Holy Land, and support for Jewish settlement there. In the same chapter, Schiper goes on to discuss the function of folk beliefs, oaths, and the activities of itinerant holy men in the culture that proved so receptive to hasidism. Another factor adduced here by Schiper to account for the rapid spread of hasidism was the fact that the movement reflected popular resistance to earlier ascetic trends. Finally, he devotes several pages in this section to popular Yiddish literature and its role in the dissemination of hasidism.

The fourth chapter is explicitly polemical. From the very first sentences, Schiper challenges what was then the conventional wisdom, namely that 'hasidism took up the struggle of the common man against the exploiters who tyrannized the Jewish communities together with their accomplices and the rabbis; and that the zaddikim became the people's tribunes in defending the poor.' Schiper mockingly takes issue with the portrayal of hasidism as 'some form of utopian socialism or at the very least a counterpart to Rousseauesque ideas'. He himself is sure that the sources do not support any such view. Indeed, he asserts:

As to the hasidic movement in the central Polish provinces, it is easily shown that even in its early stages of development it transcended class distinctions and included supporters from all social strata, the well-to-do and even the very rich side by side with the poor; the well educated along with the illiterate; and by the same token, the community strong men as well as those who suffered at their hands.

The entire fourth chapter is devoted to this historiographical debate and is largely based on the example of the Warsaw Jewish community. In that city the fabulously wealthy Samuel Zbytkover and his sons were conspicuous supporters of hasidism, along with many from among the poor. This state of affairs may partly explain why in central Poland, unlike Lithuania, there was never a rabbinic ban against hasidism. Citing passages from sources quoted by other students of the subject such as Dubnow, Horodecky, and Zinberg, Schiper concludes that 'religious-national elements were decisive' in the development of the movement. Among these were the principles of love for the Jewish people and for the Land of Israel.

Drawing once again upon the Warsaw experience, Schiper also points to the hasidic campaign against the Frankist heresy as an important factor in the crystallization of Polish hasidism. He notes, in passing, that the Frankists who remained in Warsaw following Frank's baptism were not local figures but had come from the south-eastern frontier of pre-partition Poland.

In summing up this chapter, Schiper draws our attention to the characteristic institutional forms of hasidism: the *shtibl*, or prayer-room, and the zaddik's court. He asserts, somewhat surprisingly, that these 'represented neither a challenge to the inherited modes of Jewish communal organization nor a violation of Polish laws governing Jewish communities and religious societies; hence they were tolerated by both the community and the local authorities.'

In his fifth chapter, Schiper takes up the history of hasidism in central Poland from 1796 to 1815. He sketches several important figures: the Maggid of Kozienice, the Seer of Lublin, 'the Jew' of Przysucha, R. Abraham Joshua Heschel of Apt, and R. David of Lelów. A central issue which emerges here is the political stance of the hasidic movement during the Napoleonic wars, including the measures taken by the hasidic leadership to forestall such adverse legislation as compulsory military service for Jews (in 1808), the exclusion of Jews from government leaseholding, and the prohibition against Jewish innkeeping and liquor production (in 1812). The successes of the hasidic leaders in lobbying for Jewish interests tended to reinforce their authority and enhance their reputations, Schiper contends.

Further along in this chapter, Schiper discusses the beginnings of the Haskalah, the Jewish Enlightenment, in Poland. He pinpoints four early centres of the Enlightenment in this period: Hrubieszów, Zamość, Lublin, and Warsaw. Using Warsaw as his prime example, he describes the tension between the traditionalist camp, including the hasidim, and the maskilim or 'progressives', among whom there were already numerous cases of baptism. As for the hasidim, their momentum was temporarily checked in 1814 by the deaths of R. David of Lelów, the Maggid of Kozienice, and the Jew of Przysucha, while the Seer of Lublin died in the following year.

The sixth chapter, which is the last one in our possession, bears the title 'Hasidism in the Era of Reforms in Ethics and Customs, 1815–1830'. The longest among the chapters recovered, it is subdivided into three sections. The first of these is devoted to the development of the hasidic movement in the years prior to the Polish revolt of November 1831. It focuses on several of the outstanding figures in the movement and on the emergence of the first dynasties of zaddikim. Special mention is made of R. Simḥah Bunem of Przysucha, R. Menahem Mendel of Kock, R. Isaac Meir Kalish of Warka, and of Isaac Meir Alter of Gur, the author of *Ḥidushei haRim*, who founded the hasidic dynasty of Gur (Góra Kalwaria). Each one is discussed for several pages, though without any great depth of detail and without any analysis of their philosophies.

The second section deals with attitudes to the hasidic movement in Polish society and in Polish governmental circles. Here Schiper reviews the essay by O. Radominski, *Co wstzymuje reformę Żydów w kraju naszym i co ją przyśpieszyć powinno* ('What is responsible for the delay in our country of the reform of the Jews and how may it be hastened?'), published in Warsaw in 1820. Radominski compared the situation of Polish Jewry to that of German Jewry, and took hasidism to task for obstructing the spread of the Enlightenment. He therefore urged that a campaign be waged against the hasidic movement and its leaders.

The writer Julian Ursyn Niemcewicz also took note of hasidism in his 'Jewish' novel *Lejbe i Siora* ('Leib and Sarah'), which appeared in Warsaw in 1821. This was the first work of Polish fiction to deal with the Jewish issue from an Enlightenment point of view, and it too called for a struggle against hasidism. The book is filled with inaccuracies and utter fantasies about hasidim and hasidism. It is no accident that Niemcewicz quotes from and praises Radominski's pamphlet. In the course of his discussion of this theme, Schiper also cites Polish sources regarding the relationship between Prince Adam Czartoryski and the Maggid of Kozienice.

The local administration took an interest in hasidism well before the central authorities in Warsaw did so. During the years 1817–19 an anti-hasidic trial took place in Olkusz. In 1823 an investigation was conducted against the hasidic group in Płock. The interest of the central authorities was finally aroused by an investigation into the spread of the new 'sect' in the provinces of Cracow and Podlasie. At the end of 1823 the ministerial Committee for Religious Affairs asked the Supervisory Board in Warsaw to submit a documented report on hasidism. The resultant report was moderate in tone, even sympathetic, and allayed initial government fears. Further information about hasidism came from the Jewish censor Jacob Tugendhold, and from the baptized Jew and missionary Yeḥezkel-Stanislaw Hoge.

The final subsection in the sixth chapter is entitled, 'On the External Front'. Paragraph headings in this section refer to such topics as accusations of ritual murder; reforms in Jewish communal organization; the controversy over traditional Jewish garb; elementary schools for Jewish children; the government rabbinical seminary; the Jewish committee (Komitet Starozakonnych); liquor sales in inns; and the 'hasidic' extortion by the Jewish informer Y. M. Birnbaum. All are discussed in light of their ramifications for the hasidic movement.

The chapter, as we have it, is incomplete and, as I noted earlier, we do not know what other topics were addressed in the rest of Schiper's study. What we can say is that the book is an attempt to present the history of hasidism in Poland from its earliest 'focal points' in the 1760s at least until the November rising of 1831.

Schiper's interest in the history of hasidism may seem altogether surprising to those who are familiar with the main fields in which he worked. In the bibliographies included in both the Schiper memorial volumes we find only one item directly related to the history of hasidism: an essay on R. Israel Baal Shem Tov which was published in Yiddish in 1938.[2] Gershom Scholem's comments on that essay are well enough known and there is no need to dwell on them here.

Nevertheless, it now seems quite clear that during the 1930s Schiper undertook a number of studies that led him to attempt a general history of Polish hasidism. In his book *zydzi Królestwa Polskiego w dobie powstania listopadowego* ('The Jews of the Kingdom of Poland during the November Rising'), published in Warsaw in 1932, Schiper devoted part of one chapter to the hasidim and their Jewish opponents and presented previously unknown material from Warsaw. It is also not widely known that in 1939 Schiper published the first volume of a two-volume study on Jewish cemeteries in Warsaw. This book, whose date of publication is given as 1938, was never seen outside Poland, and I must thank Jerzy Tomaszewski of the University of Warsaw, who was able to locate a copy of the book and who supplied me with a photocopy of it.[3] In this book, too, we find a good deal of scattered material on hasidim in Warsaw from the end of the eighteenth century to the 1930s. The book is primarily based on the archives of the Warsaw Jewish community, which were lost during the Holocaust.

We may surmise that it was in the course of researching these two studies that Schiper found the material on hasidism that he would later use to write a separate monograph on the subject. Indeed, it is possible that the work on hasidism is but an expansion of the material which he included in his book on the Jews in the 1831 revolt.

Simon Dubnow's history of hasidism had already pointed to the need for a separate study of hasidism in central Poland. He himself devoted special attention to the subject in two sections of his book: section 36, which bears the title 'The New Center in the Polish Interior'; and section 46, 'The Napoleonic Conquest and the Hasidic Conquests in Central Poland'. These two sections, along with other material scattered throughout Dubnow's work, seem to have furnished Schiper with a good deal of the data for his own study. He also culled information from the works of Horodecky and Zinberg. Indeed, in the second chapter of his book Schiper openly states: 'We note at the out-set that our picture will not contain any facts that are not already known from the research of Dubnow, Horodecky, and Zinberg.' In that chapter in particular, which deals with the various schools of hasidic thought, the reader will not find much that is new. The same may be said of other sections in the book, which rely heavily on Schiper's predecessors.

Schiper was well aware of this, and that is why he was at pains to point out that it was chiefly in methodology that his own book differed from that of Dubnow. Whereas Dubnow based his work on hasidic and anti-hasidic literature, without having recourse to archival material, he, Schiper, placed his emphasis on external corroboration from

[2] The original Yiddish version of this essay, published in the jubilee volume of the newspaper *Heint* (1908–38) is not readily accessible and I have been unable to consult it. A Hebrew version appeared posthumously as Y. Schiper, 'R. Yisrael Baal Shem Tov udemuto basifrut haḥasidit hakedumah', *Hado'ar*, 35 (1960), 27: 525–6, 531–2; 28: 551–3.

[3] I. Schiper, *Cmentarze żydowskie w Warszawie: Wydawnictwo Gminy wyznaniowej Zydowskiej w Warszawie* (Warsaw, 1938).

other records, especially those of the Warsaw community, and on material in the library of the Krasinski family (Biblioteka Ordynacji Krasinskich).

In his introduction Schiper bemoans the destruction of the Warsaw community archives, apparently as a result of the bombing of Warsaw in September 1939. Since the Krasinski library was also later destroyed (in the course of the Warsaw uprising of 1944), we ought to regard the material that Schiper cites from these collections as the major contribution of Schiper's study, certainly as it stands in its present form: his work on the basis of that material now constitutes the only remnant we have of two major repositories of historical data. From that point of view, the most important parts of Schiper's study are undoubtedly the fifth and sixth chapters, in which he cites archival and Polish literary sources, rather than the earlier chapters, which are largely based on secondary literature. In addition, as I have already pointed out, the fourth chapter, which deals with the question of the alleged class character of the hasidic movement, also bears particular interest for the historian.

It is clearly impossible to evaluate Schiper's monograph properly, given its present, incomplete state and our ignorance of what the third notebook contained. None the less, we may be permitted to raise the question of the historical validity of an attempt to treat the hasidic movement in Poland as a separate entity. Can the movement's origins and development in central Poland be justifiably isolated from the history of hasidism throughout the rest of pre-partition Poland? In addressing this issue, we can hardly do better than to quote from Aaron Ze'ev Aescoly's well-known essay 'Hasidism in Poland':

> When we say 'Hasidism in Poland' we thereby mean to imply a distinction, a contrast with Hasidism outside Poland. There is some validity in this kind of distinction when we refer to the last hundred years of Hasidism: from the time of Napoleon to the First World War. During these hundred years the Hasidism of Poland was indeed distinctive, and Poland became the center for that kind of Hasidism.[4]

Without knowing of Schiper's work on Polish hasidism or of the recovery of part of his text, the Hebrew University's Center for Research on the History and Culture of Polish Jews decided some years ago to prepare a collection of essays on hasidism in Poland.[5] Together with my late friend and colleague Shmuel Ettinger, I felt that the subject deserved to be studied in its own right, in order to seek some understanding of its history and particular qualities. Our idea was to follow Aescoly's lead, though in greater depth. We defined our task chronologically and geographically as a study of hasidism in ethnic Poland in the post-partition period.

Now that we have before us Schiper's contribution, we can compare his approach with Aescoly's. Aescoly focused on portraits of the hasidic masters and their religious doctrines, based on hasidic literature. Schiper, in contrast, relied in his last chapters largely on Polish archival and literary sources, an area that was his forte. One may say, therefore, that in so far as Aescoly and Schiper overlap chronologically, they comple-

[4] A. Z. Aescoly, 'Haḥasidut bePolin', in I. Halpern (ed.), *Beit Yisrael bePolin* (2 vols.; Jerusalem, 1948–53), ii. 92.

[5] This has now been published as I. Bartal, R. Elior, and C. Shmeruk (eds.), *Tsadikim va'anshei ma'aseh: Meḥkarim baḥasidut Polin* (Jerusalem, 1994).

ment one another. Moreover, Schiper's sixth chapter, by focusing on Congress Poland, adds significantly to what we know of government attitudes toward hasidism from Pesach Marek's study regarding Russia and Raphael Mahler's book on Galicia and Poland.[6]

I view the collection of essays published in Jerusalem as a continuation of the work carried out by Dubnow before the war, of Schiper's book completed in 1942, and of Aescoly's essay of 1954. The collection includes a translation of Schiper's fourth and sixth chapters, saved from the ruins of the Warsaw ghetto. That has been our way of paying final tribute to a great historian.

[6] P. Marek, 'Krisis yevreiskovo samoupravliennie i khasidism', *Yevreiskaya Starina*, 12 (1928); Raphael Mahler, *Hasidism and the Jewish Enlightenment* (Philadelphia, 1985).

PART VII

CONTEMPORARY HASIDISM

TWENTY-SIX

Hasidism: The Third Century

JOSEPH DAN

I

THERE are various alternative dates for the beginning of the hasidic movement. One is from the probable start of the career of Israel b. Eliezer Besht as an itinerant preacher, usually set at around 1736. Another is from the establishment of the first hasidic 'court' by Dov Ber of Mezhirech after the Besht's death in 1760. Still another is from the beginning of the conflict between hasidism and its opponents, a conflict that started with the proclamation of the ban against the movement in 1772, and turned hasidism into a distinct historical phenomenon. From the literary point of view, the year 1780 could be seen as the beginning of hasidism, with the publication of *Toledot Ya'akov Yosef* by R. Jacob Joseph of Polonnoye, the first hasidic work to appear in print. But whichever date one chooses, there is no doubt that eventually hasidism became a major religious movement in Judaism. Now well into its third century, it is the most enduring phenomenon in Orthodox Judaism in modern times.

Taking into account both its longevity and the profound impact it has made on Jewish society, it seems remarkable that virtually all the histories of hasidism written in the present century have been focused on a short period, from the middle of the eighteenth century to no later than 1815. Moreover, some of the most important studies of hasidism, such as those by B. Dinur,[1] J. G. Weiss[2] and S. Ettinger,[3] were confined to the beginnings of the movement, while others, most notably S. Dubnow's,[4]

The lecture on which this chapter is based was delivered at a public session on the second evening of the conference of which this volume records the proceedings. I shared the platform with the late Professor Shmuel Ettinger. No one could imagine at the time that his contribution to the session was to be his last lecture on hasidism, and his untimely death a few months later was a blow to us all. I would like to offer this essay as a modest tribute to the memory of a great teacher and scholar whose insights and erudition were instrumental in shaping my own understanding of hasidic history.

[1] *Bemifneh hadorot* (Jerusalem, 1955), 81–227. Dinur was the first to produce, on the basis of ethical and homiletic sources, a balanced historical account of the social and spiritual forces which combined to create hasidism.

[2] J. Weiss, 'Reshit tsemiḥatah shel haderekh haḥasidit', *Zion*, 16 (1951), 46–105, repr. in A. Rubinstein (ed.), *Perakim betorat haḥasidut vetoledoteihah* (Jerusalem, 1977), 122–81, and compare Dinur, *Bemifneh hadorot*.

[3] S. Ettinger, 'The Hasidic Movement: Reality and Ideals', in H. H. Ben-Sasson and S. Ettinger (eds.), *Jewish Society through the Ages* (New York, 1971), 251–66, orig. pub. in *Cahiers d'histoire mondiale: Journal of World History*, 11: 1–2 (1968), 251–66, repr. in G. D. Hundert (ed.), *Essential Papers on Hasidism* (New York, 1991), 226–43.

[4] S. Dubnow, *Toledot haḥasidut* [Tel Aviv, 1930–1] (Tel Aviv, 1960). See esp. p. 37, where the period after 1815 is described as one in which 'the doctrines of Hasidism are subsumed under the cult of Zaddikism',

which purport to offer a comprehensive history of hasidism in fact dealt with it only up to the beginning of the nineteenth century. Dubnow wrote also a general history of the Jewish people, but the volume he dedicated to the nineteenth and twentieth centuries made only few and cursory references to the hasidic movement.[5] The entries on hasidism in modern Jewish encyclopedias, while attempting to cover the entire history of the movement, similarly concentrate almost exclusively on the early decades; chronological and genealogical charts are sometimes substituted for proper historical discussion of the last 150 years of hasidism.[6] The movement is often portrayed as a 'late medieval' or 'early modern' phenomenon, totally irrelevant to contemporary Jewish life.

Gershom Scholem described hasidism as the 'last phase' in a Jewish mystical tradition that spanned nearly two millennia. Yet at the conclusion of his account of the movement in the last chapter of *Major Trends in Jewish Mysticism*,[7] he appeared, with some regret, to view his subject as a phenomenon of the past. It was as if hasidism, indeed Jewish mysticism in general, had lost its vitality, and all that one could do with it now was to record its traditions and write its history. When he wrote this chapter of the book in or around 1939, Scholem clearly could not conceive of hasidism as a relevant, vital part of Jewish history in the twentieth century. Indeed, the last paragraphs of the chapter read like a eulogy for a vanishing world.

The contrast between this view of hasidic history and the reality of Jewish life in the late twentieth century could not be greater. The hasidism of today cannot be treated as a lifeless relic from the past. It appears to have made a complete adjustment to twentieth-century technology, the mass media, and the intricate politics of democratic societies without surrendering its traditional identity in the process. Unlike other rigorously orthodox societies and groups grappling with the problem of integration into contemporary life, hasidism has succeeded in keeping its young within the fold despite the allures of Western society and its modern lifestyle, and it has even managed to attract new adherents from all walks of life, including senior academics, scientists, economists, and members of the armed forces, both in Israel and in the United States. The hasidic way of life, so at odds with the life of the contemporary megalopolis, has demonstrated not only resilience but even spiritual superiority to twentieth-century Western culture.

This becomes even more remarkable if we consider the conditions from which the hasidic movement emerged in eastern Europe in the middle and second half of the eighteenth century. Hasidism is often said to have been the most authentic product of

while in 1870 begins the period of 'complete decline'. But compare the concluding paragraph of the preface where Soviet tyranny, administered by the grandchildren of hasidic rabbis, is described as causing the physical destruction of hasidism.

[5] S. Dubnow, *Divrei yemei am olam* (10 vols.; Tel Aviv, 1929–39; 1958), ix. 127–30. Dubnow hardly mentions hasidism in either of the two volumes (ix and x) which deal with the 19th and 20th cents.

[6] The two general outlines of the history of hasidic thought which appeared in the last generation are I. Tishby and J. Dan, 'Torat haḥasidut vesifrutah', *Hebrew Encyclopaedia*, xvii (1969), 769–821, repr. as a pamphlet by Academon, Jerusalem, and in Rubinstein (ed.), *Perakim betorat haḥasidut*, 250–312, and R. Schatz-Uffenheimer, 'Teachings of Hasidism' and 'Interpretations of Hasidism', *Encyclopaedia Judaica*, vii (1971), 1403–20.

[7] 1st pub. 1941, 2nd edn. New York, 1954, 345–50. But in an essay pub. in 1964 (see 'Mistikah yehudit beyameinu', in id., *Devarim bego* (Tel Aviv, 1975), 75–7) Scholem acknowledged the revival of hasidism after the Holocaust.

the Jewish *shtetl*—that environment in which the Jews often constituted the majority of the population, and where they formed an autonomous social and cultural entity. This entity was distinguished by a number of peculiar features, which included the impact of kabbalistic symbolism and kabbalistically charged ethical works and sermons,[8] the residue of Sabbatean ideas, the tension between the wealthy, learned élite and the poor (especially the articulate poor—itinerant preachers and teachers), as well as other social and economic divisions. These and other factors had combined to infuse hasidism with an original, revivalist vigour which enabled it, in the course of the last decades of the eighteenth century and the first two decades of the nineteenth, to become a major spiritual and social force, engulfing hundreds of thousands of adherents. It seems that every single one of the distinctive features that marked the hasidic movement from the very start was directly and authentically a product of the peculiar circumstances of eastern European Jewry at that time; most of these circumstances did not obtain anywhere else in the Jewish world nor in any other period in the history of the Jews in eastern Europe. The Yiddish language, the popularity of kabbalistic symbolism, itinerant preachers, the *shtetl*—this was the unique landscape of the region in which alone, so it seemed, the growth of hasidism was possible.

How could a movement so rooted in a specific historical environment be expected to survive in contemporary Manhattan, Amsterdam, or Tel Aviv? What could be common to the *shtetl* of two and a half centuries ago and the modern, international culture of the United States, Europe and Israel? Yet hasidism has not only survived, but has been able to grow and flourish in the utterly alien environments in which history has forced it to make its new home.

Two interconnected questions present themselves to the historian of religion who is faced by this remarkable phenomenon: (*a*) What was it that enabled hasidism to make the adjustment and flourish in new circumstances? (*b*) Should the history of hasidism from its early beginnings be reviewed in the light of the contemporary achievements of the movement? If this history is to be considered a continuous whole, then surely, just as the early beginnings can provide a key to the understanding of later developments, so recent developments may well shed light on hasidism when it first began.

II

As little as forty or even thirty years ago, it was indeed possible to claim that hasidism was a phenomenon of the past, irrelevant to Jewish life in the postwar era. The hasidic communities still active at that time, mostly in Jerusalem and New York, were very small, and they seemed to function as anachronistic remnants of a world which no longer existed. The recent hasidic revival has come as a complete surprise; I am not aware of anyone who anticipated such a turn of events.

In the past hundred years, hasidism has faced and overcome extraordinary hardships. The upheavals in eastern Europe during the last two decades of the nineteenth

[8] See esp. the exhaustive study by M. Piekarz, *Biyemei tsemiḥat haḥasidut: Megamot ra'ayoniyot besifrei derush umusar* (Jerusalem, 1978).

century, followed by the emigration of hundreds of thousands of Jews to western Europe and the Americas, eroded, both economically and socially, the communities in which hasidism had once flourished. The Enlightenment drove many hasidim, especially the young, away from the traditionalist fold into modern secularism. This was followed by the pogroms of the 1905 revolution which further undermined the existence of hasidic communities in Russia; new ideologies such as socialism and Zionism offered visions of quasi-messianic redemption, and many youngsters responded by deserting their hasidic families. This erosion culminated with the upheavals of the First World War, the Russian revolution and civil war, and the annihilation of Jewish culture in the Soviet Union under Stalin. The traditional basis of the hasidic movement was completely wiped out, and the Jewish *shtetl* of the nineteenth century vanished without a trace. From every point of view, it seemed that hasidism could not survive as a spiritual force in post-1917 Europe.

Yet it survived, if not in Russia then in the relatively new hasidic communities in other east European countries, especially Hungary and Romania, where hasidism flourished and grew. Hasidic courts that had been banished from Belorussia and Ukraine found new homes in Warsaw and other Polish cities. Hasidic leaders who escaped from the Soviet Union set up new synagogues, schools, and community centres for their followers in the large, Westernized cities of Poland, ignoring the presence of Jewish secularism all around them. They continued to be identified by the names of the old towns in which they had been established during the previous century, so that the same dynasties continued to attract hasidic followers to the newly founded centres in Poland. By the fourth decade of the present century it seemed as though hasidism had overcome the crisis and re-established itself successfully on new grounds.

However, at the height of this process of rehabilitation, the hasidic world of eastern Europe was destroyed once again, this time with the efficiency and thoroughness of the Nazi murder machine. The Holocaust engulfed virtually the whole of Europe, and now there was nowhere to go, no alternative to the burning centres in Poland, Hungary, and Romania. A handful of hasidic leaders managed to escape to the United States or Erets Yisrael, but in most cases entire hasidic communities, including their leaders and their families, were murdered in gas chambers or shot.

In 1945 there seemed no hope for the hasidic movement. The Jewish people was now directing its energies to the struggle for the establishment of the State of Israel: Zionism seemed to be the only effective Jewish answer to the Holocaust. Thus by 1950 the few remnants of hasidic communities that survived the Holocaust—mostly elderly survivors who could not find their place in the new reality of the postwar era—seemed totally out of line with the main current of Jewish history.

And yet, as little as one generation later, hasidism has become the most vigorous and fastest-growing force in religious Judaism. Hundreds of hasidim fly regularly to meet their leaders across continents; video cassettes carry the leaders' sermons to their followers all around the globe; young hasidim are making careers in computing, the diamond trade, Israeli or American politics. Hasidic communities flourish, both demographically and economically, and they are accepted by governments and municipal authorities (for example, in Jerusalem and New York) as an integral part of society and a political force to be reckoned with. The most remarkable phenomenon is, I believe, that hasidism has achieved this integration into Western society in the final decades of the twentieth century without forfeiting either its traditionalist way of life or its traditional spiritual values; rather, its adherence to the old norms seems firmer than ever before. Hasidic communities exhibit self-confidence and are firm in the belief that the surrounding world should not only accommodate them but even surrender some of its own values to suit their needs. The status and image of hasidism within Judaism has been completely transformed in a brief period of no more than thirty years.

One of the most significant indications of this change is the new relationship between hasidism and Oriental Jewry, communities with which the movement had no connection whatsoever prior to the Second World War. Most hasidic communities are still predominantly Ashkenazi, consisting almost exclusively of the descendants of hasidic families from eastern Europe. But some hasidic groups—especially Habad—have managed to integrate many of those who came to Israel from the Mediterranean countries soon after its establishment. Habad is very active among North African Jews, not only in Israel but also in Morocco and France, where they have succeeded in absorbing them into their network of schools and religious academies. Other hasidic groups with an interest in spreading their message more widely (many do not share this interest) followed Habad by establishing close connections with various Oriental Jewish communities. As a result, the colourful robes traditionally worn by the Jews of the Levant are gradually disappearing from the streets of Jerusalem to be replaced—especially among the young—with the black eighteenth-century attire of east European hasidism. Moroccans and Yemenites alike are forsaking their traditional customs not, as one might have expected, in favour of the international culture of the late twentieth century, nor for the 'Israeli' kibbutz or military styles of life, but rather for the customs created in the hasidic courts of Mezhirech and Lyady and preserved by their descendants long after the destruction of the world in which they had originated. It is as if the landscape of the Moroccan Diaspora has been replaced by the landscape of the Ukraine in the streets of the capital of the State of Israel. Jews of Sefardi origin who have been educated in hasidic yeshivot now use Yiddish as the language of their religious life, while Hebrew is confined to everyday, non-religious purposes—a total reversal of the traditional relationship between the two languages. It seems that nothing can better illustrate the spiritual strength of hasidism today.

This phenomenon is closely related to another which is no less significant. I refer to the impact of the hasidic revival on the traditional opponents of hasidism, the mitnaggedim. Immediately after the Holocaust it appeared as though the long tradition of enmity between hasidim and non-hasidim (often called 'Litvaks', since it was in Lithuania that the struggle against hasidism began and was most successful) had become a historical memory of little relevance to the present. Intermarriage between the two groups was on the increase, and the sense of solidarity among those who had suffered together and survived the great hardships of the Holocaust appeared to be displacing traditional animosities. What happened, in fact, was precisely the opposite. In the past two decades the controversy between hasidim and mitnaggedim has come to life, once again dividing the two strictly Orthodox groups from one another. In the elections in Israel in November 1988 this was given clear political expression, when the two Ashkenazi Orthodox parties were divided precisely in terms of their hasidic–

mitnaggedic orientation (with the exception of one hasidic group, whose enmity towards all fellow hasidic groups had outweighed its traditional hostility to the mitnaggedim). The much publicized controversy between Rabbi Shach, the leader of the mitnaggedim in Jerusalem, and Rabbi Menachem Mendel Schneerson, the late Brooklyn-based leader of Habad, is the clearest manifestation of the revival of the old east European schism.

While the open conflict between the two camps has intensified, they have begun—paradoxically and unexpectedly—to resemble each other in a number of significant ways. On the one hand, the hasidic communities continue today the process which began in early nineteenth-century hasidism of re-embracing the 'mitnaggedic' values of talmudic study and meticulous observance of halakhah; so much so that the most extreme forms of Orthodoxy in halakhic matters today are more likely to be championed by the hasidim than by the somewhat more lax mitnaggedic rabbis. On the other hand, the opponents of hasidism are increasingly inclined to adopt some of the most distinct characteristics of hasidic life, notably the veneration of the leaders. The 'doctrine of the zaddik'—the belief in the need to affiliate with a living representative of the divine world on earth—has been the most important ideological distinction between hasidim and mitnaggedim, and the hasidim were accused by their traditional opponents of practising idolatry by their excessive veneration of fellow human beings. But in reality, scenes which were once peculiar to the hasidic 'court' are now commonly witnessed in the mitnaggedic yeshivot: hundreds of disciples and students follow the head of the *yeshiva*, the venerated teacher wherever he goes, eager for a glance or a touch; they ascribe to him superhuman qualities, believe him to be in possession of divine secrets, and, most significantly, value personal loyalty to the teacher above any ideological commitment.

Furthermore, the mitnaggedim, like the hasidim, are striving to integrate Sefardi Jews into their ranks, and to this end form alliances with their traditional rabbinic leadership. Hasidim and mitnaggedim are thus competing to gain followers among the same groups, enhancing both the similarity and the enmity between them. Those hasidic groups (again, Habad takes the lead) which have become engaged during the past two decades in encouraging secular Jews to 'return' to orthodoxy—the *ba'al teshuvah* movement—have clashed with mitnaggedim who are active in the same field, again contributing to the blurring of distinctions while increasing rivalry and conflict between the two groups.

It is not unusual in the history of ideological conflicts for the opposing sides to adopt each other's norms and mannerisms. The interesting fact in the case of the hasidic–mitnaggedic schism is that, while in the past the hasidim were the ones who found it necessary to adopt many mitnaggedic norms, today it seems that the mitnaggedim are adopting hasidic values and traditions; their rabbis are now expected to be not only Talmud scholars but also charismatic leaders in the hasidic style. This is yet another indication of the impact of modern hasidism on the contemporary Jewish world.

The renewed force and vitality of the hasidic movement appear to be increasing, and it seems likely that the processes outlined above will continue in the coming decades. The hasidic community enjoys a high birth rate; college-graduate hasidic women in

Brooklyn and Jerusalem commonly raise six to eight children and educate them to a high standard. Integration into the modern technological economy has not had an adverse effect on the hasidic family; middle- and high-income families have become increasingly common, testifying to the sound financial basis of the hasidic revival. This has led Israeli and American politicians to treat the hasidic communities with respect, investing them with legitimacy in the wider non-Orthodox or non-Jewish community. The attraction of hasidism to secular or non-hasidic Jews, whether of Ashkenazi or of Oriental origin, has shown no sign of abating, even though the numbers involved in the various *ba'al teshuvah* movements are never large; a few cases of prominent people who have joined the hasidic community are enough to give hasidism the image of an ascending power in Judaism.

It seems, therefore, that the growing impact of hasidism on the Jewish world is not a transient phenomenon but a major trend in contemporary Judaism. Well into its third century of existence, hasidism stands out as one of the most enduring religious movements in Jewish history, with no other rival but the Reform movement for the status of the most significant development in modern Judaism. It is impossible, therefore, to go on viewing it today as a movement which reached its peak before 1815 and has been declining ever since. The time is ripe for a revaluation of hasidic history as a whole, and the essential nature of hasidism must be redefined in the light of its recent achievements.

III

Historians of hasidism were right to stress that the hasidic phenomenon was deeply rooted in the unique social, economic, and spiritual conditions of the Jewish *shtetl* of eighteenth-century eastern Europe.[9] Hasidism was indeed the product of social tensions, the influence of heretical groups and various kabbalistic ideas popularized by itinerant preachers. While this reconstruction of the background to the rise of hasidism is essentially accurate, it seems totally irrelevant to the development of the movement in the twentieth century, and cannot account for the hasidic revival of the past two decades. A new evaluation of the factors that combined to give rise to the hasidic movement in the middle of the eighteenth century is called for so as to highlight those that can be shown to have led directly to the unexpected turn of events in our own time.

In attempting to explain the emergence, or the revival, of any popular religious movement, the historian of ideas would naturally tend to search for an original set of concepts or ideology which may account for its popular appeal. Accordingly, the present revival of hasidism, which has expressed itself primarily in terms of communal organization and political power, would suggest to the historian the underlying presence of new ideological and spiritual drives that may be related in some way to the cataclysmic events in Europe in the twentieth century, culminating with the Holocaust (if not necessarily with the establishment of the State of Israel).

Surprisingly, and somewhat disappointingly, the search for the spiritual or ideological foundations of the present revival of the hasidic movement has yielded virtually

[9] See above, nn. 1–4, 7–8.

nothing. Not only are new ideas apparently absent, but the old spiritual teachings are giving way to a new emphasis on the external features of Jewish life. The insistence on a strict code of dress, for example, which provides subtle differentiation of particular hasidic affiliation, status and rank, and which has turned hasidic dress into something of a military uniform, directs all spiritual energy towards the preservation of external minutiae rather than towards any religious ideology, traditional or novel. What contemporary hasidism communicates to the diverse groups and communities within its orbit of influence is the message of unrelenting adherence to the behavioural patterns of the past two centuries. These are regarded as the timeless, essential core of authentic Judaism. It is paradoxical that such a nostalgic adherence to the past is coupled with a complete economic and political integration in contemporary reality. To operate within this dichotomy of orientations towards the present and the past requires a great deal of confidence in the values inherent in the way of life dictated by the hasidic leaders.

The achievements of contemporary hasidism, then, cannot be attributed to any fresh ideological response to the course of Jewish history in the twentieth century. The unexpected strength of the reinvigoration of hasidism must have its origins in a different realm: that of hasidic spirituality and tradition. There seems to me little doubt that this has been the profound belief in the supernatural powers of the mystical leader, the zaddik. The success of contemporary hasidism is based almost exclusively on the charismatic allure of the leader.

The union between mysticism and communal leadership is relatively recent in the history of Judaism. Its first systematic expression was the belief in the mystical messiah, Shabbetai Zevi, in the second half of the seventeenth century. The theology of Nathan of Gaza, Shabbetai Zevi's prophet, based the relationship between the messiah and the People of Israel on the principles of faith and redemption: the messiah acquires spiritual force from the personal faith invested in him by the people. He employs this power in the struggle to overcome the forces of evil, and thus he enhances both individual and national salvation for the Jews. Using kabbalistic symbolism, Nathan describes the process whereby a divine power, the messiah, is sent forth by God to lead the people in the struggle for redemption.[10] Charismatic leadership and mystical symbolism combine to create a structure in which the leader achieves the aims of the people by using their faith as his main weapon.

The hasidic doctrine of mystical leadership by the zaddik reflects some aspects of Nathan's theory of mystical leadership by the messiah but departs from it in a number of significant ways. The zaddik, according to R. Elimelekh of Lyzhansk and other disciples of the Maggid of Mezhirech[11] is responsible for the well-being of his particular community during his own lifetime, unlike the Sabbatean messiah, who was responsible for all the people of Israel throughout history. It is as if the hasidic teachers had fragmented the Sabbatean concept of leadership, each fragment retaining some characteristics of the whole. The zaddik, like the messiah, moves spiritually between the

[10] G. Scholem, *Sabbatai Sevi: The Mystical Messiah*, trans. R. J. Z. Werblowsky (Princeton, 1973), 45–80, and compare J. Dan, 'The Problem of Mystical Leadership' (Heb.), in A. Belfer (ed.), *Manhigut ruḥanit beyameinu* (Tel Aviv, 1982), 63–9.

[11] See esp. R. Schatz-Uffenheimer, 'Lemahuto shel hatsadik baḥasidut', *Molad*, 18: 144–5 (1960), 365–78.

material worlds and the divine, driving evil out from his followers and bringing them salvation both on the spiritual level—in terms of repentance, for instance—and on the material level by securing their health and prosperity ('sons, health and livelihood', following the ancient rabbinic formula). The community on its part assists the zaddik spiritually by placing its faith in him, while assisting him materially by supplying his worldly needs. The cosmic dimensions of the Sabbatean redemption process were reduced in the hasidic doctrine of the zaddik to an everyday structure of interdependence between the leader and the community, who supply each other with all their needs, spiritual and worldly.[12]

It seems that adherence to their hereditary zaddikim was the main factor, if not the only one, which secured the preservation and renewal of the hasidic communities after the upheavals of recent history. Wherever an effective heir to a dynastic line of leaders could be found, the community was rebuilt around him and revived its old tradition. But wherever the line had died out, or the dynastic heirs were ineffective, the community declined and eventually vanished. The strongest link between contemporary hasidic communities and their eastern European origins is the unbroken line of succession to the office of zaddik which serves as a bridge between pre-Holocaust and post-Holocaust existence. The specific characteristics of each hasidic community seem to be determined more by the personalities of their leaders in recent times than by the ideology of their eighteenth- and nineteenth-century forebears.

After the First World War, and again after the Second, hasidic communities were re-established wherever their leaders chose to reside, whether in Israel, New York or elsewhere. Hasidic centres overlap to a large extent with the places of residence of the zaddikim. The personal attitudes of the leaders towards such issues as the State of Israel, modern technology, secular Jews, and the like determine the social character of their communities. Their personal relationships with other Jewish leaders dictate the precise positions of their communities on the political map of the State of Israel.

In general, the hasidic communities of today differ from non-hasidic ultra-Orthodox communities inasmuch as they subscribe to the doctrine of the zaddik, expressing their faith in his redemptive powers by a variety of practices which constitute his 'cult'. Individual hasidic communities may differ from one another in particular norms and customs, but no more significantly than do other ultra-Orthodox groups. Indeed, the term 'hasid' itself cannot be used in the absolute, traditional sense of 'pious' but is always constructed with the name of a specific community and its leader: 'Satmar hasid', 'Lubavitch hasid', 'Gur hasid', and so forth, a construction in which the term 'hasid' has acquired in Hebrew the meaning of 'follower of' rather than 'pious'. Hasidism today constitutes a distinctive current in Orthodox Judaism only inasmuch as its leadership is based on mystical ideas and symbols; it does not possess a religious ideology of its own. Without the mystical dimension of the leadership and its cultic manifestations, hasidism would be virtually indistinguishable from ultra-Orthodox Judaism in general.

[12] A new dimension of the doctrine of the zaddik was opened up recently by R. Elior in her study 'Between *Yesh* and *Ayin*: The Doctrine of the Zaddik in the Works of Rabbi Jacob Isaac, the Seer of Lublin', in A. Rapoport-Albert and S. J. Zipperstein (eds.), *Jewish History: Essays in Honor of Chimen Abramsky* (London, 1988), 391–456.

Some of the early historians of hasidism were inclined to minimize the role of the zaddik in hasidism, or even to see in it one of the early signs of hasidic decline. A doctrine which denied the individual direct contact with God, and insisted that religious fulfilment could be achieved only through the intermediacy of a spiritual leader who was himself a human manifestation of the Divine, seemed to them intolerable and could not be admitted as an authentic and integral part of what was evidently an important development in early modern Judaism.

For hundreds of thousands of Jews to have adopted this concept of mystical leadership and to have shaped their lives accordingly in the Age of Reason, after Mendelssohn, was anachronistic. This assessment appeared to be supported by the fact that the doctrine of the zaddik was not central to the teaching of hasidism in the first two generations of the leadership. In the traditions associated with the founder of the movement, Israel Baal Shem Tov, and in those associated with his disciples, R. Jacob Joseph of Polonnoye and R. Dov Ber of Mezhirech, the doctrine of the zaddik was present only in abstract terms, unrelated to any actual social structure of leadership within any particular community. Moreover, the hereditary aspect of the cult of the zaddik did not develop in the hasidic movement until the early decades of the nineteenth century. It was possible to assume, therefore, that the notion of mystical leadership was not an integral element of the teaching of early hasidism. The centrality of the doctrine of hereditary zaddikism in later generations was regarded by many as a distortion of the original spirit and a debasement of hasidism.

The vast literature of quasi-hasidic tales assembled or written by modern, non-hasidic authors has also tended to understate the significance and full implications of the doctrine of the zaddik in hasidism. Many of the tales by Y. L. Peretz, for example, are focused on the simple hasid while neglecting the all-important role of the zaddik in his life. Other authors have depicted the zaddik as a wise and pious individual, altogether ignoring his divine dimension and hereditary status. This, coupled with the negative attitude of the historians towards the phenomenon of the 'cult' of zaddikism, has created a false image of early hasidism as a movement headed by pious and dedicated leaders whose mystical dimension is totally obscured. This may explain, at least in part, the surprise with which the non-hasidic public has greeted the emergence of a powerful new leadership in the hasidic movement of the last generation.

If contemporary hasidism has indeed drawn its dynamism and vitality from no other source but this charismatic mystical leadership, then the following historical question may be asked: can the hasidic revival in the twentieth century provide any insight into eighteenth-century hasidism? Is it possible that the same source of power and energy which has nourished contemporary hasidism in New York and Bnei Brak fuelled it during its period of rapid growth in pre-Napoleonic Russia? Can the third century of hasidism teach us anything about the first? I believe that this direction of enquiry may prove to be one of the most interesting and productive in the historiography of early hasidism.

Nearly twenty-five years ago, when I was assisting Professor Isaiah Tishby in the preparation of the essay on the doctrines and literature of hasidism for the first Hebrew encyclopedia,[13] we asked ourselves the same question, albeit from a different point of view: what are the essential teachings which originate in hasidism, are shared by all its

[13] Tishby and Dan, 'Ḥasidut'.

factions, and distinguish it from the tradition in which it emerged? The doctrine of the zaddik presented itself as an obvious answer, and we dealt with it at length, but was it the only hasidic teaching to qualify by these criteria? At that time, several studies had already been published which stressed the traditional character of some seemingly 'new' hasidic ideas, such as the call to rejoice during worship, or the ideal of the *devekut* (communion with God) of the simple believer.[14] We could find only one other hasidic doctrine which appeared to be central and distinctive enough: the 'elevation' of evil thoughts and the utilization of 'evil inclinations' in divine service. Professor Tishby analysed the development of this idea in hasidic literature (the published version was only an abridgement of his detailed work), but his conclusions had to be qualified to some extent a few years later, when Dr Mendel Piekarz published the results of his own study (which originated as a Ph.D. dissertation written under the supervision of Professor Tishby),[15] proving that the same idea could be found in pre-hasidic and non-hasidic homiletic literature and was often expressed there more forcefully than in any hasidic work. There is no doubt that hasidism contributed significantly to the development in Judaism of the notion that evil thoughts could be 'elevated' and the evil inclination used as a vehicle for holiness, especially through the concept of 'worship through corporeality'. Nevertheless it seems that here, too, hasidism had merely revitalized or re-enforced an older tradition rather than generating an original idea.

In retrospect, it seems to me that even a generation ago it might have been possible to arrive at the conclusion that, while hasidism undoubtedly contributed to the enrichment of many Jewish symbols, customs, and ideas, its originality and distinctiveness rested solely on the doctrine of the zaddik. The history of twentieth-century hasidism provides further confirmation of this view. In other words, at least since its third generation of existence, after 1772, hasidism has presented the Jewish communities of eastern Europe with a new type of mystical leader who promised them the experience of everyday redemption through personal adherence to him. It was this promise that won hasidism hundreds of thousands of followers in the course of the nineteenth century and provided the vitality that enabled the movement to overcome the catastrophes of the late nineteenth and twentieth centuries. The destruction of the Jewish *shtetl* in eastern Europe could not disrupt this flow of energy and vitality since it was present wherever a capable, energetic heir to one of the dynastic 'seats' could be found. If mystical leadership is the core of hasidism, then it hardly matters whether one travels to the zaddik by mule or by jetliner, whether one gazes at his hand-drawn portrait or at his video cassette. Faith in the zaddik, and the belief in the intricate, mystical relationship between the ordinary hasid and his family on the one hand, and the soul of the leader on the other, can withstand political, geographical, and technological change. This may explain the fact that Oriental Jews in Israel and elsewhere have been drawn to such leaders either within hasidism or elsewhere in Orthodox Judaism, leaders who have been invested with the charismatic authority of the hasidic zaddik.

[14] Several scholars, from A. Shoḥet to I. Tishby, have identified the origins of apparently hasidic ideas in earlier strands of the Jewish tradition, especially in Hebrew ethical works. A general survey of recent developments in the study of hasidism is to be found in Z. Gries, 'Hasidism: The Present State of Research and Some Desirable Priorities', *Numen*, 34: 1 (1987), 97–108, 179–213.

[15] Piekarz, *Biyemei tsemiḥat haḥasidut*.

Every scholar in the field of Jewish mysticism must face the question of whether Jewish mysticism has a meaning in the contemporary world. Is there a form of Jewish mysticism that is alive today? Gershom Scholem, who devoted a profound essay to this question, could not supply a clear answer.[16] If there is any true insight in the brief analysis offered above, then it may provide at least a partial answer. Since the late eighteenth century, a significant segment of the Jewish people has been expressing the need for a mystical leadership that would bridge the gap between man and God and make redemption an everyday experience. Despite the enormous changes brought about by the processes of secularization and Enlightenment in the past two centuries, this need has not diminished, and in recent decades it seems to have increased. Mystical leadership is therefore an essentially modern Jewish phenomenon that has found its fullest expression in the nineteenth and twentieth centuries. While mystical schools of thought such as kabbalah, which lacked the social dimension embodied in the zaddik, could not adjust to modern circumstances, hasidism, which promoted the idea of mystical leadership, has been thriving, and seems destined to participate in the shaping of Judaism for the future.

[16] Scholem, *Devarim bego*, 71–83.

TWENTY-SEVEN

Differences in Attitudes to Study and Work between Present-day Hasidim and Mitnaggedim: A Sociological View

DANIEL MEIJERS

1. INTRODUCTION

ERNST TROELTSCH'S church–sect typology, a well-known attempt to characterize distinct types of religious organization, uses as its point of departure the extent to which Christianity is able to compromise with the material world.[1] Michael Hill has shown that this depends on whether the emphasis is being placed on a radical or a conservative element of Christianity: the church-type organization represents the conservative element, the sect the radical.[2] However, the entire question applies specifically to Christianity and cannot be seen independently of Christian theological values, ideals, and concepts. For this reason, Troeltsch's typology cannot be used directly in the analysis of other religious traditions. This does not mean that the dilemma of conservatism versus radicalism never plays a role in other religions, but it is not necessarily as basic to the understanding of the emergence and development of many non-Christian religious collectivities as it probably is to the understanding of Christianity. In itself, however, the idea that doctrinal systems are marked by inherent contradictions and present their adherents with dilemmas which force them to make choices depending on time and circumstances is one which can undoubtedly provide some insight into non-Christian religions as well, including Judaism. An example of this kind of contradiction in Judaism is, in my opinion, the clash between the values of study and work, a clash which has its roots in the more fundamental distinction between the realms of the spiritual and the physical, the sacred and the profane.

I would like to thank my colleagues Mart Bax, Hans Tenekes, and Jojada Verrips for their comments on an earlier version of this chapter. In particular I am grateful to Dr Ada Rapoport-Albert whose numerous suggestions have led to an enormous improvement of both style and content. I am also indebted to the Free University of Amsterdam for subsidizing the translation of the chapter into English by Derek Rubin. Finally I would like to thank the Netherlands Organization for the Advancement of Pure Research for their financial sponsorship of my research in Israel in 1978, upon which the present chapter is based in part.

[1] Ernst Troeltsch, *The Social Teaching of the Christian Churches* [2 vols.; 1911 (Ger.); 1931 (Eng.)] (Chicago, 1976).

[2] Michael Hill, *A Sociology of Religion* (London, 1973), 52.

2. THE SACRED AND THE PROFANE: A FUNDAMENTAL CONTRAST IN JUDAISM

The ideal (male) Jew is one who devotes himself 'night and day' to the study of Torah. Naturally, this ideal can be realized only by a restricted élite. In order to be able to devote oneself to study, one must possess the necessary intelligence. Secondly, in order to receive the required schooling as a child, and to be able to study instead of having to work as an adult, one must have the necessary financial means. The first condition is of particular importance, since without intellect the study of Torah is impossible. Money, on the other hand, can be acquired. For this reason, throughout the centuries, Jewish communities the world over have made funds available to scholars to enable them to continue their talmudic studies. This, of course, has been possible only because there are always some Jews who do not study but provide the funds by engaging in mundane activity. Thus the Jewish community can be divided into scholars and those who support the scholars financially.[3]

The issue here is one of study versus work. The antithesis is modified somewhat by the view that those who support scholars have an equal share in the study of Torah.[4] Nevertheless, one can justly speak of an inherent contrast in Judaism between sacred study and mundane work. This contrast reflects a fundamental antithesis between the spiritual and the material. Study means devoting oneself to things of the spirit, while work means dealing with material things. It is important to examine the place of spirit and matter in Judaism in greater depth. They form two different and even completely opposed categories both of which, according to tradition, were brought into existence during the Creation. The Creation was conceived as having occurred in a number of stages, and these were called 'worlds' in Jewish mysticism. Some of these worlds were perceived as consisting only of spirit (*ruḥaniyut*) while the lowest, the human world, consisted of both spirit and matter (*ḥomer; gashmiyut*).[5]

The dilemma with which the Orthodox Jew is confronted is which to choose, spirit or matter? It is traditionally self-evident for him that the religious ideal requires him to devote himself exclusively to the spiritual, but practical considerations force him to be involved with the material world through work. Legitimate though this may be, particularly since his earnings would make it possible for others to devote all their time to the study of Torah, the Orthodox Jew still perceives a dilemma. To put it another way, emphasizing the spiritual relegates work to a subordinate position. The scholar can fulfil the religious ideal while the non-scholar is obliged to work. On the other hand, because 'matter' and the material world are valued, the ordinary everyday life of the non-scholar is made meaningful and relevant in its own right. In my opinion, this dilemma is the

[3] This distinction is not the same as between scholars and non-scholars. In the Middle Ages, for instance, 'there was no learned caste in Judaism, for every Israelite studied the Law'; see Israel Abrahams, *'Jewish' Life in the Middle Ages* (New York, 1973), 357. In later times, however, a split arose between 'religious virtuosi and mass': Charles Bosk, 'Cybernetic Hasidism: An Essay on Social and Religious Change', *Sociological Inquiry*, 44: 2 (1974), 131–44. The Jewish community became divided into scholars and their supporters on the one hand, and the unlettered masses on the other.

[4] See Rashi's comment on Deut. 33: 18.

[5] L. D. Meijers and J. Tennekes, 'Spirit and Matter in the Cosmology of Chassidic Judaism', in P. E. de Josselin de Jong and Erik Schwimmer (eds.), *Symbolic Anthropology in the Netherlands*, Verhandelingen van het Koninklijk Instituut voor Taal-, Land- en Volkenkunde 95 (The Hague, 1982).

common denominator of all the main trends in Orthodox Judaism and their particular types of community organization.

3. TWO CURRENTS IN JUDAISM

Two major currents in contemporary Orthodox Ashkenazi Judaism are the hasidic and the mitnaggedic.[6] This distinction is made exclusively on the basis of religious orientation, although various political and sociological orientations may be connected with it to varying degrees. According to one of the major leaders of modern hasidism, the late Rabbi Menahem Mendel Schneerson of Lubavitch, the conflict between the two orientations originated in conflicting interpretations of certain kabbalistic views.[7] These focused on the concept of *tsimtsum* ('contraction' or 'concentration') in the teaching of the kabbalist R. Isaac Luria (1534–72). This concept is of particular importance to the problem of how the finite world was created by an infinite G-d:[8] how could a finite world exist within a finite space while G-d is infinite in all dimensions, and therefore also in space? To solve this problem, Luria employed the concept of *tsimtsum*—a process underlying the work of Creation through which G-d was concealed on various levels in the process of creation. Thus, G-d withdrew Himself, as it were, in order to make room for Creation.

This view was accepted in principle by both hasidim and mitnaggedim, but each group gave it a completely different interpretation. According to the mitnaggedim, G-d had withdrawn His essence from the world, so that the material world that remained was less divine. Consequently, any real relationship with G-d could be established only through the spiritual activity of studying the Torah in which He had revealed Himself. According to hasidic teachings, on the other hand, *tsimtsum* refers only to the concealment of a certain divine manifestation and not to the withdrawal of G-d Himself. From this it follows that G-d's essence is present in matter as well; His infinity has not been affected by the creation of the world.

These differences of opinion have far-reaching consequences for practical conduct in daily life. According to the mitnaggedim, man's most meaningful activity is continuous study of Torah. All other activities are considered inferior. For the mitnaggedim this means an incessant preoccupation with the spiritual and a contempt for material pursuits. In practical terms it leads to contempt for all those who deal with the material world, that is, those who do ordinary work, the non-scholars.[9] The hasidim, on the other hand, hold the view that G-d Himself is still as unconcealed as before Creation,

[6] It should be noted that, since the 1960s, there has been a certain influx of Sefardi or Oriental Jews to both hasidic and mitnaggedic communities, e.g. in Israel, France, and Latin America. For the purpose of the present discussion, however, the 'Sefardis' in both camps may be assumed to have assimilated the historically Ashkenazi value systems of hasidism and mitnaggedism respectively.

[7] M. M. Schneerson, *Likutei sihot* (32 vols.; Brooklyn, NY, 1967–93), xv (1980), 470.

[8] In accordance with Orthodox Jewish practice, I do not spell out the word G-d in full.

[9] The foremost leader of the mitnaggedim was R. Elijah, the Gaon of Vilna (1720–97). According to him, the proper task of the pious Jew was to study Torah continuously. However, he deemed it permissible to earn a living in a secular manner, since not everyone was capable of studying Torah without ulterior motives (such as the desire to acquire a scholarly reputation, etc.), so the pursuit of a secular occupation would act as a barrier against sin; see H. H. Ben-Sasson, 'Ishiyuto shel HaGra vehashpa'ato hahistorit', *Zion*, 31 (1966), 39–86, 197–216. It is evident that matter, according to this view, can never be more than a means to an end rather than an end in itself. A person who occupies himself with matter will automatically belong to a different category from that of the scholar, and the scholar will be the only one truly able to realize the religious ideals.

and that the concealment of *tsimtsum* applies only to specific emanations of G-dliness. G-d is therefore fully present in both spirit and matter. While the mitnaggedic interpretation of *tsimtsum* leads to a more transcendental view of G-d, the hasidic interpretation leads to a greater emphasis on G-d's immanence. Thus, according to the hasidim, if G-d can be found not only in the spiritual but also in the material, He can be found in mundane work as well.

Another concept must be taken into account in order to understand the differences in mentality between the two groups. Not only do the hasidim regard the material world as a form of G-dliness, a manifestation of divine powers, but they view it also as the place where divine 'sparks'—particles of divine substance, as it were—landed as a result of the process of Creation. According to this view, man's task on earth is to return the sparks to their divine source, a goal that can be achieved only when man makes the correct moral choice in each of his interactions with the material world. This implies that all man's actions, in all areas of life, are subject to religious and spiritual norms. For those areas of life which are not covered by direct commandments and precepts, guidelines are available which can be applied to the specific situation of each individual.

All of this means that according to hasidism, it is precisely man's dealings with the material world that render his actions spiritually meaningful in enabling him to bring Creation to its ultimate goal. This legitimization of worldly work was extremely attractive to non-scholars—inevitably, the majority of the Jewish population at the time when hasidism was spreading.[10] Their ordinary everyday lives gained purpose, meaning, and even value. This was without doubt one of the most important contributions of the hasidic movement to traditional Jewish society, one which has not only enriched its value system but may even have secured its continued existence.

Hasidim and Mitnaggedim Today

The new hasidic movement expanded rapidly. The historian of hasidism, Simon Dubnow, went so far as to state that by the nineteenth century, the majority of eastern European Jews were hasidim.[11] However, since the Second World War, the situation has changed considerably. The major hasidic and mitnaggedic centres are now located in Israel and the USA, although representatives of both currents can be found also in a number of western European and Latin American cities. Despite the geographical accessibility of these centres, it is difficult for outsiders to obtain accurate information on them. Most hasidic and mitnaggedic communities tend to exclude all strangers, especially social scientists, as I myself and others have experienced. In the words of Sanford Pinsker: 'it might be well to remember that hasidic Jews are more than a little sceptical about the value of secular scholarship in general and of social scientists in particular.'[12] The same is true of the mitnaggedim, who probably object to secular studies just as much as if not

[10] The occupational structure of Polish Jewry in the middle of the 18th cent. has been calculated as follows: 2–3% rich merchants and financiers; nearly 40% small traders, including leaseholders and innkeepers; 32–3% artisans and other urban wage-earners; 10% employed in communal service; and 15% unemployed and paupers; see Stephen Sharot, *Judaism: A Sociology* (London, 1976).

[11] Simon Dubnow, *Geschichte des Chassidismus* (2 vols.; Berlin, 1931), i. 22.

[12] S. Pinsker, 'Piety as Community: The Hasidic View', *Social Research*, 42 (1975), 230–46.

more than do most hasidim. While some publications about a number of hasidic groups have appeared in recent years, as far as I am aware, not a single study of any mitnaggedic community has been published to date.[13] Consequently, my sketch of the typical mitnaggedic community is derived from a limited number of personal experiences and contacts with a few informants only.

The Brisk Community: A Mitnaggedic Group in Jerusalem

There are several groups of mitnaggedim in Jerusalem. One of these is the Brisk community, consisting of approximately two hundred families. This community is important because it can be regarded as the most prominent representative of the mitnaggedic tradition. The group is composed exclusively of Torah scholars. They regard the study of Torah as man's only goal, more important even than prayer. This does not mean that they do not recite the prescribed prayers; on the contrary, prayers are recited meticulously. But the emphasis is on the study of Talmud, which is regarded as a full-time occupation.

Originally, during the 1940s, when the Brisk community in Jerusalem was first established by the 'Brisker Rav'—Isaac Ze'ev Halevi (Velvele) Soloveichik (1886–1959), who settled there following escape from Lithuania at the outbreak of the Second World War—only intellectuals were attracted to this community. Even now only those who have achieved a certain intellectual standard in traditional rabbinic-scholarly terms may be admitted, and there is practically no one in the community who is not intellectually able to devote himself exclusively to the study of Torah. Heredity may also play a role in defining membership, since young scholars often marry into families of their own or a similar background.

Torah study is carried out in three yeshivot, in synagogues, and in private houses scattered throughout Jerusalem. The absence of any central and easily identifiable school discourages outsiders from associating themselves with this community, many of whose members have belonged to the Brisk community for generations. If a member of such a family does not wish to devote himself to the study of Torah, he is no longer regarded as a member of the group. According to my informant, only a few such cases are known.

On the death of Rabbi 'Velvele', the Brisker Rav, each of his five sons gathered a number of families around him. Some of the sons are still alive, and each heads his own yeshivah. They are consulted not only on matters of Jewish law but also on personal problems. Nevertheless, the charismatic nature of their leadership is less pronounced than that of the hasidic leader.[14]

[13] Egon Mayer, *From Suburb to Shtetl: The Jews of Boro Park* (Philadelphia, 1979), provides a more general description of orthodox life in the Boro Park quarter of New York. Although most of his information concerns non-hasidic life, his book focuses neither on any specific mitnaggedic groups nor on any specific hasidic groups. S. C. Heilman's *Synagogue Life: A Study in Symbolic Interaction* (Chicago, 1976) treats a so-called Modern Orthodox community. Although some of his informants certainly considered mitnaggedic leaders and mitnaggedic centres as their ideological frame of reference, generally speaking they did not adhere to 'pure' mitnaggedic ideals (*Synagogue Life*, 7–8).

[14] Several distinct, if similar, titles denote distinct types of Jewish spiritual leaders. They all derive from the title *rabi*—my teacher. *Rav* is commonly the formal leader, the rabbi of a community. His traditional task is primarily to decide in Jewish-legal matters. In less traditional communities his functions include general pastoral care. Hasidic groups refer to their leader as *rebbe*. The *rebbe* sometimes functions

The Brisk community is decidedly an élite group: men who are not educated in Talmud have no place in it. This is characteristic of other mitnaggedic communities in America and Israel, but Brisk is by far the most exclusive. The Brisk community, keenly aware of its mitnaggedic identity, can be seen as a model for similar groups. More than any other community of this type, it regards itself as an heir to the original eighteenth-century opponents of hasidism, all the more so because the leaders of the community are their direct descendants. Their influence has increased since many leaders of affiliated yeshivot had been trained at Brisk and send their best students to one of the Brisk institutions. They admit only students who identify themselves completely with the ideals of the community, to the exclusion of all other loyalties. For example, a young man who wanted to study in a yeshivah affiliated with the Brisk community was not admitted because he was in contact with a well-known hasidic *rebbe*. As a condition of admission he was asked to sever this relationship but he refused. No other mitnaggedic yeshivah would have imposed such a condition, and it is not uncommon for hasidic boys to study in mitnaggedic yeshivot, particularly those which enjoy the best academic reputation.

By contrast with the situation in Israel, in the United States the 'pure' mitnaggedic community hardly exists. There, the mitnaggedim had to recruit their postwar following from within an Orthodox community which had already been Americanized to some extent, having emigrated from eastern Europe to the United States over several decades. The Jerusalem Briskers, on the other hand, landed in an environment where Orthodox Jews had lived for several hundred years and where the demarcation lines between Orthodox and non-Orthodox were much clearer. In practice, the differences between the Brisk community and other mitnaggedic groups in Israel or abroad are quite evident. While the Jerusalem Briskers are all full-time Torah scholars, in other mitnaggedic communities non-scholars may be affiliated by attending classes taught by Torah scholars and praying with them, even though they are not regarded as fully-fledged members of the community.[15]

4. SOME HASIDIC GROUPS

More information is available about hasidic groups. A number of studies have appeared, notably George Kranzler's, Solomon Poll's, and Israel Rubin's studies of the Satmar hasidim of Williamsburg, William Shaffir's study of the Lubavitch hasidim of Montreal, Charles Liebman's work on the Lubavitch hasidim of New York, as well as wider studies of the ultra-Orthodox world in general.[16] All these studies highlight the

also as the *rav* of the community in the traditional sense, but he is primarily considered a saintly person with charismatic gifts. It is interesting to note that in Brisk—and in some other mitnaggedic communities—the *rav* has taken on some of the qualities attributed to the hasidic *rebbe*.

[15] See Heilman, *Synagogue Life*, 108–11, 248, for an illustration of this mentality, even though his study does not focus on this issue.

[16] See George Kranzler, *Williamsburg: A Jewish Community in Transition* (New York, 1961), 75; Solomon Poll, *The Hasidic Community of Williamsburg* (New York, 1969), 115–18; Israel Rubin, *Satmar: An Island in the City* (Chicago, 1972), 166; William Shaffir, *Life in a Religious Community: The Lubavitcher Chassidim in Montreal* (Toronto, 1974), 96–101; Charles Liebman, 'Orthodox Sectarians', in J. Neusner

hasidic pursuit of worldly occupations. Similarly, in my own research among the Reb Ahreleh hasidim of Me'ah She'arim[17] I detected no consistent preference for the study of Torah, although the detailed breakdown of occupations pursued within this community lay outside the scope of my study. People work in all kinds of trades and crafts. Reb Ahreleh Roth, the founder of the movement, requested repeatedly that his hasidim should be employed in secular jobs.

The same applies to the Lubavitch hasidim of New York. It is difficult to estimate the size of this community, which certainly exceeds several thousands.[18] Here, too, the study of Torah is by no means the only employment. At the Lubavitch *kolel*, where married men study, only a few dozen hasidim devote the entire day to learning, without pursuing regular employment as well, and it is assumed that all members of the *kolel* will eventually seek employment, although in many cases this would be in the religious sphere. Similar findings have emerged from my own research in Israel in 1978, which was conducted among the Lubavitch hasidim in Kfar Habad and the Viznitz hasidim of Bnei Brak.[19]

In contrast to the mitnaggedic group, the hasidic community is open to non-scholars. Indeed, many of its members would have little or no scholarly background at all. The Lubavitch movement is particularly interesting in this respect: not only are they accessible, indeed hospitable, to non-scholars, but they go out of their way to involve in their activities Jews who have been totally estranged from traditional Judaism, and they train their own hasidim to assume the spiritual leadership of Jewish communities of no particular affiliation. They also work with youth organizations outside any framework of traditional Jewish scholarship, and are engaged in welfare work among convicts and drug addicts, to whom they try to offer a new life within the Lubavitch community.[20] This is done in the name of love of one's fellow Jew, and it entails a clear and conscious involvement with the mundane realm of matter and the world.[21] The essential thing is for Lubavitch to take a stand in the world instead of turning away from it, as do the mitnaggedim. In other hasidic groups, however, the involvement with matter generally remains restricted to the pursuit of a secular occupation.

An outsider may join the hasidic group. In many such groups this means in the first instance simply conforming to the externally visible norms of daily life which distinguish each group, such as the adoption of a particular style of clothing or letting one's beard and earlocks grow in a particular way.[22] Access to outsiders is facilitated

(ed.), *Understanding American Judaism: Toward the Description of a Modern Religion* (2 vols.; New York, 1975), ii. 167–8; Samuel Heilman, *Defenders of the Faith* (New York, 1992); Amnon Levy, *Haḥaredim* (Jerusalem, 1989).

17 Daniel Meijers, *Chassidisme in Israël* (Assen, 1979); id., *Ascetic Hasidism in Jerusalem: The Guardian-of-the-Faithful Community of Mea Shearim* (Leiden, 1992).

18 Liebman, 'Orthodox Sectarians', 167–8.

19 For a description of hasidic life in Kfar Habad, see D. Meijers, *De revolutie der vromen: Ontstaan en ontwikkeling van het chassidisme: Waarin is opgenomen het verslag van reb Dan Isj-Toms reis door de eeuwigheid* (Hilversum, 1989), 188–97.

20 Merrill Singer, 'The Use of Folklore in Religious Conversion: The Chassidic Case', *Review of Religious Research*, 22: 2 (1980), 176.

21 Douglas Mitchell and Leonard Plotnicov, 'The Lubavitch Movement: A Study in Contexts', *Urban Anthropology*, 4: 4 (1975), 310.

22 Poll, *The Hasidic Community of Williamsburg*, 67.

also by the fact that, in contrast to the mitnaggedic ideal, intellectual-scholarly accomplishment, which can only be acquired in many years of uninterrupted rabbinical study, is not the main goal of the new hasidic recruit. Nevertheless, most hasidic groups appear to be closed to outsiders, although here, too, the Lubavitch hasidim constitute an exception in displaying the characteristic features of an open community. They go out of their way to enter into relationships with the outside world in order to recruit new members for their group. It is precisely for this reason that the size of the Lubavitch community is so difficult to ascertain: many individuals who are not externally recognizable as Lubavitch would nevertheless be regarded as members if they maintain a certain level of contact with the group.[23] Because of their positive emphasis on the recruitment of outsiders, which is based on a totally different attitude towards the material, secular world, Lubavitch hasidim provide the most striking contrast to the mitnaggedic groups.

Between the two extremes of Brisk and Lubavitch there is, however, a wide range of attitudes which is expressed in a variety of intermediate Orthodox groups. It is precisely through these intermediate groups that the two extremes assume meaning.

5. INTERMEDIATE ORTHODOXY

Not all Orthodox communities are clearly identified as either hasidic or mitnaggedic. Orthodox Ashkenazi Judaism can best be seen as a conglomerate of communities many of which lie somewhere between the two extremes. Individual hasidim and mitnaggedim may belong to such communities without seeking active or regular affiliation with the extreme forms of either of the two currents. Other members of such communities would be indifferent to or altogether unacquainted with the differences between them. In western Europe, the practical consequence of this has been that such communities tend to look mainly to the mitnaggedic school for their spiritual-communal leadership, while the spiritual leaders themselves—rabbis and other community functionaries—would not usually impose a clear-cut mitnaggedic orientation on their communities. The situation is different in the United States. In the past few years, the demand for leaders who have been trained at Lubavitch yeshivot has increased.[24] This is a result of the fact that Lubavitch graduates have acquired the reputation of being able to activate the community and, unlike the graduates of mitnaggedic yeshivot, have often been trained in pastoral care. In general, however, it is safe to say that many Orthodox communities show no clear preference either for hasidism of any particular

[23] Liebman, 'Orthodox Sectarians', 168. During my stay in Kfar Habad, the Israel settlement of the Lubavitchers, one of the questions I put to various inhabitants was 'Who is a Lubavitcher?' Some answered, 'Anybody who feels he is a Lubavitcher'; others said: 'Anybody who does what the *rebbe* says.' More specific answers were 'Everybody in our community who grows a beard', or 'Every person who learns daily the prescribed portions of *ḤiTaT* [the acronym of Pentateuch, the Psalms, and the hasidic classic Tanya]'. See also Charles S. Liebman, 'Orthodoxy in American Jewish Life', *American Jewish Year Book*, 66 (1965), 80.

[24] I received this information from Lubavitch youth leaders in New York during my stay there in 1985. This was confirmed by non-Lubavitch informants. In western Europe there are now signs of what may be the beginning of a trend towards a situation similar to the one prevailing in the United States. In Holland, for example, three of the six official community rabbis are Lubavitch alumni. A few other Lubavitchers have been appointed as pastoral workers.

variety or for mitnaggedism. Israel, where the differences of orientation are more apparent than in western Europe or America, may be the only exception to this rule.

The lack of clear preference for either the hasidic or the mitnaggedic orientation is closely connected to the lack of traditional Orthodox education and the consequent shortage of Torah scholars within the intermediate sector. In both hasidic and mitnaggedic centres, children are schooled in Torah at *ḥeder*—the religious primary school—continue their studies in the *yeshivah ketanah*—a lower-level talmudical school—and conclude them in the *yeshivah gedolah*—a talmudical academy. The preference is for their training to be exclusively religious. In some cases this applies to the entire educational programme and in others only to the *ḥeder* stage. The question of preference for either spirit or matter in terms of employment arises most often in those who have been exposed to this rigorously religious education. Others have no alternative but to seek secular employment.

In fact, the intermediate Orthodox sector attracts not only the fully Orthodox but also all those who, while being fully involved in the world, prefer to attend Orthodox synagogue services without necessarily practising Judaism in a fully Orthodox way. A few Torah scholars would usually be affiliated to all such communities, particularly in positions which require ritual expertise such as the rabbinate, ritual slaughtering, teaching, and so on. These scholars would also provide weekly or daily instruction in rabbinics for the benefit of the fully Orthodox members of the community, but their attitudes towards the choice between spiritual and material concerns would not vary markedly from those of the surrounding secular and non-Jewish society. This is why such communities appear to lack any clear orientation. Religion does not pervade all areas of life but is reserved for special occasions. The non-Orthodox members display this attitude by their sporadic visits to the synagogue, usually during the High Holidays (Rosh Hashanah and Yom Kippur), while the Orthodox members participate in religious activities more regularly and observe other religious duties, but, in contrast to both hasidim and mitnaggedim, their lives are not conditioned by religion to the extent that every action, be it in the material or in the spiritual sphere, has a religious value and meaning.[25]

6. DIFFERENCES AND SIMILARITIES: HASIDIC, MITNAGGEDIC, AND INTERMEDIATE ORTHODOXY

The intermediate form of Orthodoxy operates in communities into which members are usually born and where membership is inclusive. This means that the standards of admission and of religious observance are low. The community is engaged in the world, and the charisma of its leaders is the charisma of office. Generally speaking, membership is

[25] See Heilman, *Synagogue Life*, 7: 'Kehillat Kodesh is populated primarily by modern Orthodox Jews. Its members are "oriented significantly to the world outside" the Jewish one, and they regard themselves "as an integral part of that [outside] world". This cosmopolitanism may be seen, for instance, in the occupational profile of the adult males. Only about 5 per cent have jobs, such as religious school teachers or kosher butchers, which allow full-time involvement and isolation within the Jewish community. Nearly 65 per cent have careers in fields like medicine, law, university teaching, and the natural sciences, which require relatively long periods of training and initiation outside the Orthodox Jewish orbit.'

large and the leadership is professional, with leaders being recruited either from within the ranks of the community itself or from the other two groups.[26] The Israeli chief rabbinate may be seen as a formal example of leadership in the intermediate Orthodox sector. The main function of the contemporary intermediate Orthodox community is to provide religious services for its members. While in past centuries European Judaism, particularly in eastern Europe, was characterized by an autonomous organization which controlled the life of the individual, determined community policy, and maintained its own rabbinic judiciary system,[27] the intermediate form of Orthodoxy today is incapable of exerting any more than a purely religious influence on its members. It has lost its grip on the daily life of the individual.[28]

This is not the case with either the hasidic or the mitnaggedic groups. Here, the religious and other spheres of life, such as, for example, the socio-economic, are less clearly differentiated. There are also fewer variations of outlook and commitment among the individual members. Each community is marked by its own distinct features, and these are displayed fully by every member. On the other hand, in the intermediate variety of Orthodoxy, individual members often differ from one another in their religious and also in their political views.[29]

Within hasidic Orthodoxy the various groups do not all share the same characteristics. Some are closed, others more open to outsiders. For instance, the Lubavitch hasidim open their ranks even to non-Orthodox Jews, while groups such as the Reb Ahreleh hasidim do their utmost to exclude all outsiders from their meetings and institutions. All hasidic groups cultivate some form of relationship with the material world without quite endorsing it fully. Some hasidic groups are small, others larger. Personal charisma plays an important part in the leadership of all: the hasidic *rebbe* derives his authority from it, while other leaders would usually draw on the charisma of office.[30] In

[26] 'A survey of 56 rabbis in the Boro Park area of New York conducted by Mayer indicated that 41% considered themselves hasidic, and 51% considered themselves Orthodox'; see Mayer, *Suburb to Shtetl*, 77. Only a small number of these Orthodox rabbis could have served truly mitnaggedic communities, since the number of such communities is quite small. Therefore, most of the rabbis who took part in the survey must have belonged to the intermediate variety of Orthodoxy. The same, though to a lesser extent, is probably true of the hasidic rabbis. At any rate, this is the case in many other Jewish communities (in Amsterdam, Antwerp, London, Paris, and the like).

[27] See Simon Dubnow, *Weltgeschichte des jüdischen Volkes* (10 vols.; Berlin, 1925–9), vii. 170–8.

[28] The situation in Israel is different in that matrimonial law falls exclusively within the jurisdiction of the rabbinic courts, and religious groups also play a political role but they do not control the lives of individual citizens in the same way in which the pre-emancipation *kehilah* and its institutions had governed every aspect of the daily existence of its members.

[29] According to Heilman, *Synagogue Life*, 7, Jewish orthodoxy should be divided into two groups, modern and traditional: 'The first group is defined by a desire to adhere faithfully to the beliefs, principles, and traditions of Jewish law and observance without being either remote from or untouched by life in the contemporary secular society. The second group is relatively more isolated from the contemporary secular world. It is in America but not of it, concerning itself almost completely with Jewish life and seeing such aspects of reality as secular education, English language, or occupations outside the Jewish community as infringements upon their life. The most prominent, but by no means the only, representatives of this group are the Chassidim, the sect of zealots whose entire lives revolve around Jewish observance.' In fact, Heilman's second group, 'traditional' Orthodoxy, consists of hasidim and mitnaggedim alike, while his first group, the so-called 'modern' Orthodox, belongs to the intermediate variety of Orthodoxy discussed above.

[30] The institution of the *rebbe* is, on the whole, hereditary. However, it is personal rather than hereditary charisma that ultimately determines whether or not the authority of an heir will be recognized.

all three groups services are performed by both laymen and professionals. Most hasidic groups recognize other Orthodox groups, with the possible exception of some of the Satmar hasidim of Williamsburg, Brooklyn, although even they cannot be said to deny altogether the legitimacy of all other Orthodox groups.[31] Generally speaking, however, hasidic groups tend to be more exclusive than inclusive.

The mitnaggedic groups present a somewhat more coherent and uniform picture. All are exclusive. Their members are usually born into the group, although some groups have begun to engage in missionary work and recruit outsiders. Nevertheless, the new recruit has to cross a high threshold: he is expected to study for several years at one of the yeshivot before being recognized as a member of the group. These small, élite communities isolate themselves from the world, and they place more emphasis on the charisma of office than on the personal charisma of the leadership.

Among all the features which distinguish the various Orthodox groups from one another or which point to the connections between them, the choice between spirit and matter, between study and work, has had the most far-reaching consequences in shaping the distinctive character of each group within present-day Orthodoxy. In respect primarily of this choice, I propose to distinguish three different ideal types of Orthodox community: the religious learning community, the religious living community, and the synagogue community. Mitnaggedism, hasidism, and intermediate Orthodoxy can all be classified as belonging to one of these categories.

The Religious Learning Community

Members of this community devote themselves exclusively to the study of Torah; they have clearly opted for the spiritual. Their attitude can be described as 'standing above the world'. The only worthwhile occupation is the study of Torah; secular work is done only out of necessity.[32] The absence of any differentiation between the religious and the socio-economic and political spheres is an ideal. Education is exclusively or primarily religious. The community is made up of individual believers. Intellectual capabilities are highly valued. All mitnaggedic groups fit into this category.

The Religious Living Community

In this community the members pursue both religious and secular occupations. Work is combined with the study of Torah. In terms of the choice between the spiritual and the material, preference is given to matter, although the importance of the spiritual in this community must not be underestimated. One is in the world without being of it. Pre-

[31] See Liebman, 'Orthodoxy in American Jewish Life', 83–5.

[32] The obligation to study applies only to men. If the salary received from the *kolel* (the institution where married men study) is insufficient, the women work. Without realizing it, Goshen-Gottstein describes precisely such a community. Her article about 'an ultra-orthodox Jerusalem group' does not distinguish between hasidim and mitnaggedim. Nevertheless, in her discussion of the occupational status of the husbands, she speaks of 'these eternal "student-scholars" who live on grants', which suggests that she was dealing with a mitnaggedic community (E. Goshen-Gottstein, 'Courtship, Marriage and Pregnancy in Geula', *Israel Annals of Psychiatry and Related Disciplines*, 4: 1 (1966), 46). For this reason, her paper should not have been included in L. Burack's annotated bibliography of articles on hasidim, 'Hasidism: A Selected Annotated Bibliography of Articles of Ethnographic Interest (1965–75)', *Jewish Folklore and Ethnology Newsletter*, 2: 2–3 (1979), 15.

cisely because actions derive their meaning from the way in which the material world is dealt with, they are all, ultimately, ascetic. Matter has to be restored to its spiritual origin, and this is why such an emphasis is placed on dealing with matter, but materialism as such is eschewed. Differentiation between the religious and the socio-economic and political spheres is not advocated here either. Education is exclusively or primarily religious. All activities are centred around the personality of a charismatic leader and are carried out in a collective rather than an individualistic manner. Emotional capabilities are highly valued. All hasidic groups fit into this category.

The Synagogue Community

In this community secular occupations are highly valued and the study of Torah does not occupy a place of prominence. Members are not aware of the dilemma of spirit and matter, and so no choice has to be made between them. One is in and harmoniously connected with the world. A distinction is made between the religious sphere and other spheres of life. The most important religious activity is attending synagogue. Some members of the group do this daily, others only a few times a year. The purely religious leadership is professional, but the community is run by laymen. In practice, the religious functionaries are dependent on the decisions of the laymen. The organizational structure of such communities varies. In some cases groups of communities are connected by a hierarchical structure of religious authority, in other cases individual communities are centred around the synagogue, each under the leadership of a single rabbi. The intermediate Orthodox sector belongs to this type.[33]

I have tried to show that the dilemma of spirit and matter is fundamental to the understanding of present-day Orthodox Judaism. While fully realizing the limitations which are inherent in any such schematic categorization, I do believe that most Orthodox communities can be shown to resemble one or another of these types.

[33] In all three types of community, the essence of man's task is perceived as located in the earthly world. However, in the first two types, all actions are in reference to a higher world, while in the third type this is hardly the case. In the learning community, the world is identified with the community's own world. In the living community this varies from the community's own world to the larger Jewish world, while in the synagogue community the concept of the world is practically synonymous with society at large.

PART VIII

THE PRESENT STATE OF RESEARCH ON HASIDISM: AN OVERVIEW

TWENTY-EIGHT

Early Hasidism: Some Old/New Questions

ARTHUR GREEN

THE following are some general remarks on the question of where we stand in the historiography of hasidism at present, and especially after the conference of which the present volume is the proceedings. I would like to suggest, only half tongue-in-cheek, that the proceedings, dedicated to the memory of Joseph Weiss, should have been entitled '*Via Negativa* in Early Hasidism'. That seems to me an appropriate characterization of the present scholarly situation. In reopening the two great questions—hasidism's origins and its success—contemporary scholarship has negated almost all the once clearly established answers. We can no longer say that hasidism began because of persecution, especially not that it arose in reaction to the Chmielnicki massacre a century earlier or its long aftermath, as was once widely claimed.[1] Nor can we say that hasidism was primarily or necessarily a reaction to Sabbateanism.[2] We certainly do not think of it as a *necessary* reaction to Sabbateanism, as Gershom Scholem once suggested.[3] Studies included within this volume serve to diminish the importance of the Turkish–Podolian connection with hasidism's origins. We have long known that we can no longer take *Shivḥei haBesht* and its account of the early days at face value as a source for how hasidism began. Our use for historical purposes of the tales included in that work is ever being refined.[4]

Hasidism's success can no longer be attributed to poverty or oppression, as was once a commonplace in the literature. We can no longer say that the Besht and his circle rep-

[1] See S. Dubnow, *Toledot haḥasidut* [Tel Aviv, 1930–1] (Tel Aviv, 1960), 8 ff.

[2] Ibid. 24 ff; M. Buber, *The Origin and Meaning of Hasidism* (New York, 1960), 29 ff. See the important rethinking of this view in I. Tishby, *Netivei emunah uminut* (Ramat Gan, 1964), 226, where hasidism's origin is described as 'an inner shift within Sabbateanism itself' rather than as a movement born of anti-Sabbatean reaction. This is also the general position already taken by J. G. Weiss in 'Reshit tsemiḥatah shel haderekh haḥasidit', *Zion*, 16 (1951), repr. in A. Rubinstein (ed.), *Perakim betorat haḥasidut vetoledoteihah* (Jerusalem, 1977), 122–81.

[3] *Major Trends in Jewish Mysticism* (New York, 1954), 328 f.

[4] Pioneering historical studies based on the material in *Shivḥei haBesht* include those by B. Dinur in his *Bemifneh hadorot* (Jerusalem, 1955), the above-mentioned essay by J. Weiss, and the several studies on early hasidic figures by A. J. Heschel, now translated in his *The Circle of the Baal Shem Tov*, ed. S. H. Dresner, Studies in Hasidism (Chicago, 1985). Some more recent contributions include A. Rubinstein, 'Sipurei hahitgalut besefer *Shivḥei haBesht*', *Alei sefer*, 6–7 (1979), 157–86; id., 'He'arot lesefer *Shivḥei haBesht*', *Sinai*, 86: 1–2 (1980), 62–71; Y. Elbaum, 'HaBesht uveno shel Rabbi Adam', *Meḥkerei Yerushalayim befolklor yehudi*, 2 (1982), 66–79; I. Bartal, 'Aliyat R. Eleazar me'Amsterdam le'Erets Yisrael bishnat 1740', *Meḥkarim al toledot yahadut Holland*, 4 (1984), 7–25.

resented the lower classes, because the earliest roots of the movement appear to defy any social stratification. Nor was hasidism a rebellion of the unlettered—not with scholarly leaders such as R. Jacob Joseph of Polonnoye or Shneur Zalman of Lyady. We know that hasidism was not spread particularly through its books, but rather through oral teaching. It was clearly not the novelty of its ideas that caused the movement to grow. We also know that hasidism was not successful either because it was or was not messianic!

What, then, is left us by way of explanation? We have cleaned out a lot of cobwebs—a lot of claims that had long lain unexamined, but were still taken as truths because we all learnt them from Dubnow and Horodecky—whose name, interestingly, has hardly been mentioned here—the writers we all read on hasidism thirty or more years ago. Many of their explanations are finally gone, yet the questions about the beginning and success of hasidism still remain with us.

I would like to mention four of these questions. Although they are not the only questions to be answered, they seem the four most important. How and why did hasidism begin? What was the secret of its great success and rapid spread? What, if anything, is new in hasidism? How are the parameters of the movement to be defined—who is and who is not a hasid? From the perspective of the current state of research, and acknowledging our *via negativa*, I would like to say something brief about each of these questions, identifying our present stand and pointing to where I think we should go in considering them further.

Regarding the origins of hasidism: we have lost much of our confidence in the historical explanations proffered by the scholarship of the past. I think that is to the good, because it forces us to turn to a question too long avoided by the historians of hasidism. I refer to the phenomenology of the religious experience of the Baal Shem, the Maggid, and those around them. What types of mystics were they? What kinds of inner experiences did they have and seek to express? Can we read their homiletic or aphoristic writings in such a way that we will achieve some greater insight into the nature of their inner world?

We students of hasidism sometimes forget that we are dealing with *mystics*, people who see the inner life as primary and who come to 'know God' through inner experience.[5] If we are dealing with mystics, we are dealing with people whose inner lives not only are the *product* of the cultural world from which they come, but also *affect* the culture that they create. It is time for scholars of hasidism to study the psychology of mysticism and to familiarize themselves with typologies of mysticism that can be drawn from a broad study of world religions. Hasidism is an outbreak of radical immanentist mysticism in eighteenth-century Ukrainian Judaism. Rather than look for its cause exclusively in political or social history (the writings of Dubnow and others), or in the

[5] I recognize the well-known reticence of Jewish mystics to write of personal experiences as well as the highly traditional nature of Jewish mysticism and the interpretative form generally taken by its literature. Such emphases within scholarship have at times led, however, to an inadequate appreciation of the essential pneumatic quality of hasidism, that which drives both its social and its intellectual/literary efforts. Cf. M. Idel, *Kabbalah: New Perspectives* (New Haven, 1988), 241 ff. The range of phenomena, whether described as *devekut*, as *da'at*, as *bitul*, or as a *nekudah penimit*, depending on schools or generations within hasidism, is to be taken as primary. I am suggesting that the striving for and attainment of such inner states should play an important role in any explanation of hasidism on the 'outer' historical plane as well.

religious-literary history of ideas (Scholem), let us take this outbreak as a phenomenon and try to understand what it is by considering its parallels in other contexts, places, and cultures. Then we might ask how such a religious phenomenon—a radically immanentist mysticism that borders on pantheism and is closer to nature mysticism than is usually the case among Jews—interacted with a new selective reading of the sources of Judaism to create a movement ideology.

Like medieval Jewish philosophy and kabbalah before it, hasidism represents a new selection and interpretation of earlier Jewish sources, reread in the light of a particular set of life experiences, and particularly inner experiences. While hasidism theoretically sanctified everything in the tradition it had inherited, there were some elements of this tradition that it quietly set aside. The detailed system of Lurianic kabbalah was revered but mostly ignored.[6] Medieval Jewish philosophy, with some exceptions, was put aside and sometimes even denounced—though it was selectively mined for terminology.[7] There were other elements that acquired greater importance than in former ages, such as certain aggadic traditions, especially those relating to the notion of the zaddik.[8] As we all know, there were certain pages of the talmudic aggadah that were very well worn in the Gemaras owned by hasidic authors. Those key passages are quoted again and again. On the other hand, one can manage to read hasidic literature perfectly well without knowing certain other pages of the Talmud, sections on which little if any comment is offered in hasidic works, at least not until the later and often more scholarly Polish authors. We have to learn to study how the inner experience that was the core of the early movement and the selection it made from the readings of Judaism interplayed with one another in creating the particular and often elusive religious texture of hasidism.

On the success of hasidism: hasidism is a typical revival or revitalization movement, marked primarily by its charismatic leadership, and its success is comparable to the success of other charismatically led revival movements—the Great Awakening, Methodism, southern United States revivalism after Reconstruction, and so forth. It may even have some features in common with revivalism in Iran in recent times. This is not to say that all these movements are the same. But one can learn something about hasidic revivalism as a religious phenomenon and understand how it spread by studying revivalism and revitalization movements in other cultures, through a study of the rather extensive anthropological literature on these matters. An examination of other revival movements and their characteristics will also provide a new background against which that which is distinctive in hasidism will stand out in clear relief.

In Judaism, which is among the most verbally self-conscious of humanity's cultural

[6] See Scholem, *Major Trends*, 337 ff.; J. G. Weiss, 'The Kavvanoth of Prayer in Early Hasidism', *Journal of Jewish Studies*, 9 (1958), 163–92 (repr. in id., *Studies in Eastern European Jewish Mysticism* (Oxford, 1958), 95–125); A. Green, 'Hasidism: Discovery and Retreat', in P. Berger (ed.), *The Other Side of God: A Polarity in World Religions* (New York, 1981), 110 ff.

[7] On hasidic (and esp. Bratslav) opposition to philosophy see my *Tormented Master: A Life of Rabbi Nahman of Bratslav* (University of Alabama Press, 1979), 285 ff. On some of the uses made of philosophical vocabulary in hasidism see J. Dienstag, 'Ha*Moreh nevukhim* ve*Sefer hamada* besifrut haḥasidut', in *Sefer yovel likhvod harav Dr Avraham Weiss* (New York, 1964).

[8] I have written on this elsewhere. See 'The Zaddik as *Axis Mundi* in Later Judaism', *Journal of the American Academy of Religion*, 45 (1977), 327–47, and 'Typologies of Leadership and the Hasidic Zaddiq', in *Jewish Spirituality* (New York, 1987), ii. 127–56.

traditions, the *language* in which the desire for renewal was expressed played a vital role. Part of hasidism's success lay in its ability to communicate revitalized or novel ideas in a language that was entirely familiar and unthreatening to its hearers. Scholem has taught us that the kabbalists were more successful than the philosophers in integrating their teachings with the language of Judaism.[9] Hasidism was similarly highly successful in expressing radical ideas in an entirely traditional language, or at least in generating daring formulations within the old language. This is something that needs to be studied. We need a greater understanding, both structural and functional, of the specific nature of hasidic homiletics within what is to a large extent an interpretative tradition. Almost all the Hebrew literature of hasidism is interpretative. We have done very little to find out how the hasidim interpreted, how their hermeneutic worked (and changed or grew?), and how they used *derush* (homilies) as an agent of social change.[10] Here, too, there is much to be learnt from comparative studies: Luther and the Protestant Reformation, for example, are likely to offer interesting parallels.

What is new in hasidism? Here we tread on more dangerous ground, and I fear that we face the risk of a new reductionism in our study. In Hebrew I have a term for such reductionism: *yesh-kevar-etsel-ism*, a rush to find early parallels as a substitute for interpretation. I am not suggesting that tracing ideas to their original sources is not important. Of course it is. We should be aware, however, that this type of scholarly work is not an end, but only a beginning. Once we have recognized that a particular idea is to be found in Baḥya, Abulafia, or the *Shenei luḥot haberit*, we still have to deal with it in the particular phenomenological context of hasidism, which chose to incorporate rather than discard this particular idea. Often the ideas themselves change in the course of integration in a new context. We have not explained anything by saying that many hasidic themes or the terms in which they are expressed are of earlier origin.

A prime example of this is the history of the hasidic doctrine of the zaddik. As I have tried to show elsewhere,[11] this is an ancient doctrine in Judaism and not a new contribution of the hasidic movement. It is based on ideas, images, and attitudes that go back ultimately to rabbinic sources, and perhaps even to the narratives about Elijah and Elisha in the Bible. The concept of zaddik in hasidism is rooted in rabbinic statements on the power of the righteous who stand as pillars of the cosmos, who have the power to negate God's decrees, and so forth. I believe that the claims for Simeon bar Yohai in the Zohar are already based on these old rabbinic paradigms, and those claims in turn affected both the Safed kabbalists and early hasidism. The folk traditions also have a place in this history, including such notions as the thirty-six zaddikim, intercession by deceased zaddikim, and so forth. What is new in hasidism is the centrality accorded to what was previously a side-stream in Judaism. The doctrine of the zaddik is something that had been there for a long time but was never dominant. Faith in the power of the righteous surely had a long history among Jews, but remained secondary to faith in Torah and in the direct accessibility of God in prayer. Here Judaism's system of values

[9] See 'Kabbalah and Myth', in his *On the Kabbalah and its Symbolism* (New York, 1965), 87–117, esp. 99f.

[10] In general, remarkably little work has been done on hasidic homiletic as such. See my remarks in 'On Translating Hasidic Homilies', *Prooftexts*, 3 (1983), 63–72, and some other general comments in 'Teachings of the Hasidic Masters', in B. Holtz (ed.), *Back to the Sources* (New York, 1984), 361 ff.

[11] Green, 'The Zaddiq as *Axis Mundi* in Later Judaism'.

is *reordered*, with the zaddik being given a position of supremacy. Moreover, the zaddik is *identified*. The claim is no longer that there are zaddikim about in the world who can negate the decrees of God; this claim now refers to a particular zaddik: his name is Naphtali, he lives in Ropczyce, and one can go to him, or to any one of a number of others like him. The belief in the 'zaddik-idea' is now identified with particular living individuals. It seems to me that what is new here is the *institutionalization* of the zaddik. Consequently, the teachings about the zaddik proliferate and develop much more than ever before. The thread of zaddik is drawn forth from the fabric of traditional Jewish civilization, but I would not say that the idea of the zaddik is new; the change lies rather in its centralization and its institutionalization.[12]

But this is not all that is new in hasidism. I believe there is a new religious *Gestalt* in Judaism that takes place in hasidism. It is hard to characterize but is nevertheless present. I would say that it is a focusing of Judaism on worship—a sense that the simple prayer life (I say 'simple' to exclude the *kavanot* of the kabbalists) is the very centre of Judaism. For the hasidic masters, Judaism is all about the act of devotion, and especially prayer. This is the heart of Judaism as far as they are concerned, and everything else, including both study and ritual observance, is centred around this spiritual core in a simple way, open to the unlearned as well as to the learned. This seems to constitute a core that is unique and definable, a *Gestalt* of hasidic piety as distinct from that of other Judaisms. The typology of this view of Judaism *al derekh ha'avodah* is in need of further clarification and definition.[13]

Finally, the question of borders: who is in and who is out of the phenomenon we call hasidism? Scholarship is well aware that there are certain borderline figures—R. Hayyim of Chernovtsy and R. Baruch of Kosov come to mind. It would be useful to characterize the relationship of such figures with hasidism. Surely, not everyone who could be defined as a zaddik was necessarily a follower of hasidism. There were also some hasidim without a *rebbe*, especially in Erets Yisrael. There, it was possible to be a *ḥasid* (pietist) without necessarily being a *ḥasid* (disciple) *of* someone. After the Holocaust, certain hasidic groups whose ruling dynasties had died out became 'hasidic' in this sense, without a *rebbe*. There are individuals who consider themselves hasidim, who follow the hasidic liturgy, who wear a *gartel* and perhaps even a *shtrayml*, but who do not have a *rebbe*. Our phenomenological description of hasidism has to include them, too. For a working definition of the movement I would suggest *a traditionalist Jewish pietism bound by the authority of both halakhah and aggadah that traces its spiritual lineage to the Baal Shem Tov*. The person who declares that his spiritual lineage goes back to the Besht, whether his own *rebbe*'s ancestry goes as far back as a disciple in the second generation or no further than, say, R. Ahreleh Roth, accepting the authority of halakhah and aggadah as well as something of the style of hasidic life, is, I suggest, a hasid. It seems to me that this is as close as we are going to get to a good working definition at present.

12 See my remarks in 'Typologies of Leadership', 127–56.

13 On this level the most profound readers of hasidism are still Martin Buber and Hillel Zeitlin. Nothing in contemporary Jewish theological writing has surpassed them. For Buber, I believe it is his earlier essays (esp. 'The Life of the Hasidim', included in his *Hasidism and Modern Man* (New York, 1958)) that are most insightful. Zeitlin's 'Yesodot haḥasidut', in id., *Befardes haḥasidut vehakabalah* (Tel Aviv, 1965), 11–52, is also very useful.

One final remark: I certainly agree with Joseph Dan about the need to consider later hasidism and even present-day hasidism as an integral part of what we study.[14] This is an important revision of the earlier historiography of hasidism. I would demur, however, at Dan's remarks on the vitality and creativity of the contemporary hasidic community. While I agree that contemporary hasidism is vital, I believe there is room to question its creativity. Most of its efforts seem directed, as is quite understandable, to rebuilding communal infrastructure and debating degrees of accommodation to life in a new environment, one hostile to hasidism in new and different ways from the hostility that may have existed in the Polish or Hungarian countryside.

Hasidism today displays two sorts of vitality. One has allowed it to continue to exist and to recover after the Holocaust. Here I have in mind the postwar dynasties in Israel and America: the Bobover Rebbe, for example, who seemed to be struggling for survival after the war with a very few surviving hasidim, has now rebuilt a tremendous following. The history of this extraordinary recovery has not yet been written. Its social, political, and religious implications for the future of Judaism may be very great.

But there is another sort of vitality rooted in hasidism. I refer to the remarkable ability of hasidism to inspire people who are either altogether remote or estranged from hasidic practice. This includes non-Jews as well as Jews. It is significant, for example, that of the four or five major theological figures in twentieth-century Judaism, two—Martin Buber and Abraham Joshua Heschel—were nourished primarily by the vision of hasidism. The two fiction writers who have been recognized by the international community as the greatest Jewish novelists of the twentieth century—S. Y. Agnon and I. B. Singer—came from a hasidic milieu and were clearly inspired by hasidism. Hasidic influence or inspiration can be observed in virtually every field of Jewish creativity—in music, art, poetry, and theatre. The impact of hasidism on the non-hasidic Jewish community in the twentieth century has been tremendous. This, surely, testifies to the vitality of the hasidic tradition from its earliest beginnings. I urge scholars to take notice of this vitality and the ability of hasidism to affect Jews and others beyond its own borders. Of course, the product created in the course of such influence is not properly to be called hasidism. It clearly stands outside the definition suggested above. But in evaluating the importance of hasidism and its place in Jewish history, this influence beyond the movement's borders cannot be ignored. The Besht devoted himself to the uplifting of fallen and lost souls. What is more appropriate than to consider his influence on people like ourselves, who are far removed, in many ways, from the inner world of the historic hasidic community, but yet have been uplifted—and perhaps even transformed—by our study of it.

[14] See Ch. 26 above.

TWENTY-NINE

The Study of Hasidism: Past Trends and New Directions

IMMANUEL ETKES

It is not my purpose here to present a comprehensive and exhaustive survey of research into hasidism from its beginnings to the present. Rather, I propose to review the present state of the art in the field. I shall attempt to identify the major trends in the scholarly historiography of hasidism over the past few decades, to assess the impact that recent developments in the field have had on these established trends, and to map out some new research directions for the future.

Before embarking on any of these tasks, however, I would like to draw attention to an important and often overlooked point: we who have made it our business to study the history of the Jewish people as an academic discipline, who regard ourselves as critical scholars, guided by the rigours of our methodology and common sense, do not always realize that our scholarly endeavours are restricted by the bonds of tradition. I refer to the research tradition imparted to us by our teachers, a tradition which guided our first steps as independent scholars and in which we continue to follow, whether consciously or not, even when we venture into previously unexplored territories. This tradition serves us as the giant's shoulders on which we pygmies stand—a natural and essential condition of scholarly research. At the same time, however, it poses the danger that our intellectual and emotional fetters to the scholarly legacy of the past may inhibit our capacity to generate new insights. My intention, therefore, is to look more soberly and somewhat more critically at the tradition upon whose achievements we are trying to build our new edifices.

In the following pages I shall concentrate on a number of issues which are, to my mind, of central importance. The exclusion of other issues, and of the many scholarly studies which address them, is unavoidable within the limited scope of the present discussion, and does not aim to belittle their significance for the modern historiography of hasidism.

I

One question which has dominated the study of early hasidism is what factor or factors may account for the emergence and rapid spread of the movement. The mere fact that this question has occupied so many minds for so long needs no justification, in so far as

This chapter is an extended version of a lecture delivered at a memorial evening for the late Prof. Shmuel Ettinger, on the first anniversary of his death. I am indebted to Dr Ada Rapoport-Albert, who read the original Hebrew manuscript and offered some valuable comments.

the endeavour to discover the causal relationships between phenomena and events is a *sine qua non* of historical thinking. Nevertheless, what has lent this question its particular poignancy is the extraordinary speed with which hasidism gained acceptance throughout eastern Europe, and the persistence of this process despite the vehement opposition encountered by the new movement. The most influential attempts to answer this question have been those of Simon Dubnow, Benzion Dinur, and Raphael Mahler. All three historians sought to explain the emergence of hasidism and its rapid dissemination against the background of what Dubnow called the 'historical framework', that is to say, the political, economic, and social circumstances of eastern European Jewry during the eighteenth and nineteenth centuries.

Dubnow saw hasidism as history's response to the crisis besetting Polish Jewry in the first half of the eighteenth century. Generally speaking, he perceived it as a crisis of the proper functioning of 'rabbinic' religion. For Dubnow, religion's task was to offer spiritual and intellectual support to the Jews suffering under the burdensome yoke of Diaspora life. Although this yoke had become steadily heavier during the period in question, the rabbis were failing to offer solace to their oppressed flock. Instead, they aggravated the situation by demanding uncompromising observance of all the commandments of the Torah, and by ascribing absolute priority to the study of Torah in its driest and most casuistic vein. Hasidism came to fill a certain vacuum in the practice of 'rabbinic' religion, advocating preference for naïve faith, devotion, joyous fervour and belief in the zaddik's power to work miracles over the minutiae of religious observance and Torah study. In sum, Dubnow understood hasidism as a religion 'made to order' for the persecuted Jewish masses. Although it was not capable of modifying the harsh conditions of eastern European Jewish life—and indeed it made no claim to that effect—hasidism discharged its task by diverting attention from this sorry state.[1]

Dinur, too, saw hasidism as a reaction to a crisis. For him, however, the crisis was one of communal organization rather than of religious values. Negative elements—known in the Hebrew of contemporary documents as *takifim* or *alimim*, that is, 'violent persons'—exploited their personal connections with the Polish aristocracy and usurped all positions of communal power. They used this power to oppress the communities both politically and economically. In reaction to the tyrannical rule of the *takifim*, a political and economic 'opposition' emerged among the downtrodden Jews. Its spokesmen had come from the ranks of the common folk, particularly the artisans and craftsmen; at its head stood a number of *maggidim*—preachers who belonged to the 'secondary intelligentsia' of Jewish society. Although they never succeeded in ousting the corrupt leadership, it could be argued that hasidism, which did effectively replace it, was an offshoot of the same oppositionary tradition. The founders of hasidism originated in the same social circles as the opposition spokesmen. Moreover, the hasidic leaders provided relief from the social tension generated by the clash between the established leadership of the community and the Jewish masses. They showed special sensitivity to social injustice which they expressed in their writings. In fact, some hasidic leaders can be shown to have embarked on various social reforms.[2] Admittedly, Dinur did not see

[1] S. Dubnow, *Toledot haḥasidut* [Tel Aviv, 1930–1] (Tel Aviv, 1960), introd. 1–38.

[2] B. Dinur, 'Reshitah shel haḥasidut viyesodoteihah hasotsialiyim vehameshiḥiyim', in id., *Bemifneh hadorot* (Jerusalem, 1955), 81–227, esp. 92–159.

the social goals of hasidism as the sole cause of its ultimate success; on the contrary, he attributed greater weight to the messianic ideals of the movement.[3] Nevertheless, he believed that hasidism's response to the social distress of the Jewish masses went at least some way toward explaining its relatively rapid transformation into a broad-based popular movement.

Unlike Dubnow and Dinur, who were concerned with the rise and early development of hasidism, Mahler was interested in the movement's diffusion throughout Galicia toward the end of the eighteenth century and during the first decades of the nineteenth.[4] He differed from them also in his historiographical vocabulary. As a Marxist and an avid proponent of historical materialism,[5] Mahler saw hasidism as reflecting the economic and political sufferings of Galician Jews, particularly during the period of the 'Reaction' in the wake of Napoleon's defeat. As far as its social background was concerned, hasidism according to Mahler had a readily identifiable class identity: it was a movement of the *petite bourgeoisie* and the masses. However, in contrast to Dinur, Mahler did not think that hasidism delivered explicit messages of social reform. Instead, the hasidic leaders answered the people's economic and political needs by expounding in their sermons and teachings such concepts as the divine attribute of *ḥesed* (love) and the ways in which to reinforce it in order to counteract the effects of the harsh attribute of *din* (judgement); the merit of *bitaḥon* (trust in God) and belief in the zaddik; the importance of charity and love of one's fellow Jew; the meaning of Diaspora life and the hope of redemption. Despite their different styles and terminologies, one cannot but note the similarity between Mahler and Dubnow: both believed that hasidism had come about to alleviate the sufferings of the Jewish masses by diverting their attention from the material causes of their hardship and by providing them instead with spiritual sustenance.

All three scholars—Dubnow, Dinur, and Mahler—have enough in common to justify their categorization as a single trend. All argued in favour of a causal relationship between the emergence and expansion of hasidism, on the one hand, and the oppressive political, economic, and social conditions in which the Jewish masses of eastern Europe were living, on the other. Moreover, in the view of all three it was this 'oppression' or 'crisis' that conditioned the character and essence of hasidism. All three described hasidism as originating in the lower strata of Jewish society, and they shared the assumption that the rise of hasidism could have an overall causal explanation, that is, that a relatively small number of factors, taken together, could explain everything. Finally, as captives of their social-materialist—and, in Dinur's case, national-messianic—interpretations of hasidism, all three scholars failed to recognize the power of religious experience as a factor in the development of hasidism.

Dinur's view of the alleged social reform message of hasidism has been contested by several scholars. The first critique appeared in a paper by Israel Halpern, in the context of—as usual for Halpern—his analysis of a seemingly minor matter: the tax ordinances enacted in 1769 in the community of Nesvizh, one of the signatories to which was R. Aaron 'the Great' of Karlin, disciple and emissary of the Maggid of

[3] Ibid. 170–227.

[4] R. Mahler, *Hasidism and the Jewish Enlightenment* (Philadelphia, 1985), 3–67.

[5] For Mahler's historical method see J. Katz, *Le'umiyut yehudit* (Jerusalem, 1979), 243–51.

Mezhirech. This minor episode has served as the cornerstone of the thesis advanced by Dinur and others regarding the social reform aspirations of hasidism. For Dinur, these ordinances, interpreted as an attempt to avert the social evil of unjust taxation, were a perfect example of the social reforms allegedly initiated by hasidic leaders. However, a careful examination of these particular ordinances brought Halpern to the following conclusions: (*a*) the ordinances were initiated not by R. Aaron of Karlin but by the communal leaders of Nesvizh; (*b*) the ordinances did not go beyond what was customary in many communities at the time; they can hardly be considered a new departure in terms of social reform; (*c*) R. Aaron's purpose in travelling from community to community as the Maggid's emissary was to discharge a religious, not a social, mission; since he happened to be in Nesvizh at the time and to agree with the substance of the ordinances, he was willing to add his signature to the list of local signatories in order to enhance their authority.[6]

Another objection to Dinur's thesis came from one of Halpern's students, Yeshayahu Shachar, who, in a master's thesis written under Halpern's supervision, critically examined the argument that hasidic literature is exceptionally sensitive to social issues. Shachar compared hasidic homiletic works with homiletic and ethical tracts written concurrently with the beginnings of hasidism and in its area of expansion, by authors who were not associated with the hasidic movement. His findings were surprising: the non-hasidic authors were far more sensitive to social injustice than their hasidic contemporaries.[7]

An alternative to Dinur's explanation of the alleged 'social activism' of the hasidic leaders was proposed by Chone Shmeruk in a paper on hasidism and the *arenda* system, which, incidentally, also grew out of a master's thesis written under Halpern's supervision. The *arenda* leases were a major source of income for many Polish Jews. Naturally, the Polish nobles preferred to grant these leases to the highest bidders. As a result, every Jewish lessee was always at risk of losing his home, and indeed his source of income, to another Jew who was able to undercut him, offering the Polish landlord a higher payment for the lease. As a countermeasure the *kahal* enacted an ordinance forbidding Jews to compete with one another for *arenda* leases. However, by the second half of the eighteenth century *kahal* officials found it difficult to enforce this ordinance and the number of infractions increased. One reason for this was that in many cases the Polish landlord was not only the lessor but also the political overlord, with the Jewish community and its *kahal* being subject to his jurisdiction. Under these circumstances many hasidic leaders, by virtue of their charismatic authority which did not derive from or depend on their relationship with the Polish nobility, were able to take over some of the traditional law enforcement functions of the *kahal*, whose own authority was in decline.[8]

Combining these findings of Halpern, Shachar, and Shmeruk, we may be permitted to draw a conclusion of general significance: Originally, the hasidic leadership had no particular message of social reform; it confined itself to the religious, spiritual realm.

[6] I. Halpern, 'Yaḥaso shel R. Aharon hagadol miKarlin kelapei mishtar hakehilot', *Zion*, 22 (1957), 86–92, repr. in id., *Yehudim veyahadut bemizraḥ Eiropah* (Jerusalem, 1969), 333–9.

[7] Y. Shachar, *Bikoret haḥevrah vehanhagat hatsibur besifrut hamusar vehaderush bePolin bame'ah hashemoneh esreh* (Jerusalem, 1992), orig. MA thesis (Hebrew University of Jerusalem, 1963).

[8] C. Shmeruk, 'Haḥasidut ve'iskei haḥakhirut', *Zion*, 35 (1970), 182–92.

However, when the traditional communal leadership found itself unable to enforce its own social policies, the hasidic leaders leapt into the breach.

Recent research findings have clarified an additional aspect of the problem. Moshe Rosman has unearthed material from Polish archives which throws considerable light on social and economic conditions in the Medzibezh community of the eighteenth century. Not surprisingly, Rosman's research has revealed a far more complex situation than was suggested by Dinur's black and white picture of social conflict. As it turns out, the traditional conception of the Besht as a leader of the downtrodden masses in their struggle against the establishment cannot be upheld; in fact, for as long as he resided in the town of Medzibezh, the Besht enjoyed the economic support of the very establishment he is alleged to have opposed.[9]

As we have seen, both Dubnow and Dinur posit a causal connection between the crisis of Polish Jewry in the first half of the eighteenth century and the emergence of hasidism. Moreover, although each of the two scholars takes a different view of the essence of the crisis and of its resolution by hasidism, both are convinced that the crisis *per se* predetermined the nature and values of hasidism. It was Jacob Katz, in his book *Tradition and Crisis*, who challenged this conception and suggested an alternative. Katz objected on two counts to the thesis that the crisis itself promoted the growth of hasidism. First, he argued, traditional Jewish society had already weathered serious crises and emerged successfully from their aftermaths. Second, if hasidism were indeed a necessary outcome of the crisis, it should have spread through the entire geographical region within which the crisis took place, including those areas in which the movement's opponents were predominant. Katz's alternative explanation takes a closer look at the crisis itself. Its main manifestation was a weakening of the bonds that tied individuals—the constituents of society—to its institutions, values, and leadership. Although these circumstances did not necessitate the rise of hasidism, they made it easier for the movement to take root and expand. In other words, early hasidism ascended the stage of history independently of the crisis; but it was the crisis that facilitated its evolution into a broad-based movement.[10]

The advantage of Katz's approach is its careful assessment of the nature of the causal relationship between the rise of hasidism and the crisis of Polish Jewry. Katz does not view hasidism as predetermined by the nature of the crisis. The looser relationship he sees between cause and effect is a natural outcome of his sociological interpretation of the crisis: the crisis resulted from the diminished efficacy of social institutions rather than from a depreciation of the values which these institutions upheld. Katz was thus free from the need to attribute spurious notions and values to hasidism. Moreover, he did not detract from the significance of religious experience as a motive force behind the growth of hasidism.

Clearly, any attempt to account for the emergence of hasidism and its subsequent expansion must take into consideration the inherent appeal of the hasidic religious experience, and place it in the context of the crisis of the scholarly ethos in eastern European Jewry at the time. Indeed, contrary to the commonly held view, those who

[9] M. Rosman, 'Miedzyboz veRabi Yisrael Ba'al Shem Tov', *Zion*, 52 (1987), 177–89.

[10] J. Katz, *Masoret umashber* (Jerusalem, 1958), pub. in Eng. as *Tradition and Crisis*, trans. B. D. Cooperman (New York, 1993), 195–201.

flocked in great numbers to the new movement in its early stages were primarily members of the scholarly intelligentsia.[11] I believe that it was no accident that the method of casuistic Talmudic analysis known as *pilpul* and *ḥilukim*—the very pinnacle of the scholarly ethos—was a prime target of criticism in the early days of hasidism.[12] Such criticism came not only from hasidic circles,[13] but also from the chief opponents of hasidism, the Gaon of Vilna and his disciples as well as the harbingers of the Haskalah movement.[14] It follows that in order to understand how hasidism could attract large numbers of well-educated Jews who sought a better way than talmudic scholarship of expressing their religious feelings, it is not sufficient merely to analyse the novel spiritual teachings of hasidism as compared with those of earlier stages in the history of Jewish mysticism; one must also consider the attraction of hasidism against the background of the dominant trends in the spiritual lives of east European Jews in the period preceding the emergence of the new movement.

II

Another important trend in the study of hasidism is represented by the work of Gershom Scholem and his followers. Unlike all the historians mentioned above, whose interests centred on the causes of the rise of hasidism, the crucial question for Scholem was the religious and spiritual identity of the new movement. It was only natural that Scholem, as the leading student of all brands of Jewish mysticism, who was the first to illuminate the profound and complex relationship between hasidism and kabbalah, should try to examine the nature of hasidism against the backdrop of earlier trends in the history of Jewish mysticism. Scholem proposed the thesis that hasidism was the 'latest phase' in the history of Jewish mysticism, and as such was dialectically related to the two immediately preceding stages, Lurianic kabbalah and Sabbateanism. In Scholem's own

[11] That this was the case may be shown, *inter alia*, from the writings of the mitnaggedim; see e.g. M. Wilensky, *Hasidim umitnaggedim* (2 vols.; Jerusalem, 1970), i. 38, 59; Hayyim of Volozhin, *Nefesh haḥayim* (Vilna, 1824), gate 4, ch. 1.

[12] See M. Breuer, 'The Rise of *pilpul* and *ḥilukim* in German *yeshivot*' (Heb.), in *Sefer hazikaron laRav Yeḥiel Ya'akov Weinberg* (Jerusalem, 1970), 241–55; I. Ta-Shma, 'Tosafot gurnish', *Sinai*, 68 (1971), 153–61; C. Z. Dimitrovsky, 'Al derekh hapilpul', in *Salo Wittmayer Baron Jubilee Volume* (3 vols., i, ii in Eng., New York, 1974; iii in Heb., Jerusalem, 1974), iii. 111–81; D. Rapel, *Havikuaḥ al hapilpul* (Jerusalem, 1980); E. Reiner, 'Temurot biyeshivot Polin veAshkenaz bame'ot hatet-zayin-yud-zayin vehavikuaḥ al hapilpul', in I. Bartal, E. Mendelsohn, and C. Turniansky (eds.), *Keminhag ashkenaz uPolin: Sefer yovel leChone Shmeruk* (Jerusalem, 1993), 9–80.

[13] The following saying, attributed to R. Jacob Joseph of Polonnoye, represents the change in values reflected by the disparagement of *ḥilukim* as against the merit of devotion in prayer: 'The zaddik R. Jacob Joseph . . . used to say: It is easier for him to say ten *ḥilukim* than to recite one *shemoneh esreh* prayer' (Dov Ber b. Shmuel of Linits (Luniets), *Shivḥei haBesht* (Kopys, 1814), 16*d*). Most likely, the Besht's blunt charge that the rabbis were inventing 'false premisses' referred to *pilpul* (ibid. 7*c*). For an instructive example of hasidic criticism of excessively formalistic study see R. Meshullam Phoebus Heller of Zbarazh, *Yosher divrei emet*, in *Likutim yekarim* (Jerusalem, 1974), 112–13.

[14] For the Gaon's attitude to *pilpul*, see R. Joshua Heschel Levin, *Aliyot Eliyahu* (Vilna, 1856), 19–20; J. L. Maimon, *Toledot haGra* (Jerusalem, 1970), 37–52. For the view of the harbingers of the Haskalah movement, see I. Etkes, 'On the Question of the Harbingers of the Haskalah in Eastern Europe' (Heb.), *Tarbiz*, 57 (1988), 95–114.

words: 'Lurianic Kabbalism, Sabbatianism and Hasidism are after all three stages of the same process.'[15]

Lurianic kabbalah aimed to capture the imagination of the masses; it succeeded because it enabled the common folk to express their yearning for redemption. Sabbateanism, however, tried to realize those yearnings 'in our time' and therefore culminated in catastrophe. Hasidism, in Scholem's view, was a sequel to both in that it attempted 'to make the world of Kabbalism . . . accessible to the masses of the people'. However, in order to do so it had first to relieve Lurianic kabbalah of its messianic 'sting'. This hasidism proceeded to do by replacing the Lurianic messianic ideal of *tikun* with the mystical ideal of *devekut*, communion with God, thereby neutralizing the acute messianic element that pervaded both Lurianic kabbalah and Sabbateanism.[16] At this point, incidentally, one should note that Scholem's famous thesis regarding the 'neutralization' of the messianic element in hasidism is simply a more profound and sophisticated version of what Dubnow had earlier defined as a shift of emphasis from the messianic-historical to the spiritual-personal type of redemption.[17]

For Dinur, on the other hand, hasidism was a messianic movement *par excellence*. His main arguments are as follows. Hasidism emerged at a time when Polish Jewry was pervaded with messianic expectations and religious uncertainties. Both sentiments could be traced to Sabbateanism—to the messianic hopes that the movement had aroused, and to its failure to realize them. Hasidism's response was embodied in the messianic-prophetic mission of the Besht, a mission which had its source in a revelatory experience which the Besht described in a letter to his brother-in-law in 1751. In it he relates that he experienced a 'spiritual ascent' in 1747, during which he encountered the messiah. To the question 'When will you come?' the messiah replied, 'When your learning becomes known and revealed to the world and your springs gush forth as I have taught you.' The messiah's words, as well as his own aborted attempt to travel to the Holy Land, convinced the Besht that in order to accelerate the coming of the redemption, it was no longer necessary to engage in the mystical speculations and esoteric practices which were common in the kabbalistic circles of his day; what was needed now was to strive for repentance, to raise the whole nation of Israel to the level of a 'knowledgeable generation' and a 'holy congregation'. Thus, all the efforts of the Besht and his disciples to disseminate hasidic doctrines were designed to pave the way for the advent of the messiah. Faced with the fact that the alleged messianic mission of hasidism was not explicit in its literature, Dinur argued that the public disclosure of this mission would have played into the hands of the opponents of hasidism, as they would have accused the movement of crypto-Sabbateanism. Hasidic leaders preferred, therefore, to keep their messianism secret and merely hinted at it in their writings. Dinur, for his part, undertook to 'decode' the messianic 'allusions' and reconstructed on that basis what he called the 'doctrine of redemption' of the Besht and his school.[18]

Scholem rejected these arguments in his essay on the 'neutralization' of the messianic

[15] G. Scholem, *Major Trends in Jewish Mysticism* (New York, 1954), 325–50.

[16] See ibid., and in greater detail in Scholem's essay 'The Neutralization of the Messianic Element in Early Hasidism', *Journal of Jewish Studies*, 20 (1969, 25–55, repr. in id., *The Messianic Idea in Judaism* (London, 1971), 176–202.

[17] Dubnow, *Toledot haḥasidut*, 2.

[18] Dinur, 'Reshitah shel haḥasidut'.

element in hasidism.[19] Stressing that it never abandoned the traditional belief in the messiah and eagerly awaited his coming, Scholem argued nevertheless that hasidism was not a messianic movement inasmuch as it did not strive to accelerate the messianic redemption. The Besht's letter to his brother-in-law, with its account of his conversation with the messiah, was in no way evidence of any messianic urge in early hasidism; indeed, the letter remained concealed for many years in the possession of R. Jacob Joseph of Polonnoye, who had received it from the Besht in 1751 but 'revealed' it only in 1781, when he included it in his book *Ben porat Yosef.* Nor did Dinur's so-called hasidic 'doctrine of redemption' prove his point, since it was merely an artificial construct, made up by combining quotations from the works of many different hasidic authors. It follows that the 'doctrine of redemption' was an invention of Dinur: no real hasid had ever been acquainted with it. Scholem based his arguments on the thesis that the main concerns of hasidism were quite different from those of the Lurianic kabbalah. In place of the Lurianic *tikun,* suffused as it was with messianic meaning, hasidism upheld the mystical ideal of *devekut*, communion with God, which bore no relation to messianism.

Scholem's critique of Dinur, and the rejection of Dinur's claims by other scholars,[20] leave no room for doubt that the conception of hasidism as a messianic movement is less of an insight into the history of hasidism than it is a contribution to our understanding of Dinur's own nationalist historical outlook.[21] Ultimately, even if we follow Isaiah Tishby in modifying Scholem's 'neutralization' thesis and concede that some of the earliest hasidic leaders were messianically inclined as individuals,[22] it seems that Scholem was correct with regard to the limited role of the messianic element in early hasidism.

III

If Scholem's thesis of the neutralization of the messianic element in hasidism is generally accepted today, other aspects of his view of the relationship between hasidism and Sabbateanism have fared less well. This dialectic relationship expressed itself, according to Scholem, not only in the rejection of the messianic element, but also in other links—literary, ideological, and personal—between the pioneers of hasidism and the Sabbatean movement. As his grounds for this claim Scholem cited the fact that hasidism began in those parts of eastern Europe in which there were known to be large numbers of crypto-Sabbateans. In view of the common geographical ground of Sabbateanism and hasidism, as well as the chronological proximity of hasidism's early stages to the Frankist eruption, Scholem concluded that

> [the] founder of Hasidism and his first disciples, therefore, must have been fully aware of the destructive power inherent in extreme mystical Messianism . . . They were active among the

[19] See Scholem, 'Neutralization of the Messianic Element'.

[20] See e.g. A. Rubinstein, 'Igeret haBesht leR. Gershom miKutov', *Sinai*, 67 (1970), 120–39 (critique of Dinur on 133 ff.).

[21] See Katz, *Le'umiyut yehudit*, 230–9.

[22] I. Tishby, 'Hara'ayon hameshiḥi vehamegamot hameshiḥiyot bitsemiḥat haḥasidut', *Zion*, 32 (1967), 1–45.

same people whom Sabbateanism had tried [to convert] . . . and it is by no means impossible that there was at first a certain passing over of members from one movement to the other.[23]

Scholem reported what he considered important evidence for the link between Sabbateanism and hasidism in an 'unexpected find' (his own phrase), which greatly excited him. This was the discovery, in the archives of the Karlin dynasty, of a manuscript of the work *Sefer hatsoref* by the kabbalist R. Heshel Tsoref, who died in Vilna in 1700. Scholem was convinced that Tsoref was 'one of the outstanding prophets of moderate Sabbateanism', who had kept his belief in Shabbetai Zevi secret during the last years of his life. The copyist of the manuscript told its history in detail, and Scholem saw 'no reason to disbelieve him'. It seems that after Tsoref's death one of the manuscripts of his work fell into the hands of the Besht, who held it in great regard and hoped but never managed to have it copied. This was eventually accomplished by one of the Besht's grandsons. Scholem juxtaposed this account of the history of the manuscript of *Sefer hatsoref* with the well-known tale which appears at the beginning of *Shivḥei haBesht*, of 'R. Adam Ba'al Shem' and the secret writings he had left to the Besht. This tale, which Scholem himself had first considered a legend devoid of factual corroboration, now took on a major historical significance: it reflected the link between the founder of hasidism and *Sefer hatsoref*. The unusual name 'Adam', Scholem suggested, was invented by the hasidim in order to camouflage the relationship to Heshel Tsoref after his Sabbatean connections had come to light.[24]

As an expression of the ideological continuity between Sabbateanism and hasidism, Scholem pointed to their respective conceptions of 'the ideal type of man to which they ascribe the function of leadership'. This was no longer the scholar, the man of halakhah, as envisaged by rabbinic Jewry; rather 'the illuminate . . . the prophet' was the ideal leader of the community.[25]

A number of Scholem's students followed in his footsteps, most notably Isaiah Tishby and Joseph Weiss. Tishby, for his part, exposed the link between the pioneers of hasidism and Sabbateanism in the writings of the kabbalist Jacob Koppel Lifshitz of Mezhirech (d. 1740).[26] Lifshitz's books were printed at the same time as hasidism was gaining ground in eastern Europe, and several hasidic leaders wrote *haskamot* (approbations) for them. On the title-page of one of Lifshitz's kabbalistic books, and also in a *haskamah* by the 'scholars (*lomedim*) of Mezhirech', we are told that the Besht, upon being shown Lifshitz's works during his visit to the town, embraced and kissed them. There is nothing suspicious in this: the implication is that the Besht admired the writings of a kabbalist who was renowned as a saint; moreover, Lifshitz himself reviled Sabbateanism as an evil, foolish heresy. However, Tishby was able to identify various indications in Lifshitz's writings to the effect that he was a crypto-Sabbatean; as Tishby writes, 'In his clever self-disguise he successfully misled the scholars of later generations; but his cunning cannot withstand the test of critical scholarship.'[27]

At this point, of course, it is quite natural to ask, were the Besht and his disciples aware that Lifshitz was a crypto-Sabbatean? Tishby entertained few doubts on that

[23] Scholem, *Major Trends*, 330–1. [24] Ibid. 332–3. [25] Ibid. 333.

[26] I. Tishby, 'Between Sabbateanism and Hasidism: The Sabbateanism of the Kabbalist R. Jacob Koppel Lifshitz of Mezhirech' (Heb.), in id., *Netivei emunah uminut* (Ramat Gan, 1964), 204–26. [27] Ibid. 215.

count: he thought it hardly possible that the Besht could not have known the Sabbatean identity of the author whose works he had so praised. First, Tishby argued, the Besht had visited Mezhirech, Lifshitz's home town. Moreover, the persons who had presented Lifshitz's writings to the Besht 'were surely members of the author's Sabbatean-hasidic circle, who knew him well and revered him'. Tishby went on to propose an important conjecture:

> As they had asked the Besht for a kind of approbation, while the Besht himself was at that time a relatively unknown figure, there are good grounds for the assumption that they were adherents of his new type of hasidism. This points to an important conclusion: the circle of the first hasidim in Mezhirech had opened its ranks to several Sabbatean believers.[28]

Joseph Weiss, too, kept to the path mapped out by Scholem, making his own contribution to the thesis concerning the Sabbatean connections of the founders of hasidism. In a paper on the circle of pre-Beshtian hasidim in the town of Kutow, he located his subjects on the borderline between Sabbateanism and hasidism.[29] He based this, first and foremost, on the fact that the circle reportedly engaged in 'prophesying', that is, divulging the secret sins of their fellow-men, a pattern of behaviour which had been known since the time of Nathan of Gaza as a hallmark of the Sabbateans. Weiss presented further, and more radical arguments to this effect in his celebrated paper, 'The Early Emergence of the Hasidic Way',[30] in which he attempted to paint a spiritual and social portrait of the circle of *maggidim* which he identified with the Besht's associates. It will suffice to mention here only three of his points. First, Weiss argued that the idea of the 'descent of the zaddik' as formulated by the circle of *maggidim*—that is, the idea that the zaddik must ally himself with sinners in order to raise them up and restore them to purity—was 'a development of the Sabbatean conception of the Messiah's descent to the depths of the *kelipot*'.[31] Second, he pointed to certain affinities between the leaders of both movements: both opposed rabbinic authority; both belonged to the 'unofficial intelligentsia', which challenged the power of the rabbis and *parnasim*.[32] And, finally, Weiss cited a sermon in which one of the *maggidim*, R. Menahem Mendel of Bar, likened the *maggidim* to the prophets, though pointing out the difference between them; in Weiss's opinion, this constituted 'philological proof in support of the view that the typological origins of the hasidic zaddik lay in the Sabbatean prophet'.[33]

Did Sabbateanism indeed play such a crucial role in the early stages of hasidism as Scholem and his disciples would have us believe? In view of the difficulties and objections that have been raised in connection with this thesis over the past few years, it has now become rather difficult to defend.

One of the first scholars who dared to challenge the alleged link between hasidism and Sabbateanism was Abraham Rubinstein. Rubinstein devoted the beginning of one

[28] Tishby, 'Between Sabbateanism and Hasidism', 225–6.

[29] J. G. Weiss, 'A Circle of Pneumatics in Pre-Hasidism', *Journal of Jewish Studies*, 8 (1957), 199–213, repr. in id., *Studies in Eastern European Jewish Mysticism* (Oxford, 1985), 27–42.

[30] 'Reshit tsemiḥatah shel haderekh haḥasidit', *Zion*, 16 (1951), 46–105. Repr. in A. Rubinstein (ed.), *Perakim betorat haḥasidut vetoledoteihah* (Jerusalem, 1977), 122–81.

[31] Ibid. 75. [32] Ibid. 57. [33] Ibid. 51.

of his papers to questioning Tishby's findings.[34] How, he asked, could Tishby be sure that the Besht was aware of Koppel Lifshitz's Sabbateanism? One of the approbations of Lifshitz's kabbalistic work was written by R. Ephraim Zalman Margolioth; and if this learned personage, known as a vehement anti-Sabbatean, who had moreover exposed the Sabbatean leanings of *Sefer hatsoref* and thwarted plans to publish it, had failed to realize that the book was Sabbatean, 'why should we blame the Besht for not noticing this after reading only "two or three lines," i.e., after only glancing into the book?' As against Tishby's hypothesis, Rubinstein argued that there was no shred of evidence to support the notion of the direct connection between Lifshitz's Sabbatean circle and the hasidic group of the Maggid of Mezhirech. On the contrary, the only knowledge we have of any link between the two men—in the memoirs of the maskil Abraham Ber Gottlober—concerns a reported quarrel between them.[35]

Rubinstein's objections to Tishby's views may be applied to Scholem's argument: Scholem asserted that the Besht knew of Heshel Tsoref's Sabbateanism on the basis of the Adam Ba'al Shem tale in *Shivḥei haBesht*, which according to him was meant to conceal the relationship between the founder of hasidism and the Sabbatean kabbalist. That this argument is untenable has been demonstrated by Shmeruk, who showed that the Adam Ba'al Shem tales of *Shivḥei haBesht* first appeared independently in a seventeenth-century pamphlet, from which they were borrowed and inserted in *Shivḥei haBesht*.[36]

Rubinstein went on to challenge the argument that the hasidic doctrine of the zaddik was related to Sabbatean ideas, pointing out the differences between them. He also examined the Besht's attitude to Shabbetai Zevi, and demonstrated that the well-known tale from *Shivḥei haBesht* about the encounter between them furnished no proof of a positive attitude to Sabbateanism. Despite his well-reasoned arguments, Rubinstein was cautious in his conclusions. While imposing certain limits on Scholem's thesis, he did not reject it outright. On the one hand, he asserted, it is inconceivable 'that hasidism had emerged or could persist within the historical or ideological framework of Sabbateanism'. On the other, he admitted that

> the chronological and geographical proximity of Sabbatean groups and groups of hasidim gathered round the Besht, as well as the typological similarity between them, and the popularity among the hasidim of Sabbatean writings whose secret Sabbatean nature was not recognized at the time—all these prove that hasidism in its early stages had some connections with Sabbateanism in its period of decline.

As to the nature of this connection, Rubinstein wrote: 'Certain Sabbatean notions reverberated in the teachings of hasidism. But the intensity of the reverberation and the compensating effect of the complex of other influences on hasidism still await proper investigation and clarification. Much remains to be done.'[37]

[34] A. Rubinstein, 'Between Hasidism and Sabbateanism' (Heb.), in *Sefer hashanah shel universitat Bar Ilan*, 4–5 (Ramat Gan, 1967), 324–39, repr. in id. (ed.), *Perakim betorat haḥasidut vetoledoteihah* (Jerusalem, 1977), 182–97.

[35] Ibid. 327.

[36] C. Shmeruk, 'Hasipurim al R. Adam Baal Shem vegilguleihem benusḥe'ot sefer *Shivḥei haBesht*', *Zion*, 28 (1963), 86–105, repr. in id., *Sifrut yidish bePolin* (Jerusalem, 1981), 119–46.

[37] Rubinstein, 'Hasidism and Sabbateanism', 338–9.

Although Rubinstein's cautious conclusions refute the core of Scholem's thesis, they constitute a partial acceptance of his claims: one point that Rubinstein did not contest was the alleged geographical coincidence of the beginnings of hasidism and Sabbateanism. However, this point too has now been challenged: Michael Silver, in a detailed historical-geographical study, has proved beyond a doubt that the regions in which hasidism first emerged were not the same as those that harboured crypto-Sabbateans. In fact, the very opposite was true: the founders of hasidism took care to concentrate their activities in non-Sabbatean areas.[38] This unequivocal conclusion may support one constituent of Scholem's thesis, namely, that hasidism indeed turned its back on Sabbateanism; but at the same time it disproves his claim as to the geographical affinity between the two movements.

Silver's study also refuted Weiss's findings as to the alleged personal relationship between the first hasidim and the last Sabbateans. As for Weiss's claim that there were phenomenological similarities and ideological affinities between the two movements, for all its intellectual brilliance, it lacks a proper textual basis, as has already been observed by Haim Lieberman and Mendel Piekarz.[39] However, without going into the finer points of their textual criticism, we may ask: is it really necessary to associate the hasidic leadership's critique of the rabbinic establishment with Sabbateanism? Moreover, even if we admit to a certain phenomenological similarity between the movements—which in itself is rather questionable—does this really attest to ideological affinities and influence? In addition, the argument whereby the hasidic idea of the zaddik's descent to the level of ordinary sinners in order to redeem them must have developed from the Sabbatean notion of Shabbetai Zevi's descent to the depth of the *kelipot* is untenable. As against Scholem's tendency (emulated by his followers) to attribute any hasidic expression of religious radicalism to Sabbatean influence, we have Piekarz's striking findings to the effect that such aberrant ideas were already present in non-Sabbatean kabbalistic homiletic literature which was readily available in print when hasidism was in its infancy.[40] Thus, such radical notions as 'the descent of the zaddik' may well have entered hasidism directly from Lurianic kabbalah, totally bypassing the heretical aberrations of Sabbateanism.

Today's reader of Scholem, Tishby, and Weiss cannot but wonder at how these distinguished scholars could have been misled by such tenuous analogies. I venture to suggest that the exciting thesis of a dialectic relationship between hasidism and Sabbateanism must have dulled their critical faculties. It seems to me that the determining factor here was not only the fascination which the thesis itself must have held for this generation of scholars, but also its underlying methodological assumption—that the development of hasidism must be explained by reference to earlier stages in the history of Jewish mysticism. Against this methodological premiss we now have Moshe Idel's view, that the founders of hasidism could have drawn their inspiration from a wider range of diverse sources among the religious and spiritual traditions of

[38] Silver reported his as yet unpublished findings to the conference of which the present volume is the proceedings.

[39] See H. Lieberman, 'Keitsad ḥokerim ḥasidut beYisrael?', *Bitsaron*, 14, 27: 3 (1953), 165–73, repr. in id., *Ohel Raḥel* (3 vols.; New York, 1980–4), i. 1–11, and M. Piekarz, *Biyemei tsemiḥat haḥasidut: Megamot ra'ayoniyot besifrei derush umusar* (Jerusalem, 1978), 96–8.

[40] Piekarz, *Biyemei tsemiḥat haḥasidut*, chs. 6, 7, 269–302.

Judaism.[41] Thus, for example, I find it difficult to accept Weiss's attempt to link the Kutow hasidim with Sabbateanism, on the sole basis of the group's engagement in 'prophecy'. Indeed, this type of 'prophetic' exposure of other people's sins pre-dates Sabbateanism; it was, in fact, one of the most prominent trends in the early development of kabbalah.[42] Moreover, some of the most noted Safed kabbalists, including R. Moses Cordovero, R. Isaac Luria, R. Hayyim Vital, and R. Joseph Caro, were also known to have engaged in such activities.[43]

Jacob Katz, who agreed with the general trend of Scholem's thesis and explored its social implications, touched on the relationship between hasidism and Sabbateanism in the following lines:

> And indeed, important elements of these two movements [i.e. kabbalistic pietism and Sabbateanism] were absorbed by Hasidism, and the rise of Hasidism cannot be understood without reference to these movements. On the other hand, such an argument from chronology to causality is satisfactory only in part. Hasidism is so radically innovative, even *vis-à-vis* Sabbateanism and kabbalistic pietism, that any attempt to explain it as the outcome of these two is virtually tantamount to intellectual evasion.[44]

In the light of subsequent developments of research in this area, I believe that we can now go even further: the rise of hasidism as we know it today can be explained without postulating any links with Sabbateanism.[45]

IV

As we have seen, Scholem sought to highlight the religious and spiritual significance of hasidism, and much of what he wrote remains valid, even if we reject his thesis of Sabbatean influence. A cardinal question that he raised in this connection was: did hasidism make any original contribution to kabbalistic theology? His answer was as follows:

> If one leaves out of account the lone effort . . . made by Rabbi Shneur Zalman of Ladi . . . Hasidism seems to have produced no truly original kabbalistic thought whatever . . . Hasidism is practical mysticism at its highest . . . Particular emphasis is laid on ideas and concepts concerning the relation of the individual to God. All this centers around the concept of what the kabbalists call *devekut*.[46]

Scholem subsequently developed this theme, which he had already formulated in the last chapter of *Major Trends in Jewish Mysticism*, in his essay on *devekut* in early hasidism.[47]

[41] M. Idel, 'Martin Buber and Gershom Scholem on Hasidism: A Critical Appraisal', in this volume.

[42] See M. Idel, *Haḥavayah hamistit etsel Avraham Abulafiyah* (Jerusalem, 1988).

[43] See e.g. M. Benayahu, *Sefer toledot ha'Ari* (Jerusalem, 1967), index, s.v. 'nevu'ah', 'navi'.

[44] Katz, *Tradition and Crisis*, 197.

[45] This thesis is contested by some students of hasidism; see e.g. Y. Liebes, 'Hatikun hakelali shel R. Nahman miBraslav veyaḥaso lashabeta'ut', *Zion*, 45 (1980), 201–45. And cf. Ada Rapoport-Albert's critique of Liebes (Heb.), in *Zion*, 46 (1981), 346–51, and Liebes's answer (Heb.), *Zion*, 46 (1981), 352–5. See also Y. Mondshine, 'On "R. Nahman of Bratzlav's *Hatikun hakelali* and his Attitude towards Sabbateanism"' (Heb.), *Zion*, 47 (1982), 198–223, and Liebes's answer (Heb.), *Zion*, 47 (1982), 224–31.

[46] Scholem, *Major Trends*, 340–1.

[47] Scholem, 'Devekut, or Communion with God', *Review of Religion*, 14 (1949–50), 115–39, repr. in id., *The Messianic Idea*, 203–27.

His conclusion was that whereas kabbalah had presented *devekut* as an exclusive ideal, fit for a small élite, hasidism considered it a challenge, a demand aimed at each and every Jew. This observation by Scholem gained wide acceptance, probably because it was in line with the common view of hasidism as a popular movement from its very inception.

In recent years, however, some scholars have rejected Scholem's contention that the Besht saw *devekut* as a spiritual ideal worthy of every Jew.[48] A close scrutiny of the individuals who made up the Besht's intimate circle of associates, those among whom he propounded his doctrine of *devekut*, has shown that most if not all of them were traditional mystics, 'hasidim' of the old stamp. In other words, the Besht operated within the exclusive framework of traditional mystical piety which was always intended for a few elect individuals. Evidence for this can be gleaned from numerous hasidic texts, as Piekarz has shown in his contribution to the present volume.[49]

Scholem, in his assertion that early hasidism aimed at putting *devekut* within the reach of every Jew, and Dubnow, with his portrayal of hasidism as a popular, almost vulgar movement, despite the considerable distance between their views shared the same misconception: both were inclined to explain hasidism at its inception in terms of its later manifestations. It is quite true that the founders of hasidism, though members of a pietist-mystic élite, appealed to the wider community and aspired to lead it. Scholem was right when he stated that hasidism had paid for this aspiration with the popularization of kabbalistic ideas and ideals. However, the transformation from an élitist circle of pietists and mystics gathered round the Besht to a broad movement embracing ordinary folk as well did not take place in one fell swoop. It was a gradual process, in which distinct stages may be discerned, with a distinctive spiritual and social dynamic. One might say that the history of the hasidic movement is essentially the history of that process. One of the most pressing tasks of research in the field of hasidism is a historical reconstruction and proper characterization of all its stages.[50]

V

Two of the foremost Jewish historians in the modern era are divided on another question of interest: the position of hasidism with respect to tradition. According to Jacob Katz, hasidism furthered the disintegration of traditional society. Shmuel Ettinger, in contrast, argued that hasidism was a 'conservative' movement *par excellence*, which had done much during the nineteenth century to reinforce the hold of tradition in eastern Europe.

[48] A. Rapoport-Albert, 'God and the Zaddik as the Two Focal Points of Hasidic Worship', *History of Religions*, 18:4 (1979), 296–325, repr. in G. D. Hundert (ed.), *Essential Papers on Hasidism* (New York, 1991), 299–329; I. Etkes, 'Hasidism as a Movement: The First Stage', in B. Safran (ed.), *Hasidism: Continuity or Innovation?* (Cambridge, Mass., 1988), 1–26.

[49] See Ch. 13.

[50] For an attempt to describe the first stage of hasidism as a movement see my paper 'Hasidism as a Movement'. For some interesting insights concerning the social characteristics and organizational structure of early hasidism see A. Rapoport-Albert's contribution to the present volume. How the esoteric elements of hasidism were imparted to the common folk—a central motif in the evolution of hasidism as a movement—is the subject of N. Loewenthal, *Communicating the Infinite: The Emergence of the Habad School* (Chicago, 1990).

Katz's view derives from his broader conception of the crisis of eighteenth-century traditional society, a crisis which was occasioned by the rise of the Haskalah movement on the one hand, and of hasidism on the other:

Hasidism and Haskalah exemplify the two forces that typically cause the disintegration of traditional social institutions: religious charisma and rationalism . . . Religious charisma and rationalism are essentially opposites, and are likely to come into conflict when they exist in the same historical framework. But they share a common attitude to traditionalism: both find the source of their authority in themselves, and tend to minimize any authority that rests solely on the force of tradition.[51]

Katz was naturally aware of the difference between the respective attitudes to tradition of the Haskalah and hasidism; accordingly, his observations on the latter were more moderate: 'If Hasidism did not destroy the accepted religious forms, it certainly shifted their spiritual basis; and if it did not destroy the accepted social framework, it certainly introduced new principles of integration into it.'[52] Katz attributed the destructive influence of hasidism on traditional society to the twofold revolution that it brought about—a religious revolution and a social revolution. The religious revolution was that *devekut* ('cleaving', i.e. subjective communion with God) was the religious goal to which the rituals of religion and tradition were totally devoted.[53] Put differently, 'the shift in emphasis from the actual performance of the precept to the attainment of ecstasy through that performance constitutes the primary religious change'.[54] Katz also pointed out the latent antinomistic potential of this transition:

after all, if the state of ecstasy was the main goal, then performance of the commandments was not the only mechanism that led to its achievement. Even the hasidic leaders, including the Besht himself, admitted that traditionally secular activities could become the means for achieving the sought-after exaltation.[55]

As to the social revolution, this was, in Katz's view, primarily the emergence of a new type of religious leadership: unlike the traditional rabbi, whose authority was drawn from his erudition and scholarship, for the hasidic leader 'the primary and ultimate prerequisite for leadership was an individual's ability to achieve communion with God and ecstatic contact with the divine sphere.[56]

Katz's view of the effect of hasidism on the role of tradition in east European Jewish society was one of the targets of Ettinger's criticism in a review of Katz's book.[57] Taking issue with Katz's notion of the 'religious revolution', in the sense of the shift in the meaning of religious observance and the function of the commandments as a means toward the achievement of ecstasy, Ettinger argued:

Even if there were such tendencies among the first, pre-Beshtian, groups of hasidim, or in the Besht's own group, these were by no means the principles of hasidism once it became a religious *movement*, governing the lives of all its 'average' members at a point at which it was about to experience an astonishingly rapid expansion. The movement had expressly rejected Sabbateanism, which was certainly not averse to the idea of personal ecstasy. Had such ideas been current within the hasidic movement, its early exponents would surely have underlined

[51] Katz, *Tradition and Crisis*, 9. [52] Ibid. 196. [53] Ibid. 204.
[54] Ibid. 206. [55] Ibid. 207. [56] Ibid. 209.
[57] S. Ettinger, review of Katz, *Masoret umashber* (Heb.), *Kiryat sefer*, 35 (1960), 12–18.

the importance of religious observance, if only in order to distance themselves from those who violated the commandments. The fact that their sermons, as Katz himself admits, contained no such exhortations, and that they took for granted the meticulous observance of all the commandments, is conclusive proof that the alleged revolution in regard to the role of tradition and the commandments had no religious or social significance.[58]

Just as he rejected Katz's notion of the hasidic 'religious revolution', so Ettinger contested his conclusions as regards the erosive effect of hasidism on Jewish society in eastern Europe:

There is no doubt that hasidism had an innovative effect on Jewish society, first and foremost because the hasidim were the first to 'change the formula stipulated by the Sages' without incurring the penalties of suppression or exclusion from the fold. However, there are surely no grounds for the contention that hasidism weakened Jewish society and its communal organization. The very opposite is true. After a brief period of inner conflict, hasidism was granted legitimacy, was accepted by all Jews, and ultimately brought about a greater degree of inner cohesion. Witness Jewish society in Russia and Poland in the first half of the nineteenth century, and even Lithuanian Jewry, on which it had its positive effect: the revival of the great yeshivot and the rise of the *musar* movement were largely a reaction to the advent of hasidism.[59]

Did hasidism generate a religious and social 'revolution', and did it contribute to the disintegration of traditional society, as Katz claimed, or was it a 'conservative movement', which buttressed the values and institutions of traditional society, as argued by Ettinger?

Essentially, there seems to be no argument between Katz and Ettinger as to the facts themselves; where they differ is in their evaluation of the facts. We can trace the difference between their respective interpretations of the place and function of hasidism in Jewish society to their divergent historical perspectives. Writing from the viewpoint of 'social history', Katz focused attention in *Tradition and Crisis* on traditional social structures and the changes they underwent. Ettinger, on the other hand, a self-avowed 'general historian',[60] took exception to Katz's use of sociological tools and emphasized the unique, non-repeatable nature of historical phenomena. Whereas Katz's book examined hasidism against the background of Ashkenazi Jewish society toward the end of the Middle Ages, Ettinger was concerned with its contribution to east European Jewish society during the nineteenth century. Katz, therefore, concentrated on the beginnings of hasidism, while Ettinger was interested mainly in its later stages of development. It is not surprising, therefore, that for Katz hasidism represented certain spiritual and social innovations which led to a radical transformation of traditional patterns of Jewish life; hence his view of it as a disintegrative factor. Ettinger, on the other hand, who had a long-standing interest in radical movements in nineteenth-century Jewry, saw hasidism, for all its innovative thrust, as a conservative force or, at most, a new instrument working to preserve the old values and patterns of communal life.

It could be argued that Katz and Ettinger, each from his own perspective and using his own methods and conceptual tools, have illuminated different aspects of hasidism. To assess their respective contributions to the field, a synthetic approach may be

[58] S. Ettinger, review of Katz, 17. [59] Ibid. [60] Ibid. 13.

adopted, which would combine the merits of both. Both scholars were trying to answer not one, but two key questions: did hasidism create a 'revolution', and did it lead to the disintegration of traditional society? According to Katz, the disintegrative effect of hasidism was no less profound than the transformation it had brought about in the patterns of religious worship and communal leadership. Ettinger, on the other hand, stressed the conservative bent of nineteenth-century hasidism, and was inclined to belittle its transformative effect. To my mind, the two questions, and the answers to them should be kept more clearly apart. Hasidism did bring about a profound change in traditional attitudes and communal organization; nevertheless, it did not further the disintegration of traditional society. In other words, while accepting Katz's analysis, I believe that one should moderate his conclusion as to the disintegrative effect of hasidism on traditional society.[61]

Katz rightly pointed out the antinomistic potential of hasidism. The leaders of the movement, however, were aware of the danger and averted it in time. Thus, for example, they restricted the application of the idea of 'worship through corporeality' to the zaddikim alone. Moreover, from the very start, hasidism was careful to channel its mystical fervour into the traditional moulds of religious worship. The most obvious example of this was the adoption of prayer as the principal medium for the achievement of *devekut*. As to the 'revolution' represented by the rise of a charismatic leadership in hasidism, it should not be viewed as exerting a destructive effect on tradition. The hasidic leaders did not use their power to undermine traditional norms. Moreover, the concept of the mystic whose authority as a religious leader is rooted in his personal experience did not begin with hasidism. The movement saw itself, with no little justification, as an heir to the kabbalistic tradition. R. Solomon of Lutsk's introduction to *Maggid devarav leYa'akov* gives concrete expression to this sense of connection to the kabbalistic past. In it he describes the Besht and the Maggid of Mezhirech as the last two links in a spiritual chain of tradition, connecting them to R. Simeon bar Yoḥai, R. Moses Cordovero, and R. Isaac Luria. Although, from the historical and social standpoints, the kabbalist who operates in a small, exclusive circle of fellow kabbalists and the hasidic leader who exercises his authority over a broad section of society are very different from one another, there is direct continuity between the two. Thus, the hasidic leadership may be seen as firmly rooted in tradition and deriving its authority from it.

For Katz, the term 'traditional society' denotes Jewish society from the time of the Mishnah and the Talmud to the eighteenth century. This society was marked by the desire to anchor its existence in traditional values and patterns of communal life. Inevitably, in the course of its long history, it experienced crisis and change but it always rebuilt itself, assuming different complexions, while retaining the conscious commitment to traditional values. According to Katz, however: 'A real break with tradition occurs only when events are accompanied by a total re-evaluation of tradition itself, and when tradition, rather than serving to justify events, becomes the point of

[61] I discussed this topic at length in a lecture entitled 'Hasidism vs. Tradition: Thoughts on Jacob Katz's Discussion of Hasidut in *Tradition and Crisis*', read at a conference held at Harvard University in 1988, on the thirtieth anniversary of the publication of the original Hebrew version of *Tradition and Crisis*. Here I mention briefly only a few of my conclusions there.

departure for reservation and criticism.'[62] I do not think that this condition was fulfilled by hasidism.

The hasidic movement did not bring about the disintegration of tradition. It was rather—to use Katz's own term—a variation within the framework of traditional society.

[62] Katz, *Tradition and Crisis*, 184.

Bibliography

AARON (the second) and ASHER of KARLIN, *Beit Aharon* (Brody, 1875).

AARON HALEVI of STAROSIELCE, *Avodat halevi* [2 vols.; Lemberg, 1842–62 (i); 1866 (ii)] (Jerusalem, 1972).

—— *Sha'arei avodah* [Shklov, 1821] (Jerusalem, 1970).

—— *Sha'arei hayiḥud veha'emunah* [Shklov, 1820] (Jerusalem, 1970).

AARON of OPATOW, *Keter shem tov* [2 vols., Zholkva (Zolkiew), 1794–5; 1 vol., Korets, 1797] (Bnei Brak, 1957; Brooklyn, NY, 1972; Jerusalem, 1975).

AARON SAMUEL HAKOHEN, *Kore merosh* [Berdichev, 1811].

ABRAHAM B. ALEXANDER KATZ of KALISK, *Ḥesed le'Avraham* [Chernovtsy (Czernowitz), 1851] (Jerusalem, 1954).

ABRAHAM B. AZRIEL, *Sefer arugat habosem*, ed. E. E. Urbach (Jerusalem, 1947).

ABRAHAM B. MORDECAI AZULAI, *Ḥesed le'Avraham* [Amsterdam, 1685] (Lemberg, 1863; Jerusalem, 1968).

ABRAHAM of GRANADA, *Berit menuḥah* [Amsterdam, 1648] (Warsaw, 1864).

ABRAHAM HAYYIM of ZLOCZEW, *Oraḥ laḥayim*. Repr in *Sefarim kedoshim migedolei talmidei Ba'al Shem Tov hakadosh* (35 + 3 vols.; Brooklyn, NY 1981–6), xxii.

ABRAHAM HAZAN of TULCHIN, 'Avaneihah barzel' (Jerusalem, 1935). Repr. in id., *Sefer kokhvei or* (Jerusalem, 1961).

—— *Sefer kokhvei or* (Jerusalem, 1961).

ABRAHAM of SLONIM, *Yesod ha'avodah* (Jerusalem, 1989).

ABRAHAMS, ISRAEL, *Jewish Life in the Middle Ages* (New York, 1973).

AESCOLY, A. Z., 'Haḥasidut bePolin', in I. Halpern (ed.), *Beit Yisrael bePolin* (2 vols.; Jerusalem 1948–53), ii.

AGNON, S. Y., *Me'atsmi el atsmi* (Tel Aviv, 1976).

AHIMAAZ B. PALTIEL, *Megilat Aḥima'ats*, ed. B. Klar (Jerusalem, 1974).

ALEICHEM, SHOLOM, *Ḥayei adam*, trans. J. Berkovitz (New York, 1920), pub. in Eng. in *From the Fair: The Autobiography of Sholom Aleichem*, trans. and ed. C. Leviant (New York, 1985).

ALEXANDER-IHME, ESTHER, '"A Yid shmadt sikh nit": Apostasie, Judenmissionsnot und Taufe in jüdischen Volkserzählungen', *Frankfurter judaistische Beiträge*, 15 (1987).

—— '"Warum wird eine Geschichte erzählt?" Überlegungen zur Bedürfnisstruktur der Erzählungen von der "Rache der Leiche" und "Rache des Toten"', *Frankfurter judaistische Beiträge*, 16 (1988).

ALFASI, I., *Bisdeh haḥasidut* (Tel Aviv, 1986).

—— *Entsiklopediah laḥasidut*, ed Y. Raphael [ii:] *Ishim* (Jerusalem, 1986).

—— *Haḥasidut veshivat Tsiyon* (Tel Aviv, 1986).

—— *Haḥozeh miLublin* (Jerusalem, 1969).

—— 'Ha*Shulḥan arukh* bikhal ḥasidim', *Maḥanayim*, 97 (1965).

ALSHEKH, MOSES, *Torat Moshe* (Amsterdam, 1777).

ALTMANN, A., "Homo Imago Dei in Jewish and Christian Theology', *Journal of Religion*, 48 (1968).

—— *Studies in Religious Philosophy and Mysticism* (New York, 1969).

ARIEH LEIB COHEN, *Derakhav, nimukav vesiḥotav shel haḤafets Ḥayim* (Warsaw, 1937).

Arvei naḥal. *See* Eybeschuetz, David Solomon.

ASHER ZEVI of OSTROG, *Ma'ayan haḥokhmah* [Korets, 1817] (Jerusalem, 1971).

ASHKENAZI, ELIEZER (ed.), *Ta'am zekenim* (Frankfurt on Main, 1854).

ASSAF, DAVID, 'MiVolin liTsfat: Deyokano shel R. Avraham Dov me'Ovruch kemanhig ḥasidi bamaḥatsit harishonah shel hame'ah hatesha'esreh', *Shalem*, 6 (1992).

—— '*Yesod Ha-Ma'ala*: A New Chapter in the Historiography of Hasidism in Erets-Israel' (Heb.), *Cathedra*, 68 (1993).

ASSAF, S., 'Lekorot harabanut', in id., *Be'oholei Ya'akov* (Jerusalem, 1943).

—— 'Sifriyot batei hamidrash', *Yad lakore*, 1: 7–9 (1946–7).

'Avaneihah barzel'. *See* Abraham Hazan of Tulchin.

Avodat halevi. *See* Aaron Halevi of Starosielce.

Avot deRabbi Natan, ed. Solomon Schechter [1887] (New York, 1967).

'Avot haḥasidut'. *See* Schneersohn, Joseph Isaac.

AZIKRI, ELEAZER, *Sefer ḥaredim* [Venice, 1601] (Jerusalem, 1980).

AZULAI, ABRAHAM B. MORDECAI, *Ḥesed le'Avraham* [Amsterdam, 1685] (Lemberg, 1863; repr. Jerusalem, 1968).

—— *Or haḥamah* [4 vols.; Przemysl, 1896] (Bnei Brak, 1973).

AZULAI, HAYYIM JOSEPH DAVID, *Ma'agal tov*, A. Freimann (Jerusalem, 1934).

BAḤYA B. ASHER, *Rabbenu Baḥya: Be'ur al hatorah*, ed. C. Chavel (3 vols.; Jerusalem, 1981).

BAḤYA IBN PAKUDA, *Ḥovot halevavot* [11th cent. (Arab.); Jerusalem, 1928 (Heb.)]. Arab. orig. trans. to Heb. as *Ḥovot halevavot*, ed. M. Hyamson (5 vols.; New York, 1925–7); Heb. version trans. as *The Book of Direction to the Duties of the Heart*, ed. and trans. M. Mansoor (London, 1973).

BALABAN, *Yidn in Poyln* (Vilna, 1930).

BARANOWSKI, BOHDAN, *Procesy czarownic w Polsce w XVII i XVIII wieku* (Lodz, 1952).

BARNAI, JACOB, 'Al aliyato shel R. Avraham Gershon miKutov le'Erets Yisrael', *Zion*, 42 (1976–7).

—— *Historiografiah ule'umiyut* (Jerusalem, 1995).

—— *Igrot ḥasidim me'Erets Yisrael* (Jerusalem, 1980).

—— *The Jews in Erets-Israel in the 18th Century* (Heb.) (Jerusalem, 1982).

—— 'Some Clarifications on the Land of Israel's Stories of "In Praise of the Baal Shem Tov"', *Revue des études juives*, 146 (1987).

—— 'Trends in the Historiography of the Medieval and Early Modern Period of the Jewish Community in Erets Yisrael' (Heb.), *Cathedra*, 42 (1987).

BARON, S. W., *The Jewish Community* (2 vols.; Philadelphia, 1945).

BARTAL, ISRAEL, "Aliyat R. Eleazar meAmsterdam Le'Erets Yisrael bishnat 1740', *Meḥkarim al toledot yahadut Holland*, 4 (1984).

—— *Galut ba'arets* (Jerusalem, 1994).

—— 'Halo-Yehudim veḥevratam besifrut ivrit veyidish bemizraḥ Eiropah bein hashanim 1856–1914' (Ph.D. thesis, Hebrew University of Jerusalem, 1980).

—— 'Le'an halakh tseror hakesef? Habikoret hamaskilit al hebeteihah hakalkaliyim shel haḥasidut', in M. Ben-Sasson (ed.), *Dat vekalkalah: yaḥasei gomelin* (Jerusalem, 1995).

—— 'Messianism and Historiography' (Heb.), *Zion*, 52 (1987).

—— 'Note' (Heb.), *Cathedra*, 31 (1984).

—— 'The Old Yishuv in Erets Yisrael' (Heb.), *Sekirah ḥodshit*, 3–4 (1981).

—— "Shimon hakofer: Perek behistoriografiah ortodoksit', in I. Bartal, E. Mendelsohn, and C. Turniansky (eds.), *Keminhag Ashkenaz uPolin: Sefer Yovel leChone Shmeruk* (Jerusalem, 1994).

—— "Tesmiḥato shel hayishuv hayashan vehatifroset hayishuvit shelo', *Hahistoriah shel Erets Yisrael*, 8 (1983).

—— 'Zikhron Ya'akov leRabi Ya'akov Lipschitz: Historiografiah ortodoxit?', *Milet: Meḥkerei ha'Universitah haPetuḥah betoledot Yisrael vetarbuto*, 2 (Tel Aviv, 1984).
—— ELIOR, R., and SHMERUK, C. (eds.), *Tsadikim ve'anshei ma'aseh: Meḥkarim baḥasidut Polin* (Jerusalem, 1994).
BARUCH of MEDZIBEZH, *Butsina dinehora* [Lemberg, 1879; Lemberg, 1884] (New York, 1956).
—— *Butsina dinehora hashalem*, ed. R. Margaliot [Bilgoraj, n.d.] (Jerusalem, 1985).
BEER, P., *Geschichte, Lehren und Meinungen aller bestandenen und noch bestehenden religiösen Sekten der Juden* (2 vols.; Brünn, 1823).
Beit Aharon. See Aaron (the second) and Asher of Karlin.
Beit Yehonatan hasofer. See Emden, Jacob.
BENAYAHU, MEIR, 'The Ashkenazi Community of Jerusalem, 1647–1747' (Heb.), *Sefunot*, 2 (1958).
—— *Hadefus ha'ivri biKremona* (Jerusalem, 1971).
—— *Haskamah ureshut bidfusei Venetsiah* (Jerusalem, 1971).
—— 'Pinkasim bikhtav-yad leḤakham miDamesek', *Kiryat sefer*, 35 (1960).
—— *Sefer toledot ha'Ari* (Jerusalem, 1967).
Ben porat Yosef. See Jacob Joseph of Polonnoye.
BEN-SASSON, H. H., *Hagut vehanhagah* (Jerusalem, 1959).
—— *Isaiah ben Abraham Halevi Horowitz*, in *Ha'entsiklopediah ha'ivrit*, vol. xiii.
—— 'Ishiyuto shel HaGra vehashpa'ato hahistorit', *Zion*, 31 (1966).
—— 'Statutes for the Enforcement of the Observance of the Sabbath in Poland and their Social and Economic Significance' (Heb.), *Zion*, 21 (1956).
—— 'Yosef Weiss, zal: An Obituary' (Heb.), *Zion*, 34 (1969).
—— and ETTINGER, S. (eds.), *Jewish Society through the Ages* (New York, 1971).
BERGER, ISRAEL, *Eser atarot* (Piotrkow, 1910).
—— *Eser kedushot* [Warsaw, 1902; Piotrkow, 1906] (Tel Aviv, 1973).
—— *Eser orot* [Piotrkow, 1907] (Warsaw, 1913).
—— *Eser tsaḥtsaḥot* (Piotrkow, 1910).
—— *Simḥat Yisrael* (Piotrkow, 1910).
BERISH, ISSACHAR, *Sefer malbush leshabat veyom tov* (Bilgoraj, 1937).
BERSHADSKI, S., *Litovskie yevrei* (St Petersburg, 1883).
BIALE, DAVID, *Gershom Scholem, Kabbalah and Counter-History* (Cambridge, Mass., 1982).
BICHOVSKY, C. E., *Ginzei nistarot* (Jerusalem, 1924).
—— and HIELMAN, H. M. (eds.), *Me'ah she'arim* [Berdichev, 1913] (Kfar Habad, 1967; Brooklyn, NY, 1975).
BLOOM, HAROLD (ed.), *Gershom Scholem* (New York, 1987).
BLUMENTHAL, D. (ed.), *Approaches to Judaism in Medieval Times* (Atlanta, 1988).
BORNSTEIN, DAVID of SOCHACZEW, *Ne'ot hadeshe*, ed. Aaron Israel Bornstein (2 vols.; Tel Aviv, 1974–8).
BOSK, CHARLES, 'Cybernetic Hasidism: An Essay on Social and Religious Change', *Sociological Inquiry*, 44: 2 (1974).
BRAWER, A. J., 'Al hamaḥaloket bein haRashaz miLiady veR. Avraham Hakohen miKalisk', *Kiryat sefer*, 1 (1924–5).
BREITSTEIN, S. Z., *Siḥot ḥayim* (Piotrkow, 1914).
BREUER, M., 'The Rise of *pilpul* and *ḥilukim* in German *yeshivot*' (Heb.), in *Sefer hazikaron laRav Yeḥiel Ya'akov Weinberg* (Jerusalem, 1970).
BROKMAN, MORDECAI, *Migdal David* [Piotrkow, 1930]. Repr. in *Sefarim kedoshim migedolei talmidei Ba'al Shem Tov hakadosh* (35 + 3 vols.; Brooklyn, NY, 1981–6), iii.
BRUELL, N., 'Beiträge zur jüdischen Sagen- und Sprachkunde in Mittelalter', *Jahrbücher für jüdische Geschichte und Literatur*, 9 (1889).

BUBER, MARTIN, *Befardes haḥasidut* (Tel Aviv, 1945).
—— *Der Jude und sein Judentum* (Cologne, 1963)
—— *Ecstatic Confessions* [1909], ed. P. Mendes-Flohr (San Francisco, 1985).
—— *Hasidism* (New York, 1948).
—— *Hasidism and Modern Man* (New York, 1958; 1966).
—— 'Interpreting Hasidism', *Commentary*, 36: 3 (Sept. 1963).
—— 'The Life of the Hasidim', in id., *Hasidism and Modern Man* (New York, 1958; 1966).
—— *Or haganuz* (Tel Aviv, 1977).
—— *The Origin and Meaning of Hasidism* (New York, 1960).
—— *Tales of the Hasidim* (2 vols.; New York, 1972).
BURACK, L. 'Hasidism: A Selected Annotated Bibliography of Articles of Ethnographic Interest (1965–75)', *Jewish Folklore and Ethnology Newsletter*, 2: 2–3 (1979).
Butsina dinehora. *See* Baruch of Medzibezh.
CALMANSON, JACOB (Jacques), *Essai sur l'état actuel des Juifs de Pologne et leur perfectibilité* (Warsaw, 1796).
CHITRIK, AARON, 'Al pegishat haBesht im Aḥiyah Hashiloni', *Sinai*, 73 (1973).
—— *Reshimot devarim* (2 vols.; Brooklyn, NY, 1981–5).
COHEN, AMNON, *Palestine in the Eighteenth Century* (Jerusalem, 1973).
COHEN, I. J., 'HaḤatam Sofer vehaḥasidut', *Sinai*, 69 (1971).
—— 'Teshuvot *Mar'eh Yeḥezkel* me'et R. Yeḥezkel Panet', *Mekorot vekorot* (Jerusalem, 1982).
CORDOVERO, M., *Tomer Deborah*, trans. as 'The Palm Tree of Deborah', in R. Ben-Zion Boxer, *An Anthology of Jewish Mysticism* (New York, 1981).
—— *Zohar im perush Or Yakar* (22 vols.; Jerusalem, 1962–92).
CYGIELMAN, SHMUEL A., 'The Proposals of M. Butrymowicz for the Correction of the Jews of Poland and Lithuania in the Late 18th Century' (Heb.), *Israel and the Nations: Essays Presented in Honor of Shmuel Ettinger* (Jerusalem, 1988).
DABROWSKA-ZAKRZEWSKA, M., *Procesy czary w Lublinie w XVII i XVIII wieku* (Lublin, 1947).
DAN, JOSEPH, 'Anafiel, Metatron and the Creator' (Heb.), *Tarbiz*, 52 (1983).
—— *Hanovelah haḥasidit* (Jerusalem, 1966).
—— *Hasipur haḥasidi* (Jerusalem, 1975).
—— 'The Historical Perceptions of the Late Professor Gershom Scholem' (Heb.), *Zion*, 47 (1982).
—— 'The Problem of Mystical Leadership' (Heb.), in A. Belfer (ed.), *Manhigut ruḥanit beyameinu* (Tel Aviv, 1982).
—— *Sifrut hamusar vehaderush* (Jerusalem, 1975).
Darkhei tsedek. *See* Zechariah Mendel of Jaroslaw.
DARNTON, R., and ROCHE, D. (eds.), *Revolution in Print: The Press in France, 1775–1800* (Berkeley, 1989).
DAVID ZEVI of NEUSTADT, *Ḥemdat David* (Bilgoraj, 1930).
DAVIES, N., *God's Playground: A History of Poland* (2 vols.; Oxford, 1981).
Degel maḥaneh Efrayim. *See* Moses Hayyim Ephraim of Sudylkow.
Derekh pikudeikha. *See* Zevi Elimelekh of Dynow.
Derekh yivḥar. *See* Panet, Hayyim Bezalel.
Devarim arevim. *See* Ehrman, D.
DE VIDAS, ELIJAH B. MOSES, *Reshit ḥokhmah* [Venice, 1579] (Jerusalem, 1972); ed. H. J. Valdman as *Reshit ḥokhmah hashalem* (3 vols.; Jerusalem, 1984).
DIENSTAG, J., 'Ha*Moreh nevukhim* ve*Sefer hamada* besifrut haḥasidut', in *Sefer yovel likhvod harav Dr Avraham Weiss* (New York, 1964).

DIMITROVSKY, CHAIM ZALMAN, 'Al derekh hapilpul', in *The Salo Wittmayer Baron Jubilee Volume* (3 vols.; i, ii in Eng., New York, 1974; iii in Heb., Jerusalem, 1974).
DINUR, BENZION, *Bemifneh hadorot* (Jerusalem, 1955).
—— 'Reshitah shel haḥasidut viyesodoteihah hasotsialiyim vehameshiḥiyim', in id., *Bemifneh hadorot* (Jerusalem, 1955).
Divrat Shelomo. See Solomon of Lutsk.
Divrei emet. See Jacob Isaac of Lublin.
Divrei Ḥayim. See Halberstam, Hayyim b. Leibush of Zanz.
DONNER, NATHAN NETA, *Derekh ha'emunah uma'aseh rav* [Warsaw, 1899].
—— *Sha'arei ha'emunah* (Warsaw, 1901).
Dor de'ah. See Kamelhar, Jekutiel Aryeh.
DOV BER of MEZHIRECH, *Maggid devarav le Ya'akov* [Korets, 1784], ed. R. Schatz-Uffenheimer (Jerusalem, 1976).
—— *Or torah* [Korets, 1804] (Jerusalem, 1968; Brooklyn, NY, 1972).
DOV BER B. SHMUEL of LINITS (Luniets), *Shivḥei haBesht* [Kopys, 1814]; ed. S. A. Horodecky [Berlin, 1922] (Tel Aviv, 1947); ed. B. Mintz (Tel Aviv, 1961); ed. Y. Mondshine; *Ketav yad* (Jerusalem, 1982); pub. in Yiddish [Ostrog, 1815] (Korets, 1816); pub. in English as *In Praise of the Baal Shem Tov*, trans. D. Ben-Amos and J. R. Mintz (Bloomington, 1970).
DOV BER SHNEURI of LUBAVITCH (the Mitteler Rebbe), *Derekh ḥayim* [Kopys, 1819] (Brooklyn, NY, 1955).
—— 'Kuntres hahitbonenut', in *Ner mitsvah vetorah or* [Kopys, 1820] (Brooklyn, NY, 1974). (Also known as *Sha'ar hayiḥud).*
—— *Kuntres hahitpa'alut* [Königsberg, 1831?], pub. in Eng. as *Tract on Ecstasy*, trans. L. Jacobs (London, 1963).
—— *Likutei be'urim* (Warsaw, 1868).
—— *Ma'amrei Admor ha'Emtsa'i* (10 vols.; Brooklyn, NY, 1985–9).
—— *Ner mitsvah vetorah or* [Kopys, 1820] (2 vols.; Brooklyn, NY, 1974).
—— *Seder tefilot mikol hashanah* [Kopys, 1816; Berdichev, 1818; Kopys, 1823] (Brooklyn, NY, 1965).
—— *Torat ḥayim* (Kopys, 1826).
DRESNER, SAMUEL H., introd. to Abraham Joshua Heschel, *The Circle of the Baal Shem Tov: Studies in Hasidism* (Chicago, 1985).
—— *The Zaddik* (New York, 1960).
DROBITSCHER, B., 'Shalosh nusḥa'ot linesi'at zekeni haBesht Le'Erets Yisrael', *Yeda Am*, 6 (1960).
DUBNOW, SIMON, *Divrei yemei am olam* (10 vols.; Tel Aviv, 1929–39; 1958).
—— *Geschichte des Chassidismus* (2 vols.; Berlin, 1931).
—— 'Haḥasidim harishonim be'Erets Yisrael', *Pardes*, 2 (1894).
—— *History of the Jews in Russia and Poland* [3 vols.; Philadelphia, 1916–20] (New York, 1975).
—— *Toledot haḥasidut* [Tel Aviv, 1930–1] (Tel Aviv, 1960).
—— *Weltgeschichte des jüdischen Volkes* (10 vols.; Berlin, 1925–9).
EHRMAN, D., *Devarim arevim* (Munkacz, 1803–4).
EICHENSTEIN, ZEVI HIRSCH. See Zevi Hirsch of Zhidachov.
EISENSTEIN, E., *The Printing Press as an Agent of Change* (New York, 1985).
ELBAUM, Y., 'HaBesht uveno shel Rabbi Adam', *Meḥkerei Yerushalayim befolklor yehudi*, 2 (1982).
ELEAZAR of WORMS, *Sefer haḥokhmah*, MS Oxford 1812, 63a.
ELIAV, MORDECHAI, *Erets-Israel and its Yishuv in the Nineteenth Century, 1777–1917* (Heb.) (Jerusalem, 1978).

ELIJAH B. SOLOMON ZALMAN (the Gaon of Vilna), *Shenot Eliyahu* (Lemberg, 1799).
ELIMELEKH of LYZHANSK, *No'am Elimelekh* [Lemberg, 1788], ed. G. Nigal (2 vols.; Jerusalem, 1978).
—— *Or Elimelekh*, ed. Alter Elisha Hacohen Pakscher (Jerusalem, 1984).
ELIOR, R., 'Between *Yesh* and *Ayin*: The Doctrine of the Zaddik in the Works of Rabbi Jacob Isaac, the Seer of Lublin', in A. Rapoport-Albert and S. J. Zipperstein (eds.), *Jewish History: Essays in Honor of Chimen Abramsky* (London, 1988).
—— 'HaBaD: The Contemplative Ascent to God', in A. Green (ed.), *Jewish Spirituality* (2 vols.; New York, 1986–7), vol. ii.
—— 'Hamaḥaloket al moreshet Ḥabad', *Tarbiz*, 49 (1980).
—— 'Hazikah shebein kabalah laḥasidut: Retsifut utemurah', *The Proceedings of the Ninth World Congress of Jewish Studies* (Jerusalem, 1986).
—— '"Kuntres hahitpa'alut" le R. Dov Ber Shne'orson', *Kiryat sefer*, 54 (1979).
—— *Torat ha'elohut bador hasheni shel ḥasidut Ḥabad* (Jerusalem, 1982).
—— 'Viku'aḥ Minsk', *Meḥkerei Yerushalayim bemaḥshevet Yisrael*, 1: 4 (1981–2).
—— BARTAL, I., and SHMERUK, C. (eds.), *Tsadikim ve'anshei ma'aseh* (Jerusalem, 1994).
EMDEN, JACOB, *Beit Yehonatan hasofer* (Altona, 1763?).
—— 'Igeret Purim', Bodleian Library, Oxford MS 2190, 7.
—— *Sefer hitabekut* [Lvov, 1877].
Emet ve'emunah. See Menahem Mendel of Kotsk.
Em lebinah. See Kamelhar, Jekutiel Aryeh.
Emunat tsadikim. See Isaac Dov Ber b. Zevi Hirsch.
Entsiklopediah laḥasidut. See Alfasi, I., Porush, S. H.
EPHRAIM SOLOMON B. AARON of LECZYCA (Luntshits), *Olelot Efrayim* [Lublin, 1590; Prague, 1619] (Jerusalem, 1989).
Eser atarot. See Berger, Israel.
Eser kedushot. See Berger, Israel.
Eser orot. See Berger, Israel.
Eser tsaḥtsaḥot. See Berger, Israel.
ESSINGEN, SAMUEL, *Ma'aseh nora zakah berurah* (n. p., n.d.). Repr. in G. Nigal, *Sipurei dibuk besifrut Yisrael* (Jerusalem, 1983).
ETKES I., 'Aliyato shel R. Shne'ur Zalman MiLiadi le'emdat manhigut', *Tarbiz*, 54 (1985).
—— 'Darko shel R. Shne'ur Zalman miLiadi kemanhig shel ḥasidim', *Zion*, 50 (1986).
—— 'HaGera vereshit hahitnagedut laḥasidut', in S. Almog *et al.* (eds.), *Temurot bahistoriah hayehudit haḥadashah: Kovets ma'amarim shai liShmuel Ettinger* (Jerusalem, 1987).
—— 'Hasidism as a Movement: The First Stage', in B. Safran (ed.), *Hasidism: Continuity or Innovation?* (Cambridge, Mass., 1988).
—— 'On the Question of the Harbingers of the Haskalah in Eastern Europe' (Heb.), *Tarbiz*, 57 (1988).
ETTINGER, S., 'The Crystallisation of the Hasidic Movement: The Maggid of Mezhirech and his Disciples', in H. H. Ben-Sasson (ed.), *A History of the Jewish People* (London, 1976).
—— 'The Hasidic Movement: Reality and Ideals', in H. H. Ben-Sasson and S. Ettinger (eds.), *Jewish Society through the Ages* (New York, 1971). Orig. pub. in *Cahiers d'histoire mondiale: Journal of World History*, 11: 1–2 (1968). Repr. in G. D. Hundert (ed.), *Essential Papers on Hasidism* (New York, 1991).
—— Review of Katz, *Masoret umashber* (Heb.), *Kiryat sefer*, 35 (1960).
EYBESCHUETZ, DAVID SOLOMON, *Arvei naḥal* [2 vols.; Sudylkow, 1825–6] (Josefov, 1868).
FAIERSTEIN, M., *All Is in the Hands of Heaven: The Teachings of Rabbi Mordecai Joseph Leiner of Izbica* (New York, 1989).
—— 'Gershom Scholem and Hasidism', *Journal of Jewish Studies*, 38 (1987).

FAIGIN, YEKHEZKEL, 'Reply' (Heb.) , *Hatamim*, 8 (Warsaw, 1937).

FINE, L., 'The Study of Torah as a Rite of Theurgical Contemplation in Lurianic Kabbalah', in D. Blumenthal (ed.), *Approaches to Judaism in Medieval Times* (Atlanta, 1988).

FISHMAN, DAVID E., 'Preserving Tradition in the Land of Revolution: The Religious Leadership of Soviet Jewry, 1917–1930', in J. Wertheimer (ed.), *The Uses of Tradition: Jewish Continuity in the Modern Era* (New York, 1992), 85–118.

FRIEDBERG, H. D., *Toledot hadefus ha'ivri bePolaniah* [Antwerp, 1932] (Tel Aviv, 1950).

FRIEDMAN, M., 'Interpreting Hasidism: The Buber–Scholem Controversy', *Leo Baeck Institute Year Book*, 33 (1988).

GARTNER, J., 'Se'udah shelishit: Hebetim hilkhatiyim', *Sidra*, 6 (1990).

GEDALIAH OF LUNIETS, *Teshu'ot ḥen* [Berdichev, 1816] (Brooklyn, NY, 1982).

GERSHONI, A. A., *Yahadut beRusiah haSovietit: Lekorot redifot hadat* (Jerusalem, 1961).

GERTENSTEIN, YEHIEL, *The Besht's Pupils in Erets Yisrael* (Heb.), (Tel Aviv, 1982).

GESHURI, M. S., 'Lancut ir hilulah', in *Sefer Lancut* (Tel Aviv, 1963).

GIKATILLA, JOSEPH, *Sha'arei orah* [Riva di Trento, 1561] (Warsaw, 1883).

GINZBERG, LOUIS, 'Ba'al Shem Tov, Israel B. Eliezer', in *Jewish Encyclopaedia* (12 vols.; New York, 1901–6), vol. ii.

—— *The Legends of the Jews* (7 vols.; Philadelphia, 1968).

GLITZENSTEIN, A. H., *Sefer hatoledot Rabbi Shalom Dovber: Admor Rashab* (Kfar Habad, 1972).

—— *Sefer hatoledot Rabbi Yosef Yitsḥak Schneersohn miLubavitch: Admor Moharits* (4 parts in 3 vols.; 1971–4).

—— *Tomekhei temimim* (Brooklyn, NY, 1969).

GOLDBERG, JACOB, 'The Attitude of Polish Society toward the Jews in the Time of the Enlightenment', in J. Micgiel, R. Scott, and H. B. Segel (eds.), *Proceedings of the Conference on Poles and Jews: Myth and Reality in the Historical Context* (New York, 1986).

GORDON, Y. L., 'Aḥarit simḥah tugah', in id., *Kol kitvei Y. L. Gordon* (2 vols.; Tel Aviv, 1953–60).

GOSHEN-GOTTSTEIN, E., 'Courtship, Marriage and Pregnancy in Geula', *Israel Annals of Psychiatry and Related Disciplines*, 4: 1 (1966).

GOTTLIEB, EPHRAIM, *Meḥkarim besifrut hakabalah* (Tel Aviv, 1976).

GOTTLOBER, Abraham Ber, *Zikhronot umasa'ot*, ed. R. Goldberg (2 vols.; Jerusalem, 1976).

GRAETZ, H., *Geschichte des Juden* (11 vols.; Leipzig, 1853–70), pub. in Eng. as *History of the Jews* (5 vols.; London, 1901).

GREEN, A., 'Hasidism: Discovery and Retreat', in P. Berger (ed.), *The Other Side of God: A Polarity in World Religions* (New York, 1981).

—— (ed.), *Jewish Spirituality*, (2 vols.; New York, 1986–7) i: *From the Bible through the Middle Ages*; ii: *From the Sixteenth Century Revival to the Present.*

—— 'Neo-Hasidim and our Theological Struggle', *Ra'ayonot*, 4: 3 (1984).

—— 'On Translating Hasidic Homilies', *Prooftexts*, 3 (1983).

—— 'Teachings of the Hasidic Masters', in B. Holtz (ed.), *Back to the Sources* (New York, 1984).

—— *Tormented Master: A Life of Rabbi Nahman of Bratslav* (University of Alabama Press, 1979).

—— 'Typologies of Leadership and the Hasidic Zaddiq', in A. Green (ed.), *Jewish Spirituality* (New York, 1986–7), vol. ii.

—— 'The Zaddiq as *Axis Mundi* in Later Judaism', *Journal of the American Academy of Religion*, 45 (1977).

GREENWALD, YEKUTIEL JUDAH, *Harav R. Yehonatan Eybeschuetz* (New York, 1954).

GRÉGOIRE, H., *Histoire des sectes religieuses* (2 vols.; Paris, 1810).
GRIES, Z., 'Arikhat tsava'at haRivash', *Kiryat sefer*, 52 (1977).
—— 'Bein sifrut lehistoriah: Hakdamot lediyun ve'iyun be*Shivḥei haBesht*', *Tura*, 3 (1994).
—— 'Between History and Literature: The Case of Jewish Preaching', *Journal of Jewish Thought and Philosophy*, 4: 1 (1994).
—— 'Der jüdische Hintergrund für Bubers Vorgehen bei seiner Gestaltung der chassidischen Erzühlungen', in M. Buber, *Die Geschichten des Rabbi Nachman* (Heidelberg, 1989). Trans. into Heb. as 'Hareka hayehudi life'ulato shel Buber be'itsuv hasipur haḥasidi', *Meḥkerei Yerushalayim befolklor yehudi*, 11–12 (1990).
—— 'Hasidism: The Present State of Research and Some Desirable Priorities', *Numen*, 34: 1 (1987).
—— 'Kuntres hanhagot ne'elam leRabi Naḥman miBraslav?', *Kiryat sefer*, 53 (1978).
—— 'Mimitos le'etos: Kavim lidmuto shel R. Avraham miKalisk', in *Umah vetoledoteihah* (2 vols.; Jerusalem, 1984).
—— 'Rabbi Yisrael b. Shabbetai haMagid miKozienice uferushav lemasekhet avot', in R. Elior, I. Bartal, and C. Shmeruk (eds.), *Tsadikim va'anshei ma'aseh: Meḥkarim baḥasidut Polin* (Jerusalem, 1994).
—— Review of M. Meged's *Ha'or haneḥshakh*, *Kiryat sefer*, 55 (1980).
—— *Sefer, sofer, vesipur bereshit haḥasidut* (Tel Aviv, 1992).
—— *Sifrut hahanhagot* (Jerusalem, 1989).
—— 'Sifrut hahanhagot haḥasidit', *Zion*, 46 (1981).
GROSSMAN, A., 'Hagiratah shel mishpaḥat Kalonymos me'Italiah leGermaniyah', *Zion*, 40 (1975).
—— 'Yiḥus mishpaḥah umekomo baḥevrah hayehudit be'Ashkenaz hakedumah', in E. Etkes and Y. Salmon (eds.), *Perakim betoledot haḥevrah hayehudit biyemei habeinayim uva'et haḥadashah, mukdashim le Ya'akov Katz* (Jerusalem, 1980).
GRÖZINGER, K. E., 'Baal Shem oder Ba'al Hazon, Wunderdoktor oder Charismatiker: Zur frühen Legendenbildung um den Stifter des Hasidismus', *Frankfurter judaistische Beiträge*, 6 (1978).
—— 'Die Gegenwart des Sinai: Erzählungen und kabbalistische Traktate zur Vergegenwärtigung des Sinai', *Frankfurter judaistische Beiträge*, 16 (1988).
—— 'Die hasidischen Erzählungen: Ihre Formen und Traditionen', *Frankfurter judaistische Beiträge*, 9 (1981).
—— 'Himmlische Gerichte, Wiedergänger und Zwischenweltliche in der ostjüdischen Erzählung', in K. E. Grözinger, S. Moses, and H. D. Zimmermann (eds.), *Franz Kafka und das Judentum* (Frankfurt on Main, 1987).
—— 'Neoplatonisches Denken in Hasidut und Kabbala', *Frankfurter judaistische Beiträge*, 11 (1983).
—— 'Sündenpropheten: Halachaprophetie im Judentum Osteuropas', *Frankfurter judaistische Beiträge*, 15 (1987).
GUENZIG, J., *Die 'Wundermänner' im jüdischen Volke* (Antwerp, 1921).
HABERMAN, JACOB, *Maimonides and Aquinas* (New York, 1979).
HABERMANN, A. M., 'Sha'arei Habad', in *Alei ayin: Minḥat devarim liShelomo Salman Schocken* (Jerusalem, 1948–52).
—— 'Shenei talmidei ḥakhamim shehalekhu le'olamam', in id., *Anshei sefer ve'anshei ma'aseh* (Jerusalem, 1974).
Halakhot gedolot, ed. Azriel Hildesheimer (Berlin, 1850–2).
HALBERSTAM, HAYYIM B. LEIBUSH of ZANZ, *Divrei Ḥayim* [Munkacz, 1877] (Jerusalem, 1988).
HALEVI, A. SCHISCHA, 'Al hasefer *Butsina Dinehora*', *Alei sefer*, 8 (1980).

HALLAMISH, M., 'Mishnato ha'iyunit shel Rabbi Shne'ur Zalman miLiadi: Mekorotav bakabalah veyaḥaso lereshit haḥasidut', (Ph.D. thesis, Hebrew University of Jerusalem, 1976).
—— 'On the Origin of a Proverb in Kabbalistic Literature' (Heb.), *Bar Ilan*, 13 (Ramat Gan, 1970).
—— *Nativ laTanya* (Tel Aviv, 1987).
—— 'Yaḥasei tsadik ve'edah bemishnat R. Sh. Z.', *Ḥevrah vehistoriah* (Jerusalem, 1980).
HALPERN, I. (ed.), *Beit Yisrael bePolin* (2 vols.; Jerusalem, 1948–53).
—— 'Gezerot Woszczylo', *Zion*, 22 (1957). Repr. in id., *Yehudim veyahadut bemizraḥ Eiropah* (Jerusalem, 1969).
—— *Ha'aliyot harishonot shel haḥasidim le'Erets Yisrael* (Tel Aviv, 1947).
—— 'Ḥavurot letorah umitsvot vehatenu'ah haḥasidit behitpashetutah', in id., *Yehudim veyahadut bemizraḥ Eiropah* (Jerusalem, 1969).
—— 'R. Levi Yitsḥak miBerdichev ugezerot hamalkhut beyamav', in id., *Yehudim veyahadut bemizraḥ Eiropah* (Jerusalem, 1969).
—— 'Yaḥaso shel R. Aharon hagadol miKarlin kelapei mishtar hakehilot', *Zion*, 22 (1957). Repr. in id., *Yehudim veyahadut bemizraḥ Eiropah* (Jerusalem, 1969).
—— *Yehudim veyahadut bemizraḥ Eiropah* (Jerusalem, 1969).
HANNOVER, NATHAN NATA, *Sha'arei tsion* [Prague, 1662] (Jerusalem, 1980).
HARAN, RAYA, 'The Authenticity of Letters Written by Hasidim in Erets Yisrael' (Heb.), *Cathedra*, 55 (1990).
—— 'On the Copying and Transmission of Hasidic Letters' (Heb.), *Zion*, 56 (1991).
—— 'What Motivated Hasidic Jews to Emigrate to Erets Israel?' (Heb.), *Cathedra*, 76 (1995).
HARSHOSHANIM, H. *et al.* (eds.), *Radomshil rabati* (Tel Aviv, 1971).
Hatamim, Habad periodical pub. in Warsaw in the 1930s (repr. 2 vols., Kfar Habad, 1971).
HAVELOCK, E. A., *The Muse Learns to Write* (New Haven, 1986).
HAYIM HAKOHEN of ALEPPO, *Tur bareket* (Amsterdam, 1654).
HAYYIM HAIKEL B. SAMUEL of AMDUR, *Ḥayim vaḥesed* [Warsaw, 1891] (Jerusalem, 1975).
HAYYIM of VOLOZHIN, *Nefesh haḥayim* (Vilna, 1824).
He'arot uve'urim (Brooklyn, NY, 1983).
Heikhal haberakhah. See Isaac Judah Jehiel Safrin of Komarno.
HEILMAN, S. C., *Defenders of the Faith* (New York, 1990).
—— *Synagogue Life: A Study in Symbolic Interaction* (Chicago, 1976).
HEILPRIN, S. A., *Sefer hatse'etsa'im* (Jerusalem, 1980).
HELLER WILENSKY, SARA ORA, 'Igrot Gershom Scholem veYosef Weiss el Orah', in N. Zach (ed.), *Igra: Almanakh lesifrut ve'omanut*, 3 (1990–1).
—— 'Lishe'elat meḥabero shel sefer *Sha'ar hashamayim* hameyuḥas leAvraham ibn Ezra', *Tarbiz*, 32 (1963).
—— *R. Yitsḥak Arama umishnato* (Jerusalem, 1956).
HELMREICH, WILLIAM B., *The World of the Yeshiva: An Intimate Portrait of Orthodox Jewry* (New Haven, 1986).
Ḥemdat David. See David Zevi of Neustadt.
Ḥemdat yamim [3 vols.; Smyrna, 1731–2; Constantinople, 1735–7] (4 vols.; Jerusalem, 1970).
HESCHEL, A. J., *The Circle of the Baal Shem Tov: Studies in Hasidism*, ed. S. H. Dresner (Chicago, 1985).
—— *Kotsk: In Gerangel far Emesdikeit* (2 vols.; Tel Aviv, 1973).
HIELMAN, HAIM MEIR, *Beit rabbi* [Berdichev, 1903] (Tel Aviv, n.d.).
HILL, MICHAEL, *A Sociology of Religion* (London, 1973).
HILLEL HALEVI of PARICHI, *Pelaḥ harimon* [3 vols.; Vilna, 1847] (Brooklyn, NY, 1954–7).
—— 'Sha'ar hayiḥud', in Dov Ber Shneuri of Lubavitch, *Likutei be'urim* (Warsaw, 1868).
HILLMAN, DAVID ZEVI (ed.), *Igrot ba'al haTanya uvenei doro* (Jerusalem, 1953).

HILSENRAD, ZALMAN ARYEH, *The Baal Shem Tov: His Birth and Early Manhood* (New York, 1971).

HIRSCH, P. H., *Printing, Selling and Reading, 1450–1550* (Wiesbaden, 1967; rev. edn., 1974).

HISDAI, Y. 'Early Settlement of "Hasidim" and of "Mitnaggedim" in Palestine' (Heb.), *Shalem*, 4 (1984).

—— 'The Emergence of Hasidim and Mitnaggedim in the Light of the Homiletical Literature' (Heb.) (Ph.D. thesis, Hebrew University of Jerusalem, 1984).

—— 'The Origins of the Conflict between Hasidim and Mitnagdim', in B. Safran (ed.), *Hasidism: Continuity or Innovation?* (Cambridge, Mass., 1988).

HORODECKY, S. A., 'Haḥasidim beErets Yisrael', *Hashiloaḥ*, 8 (1901–2).

—— *Haḥasidut vehaḥasidim* [4 vols.; Tel Aviv, 1928–43] (Tel Aviv, 1951).

—— *Olei Tsion* (Jerusalem, 1947).

HOROWITZ, ISAIAH B. ABRAHAM HALEVI, *Shenei luḥot haberit (Shelah)* [Amsterdam, 1648] (2 vols.; Warsaw, 1862).

HUNDERT, G. D. (ed.), *Essential Papers on Hasidism* (New York, 1991).

—— 'Jewish Children and Childhood in Early Modern East Central Europe', in D. Kraemer (ed.), *The Jewish Family: Metaphor and Memory* (New York, 1989).

—— 'On the Jewish Community in Poland during the Seventeenth Century: Some Comparative Perspectives', *Revue des études juives*, 152 (1983).

—— 'The Role of the Jews in Commerce in Early Modern Poland–Lithuania', *Journal of European Economic History*, 16 (1987).

—— 'Shekiat yirat kavod bikehilot Beit Yisrael bePolin–Lita', *Bar Ilan*, 24–5 (1989).

—— 'Some Basic Characteristics of the Jewish Experience in Poland', *Polin*, 1 (1986). Repr. in A. Polonsky (ed.), *From Shtetl to Socialism: Essays from Polin* (London, 1993).

IBN GABIROL, SOLOMON, *Shirei hakodesh*, ed. D. Jarden (2 vols.; Jerusalem, 1971–3).

IDEL, M., 'Abraham Abulafia's Works and Doctrine' (Heb.) (Ph.D. thesis, Hebrew University of Jerusalem, 1976).

—— 'Die Rezeption der Kabbala in der zweiten Hälfte des 18. Jahrhunderts', *Hebräische Beiträge zur Wissenschaft des Judentums*, 1–2 (1986). Trans. as 'Perceptions of the Kabbalah in the Second Half of the Eighteenth Century', *Journal of Jewish Thought and Philosophy*, 1 (1991), 56–114.

—— *Golem: Jewish Magical and Mystical Traditions on the Artificial Anthropoid* (Albany, NY, 1990).

—— *Haḥavayah hamistit etsel Avraham Abulafiyah* (Jerusalem, 1988). Pub. in Eng. *The Mystical Experience in Abraham Abulafia* (Albany, NY, 1988).

—— 'Hahitbodedut kerikuz bakabalah ha'ekstatit vegilguleihah', *Da'at*, 14 (1985).

—— 'Jewish Magic from the Renaissance Period to Early Hasidism', in J. Neusner, E. S. Frerichs, and P. V. McCracken Flesher (eds.), *Religion, Science, and Magic* (New York, 1989).

—— *Kabbalah: New Perspectives* (New Haven, 1988).

—— 'The Land of Israel in Medieval Kabbalah', in Lawrence A. Hoffman (ed.), *The Land of Israel: Jewish Perspectives* (Notre Dame, Ind., 1986).

—— 'The Magical and Neoplatonic Interpretations of the Kabbalah in the Renaissance', in B. D. Cooperman (ed.), *Jewish Thought in the Sixteenth Century* (Cambridge, Mass., 1983).

—— 'The Magical and Theurgical Interpretation of Music in Jewish Sources from the Renaissance to Hasidism' (Heb.), *Yuval*, 4 (1982).

—— 'One from a Town, Two from a Clan: The Question of the Diffusion of Lurianac Kabbalah and Sabbateanism: A Re-examination', *Jewish History*, 7 (1993).

—— On the History of the Interdiction to Study Kabbalah before the Age of Forty', *AJS Review*, 5 (1980).

—— 'The Problem of the Sources of the *Bahir*' (Heb.), in J. Dan (ed.), *The Beginnings of Jewish Mysticism in Medieval Europe*, *Meḥkerei Yerushalayim bemaḥshevet Yisrael*, 6 (Jerusalem, 1987).

—— 'Some Conceptions of the Land of Israel in Medieval Jewish Thought', in Ruth Link-Salinger (ed.), *A Straight Path: Studies in Medieval Philosophy and Culture: Essays in Honor of Arthur Hyman* (Washington, 1968).

—— *Studies in Ecstatic Kabbalah* (Albany, NY, 1988).

—— 'Types of Redemptive Activity in the Middle Ages' (Heb.), in Zvi Baras (ed.), *Messianism and Eschatology* (Jerusalem, 1983).

—— 'Universalism and Particularism in Kabbalah: 1480–1650', in D. B. Ruderman (ed.), *Essential Papers on Jewish Culture in Renaissance and Baroque Italy* (New York, 1992).

—— 'Universalization and Integration: Two Conceptions of Mystical Union in Jewish Mysticism', in M. Idel and B. McGinn (eds.), *Mystical Union and the Monotheistic Faith: An Ecumenical Dialogue* (New York, 1989).

Igeret hakodesh. See Shneur Zalman of Lyady.

Igrot kodesh, See Levine, S. B.

Imrei shefer. See Naphtali Zevi Horowitz of Ropczyce.

In Praise. See Dov Ber b. Shmuel, *Shivḥei haBesht.*

Isaac of Acre, *Sefer me'irat einayim leRabi Yitsḥak demin Ako*, ed. A. Goldreich (Jerusalem, 1984).

Isaac b. Leib Landau, *Zikaron tov* [Piotrkow, 1892].

Isaac Dov Ber b. Zevi Hirsch, *Emunat tsadikim* [Warsaw, 1900], pub. as *Kehal ḥasidim heḥadash* [Lemberg, 1902].

Isaac Jacob (the *admor* of Biala), *Yishrei lev* [Lublin, 1906].

Isaac Judah Jeḥiel Safrin of Komarno, *Ḥamishah ḥumshei torah* (5 vols.; Lemberg, 1869–74), i. *Heikhal haberakhah.*

—— *Megilat setarim*, ed. N. Ben-Menahem (Jerusalem, 1944).

—— *Netiv mitsvoteikha* [Lemberg, 1858] (Jerusalem, 1983).

—— *Notser ḥesed* [Lemberg, 1855].

—— *Shulḥan hatahor* (Tel Aviv, 1963).

—— *Zohar ḥai* (5 vols.; Lemberg and Przemysl, 1875–88).

Isaac of Radzwillow, *Or Yitsḥak* (Jerusalem, 1961).

Israel b. Shabbetai the Maggid of Kozienice), *Avodat Yisrael* (Josefov, 1842).

Israel Dov Ber of Weledniki, *She'erit Yisrael* [Zhitomir, 1868].

Israel of Ruzhin, *Keneset Yisrael* [Warsaw, 1906] (Bnei Brak, n.d.).

Jacob b. Mordecai Joseph Leiner of Izbica, *Beit Ya'akov* [Warsaw, 1890] (New York, 1978).

Jacob Isaac of Lublin, *Divrei emet* [Zolkiew, 1830–1] (Munkacz, 1942).

—— *Zikaron zot* [Warsaw, 1869] (Munkacz, 1942).

—— *Zot zikaron* [Lemberg, 1851] (Munkacz, 1942).

Jacob Joseph of Polonnoye, *Ben porat Yosef* [Korets, 1781; Piotrkow, 1884] (New York, 1954; Brooklyn, NY, 1976).

—— *Ketonet pasim* [Lemberg, 1866] (New York, 1954), ed. G. Nigal (Jerusalem, 1985).

—— *Toledot Ya'akov Yosef* [Korets, 1780] (repr. Jerusalem, 1966).

—— *Tsafenat pa'neaḥ* [Korets, 1782; Piotrkow, 1884] (New York, 1954), ed. G. Nigal (Jerusalem, 1989).

Jacobs, Louis, 'Aspects of Scholem's Study of Hasidism', in Harold Bloom (ed.), *Gershom Scholem* (New York, 1987).

—— 'The Doctrine of the "Divine Spark" in Man in Jewish Sources', in R. Loewe (ed.), *Studies in Rationalism, Judaism, and Universalism in Memory of Leon Roth* (New York, 1966).

JACOBS, LOUIS, 'Eating as an Act of Worship in Hasidic Thought', in S. Stein and R. Loewe (eds.), *Studies in Jewish Religious and Intellectual History Presented to Alexander Altmann on the Occasion of his Seventieth Birthday* (University of Alabama Press, 1979).
—— *Hasidic Prayer* (London, 1972; paperback edn. London, 1993).
—— 'Honour thy Father: A Study of the Psychology of the Hasidic Movement', in M. Zohar and A. Tartakower (eds.), *Hagut ivrit be'Eiropah* (Tel Aviv, 1969).
—— *Seeker of Unity: The Life and Works of Aaron of Starosselje* (London, 1966).
—— 'The Uplifting of the Sparks in Later Jewish Mysticism', in A. Green (ed.), *Jewish Spirituality*, ii: *From the Sixteenth Century Revival to the Present* (New York, 1987).
JEPHTHAH JOSEPH YOZPA SHAMASH, *Ma'aseh nisim* (Amsterdam, 1696).
JOSEPH B. HAYYIM TSARFATI, *Yad Yosef* (Venice, 1617; Amsterdam, 1700).
JOSEPH CARO, *Maggid meisharim* [Lublin 1645; Venice, 1654; Amsterdam, 1708] (Jerusalem, 1960).
JOSEPH DAVID RUBIN, *Atsei Levanon al hatorah* (Lvov, 1928).
JOSEPH OF HAMADAN, *Sefer tashak*, critical text edn. with introd. by J. Zwelling (Ph.D. thesis, Brandeis University, 1975).
JUDAH LEIB EGER, *Torat emet* (Lublin, 1890).
JUDAH LEIB OF GUR, *Otsar mikhtavim uma'amarim* (Jerusalem, 1986).
JUDAH LOEB of ANNOPOL, *Or haganuz* (Lemberg, 1866).
JUDAH LOEW B. BEZALEL (the Maharal) of Prague, *Be'er hagolah* [Prague, 1598]. Repr. in *Kol sifrei Maharal miPrag* (12 vols.; New York, 1969).
—— *Gur Aryeh* [Prague, 1578] (5 vols.; Bnei Brak, 1972).
—— *Netivot olam* [Prague, 1595–6]. Repr. in *Kol sifrei Maharal miPrag* (12 vols.; New York, 1969).
KAHANA, A. *Sefer haḥasidut* (Warsaw, 1922).
KAHANA, D., *Toledot hamekubalim hashabeta'im vehaḥasidim* [Odessa, 1913–14] (2 vols.; Tel Aviv, 1926–7), ii.
KAHN, R., *Lubavitch veḥayaleihah* (Kfar Habad, 1983).
[KAIDANER, JACOB?], *Matsref ha'avodah* (Königsberg, 1858).
—— *Sipurim nora'im* [Lemberg, 1875], ed. G. Nigal (Jerusalem, 1992).
KALONYMUS KALMAN EPSTEIN of CRACOW, *Ma'or vashemesh* [Breslau, 1842] (Brooklyn, NY, 1985).
KAMELHAR, GERSHON, *Mevaser tov* (Podgorze, 1900).
KAMELHAR, JEKUTIEL ARYEH, *Dor de'ah* [Bilgoraj, 1933] (Jerusalem, 1970).
—— *Em lebinah* (Warsaw, 1904).
—— letter in *Yagdil torah* , 63 (New York, Kislev Tevet 5745 [1985–6]).
KARLINSKY, N., 'The Hasidic Epistles from Erets Yisrael; The Text and Context: A Reconsideration, (Heb.) (MA thesis, Hebrew University of Jerusalem, 1989).
KATZ, J., *Le'umiyut yehudit* (Jerusalem, 1979).
—— *Masoret umashber* (Jerusalem, 1958), pub. in Eng. as *Tradition and Crisis*, trans. B. D. Cooperman (New York, 1993).
KATZ, S. T., 'Models, Modeling and Mystical Training', *Religion*, 12 (1982).
Kedushat Levi. See Levi Isaac of Berdichev.
Kehal ḥasidim heḥadash. See Isaac Dov Ber b. Zevi Hirsch.
KEPNES, STEVEN D., 'A Hermeneutic Approach to the Buber–Scholem Controversy', *Journal of Jewish Studies*, 38 (1987).
Keter shem tov. See Aaron of Opatow.
Ketonet pasim. See Jacob Joseph of Polonnoye.
KIENIEWICZ, S., *et al.* (eds.), *History of Poland* (Warsaw, 1968).

KLAUSNER, I., 'Hama'avak hapenimi bikehilot Rusiah veLita vehatsa'at Rabbi Shimon b. Wolf letikunim', *He'avar*, 19 (1972).

—— *Vilna bitekufat haGa'on* (Jerusalem, 1942).

KLIER, J. D., *Russia Gathers her Jews* (Dekalb, Ill., 1986).

Kol simḥah. See Simḥah Bunem of Przysucha.

Kore merosh. See Aaron Samuel Hakohen.

KORF, Y., *Likutei be'urim besefer haTanya* (2 vols.; Brooklyn, NY, 1968–73).

KRANZLER, GEORGE, *Williamsburg: A Jewish Community in Transition* (New York, 1961).

KREGLUSZKER, AARON, *Leḥem terumah* (Fürth, 1781).

KRESSEL, G., *Leksikon hasifrut ha'ivrit badorot ha'aḥaronim* (2 vols.; Tel Aviv, 1967).

Kuntres ha'avodah. See Shalom Dober of Lubavitch.

Kuntres hatefilah. See Shalom Dober of Lubavitch.

LAWAT, ABRAHAM DAVID B. JUDAH LEIB, *Sidur torah or im perush sha'ar hakolel* [Vilna, 1887] (Brooklyn, NY, 1987).

LEDERHENDLER, E., *The Road to Modern Jewish Politics* (New York, 1989).

LEVI ISAAC of BERDICHEV, *Kedushat Levi* [Slavuta, 1798] (Jerusalem, 1958; Brooklyn, NY, 1978).

LEVIN, M., *Erkhei ḥevrah vekalkalah ba'ideologiah shel tenu'at haHaskalah* (Jerusalem, 1975).

LEVIN, Rabbi JOSHUA HESCHEL, *Aliyot Eliyahu* (Vilna, 1856).

LEVIN, J. L., *Ḥasidim mesaperim* (3 vols.; Jerusalem, 1979).

LEVINE, S. B. (ed.), *Igrot kodesh Admor haZaken, Admor ha'Emtsa'i, Admor haTsemaḥ Tsedek* (Brooklyn, NY, 1980).

—— (ed.), *Igrot kodesh: Kuntres milu'im* (Brooklyn, 1981).

—— *Igrot kodesh me'et kevod kedushato Admor moreinu verabeinu harav R. Yosef Yitshak nuḥo eden miLubavich. See* Schneersohn, Joseph Isaac.

—— 'Note on R. Elior's "Kuntres hahitpa'alut leR. Dov Ber Shne'orson"', *Kiryat sefer*, 54 (1979).

LEVINGER, J., 'Imrot otentiyot shel haRabbi miKotsk', *Tarbiz*, 55 (1986).

LEVINSOHN, I. B. (Ribal), 'Emek refa'im', in id., *Yalkut Ribal* (Warsaw, 1878).

LEVITATS, I., *The Jewish Community in Russia, 1772–1884* (New York, 1943).

LEVY, AMNON, *Haḥaredim* (Jerusalem, 1989).

LEWIN, BENJAMIN MENASSEH, *Otsar hage'onim* (13 vols., Haifa–Jerusalem, 1928–62).

LIEBERMAN, H., 'Keitsad ḥokerim ḥasidut beYisrael?', *Bitsaron*, 14, 27: 3 (1953). Repr. in id., *Ohel Raḥel* (3 vols.; New York, 1980–4), vol. i.

—— *Ohel Raḥel* (3 vols.; New York, 1980–4).

LIEBES, Y., 'Hamashiaḥ shel haZohar', in *Hara'ayon hameshiḥi beYisrael: Yom iyun leregel melot shemonim shanah leGershom Scholem* (Jerusalem, 1982). Pub. in Eng. as 'The Messiah of the Zohar: On R. Simeon bar Yohai as a Messianic Figure', in id., *Studies in the Zohar* (Albany, NY, 1993).

—— 'Hatikun hakelali shel R. Naḥman miBraslav veyaḥaso lashabeta'ut', *Zion*, 45 (1980). Pub. in Eng. as '*HaTikkun Hakelali* of R. Nahman of Bratslav and its Sabbatean Links', in id., *Studies in Jewish Myth and Jewish Messianism* (Albany, NY 1993).

—— 'Jonah as the Messiah ben Joseph' (Heb.), in J. Dan and J. Hacker (eds.), *Studies in Jewish Mysticism, Philosophy, and Ethical Literature Presented to Isaiah Tishby* (Jerusalem, 1986).

—— 'Mysticism and Reality: Towards a Portrait of the Martyr and Kabbalist, R. Samson Ostropoler', in I. Twersky and B. Septimus (eds.), *Jewish Thought in the Seventeenth Century* (Cambridge, Mass., 1987).

—— 'Rabbi Solomon Ibn Gabirol's Use of the *Sefer yetsirah* and a Commentary on the Poem "I Love Thee"' (Heb.), *Jerusalem Studies in Jewish Thought*, 6: 3–4 (1987).

LIEBES, Y.,'Response to the Critique of Mondshine' (Heb.), *Zion*, 47 (1982).

—— 'Response to the Critique of Rapoport-Albert', (Heb.), *Zion*, 46 (1981).

LIEBMAN, CHARLES, 'Orthodox Sectarians', in J. Neusner (ed.), *Understanding American Judaism: Toward the Description of a Modern Religion* (2 vols.; New York, 1975), vol. ii.

—— 'Orthodoxy in American Jewish Life', *American Jewish Year Book*, 66 (1965).

—— *Studies in Jewish Myth and Jewish Messianism* (Albany, NY 1993).

—— *Studies in the Zohar* (Albany, NY, 1993).

Likutei amarim. See Menahem Mendel of Vitebsk.

Likutei be'urim. See Dov Ber Shneuri of Lubavitch.

Likutei Mahartsa. See Zevi Elimelekh of Dynow.

Likutei Moharan. See Nahman of Bratslav.

Likutei R. Hai Ga'on im perush Ner Yisrael [Lemberg, 1800] (Warsaw, 1840).

Likutim yekarim [Lemberg, 1792], ed. Abraham Isaac Kahan (Jerusalem, 1974).

LIPSCHITZ, JACOB, *Zikhron Ya'akov* (3 vols.; Kovno, Slobodka, 1924–30).

LOEBEL, ISRAEL, *Sefer vikuaḥ* [Warsaw, 1798]. Repr. in M. Wilensky, *Ḥasidim umitnaggedim* (2 vols.; Jerusalem, 1970), ii.

—— 'Yedi'ot meheimanot al kat ḥadashah bePolin veLita hamekhunah ḥasidim', in M. Wilensky, *Ḥasidim umitnaggedim* (2 vols.; Jerusalem, 1970), ii.

LOEWENTHAL, N., *Communicating the Infinite: The Emergence of the Habad School* (Chicago, 1990).

—— 'Early Hasidic Teachings: Esoteric Mysticism or a Medium of Communal Leadership?', *Journal of Jewish Studies*, 37 (1986).

—— 'Self-Sacrifice of the Zaddik in the Teachings of R. Dov Ber', in A. Rapoport-Albert and S. J. Zipperstein (eds.), *Jewish History: Essays in Honor of Chimen Abramsky* (London, 1988).

LURIA, ISAAC, *Sefer hakavanot* (Korets, 1784). *See also* Vital, Hayyim.

LUZZATTO, MOSES HAYYIM, *Mesilat yesharim* [Amsterdam, 1740], pub. in biling. edn. as *Mesillat Yesharim: The Path of the Just*, trans. S. Silverstein (Jerusalem, 1966).

Ma'amrei Admor haZaken. See Shneur Zalman of Lyady.

Ma'aseh nisim. See Jephthah Joseph Yozpa Shamash.

Ma'ayan haḥokhmah. See Asher Zevi of Ostrog.

Maggid devarav le Ya'akov. See Dov Ber of Mezhirech.

Mahadura kama. See Shneur Zalman of Lyady, *Likutei amarim: Mahadura kama mikitvei yad.*

Maharal of Prague. See Judah Loew b. Bezalel.

MAHLER, R., *Divrei yemei Yisrael: Dorot aḥaronim* (5 vols.; Tel Aviv, 1976).

—— *Haḥasidut vehaHaskalah* (Merhavya, 1961). Pub. in Eng. as *Hasidism and the Jewish Enlightenment* (Philadelphia, 1985).

—— *Toledot hayehudim bePolin* (Merhavya, 1946).

MAIMON, J. L., *Toledot haGra* (Jerusalem, 1970).

MAIMON, SOLOMON, *Salomon Maimons Lebensgeschichte* [Berlin, 1793] (Munich, 1911), pub. in Eng. as *The Autobiography of Solomon Maimon*, trans. J. Clark Murray (London, 1954), pub. in Heb. as *Ḥayei Shelomo Maimon* (Tel Aviv, 1942).

Maise bukh [Basle, 1602] (Nuremberg, 1863).

MANNA, ADEL, 'The Rebellion of Nakib Al-Ashraf in Jerusalem' (Heb.), *Cathedra*, 53 (1989).

MANTEL, MARTIN, 'Rabbi Nachman of Bratzlav's Tales: A Critical Translation from the Yiddish with Annotations and Commentary' (Ph.D. thesis, Princeton University, 1975).

Ma'or vashemesh. See Kalonymus Kalman Epstein of Cracow.

MAPU, ABRAHAM, *Mikhtevei Avraham Mapu*, ed. B. Dinur (Jerusalem, 1970).

MARCUS, IVAN, 'Beyond the Sefardic Mystique', *Orim*, 1 (1985).

MAREK, P., 'Krizis yevreiskovo samoupravliennie i khasidism', *Yevreiskaya Starina*, 12 (1928).

—— 'Vnutrennyaya bor'ba v yevreistve v XVIII veke', *Yevreiskaya Starina*, 12 (1928).

MARGALIOT, R., *Malakhei elyon* (Jerusalem, 1945).
MARGOLIES, H. S., *Dubna rabati* (Warsaw, 1910).
MARGULIES, MEIR *Sod yakhin uvo'az* (Ostrog, 1794).
MARMORSTEIN, A., 'Beiträge zur Religionsgeschichte und Volkskunde', in *Jahrbuch für jüdische Volkskunde* (Berlin, 1923).
—— 'Imitation of God in the Haggada', in id., *Studies in Jewish Theology* (Oxford, 1950).
Matsref ha'avodah. See Kaidaner, Jacob.
MATT, D. C., 'Ayin: The Concept of Nothingness in Mystical Judaism', *Tikkun*, 3: 3 (1988). Repr. in R. K. C. Forman (ed.), *The Problem of Pure Consciousness* (New York and Oxford, 1990), 121–59.
MAYER, E., *From Suburb to Shtetl: The Jews of Boro Park* (Philadelphia, 1979).
Me'ah she'arim. See C. E. Bichovsky and H. M. Hielman.
Mei hashilo'aḥ. See Mordecai Joseph Leiner of Izbica.
MEIJERS, DANIEL, *Ascetic Hasidism in Jerusalem: The Guardian-of-the-Faithful Community of Mea Shearim* (Leiden, 1992).
—— *Chassidisme in Israël* (Assen, 1979).
—— *De revolutie der vromen: Ontstaan en ontwikkeling van het chassidisme: Waarin is opgenomen het verslag van reb Dan Tsj-Toms reis door de eeuwigheid* (Hilversum, 1989).
—— and TENNEKES, J., 'Spirit and Matter in the Cosmology of Chassidic Judaism', in P. E. de Josselin de Jong and Eric Schwimmer (eds.), *Symbolic Anthropology in the Netherlands*, Verhandelingen van het Koninklijk Instituut voor Taal-, Land- en Volkenkunde 95 (The Hague, 1982).
MEIR B. AARON LEIB of PEREMYSHLANY, *Divrei Me'ir* (Bartfeld [Bardejov], 1901).
MEIR, Y., *Gedolim tsadikim* (Kalusz, 1932).
MEIR ZEVI of ZAMOSC, *Yad avi shalom* (Warsaw, 1882).
MENAHEM B. AARON IBN ZERAḤ, *Tseidah laderekh* (Ferrara, 1554).
MENAHEM MENDEL BODEK, *Seder hadorot heḥadash* (Lublin, 1927).
MENAHEM MENDEL HAGER of KOSOV, *Ahavat shalom* (Lemberg, 1833).
MENAHEM MENDEL of KOTSK, *Emet ve'emunah*, ed. Israel Jacob Araten (Jerusalem, 1948).
—— *Lahavot kodesh* (Jerusalem, 1980).
MENAHEM MENDEL of LUBAVITCH (the Tsemaḥ Tsedek), *Be'urei haZohar* (2 vols.; Brooklyn, NY, 1978).
—— *Or hatorah*: *Bereshit–Devarim* (24 vols.; Brooklyn, NY, 1950–74).
—— *Or hatorah*: *Ma'amrei Razal ve'inyanim* (Brooklyn, NY, 1983).
—— *Sefer halikutim*: *Tsemaḥ Tsedek* (26 vols.; Brooklyn, NY, 1977–83).
MENAHEM MENDEL of PEREMYSHLANY, *Darkhei yesharim* [Zhitomir, 1805] in *Torat haḥasidim harishonim* (Bnei Brak, 1981).
MENAHEM MENDEL of VITEBSK, *Ets peri* (Safed, n.d.; the approbation is dated 1873), apparently a copy from a corrupt MS of *Peri ets* (Zhitomir, 1874, Lvov, 1880).
—— *Likutei amarim* (Lemberg, 1911).
—— *Peri ets* [Zhitomir, 1874] (Cracow, 1937).
—— *Peri ha'arets* [Kopys, 1814] (Jerusalem, 1965, 1970, 1974). Repr. in *Sefarim kedoshim migedolei talmidei Ba'al Shem Tov hakadosh* (35 + 3 vols.; Brooklyn, NY, 1981–6), xviii.
MENAHEM NAHUM OF CHERNOBYL, *Me'or einayim* [Slavuta, 1798] (Polonnoye, 1810; Jerusalem, 1966). Pub. in English as *The Light of the Eyes*, trans. A. Green (New York, 1982).
MENDES-FLOHR, PAUL, 'Fin-de-Siècle Orientalism, the Ostjuden and the Aesthetics of Jewish Affirmation', in *Studies in Contemporary Jewry* (Bloomington, Ind., 1984).
Me'or einayim. See Menahem Nahum of Chernobyl.
MESHULLAM PHOEBUS HELLER of ZBARAZH, *Yosher divrei emet* [Munkacz, 1905] (New York, 1974). Repr. in *Likutim yekarim*, ed. A. I. Kahan (Jerusalem, 1974).

MICHAEL, REUVEN, *I. M. Jost: Avi hahistoriografiah hayehudit hamodernit* (Jerusalem, 1983).
—— 'Jost, Graetz, and Dubnow on the Singularity of Jewish History' (Heb.), in S. Almog *et al.* (eds.), *Transition and Change in Modern Jewish History: Essays Presented in Honor of Shmuel Ettinger* (Jerusalem, 1987).
—— 'Terumat ketav ha'et *Shulamit* lahistoriografiah hayehudit haḥadashah', *Zion*, 39 (1974).
MICHELSOHN, ABRAHAM HAYYIM SIMḤAH BUNEM, *Ateret Menaḥem* (Bilgoraj, 1910).
—— *Ohel Elimelekh* [Przemysl, 1910] (Jerusalem, 1948).
—— *Ohel Naftali* (Lemberg, 1911). Repr. in David Solomon b. Samuel of Tulchin, *Hitorerut hatefilah* [Piotrkow, 1911] (New York, 1982).
MIESIS, JUDAH LEIB, *Kin'at ha'emet* (Vienna, 1828).
'Migdal David'. *See* Brokman, Mordecai.
Mikhtavim kedoshim mehaBesht vetalmidav, ed. I. Margulies and A. H. Bierbrauer (Czernowitz, 1921).
MILLER, PERRY, *Errand into the Wilderness* (New York, 1964).
MITCHELL, DOUGLAS, and PLOTNICOV, LEONARD, 'The Lubavitch Movement: A Study in Contexts', *Urban Anthropology*, 4: 4 (1975).
MONDSHINE, YEHOSHUA, 'The Authenticity of Hasidic Letters' (Heb.), *Cathedra*, 63 (1992); 64 (1992).
—— 'Ha'omnam shevaḥ mi*Shivḥei haBesht*', *Tarbiz*, 51 (1982).
—— 'Hasefarim *Matsref ha'avodah* u *Vikuḥa rabah*', *Alei sefer*, 5 (1978).
—— *Hatsofeh ledoro* (Jerusalem, 1987).
—— 'Igrot Erets Yisrael', in id. (ed.), *Kerem Habad*, 4/2 (1992).
—— *Migdal oz* (Kfar Habad, 1980).
—— 'Nusaḥ kadum shel igeret aliyat haneshamah lehaBesht', in *Migdal oz* (Kfar Habad, 1980).
—— 'On "R. Nahman of Bratslav's *Hatikun hakelali* and his Attitude towards Sabbateanism"' (Heb.), *Zion*, 47 (1982).
—— *Shivḥei haBesht: Ketav yad* (Jerusalem, 1982).
—— *Torat ḥabad: Bibliografiah* (2 vols.; Kfar Habad, 1981–4).
MORDECAI B. SAMUEL, *Sha'ar hamelekh* (Zolkiew, 1774).
MORDECAI JOSEPH LEINER of IZBICA, *Mei hashilo'aḥ* (2 vols. in 1; Brooklyn, NY, 1973; vol. i., repr. of Vienna, 1860 edn.; vol. ii., repr. of Lublin, 1922 edn.).
MORGENSTERN, ARYEH, *Messianism and the Settlement of Erets Yisrael* (Heb.) (Jerusalem, 1985).
—— *Redemption in a Natural Way* (Heb.) (Elkana, 1989).
—— 'Tsipiyot meshiḥiyot likrat shenat haTar' [1840], in Z. Baras (ed.), *Meshiḥiyut ve'eskhatologiah* (Jerusalem, 1983).
MOSES CORDOVERO, *Pardes rimonim* [Cracow, 1592] (Jerusalem, 1962).
MOSES DE LEON, *The Book of the Pomegranate. See* Wolfson, E. R.
—— *Sefer hamishkal*, ed. J. Wijnhoven (Ph.D. thesis, Brandeis University, 1964).
—— *Shushan edut*, ed. G. Scholem, *Kovets al yad*, NS 8 (1975).
MOSES ELIAKIM BRIAH, *Da'at Moshe* (Lemberg, 1879).
MOSES HAYYIM EPHRAIM of SUDYLKOW, *Degel maḥaneh Efrayim* [n.p., 1808] (Korets, 1810; Zhitomir, 1875; Szinervavalja, 1942; Jerusalem, 1963).
MOSES SHOHAM B. DAN of DOLINA, *Divrei Moshe* (Zolkiew, 1865).
MOSKOVITCH, ZEVI, *Ma'aseh Neḥemiah* (Jerusalem, 1956).
NADAV, M., 'Kehilot Pinsk–Karlin bein ḥasidut lehitnaggedut', *Zion*, 34 (1969).
NAHMAN of BRATSLAV, *Likutei Moharan* [2 vols.; Ostrog, 1808; Mogilev, 1811] (1 vol.; New York, 1966; Jerusalem, 1969; Bnei Brak, 1972).
—— *Sefer hamidot* [Mogilev(?), 1811] (New York, 1948).

NAHMAN GOLDSTEIN of TCHERIN (Chigirin), *Derekh ḥasidim* [Lemberg, 1876] (facsimile, Israel, n.d.).
—— *Leshon ḥasidim* [Lemberg, 1876] (facsimile, Israel, n.d.).
NAPHTALI ZEVI HOROWITZ of ROPCZYCE, *Ayalah sheluḥah* [Lemberg, 1862] (Podgorze, 1903; Budapest, 1943; Bnei Brak, 1972).
—— *Imrei shefer* (Lemberg, 1884).
—— *Zera kodesh* (Lemberg, 1868).
NATHAN STERNHARTZ of NEMIROV *Ḥayei Moharan* [2 vols.; Lemberg, 1874] (Jerusalem, 1947), ii: *Shivḥei Moharan*.
—— *Likutei halakhot* [8 vols.; Zolkiew (Zholkva), 1846; Lemberg, 1861] (Jerusalem, 1970).
—— *Shivḥei haRan* (with *Siḥot haRan*) [Lemberg, 1864; 1901] (Brooklyn, NY, 1972), pub. in Eng. as *Rabbi Nachman's Wisdom,* trans. A. Kaplan (Brooklyn, NY, 1973).
—— *Yemei Moharnat* [2 vols.; Lemberg, 1876, Jerusalem, 1904] (2 vols. in 1; Bnei Brak, 1956).
Netiv mitsvoteikha. See Isaac Judah Jeḥiel Safrin of Komarno.
NEUBAUER, A., *Seder haḥakhamim vekorot ha'itim* [2 vols.; Oxford, 1877–95] (2 vols. in 1; Jerusalem, 1967).
Nietolerancja i zabobom w Polsce w XVII i XVIII w. (Warsaw, 1950).
NIGAL, GEDALIAH, 'Al mekorot hadevekut besifrut reshit haḥasidut', *Kiryat sefer*, 46 (1971).
—— 'Al R. Aharon Shemuel Hakohen: Mitalmidei haMagid miMezhirech', *Sinai*, 78 (1976).
—— 'Al R. Naftali Kats miPosen', *Sinai*, 92 (1983).
—— *Hasiporet haḥasidit: Toledoteihah venose'eihah* (Jerusalem, 1981).
—— *Magic, Mysticism and Hasidism* (Northvale and London, 1994).
—— 'Makor rishoni lesifrut hasipurim haḥasidit: Al sefer *Keter shem tov* umekorotav', *Sinai*, 79 (1976).
—— *Manhig ve'edah* (Jerusalem, 1962).
—— 'Moro verabo shel R. Yisrael Ba'al Shem Tov', *Sinai*, 71 (1972).
—— 'Perek betoledot hasipur haḥasidi', in *Sefer sipurei kedoshim* [Leipzig, 1866], ed. G. Nigal (Jerusalem, 1977).
—— 'Sipurei dibuk basipur haḥasidi', *Sefer Bar-Ilan*, 24–5 (1989).
—— *Sipurei dibuk besifrut Yisrael* (Jerusalem, 1983).
—— *Sipurei Michael Levi Rodkinson* (Jerusalem, 1989).
—— *Torot ba'al hatoledot* (Jerusalem, 1974).
No'am Elimelekh. See Elimelekh of Lyzhansk.
Notser ḥesed. See Isaac Judah Jeḥiel Safrin of Komarno.
Ohel Elimelekh. See Michelsohn, Abraham Hayyim Simḥah Bunem.
Ohel Naftali. See Michelsohn, Abraham Hayyim Simḥah Bunem.
ONG, W. J., *Orality and Literacy: The Technologizing of the Word* (New York, 1987).
OPPENHEIM, MICHAEL, 'The Meaning of Hasidut: Martin Buber and Gershom Scholem', *Journal of the American Academy of Religion*, 49: 3 (1981).
ORSHANSKI, I., *Yevrei v Rossii* (St Petersburg, 1877).
ORTNER, NATHAN, *Rabbi Tsevi Elimelekh miDinov* (Bnei Brak, 1972).
Or torah. See Dov Ber of Mezhirech.
Or Yitsḥak. See Isaac of Radziwillow.
PANET, EZEKIEL, *Mareh Yeḥezkel* (Siget, 1875).
—— 'Responsum Mareh Yeḥezkel', in *Ayalah sheluḥah* (Budapest, 1943).
PANET, HAYYIM BEZALEL, *Derekh yivḥar* (Munkacz, 1893).
Pardes rimonim. See Moses Cordovero.
PECHTER, M., 'The Concept of Devekut in the Homiletical Ethical Writings of Sixteenth Century Safed', in Isador Twersky (ed.), *Studies in Medieval Jewish History and Literature* (2 vols.; Cambridge, Mass., 1979–84), vol. ii.

PECHTER, M., 'Homiletical and Ethical Literature of Safed in the Sixteenth Century' (Heb.) (Ph.D. thesis, Hebrew University of Jerusalem, 1976).

—— 'Ikvot hashpa'ato shel sefer *Reshit ḥokhmah* leR. Eliyahu de Vidas bekitvei R. Ya'akov Yosef miPolonoyeh', in J. Dan and J. Hacker (eds.), *Studies in Jewish Mysticism, Philosophy and Ethical Literature Presented to Isaiah Tishby* (Heb.) (Jerusalem, 1986).

—— 'Sefer *Reshit ḥokhmah* leRabi Eliyahu deVidas vekitsurav', *Kiryat sefer*, 47 (1972).

Peri ets ḥayim. See Vital, Hayyim.

Peri ha'arets. See Menahem Mendel of Vitebsk.

PERL, JOSEPH, *Megaleh temirin* (Vienna, 1819).

—— *Über das Wesen der Sekte Chassidim* [1816], ed. A. Rubinstein (Jerusalem, 1977).

Pe'ulat hatsadik (Jerusalem, 1981).

PHINEHAS of KORETS, *Midrash Pinḥas* [Warsaw, 1876]. Repr. in *Sefarim kedoshim migedolei talmidei Ba'al Shem Tov hakadosh* (35 + 3 vols.; Brooklyn, NY, 1981–6), i.

PIEKARZ, M., *Biyemei tsemiḥat haḥasidut: Megamot ra'ayoniyot besifrei derush umusar* (Jerusalem, 1978).

—— 'Hamifneh betoledoteihah shel hameshiḥiyut haḥasidit haBraslavit', in Z. Baras (ed.), *Meshiḥiyut ve'eskhatologiah* (Jerusalem, 1983).

—— 'Hara'ayon hameshiḥi biyemei tsemiḥat haḥasidut', in *Hara'ayon hameshiḥi beYisrael: Yom iyun leregel melot shemonim shanah leGershom Scholem* (Jerusalem, 1982).

—— *Ḥasidut Braslav* (Jerusalem, 1972).

—— *Ḥasidut Polin: Megamot ra'ayoniyot bein shetei hamilḥamot uvigezeirot 1940–1945* (Jerusalem, 1990).

PINSKER, S., 'Piety as Community: The Hasidic View', *Social Research*, 42 (1975).

POLL, SOLOMON, *The Hasidic Community of Williamsburg* (New York, 1969).

PORUSH, S. H., *Entsiklopediah lahasidut*, i: *Sefarim* (Jerusalem, 1980).

RABINOWICZ, Z. M., *Rabbi Simḥah Bunem miPeshisḥah* (Tel Aviv, 1944).

—— *Rabbi Ya'akov Yitsḥak miPeshisḥah: HaYehudi haKadosh* (Piotrkow, 1932).

RABINOWITSCH, W. Z., *Lithuanian Hasidism* (London, 1970).

RADOMINSKI, O., *Co wstzymuje reformę, Żydów w kraju naszym i co ją, przyśpieszyć powinno* (Warsaw, 1820).

RAPEL, D., *Havikuaḥ al hapilpul* (Jerusalem, 1980).

RAPHAEL NAHMAN B. R. BARUKH SHALOM HAKOHEN, *Shemu'ot vesipurim meraboteinu hakedoshim* (3 vols.; Kfar Habad, 1974–7).

RAPOPORT, HAIM B. BERISH, *She'elot uteshuvot mayim ḥayim* (3 vols.; Zhitomir, 1857).

RAPOPORT-ALBERT A., 'God and the Zaddik as the Two Focal Points of Hasidic Worship', *History of Religions*, 18: 4 (1979). Repr. in G. D. Hundert (ed.), *Essential Papers on Hasidism* (New York, 1991).

—— 'Hagiography with Footnotes: Edifying Tales and the Writing of History in Hasidism', *History and Theory, Beiheft 27: Essays in Jewish Historiography* (1988).

—— 'Hatenu'ah haḥasidit aḥarei shenat 1772: Retsef mivni utemurah', *Zion*, 55 (1990); Eng. trans. in this volume.

—— 'On Women in Hasidism: S. A. Horodecky and the Maid of Ludmir Tradition', in A. Rapoport-Albert and S. J. Zipperstein (eds.), *Jewish History: Essays in Honor of Chimen Abramsky* (London, 1988).

—— 'Polish Hasidism in the Habad Perspective: The Admor Yosef Yitzḥak Schneersohn in Otwock and Warsaw' (forthcoming).

—— critique of Liebes (Heb.), *Zion*, 46 (1981).

Rashab, the. *See* Shalom Dober of Lubavitch.

REDDAWAY, W., *et al.* (eds.), *The Cambridge History of Poland* (2 vols.; New York, 1978).

REINER, ELCHANAN, 'Temurot biyeshivot Polin veAshkenaz bame'ot hatet-zayin–yod-zayin vehavikuaḥ al hapilpul', in I. Bartal, E. Mendelsohn, and C. Turniansky (eds.), *Kem-inhag Ashkenaz, uPolin: Sefer yovel leChone Shmeruk* (Jerusalem, 1993).

Ribal. *See* Levinsohn, I. B.

RINGELBLUM, E., 'Johann Anton Krieger der Nayhofer Druker fun Hebreishe Sforim', *Yivo Bleter*, 7 (1934).

RIVKIND, I., 'Letoledot hadefus ha'ivri bePolin', *Kiryat sefer*, 11 (1934–5).

RIVLIN, YOSEF YOEL, 'HaGra vetalmidav beErets Yisrael', in J. L. Maimon (ed.), *Sefer Hagra* (2 vols.; Jerusalem, 1964), vol. i.

RODKINSON, MICHAEL LEVI, *Adat tsadikim* [Lemberg, 1864]. Repr. in G. Nigal (ed.), *Sipurei Michael Levi Rodkinson* (Jerusalem, 1989).

—— *Shivhei haRav* [Lemberg, 1864] (Jerusalem, n.d.).

—— *Toledot amudei Ḥabad* (Königsberg, 1876).

ROKOTZ, Y. K. K., *Si'aḥ sarfei kodesh* [Lodz, 1928–31] (Jerusalem, n.d.).

—— *Tiferet hayehudi* (Piotrkow, 1912).

ROSMAN, M., 'An Exploitative Regime and the Opposition in Międzybóż *c.*1730' (Heb.), in S. Almog *et al.* (eds)., *Transition and Change in Modern Jewish History: Essays Presented in Honor of Shmuel Ettinger* (Jerusalem, 1987).

—— *The Lord's Jews Magnate–Jewish Relations in the Polish–Lithuanian Commonwealth during the 18th Century* (Cambridge, Mass., 1990).

—— 'Międzybóż veRabi Yisrael Ba'al Shem Tov', *Zion*, 52 (1987). Eng. trans. 'Miedzyboz and Rabbi Israel Baal Shem Tov', in G. D. Hundert (ed.), *Essential Papers on Hasidism* (New York, 1991).

—— 'The Quest for the Historical Ba'al Shem Tov', *Tradition and Crisis Revisited* (forthcoming).

—— 'The Relationship between the Jewish Arrendator and the Polish Nobleman: The Other Side' (Heb.), in N. Gross (ed.), *Hayehudim bakalkalah* (Jerusalem, 1985).

ROTH, AARON, *Shulḥan hatahor* [Satu-Mare (Satmar), 1933] (Jerusalem, 1989).

ROTHENBERG, J., *The Jewish Religion in the Soviet Union* (New York, 1971).

ROZEN, MINNA, 'The Nakib al Ashraf Mutiny in Jerusalem (1702–1706)' (Heb.), *Cathedra*, 11 (1982).

RUBIN, ISRAEL, *Satmar: An Island in the City* (Chicago, 1972).

RUBIN , JOSEPH DAVID, *Atsei Levanon al hatorah* (Lvov, 1928).

RUBINSTEIN, ABRAHAM, 'Al rabo shel haBesht ve'al haketavim shemehem lamad heBesht', *Tarbiz*, 48 (1978–9).

—— 'Between Hasidism and Sabbateanism' (Heb.), in *Sefer hashanah shel universitat Bar Ilan*, 4–5 (Ramat Gan, 1967). Repr. in id. (ed.), *Perakim betorat haḥasidut vetoledoteihah* (Jerusalem, 1972).

—— 'He'arot lesefer *Shivḥei haBesht*', *Sinai*, 86: 1–2 (1980).

—— *Hebrew Encyclopaedia*, xx (1971), s.v. 'Rabbi Israel b. Eliezer Ba'al Shem'.

—— 'Igeret haBesht le R. Gershom miKutov, *Sinai*, 67 (1970).

—— 'Perakim betoledot haḥasidut', in *Hebrew Encyclopaedia*, vol. xvii (1965), s.v. 'Hasidut'. Repr. in id. (ed.), *Perakim betorat haḥasidut vetoledoteihah* (Jerusalem, 1977).

—— (ed.), *Perakim betorat haḥasidut vetoledoteihah* (Jerusalem, 1977).

—— 'Shevaḥ mi*Shivḥei haBesht*', *Tarbiz*, 35 (1966).

—— 'Sipurei hahitgalut besefer *Shivḥei haBesht*', *Alei sefer*, 6–7 (1979).

SAADYA GAON, *Commentary on Genesis*, ed. M. Zucker (New York, 1984).

SACK, B., 'Al perushav shel R. Avraham Galante: Kamah he'arot al zikatam lekhitvei rabotav', *Misgav Yerushalayim Studies in Jewish Literature* (Jerusalem, 1987).

SACK, B., 'Galut Yisrael vegalut haShekhinah be'*Or yakar* leR. Moshe Cordovero', *Meḥkerei Yerushalayim bemaḥshevet Yisrael*, 4 (1982).
—— 'Ha'adam kemarah vera'ayon ha'arevut hahadadit', *Da'at*, 12 (1984).
—— 'An Inquiry into the Influence of R. Moses Cordovero on Hasidism' (Heb.), *Eshel Be'er Sheva*, 3 (1986).
—— 'R. Moshe Cordovero's Theory of Prayer' (Heb.), *Da'at*, 9 (1982).
—— 'Sheloshet zemanei ge'ulah be'*Or Yakar* leR. Moshe Cordovero', in Z. Baras (ed.), *Meshiḥiyut ve'eskhatologiah* (Jerusalem, 1984).
—— 'The Theory of Tsimtsum of R. Moses Cordovero' (Heb.), *Tarbiz*, 58 (1989).
SAFRAN, BEZALEL, 'Maharal and Early Hasidism', in id. (ed.), *Hasidism: Continuity or Innovation?* (Cambridge, Mass., 1988).
SAMUEL SHEMARIAH of OSTROWIEC, *Zikhron Shemuel* (2 vols.; Warsaw, 1908, Bardejov, 1925).
SAMUEL SHMELKE of NIKOLSBURG (Mikulov), *Divrei Shemuel* (Lemberg, 1862).
SCHAEDER, GRETE, *The Hebrew Humanism of Martin Buber*, trans. N. J. Jacobs (Detroit, 1973).
SCHÄFER, P. (ed.), *Synopse zur Hekhalot-Literatur* (Tübingen, 1981).
SCHATZ-UFFENHEIMER, RIVKA, 'Antispiritualizm baḥasidut', *Molad*, 20: 171–2 (1962).
—— 'Autonomiah shel haru'aḥ vetorat Mosheh', *Molad*, 21: 183–4 (1963).
—— 'The Ba'al Shem Tov's Commentary to Psalm 107: Myth and Ritual of the Descent to She'ol', in R. Schatz-Uffenheimer, *Hasidism as Mysticism* (Princeton, 1933).
—— 'Contemplative Prayer in Hasidism', in E. E. Urbach, R. J. Z. Werblowsky, and C. Wirszubski (eds.), *Studies in Mysticism and Religion Presented to Gershom G. Scholem* (Jerusalem, 1967).
—— *Haḥasidut kemistikah* (Jerusalem, 1968). Pub. in Eng. as *Hasidism as Mysticism* (Princeton, 1933).
—— 'Lemahuto shel hatsadik baḥasidut', *Molad*, 18: 144–5 (1960).
—— *Maggid devarav le Ya'akov. See* Dov Ber of Mezhirech.
—— 'Man's Relationship to God and World in Buber's Rendering of Hasidic Teachings', in Paul Schilpp and Maurice Friedman (eds.), *The Philosophy of Martin Buber* (La Salle, Ill., 1967).
—— 'Perush haḥasidut kevitui lahashkafah ha'idealistit shel Gershom Scholem', in *Gershom Scholem: al ha'ish ufo'olo* (Jerusalem, 1983). Trans. as 'Gershom Scholem's Interpretation of Hasidism as an Expression of his Idealism', in Paul Mendes-Flohr (ed.), *Gershom Scholem: The Man and his Work* (New York, 1994).
—— 'Perusho shel haBesht lemizmor 107', *Tarbiz*, 42 (1972–3). Trans. as 'The Ba'al Shem Tov's Commentary to Psalm 107: Myth and Ritual of the Descent to She'ol', appendix in R. Schatz-Uffenheimer, *Hasidism as Mysticism* (Princeton, 1993).
—— 'Self-Redemption in Hasidic Thought', in R. J. Z. Werblowsky and C. J. Bleeker (eds.), *Types of Redemption* (Leiden, 1970).
—— 'Teachings of Hasidism' and 'Interpretations of Hasidism', in *Encyclopaedia Judaica*, vii (1971).
SCHECHTER, SOLOMON, *Studies in Judaism* (3 vols.; Philadelphia, 1896–1924).
SCHIPER, IGNACY, *Cmentarze żydowskie w Warszawie: Wydawnictwo Gminy wyznaniowej Zydowskiej w Warszawie* (Warsaw, 1938).
—— *Przyczynki do dzijów chasydyzmu w Polsce*, with introd. and notes by Zbigniew Targielski (Warsaw, 1992).
—— 'R. Yisrael Baal Shem Tov udemuto basifrut haḥasidit hakedumah', *Hado'ar*, 35 (1960), 27: 525–6, 531–2, 28: 551–3.
—— *Zydzi królestwa Polskiego w dobie powstania listopadowego* (Warsaw, 1932).
SCHNEERSOHN, JOSEPH ISAAC, 'Avot haḥasidut', in *Hatamim* [Warsaw, 1936] (Kfar Habad, 1975).

—— *Hayom yom*, ed. M. M. Schneerson (Brooklyn, NY, 1942).
—— *Igrot kodesh me'et kevod kedushato Admor moreinu verabeinu harav R. Yosef Yitshak nuho eden miLubavich* (12 vols.; Brooklyn, NY, 1982–5).
—— *Sefer hazikhronot* (2 vols.; Kfar Habad, 1985). Pub. in Eng. as *Lubavitcher Rebbe's Memoirs* (Brooklyn, NY, 1956).
SCHNEERSON, M. M. *Likutei sihot* (32 vols.; Brooklyn 1967–93).
SCHOLEM, G., 'Buber and Hasidism', *Commentary*, 33 (1962).
—— 'Demuto hahistorit shel R. Yisrael Baal Shem Tov', *Molad*, 18: 144–5 (1960). Repr. in id., *Devarim bego* (Tel Aviv, 1975).
—— *Devarim bego* (Tel Aviv, 1975).
—— 'Devekut, or Communion with God', *Review of Religion*, 14 (1949–50). Repr. in id., *The Messianic Idea in Judaism* (New York, 1971). Pub. in Heb. as 'Devekut o hitkasherut intimit im Elohim bereshit hahasidut: Halakhah uma'aseh', in id., *Devarim bego* (Tel Aviv, 1975).
—— 'Hapulmus al hahasidut umanhigeihah besefer *Nezed hadema'*, *Zion*, 20 (1955).
—— 'Hashekhinah', in *Pirkei yesod behavanat hakabalah usemaleihah* (Jerusalem, 1976). Pub. in Eng. as 'The Feminine Element of Divinity', in id., *The Mystical Shape of the Godhead* (New York, 1991).
—— 'Hatsadik', in *Pirkei yesod behavanat hakabalah usemaleihah* (Jerusalem, 1976). Pub. in Eng. as 'The Righteous One', in id., *The Mystical Shape of the Godhead* (New York, 1991).
—— 'Hitpatehut torat ha'olamot bekabalat harishonim', *Tarbiz*, 3 (1932).
—— *Jewish Gnosticism, Merkabah Mysticism, and Talmudic Tradition* (New York, 1960).
—— 'Kabbalah and Myth', in id., *On the Kabbalah and its Symbolism* (New York, 1965).
—— 'Le'inyan R. Yisrael Leibel ufulmuso neged hahasidut', *Zion*, 20 (1955).
—— 'Ma'amar al ha'atsilut hasemalit leR. Yitzhak Hakohen b. R. Ya'akov z.l.: Mofet hador', *Mada'ei hayahadut*, 2 (Jerusalem, 1927).
—— *Major Trends in Jewish Mysticism* (New York, 1954).
—— 'Martin Buber's Hasidism: A Critique', *Commentary*, 32 (1961). Revised as 'Martin Buber's Interpretation of Hasidism', in id., *The Messianic Idea in Judaism* (New York, 1971).
—— 'Martin Buber's Interpretation of Hasidism', in id., *The Messianic Idea in Judaism* (New York, 1971). Expanded version of article orig. pub. in *Commentary*, 32 (1961).
—— 'The Meaning of the Torah in Jewish Mysticism', in id., *On the Kabbalah and its Symbolism* (London, 1965).
—— *The Messianic Idea in Judaism* (New York, 1971).
—— 'Mistikah yehudit beyameinu', in id., *Devarim bego* (Tel Aviv, 1975).
—— 'Mitsvah haba'ah ba'averah', *Keneset*, 2 (1937). Pub. in Eng. as 'Redemption through Sin', in id., *The Messianic Idea in Judaism* (New York, 1971).
—— *The Mystical Shape of the Godhead* (New York, 1991).
—— 'Mysticism and Society', *Diogenes*, 58 (1967).
—— 'The Neutralization of the Messianic Element in Early Hasidism', *Journal of Jewish Studies* , 20 (1969). Repr. in id., *The Messianic Idea in Judaism* (New York, 1971).
—— *On the Kabbalah and its Symbolism* (London, 1965).
—— 'The Paradisic Garb of Souls and the Origin of the Concept of Haluka de-Rabbanan' (Heb.), *Tarbiz*, 24 (1955).
—— 'Perusho shel Martin Buber lahasidut', *Amot*, 1 (1962–3). Repr. in *Devarim bego* (Tel Aviv, 1975).
—— *Pirkei yesod behavanat hakabalah usemaleihah* (Jerusalem, 1976).
—— *Sabbatai Sevi: The Mystical Messiah*, trans. R. J. Z. Werblowsky (Princeton, 1973).
—— 'Shetei ha'eduyot harishonot al havurot hasidim vehaBesht', in A. Rubinstein (ed.), *Perakim betorat hahasidut vetoledoteihah* (Jerusalem, 1978).

SCHOLEM, G., 'Three Types of Jewish Piety', *Eranos Jahrbuch*, 38 (1969).
—— 'Tradition and New Creation in the Ritual of the Kabbalists', in id., *On the Kabbalah and its Symbolism* (London, 1965).
—— 'Tradition und Kommentar als religiöse Kategorien in Judentum', *Eranos Jahrbuch*, 31 (1962). Pub. in Eng. as 'Tradition and Commentary as Religious Categories in Judaism', *Judaism*, 15: 1 (1966).
—— 'Zehn unhistorische Sätze über Kabbala', in *Geist und Werk: Zum 75. Geburtstag von Dr Daniel Brody* (Zürich, 1958).
SCHULTZE-GALLÉRA, SIEGMAN, *Fuss- und Schusymbolik und -Erotik* (Leipzig, 1909).
Seder hadorot heḥadash. See Menahem Mendel Bodek.
Sefarim kedoshim migedolei talmidei Ba'al Shem Tov hakadosh (35 + 3 vols.; Brooklyn, NY, 1981–6).
Sefat emet uleshon zehorit (n.p., 1772).
Sefer arugat habosem. See Abraham b. Azriel.
Sefer Ba'al Shem Tov, ed. Simon Menahem Mendel of Govartchov (Gowarczow) (2 vols.; Lodz, 1938).
Sefer habahir, ed. R. Margaliot (Jerusalem, 1978).
Sefer ha'otsar misipurei tsadikim (Warsaw, 1937).
Sefer hapeli'ah (Korets, 1784).
Sefer ḥaredim. See Azikri Eleazar.
Sefer hazikhronot. See Schneersohn, Joseph Isaac.
Sefer me'irat einayim. See Isaac of Acre.
Sha'ar hagilgulim. See Vital, Hayyim.
Sha'ar hayiḥud. See Dov Ber Shneuri of Lubavitch, *Kuntres hahitpa'alut* .
Sha'ar ma'amrei Rashbi. See Vital, Hayyim.
Sha'arei avodah. See Aaron Halevi of Starosielce.
Sha'arei orah. See Gikatilla, Joseph.
Sha'arei tsion. See Hannover, Nathan Neta.
SHACHAR, Y., *Bikoret haḥevrah vehanhagat hatsibur besifrut hamusar vehaderush bePolin bame'ah hayod ḥet* (Jerusalem, 1992). (Originated as MA thesis, Hebrew University of Jerusalem, 1963).
SHAFFIR, WILLIAM, *Life in a Religious Community: The Lubavitcher Chassidim in Montreal* (Toronto, 1974).
SHALOM DOBER of LUBAVITCH, *Kuntres ha'avodah* (Brooklyn, NY, 1946).
—— *Kuntres hatefilah* [Vilna, 1924] (Brooklyn, NY, 1956). Pub. in Eng. as *Tract on Prayer*, trans. Y. A. Danziger (Brooklyn, NY, 1992).
SHAPIRO, NATHAN, *Maḥberet hakodesh* (Korets, 1783).
SHAROT, STEPHEN, *Judaism: A Sociology* (London, 1976).
—— *Messianism, Mysticism and Magic: A Sociological Analysis of Jewish Religious Movements* (Chapel Hill, NC, 1982).
SHERWIN, BYRON L., *Mystical Theology and Social Dissent: The Life and Works of Judah Loewe of Prague* (London, 1982).
SHIHOR, RAHEL, 'Buber's Method in his Research of Hasidism' (Heb.), *Da'at*, 2–3 (1978–9).
Shivḥei ha'Ari (Ostrog [Ostraha], 1794).
Shivḥei haBesht. See Dov Ber b. Shmuel.
SHMERUK, CHONE, 'Haḥasidut ve'iskei haḥakhirut', *Zion*, 35 (1970).
—— 'Hasipurim al R. Adam Baal Shem vegilguleihem benusḥe'ot sefer *Shivḥei haBesht*', *Zion*, 28 (1963). Repr. in id., *Sifrut yidish bePolin* (Jerusalem, 1981).
—— 'Mashma'utah haḥevratit shel hasheḥitah haḥasidit', *Zion*, 20 (1955).
—— *Sifrut yidish bePolin* (Jerusalem, 1981).

SHNEUR ZALMAN OF LYADY, *Hilkhot talmud torah* (Shklov, 1794).

—— *Igeret hakodesh* [Shklov, 1814]. Repr. in *Likutei amarim: Tanya,* bilingual edn., trans. N. Mindel, N. Mangel, Z. Posner, and J. I. Schochet (London, 1973).

—— *Likutei amarim: Mahadura kama (mikitvei yad)*, ed. S. B. Levine (Brooklyn, NY, 1982).

—— *Likutei amarim: Tanya* [Slavuta, 1796; Vilna, 1900], bilingual edn., trans. N. Mindel, N. Mangel, Z. Posner, and J. I. Schochet (London, 1973).

—— *Likutei torah* [Zhitomir, 1848] (Brooklyn, NY, 1984).

—— *Ma'amrei Admor haZaken: 5562* [1801–2] (2 vols.; Brooklyn, NY, 1964–81).

—— *Ma'amrei Admor haZaken: 5564* [1803–4] (Brooklyn, NY, 1980).

—— *Ma'amrei Admor haZaken: 5565* [1804–5] (2 vols.; Brooklyn NY, 1980–1).

—— *Ma'amrei Admor haZaken: 5566* [1805–6] (Brooklyn, NY, 1979).

—— *Ma'amrei Admor haZaken al parshiyot hatorah vehamo'adim* (2 vols.; Brooklyn, NY, 1982–3).

—— *Ma'amrei Admor haZaken: Ethalekh liozno* (Brooklyn, NY, 1957).

—— *Ma'amrei Admor haZaken: Inyanim* (Brooklyn, NY, 1983).

—— *Seder tefilot mikol hashanah im perush hamilot* [Kopys, 1816, 1822; Zhitomir, 1863] (Brooklyn, NY, 1965).

—— *Torah or* [Kopys, 1836; Zhitomir, 1862] (Brooklyn, NY, 1984).

SHRAGA FEIVEL B. R. MOSES SEGAL, *Safah berurah* (Zholkva (Zolkiew), 1778).

SHULVASS, A., 'Hatorah velimudah bePolin veLita', in I. Halpern (ed.), *Beit Yisrael bePolin* (2 vols.; Jerusalem 1948–53), ii.

SHWERDSHARF, JACOB, *Geza tarshishim* (Lemberg, 1905). Repr. in *Naḥalat tsevi: Bamah lemishnat haḥasidut vetoledoteihah*, i (Bnei Brak, 1989).

Sidur torah or. See Lawat, Abraham David b. Judah Leib.

SIMḤAH BUNEM of PRZYSUCHA, *Kol simḥah* (Breslau, 1859).

Simḥat Yisrael. See Berger, Israel.

SINGER, MERRILL, 'The Use of Folklore in Religious Conversion: The Chassidic Case', *Review of Religious Research*, 22: 2 (1980).

Sipurei nifla'ot (Tel Aviv, 1969).

SLOTKI, A., *Yad Eliyahu* (Jerusalem, 1963).

SOLOMON OF LUTSK, *Divrat Shelomo* [Zolkiew, 1849] (Jerusalem, 1972).

—— introd. to *Maggid devarav le Ya'akov*, ed. R. Schatz-Uffenheimer (Jerusalem, 1976).

SOLOMON RABINOWITZ OF RADOMSK, *Tiferet Shelomo* (2 vols.; Warsaw, 1867, Piotrkow, 1890).

SOLOVEITCHIK, H., 'Three Themes in the *Sefer ḥasidim*', *AJS Review*, 1 (1976).

SONNE, I., 'Expurgation of Hebrew Books: The Work of Jewish Scholars: A Contribution to the History of Censorship of Hebrew Books in Italy in the Sixteenth Century', *Bulletin of the New York Public Library*, 46 (1942).

SPERLING, ABRAHAM ISAAC, *Ta'amei haminhagim umekorei hadinim* (Jerusalem, 1957).

STAMPFER, S., 'Rabi Ḥayyim miVolozhin vehaskamotav', *Alei sefer*, 4 (1977).

STANISLAWSKI, M., *For Whom Do I Toil? Judah Leib Gordon and the Crisis of Russian Jewry* (New York, 1988).

STEIN, S., AND LOEWE, R., 'In Memoriam: Joseph George Weiss', *Journal of Jewish Studies*, 20 (1969).

STEINFELD, SARA, 'The Hassidic Teachings of Rabbi Israel, the Maggid of Koznitz' (DHL Thesis, Jewish Theological Seminary, 1981).

STEINMAN, E., 'Bedikat ḥamets bemishnat haḥasidut', *Molad,* 11: 65–6 (1953).

—— *Be'er haḥasidut* (10 vols.; Tel Aviv, 1951–62).

—— 'Ha'im hayah Rabbi Yisrael Ba'al Shem Tov lamdan?', *Hado'ar,* 34: 16 [1536] (19 Feb. 1954).

STEINSALTZ, A., *Be'ur lesha'ar hayiḥud veha'emunah* (Jerusalem, 1987).
STERN, SAMUEL, *Les Chansons mozarabes* [Palermo, 1956] (Oxford, 1964).
STIMAN-KATZ, HAYA, *Reshitan shel aliyot ḥasidim* (Jerusalem, 1987).
SURASKY, AARON, *Yesod hama'alah* (2 vols.; Bnei Brak, 1991).
TAL, S., *Rabbi Naftali meRopshits* (Jerusalem, 1983).
Tanya. *See* Shneur Zalman of Lyady, *Likutei amarim: Tanya* .
TA-SHMA, I., 'Hadefus ha'ivri be'Ostraha: Tikunim vehashlamot', *Alei sefer*, 6–7 (1979).
—— 'Tosafot gurnish', *Sinai*, 68 (1971).
TAUBER, A., 'Defusei Korets', *Kiryat sefer*, 1 (1924–5).
—— 'Defusei Korets: Hemshekh', *Kiryat sefer*, 2 (1925–6).
TAZBIR, JANUSZ, 'Procesy o czary', *Odrodzenie i Reformacia w Polsce*, 23 (1978).
TEITELBAUM, M., *HaRav miLiadi umifleget Ḥabad* [2 vols.; Warsaw, 1910–13] (Jerusalem, 1970).
TELLINGATOR, SOLOMON, *Tiferet Yisrael* (Jerusalem, 1945).
Tikunei zohar, ed. R. Margaliot (Jerusalem, 1948).
TISHBY, ISAIAH, 'Between Sabbateanism and Hasidism: The Sabbateanism of the Kabbalist R. Jacob Koppel Lifshitz of Mezhirech' (Heb.), in *Netivei emunah uminut* (Ramat Gan, 1964).
—— 'Hara'ayon hameshiḥi vehamegamot hameshiḥiyot bitsemiḥat haḥasidut', *Zion*, 32 (1967).
—— 'The Influence of R. Moses Hayyim Luzzatto on Hasidic Teaching' (Heb.), *Zion*, 43 (1978).
—— *Mishnat hazohar* (2 vols.; Jerusalem, 1971). Pub. in Eng. as *The Wisdom of the Zohar* (3 vols.; Oxford, 1989).
—— *Netivei emunah uminut* (Ramat Gan, 1964).
—— *Torat hara vehakelipah bekabalat ha'Ari* (Jerusalem, 1942).
—— *The Wisdom of the Zohar* (3 vols.; Oxford, 1989).
—— and DAN, J., 'Torat haḥasidut vesifrutah', *Hebrew Encyclopaedia*, xvii (1965). Repr. as pamphlet by Academon, Jerusalem, and in A. Rubinstein, *Perakim betorat haḥasidut vetoledoteihah* (Jerusalem, 1977).
Toledot Ya'akov Yosef. *See* Jacob Joseph of Polonnoye.
Torat haḥasidim harishonim (Bnei Brak, 1981).
Tract on Ecstasy. *See* Dov Ber Shneuri of Lubavitch, *Kuntres hahitpa'alut*.
TROELTSCH, ERNST, *The Social Teaching of the Christian Churches* [2 vols.; 1931 (Eng.); 1911 (Ger.)] (Chicago, 1976).
Tsafenat pa'neaḥ. *See* Jacob Joseph of Polonnoye.
TSARFATI, JOSEPH B. HAYYIM. *See* Joseph b. Hayyim Tsarfati.
Tsava'at haRibash [n.p. (Ostrog?), 1793; Zolkiew, 1795], ed. J. I. Schochet (Brooklyn, NY, 1975).
Tsemaḥ Tsedek, the. *See* Menahem Mendel of Lubavitch.
Tur bareket. *See* Hayim Hakohen of Aleppo.
TURNIANSKY, C., *Sefer masah umerivah leRabbi Alexander beRabbi Yitsḥak Pfaffenhofen* (Jerusalem, 1985).
TYRNAU, ISAAC, *Sefer minhagim* (Korets, 1781).
URBACH, E. E., *The Sages: Their Concepts and Beliefs* (Jerusalem, 1979).
—— WERBLOWSKY, R. J. Z., and WIRSZUBSKY, C. (eds.), *Studies in Mysticism and Religion presented to Gershom G. Scholem* (Jerusalem, 1967).
URI B. PHINEHAS of STRELISK, *Sefer imrei kodesh hashalem* (Jerusalem, 1961).
VERMAN, M., 'Aliyah and Yeridah: Journeys of the Besht and R. Nachman to Israel', in D. Blumenthal (ed.), *Approaches to Judaism in Medieval Times* (Atlanta, 1988).
Vilna Gaon, the. *See* Elijah b. Solomon Zalman.

VITAL, HAYYIM, *Ets ḥayim* (Korets, 1784).
—— *Peri ets ḥayim* [Korets, 1782] (Jerusalem, 1980).
—— *Sha'ar hagilgulim* [Jerusalem, 1912] (Tel Aviv, 1963).
—— *Sha'ar hakavanot* (Jerusalem, 1963).
—— *Sha'ar hamitsvot* (Tel Aviv, 1962).
—— *Sha'ar ma'amrei Rashbi* (Jerusalem, 1898).
VOET, L., *The Golden Compasses: A History and Evaluation of the Publishing Activities of the Officina Plantiniana at Antwerp* (2 vols.; Amsterdam, 1969–72).
WALDEN, AARON, *Shem hagedolim heḥadash* (Warsaw, 1870).
WARD, W. R., 'Power and Piety: The Origins of Religious Revival in the Early Eighteenth Century', *Bulletin of the John Rylands University Library of Manchester*, 63 (1980).
—— 'The Relations of Enlightenment and Religious Revival in Central Europe and in the English Speaking World', in Derek Baker (ed.), *Reform and Reformation: England and the Continent* (Oxford, 1979).
WEINBERG, R. Y., *Shi'urim besefer haTanya* (Brooklyn, NY, 1984).
WEINRYB, B. D., *The Jews of Poland* (Philadelphia, 1972).
—— *Texts and Studies in the Communal History of Polish Jewry*. Proceedings of the American Academy of Jewish Research, 19 (New York, 1951).
WEISS, JOSEPH G., 'A Circle of Pneumatics in Pre-Hasidism', *Journal of Jewish Studies*, 8 (1957). Repr. in id., *Studies in Eastern European Jewish Mysticism* (Oxford, 1985).
—— 'Eine spätjüdischer Utopie religiöser Freiheit', *Eranos Jahrbuch*, 32 (1964). Pub. in Eng. as 'A Late Jewish Utopia of Religious Freedom', in id., *Studies in Eastern European Jewish Mysticism* (Oxford, 1985).
—— 'The Great Maggid's Theory of Contemplative Magic', *Hebrew Union College Annual*, 31 (1960).
—— 'Ha"kushiya" betorat R. Naḥman miBraslav', *Alei ayin: Minḥat devarim liShelomo Salman Schocken* (Jerusalem, 1948–52).
—— 'Ḥasidut shel mistikah vaḥasidut shel emunah', in id., *Meḥkarim baḥasidut Braslav*, ed. M. Piekarz (Jerusalem, 1974). Rev. and pub. in Eng. as 'Contemplative Mysticism and "Faith" in Hasidic Piety', *Journal of Jewish Studies*, 4: 1 (1953). Repr. in id., *Studies in Eastern European Jewish Mysticism* (Oxford, 1985).
—— 'Iyunim bitefisato ha'atsmit shel R. Naḥman miBraslav', *Tarbiz*, 27 (1958). Repr. in id., *Meḥkarim baḥasidut Braslav*, ed. M. Piekarz (Jerusalem, 1974).
—— 'The Kavvanoth of Prayer in Early Hasidism', *Journal of Jewish Studies*, 9 (1958). Repr. in id., *Studies in Eastern European Jewish Mysticism* (Oxford, 1985).
—— 'Ko'aḥ hamoshekh shel hagevul', in id., *Meḥkarim baḥasidut Braslav*, ed. M. Piekarz (Jerusalem, 1974).
—— *Ma'aglei si'aḥ: Leket siḥot vehanhagot shel R. Naḥman miBraslav* (Tel Aviv, 1947).
—— *Meḥkarim baḥasidut Braslav*, ed. M. Piekarz (Jerusalem, 1974).
—— 'Petitionary Prayer in Early Hasidism', *Hebrew Union College Annual*, 31. Repr. in id., *Studies in Eastern European Jewish Mysticism* (Oxford, 1985).
—— 'R. Abraham Kalisker's Concept of Communion with G-d and Men', *Journal of Jewish Studies*, 6 (1955). Repr. in id., *Studies in Eastern European Jewish Mysticism* (Oxford, 1985).
—— 'Reshit tsemiḥatah shel haderekh haḥasidit', *Zion*, 16 (1951). Repr. in A. Rubinstein (ed.), *Perakim betorat haḥasidut vetoledoteihah* (Jerusalem, 1977).
—— *Studies in Eastern European Jewish Mysticism* (Oxford, 1985).
—— 'Talmud torah leshitat R. Yisrael Besht', in *Sefer hayovel tiferet Yisrael likhvod R. Israel Brodie* (London, 1967).
—— *Tarbut ḥatsranit veshirah ḥatsranit* (Jerusalem, 1947).

WEISS, JOSEPH G., 'Torat hadeterminism hadati le R. Mordekhai Yosef Leiner me'Izbica', in *Sefer yovel le Yitshak Ber* (Jerusalem, 1961).
—— '*Via Passiva* in Early Hasidism', *Journal of Jewish Studies*, 11 (1960). Repr. in id., *Studies in Eastern European Jewish Mysticism* (Oxford, 1985).
WERBLOWSKY, R. J. Z., *Joseph Karo: Lawyer and Mystic* (Philadelphia, 1977).
—— 'Mysticism and Messianism: The Case of Hasidism', in *Man and his Salvation: Essays in Memory of S. G. F. Brandon* (Manchester, 1973).
WERFEL [RAPHAEL], YITSHAK, *Hahasidut ve'Erets Yisrael* (Jerusalem, 1940).
WERTHEIM, A., *Halakhot vahalikhot bahasidut* (Jerusalem, 1960).
WETTSTEIN, F. H., 'Letoledot gedolei Yisrael', in *Sefer hayovel likhvod Nahum Sokolov* (Warsaw, 1904).
WILENSKY, MICHAEL, 'Note', *Kiryat sefer*, 1 (1924–5).
WILENSKY, MORDECAI, 'Bikoret al sefer *Toledot Ya'akov Yosef*', in *The Joshua Starr Memorial Volume* (New York, 1953).
—— *Hasidim umitnaggedim* (2 vols.; Jerusalem, 1970).
—— *Hayishuv hahasidi biTeveriah* (Jerusalem, 1988).
WOLFSON, E. R., *The Book of the Pomegranate: Moses de Leon's Sefer Ha-Rimmon* (Atlanta, 1988).
—— 'Female Imaging of the Torah: From Literary Metaphor to Religious Symbol', in J. Neusner, E. Frerichs, and N. Sarna (eds.), *From Ancient Israel to Modern Judaism: Intellect in Quest of Understanding. Essays in Honor of Marvin Fox* (4 vols.; Atlanta, 1989), ii.
—— 'Images of God's Feet: Some Observations on the Divine Body in Judaism', in Howard Eilberg-Schwartz (ed.), *People of the Body: Jews and Judaism from an Embodied Perspective* (Albany, NY, 1992).
WUNDER, M., *Entsiklopediah lehakhmei Galitsiah* (Jerusalem, 1984).
YA'ARI, A., *Igrot Erets Yisrael* (Jerusalem, 1950).
—— 'Likutim bibliografiyim 49: Hadefus ha'ivri bePoritsk', *Kiryat sefer*, 20 (1943–4).
—— 'Serefat haTalmud beKamenets Podolsk', *Sinai*, 42 (1957–8).
—— 'Shetei mahadurot yesod shel *Shivhei haBesht*', *Kiryat sefer*, 39 (1964).
Yad Yosef. See Joseph b. Hayyim Tsarfati.
YEHIEL MICHEL of ZLOCZOW, *Mayim rabim* (Warsaw, 1899).
Yemei Moharnat. See Nathan Sternhartz of Nemirov.
Yishrei lev. See Isaac Jacob.
YIZRA'ELI, M., *Hahasidim harishonim beyishuv Erets Yisrael* (Jerusalem, 1995).
YOSHE SHOHET of BRISK, *Kitvei R. Yoshe Shohet* (Jerusalem, 1981).
Yosher divrei emet. See Meshullam Phoebus Heller of Zbarazh.
YSANDER, TORSTEN, 'Zur Frage der religionsgeschichtlichen Stellung des Hasidismus', *Studien zum bestischen Hasidismus in seiner religionsgeschichtlichen Sonderart* (Uppsala, 1933).
YUDLOV, I., *Ginzei Yisrael* (Jerusalem, 1985).
ZADDOK HACOHEN of LUBLIN, *Peri tsadik* (Lublin, 1934).
—— *Tsidkat hatsadik* (Lublin, 1902; 1913).
ZECHARIAH MENDEL of JAROSLAW, *Darkhei tsedek* (Lemberg, 1796).
ZE'EV WOLF of ZHITOMIR, *Or hame'ir* [Korets, 1798] (Lemberg, 1871; Warsaw, 1883; New York, 1954).
ZEITLIN, HILLEL, *Befardes hahasidut vehakabalah* (Tel Aviv, 2 vols., 1960; 2 vols. in 1, 1965).
—— 'Yesodot hahasidut', in id., *Befardes hahasidut vehakabalah* (Tel Aviv, 1960; 1965).
Zera kodesh. See Naphtali Zevi Horowitz of Ropczyce.
ZEVI ELIMELEKH of DYNOW, *Agra defirka* (Munkacz, 1942).
—— *Agra dekhalah* [Lemberg, 1868] (Przemysl, 1910).

—— *Benei Yisakhar* (Munkacz, 1940).
—— *Derekh pikudeikha* [Lemberg, 1851] (Jerusalem, n.d.).
—— *Likutei Mahartsa* (Jerusalem, 1972).
—— *Maggid ta'alumah* (Przemysl, 1876).
ZEVI HIRSCH B. SAMUEL ZANVIL SEGAL, *Margaliyot hatorah* (Poritsk, 1788).
ZEVI HIRSCH of ZHIDACHOV, *Beit Yisrael* (Lemberg, 1865).
—— *Hakdamah vederekh le'ets haḥayim* [Lemberg, *c.*1832]. Repr. with commentary by Zevi Elimelekh of Dynow as *Sur mera va'aseh tov* [Lemberg, 1840] (Munkacz, 1901). Trans. and annotated by Louis Jacobs as *Turn Aside from Evil and Do Good: An Introduction and Way to the Tree of Life* (London, 1995).
—— *Peri kodesh hilulim* (Lemberg, 1865).
ZEVIN, S. Y., *Sipurei ḥasidim* (Tel Aviv, 1955).
Zikaron tov. See Isaac b. Leib Landau.
Zikaron zot. See Jacob Isaac of Lublin.
ZINBERG, I., *Toledot sifrut Yisrael* (6 vols.; Tel Aviv, 1955–60).
Zohar, ed. R. Margaliot (3 vols.; Jerusalem, 1940–7).
Zohar ḥadash, ed. R. Margaliot (Jerusalem, 1978).
Zot zikaron. See Jacob Isaac of Lublin.

Index